MAKING CELL GROUPS WORK

Navigation Guide

MAKING CELL GROUPS WORK

Navigation Guide

A Toolbox of Ideas and Strategies for Transforming Your Church

M. SCOTT BOREN

WILLIAM A. BECKHAM

JOEL COMISKEY

RALPH W. NEIGHBOUR, JR.

RANDALL NEIGHBOUR

Cell Group Resources™, a division of TOUCH Outreach Ministries
Houston, Texas, U.S.A.

Published by Cell Group Resources™
10055 Regal Row, Suite 180
Houston, Texas, 77040, U.S.A.
(713) 896-7478 • Fax (713) 896-1874

Cover design by Don Bleyl

International Standard Book Number: 1-880828-48-0

All Scripture quotations, unless otherwise indicated,
are from the Holy Bible, New International Version, Copyright © 1973,
1978, 1984 by International Bible Society. Used by permission.

Cell Group Resources™ is a book-publishing division
of TOUCH Outreach Ministries, a resource and consulting ministry for
churches with a vision for cell-based local church structure.

Find us on the World Wide Web at
http://www.touchusa.org

To access special web resources only available to users of this
Navigation Guide, visit <www.makingcellgroupswork.com>. The username is "nautical" and the password is "navigation".

TABLE OF CONTENTS

Stage 8: Expand the Cell Groups To Reach the Unreached

ABOUT THE AUTHORS

M. Scott Boren is the Director of Research and Development for TOUCH® Outreach Ministries, The Cell Group People™ , where he has worked for over ten years. He has served as a cell group leader, coach and pastor. He has traveled across the country to visit cell churches, train cell leaders and consult with pastors. He is the author of *Making Cell Groups Work* and *Cell Group Leader Training.* He holds a Master's degree in New Testament studies from Regent College. He and his wife, Shawna, work together in cell ministry in Houston, Texas. They are the proud parents of their new son Deklan.

William A. Beckham is president of TOUCH Global, a catalytic ministry to help birth the cell church movement around the world. He speaks and consults with churches and organizations looking to embrace the cell group church model. For over 15 years, he served as a Southern Baptist church planter in Thailand. Prior to that, he pastored three churches in Texas. He has authored two books, *The Second Reformation* and *Redefining Revival.* Currently, Bill is working with Dr. Neighbour in developing the TOUCH Family. He is also the primary instructor at TOUCH Glocal, an internet - based training for cell church equipping. He and his wife Mary have been married for over 35 years and are watching their family grow with grand-children.

Joel Comiskey is an internationally recognized cell group and cell church consultant. He has served as a missionary with the C&MA in Quito, Ecuador and is now planting a cell-based church in Southern California. Joel has written best-selling books including *Home Cell Group Explosion, How To Lead a Great Cell Group Meeting* and *Reap the Harvest.* He holds a Ph.D. from Fuller Seminary in Intercultural Studies. He teaches as an adjunct professor at several theological seminaries. Joel and his wife, Celyce, have three daughters.

Dr. Ralph W. Neighbour, Jr. has been a pioneering pastor, writer, researcher and teacher for over 50 years. He has personally tested his methods in many churches, including those in Houston and Singapore. He has written over 30 books that are used worldwide, including *Where Do We Go From Here, The Shepherd's Guidebook,* and *The Arrival Kit.* He has held numerous teaching positions in seminaries and has consulted with churches on every continent. Currently, Dr. Neighbour continues to consult with churches while planting a church in Houston and starting TOUCH Glocal, a unique training center for equipping pastors and leaders in cell group church concepts and skills.

Randall Neighbour serves as the the President of TOUCH Outreach Ministries, and has been with the organization for more than ten years. Randall took the reigns of the organization from his father, Ralph, in 1995. Desiring to multiply the resources, training and ministry his father and other staff members produced through the years, he worked with key leaders from the US and pastors overseas to create sister organizations in Hong Kong, Australia, Brazil, Russia, South Korea, Germany and England. Due to this effort, many of the original published works are in numerous languages, and cell movements have been successfully resourced around the world. He has been the editor of *CellChurch Magazine* and *Cell Group Journal.* In addition to his contribution to this Navigation Guide, Randall is the author of *Are You Fishing With A Net?* and *Answers To Your Cell Group Questions.* Randall and his wife Etna, who also works for TOUCH, are the proud parents of Lady, their golden retriever, and he loves to spend his spare time on his marine aquarium.

Other Contributors Include:

Alan Corrick, cell group pastor at Door of Hope Church in Fairbanks, AK
Twyla Brickman, cell church trainer and author
Les Brickman, cell church consultant, author, and professor
Jim Egli, cell group pastor at the Urbana Vineyard Christian Fellowship
Ben Wong, pastor of Shepherd Community Church in Hong Kong
Larry Stockstill, senior pastor of Bethany World Prayer Center
Daphne Kirk, expert consultant and trainer on children's cell groups
Laurence Singlehurst, cell group church consultant and trainer in the United Kingdom
Michael Mack, small group pastor at Northeast Christian Church in Louisville, KY

Introduction

NAVIGATING YOUR JOURNEY

M. Scott Boren

The body of Christ is made up of many different parts, with Christ as its head. Every individual church has an organizational structure to organize these parts—some structures being better than others, of course. Many churches around the world are discovering the power of organizing the body around cell groups that provide a place for individuals to enter into community with others.

Cell groups work. They provide a context for connecting, ministering to, and mobilizing people. They open doors for friendships between people who've never had true friends. They facilitate ministry through and to ordinary people who are often overlooked in other church structures. They serve as a seedbed for mobilizing ministers and leaders, resulting in reaching more people and starting more groups. They promote an atmosphere of love, the kind of love every human being longs to receive and give. Cell groups work because God works through relationships based in this kind of love.

The journey toward making cell groups work in a church is full of excitement and dreams, the joy of fulfillment and the sense of accomplishment. There's nothing like the experience of community in a cell group. The first time I experienced it, I remember thinking that I felt like I was living in Acts 2. I sensed such a love for others. We were serving one another and seeing God move in our lives. We were challenging one another and seeing the unchurched being transformed. I couldn't wait to see the next step he would have us take.

At the same time, the journey has its fair share of challenges and disappointments, and even heartache and pain. Cell groups are about people, and whenever people are involved, there will be struggle. Cell groups are based on love. And love involves risk. The journey toward making cell groups work is not a journey without risk. Whenever a ship sets sail, it always takes a risk. Therefore, a wise ship captain will take every measure necessary to ensure that he's not taking any unnecessary risks. One way he does it this is to study the captain's logs from previous journeys.

Whenever a church sets sail toward the destination of cell groups, the pastor and leaders should follow a similar pattern. Too many churches have had too many experiences for others to make the same mistakes. The cell group strategy is no longer in its infancy. Those who are about to set sail toward cell groups, and those in the middle of their journey, can learn from the experiences of those who've gone before them. This *Navigation Guide*, and the book, *Making Cell Groups Work*, serve as captain's logs for those who are navigating the journey to making cell groups work.

PRACTICAL TOOLS FOR THE JOURNEY

While writing *Making Cell Groups Work*, it became obvious that one book couldn't hold all the practical tools and resources pastors, church planters, and church leaders need. In fact, as I completed the book, I saw a need for something very different from a traditional book. As we prayed and brainstormed about what we could do, a vision for something unique took shape, a toolbox or resource kit that would provide practical tools to equip church leaders in the necessary skills for developing cell groups.

Making Cell Groups Work outlines eight stages of navigating the journey from no cell groups to an expanding cell group base. This *Navigation Guide* follows the organization pattern established by *Making Cell Groups Work*, but it has a different purpose. It fleshes out the topics introduced in the book and it provides tools, exercises, assessments, resources, and teaching outlines, so church leaders can move through the eight stages of *Making Cell Groups Work*.

HOW THESE TOOLS WERE DEVELOPED

In 1973, Dr. Ralph W. Neighbour, Jr. founded TOUCH Outreach Ministries to provide resources and consulting to churches that wanted to experiment with alternative church models that included evangelistic small groups. Dr. Neighbour is a pioneer thinker and leader whose nature is to think outside the box first. He traveled to Korea and Africa to understand the cell group churches there. He synthesized the principles he learned from those churches, and tried to communicate those principles so others might understand them and implement them. During the 1970s and 1980s, few churches in North America were ready to venture down the road of experimentation. Those that did found only marginal success

The 1990s proved quite different. With the publication of Dr. Neighbour's book, *Where Do We Go From Here?*, the vision for the cell group based church took off in North America. Meanwhile, he was working with a large church in Singapore, and of course developing tools to help other churches implement what they were doing. When the Singapore church proved itself as a viable model, Dr. Neighbour began receiving calls from around the world to teach them how to develop cell group churches. This resulted in his developing of a four-part course entitled, *The Year of Transition.* After three revisions, it was further adapted into a new four-part course, *Advanced Cell Training.*

The editions of *The Year of Transition* and *Advanced Cell Training* had many hands working on it in addition to Dr. Neighbour: Bill Beckham, Jim Egli, Les Brickman, Twyla Brickman, and Randall Neighbour.

Randall Neighbour assumed the role of president of TOUCH Outreach Ministries upon the retirement of his father. In 1998, Randall invited me to join the TOUCH team as the Director of Research. *Advanced Cell Training* was in its final stages of development. That final form of the course has been taught around the world, including the countries of Russia, England, Australia, Korea, Brazil, Argentina, South Africa, the United States, and many more.

After four years of presenting this material in the United States, we decided to ask hard questions of churches that had developed effective cell groups. This led me down a path to discover why some churches effectively transition from the old way of doing church into the new cell group way, while others fail. This research on churches large and small from many different traditions led to the development of the eight-stage process outlined in *Making Cell Groups Work.*

Even with the development of the eight-stage process, pastors still need tools to move the church through those stages. While brainstorming the various tools and resources needed for this *Navigation Guide,* the enormity of the project became overwhelming. It became quite clear that it would take years for anyone to develop such tools. Serendipitously, the years of work had already been done. I only had to put the pieces together, and the eight-stage process of *Making Cell Groups Work* provided the logical organizational rubric.

The logical starting place was the material found in *The Year of Transition* and *Advanced Cell Training.* In these manuals were practical nuggets that are still needed by pastors but had never been developed into an accessible format. Dr. Neighbour was the primary author of this material in its original form. Randall Neighbour has led the way in updating and revising this excellent material. His passion for cell leadership and evangelism has led him to equip many around the world in the principles of cell groups that he writes about.

The second major contribution came from Bill Beckham. After traveling the globe teaching *Advanced Cell Training*, as a part of a sister organization called TOUCH Global, he began developing new training pastors could use to explain the vision of cell groups to their primary leaders. Bill has the ability to conceptualize the cell group vision and provide theological roots for it. Independently, he was writing new training material to help church leaders attain a conceptual and theological foundation for leading people into cell groups. After reviewing his material, I immediately saw the natural fit of his work within this *Navigation Guide*.

Over the last few years, Joel Comiskey has performed more research on the worldwide cell group church than anyone else. After writing, in multiple books, about eight of the most prominent cell group churches, he began to write about practical ways to implement the principles that are common to these churches.

Joel originally wrote a manuscript that aims to equip churches that have started cell groups to take those groups to the next level. After completing the draft, he set it aside to work on some other writing projects. When we started working on the *Navigation Guide*, we discovered how the practical nature of his chapters fit perfectly into the vision of it.

Upon completion of *Making Cell Groups Work*, I found many topics I wanted to address, but didn't have the room to do so. This *Navigation Guide* has provided a medium for me to fill in some of the holes left in the first work.

In addition to the primary authors, others have graciously contributed their expertise. They include Jim Egli, Lawrence Singlehurst, Michael Mack, Alan Corrick, and Daphne Kirk.

The goal of this *Navigation Guide* is to provide a multi-faceted toolbox that will guide pastors, church planters, and church leaders step-by-step through the process of making cell groups work.

NAVIGATING THE EIGHT-STAGE JOURNEY

The eight-stage process of *Making Cell Groups Work* breaks down the journey from no cell groups to an expanding cell group base into manageable parts. For many, they see the final destination of the cell group vision and become overwhelmed by its enormity. Therefore it becomes difficult to actually work toward the vision.

Image you're the captain of a ship. You receive orders to sail to a new destination, the port of London. Because you and your crew have never sailed to London, you must do your homework and discover as much as you can about this new destination. But determining where you're going isn't enough. You must also determine your point of origin. For instance, a ship in the port of New York will take a much different route to London than a ship in the port of Hong Kong. Therefore, the journey of each ship will be unique, even though they have the same vision. This is called navigation.

Likewise for churches. Imagine your church is a ship and you've received orders from God to develop cell groups. How you navigate your ship toward the vision of cell groups will be different than other churches. Two churches with the same vision for developing a cell group church will each take unique journeys to that vision. One church might have a quite easy journey with a direct path and few storms. Another might have to navigate around large islands, sail through a narrow strait, and endure a rough storm.

At the same time, the basic principles of sailing all ships are the same. When a captain and crew understand the principles of navigating a ship, they can apply those principles to each unique journey. When pastors understand the principles of guiding a church toward the cell group vision, they can implement these principles in many different navigational situations. These eight stages are navigation rules for sailing the ship of your church from its point of origin today to its point of destination—an expanding cell group base.

The eight stages are designed to answer eight broad questions pastors ask about cell groups. These questions are:

1. What is my first step?
2. How do I get people on board with the vision?
3. Will cell groups work in my church?
4. How do we prepare the church for cell group success?
5. How do we start the first groups?
6. How do we experience dynamic cell group community?
7. How do we establish cell groups as a base of the church?
8. How do we mobilize groups to reach people?

Each of the eight stages addresses the eight corresponding questions:

Stage 1: Discover the Cell Group Vision

This is the place where the pastor and key leaders learn as much as possible about the cell group destination. The leaders must know where God is leading them, if the church is going to sail in the right direction.

Stage 2: Develop Vision and Strategy as a Team

A Cell Group Vision Team must be convened to work on leading people toward the destination of cell groups.

Stage 3: Assess Your Current Reality

The Cell Group Vision Team must clearly define the church's point of origin, so they can articulate a clear strategy and set specific goals that fit the unique situation of the church.

Stage 4: Prepare the Church through Transformation

It's not enough to change the structure of a church. Leading people into cell group community is about transformation of the heart. The church will need heart preparation as the structure is being changed. The two work together. Without new wine, new wineskins (structures) are not needed.

Stage 5: Launch the First Groups with Kingdom-seekers

The first four stages focus on building a strong foundation. Stage 5 focuses on starting strong groups with people committed to the Kingdom of God. The first group members should be the cream of the crop, so that future groups are built upon a strong foundation.

Stage 6: Generate Cell Group Momentum

At this point in the journey, cell groups must gain momentum in order to move from a novel idea to a broadly accepted vision. To generate this momentum, the church must focus on specific support activities that have proven to produce cell group health and growth.

Stage 7: Establish the Hidden Systems that Support Cells

To ensure the long-term health of cell groups, the church must develop support systems that are often unseen. Without these systems, cell group growth stymies, cell leaders burn out, and few new leaders are developed.

Stage 8: Expand the Cell Groups to Reach the Unreached

It's not enough to start cell groups and get them full of church members. Cell groups must be on mission if they're going to be lining up with the heart of God. In this stage, the cell groups focus on developing ways to reaching the unchurched.

One might assume these eight stages are linear in nature, that one stage must be completed before moving on to the next. In reality, they're overlapping. A church won't complete Stage 1 before moving to Stage 2, but the leaders will start Stage 1 before starting Stage 2. Therefore, how a church moves through these eight stages over time might look something like this:

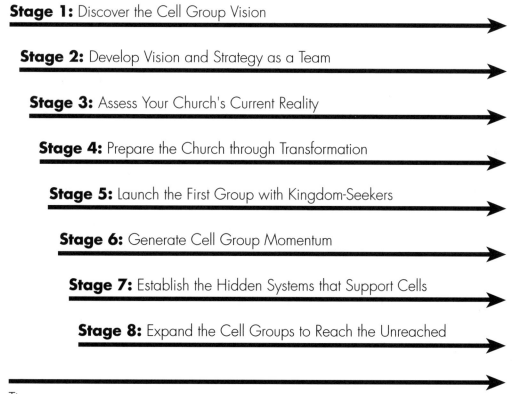

Stage 1: Discover the Cell Group Vision

Stage 2: Develop Vision and Strategy as a Team

Stage 3: Assess Your Church's Current Reality

Stage 4: Prepare the Church through Transformation

Stage 5: Launch the First Group with Kingdom-Seekers

Stage 6: Generate Cell Group Momentum

Stage 7: Establish the Hidden Systems that Support Cells

Stage 8: Expand the Cell Groups to Reach the Unreached

Time

HOW TO GET THE MOST OUT OF THIS GUIDE

• Read Making Cell Groups Work

This *Navigation Guide* will make much more sense if you first attain an understanding of the eight-stage process by reading *Making Cell Groups Work*. We designed the book and the *Navigation Guide* to work together, the former pointing you in the right direction, and the latter providing practical tools for moving in that direction.

• Use What You Need

Unlike most books, we've organized this *Navigation Guide* so you can find what you need and use it. This is not a book you'll read from start to finish. We designed it for repeat uses and return references.

• Getting Started

Read the section about the four different kinds of churches below and you'll see places to get started. Once you determine the stage of your church, turn to that part of the book and work through the material that piques your interest. Here are some other general starting points:
- "Form Follows Function" page 39
- "A Cell Group Model to Fit Your Church" page 25
- The Stage 3 assessments page 199

• Evaluate Progress

The goals found in the chapter, Leading People through Stages 4-8, (page 227) are designed for repeated use by the Cell Group Vision Team. This evaluation instrument will help the team assess the progress toward the goal, and plan ways for moving forward toward the goal.

• Read Suggested Resources

In the margins of many chapters, you'll find other books and resources that go deeper into the topic of the chapter. Invest the time to learn as much as you can. Don't shortchange yourself and make unnecessary mistakes.

• Visit <www.cellgrouppeople.com >

Click on the box that reads "Navigation Guide Resources" for additional articles on related subjects found in this Guide. In the margins of many chapters, an icon highlights specific web resources. New web articles will be added as new insights are discovered. The username is "nautical" and the password is "navigation".

• **Work on the Suggested Activities**

In the margins of many chapters are activities—some are personal in nature, while others are team oriented. These activities are designed to facilitate the implementation of the material, so that reading this *Guide* will prove to be more than an academic exercise.

• **Follow the Icons**

Not only does this book provide practical tools, it also points to other resources not included within its pages. The following icons will guide you through the book, highlighting tools within this *Navigation Guide* and resources outside of it:

Written Resources: Books, booklets, and articles that provide further information about the topic are highlighted in the margins.

Cell Group Vision Team Exercise: Some of the articles are designed specifically as exercises for the Cell Group Vision Team. Others are inserted in the margins.

Personal Exercise: These exercises are designed for the senior pastor or the cell group champion who's overseeing cell group development.

Web Resource: Many additional articles, tools, and resources are available on our website <www.cellgrouppeople.com> or the special website only for users of this *Navigation Guide* <www.makingcellgroupswork.com>. When you visit the special *Navigation Guide* page. This page will be updated with new articles periodically. The username is "nautical" and the password is "navigation".

Tool: These practical techniques are scattered throughout the eight stages.

FOUR KINDS CHURCHES THAT WILL BENEFIT FROM THIS NAVIGATION GUIDE

This *Guide* walks churches through the entire process of developing cell groups from start to finish. Because different churches are at different places on their journey, they require different tools and resources. This *Guide* provides such tools, no matter where a church is on its journey.

1. Churches that want to start cell groups

Churches in this category are the most natural fit for the *Navigation Guide*. Pastors and leadership should work through this book stage by stage, applying the tools that apply to their situation.

2. Church planters

Planters should also walk through the *Navigation Guide* stage by stage. There are a few sections which specifically target the church planter, but most of the tools apply to starting cell groups in an established church, as well as a church plant.

3. Churches that already have cell groups

How these churches will use the *Navigation Guide* is quite different. If you're in this category, go to the assessment in Chapter 21. Take this self-evaluation. To what degree have you completed the goals of each stage? You'll find some of the specific stage goals have been completed, while some have been skipped or only partially addressed. Work through this assessment with your team (See Stage 2 on developing a team), thanking God for what you've accomplished. Most will discover they need to go back to complete some of the goals of earlier stages that they haven't addressed. In addition, you'll find the articles by Joel Comiskey in Stage 6 and Stage 7 especially helpful to your journey.

4. Pastors who are coaching other churches through the process

For pastors of churches with growing cell group systems, they may find themselves answering many questions about cell groups from other pastors. The *Navigation Guide* is a resource for such pastors, as they can use the tool to walk pastors through the eight-stage process and feel confident they're providing excellent answers to the questions.

Stage 1:
Discover the
Cell Group Vision

A CELL GROUP MODEL TO FIT YOUR CHURCH

M. Scott Boren

During my senior year of university, I was taking a writing course where I was required to write a manual of some kind. At that time, I served as the student president of a large campus ministry that was built upon small groups. I decided to write a training manual for its small group leaders.

To write this manual, I begged and borrowed every book on church small groups I could find. It wasn't easy, as there were only a handful of them. I read David Yonggi Cho's book, *Successful Home Cell Groups*, and my heart was moved. I couldn't believe how God moved through the spontaneous development of organic groups like those Cho wrote about.

I remember thinking: "These groups are different from the Bible studies I knew. These groups were life-giving, spontaneous platoons that did more than discuss the Bible. They even do evangelism." Then I read Dr. Ralph Neighbour's, *The Shepherd's Guidebook*, which helped put some structure and strategy to the inspiring stories Cho presented. As I read these books, I felt God saying, "This is your life." After reading two books on cell groups, I knew God was calling me to enter into this dynamic relational life about which I was reading.

To hear God's call to this life was somewhat disturbing, as I hadn't participated in the kind of cell groups presented by Cho or Neighbour, nor had I even seen such a church. In fact, to find an American church that had developed a model for others to follow seemed impossible. I met one pastor who was trying cell groups—he had loaned me these books—but he couldn't figure out how to make them work. I wanted to see a church that modeled in America how the vision of Cho and Neighbour works.

FOLLOWING MODELS

In 1993, I started working for Dr. Neighbour at TOUCH Outreach Ministries, a dream come true. I was beginning to see the fulfillment of

God's call to cell groups. I was getting to work for the primary purveyor of cell group resources. But the problem was that there were no cell group models in North America. Dr. Neighbour had worked with churches throughout the 1980s and had finally become so frustrated that he concluded the church in America wasn't ready for cell group life. He wrote in his first edition of *Where Do We Go from Here?*:

> Finally, in 1985, when the twenty-first pastor called me from California to tell me his three-year struggle to develop relational church structures had ended in his forced resignation, I began to ask myself a serious question: can new wine be put into old wineskins? The answer is "No!"[1]

In the late 1980s, Dr. Neighbour started working with Faith Community Baptist Church in Singapore. As groups developed and the church grew to more than five thousand, this church became the primary cell group model for others to follow. Pastors from around the world, including America, flocked to the annual cell church conferences hosted by Dr. Neighbour and the senior pastor, Lawrence Khong. The vision came to life for many as they attended services, visited real cell groups, and interacted with staff pastors.

When I visited the church's 1994 Annual Cell Church Conference, I learned much about how the church operated through the general sessions, but the most powerful learning experiences came as I attended a regular cell group meeting, observing how they loved and ministered to one another. Beyond that, I had the additional privilege of staying for a few extra days to visit with multiple staff members, asking questions about the differences between their ministry now in cell groups and their former ministry in the traditional church.

The first major American model exploded on the scene in the fall of 1994, in the form of Bethany World Prayer Center, with its first cell church conference, featuring Lawrence Khong and Ralph Neighbour. This model blossomed from 54 groups to 108 groups in six months. From there, they soon grew to 310 groups. Immediately, pastors from across the nation converged upon Baton Rouge, Louisiana, for the conferences hosted by this cell group model.

In 1995, Faith Community Baptist Church, in partnership with TOUCH Outreach Ministries, sponsored three major cell church conferences in the United States: in California, Tennessee and Virginia. In these conferences, the staff of FCBC provided a thorough explanation of how their model worked so that other churches could adopt it. After these conferences, TOUCH Outreach Ministries began a series of four conferences which explicated the Singapore model in detail.

In 1997, a new model burst forth from South America. Pastor Cesar Castellanos, of the International Charismatic Mission, which had developed over 15,000 cell groups at the time, held a conference on his model, which he calls Groups of 12. Subsequently, Bethany World Prayer Center has adopted this model and now hosts major G-12 conferences to explain how this model works.

Since 1997, cell group models have proliferated. Victory Christian Center in Tulsa, Oklahoma hosts an annual conference. Free-market groups have sprung up in Life Christian Center in Colorado Springs, Colorado. Willow Creek Community Church has developed a very popular model its leaders have called a Church of Small Groups.

TWO APPROACHES TO CELL GROUP MODELS

The easiest way to learn about cell groups is to see what other churches have done to make their cell groups work. Over the last ten years, I've observed that churches take one of two approaches when they visit cell group models.

Observe, experience, and adopt. The first approach follows this scenario: a pastor reads a book on a model. He then attends a conference hosted by this model church. He purchases the training resources developed by the model, and then returns to his home church with the intent of emulating everything the model church has modeled. The theory is that this model church has become successful because of its model and that the model will work in many different contexts.

The "adopt the model" approach works well when three pieces line up. First, the senior pastor must feel a calling from God to follow a specific model. Second, the model fits the church culture and the social setting in which the church is located. Third, the church is willing to not only observe the structures, but also experience the life of the model.

In other words, the leadership must be willing to catch the life of the model by participating in the activities of the model. They can't just copy its structures and hope to make it work. One staff pastor of a church that has a vision for following the pure Groups of 12 model as established by

Cell Group Vision Team Exercise

Why do you think that church leaders are so vulnerable to Model Idolization Disease?

the International Charismatic Mission has made more than fifteen trips to Bogota, Colombia to experience the dynamics of the church and learn how the model works.

Even when these three things line up, it's still quite easy to succumb to Model Idolization Disease, which causes people to follow other people rather than God.

Observe, understand, and adapt. The second approach follows a different scenario: a pastor learns about cell groups. He reads not only about one model church, but about many model churches. He attends multiple conferences held on these different models. He purchases training resources produced by these models, and then he returns to his home church with the intent of discovering what kind of model God wants to create in his church.

The theory of this approach is that each church is like a snowflake: no two are exactly alike. At the same time, snowflakes have much in common and have the same basic structure and composition.

This approach to a model works for a church when these things line up. First, the senior pastor and a team of key leaders are committed to discovering the kind of cell groups that will work in their church. Second, this team is determined to learn not only about how the models work but also to understand the principles that are common among all models. This will allow the church to develop a unique model based upon those principles. Third, the senior pastor is ready to lead the church into a shift of values to experience biblical community. In other words, the leadership has a vision to lead people into small group community, not just to create a small group structure.

Rob Campbell started his church in 1993 in rural Texas with about 40 people meeting in his home. As the church grew he started implementing the cell structure outlined by Ralph Neighbour. Over the last few years, the church has incorporated aspects of different models. Leaders have attended conferences at Bethany World Prayer Center and read books on all the different cell/small group models. The senior pastor took a sabbatical to visit Korea, Singapore, and Bogota to learn firsthand from these great models.

The church has learned from many different models. What its leaders chose to adapt to their church from these models was based upon an understanding of principles that make all model cell group churches work and the vision to create biblical community. Now more than 100 cell groups and 1000 people meet in weekly worship, and this is happening in a rural community.

Cell Group Vision Team Exercise

What are the advantages to adapting models as compared to adopting a model?

Rob Campbell understands that there's much more to a cell group model than the structures and methods. He knows the structures and methods are built upon principles.

Because he understands that all successful models are built upon principles, he can learn from other models and adapt aspects of those models to his situation.

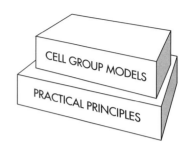

UNIQUE CONTRIBUTIONS OF MAJOR CELL GROUP MODELS

While the most prominent cell group models have principles in common, each model tends to emphasize something unique, focusing on a different piece of the pie. Churches which are learning about these models would be wise to learn about all these different models so that they can discover how all the pieces work together to make a complete pie.

Cho Model: Small Groups for Spiritual Growth and Evangelism

In 1964, Yonggi Cho, then a pastor of a small church of twenty-four hundred people, hit a physical wall that was a result of carrying the entire load of the church's ministry. After insisting on baptizing 300 people without any help, his body collapsed while interpreting a message from a visiting evangelist. He had worked so hard that he had exhausted his body to the point that doctors told him he could not continue to pastor. This caused him to seek other ways to lead the church. He writes about searching in the book of Acts to find new ways to be the church,

Written Resources

- *Successful Home Cell Groups* by David Yonggi Cho
- *Growing the World's Largest Church* by Karen Hurston

> Until then my idea of church was always a public building; I had never even considered the possibility of turning a house into a church. Yet the Bible clearly and specifically mentioned the church meetings in houses.
>
> And I thought to myself, here I have been stressing only temple ministry. We have no house-to-house ministry. I've just been telling our people to come to church on Sundays and Wednesdays. There is something we have been lacking.[2]

From this search, he concluded that releasing lay leaders to lead small groups of people to meet in homes was God's plan for His church. Such a plan might not seem radical at the beginning of the twenty-first century, but in 1964, pastors did not release average lay people into this kind of ministry. On an even more radical level, after Dr. Cho presented his idea to his all male deacons, they failed to step up and help him pastor the church. Therefore, he went to his women and released them to lead cell groups. Again, this might not seem radical in an egalitarian period in which we now live in North America, but Korea is far from an egalitarian culture. Women are not released into leadership in Korea, much less in the church.

The purpose of these groups is twofold: evangelism and spiritual growth. In other words, these groups are not Bible study care groups. They're organic life-centers that will grow and multiply. Again, this was very radical for that time.

Many churches have tried to copy Cho's model of releasing ordinary people into ministry, but they failed to see a secret that made this model work. Cho did not send his new cell group leaders out to the wolves to minister in isolation. Instead he developed a team of staff pastors who focus on supporting the leaders and the ministry in these cell groups. This ministry is not one of administration from an office, but one of spending time with the people, praying for them outside the church office. Karen Hurston, whose father was Dr. Cho's mentor, writes:

> During the week the typical staff pastor administrates various programs or departments, making several telephone calls, and doing a limited amount of counseling in the church office. Most staff pastors teach a Sunday School or Bible study class once or twice a week, sometimes training the lay leaders in their respective programs. By contrast, YFGC staff pastors spend four and one half days each week making home and business ministry visits. During most days a staff pastor visits 5-7 homes or businesses; during Grand Home Visitation he visits about 10 homes a day. In each visit, he preaches a different mini-sermon or devotional to correspond with specific concerns. During most days of visitation, staff pastors officiate at major birthday parties or go with lay leaders to requesting businesses, for a service of dedication and prayer. One observant Westerner said, "A minister with a 'preaching itch' would love to serve on this staff."[3]

Dr. Cho opened the door in the twentieth century for radical ministry through cell groups. There are many unique components to the Cho model that are used around the world. *But the primary contribution of this model is the cell group itself, along with the pastoral support that's provided to make these groups work.*

Neighbour Model: Equipping Every Cell Member for Ministry

Ralph W. Neighbour, Jr. moved to Houston, Texas in 1969 to start an experimental church based upon evangelistic small groups. Within three years the church had grown to over 300 people. In his book, *The Seven Last Words of the Church,* he wrote, "Evangelism would have to be the life-force of the group—but not evangelism in the sense of meetings where a preacher preached and an audience listened. It must be evangelism in the way Daniel T. Niles defined it: 'One hungry beggar telling another hungry beggar where to find bread.'"[4]

Written Resources

- *Where Do We Go From Here?* by Ralph W. Neighbour, Jr.
- *The Second Reformation* by William A. Beckham

The purpose of a cell group in Dr. Neighbour's mind extended beyond fellowship. A vision captured him to equip every cell group member for more than cell group attendance. He wanted to equip them for ministry. Over the next thirty years, he wrote, rewrote, refined, and re-refined a cell member discipleship process that leads a person from the first steps as a new Christian and through various steps that eventually prepares that person to become a cell group leader. This equipping process is not discipleship for the sake of discipleship. It is discipleship for the sake of equipping people for ministry.

The current edition of this process is called *Your Equipping Journey* and is thoroughly discussed in Chapter 49.

Many churches have tried cell groups and have put all of the pressure upon those groups to raise up disciples. This approach produces groups that are ungrounded in the Word, with new Christians having no place to learn the Bible. Dr. Neighbour's unique contribution has been the development of a comprehensive cell group member equipping process that guides people into ministry and eventually leadership. Many churches have taken Dr. Neighbour's material and have adapted it for their settings. Other churches have developed cell member equipping that has taken a different form. *The principle is that cell group members need to be trained as disciples and such a process helps to facilitate discipling.*

Written Resources

- *Groups of 12* by Joel Comiskey
- *From 12 to 3* by Joel Comiskey
- *The Jesus System* by Rocky Malloy
- *The Ladder of Success* by Cesar Castellanos
- *Successful Leadership* by Cesar Castellanos

Groups of 12 Model: Mentoring

This model emphasizes releasing ordinary people to lead cell groups just as Cho's model does. It also places a heavy emphasis on equipping and discipling cell group members, with the goal of preparing every member to eventually lead a cell group. *But the unique contribution of this model lies in a different area: how the cell group leaders are supported.*

Every successful cell group model has a coaching structure. A coach is a person who has direct oversight of cell group leaders, who plays the role of mentor, encourager, and friend to those who are on the front lines of ministry. In this model, the coach is called a G-12 leader. A G-12 leader coaches up to 12 leaders, all of whom have been birthed out of his or her cell group. This model places such high emphasis upon the relationship between the G-12 leader and his cell group members that the entire Group of 12 meets once per week in a leader huddle. This meeting is a closed group open only to those cell group leaders under a specific G-12 leader's care.

Not only does this model emphasize mentoring between the coach (G-12 leader) and cell group leaders, it's based on mentoring that flows from the senior pastor all the way down the entire structure of leadership. The senior pastor would then have a G-12 comprised of his primary leaders. (Note: these are leaders who work within the cell group system, either G-12 leaders or cell group leaders.) This group would meet every week, for the purpose of building relationships, ministering to one another, and mentoring by the pastor. This model is dependent upon the senior pastor establishing the flow of ministry that will move throughout the entire body.

The members of the pastor's G-12 would then also meet weekly with their Groups of 12, whom they mentor and minister to, so they can be effective leaders in the church. The more cell groups there are in the church, the more G-12 layers there are. But the unique contribution of this model isn't found in the method of gathering 12 leaders to meet weekly. *It's found in the principle of mentoring that starts with the senior leader and flows down through the entire structure.*

Department Model: Support Ministries

In 1975, a former police detective in the Ivory Coast started a church. In the early days of the church, growth was very slow. Then after six years, it exploded with growth. Now the church has over 150,000 people meeting in cell groups.

What's the unique contribution of this church? *It's found in how the church has developed ministries that support the life of the cell groups.* Some have argued that cell groups should do everything in a church and that no ministries or programs are required. While that is an option, most model churches have developed ministries that are separate from the cell groups. The Works and Mission Baptist Church is a glowing example of how this functions.

When you view the structure of this model on paper, it looks as though the different departments compete with one another, much like has been the case in the traditional church. But the departments don't form the backbone of the church. The cell groups do. The departments are designed to support the life of the cell groups. All department ministers are members of a cell group. Participation in one of the department ministries is dependent upon gifting and calling.

Therefore, if cell members feel called to work in the evangelism department where they plan evangelistic campaigns and follow up with converts for a 30-day period, they work with the team to facilitate evangelistic ministry which will feed the cell groups. The same applies to the demonology department, marital care department, prison ministry, etc.

Elim Model: Cell Group Teams

Elim Church is located in San Salvador, El Salvador. Every week over 130,000 people gather in cell groups throughout the city. Hundreds of Elim churches have been started around the world based upon the mother church's model.

The primary contribution of this model to the church is found in how they organize their cell groups. Most churches operate from a theory of one leader + one apprentice/intern = one group. This is not the approach of Elim. They operate from a cell group team theory. Every cell group has a group of four or five people who work together as a team to lead the group. One person serves as the primary leader. Another serves as an intern who is being trained to lead the next group. All cell group members who are committed to discipleship and reaching others for Christ are invited to participate in this team.

All cell groups at Elim meet on Saturday nights. All cell group leadership teams meet on Thursday nights to prepare and pray for the Saturday night cell group meetings.

Some people see how the core leaders of every cell group must partici-

Written Resources

• *Preparing the Church for the 21st Century* by Les Brickman

Written Resources

• *The Elim Story* by Joel Comiskey with Mario Vega

pate in two meetings per week and conclude that the Elim model won't work for them. *But again, the key contribution of this model is not found in the two meetings per week, but in the team leadership approach.* When cell leaders learn to gather a team and work together with those team members, it takes the pressure off and actually requires less work in the long run. It also develops and multiplies leaders faster.

Mixed Model: Creativity

Victory Christian Center in Tulsa, Oklahoma has developed an attractive model that has grown to over 1000 cell groups and 13,000 people gathering for worship on Sundays. The primary contribution of this church is found in its cell group creativity. This church has discovered how to create many different kinds of cell groups, while at the same time keeping these groups on the same page with one another.

For instance, there are family groups that are geographically based, but there are also men's groups, women's groups, singles' groups, college groups, youth groups, and children's groups. There are groups that meet in businesses over lunch, prison outreach groups, groups that meet in nursing homes, worship team members that meet as groups, and young couples' groups that meet to deal with their specific struggles. Victory Christian Center has learned how to be creative with its cell groups so it can reach people where they are.

At the same time, it doesn't allow this creativity to cross over into chaos. While the groups might look very different in their structures, each group has the same goal of living out the "five-fold vision": Worship and Praise, Prayer, Word of God, Fellowship and Interaction, and Ministry and Evangelism. Karen Hurston writes about these diverse groups,

> Victory's cell leaders guide their meetings by [Pastor Billy Joe] Daugherty's 'five-fold vision.' Groups that can take ninety minutes for a meeting, such as the home-based 'zip-code cells' and the G-12 groups, do all five parts of the vision. Groups more limited in their time, such as cells that meet during a lunch hour in an office setting, must do at least three parts of the vision—typically including prayer, the Word and fellowship with interaction.[5]

Congregationally-Focused Model: Mid-sized Groups

Pastor Randy Frazee of Pantego Bible Church, located in Fort Worth,

Written Resources

- *Breakthrough Cell Groups* by Karen Hurston

Texas, has developed a model, which he writes about in his book, *The Connecting Church.* He has built his model upon a three-fold biblical call to help people share common purpose, common place, and common possessions. By common purpose he means that those in the cell groups should be working in unity under the vision of the church leadership and discussing the same material other groups are discussing. By common place, he means that groups will experience more powerful community when the group members live in close proximity to one another. By common possessions, he means that people today practice what is seen in Acts where people were "more than willing to share or sell what they had so that those in need would be cared for." To facilitate these three values, this model organizes all cell groups geographically to meet in homes and discuss the same topic.

But the truly unique feature of this model is that it isn't just about developing cell groups. This model also focuses on developing biblical community at a mid-size group level. Every Sunday morning, adults from five to seven groups, which are located in relatively close geographic proximity, gather for fellowship and biblical instruction.

This model highlights the importance of mid-sized group gatherings. Many other cell group models have also recognized the importance of this mid-sized gathering. While Pantego gathers people on a weekly basis, many do this monthly. It's a great way for cell group members to connect with other people from other cell groups. It relieves some of the pressure of multiplying groups, as cell members realize they'll see their friends in these mid-sized gatherings. It also provides a place where gifted teachers can instruct people in the Word.

Free-Market Group: Evangelistic Interest Groups

The Free-Market model is based upon the desire to release people to lead any kind of group that individuals have an interest to lead. Potential participants in these groups gather around an interest for a short-term commitment of one semester. The goal of these groups is to involve the unchurched and help them take one step closer to the knowledge of Christ. One leader might gather a group of non-Christians around the interest of fly fishing, meeting once per month. His goal is to build relationships with them and help them become more open to the message of the Gospel.

Another group might meet to discuss the threat of terrorism, still

Written Resources

- *The Connecting Church* by Randy Frazee

Written Resources

- *Fly Fishing, Dog Training and Sharing Christ in the 21st Century* by Ted Haggard

another to play volleyball, and another to discuss evolution. Some groups meet around the desire to study a book of the Bible or to discuss a biblical topic like Christian leadership.

Each group is designed to meet people at different points on a continuum. The Engel scale is used to identify how far an unchurched person is away from receiving Christ. "Every small-group leader knows that his job is to bring the people in his group up one point on the Engel scale every semester."

This model contributes a vital piece to a complete understanding. *It recognizes that people are more likely to gather around a common point of interest, which serves as a great way to connect Christians with non-Christians.* Such groups are very different than those designed by Dr. Cho and form the basis for all of the major models listed above. The goal of those groups is to build biblical community that results both in edification of one another and evangelizing the lost. The goal of these groups is to use an interest to connect people and lead them one step closer to accepting Christ.

Free-market groups are low-commitment ways to build relationships with the unchurched. Dr. Neighbour developed a similar group in the 1970s called an interest group. But unlike the Free-Market model, Neighbour's groups recognize the difference between a holistic cell group and an interest group designed for outreach. The interest group is a sub-group of the cell group.

COMMON COMPONENTS FOUND IN THE DIFFERENT MODELS

The major models highlighted above each contribute something unique to the cell group church vision. There are many different ways to organize each component. There is no ideal structure. Instead it's crucial to understand the common components found in effective cell group structures.

The diagram on the next page provides a visual for these various components:

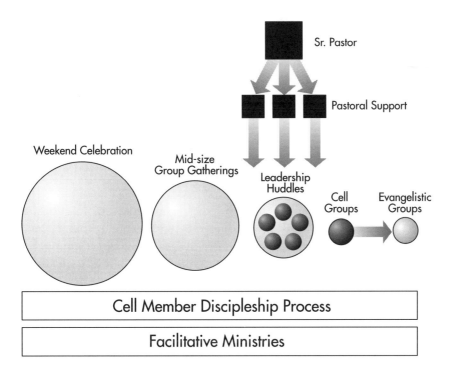

- **Weekend Celebration**—The first component is found in all major models. They all have outstanding worship, teaching, and ministry. The cell groups don't replace what occurs in large group worship services. These services are designed to equip the believer and serve as a door for unbelievers to learn about Christ and even receive him.
- **Mid-size Group Gatherings**—Pantego Bible Church illustrates this component. Peter Wagner calls this group the congregation. Some, like Pantego, hold this gathering on a weekly basis. Most hold it monthly. For instance, in many churches that have men's groups, women's groups, college, etc., they'll have a monthly gathering for all the men, another for all the women, another for college students, etc.
- **Senior Pastor Mentoring**—The Groups of 12 model emphasizes the mentoring that's modeled by the senior pastor, who establishes the pattern for ministry in the church and then passes that leadership down to his key leaders. In the G-12 model, the senior pastor will gather 12 people, based on the number Jesus chose. The key isn't

found in the number of people mentored, but in the fact that the senior pastor is mentoring leaders who can pass on life to others.

- **Pastoral Support**—The Cho model depends upon staff cell pastors who are out of the office, free from all kinds of administrative duties to spend their time in relational ministry. They focus on mentoring the cell coaches under their care. They work with cell group leaders, helping them develop their groups. They're not stuck in the office waiting for ministry to occur. They're out with the people seeing where they can minister to needs.

- **Leadership Huddles**—All the cell group models recognize the importance of leadership huddles. The Groups of 12 model elevates them to the level of needing a weekly meeting. Others hold these huddles on a biweekly or monthly basis. The key is found in the mentoring provided by the cell coach to the cell group leader, which can take a variety of forms.

- **The Cell Group**—The Cho model gets the credit for this contribution. The cell group isn't just a small group that happens to meet together. It's a group of 4-15 people who experience life-transforming community around the presence of Christ. These aren't just home Bible studies or recovery groups, but a place where people find "home" with others.

- **Evangelistic Groups**—The Free-Market model emphasizes this group, equating it with a cell group. While some of these evangelistic groups experience the dynamic of a cell group, the intent is different from that of a cell group. Therefore, it works best when people experience biblical community with others in a cell group and then start an evangelistic group from the overflow of that experience.

- **Equipping Every Member for Ministry**—The Neighbour model highlights the need to equip every cell group member for ministry. The most effective cell group models each have developed a way to disciple cell group members to the point of being ready for cell group internship.

- **Facilitative Ministries**—The Works and Mission Baptist Church has developed ministries that facilitate, rather than compete with, the life of cell groups. Every major cell group model has developed ministries that are separate from the cell groups, but are manned by people who participate in cell groups. These might include prayer ministry, evangelism ministries, etc.

Form Follows Function: Moving Beyond the Models to Biblical Community

M. Scott Boren

When pastors survey the different cell group models, most will find themselves more attracted to one model over the others. They read more about that model than they do the others. They search the web for articles on that model and enter chat rooms to discuss how it works. They make pilgrimages to model churches for annual conferences.

Model cell group churches are working and they want to help other churches work as well as they do. No one can blame pastors of these model churches for being excited and promoting what God has shown them to do. If what they're doing doesn't get their blood pumping, then we must ask why they'd do it in the first place.

But the promotion of models often leads to model infatuation. Pastors fall prey to the "right model theory" thinking: "If I find the right model, then cell groups in my church will take off just like they have in that model." Yet most find they're not able to replicate the "magical" success of these models. The cells grow with enthusiasm at first, but then they stagnate. When this occurs, pastors look on the horizon for the next model, because they assume they've yet to find the "right model."

Many churches have done just this. They traveled to Korea and learned about the Cho model. Then they gathered some practical resources from the Neighbour model. For a few years this worked, but the groups didn't multiply as expected. Then they learned about Groups of 12 and when they implemented this model cells took off again, only to take a nosedive six months later. After this, they embraced Free-market groups and the different kinds of groups found in the Meta-group model.

What happens tomorrow when another ideal model promises cell group salvation? Let me shoot straight: no such model exists. Models do not make cell groups work. The life of Jesus through people makes groups work. Should we learn from models? Yes! I read about and study different models on a weekly basis. This learning helps me greatly in my church and as I work with other churches. But as I study different model churches, I find two things in common. First, they're all distinct in their methods and structures; they have different forms. Second, their unique forms are based on common functions.

This leads to one conclusion: every church will have different forms, even when they follow a similar pattern established by a specific model church. The key then to success isn't found in learning about these forms, but in discovering the function that drives the creativity needed to develop forms that work in specific churches.

FORM FOLLOWS FUNCTION

Most pastors who are seeking to build a cell group system begin with questions of form. These questions include:

- What happens in your groups?
- How do you train leaders?
- Where do your groups meet?
- What do your groups discuss in their meetings?
- What does your oversight structure look like?
- How often do your oversight groups meet?
- What kind of reporting system do you use?

Cell group enthusiasts aren't the only ones who become enamored with forms. How many evangelism programs have worked in one church only to prove fruitless when transferred to other churches? Youth programs have risen to prominence, only to have dreams shattered when other youth pastors couldn't make them work.

The same is true of prayer plans, mission strategies, children's ministries, etc. It isn't enough to have the right materials, to have all the instructions on how to use those materials, and to follow them to a T. God didn't create the church to operate as computers following code. He designed the church to develop organically, to allow the form to flow out of the function.

Prayer in the church can serve as an excellent model of form and function. All the major cell group churches around the world are known for their commitment to prayer. This is especially true of the Cho model. This church has developed a form of prayer they call concert prayer. In their worship services, they have times of prayer where the entire church prays aloud. It sounds like waves crushing against a rocky shore.

In addition, they have another form they call Prayer Mountain. Located one hour north of Seoul, the church has a retreat center where people visit every day to fast and pray. The function is fervent, diligent prayer. The forms come in concert prayer and prayer mountain. But these two forms don't translate well to every church.

Cell church advocates have been guilty of proclaiming that they've discovered "the New Testament" model for the church—some implying and others accusing that any structure that varies from their cell church model is less than biblical. Yet within the cell church world, there are as many different models for how they do church as there are churches. No two churches do it exactly the same.

The same can be said for the specific structures found in a cell group model. The G-12 model has a form of gender-based groups. Other models only have intergenerational groups—Pantego Bible Church is the primary example. Still others have a mixture of both. But the magic isn't found in the form. God isn't sitting in heaven, waiting for churches to find the magical formula before he pours out his blessings of growth. He isn't interested in developing a perfect model. No such model exists. He wants us to discover and live out his function for cell groups.

THE FUNCTION OF A CELL GROUP SYSTEM

If you were to ask ten pastors their opinion on the function of a cell group, you'd most likely receive ten different answers. These answers usually include:

- To close the back door
- To connect people in relationships
- To grow the church
- To reach the lost who won't come to a church building
- To facilitate the use of spiritual gifts
- To learn the Word together
- To raise up leaders
- To get to know others in the church
- To follow the pattern established by the early church
- To pray for and encourage one another

Cell Group Vision Team Exercise

List some things that you desire to see occur through cell groups.

None of these answers is wrong. Healthy cell groups produce all of them. At the same time, this list fails to articulate the primary function of cell groups. For instance, if cell groups are built upon the function of closing the back door, then groups will be seen as a non-essential necessity so people won't leave the real church. If groups are viewed as a way to grow the church, then people will eventually feel used by the growth-hungry senior pastor. If the function is Bible study to learn the Word, then people will feel they have to get the right answers and the groups won't be very relational. There must be a function that drives the form of cell groups beyond these sub-functions.

Most of the functions for cell groups listed above relate to practical concerns pastors face everyday. Practical concerns will motivate people to develop a nice cell group program, but they won't stir people to revamp their lives around the call of God. Practical concerns will cause people to attend meetings, but they won't push them out of their comfort zones to move into a new way of being the church.

The function of cell groups isn't to create a cell group ministry that grows and multiplies. It's not enough to get people together in a small group once a week, even if it does meet in a home. Too many churches have created the form of a cell group, going through the motions because they don't understand their true function.

The function of cell groups can be summarized in two words: *biblical community*. Church members generally don't need another meeting to add to their weekly schedule. They don't want another Bible study. They don't care about church growth. And they don't really understand what "closing the back door" means. But there is an experience for which the dormant parts of most hearts cry. This is the experience of true biblical community.

Church leaders visit a cell church model and see the form of cell groups and they see the weekly meetings. They hear the statistics. They visit a worship service. They might even visit a couple of cell group meetings. But there's no way to capture the biblical community that stimulates those meetings. Cell groups don't develop biblical community in a 90-minute meeting held once a week. The meeting is only a starting point of edification and evangelism through the group.

Most pastors think they don't have time to experience "community" before implementing the form of cell groups. They have sermons to prepare, committee meetings to lead, budgets to develop, elders and deacons to please, and hurting people to counsel. They have to fix the church and make something happen before it's too late. They only have time to experience a short conference or a quick read of a book.

Because both my father and my uncle worked in construction, I learned how houses were built. I watched houses rise from stage to stage in their development. Obviously there's more to a house than what the eye can see. The façade is supported by a basic structure, and this structure is built upon a foundation. Likewise, when visiting a model cell group church, pastors see the façade. Beneath this façade are the practical principles common to all model churches. But the unseen foundation is that of biblical community.

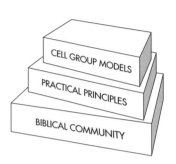

Cell groups are simply a form designed to create a place where people experience a radical connection with other brothers and sisters, where they enter into a life of unity with one another, where they learn to sacrifice for one another. This is the experience Paul described when he instructed the believers in Ephesus: "Be completely humble and gentle; be patient, bearing with one another in love. Make every effort to keep the unity of the Spirit through the bond of peace" (Ephesians 4:2-3).

WHAT IS BIBLICAL COMMUNITY?

Biblical community is a great idea, but few today have an inkling of what it looks like. To describe it is like trying to describe the taste of my grandmother's chocolate pie. The only way to understand it is to eat it. Jesus knew this to be true. In order to establish his Kingdom, he did much more than teach about it; he demonstrated it so others could experience it. He provided a three-year experience in Kingdom community for the disciples so they'd understand his kind of life. His teachings were brief explanations of what they were experiencing with him. Jean Vanier says this about community:

> Community is a place where people can live truly as human beings, where they can be healed and strengthened in their deepest emotions, and where they can walk towards unity and inner freedom. As fears and prejudices diminish, and trust in God and others grows, the community can radiate and witness to a style and quality of life which will bring a solution to the troubles of our world.[6]

Jesus did much more than mentor twelve (really eleven) men to be his future for the church. He took four uneducated fishermen, a tax collector, a rebellious zealot and six other men—men who had little in common in the natural world—and prepared them to enter into community. He didn't try to create this community in a classroom, through books, but instead used the hard teacher of experience with one another and with him. He provided the experiences of feeding the thousands, walking on water, healing the sick, forgiving the prostitute, and ultimately going to the cross. Jesus had to lead them to experience the reality that following him meant something totally different than what they expected. They expected a King to rule with a scepter in Jerusalem just as David did, but they experienced the community formed around a servant who ruled with a basin and a towel.

In John 13, Jesus modeled biblical community to the disciples, concluding with this instruction: "Now that I, your Lord and Teacher, have washed your feet, you also should wash one another's feet. I have set you an example that you should do as I have done for you." In John 17, Jesus took community to another level as he prayed for the church that would follow his disciples:

> My prayer is not for them alone. I pray also for those who will believe in me through their message, that all of them may be one, Father, just as you are in me and I am in you. May they also be in us so that the world may believe that you have sent me. I have given them the glory that you gave me, that they may be one as we are one: I in them and you in me. May they be brought to complete unity to let the world know that you sent me and have loved them even as you have loved me (John17:20-23).

Jesus not only modeled community, he established it as a model for how to live as church. He prayed prophetically for the church that would follow his ascension to operate in the same unity he demonstrated with the basin and the towel. He prayed this prayer for the church in the twenty-first century. He prayed this prayer for cell groups around the world who think they have it right, but they only have weekly meetings. He prayed this prayer for church members who are isolated from other Christians, even though they work hard to serve the Lord. He prayed this prayer for hurting people who have never known love and are looking for a place to belong.

This is an incredibly radical prayer if you think about it. To understand this prayer, the unity of the Father and the Son must be made clear. Jesus prayed that the members of his church would be one, "just as you are in me and I am in you." As Jesus and the Father are one, so shall the church be when this prayer is answered. According to the church fathers who established the orthodox doctrine of the Trinity, Jesus and the Father, "of the same nature," are absolutely unified in being. Jesus said, "When you see me, you see the Father." They are one in being. Jesus wasn't a man filled with God; he was God, who operated in totally unity with his Father in heaven.

At the same time, God the Son is distinct from God the Father. They are not the same person. The Father did not become flesh, the Son did. Therefore, we must conclude that the Son and the Father experienced unity that did not cross over the line into uniformity. They're not exactly the same, even though they're the same in being.

Gregory of Nazianzen, one of the Cappadocian Fathers, wrote this about the Trinity in the fourth century:

> No sooner do I consider the One than I am enlightened by the radiance of the Three; no sooner do I distinguish them than I am carried back to the One. When I bring any One of the Three before my mind I think of him as a Whole, and my vision is filled, and the most of the Whole escapes me. I cannot grasp the greatness of that One in such a way as to attribute more greatness to the rest. When I contemplate the Three together, I see but one Torch, and cannot divide or measure out the undivided Light.[7]

The unity of the Father and the Son is radical unity. They are distinct, but they are one. This unity is characterized by love. This love isn't some kind of emotive feeling between the Father and the Son; love is the very nature of who God is. This love is defined for us not by what we call love today, but by the cross. Jesus demonstrated the nature of this love through sacrifice, by suffering as a man, bearing the burden on the cross, taking man's shame and sin upon himself.

The Father and the Son share this kind of love for one another. The Father loves the Son and the Son loves the Father. Love is not lordship; it is mutual life together, with no one of them claiming power or authority over the other. The Son willingly submits to the Father and the Father blesses the Son.

Theologians through the centuries have pontificated about the inner workings of the Trinity. But few have explicated what it means for the church to operate in the kind of unity Jesus prayed for here. Some have applied this prayer to ecumenical cooperation between churches and denominations. This verse has been used to promote inter-faith conferences, councils to discuss theological differences, and cooperative ministry efforts. While not inappropriate, such an application seems premature. How can churches that aren't unified within become unified with other churches?

It seems the definition of "one" must be interpreted by other scriptures, not by the modern desires to establish networks between churches. When Jesus prayed this prayer, he probably knew it would apply to the theological differences and church schisms, but the setting of John 17 seems best interpreted in the light of Jesus' previous discourse in earlier chapters.

In John 15, Jesus teaches on the vine and the branches. In the first eight verses, Jesus explains how his disciples cannot live apart from him, just as a branch cannot live apart from the vine. As a result of being in Christ, the disciples would bear much fruit (v. 8). On the heels of the vine and branches teaching, Jesus shifts to an emphasis on love. He says: "If you obey my commands, you will remain in my love, just as I have obeyed my Father's commands and remain in his love … My command is this: Love each other as I have loved you. Greater love has no one than this, that he lay down his life for his friends" (John 15:10-13).

The relationship between the Son and the Father is characterized by personal interaction, mutual submission, and mutual love. Jesus commands his disciples to operate the same way with one another. The church is only the church when it enters into this love for one another. It is not the church because it preaches orthodox doctrine. It falls short of being the church when it only meets for worship. Just because people meet in small groups doesn't mean the church has come to life. The full expression of the church includes teaching, it includes worship, it includes small groups; but these are not the cornerstones of the nature of the church. Life in Christ and love for one another characterize the true church of God.

Some of the more practically minded might ask: Where's the evangelism? Where's the church growth? Where's the group multiplication? What about assimilation and closing the back door? According to John 17, all these are found in biblical community. Jesus prayed that we would be one, "so that the world might believe that you have sent me." True biblical unity leads to evangelism. It results in church growth. Groups will multiply.

When God is truly flowing through a cell group, it will spontaneously grow. It's difficult to realize this because so many leaders are so focused on the forms of cell group growth that they don't realize that if they focus on developing biblical community, the results will be spectacular.

INDIVIDUALISM VS. COMMUNALISM

John 17 unity so dynamically opposes the westerner's view of life that most Christians don't know what to do with it. It reads like a foreign language. It's definitely a foreign way of living for those of us in North America and Europe. When Joel Comiskey was living in Ecuador, he flew through Houston and I met him for coffee during his layover. Our meeting lasted for about three hours. We talked about family, dreams, struggles, and work. We shared ideas and opinions. As we drank coffee, Joel said, "In South America, people do what we've been doing for the last three hours almost every day. The church uses the cell group structure to help guide what they already do with one another toward the purposes of Christ." People in non-Western countries already understand community. They just need church leadership to guide them in living out biblical community.

Written Resources

- *Making Room for Life* by Randy Frazee
- *The Safest Place on Earth* by Larry Crabb

Westerners understand individualism. We understand how to get ahead by winning, which means someone else loses. Society's push toward rootless mobility, marital uncertainty, and consumerism drives individuals to live isolated lives. John Wayne may be dead, but his spirit is alive and well in twenty-first-century life. People define themselves by how they compare to others. Making more money, accumulating more toys, buying bigger houses all are signs that "I," as an individual have succeeded. We've learned how to "pull ourselves up by the bootstraps," how to "watch out for Number One," how to "take care of ourselves because no one else will."

Sometimes pastors allow the lie to slip in that cell groups won't work in America. In reality, Satan's using a half-truth to distract pastors from the real issue. Cell groups won't work in Western society like they work in Korea or South America. The form will be different. But biblical community is God's design for every church, no matter the location.

Paul wrote: "It was he who gave some to be apostles, some to be prophets, some to be evangelists, and some to be pastors and teachers, to prepare God's people for works of service, so that the body of Christ may be built up until we all reach unity in the faith, and in the knowledge of the son of God and become mature, attaining to the whole measure of the fullness of Christ" (Ephesians 4:11-14).

The call of pastors is to facilitate the "unity in the faith," not the individuality in the faith. The church isn't designed to be a disparate group of individuals who lack intimate connection with one another as they go about their individual service for God. The John Wayne mentality works on the frontier, but it fails in the church.

Often when Americans, who've been trained in the culture of individualism, read about biblical community, they envision communalism. Images of David Koresh and the Branch Davidians or communist control come to mind, where everyone is forced to sell all they have, give it to a leader, and deny any personal freedoms for the sake of the whole. Communalism requires people to give up their individuality and forces people to align under the control of the establishment.

Community doesn't strip people of their individuality. Peter was still the bombastic, impetuous Peter even after entering community, although refined and more balanced. In community, people are free to participate at whatever level they choose. No one forces anyone else to agree or to submit. Jesus never forced Judas to believe; his love for Judas freed him to make his own decision.

Sects force people into a belief system. Community loves people into life. Sects control people's actions. Community frees people to become who they really want to be. Sects tell people what they will do. Community opens possibilities for people to discover what they want to do.

FORMS MUST PROMOTE BIBLICAL COMMUNITY

John 17 is a chapter solely dedicated to prayer. Prayers are offered to God because action is required by God to do what man cannot do. Man cannot make biblical community. It cannot be produced with machines. There's no blueprint model for it. It's alive. It's organic. It's too free to be limited by any model.

Cell Group Vision Team Exercise

Compile a list of words to describe biblical community.

From a practical perspective, we operate in the church via forms of ministry. Forms are necessary, and much can be learned from the forms of cell group models. But forms are secondary. Forms are flexible. All cell group forms should be measured against this standard: Does it facilitate the answer to Jesus' prayer or does it detract from it?

A THEOLOGICAL FOUNDATION FOR CELL GROUPS

3

Bill Beckham

Many church strategies today start with the pragmatic questions of: What will work in the church? Or: What will make my church grow? While such questions aren't evil or wrong, they don't go deep enough. Pragmatic questions deal with surface issues, which must be rooted in much deeper questions. Specifically, answering the question of what the church should do strategically must be rooted in the question of what kind of life God wants the church to live.

To properly answer this question, one must look at the kind of life God lives. Man is created in God's image, but has become tarnished and deformed by sin. The church must be a place where people rediscover their image before God. Therefore, the nature of God is the starting point for developing a theological foundation for church structure and cell groups.

GOD IS TRINITY

Francis Schaeffer said, "Let us understand that the beginning of Christianity is not salvation: it is the existence of the Trinity. Before there was anything else, God existed as personal God in the high order of Trinity. So, there was communication and love between the persons of the Trinity before all else. This is the beginning."[8] The Trinity is the central theological principle for the church and it models the essential structural design for how the church should be organized.

Therefore, in order to understand the life of the church, we must go back to the beginning point of Trinity. Whatever its form on earth, the church must be able to be the dwelling place of God in his full Trinitarian expression.

God revealed himself as Trinity to the early Christians and therefore the concepts of the Trinity were expressed naturally in the life of the church. Paul's benediction to the Corinthians is one of the oldest, simplest, and most popular expressions of the Trinity. "The grace of the Lord Jesus

Christ, and the love of God, and the fellowship of the Holy Spirit be with you all."

By the second century, using a guide called the Didache, converts were baptized into the Threefold Name with questions and answers.

QUESTION: Do you believe in God the Father?
ANSWER: I believe in God the Father!
QUESTION: Do you believe in Jesus Christ, His only Son, our Lord?
ANSWER: I believe in Jesus Christ, His only Son, our Lord!
QUESTION: Do you believe in the Holy Spirit?
ANSWER: I believe in the Holy Spirit! [9]

Tertullian, an early theologian of the third century, is credited with first using the actual word "Trinity." He also gave the definition of the Godhead as "one substance in three persons." Today we sing the Trinitarian truth:

Holy, Holy, Holy! Merciful and Mighty!
God in Three Persons, blessed Trinity!

Why a Trinity? If God were one person, there could be power. If God were two persons there could be love. But God is three. And with the Trinity, there is now community. The highest Life Form in the universe has chosen to live in community.

No other religion has ever dreamed of a concept like the Trinity. The Muslims, Jews, and Unitarians believe God is one and only one. Therefore, God is authority. Dualism, as seen in Zoroastrianism and Gnosticism, taught that God is two: good god and evil god. Therefore, God is an adversarial relationship. This adversarial concept of deity is also seen in the "Ying" and "Yang" of Chinese philosophy. On the other hand, Hinduism has many gods and is, therefore, a crowd.

TRINITY MEANS GOD IS COMMUNITY

To say, "God is Trinity" is to say, "God is community." God is Father, God is Son, and God is Spirit. Community is not just an activity of God. Community is the nature of God. Just as God is holy, God is community. Just as God is love and righteousness, God is community. Just as God is power, God is community. Within his very nature, God is community.

This means God is different in nature from Adam and the race of

Adam. Man was created in the image of God, but not with the Trinitarian nature of God. This is why it's so difficult for us to understand the Trinity.

Within my nature, I am not community. I am an individual. If I am to experience God's kind of community, I must be in association with another, and several others. Then, I begin to participate in God's kind of community life. Only in small group community can I experience the most basic nature of God. God created me for community, and I know God best in community. But a human being only experiences the full nature of God in community with at least two other humans.

Each member of the Godhead participates in community in a special way. God the Father created community. Christ died on the cross in order to break down all the barriers between God and man to restore community. The Spirit has been given as the witness to the Father and Son to nurture and empower community. We might say the work of the Spirit is to form Christians into the divine community of the Father, Son, and Spirit and to teach Christians how to be God's family within the Trinity.

The church and Christians do not build spiritual community. We enter into the eternal community of the Father, Son, and Spirit that has always existed, that was redeemed at Calvary, and that will never cease to exist.

Ralph Neighbour states that "the serious error of the twentieth-century church has been its blindness to the importance of being a community, where people become responsible to and for one another." Unfortunately, the error has been carried over into the twenty-first century.

THE TRINITY IS MYSTERY

The Trinity is an intellectual and theological mystery that the mind of man cannot completely grasp. To understand the Trinity, we're left to analogies and pictures that are all inadequate and even dangerous when used alone.

In the fourth century, Augustine used an analogy from the human mind to explain the Trinity. The Trinity is like the memory, intelligence, and will in the mind of a man. Father, Son, and Holy Spirit are like the sun, the rays of the sun, and the heat generated by the sun. The Trinity is like a spring, a stream, and a lake, which as a single whole make up a river.

The Trinity is like the properties of water. Water is a solid, a liquid, and steam. But all three forms are still water and are of one substance. This illustration is applied to the Trinity in various ways. The Father may be understood as the solid aspect of the Godhead, the Son is the liquid, the living water, and the Spirit is the steam or vapor.

Relationships have also been used to try to explain the Trinity. I am father to my children. I am son to my father. And, I am husband to my wife. But I am still one person.

Objects have also been used to try to explain Trinity. It is said that Saint Patrick in the fifth century used the shamrock (a cloverleaf) to explain the concept of Trinity to the pagan Celts in Ireland. A cloverleaf has three parts but is still one "leaf." An egg is made up of three parts but is still one egg. The egg consists of a yolk, the white, and the shell.

THE TRINITY IS EXPERIENCE, NOT DOCTRINE

For many, the concept of the Trinity is an academic or doctrinal exercise. For those disinclined toward such theological ideas, they often miss the riches of the Trinity. Such Christians experience the Trinity in relationship; they don't study it academically. Even Paul didn't attempt to explain the Trinity intellectually as a doctrine. We accept the Trinity because we experience God as God the Father, God the Son, and God the Spirit. And we experience God in these three ways in our daily lives, not just in the pages of the Bible or theological treatises.

Therefore, the New Testament explains the Trinity experientially rather than doctrinally. The followers of Christ experienced God as Father. But, when they said, "God is Father," they had not said all they had experienced about God. They also had to say, "God is Son." But when they said, "God is Father and God is Son," they still had not explained their total experience with God. They also had to say, "God is Spirit." Then, when the followers of Christ had said, "God is Father, Son, and Spirit," they had explained their complete experience with God.

Instead of trying to understand the Trinity intellectually and logically, we should begin to experience and enjoy the Trinity. We enjoy God as our loving Father. We enjoy God as Son: our Savior, Brother, and Friend. We enjoy God as omnipresent Spirit who indwells us, walks beside us, and empowers us.

PERSONAL AND CORPORATE EXPRESSIONS OF THE TRINITY

The Trinity is a glorious and blessed mystery in which the Christian shares the life of God in two venues. In the Trinity, the Christian is part of a personal relationship with God and part of a corporate experience with God.

The personal relationship of the Christian to the Trinity is explained in John 14:20. "In that day you shall know that I am in My Father, and you in Me, and I in you." The Father, Son, and Spirit indwell the individual Christian. Each Christian is "in" Christ, who is in the Father.

The corporate relationship is explained in Matthew 18:20. "For where two or three have gathered together in My name, there I am in their midst." The Father, Son, and Spirit indwell a group of Christians.

The picture in John 14:20 of our individual relationship with God reaches from earth to heaven. Christ is in me on earth and I am in Christ who is in the Father in heaven. The believer's personal and individual relationship with Christ is sealed in the Trinity all the way from earth to heaven. This personal and individual relationship in the Trinity is a great mystery, but Christians accept it as a reality of the Christian life.

The Christian's corporate relationship with the Trinity is lived out in the New Testament in either a small group or a large group setting. Today the presence of God in the large group is almost automatically accepted because the large group has been so dominant for so long in the life of the church. However, how Christ relates to Christians in a small group experience often raises questions. The Christian's small group relationship with the Trinity is often misunderstood and neglected.

TWO SIDES OF GOD'S NATURE

Transcendence is a theological word that means God is great. Transcendence suggests that God is far from man. God is inaccessible. God is above man, distant from man, and unapproachable by man. God is glory, majesty, and holiness—totally different from man. God is up there and exists outside of man.

Immanence is a theological word that means God is caring and able to touch man. Immanence suggests that God is near to man. God is accessible. God is below with man, intimate, and approachable by man. God is here and indwells man. God as Father is protector and loving parent. God in Jesus is brother and friend. God in the Spirit is teacher and daily companion.

Old Testament writers knew God in transcendence and immanence. Isaiah places these two encounters together in Isaiah 57:15 when he describes God as the "Most High God" and the "Most Nigh God." "For thus says the high and exalted One Who lives forever, whose name is Holy. I dwell on a high and holy place, and also with the contrite and lowly of spirit in order to revive the spirit of the lowly and to revive the heart of the contrite."

MOUNT SINAI AND THE TENT OF MEETING

God expressed Himself in transcendence and immanence to the children of Israel at Mount Sinai. There, on the mountain where God had first revealed his name to Moses at the burning bush, the children of Israel saw evidence of the transcendent God. The earthquakes, smoke, thunder, and lightning reminded them that the God of Abraham, Isaac, and Jacob was there on the mountain. They built a barrier around the mountain to keep humans and animals from wandering upon that mountain, because any living thing that went too close would die. To the children of Israel, the mountain was a terrifying reminder of transcendent holiness.

In Exodus 33 and 34 we learn that God met Moses below the terrifying mountain at the "Tent of Meeting." The tent was so named because it was the place outside the camp where God would meet Moses. "As Moses went into the tent, the pillar of cloud would come down and stay at the entrance, while the Lord spoke with Moses." The Lord would speak to Moses "face to face, as a man speaks with his friend" (Exodus 33:11). This is an immanent encounter between God and Moses.

After God spoke to Moses "face to face, as a man speaks with his friend," Moses made a strange request of God. "Now show me your glory (face)" (Exodus 33:18). God said to Moses, "You cannot see my face, for no one may see me and live."

Why can Moses meet God "face to face" at the Tent of Meeting and yet not live if he sees God's face (glory) on the mountain as he requests? Is Moses confused about what happened in the tent when God spoke to him "face to face?" Or, has God discounted the importance of that "face to face" tent experience?

God knows what Moses is asking and Moses knows what he is requesting of God. Moses is saying, "In the Tent of Meeting I have seen your face immanent. Now show me your face transcendent." That is why God said, "No man can see my face (transcendent) and live."

But God told Moses to go to "a place near me (high on Mount Sinai) where you may stand on a rock. When my glory passes by, I will put you in a cleft in the rock and cover you with my hand until I have passed by. Then I will remove my hand and you will see my back; but my face must not be seen" (Exodus 33:20-23). God protects Moses with his hand, his immanence, in order to reveal a passing view of his transcendence. God in his love and grace always mediates his transcendent nature in his immanent nature. The incarnation is the moment of greatest mediation and miracle when God emptied himself and became man. "The word became flesh." The eternal became temporal. Power became weakness. Transcendence became immanence.

CHRIST'S PARADIGM OF TRANSCENDENCE AND IMMANENCE

Christ built transcendence and immanence into the practical design of the church. Every Christian personally experiences God in a transcendent and immanent way through the work of the Holy Spirit. A Christian can be alone or with thousands and still personally experience the greatness (transcendence) and nearness (immanence) of God.

As a corporate body Christians experience the transcendent and immanent nature of God together in a special community way we call church. Within a large group setting of scores, hundreds, or thousands, Christians uniquely experience the transcendence of God. Within a small group setting of no more than ten to twelve people, Christians uniquely experience the immanence of God.

Cell Group Vision Team Exercise

Why is it important to have a theological foundation for cell groups?

This is not a debate about structure or place of meeting. It is a truth about how God chooses to be his body on earth, express himself to mankind, and operate his Kingdom in this world. The first-century Christians met in small groups not because of culture or convenience, but because Christ was present in those small groups.

Think about the directional thrust of worship and singing in the two meetings. In the large-group setting, the focus is most often upward toward God in his transcendence. God is on his throne in heaven. However, in the small group the directional focus seems most often to be within the room or circle. Christ is in the midst of his people on earth.

For the church to meet only in small-groups is not enough. God's transcendent nature will be lacking. For the church to meet only as a large-group is not enough. God's immanent nature will be slighted. Only Jesus' simple design will allow God to express his full transcendent and immanent nature to and through his church. The church that refuses to use Jesus' simple large-group and small-group design is not only rejecting the New Testament design of the church, but is in danger of distorting the nature of God.

THE LIFE OF TRINITY AND THE APPLICATION OF TRANSCENDENCE AND IMMANENCE

Ephesians 2:22 is an example of the relationship between the Trinity and church. "In Whom (Christ) you also are being built together into a dwelling of God in the Spirit." In this verse Paul explains the Trinitarian nature of the church. Christians are being built by Christ into a dwelling of God! Christ is building the church. The church is a dwelling of God the Father. And the church is "in the Spirit."

The triune God manifests himself in his transcendence as the church gathers together in corporate worship. The Father, Son, and Spirit manifest in immanence as they come close to people and build them up. In the large group setting, people learn about the nature of God, they discover the mystery and wonder of his greatness, they see the great depths of his call on their lives. But without the small group setting, people miss the opportunity to apply the truth of God to their lives.

The book of Ephesians is full of practical application. The small group meeting is the place for doctrinal application within the church. Doctrines are not just to be studied in seminary but truths to be experienced in community. In large-group meetings, people study these doctrines. In personal relationships with Christ, they begin to understand the implications of these doctrines. In small groups, they apply these doctrines to their lives. Without life in small groups, people fail to experience the great doctrines of the church.

The continuing presence of Christ in the world (incarnation, Trinity, omnipresence) is lived out in community. The power of God released in the world (omnipotence) is experienced in community. The divine purpose of God (redemption, sanctification, and eschatology) is applied in community. A small group is the bridge from doctrinal information to doctrinal application and spiritual transformation. Therefore, small group community is not optional. It is absolutely essential for Christians who desire to live out the truths of Scripture.

CHURCH DESIGN

Bill Beckham

The New Testament church was an amazing movement that "turned the world upside down." How was this possible? The first century church had no buildings, no seminaries, no support ministries, no organized Sunday school, no boards or societies, no professional clergy or television.

The first century revolution was possible because Jesus designed the New Testament church with a special wine and wineskin paradigm that he explains in Matthew 9:17. "Nor do men put new wine into old wineskins; otherwise the wineskins burst, and the wine pours out and the wineskins are ruined; but they put new wine into fresh wineskins and both are preserved." Jesus inaugurated a new day with his presence. He is the new wine and he sent the Holy Spirit to continue pouring his new wine into the church.

As the church seeks his new wine, it must also develop a wineskin to hold the new wine. The wineskin that was at work immediately after Pentecost met publicly at the Temple and met house to house (Acts 2:46; Acts 5:42; Acts 20:20). Today, God is renewing his church by his Spirit. But in most cases, churches are not designed to hold what God is doing because they're wineskins of leaky design.

THE CELL GROUP CHURCH SYSTEM

Jesus lived in community with twelve men. He chose to model a way of living together. He couldn't model this lifestyle with the masses. He had to focus his energy and show a small group his way of living in love for one another.

Small group researchers have demonstrated that as a small group grows in size, it becomes harder to develop a sense of community. In fact, when a group becomes larger than fifteen people, relating in community becomes quite difficult. Intimacy decreases as the number of communication lines increase.

Communication lines are the points of interaction between people in a group. The more people there are in the group, the greater number of communication lines. For instance, two people have two communication lines;

Tool

The formula to compute the number of communication lines is:

N X N – N = CL

N= Number of people
CL= Communication Lines

four people have 12 communication lines; 10 people have 90; 15 people have 210 communication lines.

After fifteen persons, there's no longer the opportunity for people to know each other intimately. Because Jesus valued intimacy and transparency, he chose to equip a community of twelve. The New Testament church is an extension of a system Jesus carefully built during the last three-and-a-half years of his life on earth.

We should not be surprised that when God created the church, he designed it as a system. Everything God has created, man refers to as a system: the solar system; the nervous system; the cell system. Some in the church believe systems to be unspiritual. Systems are associated with dead programs and rigid institutions. However, the opposite of system is chance, randomness, nothingness, and chaos. A system gives freedom while chaos restricts, limits, and distorts. Satan loves chaos and fragmentation and causes it at every opportunity. God unifies, integrates, and systematizes everything he touches.

The traditional church has an effective system for being the church on Sunday. However, the traditional church lacks a system for operating as the church the other six days of the week. The cell group church offers an effective seven-day-a-week system that mobilizes and multiplies every member for discipleship, ministry, leadership, and expansion.

Paul's picture of the church in Ephesians 4:16 describes this integrated quality. "From whom the whole body, being fitted and held together by that which every joint supplies, according to the proper working of each individual part, causes the growth of the body for the building up of itself in love." That's a classic description of systems integration.

An effective system consists of three elements: methods, mentors, and materials. A system will have a method for completing every task. An effective system also has a mentor: a way to oversee the method. The key mentor for a cell group church is the cell leader. The cell leader monitors tasks through the cell. And finally, a system has materials and tools to help accomplish the task. Without these materials and tools, we're asking people to "make bricks without straw."

THE SYSTEM DESIGN OF ISRAEL

God commanded Moses to develop the system of the nation of Israel around tens, fifties, hundreds, and thousands. These were God's numbers, selected because they represent universal principles of how people interconnect with each other. The numbers represent four roles or principles of leadership: Coordination (1000), Support (100), Supervision (50) and Implementation (10).

Within Old Testament Israel, the basic building block of life was the "household," which averages ten people. Households formed communities of fifties. These clusters of five households were to be supervised by one person. The next cluster was to be by "hundreds" (plural). We may understand this to be about 200-250 persons, thus once again assigning a cluster of four or five communities to be supervised. Finally, these clusters of "hundreds" were formed into groups of "thousands"—the final size for structuring the people of Israel.

With a conservative estimate of 1.5 million Israelites, this would mean there were 150,000 cells, or households, 30,000 clusters of fifties, 6,000 clusters of hundreds, and according to Exodus 24:9, seventy elders who would have been over the thousands.

JESUS DESIGNED THE CHURCH WITH A LARGE AND A SMALL GROUP BALANCE

The New Testament church was balanced between corporate community and cell community: between a large group expression and a small group expression. Today God is restoring this balance through key churches that have been experimenting with small groups for more than forty years.

This design of the church can be visualized in the analogy of a bird with two wings. The two wings mutually support each other and create a divine synergism that results in holiness and harvest. This simple design integrates the pieces and parts of the church into a cohesive whole. The following story of the two-winged church is a paradigm picture of the large group and small group design of the church.

Once upon a time, God created a church with two wings. One wing was a large-group wing, and the other was a small-group wing. With these two wings the church could soar high into the heavens, come into the presence of the Creator, and do his bidding over all the earth.

One day the wicked serpent, which had no wings, came to the two-winged church and said, "Do you know you can fly with just one wing? Yes! You can fly with just a large-group wing." The church that had been created with two wings began trying to fly with just the large-group wing. Sure enough, if it beat its large-group wing long enough and hard enough, it could get airborne. But it never flew very high, never went very far from its original takeoff point, and as one-winged things are prone to do, many times it went in circles.

This happened sometime in the fourth century.

From that time forward, the church that had been created as a two-winged church used only the large-group wing. Finally the small-group wing atrophied at the side of the two-winged church.

From time to time, the church remembered those days when it was able to soar high into the heavens, come into the presence of the Creator, and do his bidding over all the earth. But now it was too late. The two-winged church had become a one-winged, earth-bound institution.

One day the Creator returned and recreated another two-winged church—with a large-group wing and a small-group wing. Once again the church could soar high into the heavens, come into the presence of the Creator, and do his bidding over all the earth.

SATAN DESIRES TO DESTROY THE CHURCH'S COMMUNITY DESIGN

The conflict of the ages is Satan's determination to thwart God's plan for man to live in community. Satan has tempted man to build significance upon achievements, not primary relationships. The lineage in Genesis 4 reveals this attempt of man to find meaning in achievements rather than in relationships.

- Cain's significance was that he built a city (v. 17).
- Jabal's significance was that raised livestock (v. 20).
- Jubal's significance was that he was a musician (v. 21).
- Tubal-Cain's significance was that he forged tools (v. 22).
- Lamech's significance was that he murdered two people (v. 23).

Then, the Bible records a new lineage that goes back to Adam and Eve (v. 25). This lineage was based on community: "At that time men began to call on the name of the Lord" (v. 26). For seven generations, we know nothing about the achievements of this new blood line. All we're told is how long each man lived. This is important because when man is living in community with God, every year is precious!

Finally, parallel to Lamech, the crazed murderer, we have Enoch, who "walked with God" three hundred years. Then he was no more, because "God took him away." Thus, in these earliest accounts of man, we see the gulf between those who chose God and lived in community with him and one another, and those who sought self-aggrandizement and personal power.

But Satan's greatest *coup d'etat* was when he inspired the Edict of Bishops, which permanently divided the "clergy" from the "laity" and removed ministry from the body of Christ. No longer would the people of God become responsible to and for each other. This changed the divine design of the church, but God has prepared the way, through the cross, to restore his divine design of the church in order to demonstrate his divine nature through the church.

RESULTS OF THE FLAWED DESIGN

One author has argued, "All the major problems of the church today, other than sin, can be traced back 1700 years, to when the church became an audience."[10]

The one-winged church is often called the traditional church. Ralph Neighbour refers to it as the PBD church: the program-based design church. The cell church movement in Brazil uses the term auditorium church.

In the popular devotional booklet, *Our Daily Bread*, Henry G. Bosch tells the amusing story of what happened when a customer in a small store discovered that Eddie, a slow-moving clerk, wasn't around.

"Where's Eddie? Is he sick?"

"Nope," came the reply. "He ain't workin' here no more."

"Do you have anyone in mind for the vacancy?" inquired the customer.

"Nope! Eddie didn't leave no vacancy!"

Then Bosch applies the story to the church. "There are quite a few Eddies in most churches today. They leave, and no one even notices. Why? First, because there's no real sense of the body of Christ in which members are involved in a functioning manner. Second, many, by their own decision have chosen to sit on the church bench on the sidelines of the action."[11] "Eddies" exist under the radar screen of giving ministry but are highly visible when it comes time to receive ministry.

The author of this amusing story is describing a prevailing illness of the institutional church that still infects creative churches. A large percentage of church members (often estimated to be eighty percent or more) contribute little to the life and ministry of the church. Like "Eddie," these members are consumers, not producers. They're consumer Christians because the traditional church has no viable context in which to make them producers, or use them in a productive way. Staff-based churches mass-produce consumers rather than producers.

The more successful a church is in attracting members, the more pressure is placed upon the staff to minister to all the new consumer members. In addition to providing the church's spiritual ministry, the staff must also organize, oversee, and motivate twenty percent of the productive members to provide the programs and activities necessary to attract and keep the other eighty percent who are consumers.

This is an "upside-down" consumer system. The program system exists because twenty percent of its members maintain programs for the other eighty percent. This is a classic distribution system.

This consumer system creates a weight upon a small number of members in the church who are responsible for maintaining the system for the others. Without the twenty percent who are producers, the church cannot exist. The other eighty percent will let the church die. Hired professionals and volunteer members sacrificially give their time, money, and energy in order to keep the system running.

The church must change from a consumer to producer system, from a distribution system to a contribution system. Return to the church as Jesus designed it, and then "impossible" suggestions become possible. This is not easy, but it is possible!

COMBINING CONSUMER AND PRODUCER SYSTEMS

The cell church system depends upon twenty percent of its people equipping the other eighty percent to "do the work of ministry" in and through cell life. This system operates around three primary functions: weekly celebratory worship, weekly cell group community, and leadership coordination.

The old and new systems overlap in the functions of celebratory worship and leadership coordination. But the focus of the cell group church design rests upon the cell units where the members do the work of ministry. This mobilizes the entire membership and provides a basic unit with its own energy, resources, leaders, growth, nurture, and care.

ONE CHURCH DESIGN WITH MANY MODELS AND METHODS

During the last half of the twentieth century, the church has been challenged to function in the two dimensions of the New Testament: the gathered "whole church" and the "scattered" church in the home. Simply stated, God has asked the traditional large group church to include the cell group structure. With this balanced approach, the elements of the church that work best in the large-group wing function there and the elements of the church that work best in the small-group wing operate there.

The large group supports the small group and the small group supports the large group. This mutual support results in divine synergism as the power of God flows between the transcendent nature of God in the large-group expression and the immanent nature of God in the small-group expression.

Proponents of the modern cell-based church believe this design is THE intentional New Testament pattern of the church. But, is it presumptuous to claim one pattern as THE pattern? I don't believe so. To claim one method or set of materials or organizational structure as THE way would be wrong.

No method is THE New Testament method! No materials are THE materials! No organizational structure is THE organizational structure. But, the large group and small group community design is THE pattern of the Church because that's the pattern established by Christ in the New Testament in order for his followers to live out the community nature of God.

CELL GROUPS IN THE HISTORY OF THE CHURCH

By Bill Beckham

Habakkuk is a book about historical paradigms: God's perspective of history and Habakkuk's view of history. In three brief chapters we see how the two paradigms differ and how Habakkuk's view of history changes as he focuses his attention on God. God wants us to be excited about what he is doing in history. "Look among the nations! Observe! Be astonished! Wonder! Because I am doing something in your days you would not believe if you were told."

In the book's beginning, Habakkuk complained and talked a lot! But eventually he went to his place of duty and listened. "I will stand on my guard post and station myself on the rampart and I will keep watch to see what he will speak to me."

What did Habakkuk see? What do you see when you look out upon history? It depends on which direction you look and what you're looking for! The prophet saw violence, silence, iniquity, cruelty, strife, and injustice when he was looking at Israel. He also saw the Chaldeans and was filled with dread and fear. He heard mocking insults and saw evil, treachery, and images of fierce battle horses.

Finally Habakkuk saw and heard God: his vision, glory, holiness, mercy, splendor, radiance, power, anger, voice, indignation, salvation, and strength. Only then was the prophet able to properly interpret and boldly face history as it was being written in his day. Today, we must look for God in history and interpret history from his perspective.

HOLY HISTORY AND HISTORICAL FOOTNOTES

History is important to God because history is the story of his work in and through his creation. God moves all of history toward his divine purpose and we are part of that history.

In secular history, spiritual events are often seen as insignificant footnotes to the political and sociological events in the world. Abraham, Moses,

David, and even Christ receive only passing mention in secular history and, if it were not for the Bible, would be completely left out of the history of mankind. Modern secular historians are recording September 11, 2001, and are writing about New York City, Osama bin Laden, and the first war of the twenty-first century.

However, in holy history, secular events are footnotes to what God is doing. When God gives his historical account of the early days of the twenty-first century, he may talk about the churches in China, the Christians in Indonesia, and what he's doing in your life and church. The historical events that are so important to secular historians will only be the backdrop and footnote for God's holy history.

HISTORY TODAY AND IN THE FIRST CENTURY

God's holy history is just as important in the twenty-first century as it was in the first century. Every Christian and every church in every age are part of God's holy history and are provided with his presence, power and purpose! How can God use modern Christians like he used Paul, Luther, and Wesley? God can use individuals and churches in his holy history because he's the one writing the history. This is the fulfillment of Jesus' promise that "Greater things shall you do" and, "More blessed are those who have not seen but who believe."

THE HISTORICAL ASSAULT AND COUNTERASSAULT ON THE NATURE OF GOD

For the past 2000 years, the Holy Spirit has continued to pass on Jesus' New Testament community design. Jesus established the first community model of the church. Then the apostles, early converts, and eventually Paul, continued to establish this same design in Jerusalem, Judea, Samaria, and the entire Mediterranean world. The church remembered its community nature for several hundred years after Christ. This community and corporate memory explains the presence of the community-based church throughout history, in spite of the assault of Satan and the opposition of religious structures.

For the first several centuries, Satan tried his best to deceive the early church with an attack upon the nature of God. But the early church countered Satan at every point and beat back each assault. In the end, the revelation truth about the nature of God triumphed and the church deservedly celebrated victory!

However, while the church was busy defending the faith and winning the battles against theological frontal attacks, Satan counterattacked from the rear. In the fourth century, during the time of the Roman Emperor Constantine, Satan attacked the small group: the place where the nature of God could be experienced and lived out in practical every day community. The church suffered severe damage when small group community was stopped and spiritual ministry by ordinary Christians was virtually eliminated. The church was restructured as an institution, dependent on a building and professional leaders. For good measure, the church was married to the state and became either the lord or servant of political powers.

CONNECTING THEOLOGICAL AND STRUCTURAL DOTS

A strong case can be made that a parallel large group/small group stream was flowing throughout history underneath the model established by Constantine. Several facts seem to logically support the existence of this parallel stream theory.

First, if this kind of community-based church existed in the periods of history we know about, such as with Wesley, it probably also existed someplace in the periods of history we don't know.

Second, this pattern of church was the context of everything that happened in the early church. The authors of the New Testament lived and wrote in a community environment. We should not be surprised if those who read the New Testament in the centuries that followed actually replicated not only the theology of the New Testament church, but also the community structure. The theology and nature of the church leads back to some kind of large group and small group expression.

Third, some Christians, even within the traditional church, continued to live in small group community life in orders and special ministries.

Fourth, if God has placed this essential vision within hearts of twenty-first century Christians, he could do the same in previous centuries of the church, even if the evidence isn't recorded in history.

Fifth, this model can survive persecution. Therefore, we should expect the New Testament wineskin to have survived underground during even the most severe persecution from pagan governments or the institutional church. If community Christianity has been necessary to survive persecution in China today, why wouldn't it be necessary to survive persecution during other centuries?

For several reasons, the specifics about this kind of church in history are not well documented.

First, books in general were rare. Books about alternate ways of being church weren't high on the ecclesiastical or political publishing list. Second, the people writing and editing the books were killing those who were doing church differently. Heretics don't get good press. Third, these streams had to exist out of sight from those in power in order to survive. Fourth, like Jesus with the authorities of his day, these movements were considered to be insignificant and unimportant to the "real" events of history.

Finally, modern historians with the traditional "auditorium" paradigm of church have overlooked a different model. Connecting the dots of community from the first century to modern times is difficult enough when one is looking for it. But, when Constantine's cathedral, rather than Christ's community, is the pervading paradigm, the historical community dots are almost impossible to connect.

But they are there! Reading between the lines of what history we have, one may conclude that a more New Testament structure of the church coexisted in some form with the more visible Constantine cathedral, the Catholic Church, and state churches.

PATRICK AND IRELAND

As early as the fifth century in Ireland, Patrick seems to have used a more New Testament approach that was different from the traditional Constantine model. Patrick established a community-based church in a forted monastic environment.

Comgall lived in one of these "communities" in the sixth century. Hearing of the death of his confessor, he wrote, "My soul-friend has died and I am headless … for a man without a soul-friend is a body without a head."[12] This vivid expression reveals Comgall's deep commitment to community life as the way of holiness, a conviction that resulted in his establishing one of Ireland's largest and most renowned monasteries, Bangor.

In the sixth century, the Iona community was established by the great Irish missionary Columba and is one of the best examples of this monastic community life. Missionaries traveled from that island-community to Scotland, England, Europe, (and some think) even to North America.

Written history is sketchy during these early centuries for the reasons stated above. However, hints of community life crop up during every period of awakening and revival. Sometime around the year 1000, the memory from past history, the message found in the New Testament, and the corruption in the Constantine Church, caused political and sociological reactions that were accompanied by the restoration of community life.

THE "RESTORATION" MOVEMENT

For several centuries before the Reformation, the church experienced powerful forces of restoration. These movements were intent upon restoring the life of the New Testament church, not just reforming the existing church and changing its theology. Most of the early restoration streams had a small group community expression in one form or another.

At the end of the first millennium, Waldo Valdes, a Frenchman from Lyons, founded one of the early parallel restoration movements in the Piedmont region of the Alps. The motto of the Waldensians was, "Into darkness, light."

The Catholic Inquisition found numerous Waldensian communities in the Danube Valley in Austria and in Northern Germany in the fourteenth century. An Inquisition police report written at that time stated that the Waldensians were divided into small groups with certain individuals responsible for the care of each group. "These various small groups, to a certain degree, were independent, and able to pursue their particular vision of the religious life."[13]

Other reform streams flowed out of the theology and practices of the Waldensians. John Huss, the great Bohemian (Czech) preacher, followed the theology and small group community approach of the Waldensians and had many Waldensian followers. Consequently, he was accused of being a Waldensian at his trial and was martyred in 1415. Huss had operated outside of the Constantine Church.

During the twelfth century, another group began to live out the community life of the New Testament and Waldensian model. The Brethren desired to restore New Testament community life and to escape the Constantine/Catholic model. In 1457, this group formally organized a church called the Unitas Fratrum, the Unity of the Brethren, later to be known as the Moravian Church. They suffered great persecution and only survived because of their small group community structure.

THE REFORMATION

An impressive monument stands in the city of Worms where the famous Reformation statement attributed to Luther was made. "Here I stand. I can do no other, so help me God." Luther is at the top of the monument surrounded by other men who helped set the Reformation into motion. Some of the faces are Wycliffe, Huss, Erasmus, and Zwingli.

Many of these men suffered and died not only for the theology of the church but also for the right to live out the theology of the church in a New Testament community way. A significant number of those leaders desired to restore the church to its New Testament pattern, not reform the existing church.

The New Testament memory and message being lived out around him in the restoration streams of the church undoubtedly had great influence on Martin Luther. Luther seriously considered changing the Constantine structure in the early days of the Reformation by adding a small group element to the church. "Those who want to be Christians in earnest and who profess the Gospel with hand and mouth should sign their names and meet alone in a house somewhere to pray, to read, to baptize, to receive the sacrament, and to do other Christian works."[14]

However, in the end Luther did not complete reformation at the point of structure because of personal, practical, and political reasons. The opportunity to marry reformation doctrine and restoration community life was thwarted. The two streams coexisted side by side with reformation receiving the most visible recognition in historical accounts. The restoration stream continued in its unrecognized and almost silent journey through history. Two hundred years after the Reformation, God merged the two streams of reformation and restoration in a model that could not be ignored in history.

WESLEY'S HISTORICAL MODEL

The theology of the Reformation obviously influenced Wesley's movement in the eighteenth century. Wesley's heart was "strangely warmed" as he listened to a message from Luther's Commentary on Romans. However, Wesley's movement has even stronger ties to the restoration stream of the church because it contributed to his understanding of church life, church structure, and his interpretation of church history. Wesley believed the spirit and practice of primitive Christianity could and should be recaptured.

Written Resources

- *John Wesley's Class Meeting* by D. Michael Henderson

He "did not view church history as the progressive unfolding of God's plan, but rather as deviations from the correct model of Christianity followed by occasional returns to it. He looked upon his own movement as a retrogression toward primitive church life, instead of a progressive movement coming out of Anglicanism."[15]

In 1722, Count Zinzendorf began an experiment in restoring New Testament communal and community life. He assembled Bohemian and Moravian Brethren and Pietists on his German Saxony estate in a special community called Herrnhut. John Wesley was deeply impacted by the New Testament life of these groups during a personal visit to Herrnhut. He was also influenced by the spiritual faith and life of a group of Moravians he met on his voyage to Georgia in the United States. After returning from Georgia in a state of despair, a personal study with the Moravian teacher, Peter Bohler, led Wesley to his personal conversion experience.

The gear that moved Wesley's system was New Testament holiness. Wesley's watch cry was "to spread scriptural holiness throughout the land." Secular historians credit Wesley's movement for saving England from a bloody revolution such as happened in France and other countries in Europe.

In order to live out holiness, Wesley developed what Michael Henderson calls "an interlocking group system." This system was made up of three different types of groups that resulted in harvest and holiness.

Wesley called his three interlocking groups "bands," "societies," and "classes." In modern terms, Wesley's groups were leadership and accountability groups (bands), large group worship (society) and cells (classes). Wesley put the three groups in place over a period of almost fifteen years. He began with a leadership accountability group in 1729 while at Oxford University. These bands focused on affective attitudes of the heart. Then ten years later, he added the large group worship group that he called a society. The society focused on cognitive understanding of the mind.

After developing the band and the society, Wesley was still frustrated with the lack of close pastoral oversight, especially for those who had been recently converted. He did not see the radical change in psychomotor behavior that he observed in the New Testament. Later, Wesley admitted that the solution to this problem was discovered quite by surprise. "At length, while we were thinking of quite another thing, we struck upon a method for which we have cause to bless God ever since."[16]

Evaluating the "class meeting" (cell) Henderson concludes, "The class meeting turned out to be the primary means of bringing millions of England's most desperate people into the liberating discipline of Christian faith."[17]

WARP AND WOOF

When weaving cloth, the "warp" is the vertical thread and the "woof" is the horizontal thread. These are woven together to manufacture all cloth. Because of this principle, cloth has strength and suitability. If threads run only in one direction, a finger can be poked through the cloth and it will not be of any use.

The illustration is helpful in understanding the visible and invisible aspects of the church as they were changed in the course of church history. The New Testament church operated in both the visible (warp and vertical) and invisible (woof and horizontal). In the fourth century, Constantine began the audience church, a church cloth with only vertical threads. This church design wasn't effective in doing ministry and missions because it had no small group expression.

Later in history, orders began to develop in the Catholic Church. These orders were an attempt to do the work of ministry and missions (the woof and horizontal). Even the early vertical-thread church knew the church was supposed to be involved in ministry and mission.

The Reformation continued the audience (vertical-thread) design of the church, even though Luther intended to change the structure. During this time, denominations, boards, and societies developed. These were necessary to do the work of ministry and mission that the audience church could not do.

After World War II, visionary leaders began to develop parachurch ministries which worked "alongside" the church to carry out mission and ministry functions. Campus Crusade was born to help the church witness. World Vision desired to help the church minister. The Navigators wanted to complete the church's disciple-

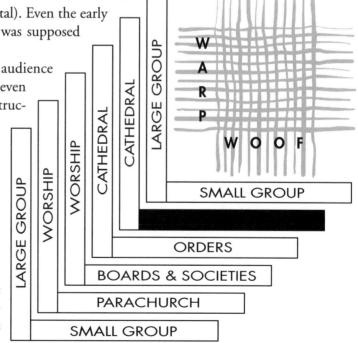

ship mandate. Youth with a Mission desired to help the church do missions.

However, today God is restoring the New Testament warp and woof design of the church. The cell-based church is visible and stable in the large group and also does ministry and missions through the small group expression. Therefore, an operating cell-based church does ministry. A cell-based church does missions. A cell-based church disciples its own members. A cell-based church witnesses and does evangelism in its small groups. A cell-based church trains its own leaders.

OUR MOMENT IN HISTORY

Billy Graham, at the 1966 World Congress on Evangelism in Berlin said: "Every generation is crucial: every generation is strategic. But we are not responsible for the past generation, and we cannot bear full responsibility for the next one. However, we do have our generation! God will hold us responsible at the judgment seat of Christ for how well we fulfilled our responsibilities and took advantage of our opportunities."

During a period of 2000 years, God has overcome all obstacles in order to preserve his church's community design. In the twenty-first century, God can once again use the modern New Testament community church to bring about first-century harvest in the world and New Testament holiness within his church. God is writing a new chapter of his holy history for this century, a significant movement that will record the greatest harvest his church has ever experienced.

Wesley wrote in his Journal on Easter Day, April 2, 1738. "I preached in our College chapel on, 'The hour cometh, and now is, when the dead shall hear the voice of the Son of God ...'"

Wesley's comment was, "I see the promise; but it is afar off ...The hour cometh: but, it is afar off ..." Then, during the next pages, Wesley had his Aldersgate experience when his heart "was strangely warmed." Afterward, he writes in his Journal on Pentecost Sunday, "Afar off? The hour cometh—and now IS!" John Wesley is changed and placed in the presence of the Holy Spirit.

James S. Stewart comments on this inner transformation. "We glorify the past, and say, 'O had I lived in that great day when Christ was really here!' But why dwell regretfully upon an age that is gone? Christ is here! The Lord and Giver of life is here. The hour cometh—and now is!"[18]

The name of God is not "I was or I will be." The name of God is "I

Am!" God is personal and present tense and living today. History is now!

CHARACTERISTICS OF CHRISTIAN MOVEMENTS

A Christian movement is birthed by God and continues as long as it focuses on him. It's a process, going through several stages before reaching its full expression. A movement may stagnate, die, or be revived at any one of the stages.

A movement is able to adapt to, and bridge, diverse cultures and ethnic differences, while maintaining the core truth that birthed it. Also, a movement is simple and perpetuates itself by meeting practical needs, rather than by teaching complex theories.

Cell Group Vision Team Exercise

How well does the cell group vision fit with your church's tradition?

A Christian movement has an historical context and is more than a temporary fad. The life of a movement is ordained by God, but determined by the degree of human vision and commitment. Jesus' movement has continued for two thousand years. Communism, on the other hand, has lasted as a worldwide movement for less than eighty years.

From a human perspective, Christian movements look messy and out of control. Is this surprising? Jesus compared the nature of the Spirit to the wind, which goes where it wants and no man can control it. Christian movements are organized and controlled by the Holy Spirit.

For five decades, the church expressed in small group community has been a 'messy' movement. Even the name is disorganized! It has been called the small group movement, the cell church movement, and the house church movement. Different streams associated with the movement include the seeker church, the mega church, the purpose-driven church, and the 'groups of twelve' church.

So is this movement winding down after fifty years? Is the shelf life of this movement about to expire? Is it imploding upon itself because of the multiplication of different streams? Or, is it just now ready to explode? Do these five decades reveal the patience of God in preparing a base for major harvest in the twenty-first century? I believe the latter is true and that in the twenty-first century God will use this movement for the greatest harvest the church, or world, has ever seen.

Questions asked about the movement's past five decades help us understand its development. Similarly, questions being asked right now reveal the direction of the movement in the twenty-first century.

EARLY QUESTIONS

What is this thing in Seoul? The modern movement was kicked off in South Korea in the ministry of Paul Yonggi Cho. In retrospect, it's obvious that Yoido Full Gospel Church was not a teaching model for the movement, but an "attention-getting" model. God attracted the attention of leaders searching for a more New Testament ministry model.

Can I transplant the system? Understandably, many pastors wanted to experience the same kind of growth they heard about in this big church. Some went to Seoul, saw the growth, and drew an obvious, but incomplete conclusion. Others drew the same conclusion by staying home and reading about the church, or listening to those who made the pilgrimage. The conclusion was, "I can experience this church's growth by using its structures."

Hundreds of churches reorganized and experienced some growth— while many others failed. The reason? You can never change a structure until you change a value. We don't transplant systems and structures. We transplant values and life. That's the first lesson God wanted the church in the twentieth century to learn.

So the next question during the life of the movement arose from these failures with structures:

Will small groups work outside of Korea? Many leaders concluded that small groups either failed, or would fail, in their country because small groups only work in certain cultures. Today, small groups 'are working' on every continent.

GROWING PAIN QUESTIONS

Where do we go from here? Visionaries like Ralph Neighbour and Carl George, along with others, attempted to understand the values and theology of small groups and to express them in practical implementation models and materials. Neighbour wrote about the cell church and George explained the movement as mega churches. Bill Hybels began with the values of small group community and developed the Willow Creek model in Illinois.

However, during the development of these early models, the new wine was often heavily influenced by the old large group structures. Moreover, Bible studies, care groups, and fellowship groups dominated the dynamics and mechanics of the new small groups. Leaders once again experienced some less-than-satisfying success with small groups, and that frustration led to other questions.

Is a small group cultural or theological? As the difficulty in changing to this kind of church became more obvious, a new question was posed. "Are small groups just the 'setting in life' of the New Testament church? Were small groups in the first century cultural structure, or essential theology?" This question gave pastors a way out of the pressure to implement New Testament groups. After experiencing difficulties in using small groups, one pastor said, "That's the way they did it in the first century. We do it in a large group today." These questions about the small groups in the New Testament and the twentieth century led to the next question.

What is the theology of small groups? A Christian movement cannot sustain itself unless it eventually defines itself theologically. Over the past decades, small group theology developed around the foundational truth of the nature of God. God in his very nature is community: Father, Son, and Spirit. Therefore, the Trinity is the primary concept used to explain the theology of community and guide the life of the church and every Christian.

Defining the theology of community has brought the movement to another level. Now leaders can no longer dismiss small groups as just a passing method. If small group community is part of the basic theology of God's nature, then being part of community is no longer just an option. Leaders can no longer debate the merits of small groups because the value of small groups is now established in the very nature of God. Leaders and churches must now find a way to live in small group community!

RECENT QUESTIONS

During the last decade a new set of questions has been asked about the movement. These questions are not about the validity of using small groups, but about the nature of such churches. What do they look like and how do they work? The house church movement reacts against the failures of the large group and asks, "Is the large group necessary?"

Another question arises because the most visible models for the movement to this point have been very large churches: "Is the small group strategy primarily a large church method?" However, a large percent of churches in the world today have less than one hundred active adult members. For no other reason than their numbers, these small churches are critical to the growth of the movement. The house church movement in China also proves that this isn't just a large church phenomenon.

Questions are being posed in other areas as well. How do church planting and support ministries fit into the movement? Several current questions in the movement deserve special attention.

Is there only one model and method? This is one of the most important recent questions about the movement. It developed because of the great success of the Groups of Twelve (or G-12) model in Bogota, Colombia. History affirms that the Holy Spirit is able to use many different models and methods in a movement he controls. There isn't one model or one method or one set of materials. In the future, the movement will have other models that look like 'the' model. But these special models are just God's way of making mid-course corrections and reminding us of forgotten or neglected values that must continue to drive the movement.

Does the movement need to be controlled from the top by entitled leaders? This is a question that has been asked with increasing frequency over the past several years. The fact is, the movement has lasted five decades with only the Holy Spirit as the divine administrator. It won't survive many more decades if human apostles tie it to themselves, box it into certain models, codify its life, or forget to lead as servants.

Leaders may be nouns or verbs. Noun leaders must have titles and positions. Verb leaders lead by example. Noun leaders say, "Listen to me" and "Obey me." Verb leaders say, "Follow me" and, "Let me serve you." A movement of God will not long survive leaders who demand titles and positions.

Is it man-made groups or God-made cells? This question is important for the expansion of the movement in the twenty-first century because it goes to the heart of the nature and DNA of a small group. Is Christ in the midst of each group in divine presence, resurrection power, and eternal purpose?

The cell church movement will not survive as a small group movement, as a church planting movement, as a church growth movement, or as a large church movement. Nor will one-dimensional Bible studies, care groups, and task groups penetrate radical religions, transform secular cultures, and change deteriorating societies. This movement will only continue if Christ shows up in these groups/cells as he promised. This question must be answered with passion and resolve that: "Every basic implementing unit of this movement must operate as a God-made, Christ-indwelled, and Spirit-empowered community."

WILL IT CONTINUE?

This movement's effectiveness in the future will be directly related to the answers of the following questions:

- Is the movement flowing out of the nature and heart of God?
- Does the Holy Spirit control the movement?
- Are Christians willing to die in order to live in community with Christ and each other?
- Are God-made, Christ-indwelled, and Spirit-empowered cells the basic implementing unit of this movement?
- Is this a local church movement?

Ultimately this movement is about God and how he expresses himself as the body of Christ on earth and how he empowers that body through the Holy Spirit. As long as the movement is about him and is empowered by him, he will use it for his purpose of creating a church of holiness and harvest in the twenty-first century.

CELL GROUP CHURCH VALUES

Bill Beckham

The values of a person dictate how he lives. Values tell us how "we want to act, consistent with our mission, along the path toward achieving our vision." And, "core values are guiding stars to navigate and make decisions day to day."[19]

A vision statement not based on right values will eventually expose itself as just a hollow document, wasting paper. A mission statement without right values will degenerate into an emotional but meaningless slogan. Strategy without right values will lack a common commitment, will be consumed by unworthy goals, and will be compromised by personal ambition and unethical behavior. An organization can have a well thought-out vision, a passionate mission statement, and an aggressive strategy. However, if the company lacks the proper value base, the end product can be a culture of destruction.

FOUR TRUTHS ABOUT VALUES

Understanding four truths about values prepares a church for the challenge that accompanies meaningful change. Leaders and members must come to grips with these truths if they're to live out the values needed to develop effective cell groups.

Truth #1: "We do what we value and value what we do."

A church doesn't do what it writes in a vision statement or mission statement. It will not do what someone persuades it to do in a slick presentation, or what someone promotes as a guaranteed success. A church doesn't do what it learns about in an exciting conference. In the end, a church will do what it values. A good church may have good values written in a good vision statement and still fail to implement those values for the following reasons.

One, the stated value is not the actual value. Another value is the real value. Perceived values are those we honor in our words but don't actually implement. Actual values are the ones lived out. "Every member a minister," and "the priesthood of every believer," may be stated values, but the church may actually value professionally trained clergy doing the ministry as hired holy priests.

The second reason for not implementing stated values is that structures formerly developed to implement a good value have become the value. For example: Sunday school was a structure developed in the United States to implement the value of Bible study. For many churches, the institution of Sunday school itself has become the actual value. Choir is a structure developed to implement music in worship. However, choir may become the value, rather than worship.

Three, no appropriate structure exists to implement the stated value. I may value evangelism but have no structure for actually doing what I really value.

Or, four, two good values are not balanced. One value neutralizes the other. For instance, a church values celebration worship and cell life. However, celebration worship receives the majority of time and resources. Cell life is neutralized!

No matter what we say, in reality, "we do what we value and value what we do!"

Truth #2: "You never change a structure until you change a value."

"The basic idea is that … everything else—the strategy, structure, systems, skills, and style—are derivatives, that is, they ought to flow with, not against, core values and stream realities."[20]

We're often ineffective in changing values because we mix up values and structures. It's impossible to change structure until a corresponding value has changed. The assumption is that a good sermon or pep talk about new structures or methods will result in meaningful change. However, reorganizing and changing structures will make no difference until we change the underlying values. We'll simple apply our old set of values to the new structures.

For centuries, leaders have tried to bring about change by rearranging existing structures, maximizing familiar activities, and increasing the amount of work. These words by Petronius Arbiter were found on a scroll written in 66 A.D. "We trained hard, but it seemed that every time we form up into teams, we would be reorganized. I was to learn later in life, we tend to meet any new situation by reorganizing and a wonderful method it can be for creating the illusion of progress while producing confusion, inefficiency and demoralization." This Roman discovered in the first century the truth about reorganizing structures. "You never change a structure until you change a value."

Truth #3: "Where the vision is unclear, the cost is always too high."

Disagreements may arise among leaders in a church about the meaning and implications of the vision, and when this occurs, people will always see the cost as being too high. "In the presence of greatness, pettiness disappears. In the absence of a great dream, pettiness prevails."[21] This is another way to say, "Without vision, the people perish." The vision must be big and compelling. It must be from God and it must be clear.

Clarity doesn't mean that everyone must understand every detail. It means people must understand the call of the vision. They must understand where the church is going. They must see a vivid picture of what it means to be the church today. They need not know every detail about how the vision works; they only need to know that the vision is so great that it will be worth the cost.

Jesus communicated his vision for over three years to his followers, and they still didn't understand. When it came time for Jesus to go to the cross, they found the cost too high. They couldn't see Jesus' vision. After the resurrection, no cost was too high for them. They became bold and sacrificial to the point of death. Before the cross, they were committed to their own vision for Jesus. After the resurrection, Jesus' vision became the focus of their commitment.

When people don't see the vision, they'll find themselves unwilling to pay the vision cost. They might say, "I don't understand the vision," but in reality, they're trying to fit the vision into their plans. They use, "I don't understand the vision," to cover up deeper feelings of, "I'm not willing to pay the price," or, "I'm not willing to submit to the leaders with the vision."

Those with hidden agendas, who try to fit God's vision into their own vision and aren't committed to a vision in the beginning, will usually bail out of the vision no matter how it's explained to them or modified for them. At the worst possible time, even friends may bail out of a vision after realizing they can't change the vision to their own agenda. The vision must be clearly restated, inviting those who are willing to count the cost. "Where the vision is unclear, the cost is always too high."

Truth #4: "Vision plus vision equals division."

Dion Robert, pastor of a large cell group church in the Ivory Coast, teaches this important value principle. A church must have one consuming vision its leaders and members are committed to implement. That one vision will include all necessary implementing values. Multiple visions create chaos and fragmentation, and spiritual values are never effectively implemented in that kind of an environment.

Multiple and independent visions are a major problem in churches today. In fact, most churches are not guided by one integrated church vision, but by multiple ministries disguised as a church vision. Some members have a vision of worship or prayer. Others have a vision about Bible study. Children, youth, women's work, and men's work define the vision of other members. Some Christians have a vision to strengthen the family through marriage conferences or family seminars. Another person or group may be driven by special political visions that are superimposed upon the church. Others focus on one particular gift, such as deliverance or healing.

All these are good ministries. However, no matter how good it is, one ministry cannot be God's vision for a church. All ministries must fit into

God's vision for a church, not the other way around. When any one of the ministries mentioned above becomes the primary vision a person or group of persons imposes upon a church, that ministry becomes a kingdom in itself. And every kingdom has a king or queen over it, with loyal subjects around them. This is devastating for the vision and unity of a church. Multiple visions create individual kingdoms in which personal ministry is elevated over community. And individual kingdoms within a church create disunity, fragmentation, and rebellion.

In a church with multiple visions and kingdoms, the leaders must negotiate a truce with every kingdom whenever a major thrust is to be made. As long as the leaders of a church honor the treaties with the individual kingdoms, everything can remain relatively peaceful. But, if the individual ministry kingdoms are expected to become submissive to one integrated church vision, then war is declared. This has resulted in the "Balkanization" of the church: multiple kingdoms living together in an uneasy peace as separate entities in the same geographical area. Vision plus vision does equal division!

On the other hand, one consuming church vision brings order out of chaos and unrestrained fragmentation. Scripture reminds us that, "Where there is no vision, the people perish (are unrestrained)." This means that where there is vision, the people are restrained and saved.

CHRISTIAN VALUES ARE BASED IN BELIEFS

The values and beliefs of the Christian life grow out of relationship and community concepts. Jesus taught sets of God-beliefs and life-values. We will first consider five God-values that produce nine life-values, shaping the vision and culture of a church. These God-beliefs are associated with special family and relationship vocabulary, which grows out of the Trinitarian nature of God.

God-belief #1: God is Father! The Holy Spirit teaches believers to say, "Abba! Father!" (Romans 8:15 and Galatians 4:6). The phrase "Abba! Father!" reassures that God is personal, near, and loving. When we know God as "Abba" (Daddy or Papa), we feel part of his family. "Abba" Father is intimate, accepting, and approachable.

God-belief #2: Jesus Christ is incarnate Son! At the Jordan River, God the Father introduced Jesus as Incarnate Son. "You are my Son, whom I love; with you I am well pleased" (Mark 1:11). The Holy Spirit also teaches us to say, "Jesus Christ has come in the flesh" (John 16:14; Romans 8:9;

1 Corinthians 12:3). This incarnation phrase means the Son has come in the flesh and therefore knows our state and nature. He knows our weaknesses and temptations. Jesus in the flesh understands us.

God-belief #3: Jesus is savior, friend, and brother! Through the personal incarnation of Jesus, we know God as a caring and personal God, as friend (John 15:14-15), and brother (Hebrews 2:11-14). The Holy Spirit teaches us Jesus sacrificed his life for us. These are community words and concepts. God is approachable.

God-belief #4: The Holy Spirit is companion, comforter, and teacher! Jesus used these words to introduce his followers to the Holy Spirit. Through the Holy Spirit, we see God as our constant companion, omnipresent and indwelling. Through the Holy Spirit, God comforts like a father and mother. Through the Spirit, God is teacher as a father, mother, brother, and sister, teaching the family's youngest.

God-belief #5: We are God's children! These value words about God establish a special relationship between Christians. We are God's children, therefore we are family. When we know God as "Abba! Father!" we see others as "brother" and "sister." When God is "Abba! Father!" to us, we can live in community with him and with each other. The Holy Spirit wants every Christian to know God's personal love as Father and God's personal friendship as Jesus, the Son.

GOD-BELIEFS PRODUCE LIFE-VALUES

Jesus wanted his disciples to internalize several important values before Pentecost. The success of his movement would depend upon how well they learned the lessons of the five relationship beliefs about God and these nine values for living the life of Christ on earth.

Life-value #1: I submit to Jesus as Lord. This is the bridge value between God-beliefs and life-values. Jesus Christ as Lord is a relationship. When Jesus is Lord, then the values of life can be lived out. The Holy Spirit teaches every Christian to say: "Jesus is Lord!" because that confession establishes authority in the church family (Romans 10:9). This statement once and for all solves the issues of loyalty and obedience that are necessary for living out the Christian life values. God is loving Father, Jesus is incarnate Son, sacrificial friend and brother, the Holy Spirit is companion and comforter, and we are God's children, brothers and sisters in his family. But he is also Lord of Lords and King of Kings. The Christian life will not work until the truth of Lordship is established.

Life-value #2: I choose to live in community. This community value naturally grows out of the basic values that Jesus taught about the nature of God. If God is Father, then we are family (community)! These family words are the context for understanding and living out all the other values in community. Everyone is responsible and accountable. Everyone ministers and is ministered to by others. Leadership is service within a family context. A family plans for and celebrates the birth of children. A family nurtures every individual member. Jesus' disciples in every period of history must experience community, learn to deal with each other in forgiveness, learn to bear each other's burdens, and learn to enter into spiritual fellowship.

Life-value #3: I live by spiritual power. Disciples of Christ must learn to depend on God's power and not on human abilities. Jesus' kind of church will simply not work on human power and ability. Therefore, the leaders and early core must learn to allow his spiritual power to direct the church.

Life-value #4: I live by faith. Jesus' disciples had to learn how to walk in faith, which was the major objective of the entire Sermon on the Mount. He took them into situation after situation where absolute faith was demanded of them. Their faith was tested while in the boat during the storm on the Sea of Galilee. Over and over again, their trust and faith were stretched beyond human limits. This was a necessary value, because Jesus knew how much faith it would require to believe he had overcome death. This was necessary because the community would not work without faith.

Life-value #5: I am unconditionally committed to following Christ. Jesus' disciples had to learn to commit to him totally and completely. There could be no conditions and reservations if his church was to succeed. "For to me to live is Christ and to die is gain." Unconditional commitment means death, which is why this value is so difficult to embrace.

Life-value #6: I receive the indwelling presence of the Spirit. The disciples had to experience the indwelling presence of Christ even after he was no longer physically with them. Jesus carefully taught about the Holy Spirit because he would be with them and teach them all things.

Life-value #7: I see Jesus' Kingdom vision. The disciples had to understand the vision of the spiritual Kingdom of God on earth and learn that the vision was not political or physical, but spiritual.

Life-value #8: I walk in unity with other believers. The disciples had to experience the meaning of spiritual unity around Christ, not around common backgrounds, beliefs, or practices, but around a common Lord.

Jesus prayed to the Father that his followers would live in unity. Unity is a precious and essential value. Jesus cherished unity over all things because God in Trinity is in unity. Unity is the nature of God. Unity is an essential value in the word "community."

Life-value #9: My ministry is one of service. The disciples had to learn to be servants and to wash each other's feet. This was the final lesson Jesus taught them in the upper room. Leaders may only really learn this lesson while the movement is still simple and small.

Jesus teaches these same essential lessons today, if we're willing to walk with him through his initial stages of growth. These God-beliefs and life-values must be learned if a church is to function as a New Testament Church.

WHY DO WE DO WHAT WE DO?

Values are defined and lived out in layers or levels of life as seen in the Levels of Life chart. These "levels" make up our personal and social culture and are reference points all humans use in interpreting life. Decisions about every facet of life (personal, social, political, and religious) are made out of these levels. However, only Christians have access to the dynamic and powerful Level 5 that is the revelation and relationship of God.

Human culture is formed out of values and principles (Levels 3 and 4), and then the traditions and precedents (Levels 1 and 2) become the visible expression, structure, and skin of culture. The danger is that traditions and precedents may eventually replace the original values and principles that formed the culture. Then a culture becomes rootless, cut away from the values and principles that produced it. This is called a "cut flower civilization."

The picture is a long-stem flower that has been cut and put in a vase. The flower will last for days but will eventually dry up because it has no roots. Even a good religion can become a "cut flower." Cultures, persons, and religions must be constantly renewed at the deeper root levels of life. Eventually, all human and religious cultures die unless they are born and reborn out of the presence of God at Level 5.

Notice that values are in the middle of these levels or layers of life. For a Christian and Christian organization, values are formed out of a revelation vision of God that's expressed in the principles of Scripture. Then those God-beliefs are organized according to priorities and lived out in appropriate traditions.

Levels of Life

Level 1
Practices
"These are our traditions"
CUSTOM

Level 2
Priorities
"We always do it this way."
PRECEDENT

Level 3
Values
"This is what I believe."
CONVICTION

Level 4
Principles
"The Bible says."
TRUTH

Level 5
GOD
"This is God."
REVELATION

JESUS' CONFRONTATIONS

The Levels of Life chart helps explain the constant confrontations between Jesus and the religious authorities of his day. Jesus and the authorities would use the same words: "Temple," "Messiah," "Kingdom," and "the Law." But, they interpreted the words in radically different ways. For instance, Jesus taught that the Messiah would suffer and die. This was offensive to the authorities because they believed the Messiah would come and set up an earthly rule and overthrow Rome. The difference in understanding these concepts was so great that it eventually led to the death of Jesus.

How could these concepts cause such confrontation? The Levels of Life chart explains this. Jesus made decisions from the most basic level of life: God (Level 5). Every decision he made and every value he lived out came from his relationship to the Father. The authorities made decisions from their own cultural paradigms that were mostly rooted in traditions (Levels 1) and precedents (Level 2).

Levels 1 through 3 aren't bad, but must be constantly interpreted out of Level 4 and 5. Organizations and movements that begin at Level 4 or 5 almost always codify themselves at Level 1 and 2 and then force their values and beliefs into their traditions, customs, and precedents. The Jewish authorities had done exactly that. The question for us is: "Out of which level do we operate today?"

LEVELS LIVED OUT

Look at the "Levels of Life" chart. Familiar practices (Level 1) are the easiest and most obvious way to determine how I'm going to live. These are the traditions I've learned from childhood. They're the familiar customs that guide me in making decisions. My practices and traditions form a culture from which I interpret life around me. For instance, a family must establish some practices so everyone gets to work and school on time in the morning. Some kind of regular routine is helpful. Over a period of time, these "practices" become traditions and then are established as part of family culture.

Life can be lived out in the paradigm of priorities (Level 2) that are formed from personal and group experiences. "We always do it this way." At this level traditions are still important. However, precedents that have worked in the near past are included with traditions to make decisions.

Life decisions can also be made from personal and group values (Level 3). "This is what I believe." Values are deeply held convictions that formed traditions and priorities in the first place. These values are handed down from generation to generation and internalized through subtle teaching and reinforced experiences, and may or may not be stated in a written form. For instance, parents value good teeth for themselves and their children. Therefore, parents set priorities and develop traditions about how and when teeth are brushed.

Principles are an important part of the process for making decisions (Level 4). For example, medical books contain the principles of hygiene and health from which the values about brushing teeth are developed. For a Christian, the principles of life are contained in the Bible. What the Bible says should be the primary consideration in making decisions and living life. These biblical principles are the truths that formed the values from which our priorities and practices evolved.

However, even biblical principles do not go deep enough for Jesus. Jesus referred to Nicodemus as the teacher of Israel, implying that he understood biblical principles. However, Jesus told Nicodemus that he had not yet gone deep enough to understand the mystery of God or the secret of salvation. Nicodemus had to go to the source of God and be "born again."

Jesus is the only person whose every thought, attitude, and decision came out of the presence of God (Level 5). He interpreted every level of life out of his relationship with the Father. This was a natural process for Jesus and is God's expectation of every Christian. However, living in the presence of God isn't natural for Christians, because of the pressure of inward sin and outward culture.

The Holy Spirit takes every Christian individually by the hand and moves that person through these levels of life until he/she experiences God personally in divine revelation. This is the continuing process of sanctification. The Holy Spirit "comes along side" and walks every Christian through traditions to priorities, and then through priorities to deeply held convictions and values. From values, the Holy Spirit moves a Christian through biblical principles until the Christian stands in the presence of God himself. At the point of God, the Christian has reached the deepest level of revelation, relationship, community, and decision making.

When the Holy Spirit moves the Christian down through these layers of life to the point of God, the journey is only half over. Then, the Holy

Spirit must take the Christian back through the other levels of life. Out of the revelation relationship with God, the Christian interprets and applies the truths of Scripture. The Christian then applies living Scripture to deeply held convictions and values. The deeply held values are applied to priorities and traditions.

Traditions, priorities, values, and beliefs are only safe for making decisions about life when they're driven out of a personal revelation and relationship with God. Terrible things happen when a culture or religion replaces God as the base reality of life and decision making.

CULTURAL VALUES CAN BLIND, DEAFEN, HARDEN, AND SILENCE CHRISTIANS

In a little village in Germany sets a huge and ancient cathedral. The structure was originally a Roman cathedral, but after the Reformation became a Protestant church building. It was then adapted for various purposes at different times in history. Among other things, the compound has been a hospital, an orphanage, and a center for the homeless and destitute. Additional buildings were built to facilitate the changing purposes of the complex.

At some point, a partition wall was built at the end of the huge cathedral nearest to the village. The result was a lovely little chapel that seats several hundred worshippers in two sections. Each Sunday the villagers would enter the compound through a special gate and then enter the chapel through a special door. Thick hedges obstructed the view of the worshippers into the other parts of the compound.

When Hitler first came to power, the compound was used as a holding center for political prisoners such as communists, Democratic Socialists, homosexuals, and gypsies. Jews and other "undesirables" from the surrounding regions were systematically arrested, sent to the facility, and processed for eventual assignment to the infamous concentration death camps. This included all the Jews, who made up thirty percent of the village's population at the beginning of the war. Not a single Jew remained in the village at the end of the war. One woman from the village, listed as a Lutheran priest, was imprisoned because she protested the arrest of her Jewish neighbors. This suggests that the people in the village knew what was going on in the compound.

To accommodate the increasing number of prisoners, the vast space in the cathedral was remodeled into several floors with rooms and holding cells. Opposite the wall where people gathered for worship in the chapel are torture rooms, where chains anchored in the walls can still be seen. Prisoners who survived the concentration camps tell the story of hearing songs of worship on Sundays coming from the chapel. If the prisoners could hear the villagers, then the villagers could surely hear the prisoners. However, these villagers had no ears to hear sounds beyond the chapel, no eyes to see what was going on, no voices to speak about it, and no hearts to show compassion.

The Nazi culture and self-preservation had become their controlling god. When we're stuck in the wrong paradigm, culture and fear can make us blind, deaf, dumb, and dead to what's happening around us. Only convictions and values lived out of the presence of God will see, hear, speak, and feel in such situations. Only a relationship with the living God will give truth and courage in the face of oppressive culture and social injustice, when punishment is possible for speaking up.

TWENTY-FIVE FACTORS THAT DEFINE VALUES

The contrasts in this section are obviously "exaggerated," but they are real. The contrasts go deeper than structure and reflect the value systems that operate in different church designs.

Location: A) The church is located in a building and cannot exist without a building. B) The church is located both in a small group setting such as houses and a large group setting. The church is the people and can exist even without a location and building.

Relationships: A) The church stresses information more than relationships and uses an information-based design. B) The church stresses intimacy and helping one another. It's a transformation-based design.

Discipleship: A) The church disciples with classes and notebooks. Values are not shaped and there is little modeling. B) The church disciples by mentoring and modeling so that values are shaped.

Spiritual Gifts: A) The church limits the use of spiritual gifts and the number of Christians using spiritual gifts by its structures. B) The church expects all members to use spiritual gifts to build up others in cell group community.

Church Motto: A) The church's motto is "come grow with us." The church is a "come structure." B) The church's motto is "Go and make disciples." It is a "go structure."

Evangelism: A) The church does personal and crusade evangelism and has a large group revival mentality. Few members are involved in evangelism. B) The church uses the cell group as an evangelism net that supports all other evangelism methods. A large number of members in the church are involved in "lifestyle" relational evangelism.

Expectation: A) The church expects members to commit to enlarging the institution and promoting the same theological system. B) The church asks members to commit to increasing the Kingdom and to live in unity and body life.

Leaders: A) The primary leadership task is to direct the programs of the church. B) The primary leadership task in a church is to model the Christian life.

Pastoral Task: A) The primary pastoral task in the church is to preach good sermons and marry and bury. B) The primary pastoral task in the church is to equip believers for ministry.

Leadership Test: A) The church tests leaders by what they know. B) The church tests leaders by how they serve.

Securing Staff: A) The source for securing staff is trained, "professional" clergy. Leadership moves horizontally, as staff level leaders are recruited from other churches. B) The source for staff is servants developed from within the system. Leaders are tested before they're set apart for ministry within the church itself. Leadership moves vertically.

Prayer: A) Prayer life in the church is an individual choice and activity, and is usually limited. B) Prayer life is a lifestyle that grows out of personal and community needs discovered in cell group life.

Organizing Focus: A) The church focuses on the congregation large-group wing. B) The church focuses on cell groups.

Teaching: A) The teaching objective in the church is to get members to subscribe to distinctive beliefs. Information is the objective. B) The objective of teaching in a church is for members to apply Scripture to needs and relationships. Application and transformation are the objectives.

Ministry: A) The ministry support system in the church is the pastor and staff. B) Ministry takes place within cell life as members build up one another.

Fellowship: A) The church fellowships weekly, after worship services or in large groups in a fellowship hall. B) Fellowship in the church is daily as cell members care for each other.

Missions: A) The church supports missions with contributions, prayers, and personnel. B) The church does missions and is a mission church in Jerusalem, Judea, Samaria, and the world.

Small Groups: A) The church uses small groups as an optional, attached program along with all other kinds of programs. B) The church sees small groups as the essential base activity for ministry.

Sunday Service: A) What happens on Sunday has the highest priority. The majority of the church's time, energy, and resources go into what happens on Sunday. B) Cell life is the primary focus of the church, even though a Sunday service is experienced.

The intent of the contrast of the evaluation on the next page is not to condemn structures but to define positions that help each person determine the values that drive his/her personal and church actions. Are these contrasting assumptions true or false? Which ones do you think are fair and which are unfair? What are the implications if they are true? What are the solutions if they are true?

EVALUATION OF PERSONAL & CHURCH VALUES

Factor	1st Value Position	Rating	2nd Value Position
Church Location	Sacred: In a building	1 2 3 4 5 6 7 8 9 10	Functional: large and small.
Relationships	Information-based design	1 2 3 4 5 6 7 8 9 10	Relationship-based design
Discipleship	Classes, little modeling	1 2 3 4 5 6 7 8 9 10	Mentoring and modeling
Spiritual Gifts	Leaders use selected gifts.	1 2 3 4 5 6 7 8 9 10	All members use gifts.
Church Motto	"Come grow with us."	1 2 3 4 5 6 7 8 9 10	"Go and make disciples"
Evangelism	Personal and crusade	1 2 3 4 5 6 7 8 9 10	Lifestyle evangelism
Expectation	Enlarge the institution	1 2 3 4 5 6 7 8 9 10	Increase the Kingdom
Leaders	Professional "Clergy"	1 2 3 4 5 6 7 8 9 10	Ordinary "Laity"
Pastoral Task	Preach, marry, and bury	1 2 3 4 5 6 7 8 9 10	Equip believers for ministry
Leadership Test	What a person knows	1 2 3 4 5 6 7 8 9 10	How a person serves
Securing Staff	Hire outside professionals	1 2 3 4 5 6 7 8 9 10	Develop within the system
Prayer	Individual and formal	1 2 3 4 5 6 7 8 9 10	Lifestyle
Organizing	Large group	1 2 3 4 5 6 7 8 9 10	Cell groups
Teaching	Subscribe to doctrines	1 2 3 4 5 6 7 8 9 10	Apply Scriptures to life
Ministry	Pastor & staff do ministry	1 2 3 4 5 6 7 8 9 10	Members do ministry
Fellowship	Weekly in large groups	1 2 3 4 5 6 7 8 9 10	Daily as cell members
Missions	Support, pray for, & send	1 2 3 4 5 6 7 8 9 10	Do and be
Small Groups	Optional attached program	1 2 3 4 5 6 7 8 9 10	The essential base activity
Sunday Service	Highest priority	1 2 3 4 5 6 7 8 9 10	Cell life is primary.
Bible Study	"Give a man a fish."	1 2 3 4 5 6 7 8 9 10	"Teach a man to fish."
Children	Taught in classroom	1 2 3 4 5 6 7 8 9 10	Nurtured in a family context
Youth	Activities-centered program	1 2 3 4 5 6 7 8 9 10	Disciple-centered lifestyle
Training	Specialized training	1 2 3 4 5 6 7 8 9 10	On-the-job training in cells
Worship	Public worship is supreme	1 2 3 4 5 6 7 8 9 10	Cluster & cell worship also

LEADERSHIP: THE KEY TO CELL GROUP DEVELOPMENT

Bill Beckham

John 17 records Jesus' high priestly prayer. In this prayer, Jesus confirmed to the Father that their strategy was going to be successful. Why was Jesus optimistic about their chances? He was still facing the cross, the betrayal of Judas, the falling away of the disciples, and the turning away of the crowds. In his report to the Father, what positive spin could Jesus put on the divine strategy to that point? Consider three different strategy reports Jesus could have presented.

Strategy Report #1: Our strategy is going to work because within the first year, huge crowds have followed me. I could not get away from them. They clamored for me to speak to them and even left their homes and jobs to hear me preach. There was great response and popularity. Our strategy is going to work because of the multitudes and early response.

Strategy Report #2: The strategy is going to work because in the near future, numerical growth is going to explode after Pentecost. Thousands are going to believe during just one week of preaching. Therefore, the strategy is going to work because of the large number of believers after Pentecost.

Strategy Report #3: The strategy is going to work because of the core disciples. These are the ones who have followed us in community. I have taught them and lived with them. They know I have come from you, Father. Our strategy is going to work because of our leaders.

Which strategy report sounds most promising and logical? In light of modern church methods, either the first or second look best. But Jesus gave Strategy Report #3 to his Father. The strategy of God the Father and God the Son was going to be successful because of leaders empowered by the indwelling presence of God the Holy Spirit.

LEADERSHIP PRINCIPLES

In his classic book, *The Master Plan of Evangelism*, Robert E. Coleman identifies eight principles that guided Jesus in his leadership strategy. "One

Written Resources

- *The Master Plan of Evangelism* by Robert E. Coleman

must decide where he wants his ministry to count ... in the momentary applause of popular recognition or in the reproduction of his life in a few chosen men who will carry on his work after he has gone."[22]

In the chart, the eight principles are listed, along with a descriptive statement and a key verse from Scripture for each leadership principle.

LEADERSHIP DEFINITIONS

John Haggai says, "Leadership is the discipline of deliberately exerting special influence within a group to move it toward goals of beneficial permanence that fulfill the group's real needs." J. Robert Clinton, professor of the School of World Mission at Fuller Theological Seminary, defines Christian leadership as "a dynamic process in which a man or woman with God-given capacity influences a specific group of God's people toward His purposes for the group."

Peter Wagner suggests the following definition of leadership. Leadership is "the special ability that God gives to certain members of the body of Christ to set goals in accordance with God's purpose for the future." Wagner concludes that leadership is then able "to communicate these goals to others in such a way that they voluntarily and harmoniously work together to accomplish these goals for the glory of God."

About leaders, Fred Smith states: "The Christian leader is primarily a servant of God, not a servant of the sheep. Many shepherds act as if they're servants of the sheep ... a faulty concept. You are a servant of God, given to absolute obedience to what he says. To extend that to say you are a servant of each sheep is a fallacy."

Charles Simpson says leadership is "courage in action." He adds "leadership is not the holding of position or office, but the pursuit of purpose. It is a battle to win hearts and minds for a cause. If you are one step ahead of the group, you are a leader. If you are two steps ahead, you are a pioneer. If you are three steps ahead, you are a martyr."

LEADERS CAN BE NOUNS OR VERBS

The traditional church tends to honor position leadership: pastor, deacon, teacher, and prophet. Noun titles are given to these positions. Then these positions and titles are sanctioned by other noun leaders and protected and perpetuated by the system.

However, action leadership is more important than positions in the New Testament. Such leadership is described by verbs: serve, shepherd,

Eight Guiding Principles of the Master's Plan

- Selection:
  Men were his method.
  "He chose from them twelve."

- Association:
  He stayed with them.
  "Lo, I am with you always."

- Consecration:
  He required obedience.
  "Take my yoke upon you."

- Impartation:
  He gave Himself away.
  "Receive ye the Holy Spirit."

- Demonstration:
  He showed them how to live.
  "I have given you an example."

- Delegation:
  He assigned them work.
  "I will make you fishers of men."

- Supervision:
  He kept check on them.
  "Do ye not yet perceive?"

- Reproduction:
  He expected them to reproduce.
  "Go and bring forth fruit."

teach, and prophesy. Jesus cared little about titles and positions and chose verb leaders who would act according to his leading, whether or not they had a title.

God first gifts a person to act as a leader before giving any titles or positions. Noun titles and positions are meaningless without verb actions. Churches make a grave mistake in giving titles and positions unless the recipient has already demonstrated the gifts of doing leadership. Then any titles are simply names of service and not badges of honor, achievement, or power.

A church operates as an institution when its leaders are serving in titles and positions rather than doing the work of ministry as a verb. A movement of God is always led by verb leaders. Verb leaders say, "Follow me," and "let me serve you." Noun leaders say, "Obey me," "listen to me," and "serve me." An organization led by nouns is doomed to becoming an institution.

Why are noun leaders so important to a church with only a large group structure? In a large-group church setting, the most important tasks are large-group activities that require highly skilled persons. Therefore, title and positions are developed to maintain the essential task of the large-group church. When the most important task of the church is to do the work of ministry through small groups, then ordinary leaders are essential. Titles and positions are unnecessary for this basic spiritual task. Today, churches that still operate with Jesus' small group community wineskin put a high value upon verb leaders.

JESUS PREPARED HIS DISCIPLES IN A LEADERSHIP STRUCTURE

Jesus followed universal principles of leadership in developing his system of training. Just before his death, he was with his disciples in the Garden of Gethsemane. In the Garden, he deployed the disciples in a special leadership arrangement used throughout his ministry. He left the nine at one point, took the inner circle of three deeper in with him, and then he himself went further into the Garden. Thus, on the last night he was to be with them, Jesus modeled the way he had been relating to his leaders for those past three years.

The use of a triangle helps us to picture Jesus' leadership approach. At the top of the triangle is the catalyst or innovator. This was Christ. In the middle of the triangle is the inner circle, consisting of Peter, James, and John. On the base line of the triangle are the remaining nine members of Jesus' core leaders. Around this core group were their extended family members. This was the way Jesus physically arranged the disciples in the Garden.

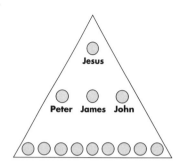

This leadership context provided Jesus with several ways to relate to his leaders. He could relate to them one on one, as he often did with Peter, Thomas, John, and even Judas.

He could also relate to the twelve as a whole unit. Much of his teaching was to the twelve and he often took them away from the crowds in order to have special time with them. Research on the Gospel of Mark reveals that forty-nine percent of the book is given to the time Jesus spent with his disciples. Jesus, by design, set aside a major portion of his time and energy to be with his chosen leaders.

The disciples could also relate to each other one on one. This leadership framework gave opportunity for personal contact with each other—both good and bad. When the disciples moved toward Jerusalem the last time, they were out of sorts with each other. James, John, and their mother were trying to gain advantage.

Jesus could relate to the three in his inner circle and did so frequently. On the Mount of Transfiguration, he took Peter, James, and John. When he healed the daughter of Jairus, it was Peter, James, and John who entered the room with him while the others remained outside.

There's at least one other possible relationship within the context of Jesus' leadership triangle. Subgroups within the twelve could have developed that modeled Jesus' relationship with the inner circle subgroup. Some biblical scholars suggest subgroups within the twelve were functioning around Peter, James, and John, or even Philip. Such subgroups would allow the principle of delegation and transference of leadership found in 2 Timothy 2:2 to be in operation in Jesus' leadership framework. "And the things which you have heard from me in the presence of many witnesses, these entrust to faithful men, who will be able to teach others also."

Though Jesus did not have this leadership triangle in his mind as he trained his disciples, he did use these triangle principles to train his leaders as a unit with natural sub-units. The triangle helps to visualize his process.

Jesus put this unit of leaders together in the beginning of his public ministry, planned his days around them, included them in his confidence, and prepared them to carry on his work. This leadership triangle applies to what God is doing in all church situations, no matter what their size or circumstances. This is the way Jesus began his church in the first century and it's the way he develops leaders today.

MOSES' LEADERSHIP

As Moses surveyed the multitudes of people surrounding him, he must have thought, "What kind of mess have I gotten myself into? How am I going to lead these people?"

He had to mold a mob of former slaves into a traveling nation and lead them to God's Promised Land. Moses was the best-educated person in that crowd, having been trained in the best schools of Egypt while his followers were slaving to make bricks. How would Moses organize this mob into a functioning nation?

Moses had several organizational options. He could govern with the pharaoh model he'd learned during the first 40 years of his life. This is a model of dictatorship based on absolute authority enforced through absolute power. Though this model is excellent for coordinating, people rebel against absolute authority. In fact, Moses had been the leader of such a rebellion, which brought him to his present leadership quandary.

Moses learned another organizational model in the desert of Midian. For 40 years Moses operated with the shepherd model, where the shepherd cares for each sheep individually and provides personal attention to every detail. This is an excellent model for a limited number of sheep, or people. Feed the sheep, lead the sheep, care for the sheep, and provide for the sheep. This leadership model eventually breaks down because of the pressure placed upon one caring person. Evidently Moses was trying to use a variation of this model at the time of his conversation with Jethro.

Moses could have chosen the prophetic model. He had successfully used this model of leadership to secure the release of the children of Israel from Egypt and had brought them to the desert. This model depends upon awe and reverence for God's prophet and the recognition that the prophetic figure has received a special word from God. The problem in this model is sustaining the awe. Paul says Moses would place a veil over his face so that the people would not "look intently at the end of what was fading away" (2 Corinthians 3:13). The glory of prophetic leadership fades and the leader must either hide his humanness or fake the glory of God.

He could have used a tribal model. This model had been used to organize the children of Israel before they were slaves in Egypt and would again be used when they moved into the Promised Land. The twelve tribes would be assigned geographical areas and each tribe would be divided into basic family units. The tribal model depended upon a sense of kinship as one family, and was excellent for administrating geographical areas. This model developed into the king model Israel used for a large portion of its history. The strength of this model is also its greatest danger. The people see themselves as separate tribes and clans and set up their own kingdoms. This eventually happened with the forming of the Northern and Southern Kingdoms of Israel.

WISE COUNSEL

Jethro, Moses' father-in-law, suggested a delegation model of shared leadership, which included some of the strengths of other models. Jethro suggested that Moses organize the nation of Israel around four different types of leaders: leaders over tens, fifties, hundreds, and thousands. These numbers represent four universal principles of leadership essential to the successful operation of any organization: coordinating, supporting, supervising, and implementing. These leaders share the burden and blessing of leadership. Each leader empowers the unique function of other leaders so that all contribute to the successful implementation of the vision.

Every military group since the time of Moses has used this leadership approach in one way or another. The military has divisions made up of battalions (thousands), companies (hundreds), platoons (fifties), and squads (tens). World War II historian, Stephen Ambrose, explains the organization of the military from the perspective of the squad. "The social bond within the Army was like an onion. At the core was the squad, where bonding could be almost mystical. After the squad came succeeding layers, the platoon, company, on up to division, all covered by the loose outermost layers of corps and army."[23]

Successful businesses are organized along this same basic leadership structure, even though different titles may be used. An organization will have CEOs, vice presidents, mid-management leaders, and working teams.

Even Jesus used a multi-level system of empowering leadership. The Master modeled the implementing role in his relationship to the twelve and, early in his movement, chose Peter, James and John to be sub-leaders at the level of supervision. After three-and-a-half years of on-the-job training, Jesus installed a leader to coordinate his movement (Peter) and instructed the others in appropriate leadership roles.

Every leader (coordinating, supporting, supervising, and implementing) uses all four of these leadership qualities to some extent. For instance, each leader will be functioning in the principle of coordination to some degree. In the broader picture of leadership, however, each one of the four leaders will be associated primarily with one leadership quality. Empowering leaders operate as a team because each leader is dependent upon the unique gifts and roles of the other leaders for success.

LEADERSHIP QUALITIES AND SUGGESTIONS

In Exodus 18, Jethro suggests four basic qualities of leadership. "Capable men" suggests that leaders should have ability to lead. "Fear God" refers to spirituality. Leaders should be "trustworthy" in their relationships and must" hate dishonest gain." These are the leadership qualities of ethical behavior.

Jethro makes several suggestions to Moses for leaders "over the people." These leaders should share the burden (18:17-18, 23) and listen to good counsel (18:19a). Leaders over the people should represent the people before God (18:19b) and teach them the statutes and laws (18:20a). Leaders are to show the people (18:20b) by modeling the way to live and the duties they're to perform.

Appoint these leaders over the people to specific units and give them freedom to do their assigned tasks. Then be available to support them in the hard problems. Finally, implement the plan (18:24b).

What should we look for in future cell leaders? Using 1 Samuel 16:6-12 as a reference scripture, Les Brickman suggests we begin where God begins, with the heart! Out of what fills the heart, the mouth speaks and the feet walk. If one has the right heart, God will, over time, take care of things like maturity, zeal, knowledge, and experience. Look for a person with God's H.I.G.H. heart standards.

John Wesley in the eighteenth century had several requirements for persons seeking to be pastoral leaders: Do they know God? Have they received gifts? Have they the graces? Have they produced fruit? Are any truly convinced of sin and converted to God by their preaching?

RESULTS OF USING THE JETHRO APPROACH

Jethro told Moses that two things would happen if he organized the children of Israel into functioning groups. First of all, Jethro assured Moses that "the people will go home satisfied." That's the goal of a good leader.

God's H.I.G.H Standards

Holiness: Is there sensitivity to sin and a heart that walks in repentance?

Integrity: Has the person proved trustworthy in the small things?

Gratitude: Do murmuring and complaining fill this person's mouth?

Humility: Does the person come as a master, or as a servant?

The people are satisfied in the vision, purpose, ministry, direction, and administration of the church.

Pastor Elias leads a Baptist church in Jales, a Brazilian city of 100,000. In 1997, the church of six hundred members began the transition to a cell group church structure and over a period of three years grew to twelve hundred. Pastor Elias was part of a year of training in the process of transition. He shared the following testimony: "For 28 years, I pretended I was able to pastor my flock and my flock pretended that I was able to pastor them. Since I died to my old pastor paradigm, I am now in a joyful time of ministry. I no longer have a make-believe ministry. I can now truly pastor my people through my cells."

Other models won't satisfy the people. They may fear the pharaoh but they won't be satisfied. They may love the shepherd as long as he's able to give individual attention, but eventually the sheep won't be satisfied. The people may be in awe of the prophet as long as his messages are pleasing and the miracles are beneficial. Tribal kings are praised until they impose taxes to pay for their palaces and privileges of power.

The old paradigms of ministry always result in a gap between the leader and the people. No matter how hard the leader tries to fill the gap between leadership and ministry, it still exists. With what is the gap filled? In the past, leaders have attempted to fill the gap with authority and power, personal care giving, reverence and respect, or strong government. The Jethro approach establishes an empowering model that fills the gap with leaders. Paul describes this leadership approach in Ephesians 4. God gives gifted leaders to the church in order to "equip the saints for the work of ministry." When this leadership system is working, then the church "builds itself up in love."

In addition to the people "going home satisfied," Jethro assured Moses that with this delegated approach he "will be able to bear it." Though Jesus promised that his "yoke is easy and His burden is light," modern pastors are weary in well doing.

A church can measure the effectiveness of its organizational leadership structure by asking these simple questions: Are the people satisfied? Is the pastor able to bear the burden of leadership? Are church pastors and leaders experiencing burnout?

JESUS AND JETHRO PRINCIPLES

Robert Coleman writes, "Men were to be His method of winning the world to God."[24] This meant that Jesus' concern "was not with programs to reach the multitudes, but with men whom the multitudes would follow."[25] "Though He did what He could to help the multitudes, Jesus had to devote Himself primarily to a few men, rather than the masses, in order that the masses could at last be saved."[26]

Coleman saw the dynamic tension in Jesus' ministry between the multitudes and the leaders. He declares that "victory is never won by the multitudes."[27] On the other hand, he asserts that "everything that is done with the few is for the salvation of the multitudes."[28] "Jesus had already demonstrated by His own ministry that the deluded masses were ripe for the harvest, but without spiritual shepherds to lead them, how could they ever be won?"[29]

Jethro and Jesus Leadership

JETHRO	ARMY	PRINCIPLE	JESUS	QUALIFICATIONS
1000	Battalion	Coordinate	3000	Elder 1 Timothy 3:1-7
100	Company	Support	120	Elder 1 Timothy 3:1-7
50	Platoon	Supervise	70	Deacon 1 Timothy 3:8-13
10	Squad	Implement	12	Deacon 1 Timothy 3:8-13

Jesus' leadership strategy follows the Jethro principles even though the exact numbers are different. The Master modeled the basic unit with the twelve disciples, who relate to the tens (implementing). Jesus tested His model with seventy, which corresponds to the fifties (supervising). Jesus established His model with 120, which represents the hundreds (supporting) and the base church. Jesus reached the thousands (coordinating) and anticipated large numbers being part of his movement. He thus provided a way to lead at the thousands level. These levels of leadership were necessary for Jesus to model leadership for his church.

The key to the New Testament system is the cell leader who facilitates the implementing groups in homes. Once the implementing unit is in place, the other principles of leadership operate naturally as a means of supporting the basic unit.

The Principle of Coordination

A leader (or team of leaders) coordinates the overall vision and directs the total project. Gathering all members and units is the primary role of a leader over thousands. The numbers represent a type of leadership, not just a number of people. A church of seventy-five members also needs someone

The leader who coordinates a cell group church must:

1. Coordinate the administration of the church
2. Cast the vision
3. Birth the concepts
4. Model the basic task
5. Mentor the leaders of hundreds
6. Have vision for growth
7. Facilitate the five-fold gifts
8. Oversee celebration

to coordinate.

The coordinating and supporting roles are linked together in overseeing larger areas of the work. They work to give direction to the coordinating units of the church, congregations. But, the two roles differ in the number and nature of people they oversee. The coordinating leader can oversee numbers in the thousands and works through leaders over hundreds. The support leader oversees numbers in the hundreds and works through leaders over fifties and tens.

The Principle of Support

Leadership is also required at the level of hundreds. This level of management interprets values, applies strategy to a designated geographical or people area, trains leaders, and sees that all support resources are passed to the basic point of implementation. This area of leadership is often associated with a congregation. The congregation has been traditionally identified with worship and a building.

However, in a cell group church, "congregation" is a unit for planning, coordinating, counseling, and training, not primarily for worship. Unfortunately, this word often confuses those trying to understand a cell group church, and so, must be redefined.

The size of the area task unit (congregation) ranges from six to twenty-five cells (70 to 250 people) depending upon the phase of development of the area unit.

The Principle of Supervision

A leader is needed to supervise the implementation of the basic task, to monitor quality control, and to mentor leaders of the basic task unit, the cell. This mid-management level is represented by the leader over fifties (three to five cells or 15 to 70 members). The leaders over fifties and tens operate as a team that focuses on the basic cell unit. The supervising leader is responsible for the overall direction of two to five basic units, while the cell leader is responsible for the specific tasks of one cell.

The Principle of Implementation

A project must have leadership at the fundamental level of implementation so the basic task can be completed. The leader over tens oversees one unit of five to fifteen adults that implements the basic tasks of holiness, har-

The support leader must:

1. Lead the flock
2. Plan for expansion in an area
3. Counsel leaders and members
4. Train leaders
5. Equip members (through special equipping encounters)
6. Shape growth in the designated area
7. Mentor the leaders over fifties
8. Administer the five support systems
9. Serve as a link to the whole church

The role of supervision requires some who can:

1. Shepherd two to five cell group leaders
2. Control quality for cell group life and ministry
3. Trouble-shoot
4. Serve as the eyes and ears for leaders of hundreds
5. Mentor cell group leaders
6. Affirm the selection of cell group interns

The profile of the implementing leader includes:

1. Following the model of Aquila and Priscilla (Romans 16:3-5)
2. Shepherding Christ's sheep
3. Tending Christ's lambs
4. Facilitating community
5. Mentoring an assistant
6. Referring to support leaders
7. Monitoring spiritual growth
8. Bringing cell members into the presence of Christ

vest, edification, and evangelism.

The basic unit of the squad in the military helps to illustrate the uniqueness of the cell. Stephen Ambrose saw the squad (cell) as the most important unit in the military. In his book, Citizen Soldiers, he explains the uniqueness of the squad: "In assessing the motivation of the GIs, there is agreement that patriotism or any other form of idealism had little if anything to do with it. The GIs fought because they had to. What held them together was not country and flag, but unit cohesion."[30]

Organization for a common and concrete goal in peacetime organizations does not evoke anything like the degree of comradeship commonly known in war. At its height this sense of comradeship is an ecstasy. Men are true comrades only when [each member of the squad] is ready to give up his life for the others without reflection and without thought of personal loss.[31]

We see this level of community and commitment to one another in the New Testament movement. As in the military, the groups (squads of ten to twelve adults) in the New Testament produced this kind of commitment.

All other leaders exist in order to support the cell group leaders. If they're successful, the leaders over fifties, hundreds, and thousands are successful. The leaders over tens (cell group leaders) make sure that the basic tasks of the church are completed.

THE JETHRO APPROACH STILL WORKS

Every successful cell group church uses some variation of the Jethro model. These churches may use different names for the leaders and have slightly different job descriptions, but they all have leaders who coordinate, support, supervise, and implement.

Thousands of years of management confirm that leadership will not work properly without each of these roles functioning in one way or the other. The proper functioning of these four leadership roles is essential for worldwide revival in the twenty-first century.

SHARING THE CELL GROUP VISION WITH KEY LEADERS

M. Scott Boren and Randall G. Neighbour

In the churches that have developed the most effective cell group systems, the senior pastor was the first to catch the vision for the groups. While there are a few exceptions where a key staff pastor or an influential lay leader caught the vision first, the senior pastor's commitment has proven to be a crucial driving force for group development. At the same time, one person cannot force cell groups upon people. Senior pastors are not controlling dictators who force their visions upon their people. Even Moses, one of the strongest leaders in the history of man, understood this. He worked with Aaron, Joshua, and seventy elders to lead the people of Israel.

THE INNER LEADERSHIP CORE

Stage 2 highlights the need to lead people into cell groups with a Cell Group Vision Team. There are people who serve as church leaders who must support the cell group vision, but who will not serve on the Cell Group Vision Team. These people comprise the inner core of the church's leadership. Usually this group is comprised of the key leaders who serve on a board of elders, a board of deacons, or a ministry management team, depending upon a church's polity.

Most likely there'll be members who, while they don't serve on an official leadership board, are very influential leaders within the church. In addition, there may be board members who are filling an official role but wield very little influence within the church. Therefore, determining who operates as a part of the Inner Leadership Core varies from church to church. We've worked with churches where the elders were the true spiritual leaders of the church and they faithfully led the people. We've also worked with quite a few churches where the official board was comprised of people who like business meetings, while the real spiritual leaders served in other capacities. In such situations, the senior pastor worked with the unofficial leaders more than the official board.

To determine the make-up of the Inner Leadership Core, ask these questions: "Who do people trust for spiritual leadership?" "Who do people follow?" "Who do people listen to?" Hopefully these people are true spiritual servant leaders who lay down their lives for people. This core is comprised of two groups of people, those with veto power and key influencers.

**Cell Group
Vision Team Exercise**

Who are the "veto power" people who need to learn about the cell vision?

"VETO POWER" PEOPLE

This group has the final word. They set the course for the church, and they model the values and direction for the rest of the church body. They most probably hold roles such as deacons, elders, committee heads or team leaders, the pastor's spouse, or perhaps a paid staff member. These men and women—when headed in a new direction in unity with the senior pastor and each other—become an unstoppable team.

To determine who has veto power, make a list of the individuals who fit into this category. Then ask yourself these questions about them. If asked, would this person:

- Know the church's current position on its course to fulfill the stated mission?
- Know with certainty if the church is growing by moving forward, remaining stationary, or falling behind?
- Know how the church should fulfill the stated mission with strong opinions?

The persons on the initial list should be able to articulate the answers to these questions with a high degree of clarity and passion. They have "veto power" due to their position, duration in that position, and respect level among the staff, key influencers, and general membership. They earned this respect because they're the backbone of your current structure.

KEY INFLUENCERS

This group is characterized as persons who have "unofficial" influence within the congregation. They may or may not hold a formal title in your current structure, which makes them all the more dangerous if not moved to the new direction of the church early in the process. These individuals can range from the little old lady in your congregation, who has seven children and twenty grandchildren, to a long-term deacon or board member.

(This group could also include a paid staff member.)

Generally, Key Influencers are not as involved as the "Veto Power" group, but they are strong tithers. Often, they'll apply subtle pressure to the staff for answers to questions they may never voice to the "Veto Power" people or you, the senior pastor.

This group often votes with their pocketbooks, then their feet. Unlike the "Veto Power" group, they're not as verbal with leadership when they're dissatisfied or disgruntled. Reduced offerings and joining another church in town may be the first indication given that they're not happy with the new direction of your church. For this reason, you must create and execute a strategy to transition this important group within your church or you'll have no funds to employ your staff!

Review the initial list of "Veto Power" people you've made. Should some of these people be moved into the Key Influencers column? Who should be added to the Key Influencers column, using the information supplied above?

The only way to know where this group stands is through open, honest dialogue. Most of them won't make lifestyle changes without a clear understanding of and a commitment to that change. The bottom line questions for this group are usually, Will it work? and What will it cost me personally? and Is God really calling us (translation = me) to make this radical change?

To effectively transition this group, you must do your homework and ensure you approach them in such a way that they feel you have their best interests at heart. While the "Veto Power" group will make personal sacrifices to fulfill the vision of the church, this group is different. Key Influencers are far more interested in how they'll feel when the change occurs or how the difference will affect them personally.

Be sure you're wearing your pastoral hat as you transition this group! It will require patience. You'll also discover it's much harder to transition this group, due to the unknown emotional factors and underlying motivations that have yet to be voiced.

SHARING THE VISION WITH THE LEADERSHIP CORE

One of the most effective ways to share the vision is to create an atmosphere where the leadership core develops shared vision. In other words, the senior pastor facilitates a time where the core can discover the vision together. A retreat setting is excellent for such purposes.

Cell Group Vision Team Exercise

Make a list of the key influencers in the church who must buy into the cell group vision for it to work.

To prepare for this retreat, it's good to enlist the help of the core members. The senior pastor can ask them to gather some information to stimulate discussion. For instance:

- One person could gather demographic data on the makeup of the community and ratio of church attendees to population. If possible, he should obtain information on what's projected over the next ten years.
- One person could gather and present the church's statistics (particularly attendance, membership, number of new members per year for past ten years). The goal is to discover trends.
- One person could prepare a short history of the church, emphasizing the ways God has worked to achieve his purposes through the church.

In addition, each core member should read a book or an article in preparation for thinking in new ways about the church. They should be challenged to think outside the box. Specifically, they need to rediscover the mission of the church. When they see that the church has a mission, then they can see how cell groups fit into that mission.

A Suggested Retreat Outline

1. Overview retreat goals. They include:
   - To recognize God's goodness to your church in the past and to seek his plans for the future, as you seek him, pray, and plan together.
   - To deepen relationships as a leadership team.
2. Lead a devotional on "reporting" and planning based on the story of the twelve spies who searched out Canaan. Ten of them gave an "evil" report. Two gave a good report. The difference between an evil and a good report is not in the accuracy. An evil report is one that lacks faith and omits God's plans and power in its consideration. Pray as a team, committing your time, yourselves, and your church to God.
3. Look at where the church has come from. Have reports presented on your church's history and on its statistical record.
4. Discuss the special purposes God has sought to achieve in your church. Talk about questions like:
   - What destinies has God spoken or built into your church?
   - Name your church's greatest strengths in the past. What are your current strengths?
   - List special things God has been teaching your church in the past five years.
5. Present how the church is no longer the respected institution of the Western culture. See pages 67-81 in *Making Cell Groups Work*.
6. Articulate the calling or mission of the church. Ask, "What were the values of the first century church?" Helpful passages include Acts 2:42-46, Romans 12:1-8, and Ephesians 4:11-16. (If there are more than five people on your leadership team, do this in smaller groups.)
   - Have people brainstorm using Post-It™ notes, writing down everything that comes to their minds.
   - Let sub-groups report.
   - The senior pastor should feel free to guide this process, adding his insights and thoughts, but not dominating the interaction.
   - Organize the values into categories.
   - If you can reduce the mission to five to ten key words, do it, and have teams work on tentative mission statements for those words.
7. Show the *Cell Church Revolution Video*. This ten-minute video provides testimonies from pastors, cell group leaders, and cell group members about how cell groups have impacted their lives and their churches. In

response to the video, ask these questions:
- What stands out to you from these testimonies?
- Which characteristics would you most like to see in our church?
- According to these testimonies, what role do cell groups play in accomplishing the mission of the church?
- Take time to pray and commit yourselves and your church's future to God. Invite the Holy Spirit to let you see new visions and dream new dreams.

8. Explore your church's future.
- What has God clearly spoken to your church about what he wants to do through it in the future? (These can be truths from Scripture, words spoken to your church in the past, or dreams God is planting in your hearts now.)
- What are some things you believe God is saying, but for which you lack clarity concerning specifics and timing?
  - The senior pastor should begin this sharing by outlining the ideas and concepts God has imparted to him.
  - Invite other team members to share their thoughts and dreams before specifically responding to yours.
  - Invite quiet members to share. They may be sitting on key concepts and principles.
  - Seek to bring a sense of clarity and consensus around a central core vision.

9. Explain what it takes to move forward.
- Explain the 8-Stage process for cell group transformation as outlined in *Making Cell Groups Work.*
- Roughly outline specific plans you're envisioning.
- Introduce the idea of a Cell Group Vision Team. The senior pastor should state that he will be talking with individuals over the next few weeks about who should form this team.
- Ask: What are they particularly excited about? What should be your specific achievable goals?
- Ask: What obstacles do they see to achieving these plans? How specifically can these obstacles be overcome?
- Discuss how united you are as a team. Will you stand together if there are setbacks or opposition?
- Spend time in prayer together.

Stage 2:
Develop Vision and Strategy as a Team

HOW TO CHOOSE A CELL GROUP VISION TEAM

M. Scott Boren

During a presentation on cell groups strategy, I noticed the dismay of an older couple named Ned and Nancy. They expressed frustration because they couldn't catch the vision in the way their pastor had hoped. Even though he'd presented the vision for over three years, they couldn't get their minds around it.

At the same time, this couple led a very effective cell group. They practiced all the ministry habits of good cell leaders. They were happy to follow their pastor into cell ministry, but they didn't concern themselves with big-picture questions of cell theology, cell vision, cell structure, or cell strategy. They were much more concerned about actually caring for the people and doing the work of ministry.

On the other hand, during that same training, there were four others who couldn't get enough information about the intricacies of the cell group vision and strategy. Even after the conference, they bombarded me with questions.

Not all leaders are the same. Not every church leader will find participating in the Cell Group Vision Team fulfilling. Different teams require different types of people. John Maxwell lists the seven types of challenges and the type of team required to meet those challenges:[1]

Type of Challenge	Type of Team Required
New Challenge	Creative Team
Controversial Challenge	United Team
Changing Challenge	Fast and Flexible Team
Unpleasant Challenge	Motivated Team
Diversified Challenge	Complementary Team
Long-term Challenge	Determined Team
Everest-sized Challenge	Experienced Team

There are aspects of all these challenges that apply to the charge given to a Cell Group Vision Team. But the one challenge that applies the most is that of a new challenge, requiring the team members to be creative, having the ability to think outside the box, and hear God's direction about how to operate differently through cell groups.

Even though people like Ned and Nancy have served as faithful leaders in the church for years, it doesn't mean they have the ability or desire to strategize and lead the charge into the future. During the seminar with Ned and Nancy, I explained how people who don't thrive on big-picture questions of vision and strategy need not concern themselves with trying to understand it. They only need to see their role in the strategy and follow God in it. Immediately, Ned and Nancy breathed sighs of relief.

In order to design an effective vision team, it must be comprised of people who like to think about these big-picture questions regarding vision and strategy. I'm energized when I serve on such a team. To help understand the differences between those who like to serve on such a team and those who don't, it helps to know the difference between "in" people and "on" people.

RECOGNIZING "ON" PEOPLE

Characteristics of "On" People
- Focus on big picture
- See things in long-range terms
- Can analyze situation objectively
- Concerned about structure and strategy

Creative people like to work "on" a project. They like to think about the possibilities of what can happen. They like to step out of the situation and analyze the big picture, without getting bogged down in the details. Such people are great at developing vision, defining what the cell groups will look like, and refining what they articulate.

Ned and Nancy were frustrated because they were being asked to participate in the Vision Team, even though they don't think like an "on" person. They're leaders in their church, respected ministers who love people, pray for people, and serve as pillars of faith for others to follow. People like Ned and Nancy are "in" people, because they like to focus their energy working inside the vision, not on the vision.

Church leaders need to determine if they're an "in" or an "on" person. When "on" pastors get excited about the cell group vision, they often spend endless hours teaching "in" people the intricacies of cell group theology, cell group theory, cell group strategy, cell group structures. For "in" people, this is boring and frustrating. They just want to know what they need to do in the new vision. The other "on" people in the room find this exciting. Understanding this distinction gives freedom to both the "in" and the "on" people to use their unique skills.

Sometimes a pastor catches a vision for cell groups, but then realizes he's an "in" person. It may be tempting for him to abdicate his responsibility to participate in the Cell Group Vision Team to others. This is a grave mistake, especially in small churches. He must be an integral part of the vision development, even though participating in such a team will be stretching for him. He'll need to recruit an "on" person who can lead the team through the process.

ADDITIONAL CHARACTERISTICS OF TEAM MEMBERS

It's not enough to be an "on" person to contribute effectively to the Cell Group Vision Team. Here are a few additional characteristics:

- Broad knowledge about, or a desire to learn about, what's happening in the church in America is essential for creating vision for cell groups.
- Credibility, connections, and stature within the church are needed for communicating the vision.
- An understanding about the internal workings of the church is used to remove the barriers that impede people from entering the vision of cell groups.
- Having formal authority and managerial skills needed to plan, organize, and oversee the process of implementing cell groups are required to create short-term wins.
- Leadership skills for developing vision, communicating that vision, and motivating people to enter that vision.
- A commitment to daily prayer and hearing God's direction.
- A hunger to see biblical community developed in the church through cell groups.
- The availability to work on a vision team.

Characteristics of "In" People
- Focus on the details they're working on today
- See things in short-range terms
- Deeply connected to current situation
- Concerned about getting the objectives done

Personal Exercise

List three to seven people who have the potential to serve as Vision Team members.

CELL CHANGE CHAMPION: FINDING A JOSHUA

Alan Corrick

Alan Corrick serves as Door of Hope Church's Body Life Pastor in Fairbanks, Alaska, ministering to the cells and their related ministries including training, church gatherings of all sizes, and interest groups. His primary passion is birthing new ministers and ministries by helping people's dreams become their destinies. He is married to Cheryl, a certified professional midwife, and God has put together their family from three continents and two generations

Transitioning a program-based or event-driven church into a cell-based, relationally-driven body poses unique challenges when compared to the process of planting a cell church. In a church plant, the leadership team need not concern itself with old structures and programs but instead can focus on establishing the new modus operandi. Established churches though, often discover more needs to be unlearned than learned, both in terms of principles and practices. The larger and more successful the church is, or the more traumatic and tumultuous its recent history, the greater the degree of challenge it faces. Many senior pastors feel overwhelmed by the sheer volume of tasks and considerations involved.

A 1956 movie, *The Ten Commandments*, narrates one of the greatest transitions in history. During the course of the tale, Moses becomes God's prophet, a mass of slaves becomes an army of warriors, and a disorganized rabble becomes a lawful nation. The Exodus even includes the Old Testament's clearest delineation of cell-based organization in Exodus 18 when Moses' father-in-law, Jethro, convinces the prophet to structure the nation into tens, fifties, hundreds, and thousands (cells, sub-zones, zones, districts).

The narrator of the movie highlights an important element of the transitional journey from Egypt to the Promised Land: "They did not know where they were going … and there went forth among them planters of vineyards and savers of seeds, each hoping to sit under his own vine and fig tree. Out of this glorious chaos, it is Joshua who brings order and purpose." It was not enough for the senior leader to have the proper vision and structure for the people. Moses needed someone who would serve him and help him bring order and purpose out of the chaos.

The same is true for churches that are making the journey from an established program-based or event-driven church to a cell-based church. The senior pastor cannot lead the people by himself. This is especially true of churches that are larger than 200 people. Senior pastors need a cell group champion, someone who wakes up every morning thinking about the journey toward the cell group destination.

WHY JOSHUA MATTERS

Like Moses, a senior pastor is the Lord's agent for shepherding His people. Regardless of church government or framework, the pastoral leader is responsible for delivering the Word, overseeing all activity, and otherwise defining and directing the life of the church. None of this responsibility goes away because you decide to transition to a cell-based church. Until people's expectations change, until the church structure changes, these basic needs must be met as always. Moses was expected to make each decision, deal with any crisis, and set every direction. The only reason he could handle these old responsibilities while ushering in the new is because he had help—and Joshua was his most significant helper.

During Moses' lifetime, Joshua's primary relationship with him was as his servant (Numbers 11:28). From spying out the land, to commanding the army, to giving counsel, whatever Moses needed done, Joshua did. A senior pastor leading a transition is also taking God's people on a journey, from what they have been, to what they are becoming. The issues of redefining identity, equipping people to be ministers, acquiring a new perspective, and people adopting and adapting at different paces are all there, just as they were in Exodus. *The senior pastor must give his limited time and energy to those core areas where his influence matters the most. Having someone else to carry other important, even critical assignments, releases the top leader to greatest effectiveness.*

WHAT JOSHUA DOES

When Door of Hope embarked on its transition to cell-based life, it was a successful program-based church of a thousand people. Moreover, it had been created less than a year earlier by a merger of two churches that had gone through some recent traumatic events. As a result, even Ralph Neighbour and Bill Beckham were concerned for our welfare. Our senior pastor, however, discerned unique issues that needed to be addressed in our journey into cell group life. One of the most significant was his recognition that he was responsible for seeing as many of our people complete the journey as possible. Therefore, he concentrated on making sure the ship stayed on course, while minimizing those who jumped—or felt pushed—overboard. At the same time, he had to be the inspirational leader, sowing the values and vision for a cell group church body. What he quickly realized was that he needed someone to implement the changes he was calling for, a leader who could cultivate what he was sowing into the church.

In structuring the role (to which I was appointed), two important things must be recognized. First, though this role carried the title "cell ministry pastor," the senior pastor remained the leader and point person for cells and the cell-based church life. As discussed repeatedly in cell group church training and literature, the highest authority must lead the transition or it won't be taken seriously. Second, though the title referenced cells, the actual commission was to serve as the church's agent for transition. By making the task one of "change" rather than simply "cells," I was given permission to address ALL of the issues involved in EVERY area of church life and how they impacted our transition to the new vision. This designation allowed me to serve the senior shepherd wherever and however needed.

The working relationship between this transition leader and the head pastor must be as symbiotic as that of Moses and Joshua. The best way to illustrate this relationship is this: the senior pastor is the driver of a 60-passenger bus trying to stay on the road as the transition leader (cell champion) tries to successively change all the tires while cruising down the highway at speed! Moses and Joshua led the nation of Israel forward while hundreds of thousands were being fed, educated, and otherwise cared for on a daily basis.

The senior pastor serves as God's messenger and motivator to His people. The values and vision are delivered by the teaching and preaching of the Word and are then ignited by Spirit-led example and Spirit-fueled passion. The change champion can reiterate and reinforce this work, but it is the top leader's place to be God's vessel in this regard. The cell change champion primarily serves the senior pastor as a mobilizer and manager, stimulating people to embrace the vision and practices of cell group life and structures. The quote from the Ten Commandments states that Joshua was used to bring "order and purpose." In the movie, the narrator reads these words while the film depicts Joshua organizing midwife wagons, directing fire bearers, and otherwise overseeing the logistics on Moses' behalf. This teamwork between God's messenger and motivator leader and the mobilizer and manager servant is perfectly illustrated.

WHO JOSHUA IS

One pastor asked us, "Should I choose a loyal servant or someone skilled with people or a person with administrative ability and insights to fulfill this role of cell change champion?" The answer we gave was "Yes!" Joshua would have been of little value to Moses if he was personally untrustworthy, relationally incompetent, or managerially lacking. There has to be a basic combination of attitudes, abilities, and attributes to effectively help others change, especially in a corporate setting.

A change agent focuses on mobilization for, and management of, transition toward the new vision. Mobilization requires the ability to exercise influence toward a particular end. Management requires the ability to coordinate people, resources, and tasks. In terms of spiritual gifting, this role requires someone who possesses Romans 12 leadership and administration abilities.

He needs to be an innovator/pioneer or at least an "early adopter" who has the ability to embrace new ideas and see the vision before it becomes real. At the same time, he should be able to relate to, and communicate with, those who do not have the ability to see a new vision easily. These are the people who will make the vision work and if he cannot work with them, the vision will never occur.

He must be committed to that local body, without any intention of moving down the road to another church or better position, at least for the next five to seven years. This person must submit his ego and agenda to the vision of the senior leader.

Finally, he must have the ability to maintain perspective (especially through humor).

HOW JOSHUA OPERATES

One of the most sobering points threaded throughout the Old and New Testaments is that people can know the principles, but fail if they don't discern the practices. Worship and praise, tithing and giving, service and sacrifice are addressed in the Bible, not just about WHAT we do, but HOW we do it. Principles and practices work together.

As the cell ministry model has spread, I see this dynamic at work in cell group churches. I've watched cells operate as programs with program-based values and structures. I've seen cell training that is entirely academic while proclaiming the need of real life experiences. I've watched events and activities displace cells while the primacy of relationship is preached from the pulpit. The job of the cell change champion is to help the leadership team connect cell principles with cell practices. Even though the senior pastor has the cell group vision, he most likely will continue to struggle with the practical ways to implement that vision.

For example, early in our transition various leaders, including pastors, expressed their lack of enthusiasm for cells, change, and me. Desiring some constructive engagement, I asked one leader what the problem was and was enlightened thusly, "I feel like we are all working in a garden. I'm working on my row of peas, and he's working on his row of carrots, and you are working on your row of corn. Now I feel that I have turned around and here you are, messing in my peas." Immediately I felt understanding and empathy. His priority was to produce the most and best "peas" (his type of ministry and ministers) possible. To him, cells were just another vegetable in the garden of ministry. As a result, his principles emphasized boundaries and departmental autonomy. The resulting practices were competitive, possessive, and defensive. In response, I shared my principle. "Actually, I'm not about corn, peas, or carrots. My call is to build the SOIL because I want everyone to grow into what God created them to be."

Joshua's calling is to practically implement Moses' vision. Moses must wake up every morning thinking about the vision and all of the other big-picture issues that fill his day. He must take care of the people who are well on the way to the new vision, as well as oversee those who are stuck in the old ways. Joshua gets up every morning thinking differently. He thinks solely about getting people on board with the new. His job is to develop practical ways to make the vision work.

CELL GROUP VISION TEAM RETREAT

M. Scott Boren

A retreat is an excellent way to begin the journey as a team. Such a retreat provides extended time for team members to dialogue about the vision, to clarify how the vision might work, and to begin to put some plans in place. In addition, it allows time for team members to connect with one another on a personal basis, thereby creating unity.

To take advantage of the retreat experience, all the team members should read a book on the cell group vision before arriving. *Making Cell Groups Work* is the best place to begin, because the team will be working through the eight stages outlined in that book.

The retreat should allow time for:

1. Processing the different visions for cell group ministry. Stage 1 material in this *Navigation Guide* can help with this.
2. Defining the purpose of the cell groups for the specific church. Chapter 12 in this *Navigation Guide* is an excellent tool for facilitating this interaction.
3. Beginning to assess where the church is today by working through Stage 3 assessments or planning when to work through those assessments.
4. Establishing how the team will work together. Some teams meet weekly, others monthly.
5. Worshiping and praying together, allowing the Spirit to guide the entire retreat.

Possible activities include:

- Discussing a book related to cell-group ministry. *Life in His Body*, by David Finnell, is a great tool for this purpose. (Team members should read the book prior to the retreat).
- Having each person reflect on his/her dreams for the future, both personally and for the church.

• Doing a Bible study of 1 Corinthians 3:9-15, and discuss its application to the present situation.
• Completing the Purpose, Vision, and Strategy Worksheets below.

The success of this retreat is dependent upon a facilitator. This person could be the senior pastor or the cell group champion. The facilitator should not see his role as that of a teacher who shares his concepts of how he thinks cell groups should work. His job is to create an atmosphere where the entire group can enter into dialogue with one another about the future of cell groups.

This doesn't mean the facilitator convenes the retreat around a blank sheet of paper, where the entire group can contribute whatever they think. Such a time is an act in futility. Instead, the facilitator should bring his ideas of the vision and offer them to the team for open dialogue. The facilitator could develop a vision for how he sees cell groups working in the church and present it in such a way that allows ample time for the group to process it and provide feedback. The following worksheet illustrates one way of facilitating this process.

CELL GROUP VISION WORKSHEET

Purpose of the Church and Cell Groups

- Use the following Scriptures to list four purposes of the church:
  Matthew 22:37-39 and Matthew 28:19-20

  1.

  2.

  3.

  4.

- In the space below, write a short statement describing your church's purpose.

The Vision of Your Church

- Imagine a picture hanging on the wall depicting your church five to seven years from now, effectively living out its purpose. What do you see?

- How do cell groups fit into that picture?

- In the space below, write a short statement describing your church's vision for cell groups. (This is meant to be a broad statement, that is, a work in progress.)

The Strategy for Your Church

- For your church to live out its purpose and achieve its vision, what must be done?

- How do cell groups fit into this strategy?

DEFINE THE CELL GROUP

M. Scott Boren

Robert sees the time and shuts down his computer so he can leave early to beat the traffic. As he pulls into the street, he remembers to swing by the grocery store to pick up a few things for the weekly small group that will meet at his house tonight. He smiles as he realizes he has true friends for the first time in his life. His marriage is improving, although he'll need prayer tonight for yelling at his children.

Steven and Janice stare at the map to Robert's house. "They seemed friendly," Janice said, "and Christine even called to see how we were doing on Tuesday. Let's give it a shot."

Terry, a divorced man, who has been off drugs for six months, lives for his weekly meeting with Robert and the gang. As he drives over, he thinks about the things he can share with the rest of the group. God has done so much.

About 110 million people, more than forty percent of the U.S. population, join Robert, Steven, Janice, and Terry as they participate in some kind of religious small group.[3] Church leaders and consultants have argued for years that small groups or cells are essential to the flourishing of a church.[4] In fact, small groups—though churches emphasize them today more than ever—aren't new to the church. The church has organized itself around small groups for decades.

From Sunday school classes, home fellowship groups, short-term discipleship groups, outreach groups, leadership groups, service committees, and choir groups, few churchgoers have lacked for small groups in their Christian experience.

Because traditional small groups and cell groups look much like one another, it's important for those with traditional small group experience to understand the differences. Without a clear definition of a cell group, people will gather in groups, reproducing their previous small group experiences. Those who have led deep Bible studies will create cell groups that are deep Bible studies. Those who have led fellowship groups will create cell groups that focus on great fellowship. Those with 12-step experience will create cell groups that resemble support groups. Cell group leaders with an unclear vision for the cell group will unknowingly revert back to their previous small group experiences because people do what they know. If the vision is unclear, each group will "do what is right in their own eyes."

SMALL GROUPS AND CELL GROUPS

First let's answer the question: what is a small group? Bible studies are small groups. Twelve-step programs are small groups. Alcoholics Anonymous uses small groups. There are book groups, cooking groups, volleyball groups, sewing groups, running groups, and weight loss groups. The list extends as far as the imagination.

Then there are deacon small groups, leadership training groups, community service groups, evangelism groups, choir groups, parking lot attendant groups, and Sunday school small groups. All these groups have one thing in common: they're groups that are small (usually less than fifteen people) who meet on a regular basis, some weekly, others less often.

Many have argued that the small group definition should recognize that people in church are already connected in small groups and therefore the leadership should promote and support the life within that group. For instance, because a church has a choir, it should be recognized as a cell group and supported. Most churches have ushers; therefore this should form an official cell group within the church because it already is a group. Likewise, Sunday school classes are naturally cell groups. People already meet together on a weekly basis and therefore are part of an intentional cell group strategy. This is the basic premise behind the popular meta-group structure.

Others have argued against this proposal. They maintain that there's a drastic difference between traditional small groups and cell groups. This chart contrasts the differences.[5]

While small in size like the traditional small group, a cell group is radically different. A cell group is much more than a weekly meeting

	Cell Groups	Traditional Small Groups
Nature	Church in nature, purpose & power	Extension of the real church
Function	Fulfills every task	Limited purpose
Focus	Person of Christ	Performance for Christ
DNA	Christ indwells & empowers	Techniques, methods, materials
Leadership	Nurture, facilitate, shepherd	Teach, promote, motivate
Witness	Transformation through relationships	Convince through information

where fewer than fifteen people gather for an activity, such as discussing the Bible. Such groups stand in contrast to groups that meet to perform a task, play a sport, share a hobby, or even pray for one another. While the foci of traditional small groups vary from group to group, all cell groups have the same focus. The focus in a cell group lies on experiencing the presence of Christ. Jesus said, "Where two or three are gathered together in my name, there I am also."

Bill Beckham emphasizes that the only thing a cell group has to offer is the presence of the incarnate Christ. Without Christ in the midst, a cell group only becomes a "little Bible discussion group," or a "fellowship group," or an "activity group." The focus of a cell group lies not on any one activity or study, but on the living presence of Christ, through the Holy Spirit.

TOWARD CELL GROUP CLARITY

The focus of Christ in the midst of the group sounds great from a biblical perspective, but when a person is leading a group, it feels too nebulous to be practical. Trying to understand a spiritual dynamic is challenging.

Trying to define "Christ in the midst" is like trying to hold Jell-O™ in your fist. As soon as you try to make it fit into a box, you suddenly learn you're squeezing too hard and making a big mess. Experiencing Christ in a cell group is about gathering with others to experience a relationship with him together. It's about coming into unity with one another by connecting first to Christ. It's about making him the hub of the group, and allowing him to connect us to one another.

Even still, this is very nebulous. Pastors and leaders want practical handles so they can "do" cell groups. These are valid concerns. But the responses to these concerns often lead people down the wrong track. Let me give an example.

Over the past few years, a battle has raged in articles, chat rooms and e-mail newsletters over what is and is not a cell group. On one side of the argument lie the cell group legalists. On the other side are the cell group abolitionists. The legalists argue that all cell groups in a church must meet in homes, study the same lesson, be intergenerational in nature, and be organized geographically.

The abolitionists argue that groups can meet anywhere (even at the church building), can study a variety of materials, can meet around common interests, and are usually not organized geographically. The legalists vouch for a definition where all the groups look identical. The abolitionists promote a variety of types of groups, varying in how often they meet and what they study.

In reality, both are wrong. The legalists state that the only way to do cell groups is by making them uniform. The abolitionists state that the only way to do cell groups is to make them diverse. Actually, most of the largest cell churches around the world have cell groups that meet in a variety of settings—they're not limited to the context of a home—they're homogeneous and/or heterogeneous in member composition, and they may be organized geographically or in homogeneous networks.

But the issues that are debated center around the practical forms cell groups take. What do cell groups study? Where do they meet? Who comprises their membership? When do they meet?

Definitions of cell groups based upon the clarification of forms create very rigid methods for ministry. It's very dangerous to argue about which form is right. Some have gotten so worked up over their definition of a cell group they've even called theirs the PURE form of what the church should be. The basis of what is or isn't a cell group can't be found in its outer forms. Cell groups can meet in homes, or they can meet in a boardroom. They can meet in coffee shops, clubhouses, or even at a park. They can be comprised of couples, only men, only college students, etc. There's no one form that defines a cell group.

DEFINE WHAT YOU WANT
CELL GROUPS TO EXPERIENCE

Instead of defining groups around forms, the best way to define a cell group is to begin to articulate what you want a group of people to experience together. Ralph W. Neighbour points us in the right direction: "The shepherd group is the cell where people are nurtured, equipped to serve and where members build up (edify) one another. It forms community where believers are called to be accountable to each other, and where they can be totally transparent with one another."[6]

Bill Beckham helps define this for us, as he says that a cell group is "a group of Christians who live together in spiritual community as the church in nature, purpose and power, resulting in edification, equipping and evangelism."[7]

Joel Comiskey helps fill in some of the gaps by demonstrating how the small groups are connected to the wider church. In his definition, "A small group or cell is a group of people (4-15), who meet regularly for the purpose of spiritual edification and evangelistic outreach (with the goal of multiplication) and who are committed to participate in the functions of the local church."[8]

These definitions don't focus on what a group looks like on the outside. Instead they reveal what a group is at its heart. They explicate the essence of the life of the group that cannot be seen. This inner essence is what makes the outer components work and propels the strategy.

The cell group vision team of a church should define the cell group around the components the groups should experience, not around the activities of how a meeting is structured or where it meets. These are crucial practical questions that should only be addressed after the nature of cell group experiences is defined.

Some of the more prominent cell group churches in the United States have taken great effort to define the essence of the life of the cell. Other churches should look at these just as clearly as they look at the various strategies and structures.

Bob Logan observes that the cell group experience is seven-fold: teaching, fellowship, worship, prayer, power, ministry, and evangelism.[9]

Billy Hornsby, formerly of Bethany World Prayer Center, states that there are seven life-giving activities that should occur during a cell group meeting. They are:[10]

1. Prayer as a group
2. Praying for the specific needs of each member
3. Worship
4. Fellowship and interaction
5. Allowing each member to express himself in a transparent manner
6. Sharing praise reports and testimonies
7. Using spiritual gifts.

Then Hornsby continues with a list of seven growth activities that should happen between the meetings:[11]

1. Spending daily time with the Lord in prayer and in devotion for personal edification
2. Praying daily for each cell member and for your city

3. Showing hospitality through social and ministry activity with members and potential members

4. Inviting people you know or meet to attend your cell meeting

5. Following up on visitors who attend your cell and/or church services with personal visits and phone calls

6. Setting clear goals for the growth of your cell and for raising up new leaders

7. Spending time in preparation for the meeting by studying the lesson and by fasting and praying on the day of the meeting.

Hornsby defines what groups should experience together, not the exact form these groups should take.

Victory Christian Center in Tulsa, Oklahoma has defined its groups around the big five:[12]

Worship and Praise: The focus is on magnifying the Lord and exalting the name of Jesus through song, praise, and worship, and often takes 10-15 minutes.

Prayer: While a group will take another 10-15 minutes to pray for the needs and requests of group participants, Victory also stresses praying for others outside the cell—including the government, pastor and church staff, schools, missionaries, and the body of Christ overall.

Word of God: During the next 10-15 minutes, the leader is to facilitate discussion based on the Scripture used in a previous sermon. Each leader is to add personal illustrations to tailor the truth given for that particular group. Victory repeatedly stresses that this is to be a short lesson, focused on applying a nugget of truth, not an extensive, in-depth teaching.

Fellowship and Interaction: Triggered by discussion questions written at the end of each lesson, during these 15-20 minutes each person in the group is to have an opportunity to share what's on his or her heart, whether that be questions, comments, insights, or testimony. It's the leader's goal to have equal participation during this time.

Outreach (ministry and evangelism): Victory encourages leaders to allow the gifts of the Spirit to operate during these closing 15-20 minutes. The leader and his/her apprentice are to minister, edify, and strengthen those gathered, and to help the group learn to flow in the Spirit's gifts. If unbelievers are gathered, this time can also be used to answer questions and communicate God's love. If no unbelievers are present, this time can also be used to strategize for more effective ways to reach the lost.

This explication by Victory's groups puts the focus on what goes on in the meeting, but it goes beyond meeting activities. It enters into the lives of people as they relate to one another as brothers and sisters in everyday life. It penetrates the places where people live and invades how people live as they leave the meetings.

Bill Donahue, from Willow Creek Community Church, uses a definition that extends beyond the bounds of the meetings. This church is known for its seeker-targeted worship services. Few realize that their small group structure is quite advanced and their leadership is directing their groups to become more and more the focus of the church. Many of their new Christians enter the church through small groups. Their groups are to fulfill the following components of group life, no matter what the group looks like in its activities:[13]

1. Love. "Love is expressed in a variety of ways in group life. First, we express love to God through prayer and worship and by giving him praise. We express love to one another as we serve one another and care for one another in our group."
2. Learn. "Learning about Christ and about his will for our lives is a key component of group life. All groups learn—they learn the Scriptures, they learn about one another, and they learn about themselves."
3. Serve. "Service and good works are part of any vibrant, healthy small group. Your group must decide how you will express Christian love to your community or to others in the body."
4. Reach. "Groups must make decisions that ensure the group's purpose and vision are carried out. That means reaching others for Christ."

HOLISTIC CELL GROUPS – EXPLAINING THE ESSENCE

Traditional small groups are uni-focused. They focus on one experience of the Christian life. Bible study groups meet to grow together in biblical knowledge. Discipleship groups meet to hold one another accountable and deepen their walk with Christ. Leadership groups meet around leadership issues. Service groups meet to do the specific task they've committed to accomplish. Evangelism groups meet to win the lost. Fellowship groups meet to develop and deepen friendship. Any additional experiences are a byproduct of the primary experience of the chosen focus of a group.

In contrast, cell groups are holistic in nature. The purpose isn't limited to one aspect of life in Christ. They're more than a group that meets to discuss the Bible. When Christ is in the midst of a group, the Bible will come to life. They're more than a discipleship group. When Christ is in the midst, discipleship will naturally occur. They're more than a group that does evangelism, or works to accomplish a task. When a group focuses on Christ in the midst, the group will reach out to the lost and will work together in projects. The form a group takes is a byproduct of the focus on Christ.

Christ manifests himself in groups through four experiences. The best way to define the experiences of a holistic cell group is found in the Great Commandment and the Great Commission. These two teachings of Christ describe the essence of what cell groups should experience, no matter what form they take.

Written Resources

• *Upward, Inward, Outward, Forward* by Jim Egli

First of all, holistic cell groups reach Upward: "Love the Lord your God with all of your heart, with all of your mind and with all of your strength." Cell groups work because they focus on the living presence of God in the midst of the group. They're not 'fellowship' groups or Bible studies that meet for the sake of being together once per week. These groups have a primary purpose of connecting to God.

Second, holistic cell groups reach Inward: "Love your neighbor as yourself." Loving one another, encouraging one another, forgiving one another, showing hospitality to one another, and exhorting one another, are examples of New Testament commands for life in the church.

Cell group members embrace these commands when they realize a cell group is much more than a weekly meeting. Some have even labeled holistic cell groups as 'Sunday sermon cells' because many churches instruct groups to discuss the Sunday sermon in their group meetings. But if a group is seen as only a meeting where a topic is discussed, then it will fail, no matter what's discussed.

Third, holistic cell groups embrace the Great Commission by reaching Outward: "Go and preach the Gospel, baptizing them in the name of the Father, the Son and the Holy Spirit." Healthy cell groups act as platoons for Christ, reaching out to the unchurched and providing a place where they can find Christ and the love of other Christians.

Finally, holistic cell groups move Forward: "teaching them to observe everything I have commanded you." It's not enough for cell members to attend a meeting every week. The ultimate goal is for them to advance in their relationship with the Lord, becoming more like him. This will result in developing new cell group leaders and birthing new cell groups.

The following diagram illustrates how the four values of Upward, Inward, Outward, and Forward, (UIOF), work together in the development of healthy holistic cell groups.

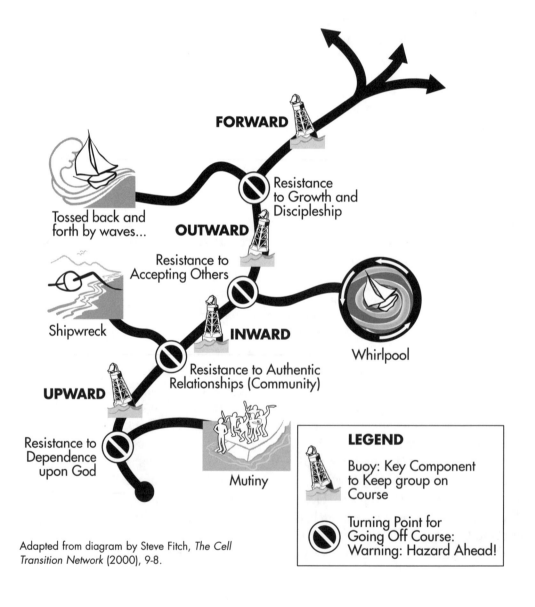

Adapted from diagram by Steve Fitch, *The Cell Transition Network* (2000), 9-8.

Such groups come in a variety of forms, including intergenerational groups that meet in homes. They also include men's groups, women's groups, and youth groups. They include groups that meet during lunch breaks, groups where workers meet at midnight after their shift ends, young mothers' groups that meet on Tuesday mornings, collegiate groups that meet in dorm rooms, and newly married couples' groups that meet on Saturday nights. The form UIOF holistic cell groups can take is unlimited.

THE EXPERIENCE OF A CELL GROUP MEETING

Few disagree with the importance of UIOF and the importance of Christ in the midst, but not everyone agrees upon the experience a group has in a meeting. Some will argue that a group can experience UIOF and only meet once per month. Some state that UIOF is possible through a study on evolution that's taught by an evolution expert. Some will state that an evangelism team can experience UIOF.

The experience of UIOF defines the life a cell group is to experience together. This life is much more than what can be contained in a meeting. But at the same time, a regular meeting is vital to the life of a group. The same could be said about the church at large. By definition, the New Testament use of the word "church" means much more than a gathering for worship and teaching.

The church isn't really entering into the fullness of its calling if it only meets on Sunday. According to the New Testament, the church is the people of God, and the life of the church only starts on Sunday mornings. It extends into the lives of those people, their homes, their work, and their play. But no church would downplay the importance of weekly worship and what should be experienced as the entire body comes together.

While UIOF defines cell group life, it doesn't diminish the role the meeting plays in the life of the group. There are certain experiences of a group meeting that promote UIOF and others that limit it. For instance, weekly meetings enhance the UIOF experience. Though some might argue that Americans are too busy to commit to a weekly meeting, it could also be argued that if a group only meets once a week, it won't experience UIOF. The meeting isn't the focus. Creating the experience of UIOF is, and this requires a deeper commitment to one another than just attending a ninety-minute meeting. The weekly meeting is only the starting point, just as Sunday morning worship is just the beginning of the experience of the church.

Opening the Word together is another experience that promotes UIOF.

Written Resources

- *How to Lead a Great Cell Group Meeting* by Joel Comiskey

Spiritual edification is crucial to group life. The group must learn how to minister to one another through the Word, not just study the Word. One conference attendee put it this way: "Limiting a group meeting to only studying the Word is like going to a cooking class where the leader passes out cookbooks and says, 'We're going to read this cookbook cover to cover. We're going to study each recipe and seek to understand the meaning and the context of each recipe. But we're not going to actually cook any of the recipes and we're not going to eat any of them either. This is a study group, not a cooking group.'"

Worshiping together and praying for one another happens in UIOF cell group meetings, and so does praying for the lost. Many include eating together as a regular practice of a cell group meeting.

Honesty and transparency are crucial components of a group that experiences UIOF. An honest group is attractive to the unchurched. A group that hides behind church rhetoric and biblical knowledge will run off those who are searching and hurting.

THREE WAYS PEOPLE MISUNDERSTAND UIOF CELL GROUPS

In the growing library of literature on small groups, authors discuss cell groups as an option and they often contrast their model of small groups against the cell group strategy. In this contrast, it seems that the cell group experts have failed to communicate clearly the essence of the cell group because it is so often misunderstood. Here are three common ways that cell groups are misunderstood:

"Sunday Sermon Cells"

Many if not most of the cell group based churches around the world write cell discussion guides that are based upon the Sunday sermon. Yet when these churches talk about their cell groups, they don't emphasize the content of their discussion. They emphasize the life that's experienced with one another in these groups. To label these groups as "Sunday sermon cells" puts the focus on the form rather than the experience of these groups. If the only thing a cell group experiences is a discussion about what the pastor preached on Sunday, it will prove to be one of the most boring experiences ever created by the church.

The cell group meeting involves much more than a discussion of a set of questions provided by the pastor. The content of the discussion is the starting point for ministry in the meeting. It doesn't comprise the culmination of the discussion. The purpose of providing uniform cell discussion guides is to free the cell leaders to pray and care for their people rather than having to write lessons for themselves, and to bring the body into unity under the leadership of the church. But the discussion around these guides is designed to be so flexible that the unique needs of each group can be met.

In fact, when cell leaders understand the purpose of the cell discussion guides, they understand how no two cell groups will be the same, even with the same questions asked. The cell group meeting is a place to encounter the presence of the living God. It's a place where cell group members edify one another, encourage one another, and pray for one another. The questions provided by the pastor are only to facilitate that edification, not become the source of that edification.

Care Groups

Another misunderstanding of holistic UIOF groups is called Care Groups. These groups limit themselves to the role of maintenance by connecting those who are already Christians. These groups meet regularly, but don't have a vision for reaching those who don't know Christ, and there's no plan for discipling the group members into Christian leadership. The goal is for the group leader to care for the group members by providing a context for fellowship, Bible discussion, and friendship.

Many churches intend to create holistic cell groups, but they inadvertently end up with care groups. In a survey conducted at a pastors' forum, the participants were polled to determine the greatest barrier to effectiveness in their cell groups. Almost everyone identified the lack of evangelism. The experience of such groups proves lifeless after all the current church members are assimilated into groups. Care for one another is not enough.

Deeper Life Bible Studies

Many have a definition of a cell group that focuses upon deep Bible discussion. In the book, *Seven Deadly Sins of Small Group Ministry*, authors Donahue and Robinson state that in the past, "The definition of small group life was often limited to several people at a table, Bible in one hand and fill-in-the-blank curriculum in the other."[14]

Such groups often meet around a table, each member with a Bible study guide and pen in hand, answering questions about the interpretation of a scriptural passage, the original meaning of a Greek word, and the context in which the passage was written. Such experiences are often labeled 301 or 401 level small groups.

The purpose of a holistic UIOF small group is not Bible study—although the Bible plays a large part. Instead, when discussing the Bible in a group meeting, members seek to enter into transparency and apply the Bible passage to their lives. It's not a place to study about the meaning of *agape*, but to demonstrate *agape* to one another. It's not a place to deeply study about the spiritual gifts, but to allow the Spirit to empower the members of the body for ministry to one another. Deep Bible study occurs in a different setting with gifted teachers. Most cell group leaders aren't equipped to lead helpful discussions in deep Bible study. But they can facilitate application of the Scripture in life and ministry to one another.

CONFUSION OVER HOW THE TERM 'CELL GROUP' IS USED

While the phrase "cell groups" was originally coined to refer to holistic cell groups as described above, many churches are now using the phrase to describe groups that are not holistic in nature. They label all kinds of groups as cell groups, without a clear definition of what should occur in those groups. For instance, many have changed the name of Sunday school classes to Sunday cells. Or evangelism groups that meet once per month are also called cell groups. Some even advocate calling groups within the choir cells, (i.e. the tenor cell, bass cell, etc.).

In other words, churches are taking the current small groups that already are formed in the church and labeling them cell groups, without evaluating whether those groups are accomplishing a predetermined vision that God is calling the church to be. The churches assume that 'small is great' no matter what its form.

The following is not a judgment on how churches use the words "cell groups." It's only designed to clear up the confusion for cell group novices who read the title "cell groups" and then assume that all the different kinds accomplish the same purposes. It seeks to look beneath the surface of the terminology and clarify that these groups are not only different in their forms, but also in their experiences.

Leadership Groups

Many churches have adopted the Groups of 12 (G-12) strategy that was first developed at International Charismatic Mission in Bogota, Colombia. Rocky Malloy states in his book, *The Jesus System Groups of Twelve: Launching Your Ministry into Explosive Growth*, that in this strategy there are two types of cell groups. First there's the open cell group that meets weekly for edification and expansion. These are the holistic UIOF groups discussed above. Malloy then states that there's a second type of cell group that meets as a closed cell group. This group meets weekly for the development of leaders.

Malloy has spent years seeking to understand the G-12 system and articulate it in his books. He properly describes the two types of groups. The first is a regular cell group, the other is a closed group. But by calling both "cells," it's confusing to the G-12 novice. It makes it sound as though the open cell group is on the same level as the closed group, allowing people to choose between the two.

After further inspection of the G-12 system, it becomes clear that the open cell group is very different in nature from a closed leadership group. The closed group is a G-12 group, which is a gathering of cell group leaders. The G-12 group is not open to anyone who wants to participate in it. In other words, the cell group leaders gather together with their leader every week to discuss their cell groups, receive prayer and encouragement, and receive leadership development training. The G-12 group is a weekly leadership huddle, not a cell group.

Recently, we called a prominent G-12 church and asked how many cell groups it has. We were given a number, and then asked if this number reflected just open groups or a combination of open groups and closed G-12 groups. It turned out to be a combination, and there was no accurate count of the open groups. G-12 churches emphasize the importance of the open cell group, and do this by developing cell group leaders through the closed G-12 groups. But calling both of these groups "cell groups" is mixing apples and oranges. They have different purposes.

Evangelistic Target Groups

Another popular type of group is the small group that seeks to reach out to the lost within a target group. New Life Church in Colorado Springs has developed and propagated this model, calling its groups "Free-Market Cell Groups." These groups, which meet for thirteen-week periods, have the purpose of reaching out to the lost through building relationships around a common interest, such as quilting, reading novels, playing basketball, or gardening.

This system uses the Engel scale to describe where a person is in his or her journey to Christ. "Engel places people on a line with twelve degrees, from –8 to +3 (including zero) where the –8 indicates a person who has no knowledge of the Gospel and the +3 indicates a person who has several years of conceptual and behavioral growth in Christ. At the 0, one is born again."[15]

Free-market groups are designed with a specific focus for different kinds of people, depending upon where people are on the Engel scale. The goal of each group is to help people take one step along the Engel scale toward Christ. This model has all kinds of "cell groups." One might meet to discuss the future of nuclear physics, another for mountain biking, and another for a discussion of Romans.

More than twenty years ago, Ralph Neighbour, Jr. tested a very similar type of group for evangelism, which he called share groups. These groups meet for about thirteen weeks and are comprised of three believers and up to nine nonbelievers. "Share groups provide the contact between the unchurched and believers, using homes of share group members as a neutral meeting place … Share groups are a special arm of evangelism, reaching out from the shepherd group (cell group) to the hardest groups to reach—the totally unchurched persons who have been ignored by [most] churches."[16]

Neighbour also developed another concept of interest groups. An experienced guitar teacher could hold a class for twelve weeks to teach people how to play the guitar. Or a couple could hold a class on parenting to reach out to the troubled parents in the neighborhood. These groups are designed to build relationships with the unchurched and lead them one step closer to Christ. Neighbour's share groups and interest groups were not placed on the same level as the UIOF cell group; rather, they're subgroups of a cell group, whose purpose is relational evangelism.

The Free-Market model is tapping into some powerful principles about how to reach the unchurched around common interests. But as churches explore how they'll define their cell groups, it's crucial to understand that a free-market cell group accomplishes different goals than a holistic UIOF cell group. To say a free-market approach works better than the holistic approach is once again comparing apples to oranges. They are two different kinds of small groups that have different experiences.

Admittedly, people who meet around an interest can experience UIOF. For instance, a group of men interested in playing volleyball might meet every Saturday morning to play. But if all they do is play volleyball, then it's a volleyball group. If they gather in a circle for forty-five minutes to an hour and encourage one another and pray for one another, then they're embracing the elements of a UIOF group.

Sunday School Cells

Ken Hemphill, former president of Southwestern Baptist Theological Seminary and pastor of multiple Sunday school-based churches, compares Sunday school classes with cell groups. He wrote, "I have frequently defined a Sunday school class as 'a cell group that meets in your church building on Sunday morning' and a cell group as 'a Sunday school class that meets outside your building at some other time.'"[17] Many have bought into this philosophy and made the transition to the cell-based church by simply changing the name of their Sunday school to "Sunday cells."

As I interviewed a staff pastor of a church with more than one hundred holistic UIOF cell groups, he shared how he served as a staff member of one of the largest and most successful Sunday school churches in North America. I asked him to share with me the differences between Sunday school and cell groups. To summarize, he said there's a night and day difference.

On the other hand, can a group that meets on the church campus on Sunday morning live out the values of UIOF? Theoretically, a group can experience UIOF anywhere. There are many Sunday cells at Victory Christian Center in Tulsa that are doing this very thing. Yet for most churches, it would be a grave mistake to label their Sunday school classes "cell groups," expecting them to produce UIOF. Most Sunday school attendees are so entrenched in a model of Sunday school that doesn't promote UIOF that it's impossible for them to change the pattern. First they'll have to change their venue before they can change their values.

Task Groups

Another type of small group that has become popular is the task group. These groups are established to work on a specific task, such as counting the offering, mowing the church lawn, parking cars, or working in the nursery. Some churches have determined that it's impossible for people to be involved in a task group and participate in a holistic UIOF cell group. Therefore, they identify these task groups as cells. The argument looks like this: "The parking lot team works together every week and they pray before they park cars. Through this task they develop deep friendships and they begin to care for one another. The key is not that they meet for an official meeting every week, but they develop a sense of community."

While this is better than nothing and many people have developed connections with other believers with this approach, how does the group experience the "where two or three are gathered in my name, there I am also?" No pastor would give permission to a church member to skip the Sunday celebration service because he serves the Lord the rest of the week by working around the church or reaching out to the homeless. A person needs to experience worship and teaching, along with everyone else in the church. In the same way, why would we give permission for a group to skip out on the experience of gathering around the Word of God to encourage one another, pray for one another, and challenge one another?

A task group can accomplish some of UIOF through one-on-one and ad hoc interaction. But it's too easy for people to skip out on ministering to one another, if there's no regular time when the group can encounter the Lord together. At the same time, if a group wants to gather around a task, like maintaining the church lawn, this is great; but there should also be a weekly time when the group can minister to one another and experience UIOF.

DEFINE YOUR GROUPS

No two churches will use the same words to define what it means to be a fruitful cell group. But all churches that are successful in cell ministry incorporate the four dimensions of Upward, Inward, Outward, and Forward. These dimensions are taught and modeled. The cell groups practice various activities to fulfill these dimensions.

A church's definition cannot be copied from Bethany World Prayer Center, Victory Christian Center, or Willow Creek Community Church. Its definition must reflect its own vocabulary, culture, and vision. It also must be birthed out of time with the Lord, interaction with key leaders, and experiencing the life of a cell group. Words are artificial and empty unless they have meaning to people. Leaders must find words and clear definitions that mean something to their people. Fill them with new meaning and make sure they incorporate the four dimensions of Upward, Inward,

Outward, and Forward.

One church has synthesized these principles into their definition of groups. They define "cell groups" as: A group of 4-15 people who gather as a sub-group of the local church around the presence of God, build community, reach out to the hurting world, and develop new leaders, which will result in the creation of new groups in the future. Bill Beckham uses the phrase "primary groups" to define the cell groups. He compares this with the "multi-group system." When cell groups are defined as primary groups, it does not limit the types of groups. It only means that other types of groups flow out of the life of the experience of community in the primary groups.

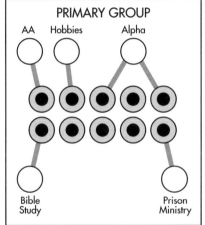

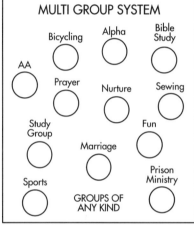

Defining a cell group based upon its intended experiences sets clear boundaries that good leaders need. These boundaries provide space to play. Leaders who don't have boundaries wonder if they're doing it right and often get overwhelmed with self-questioning about their leadership.

At the same time, leaders who have boundaries placed upon them that are too tight feel confined and frustrated. Therefore the boundaries must be clear and they must allow for flexibility. With clarity of definition and direction, the leader has permission to pray and think creatively about how a group can experience the life of UIOF. If a leader understands Upward, Inward, Outward, Forward, he can be creative and gather his group at a restaurant and pray for one another after eating.

If someone is a great volleyball player and has a heart to lead a group of other volleyball players, they can gather for a weekly game and spend an hour after the game ministering to one another. A sewing group can gather to sew and then take time to share the Word and pray for one another.

With this flexibility, it's tempting to say the group is focused upon volleyball or sewing, but the activity does not define the group. The life of Upward, Inward, Outward, Forward shapes the group and focuses it on the presence of Christ, not an activity. The activity is only an expression of the life the group has together.

CELL GROUP DEFINITION WORKSHEET

Visit a cell group church and ask to observe a cell group meeting, and to interview a cell leader to answer the following questions:

1. How does your church define "cell group?"

2. How does your cell group:
   • deepen intimacy with God?
   • grow individuals as disciples?
   • build evangelistic relationships with nonbelievers?
   • prepare group members to multiply by developing them as leaders?

3. Describe the agenda for your regular cell group meeting.

4. How do group members interact with each other during the week between meetings, both intentionally and spontaneously?

GOD-MADE CELL GROUPS

Bill Beckham

A church that will impact the twenty-first century must have a working unit that's simple, self-contained, and easily reproduced. The unit must generate fierce loyalty to its lifestyle and must be sustainable even during intense persecution and opposition. This basic unit must be able to pass on values, assimilate a harvest, mobilize members, and produce necessary leaders. This basic unit is the small group cell. It was the basic unit in the first century and it must be today.

In its New Testament form, a cell was as warm and nurturing as a family, as disciplined and focused as a squad of soldiers, and as self-contained and cohesive as a biological cell. This dynamic small group unit allows the church to be a holy church and a harvest church, no matter what its size or geographical location, the sociological conditions around it, or the culture in which it exists.

Many churches have tried cell groups. They've learned about the structure of cell groups found in the world's most evangelistic churches. But in their replication of others' structures, many churches have created manmade groups. Such groups can be effective in building relationships, promoting fellowship, and implementing a specific task, such as studying the Bible, or caring for the hurting. However, they cannot produce the life and power we see in the New Testament. The church today needs God-made cells instead of man-made groups.

THE MOST IMPORTANT ASPECTS OF A NEW TESTAMENT CELL

Where a cell meets is not most important. A cell can meet under a shade tree. When a cell meets is not most significant. A cell can meet at three o'clock in the morning with a group of shift workers. Who is in the cell is not primary. The cell can be homogeneous or heterogeneous, all men or all women, old or young, educated or uneducated, rich or poor. What the group is called is not definitive. These cells have been called cells, house churches, small groups, life groups, seeker groups, and fellowship groups. Shakespeare reminds us that "a rose by any other name will smell as sweet."

Which oversight system is used is not decisive; 5x5, G-12, J-12, G-12.3, or other leadership systems can manage these cell groups. How the cell multiplies is not the essential issue. These groups can multiply as cells by biologically splitting, or can multiply as families by beginning new generations of cells.

The importance of a cell is found in what it is and what it does. A cell is the most basic form of the spiritual body of Christ on earth. A New Testament cell is God-made, Christ-indwelled, and Spirit-led. A cell is in community, on mission, and lives as the body of Christ. The cell is the indwelling presence of the Father, the resurrection power of the Son, and the eternal purpose of the Spirit. A cell is organically, socially, and functionally organized around the Trinity. The Father makes the cell a family. A cell is not all of the body of Christ but is its most basic form.

The cell's significance is found in what it does. It lives out the life and purpose of Christ on earth between his ascension and second coming. A cell is the ministry of Christ on earth through the Spirit while Christ is in heaven.

I DON'T LIKE THE NAME "CELL!"

Many Christians around the world are suspicious, or even critical, of the word "cell." A frequent comment is that "the word cell reminds me of prison cells or communists cells." The complaint is also made that "today the word is used for terrorist cells." Why insist on using a word that's associated with such unsavory activities?

We can use any word we like for basic Christian community. It's not the word "cell," but the concept and nature of "cell" that's important. From the design and nature of the biological cell, we can learn important truths about the basic cell unit that makes up the body of Christ.

In a 1998 conference, Robert Lay, director of TOUCH Brazil, was teaching about the cell. An elderly lady approached him and said, "I understand the teaching about the DNA and RNA of the cell. DNA stands for the *Divine Nature of the Almighty.* RNA stands for *Relationships Nurtured through Amour.*" This Christian grandmother understood that a spiritual cell group is not about using the right words, but about the divine nature of love that operates around God's divine nature.

All healthy life and growth functions take place within the cell itself. Without cells, the body cannot be the body. God used this life cell principle when he created his own spiritual body on earth. Christ's body, the church, consists of cells. Cells in Christ's spiritual body fulfill the same function as cells in the physical body. Cells are spiritual units with a simple physical form.

Christ in the midst is the "DNA" of the cell: the blueprint, life force, genetic code, information highway, and catalyst, that tells the cell how to grow and what to be. Without Christ (the nucleus) at the center of every cell, the individual cells cannot function and the body cannot exist as his body.

The DNA (Christ) directs the cell to do those activities that build it up. Through its members, RNA begins new "sites" where new cells are assembled. Edification, "the building up of the body," takes place. Holiness and harvest are built into the very nature of the church's most basic unit.

The cell lives to reproduce. One primary requirement for any hereditary material is that it be able to reproduce itself. Information must be

Common Names Used by Churches for Cell Groups

- Cell Groups
- TOUCH (Transforming Others Under Christ's Hand) Groups
- Hope Groups
- LIFE (Living in Fellowship Everyday) Groups
- Small Groups
- Home Groups
- Community Groups
- Reach Groups
- Kinship Groups
- Encounter Groups (E-Groups)
- Connecting Groups
- Koinonia Groups
- Acts Groups
- Impact Groups

passed along exactly from generation to generation. New materials are brought into the cell, so it will have the ingredients to become two cells. Evangelism is the natural process of growth within the spiritual cell. At the right time, the cell "unzips" and the stairway of gifts multiplies and becomes two identical cells, each with the nucleus of Christ in its midst.

Each individual cell is self-contained, but capable of joining with other cells to be larger and more complex bodies. In a cell, Jesus himself is the one essential factor in the life of his called-out community on earth.

FIVE ELEMENTS OF CELL LIFE

The hand is a marvelously designed instrument and an excellent picture of a cell. A large number of bones in the human body are in hands. The human hand uniquely sets man apart from all animals. With the hand, a person can do both very delicate and very heavy work.

The arrangement of the four fingers with the thumb makes the human hand so special. Each finger operates in relationship to the thumb. The hand, as a tool, is effective because of its integrated design. All the fingers work independently, but also interdependently with the thumb.

The hand illustration is a useful tool for understanding the essential elements of cells. It provides an intentional and predictable system for implementing cell group life. The cell unit can be predictable when the five important elements of cell group life are used in all cells. This hand illustration is simple enough for a child to understand, but profound enough to contain the very life of Christ in community.

The thumb represents community.

Only community can integrate the other ministry elements of the church. Equipping/discipleship, accountability, leadership, and evangelism fit together as a whole when activated in community. However, no one of the other elements will unite the others. For instance, a focus on equipping often neglects evangelism. The element of accountability may become legalistic and restrictive while focusing in upon itself. Integrating the work of the church around leaders often focuses on the particular gifts of the leader and neglects the other important elements. Evangelism as the integrating element often neglects the other four.

But New Testament cell community integrates the other elements and allows them to operate in the proper way at the proper time. The thumb represents the cell meeting that's the most basic wineskin of

Christ. The thumb also represents the spiritual aspect of cell life that unites the life of all the members into the life of Christ. Jesus' concept of "abiding" (John 15 and 1 John 1) sums up the New Testament meaning of community.

The little finger represents equipping.

The little finger reminds us of the new babies, the new believers, and the "little ones." Large numbers of new Christians have been birthed over the last decades but have been neglected and lost to meaningful ministry within the church system. Churches with no small group family structure must try to care for the spiritual babies in a sterile institutional setting. New Christians are placed in a "warehouse" environment in the Sunday structure.

Christ provided for the care of his spiritual babies within spiritual families (small group family type communities). Therefore, new believers in a cell church are cared for in a small group family setting. Cell leaders are spiritual parents to new believers. The other cell members are older brothers and sisters to help guide the steps of new babies.

E. Stanley Jones, the great Methodist missionary to India, illustrates the need for a place where the weak can feed their inner spirit. "I sat alongside of Lake Massaweepie, in the Adirondacks, writing this book. Each morning a wild duck came by foraging near the shore with her brood. One duck seemed to be weaker than the rest and spent most of his time just keeping up with the others. He had no time to feed. Many of us spend most of our time keeping up with our tasks. We have no time to feed our inner spirits. We lack a plus, a margin of power that lets us meet our tasks with something left over."[18]

That weak little duck needed a place to feed without trying to keep up with the others. It needed a flock that cared for the weaker and didn't tie feeding onto the activity pace of the strongest. To continue to try to keep up, without the opportunity to feed, would doom the weak little duck to become weaker and weaker. It needed a "margin of power" to "meet its tasks with something left over."

All of us are "weak little ducks." Every Christian needs a time of personal feeding that's not tied to keeping up with the crowd's activity. Without this, the Christian grows weaker and weaker. The small group is the context in which we receive a "plus, a margin of power, that lets us meet our tasks with something left over."

Basic Christian community is the time that every little duck can feed together without the pressure of trying to keep up. Jesus provided for this feeding time within the context of the small group meeting.

The ring finger stands for accountability.

In the New Testament the concept of accountability is associated with the "one another" passages such as: "And be kind to one another, tender-hearted, forgiving each other" (Ephesians 4:32).

One of the names Jesus uses for his promised Spirit explains the meaning of accountability and removes the fear from it. The Spirit is the Advocate: "the one who comes alongside" (John 14:16). This is a beautiful picture of the work of the Spirit and the spirit of accountability. The Holy Spirit comes alongside and cares for the Christian. The Spirit's work is multiplied in a cell as he enlists each member to share in his work of "coming alongside" every member. The Holy Spirit, through one cell member, "comes alongside" others to support and encourage.

Activities associated with this finger in a cell group church begin with a mentor for a new believer. Members in a cell who aren't mentoring a new believer will partner in support pairs, men with men, and women with women. This finger also represents the accountability relationships among leaders who support each other through mentoring.

The large finger stands for leadership.

This finger represents strong and mature people in the cell who are spiritual fathers and mothers. Christ called out and prepared leaders to care for the babies and to lead his flock.

In 1 John, the writer separates this mentoring process into fathers, young men, and children. Fathers mentor young men who then mentor children. Leadership grows out of the heart of God as Father. Fathers (and mothers) are mature Christians. Young men (and women) are growing Christians. Children are new believers. Mature members in a cell live out the love and life of Father God, who parents his children in the spiritual family of the cell.

The term "father" implies reproduction. The cell's objective is to reproduce itself. This must take place first at the point of leadership. Every cell has a leader and is developing at least one other to become a leader.

The index finger represents evangelism.

This finger is good for pointing, directing, and picking up things. It represents evangelism, because this element of the cell points direction for lost people, directs cell members toward the lost, and "picks up" the lost.

Jesus came "to seek and to save the lost." This is the heart of God. It's Christ's eternal purpose. He is the center of the cell and his desire is fulfilled through the cell. Jesus promised, "If I am lifted up, I will draw all men unto myself." The beginning of evangelism is when Christ is lifted up in the cell. He then draws the lost to himself.

Evangelism in a cell group church is varied, creative, and comprehensive. Through cells, a cell group church will throw out different evangelism nets. Relationship evangelism (*oikos* evangelism) is the basic form of evangelism in a cell group church. In order to enlarge the *oikos* (extended contacts) of a cell, a church will also evangelize through special groups that target unbelievers who are outside the relationship sphere of cell members. Cell group churches also plan periodic harvest events so cells can come together and bring group contacts to a special event.

This is a simple picture of how Christ, through the Spirit, expresses his life through the most basic unit of his body—the cell. Now with your hand, you carry a picture of the cell wherever you go.

CHRIST IN THE MIDST: THE "THREE P'S"

The hand also illustrates the cell's life and dynamic. Christ can be visualized in the center of the hand. This mental image is a reminder that Christ is present in the cell, empowers the cell, and uses the cell. Christ in the cell's midst means that the full Trinitarian expression of God is present as the Father, Son, and Spirit. A healthy cell operates in the "Three P's":

The presence of Christ: "What he indwells."
The power of Christ: "He empowers."
The purpose of Christ: "What he indwells and empowers, he uses."

In discussing a cell's characteristics, we must begin with Christ. His presence is the key to the cell. Jesus is the beginning and ending of Christian community, the Alpha and Omega of the cell. Unless we start with him, we'll end up with something other than Christ and something other than New Testament community. Other tasks and works will become primary, and Christ will be a secondary influence upon what happens in the group.

THE HAND PROVIDES A PICTURE OF DEATH

In the hand illustration, the thumb and fingers represent the cell's tasks and the palm represents Christ in the midst of the cell. Imagine a scar on the wrist, which represents the nail scar on Christ's wrist. This reminds us that there's no real community apart from death.

In order to live in community, group members must die to all agendas except Christ. "Hidden agendas" can be superimposed upon a cell and a cell group church. Individuals' agendas are objects of obsessions (what I need), possessions (what I have), or professions (what I believe). These obsessions, possessions, or professions become more important to the individual than community with others. The cell group or church must meet conditions about these agendas before the individual will live in community with the group.

We have fellowship with God and with each other by way of Christ's death. On the cross, Christ broke down all the barriers that separate us from him and from each other. The work of reconciliation began in the Garden when Jesus said, "Not my will, but Your will be done," and that work of community continues as individuals enter into that same death. "Not my will, but God's will be done in my life, in my cell, and in my church." *Participation in community begins by death to selfish interests.*

THE TEST FOR GOD-MADE CELLS: DOES CHRIST SHOW UP?

How does a church know if it has God-made cells or man-made groups? Jesus said, "Where two or three gather together in my name there I am in their midst." The test of a God-made cell is whether or not Christ shows up and directs the meeting or, more correctly, whether or not group members acknowledge Christ, who is already there. He promised to be in each group that gathers in his name. The real issue is whether or not group members "see" him.

But, is it really possible for Christ to be in a group and the members not recognize and relate to him? One of Jesus' post-resurrection appearances verifies that it is possible to have him present but unrecognized. Cleopas and another disciple were walking home to Emmaus on the evening of Jesus' resurrection. "And after that, he appeared in a different form to two of them, while they were walking along on their way to the country. And they went away and reported it to the others, but they did not

**Cell Group
Vision Team Exercise**

Why is the presence of Christ the key to an effective cell group meeting?

What other things do group leaders tend to depend upon?

Why is it so easy to depend upon other things than the presence of Christ?

believe them either" (Mark 16:12-13). See Luke 24:13-35 for a more detailed account of this fascinating story.

The seven-mile walk plus the brief time Jesus was in the home must have taken at least two hours, the amount of time for a small group cell meeting. They remember that their hearts had "burned within" them as they walked with him. But here is an instance where those who knew Christ didn't recognize him, even though he was with them for at least two hours, teaching them.

Christ has promised that he will be in the midst of every group that gathers in his name, but we must have our eyes open. We must expect him and acknowledge his presence! We must keep an appointment with him, instead of attending a meeting about him. Otherwise, we do what the two disciples did. We talk about him. We even explain things to him. We recite Scriptures referring to him and even receive teaching from him. But, in all that time, we don't recognize and acknowledge him as Christ with us.

Think of the tragedy of that seven-mile walk! These two disciples could have been with the resurrected Lord for those seven miles, worshipping him, learning from him, and having fellowship with him. But all they experienced was a stimulating conversation, some good teaching, and a "burning in their hearts." They had a little spiritual indigestion instead of a wonderful experience with Christ.

Think about the modern day tragedy! Christ has been showing up in every small group meeting wherever and whenever Christians gather together in his name. Yet, for the most part, those Christians study or talk about Christ or do something in his name, but they don't experience the reality of his living presence. In a God-made cell, Christ will certainly show up in presence, power, and purpose, but we must expect him, prepare for him, acknowledge him, and talk to him.

CELL LIFE IS FAITH, NOT FEELING

How do we know Christ shows up? Some depend upon feelings and believe Christ is present when they feel he is there. But feelings can be deceiving when it comes to the things of God.

Our faith confirms and verifies the presence of Christ to us, but our faith doesn't make him present. Christ is there because he's there as the living God. He's there out of his own being, intention, omnipresence, and promise, not because of our spiritual feelings or intellectual imaginings. He's there like he was with Moses at the burning bush and in the Tent of

Meeting. He's there like he was with the women and the disciples on the resurrection morning. He's there like he was with the disciples at Pentecost.

He's there because he promised to be with us. We believe he keeps his promises. We know he's with us and within us as individuals. Therefore, when we gather together in his name, he's there with us in our small group cell meeting.

Faith is the lens through which we see and relate to the resurrected Christ. Through the Spirit's work, Christians exercise this resurrection faith when gathered together in small cell groups. Through this resurrection faith, every Christian can recognize, experience, and encounter the living Christ.

The resurrected Christ waits for each cell group member to acknowledge him when they meet. It's then that they begin to participate in a New Testament, God-made, Christ-indwelled, and Spirit-led cell.

SATAN SEEKS TO DESTROY THE CELL

Satan has always tried to destroy God's work at the most basic and vulnerable point. Satan's first century plan was twofold in nature. Striking at the point of incarnation, Satan sought to kill the baby. When that failed, the fallback plan was to strike a deathblow to Christ when he was defenseless on the cross and to win the war. That plan failed at the mouth of the open tomb.

Today, Satan's strategy once again is to attack Christ at the most basic, exposed, and vulnerable point. Destroy Christ where he manifests his presence, power, and purpose in the church, and Satan believes he'll win a significant battle on earth, even though he has already lost the war in heaven.

Satan's battle against God's Kingdom is fought in every living room where two or three gather together in Jesus' name. The plan of Satan is to keep Christ from controlling and empowering the most basic form of his body on earth; blinding the followers so they don't see him in living reality, and turning their faith toward academic doctrines, good works, and spiritual experiences rather than toward the resurrected Christ. Satan's hope is to control the practical application of the life of Christ in and through the most basic expression of his life on earth: the cell.

If Satan can't keep a church from forming small groups, he uses a fallback position. He seeks to distort the nature of the groups, by confusing the focus of the groups, emphasizing the use of human techniques, and taking the spiritual power out of the groups. He will do anything to get peo-

3 Rules for Naming Your Cell Groups

1. Choose a name that fits your church. What you call your groups should fit the language of your church. For instance, one church in Tennessee is called True Life Church. It makes sense for them to call their groups Life Groups.

2. Give new meaning to old words. Deny the urge to create new words to introduce new ideas. It's much easier to change the meaning of old, already accepted words than it is to introduce new words that are foreign. "Home cell groups" are used to describe the organic development and growth of life that resembles the organic life and growth of a biological cell. In some churches, this biological analogy communicates well. In other places, it does not.

3. Reflect the purpose of the groups. Words communicate purpose. The name chosen should reflect the stated purpose of the groups. Some names used for small groups don't communicate the purpose of holistic cell groups. The first is "Bible Study," as the group is much more than a study group. Another, "Growth Groups," tends to communicate that the group focuses on personal growth and doesn't intend to reach out to the unchurched. The same is true for "Fellowship Group." "House Church" gives the impression that the group is distinct or separate from the larger church and could tend to breed independence.

ple to focus on something other than Christ in the midst of the group. People will think a cell group is about discussing the Sunday sermon. Others will determine that the focus should be working through a book study. Still others will focus on a common interest, like cooking. While these things aren't bad, they can't compare to what God will do in a group that will gather every week to solely focus on him.

How is Satan's plan thwarted? The church must return to the New Testament cell dynamic where Christ indwells, empowers, and uses the cell to carry out his ministry purpose on earth. Satan's plans are thwarted through God-made, Christ-indwelled, and Spirit-led cells, rather than man-made groups.

GOOD AGENDAS GIVE ONLY TEMPORARY RELIEF

Even religious small groups fall far short of the small group community movement recorded in the New Testament. The modern church has become so dependent on Bible study curriculum that its leaders don't know what to do when Christ shows up to do something that wasn't in the lesson plan. Christ's presence is the one dynamic that cannot be duplicated in any other type of group. No other group expects it, prepares for it, or claims it. Only the group that lives in the presence, power, and purpose of Christ as an intentional focus experiences the incarnate, indwelling, resurrected, and living presence of Christ in their midst in a New Testament way.

Such a group is more than a meeting where ten people get together to talk about the meaning of a Bible passage and answer a set of questions asked by the leader. When Christ is in the midst of a group, he isn't looking for people to answer the questions properly and go home after drinking coffee. He wants to lead those people into an encounter with himself. He invites people to share their joys and hurts. He wants to apply the Word to their hearts. He wants to minister to people, so they might be healed of their sin.

Cell group agendas, discussion guides, and Bible lessons are only a starting point for something much more significant than getting the right answers. Agendas provide questions that probe to see how God is moving upon the hearts and minds of the people in the group.

When groups discover the power of recognizing Christ's presence, they've tapped into the power to significantly and permanently change the world around them. We must recapture what was happening in the home of Aquila and Priscilla in the first century.

EXPERIENCING CHRIST'S PRESENCE

There are no magic formulas for experiencing Christ's presence. However, some simple attitudes and activities seem to prepare the way for experiencing him in cell life.

First, exercise resurrection faith. Experiencing his presence, power, and purpose is a great act of faith. We believe that what he said he does, even though we can't physically see him or touch him. Jesus understood this when he taught his disciples during his post-resurrection appearances. He said, "Blessed are you who have seen and believe. But more blessed are those who do not see but who believe." Believe what? Believe that the resurrected Christ is in our midst.

Second, continually acknowledge his presence at the beginning of each cell group meeting. He has promised to be with us, so we should welcome him into every cell meeting. Some use an empty chair as a physical reminder of his spiritual, but real presence.

Third, prepare for his power to operate. Use the empty chair as the place of sharing needs, the place of root cause revelation, and the place of opportunity for prayer and healing. For instance, when a member has a need, he or she sits in the chair and briefly shares. Everyone listens to God and seeks his wisdom in identifying and verbalizing real root causes. The group prays specifically as God leads, expecting him to work in power. The experience is debriefed after sufficient time to evaluate what God has done.

Fourth, teach on themes that help people understand related truths about Christ's presence. These themes include the work of the Holy Spirit (how Christ relates to us between his ascension and second coming); the mystery of the indwelling Christ; the omnipresence of God; and Mary and Martha models (working for, or relating to, Christ).

Fifth, read Ray Stedman's book, *Body Life*, periodically. God taught Stedman the meaning of this great truth.

Sixth, focus eyes and hearts in the right direction. With Christ in our midst, we should look in the middle of our circle, rather than up toward heaven. Sing and pray to Christ (in the midst) rather than to God far away in heaven.

Seventh, believe, speak, and act on the promise that where two or three come together in Jesus' name, he is in the midst.

Eighth, practice the presence of Christ personally and share with others how this happens.

DEVELOPING A CELL GROUP VISION THAT FITS YOUR CHURCH

M. Scott Boren

Powerhouse Christian Center in a western suburb of Houston is a large cell-based church that has developed family cell groups, with a focus on men mentoring men and women mentoring women, and a G-12 oversight structure. Hosanna Church, a mid-sized congregation set just 10 miles east of Powerhouse, has developed a network of homogeneous groups, including men's, women's, and youth cells, with an organic oversight structure that resembles the G-12.3.

Five miles to the north of Hosanna sits a large, creative Baptist church with successful programs, which has developed cell groups that parallel the programs the church has used successfully for more than a decade. Less than three miles further is a young church, Crosspoint Church, which meets in an elementary school on Sundays, and focuses all ministry through the family cell groups that have been developed.

These churches believe passionately in what they're doing. All are building biblical community through these groups, and are reaching people for Christ. While leaders of all four churches have attended cell group conferences, read lots of books on various cell group models, and have even used professional consultants to help them develop their current approach to groups, they have slightly different visions for their operation.

That's as it should be. It's absurd to think God has created one cell group model for all other churches to emulate. Even though all four of these churches sit in a middle-class suburban area of western Houston, each one is quite distinct. To believe God created these four churches to be identical is like believing he created four men to be identical. God does not create clones. Even identical twins have distinctives that make each one unique.

The role of the Cell Group Vision Team is to articulate the unique form groups will take in a particular church. The goal is to learn from cell group models, not to copy a predetermined ideal cell group church structure. Such a structure doesn't exist. The goal is to create cell groups where people experience the life of Christ and express Upward, Inward, Outward, Forward values. The forms this will take vary from church to church.

QUESTIONS TO CONSIDER

Before embarking upon the cell group journey, the Vision Team should articulate the vision it feels God has called the church to be. In determining this vision, a church should take the following into consideration:

1. The vision of the senior pastor

The vision God has given the senior pastor will determine much about the vision for cell groups. Some have argued that if the senior pastor isn't leading the charge for groups, then don't start them. This is definitely true of churches with fewer than five hundred members. Larger churches can start cell groups within the structure of the church without the senior pastor leading the vision, but in order for the groups to take off, the senior pastor will eventually have to undertake the vision.

To illustrate, G. F. Watkins, a former high school football coach, pastors Powerhouse Christian Center, one of the churches discussed above. His vision is very bold and focuses upon the mentoring of men, and training them to be leaders of their families. Therefore, all their family groups are led by men, because it fits into the vision and focus of the pastor. His cell vision fits his approach to ministry. His church building is even located near a large high school football stadium.

Key questions for senior pastor:

- What kind of vision for cell groups has God put in the heart of the senior pastor?
- What kind of time can the senior pastor commit to learning about and developing this vision?
- What kind of cell group is the senior pastor willing to lead and/or participate in?

2. The age of the church

The older the church, the more entrenched it will be in the old ways of doing church. With more established programs in place, it might be better to develop a modest cell group transformation vision that aims not to transform the entire church, but to experiment with cell groups and allow them to develop organically. Churches that are less than ten years old are often more flexible and allow for more innovation.

Key questions regarding age:

- How entrenched is the church body in traditional forms of ministry?
- Has the church membership grown to expect the pastor to leave in less than five years, and therefore will only see cell groups as another innovation that will come and go?

3. The size of the church

In smaller churches (less than 250) it's very difficult—if not impossible—to develop cell groups unless it's the main focus of the primary leadership, including the senior pastor. In mid-sized churches (250-500), it's easier to experiment with cell groups without completely buying into the cell group vision. In churches over 500, cell groups can be developed alongside current programs until the cell groups demonstrate that they're working well.

4. The vision for children

Key questions about children:

• What's the vision for children in cell group life?
• Is there a champion for intergenerational cell group life who'll research it and train others in it?

Many churches have a vision for intergenerational groups that include children as full group members. Pastors have shared that the best thing they ever did was to start out with intergenerational groups because it taught them how to live in community. At the same time, intergenerational groups are more difficult to lead. Not only are leaders learning how to lead adults into biblical community, but they're also trying to incorporate children into the groups. It often proves overwhelming.

It also requires a person serving as part of the Cell Group Vision Team who feels called to champion the cause of children in groups. Others aren't ready to discover how children fit into cell group life until after they learn how to develop effective groups with adults. They've chosen to wait for a few years of cell group development until they incorporate children into the vision. Many of these churches have a vision for homogeneous groups of men and women.

5. The current small group system

Almost every church has some kind of small group system. Some small groups can be transitioned into cell groups. Others can be used as a preparation experience for future cell group participation. Still others should continue as they are, paralleling the new cell groups that will be developed.

COMMON VISION OPTIONS

The vision for biblical community in holistic cell groups that seek to experience both the Great Commandment and the Great Commission is common. But the vision for the structure of how these groups will be developed will vary from church to church. Here are some common visions:

A Vision to be a Fully Cell-based Church

Churches that espouse this vision are led by a pastor who has a passion for cell groups, a passion that has grabbed him to lead the church on a radical path toward biblical community. These churches tend to be more flexible and therefore tend to be younger. In more established churches that articulate this vision, the lay leaders feel a great sense of urgency to develop new forms of ministry.

A Vision for Intergenerational Cell Groups for Families

Some churches promote one kind of cell group, one that ministers across ages. Those churches that are successful with this vision have a passion for developing this kind of community, and they have the freedom to focus the entire church to support this kind of cell group.

A Vision to Organize Groups around Geography

Some churches develop cell groups where the members live in close proximity to one another. These groups tend to be heterogeneous in nature.

A Vision for Homogeneous Cell Groups

Cell groups meet around a shared trait, usually age, gender, or life situation. Men's cell groups, women's cell groups, youth cell groups, college cell groups, and children's cell groups are common when this vision is embraced.

A Vision to Experiment with Cell Groups

The leaders of these churches feel a great passion for what can happen through cell groups, but they don't know if their people are ready to embrace the concept. Cell groups are proposed as an experiment, giving room for the Vision Team and a few leaders to test out groups, without having to change everything in the church from the beginning.

A Vision to Transform Current Small Groups into Cell Groups

Churches that already have effective small groups can transform those groups into holistic cells. This tends to work when the groups are already quite healthy and those leaders are willing to change how they operate. If the old small groups have been operating as closed groups, lacking a vision for growth and multiplication for more than three years, it's probably not wise to choose this strategy.

A Vision to Develop Cell Groups alongside Current Programs

This vision works best in larger churches that have successful programs

Key questions about current small groups:

- What kind of small groups does the church currently have running?
- How entrenched are these small groups in the life of the church? Are people willing to change?
- How difficult would it be to change these groups to holistic cell groups?

running. Rather than shutting down all these programs, and thereby hurting a lot of people, cell groups are developed as a parallel option. This allows the groups to develop life and, as they do, more people from other programs can be incorporated into them.

COMMUNITY LIFE IN THE CELL GROUP

Bill Beckham

A working definition of community is "life in association with one another." Community must be experienced. It's not enough for people to meet weekly for a cell group meeting. God intends the church to provide an experience of life together with others that's radically different from life people experience outside church. There are several important characteristics of the experience of community in cell groups.

COMMUNITY IS RELATIONSHIP

Cell life can be approached in two ways: the Martha approach of performance and the Mary approach of relationship (Luke 10:38-42). The story about Mary and Martha isn't about who does the dishes, sweeps the floor, and prepares the meal. Jesus' concern (and displeasure) with Martha is at the point of her relationship and attitude toward him. Martha is so busy doing for him that she has no time to be with him.

As she was busy with her chores she may have waved at Jesus.

"Hello, Jesus. See how busy I am getting everything ready for you?"

"Look how hard I'm working to make your visit pleasant!"

"Make Mary help me!"

This is characteristic of the "doer" for Christ. Martha sees her own significance in what she does for Christ, and she judges everyone else in the same way. In Martha's mind, Mary was wrong for not helping her do for

Christ. Jesus corrected her and explained the superiority of "being" over "doing."

Jesus said Mary focused upon "what is better" and Martha upon what is secondary. What's best about our Christian life? It's our relationship with Christ. Nothing must hinder that. No work we can do, even spiritual work, can substitute for our relationship with Christ, being with him, focusing our lives and time upon him.

Many small groups that have sprung up over the past several decades have been Martha-type groups—performance-driven, task-oriented, work-consumed, activity-centered, and duty-bound. Jesus is no more pleased with performance small groups of today than he was with Martha's performance in the first century. Whether we're relating to him personally or corporately, Jesus always praises our Mary heart, not our Martha hands.

COMMUNITY IS UNCONDITIONAL

A person with an agenda says: "I will relate to you in community IF the group will accept this assumption or premise. Otherwise, I won't be part of the group."

How does a cell member know when a group is operating around personal agendas, rather than around Christ as the agenda? Look for the word "if" in the group, either spoken or lived out in actions. Agendas thrive in the atmosphere of conditional relationships.

Imagine being part of a small group where every person is defending a personal set of positions and agendas. These agendas destroy true spiritual community, because at the very root they're individualistic, selfish, unloving, controlling, and anti-community. The group can't address the real purpose (agenda) of the group, which is Christ. Instead the group must carefully tiptoe around all the personal agenda minefields.

Personal agendas drastically limit the areas into which a group dares journey and they restrict the Holy Spirit's freedom. Agendas fragment the group's focus, dissipating the spiritual dynamics and ultimately setting group members against each other. An agenda is an attempt to personally control the group rather than to trust Christ to control it. Personal agendas separate a group into enclaves of selfish interest and comfort zones that can't be touched or compromised. Personal agendas will ultimately kill the possibility of community.

Community is relationship.
Community is unconditional.
Community is transparency.
Community is confession.
Community is healing and holiness.
Community is grace.
Community is love.
Community is silence.
Community is penetration.
Community is intercession.
Community is safe.
Community is humility.
Community is covenant.

The "IF Test

"I will be part of this community IF the cell will ..."

...take care of my children.
...teach the Bible properly.
...listen to me teach the Bible.
...use the gifts as I like.
...let me use my gifts.
...make miracles happen.
...entertain me.
...motivate me.
...be comprised of people like me.
...use my formulas for worship.
...use my formulas for deliverance.
...do my style of evangelism.
...use my formulas for healing.
...agree with my political causes.
...be theologically correct.

COMMUNITY IS TRANSPARENCY

Bruce grew up in the home of a Baptist preacher, but had chosen the prodigal life. He'd made several successful business ventures in life, only to see them disappear down the bottom of a bottle. To support Bruce, I went with him to my first open Alcoholics Anonymous meeting. What impressed me in that cigarette smoke and earthy talk-filled AA group meeting room was the honest transparency. These people confessed their failures in front of everyone. They were transparent out of a desperate need, knowing that if they weren't honest and open, they'd be enslaved once again to face the consequences of both physical death and a living hell on earth. Such dire consequences tended to cut through the masks and superficial talk.

Transparency is seldom experienced in large groups where Christians are spectators. Bible study groups where members are busy ingesting information, and task groups focused on activities don't foster honesty. Masks kept on by fear of others' reaction, rejection, and ridicule are only taken off in the safety of a transformational small group context in the presence of Christ himself.

Deitrich Bonhoeffer wrote the spiritual classic, *Life Together*, which is based on his experience as a pastor and teacher with a group of seminary students in Berlin during the rise of Hitler. He wrote,

Written Resources

- *Life Together* by Dietrich Bonhoeffer

> You can hide nothing from God. The mask you wear before men will do you no good before Him. He wants to see you as you are. He wants to be gracious to you. You do not have to go on lying to yourself and your brothers, as if you were without sin; you can dare to be a sinner. Thank God for that. He loves the sinner but He hates sin.
>
> All shame was ended in the presence of Christ. Community is a place where people can experiment with vulnerability and transparency![19]

COMMUNITY IS CONFESSION

Bonhoeffer understood the need to "confess your faults one to another" (James 5:16). This section summarizes three reasons he believed confession is important for community.[20]

First, confession reveals sin and our sinfulness. Christians who participate in corporate worship, Bible study, and common prayer are often having fellowship with one another as believers and devout people. This pious fellowship permits no one to be a sinner in the fellowship of the pious. Many Christians are unthinkably horrified when a real sinner is suddenly discovered among the righteous. So everyone must conceal his sin from himself and from the fellowship.

Satan wants to keep people alone and to always separate them from the community. The more isolated a person is, the more destructive the power of sin will be over him. The more deeply he becomes involved in sin, the more disastrous is his isolation and the more he must deny or hide his sin. It shuns the light and, in the darkness of denial and repression, sin poisons the whole being of a person. This can happen even in the midst of a religious group. In community confession, the light of the Gospel breaks into, and overcomes, the darkness of sin.

Second, confession helps us understand sin. A Christian who lives beneath the cross of Jesus understands the utter wickedness of all men and of his own heart. Anyone who has once been horrified by the dreadfulness of his own sin that nailed Jesus to the cross will no longer be horrified by even the rankest confession of a brother's sin.

It isn't the experience of life, but the experience of the cross, that makes one a worthy hearer of confessions. The most experienced psychologist or observer of human nature knows infinitely less of the human heart than the simplest Christian who lives beneath the cross of Jesus. The greatest psychological insight, ability, and experience cannot grasp the meaning of sin. Worldly wisdom doesn't know that man is destroyed only by his sin and can be healed only by forgiveness. Only the Christian knows this. In the presence of a secular psychiatrist, a man can only be sick. But in the presence of a Christian brother, he can dare to be a sinner.

Third, confession opens the door so we can bear each other's sins. If people live in community, they must be willing to bear each other's sins. In community people live too close together for their sins to be individual. If one person is angry, that anger will touch others. If one is bitter, then his bitterness affects the group. Within community, group members must either bear each other's sins or ignore them. The minute they choose to ignore each other's sins, community is destroyed.

Ralph Neighbour often shares the story of Jackie Pullinger, who began her ministry in a lawless section of Hong Kong infested with drugs and gangs. When one of the residents of that area believed, he was brought into small group community. Soon after, the new believer returned to his new group in great sorrow. Gang members had threatened his life if he refused to carry out a murder contract. The new Christian confessed that because of fear for his life, he had killed another person.

When Jackie Pullinger and other group members heard this confession, they all began to sob and weep. They bore the sin of this brother. To this day, when a member of one of their groups confesses, they all weep.

"Vulnerability is a two-way street. Community requires the ability to expose our wounds and weaknesses to our fellow creatures. It also requires the capacity to be affected by the wounds of others, to be wounded by their wounds."[21]

Confession was a key to John Wesley's movement. The comment was made that "other leaders were telling people what they ought to do." However, in small group confession, Wesley and his followers were "telling each other what they were doing."[22]

COMMUNITY IS SPIRITUAL HEALING

Sigmund Freud, in the fading years of his life, observed that humans are threatened with suffering from three directions. First, our bodies are doomed and our aches and pains remind us even now that we will die. Second, the structures of society can rage against us. And, third, our relations with one another can hurt us. "The suffering," he added, "which comes from this last source is perhaps more painful than any other."[23]

Where is the place of healing and restoration of feelings, hurts, spirits, and bodies in our world? Today we desperately need an "economy of healing" in order to deal with the epidemic of emotional and spiritual sickness. In order to make a significant difference in the emotional state of society, healing on couches and chairs must be supplemented with healing in Christian groups. The community of faith doesn't take the place of Christian counseling and therapy, but can significantly increase the emotional and spiritual health of the hurting.

Jesus provided continual healing for his people through the work of the Holy Spirit in spiritual community. God's place of spiritual healing is the New Testament family: the community of faith. This community is so designed that emotional, spiritual, mental, and physical healing takes place within it. In a nurturing small group community, God is able to re-parent us.

In a God-made, Christ-indwelled, and Spirit-empowered cell, God is able to bind up wounds, apply a balm, remove cancerous feelings of past experiences, and restore spiritual health, healing both physical and spiritual aches, pains, and hurts.

COMMUNITY IS GRACE

A young Houston businessman had been a Christian for about seven years when he entered cell group life. Zealous to a fault, he had turned off most of his friends and relatives with his abrasive way of witnessing. After his conversion, his wife had seen a change in his life, but also was alarmed at his rigid attitudes. She saw him reacting in a negative and legalistic way to people outside his own religious rules. In community life, he found freedom and grace that released him from trying to prove his salvation by keeping the law and condemning others.

Grace is a community value. When we experience grace in community, we can apply grace personally. When we experience grace personally, we can live in grace in community. Grace means giving up the right to judge others. It turns legalism into love and frees Christians from the unproductive task of trying to "fix" each other.

Grace allows the Christian to let go. We let go of the sins of our parents, our grandparents, and great grandparents that have been visited upon us. After that, we have to let go of our children, so they can be on the journey of becoming themselves. Then, we learn to relinquish other Christians so they're not manipulated by our desires or needs. Only then are they free to relate to the voice and guidance of Christ within them. In every human relationship, we learn to let others go, so God can protect them in the center of his grace.

COMMUNITY IS SPIRITUAL LOVE

Exercising spiritual love means releasing another person into Christ's care and refusing to remake that person according to a personal agenda. This is the defining difference between human and spiritual love. Spiritual love refuses to regulate, coerce, and dominate another person with well-meaning human love.

God's image in others always manifests a completely new and unique form that comes solely from God's free and sovereign creation. He creates every man in the likeness of his Son. Human love constructs its own image of another person, of what he is, and what he should become. It takes the life of the other person into its own hands. But spiritual love meets others with the Word of God, not with personal opinions.

> Human love produces human subjection, dependence, constraint; spiritual love creates freedom of the brethren under the Word. Human love breeds hot-house flowers; spiritual love creates the fruits that grow healthily in accord with God's good will in the rain and storm and sunshine of God's outdoors.[24]

COMMUNITY IS SILENCE AND LISTENING

"There is a time to keep silent, and a time to speak" (Ecclesiastes 3:7). However, most of us are better at speaking than remaining silent. In fact, silence in a group meeting can be frightening. Many small group leaders evaluate their performance as a small group leader according to how much stimulating conversation or teaching takes place. Silence is feared and avoided, while conversation is valued.

Silence is taboo in a group that focuses either on information or action. If people relate to God through intellect and information, silence is suspect. In this way of thinking, when information isn't flowing and there's silence, religious things aren't really happening.

If people relate to God through what they do for him (implementation), stillness is suspect. Sitting in silence is equated with doing nothing. The feeling is, when people are talking or studying the Bible, they're at least doing something.

Silence is one of the signs and joys of true companionship. Deep relationships are a balance between companionship and communication. True companions can be comfortable even when there's silence. The relationship between a husband and wife will not survive if every waking moment must be filled with words or if one partner does all the talking and no listening. It's in quiet companionship that true depth of relationship is seen.

In our relationship with God, silence is even more necessary, because God does not usually speak through verbal communication. God communicates with us in our inner spirits and our spirits don't speak audibly. The very blessing of verbal communication can hinder our spiritual communication with God in a group. "Be still (quiet) and know that I am God." We must stop talking in order to hear. As long as we're talking, we're not listening. We must relearn this spiritual language of God that takes place in quietness.

Therefore, a small group must break the silence barrier. This doesn't mean breaking out of silence but breaking into silence—into the presence of God. When we come together with Christ in the midst, when does he talk? When do we listen? It's in our moments of silence before the Lord that he can speak to our hearts. Groups who can listen together will enter God's presence and hear him speak in life-changing ways.

COMMUNITY IS SALT AND LIGHT

Spiritual community is a preparation place for penetrating the lost world. It's a powerful light to repel darkness, salt to give taste to life, and yeast to change society. Christian community challenges people to be "in the world but not of it."

Spiritual community doesn't withdraw from the world, nor is it afraid of either being contaminated or destroyed by the world. Many Christians totally withdrew rather than penetrating the world. Some modern churches are just as isolated as the most extreme monastic orders of the past. On one special day of the week, Christians withdraw from the world into monastic structures of church buildings, clergy, institutions, and meetings. Then, on the other six days, Christians withdraw from Christian community and live a secular lifestyle at work and at home. The end result is the total isolation of the spiritual from the world.

> The test of a group's vitality does not occur primarily while the group is meeting; it occurs after the meeting is over. The vitality of the original Christian movement was not demonstrated by the meetings they held, of which we have some limited knowledge, but by the way in which Christians provided an antidote to the loss of nerve and to the moral sag of the ancient world.[25]

For Deitrich Bonhoeffer, the experience out in the world away from community, even in Nazi Germany, proved the genuineness of the community itself.

> Every day brings to the Christian many hours in which he will be alone in an unchristian environment. These are the times of testing. This is the test of true meditation and true Christian community. Has the fellowship served to make the individual free, strong, and mature, or has it made him weak and dependent? Has it taken him by the hand for a while in order that he may learn again to walk by himself, or has it made him uneasy and unsure? This is one

of the most searching and critical questions that can be put to any Christian fellowship.[26]

COMMUNITY IS INTENSE INTERCESSION

Community cannot exist apart from prayer among its members. Either a group learns to pray for and with each other, or it experiences less than true community. A New Testament group prays out of desperation and practices survival prayer. Community will not continue unless group members pray for each other. Only in intercession can members truly learn to love each other. Why? Intercession involves going to the cross and seeing one's own sin and desperate need. Intercession breaks down attitudes of pride and superiority and results in truly loving and accepting others in their need.

Consider Bonhoeffer's thoughts about the importance of intercession in community:

A Christian fellowship lives and exists by the intercession of its members for one another, or it collapses. I can no longer condemn or hate a brother for whom I pray, no matter how much trouble he causes me. His face, that hitherto may have been strange and intolerable to me, is transformed in intercession into the countenance of a brother for whom Christ died, the face of a forgiven sinner.

There is no dislike, no personal tension and no estrangement that cannot be overcome by intercession as far as our side of it is concerned. Intercessory prayer is the purifying bath into which the individual and the fellowship must enter every day.

Intercession means no more than to bring our brother into the presence of God, to see him under the Cross of Jesus as a poor human being and sinner in need of grace. Then everything in him that repels us falls away; we see him in all his destitution and need. To make intercession means to grant our brother the same right that we have received, namely, to stand before Christ and share in his mercy.[27]

COMMUNITY IS A SAFE PLACE

A man sat quietly in the cell group until he finally confessed how his life was full of fear. His group listened to him. They asked questions so they could understand how to pray. They listened to the Lord to understand his direction. They asked the man to move his chair to the center of the circle where they prayed for him and encouraged him. The next day he commented: "Last night when I was in the center of that group I never felt so naked. But I felt safe."

In true community, a feeling of safety is a common experience. Community provides a safe place for people to be themselves, to open their hearts, to share weaknesses, and to be vulnerable. In community, people are not afraid to share their deepest needs and hurts.

Elizabeth O'Connor describes her experience in a small group:

If there was somehow in this community the element of safety, it was not because there was any paternalism around. It sometimes seemed as though our feelings and sensitivities were not well enough protected, and there needed to be more people to smooth the way and give us flat green plains to walk on. The safety was not in protection from 'slings and arrows,' but in a group of people who, however poorly they might embrace it, had as the basis of their life in Christ an unlimited liability for one another.[28]

"Unlimited liability for one another" is an important characteristic of spiritual community. This gives those in the group a sense of safety and well-being in relationship with God and the group.

COMMUNITY IS HUMILITY

Philippians 2:5-11 is one of the most important Scripture passages for understanding and experiencing true spiritual community. Paul said we should, "Let this attitude be in us which was also in Christ Jesus." Christ's attitude and life is community.

- He did not grasp what was rightfully his.
- He humbled himself.
- He became a servant.
- He became obedient.
- He was willing to die.

This was the attitude Jesus modeled in the upper room community when he took towel, basin, and water to wash the feet of feuding disciples. It's the attitude we see as he died on the cross.

An important aspect of the realism of community deserves mention: humility. While rugged individualism predisposes one to arrogance, the 'soft' individualism of community leads to humility. Begin to appreciate each other's gifts, and you begin to appreciate your own limitations. Witness others share their brokenness and you will become able to accept your own inadequacy and imperfection. Be fully aware of human variety, and you will recognize the interdependence of humanity. As a group of people does these things … as they become a community … they become more and more humble, not only as individuals but also as a group … and hence more realistic. From which kind of group would you expect a wise, realistic decision: an arrogant one, or a humble one?[29]

Christian community is a place to experience and practice humility. In community, the individual members stop demanding their own way and live humbly before each other. If we can't be humble in the presence of Christ and those who love us, then how can we ever hope to live humbly before the world?

COMMUNITY IS COVENANT ACCOUNTABILITY

Accountability in the New Testament can be identified by watching for the term "one another." "Love one another." "Admonish one another." "Confess your faults one to another." "Bear the burdens of one another." "Forgive one another." These are terms of mutual care and responsibility. Accountability is formed out of my spiritual covenant with God. That covenant with God then covers my relationship to other Christians.

Accountability works as a voluntary covenant within a group. Christians living in community choose to be responsible to each other and for one another within a covenant relationship. That covenant may be written or unwritten.

When human leaders try to establish accountability standards and structures, the results can be disastrous. Leaders, even Christian ones, tend to develop legalistic accountability systems that result in bondage. Love must be the spirit of accountability, not authority and control. Christ, who operates in grace and freedom, must set the standards and spirit for accountability in my life and the life of my community. Accountability of authority and control is to be feared. Accountability of love and support is to be cherished.

Some groups have found the two written covenants below helpful in experiencing the practical benefits of accountability.

MY PERSONAL COVENANT
Knowing that Christ has brought me his peace,
I will declare him to be Lord over all my life.
My body, my possessions, and my future are his to command.
I will join my life to a cell group and consider it my basic Christian community.
I will respond to all with God's acceptance.
I will not be judgmental.
I will always remember that God works all things for the good.
I will learn to pray and seek to know how to hear his voice speaking to me.
I will prayerfully seek to know what, in each situation, God wants to address,
and to be his instrument of healing.
Knowing that my cell group may be a turning point
for my life or that of another person,
I covenant to place my commitment to its ministry
at the very top of my priority list.
As God anoints me, I shall be his instrument
to save, to heal, to deliver, and to restore others.
In this spirit, I invite his Spirit to take my life and use it for his glory.

TEN COMMANDMENTS OF
COVENANT ACCOUNTABILITY

1st Commandment (Colossians 3:4-15): Unconditional Love

I choose to love, accept, and edify you, my brothers and sisters. It doesn't matter what you say or do. I choose to love you the way you are. Nothing you've done or will do will keep me from loving you. I can disagree with your actions, but I will love you as people, and do all I can to support you in the certainty of the love of God.

2nd Commandment (Ephesians 4:25-32): Honesty

I will not hide my feelings about you, or how I experience you. Rather, if I have an issue with you, I will seek, in the timing of the Spirit, to discuss them frankly and directly with you in love and forgiveness. I will do this for your sake, seeking to edify you in your difficulties, and so that any misunderstandings do not turn to bitterness. I will try to reflect back to you what I'm hearing and feeling regarding you. I realize this may bring about personal suffering, yet knowing that in speaking the truth in love we will grow in all ways in Christ, who is the head (Ephesians 4:15), I accept this risk. I will try to express myself honestly, in sincerity, and under control according to my understanding of the circumstances.

3rd Commandment (Romans 7:15-25): Transparency

I promise to work to become a more open person, sharing my feelings, my struggles, my joy, and my pain with you in the best way possible. I will seek out at least one person in the group with whom I can share personal issues in my life, recognizing that I need the accountability and encouragement that comes from this kind of relationship.

4th Commandment (2 Thessalonians 1:11-12): Prayer

I covenant to pray for you regularly, believing our beloved Father desires that we pray for one another, seeking the blessings we need. I will not be a passive listener, but rather I choose to be a spiritual participant, desiring to enter into your situations and help you bring your burdens before the Lord.

5th Commandment (John 4:1-29): Sensitivity

In the same way I desire to be known and understood by you, I covenant to be sensitive to you and to your needs in the best way possible. I will try to hear you and feel what you're experiencing, and try to lift you out of any pit of discouragement and isolation in which you may find yourself. I will seriously seek to avoid giving trite and simplistic responses to the difficult situations you encounter.

6th Commandment (Acts 2:47): Availability

Here I am if you need me. All I have–time, energy, understanding, material possessions–is at your disposal, if you have need. I give these things to you in a covenant that you have priority over others who are not under this covenant.

7th Commandment (Proverbs 10:19; 11:9, 13; 12:23; 15:4; 18:6-8): Confidentiality

I promise to maintain in confidence everything that is shared within the group to whatever level is necessary to maintain an atmosphere conducive to transparency. I understand, however, that this confidence does not forbid my cell leader or intern from sharing any necessary information with my pastor, be it verbally or in writing. I understand leaders and interns work under the supervision of the pastoral team of this body, and have been delegated authority by them. These, in turn, are accountable to the Great Shepherd, Jesus Christ, our Lord (Hebrews 13:17).

8th Commandment (Ezekiel 3:16-21 and Matthew 18:12-20): Accountability

I covenant to study the training materials used by each cell for the growth and development of its members. In doing so, I will be accountable weekly to another member of my cell. I give you the right to question, confront, and challenge me in love when I'm failing in some aspect of my life with God, my family, my devotional life, or any aspect of my spiritual growth. I trust you to be in the Spirit and guided by him when you do this. I need your correction and reproval in a manner that will perfect my ministry before God in your midst. I promise to not react. (Proverbs 12:1, 15; 13:10, 18).

9th Commandment (Luke 9:57-62): Faithful Attendance

I will consider the normal time my group meets as a weekly opportunity to meet Christ along with you in this special time together. I will not grieve the Spirit or impede his work in the lives of my brothers and sisters by my absence, except in case of emergency. Only with his permission, in prayer, will I consider an absence a possibility. If it's impossible for me to come for whatever reason, out of consideration, I will phone my leader so the members of the cell know why I'm absent, that they may pray for me and not worry about me.

10th Commandment (Matthew 25:31-46): Reaching Others

I covenant to find ways to lay down my life for those I meet outside of our fellowship in the same way I made an alliance to lay down my life for you, my brothers and sisters. I will do my best to bring two or more unbelievers or unchurched people to my cell during its lifecycle. I want to do this in the name of Jesus so that others will be added to the Kingdom of God by his love.

THE CELL GROUP COMMUNITY CYCLE

16

Bill Beckham

In living organisms, a biological cell passes through dynamic growth stages on its journey to maturity and reproduction. The same is true for the development of community in a cell group. No group will enter into maturity from its inception. Cell groups go through a process of growth that forms a cell into true spiritual community and guarantees its survival by reproducing itself.

Secular psychologists, sociologists, anthropologists, and even theologians are in general agreement about the stages groups routinely go through on the way to experiencing true community. Not every group follows this process step by step, because community development doesn't occur by formula. However, in the process of community, there is a natural, usual order of things.

HONEYMOON OR GET-ACQUAINTED STAGE

A group usually begins with a honeymoon period because everyone's glad to be together in a new and exciting group experience. Initially, members of a newly formed cell need to get to know each other. First impressions are often based on past impressions with other people. As people get to know you they may tell you that, "You aren't a bit like I thought you were when we first met!" It can take a number of sessions before cell group members begin to overcome false impressions they may have about one another.

The first response of a group in seeking to form a community is most often to try to fake it. The members attempt to be an instant community by being extremely pleasant with one another and avoiding all disagreement. During the honeymoon/discovery period, the group may think they're in community, but are actually experiencing pseudo community.

Beware of instant community. Real community requires time, as well as effort and sacrifice. Pseudo community is attempting to purchase com-

The common stages of cell group development:

- Honeymoon or Get-Acquainted Stage
- Conflict or Confrontation Stage
- Resolution or Death Stage
- Community or Unity Stage
- Ministry or Witness Stage
- Multiplication or Closure Stage

munity cheaply by pretense. It's an inviting but illegitimate shortcut to nowhere. Pseudo community avoids conflict at all costs; true community seeks to resolve conflict. In pseudo community, individual members act as if they're operating according to the same book of etiquette, denying individual differences or points of view.

CONFLICT OR CONFRONTATION STAGE

When people finally understand each other, value systems will clash and eventually the group will come into conflict. Personalities will be different, misunderstandings will happen, differences in opinion about large and small matters will surface. This conflict comes in a multitude of ways, but it will surely come. One person may talk too much, making others in the cell feel angry by this unwanted domination. Another person may be insensitive or someone else may be too sensitive. It may become obvious that a member is using the group for a personal need or agenda. It won't be too long before these tensions begin to emerge.

I may discover you have some warts that weren't evident in our previous religious meetings in worship or Sunday school. Either we'll deny the difference, fight about it, leave the group, or honestly come to grips with our differences.

It should be borne in mind, however, that conflict of this type is not only inevitable, but is often a sign of successful group development. Leaders are encouraged to share with the cell during a meeting that conflict is a natural part of the process. They need to ensure that they gently guide the cell through such tensions, allowing members to share their concerns and work through their differences.

While this won't be an easy process, it should never be avoided. Unresolved tensions and conflicts can simmer under the surface, grow, and eventually rip cell groups apart. 'Nipping it in the bud' not only prevents this, but the process of conflict resolution often helps to draw the group together, establishing a clearer identity and fostering a greater commitment to the group within its members.

A group may look for someone to blame for the uncomfortable conflict. The leader is often singled out as the one who has caused or allowed the unpleasantness to develop. The idea, spoken or unspoken, is "If our leader was better, this wouldn't have happened!" If members insist on blaming the leader and refuse to deal with the differences, the group is stuck in pseudo community. The group meets, greets, and accomplishes some task.

However, the group does not experience real spiritual community. The group has settled for false community.

When a group faces conflict, it may go in two directions. The group may avoid conflict and focus on a lesser task. It may become a fellowship group, a Bible study group, or a ministry group. This dooms the group to experiencing pseudo community, instead of New Testament spiritual community. Or the group may face the conflict honestly and work through it, as described in the next stage.

RESOLUTION OR DEATH STAGE

Though often included as part of the community stage, this is a separate and distinct stage and must be considered alone, lest it be neglected or misunderstood. Unless individuals, and eventually the group, "fall into the ground and die," they'll be a group of individuals living alone, while gathering for a meeting together.

God prepares man to live in community with him and with other Christians in three important experiences: change, exchange, and interchange. These three experiences are revisited over and over in the development of community, and all three are part of the community phase within the cell cycle.

The Christian life begins with a dramatic personal change, which is brought about by death. "Therefore, if any man is in Christ, he is a new creature; the old things passed away; behold, new things have come" (2 Corinthians 5:17). The new birth saves man from sin, for community with God and each other. Without this initial change, it's impossible to live in God's community. Some people can't live in spiritual community because they've never been born spiritually.

Paul also teaches in Galatians 2:20 that the "changed" life is an "exchanged" life. The "exchanged" life is required for a Christian to live in body life, because it allows Christ to live in and through the individual Christian with his power. "I have been crucified with Christ; and it is no longer I who live, but Christ lives in me; and the life which I now live in the flesh I live by faith in the Son of God, who loved me and delivered Himself up for me."

An "exchanged life" doesn't mean I cease to exist as a person when I become a Christian. Christ is not me, but Christ lives in me. I'm not totally absorbed by Christ, but when making decisions I exchange my will and my preferences for that of Christ, who lives in me. This exchange is a "good swap." Jim Elliot expressed it well in his life statement: "He is no fool who gives what he cannot keep to gain what he cannot lose."

When used in a community sense, Galatians 2:20 refers to the "interchange" (sharing, connecting, bonding) of my life with you and the body of Christ. "It is no longer I who live, but Christ who lives in me … and in US!" Christ builds his church out of the lives of individual Christians who mutually share the life of Christ together. "In whom the whole building, being fitted together is growing into a holy temple in the Lord; in whom [Christ] you [plural] also are being built together into a dwelling of God in the Spirit" (Ephesians 2:21-22). Christ in and through each individual Christian builds the individual Christians into a "holy temple" and "dwelling of God."

When I voluntarily "exchange" my right to be the CEO of my life for the presence, power, and purpose of Christ, and you do the same, an "interchange" between us and the Christ who lives in us takes place. I personally live the life of Christ (exchange), and I participate in the life of Christ with another (interchange). My conversion change and my daily exchanged life in Christ prepare me for a dynamic interchange in my relationship to other Christians. This interchange of our lives in Christ is body life community.

COMMUNITY OR UNITY STAGE

The conflict and death stage is followed by a meaningful period in which the members move toward one another. When the group learns to be honest and open with each other and to solve differences, then true spiritual community can take place. It's not only a period of enrichment and empowerment, it's also a danger point! When the cell group has found meaningful relationships, it may decide it wants to close itself off, to remain undisturbed. If this is permitted, the cell group will turn in on itself, and become selfish and exclusive. As soon as strong relationships begin to develop, it's important that the group be guided to focus on and reach out to others. (See Chapter 15 for more on community.)

MINISTRY OR WITNESS STAGE

Out of community, ministry within and outside the body is a possibility. The foundations for this stage should be developed early in the life of a cell and should already be emerging. However, with relationships built up and strengthened, the cell is now at its most fruitful potential point for reaching out effectively to others. This should be any cell's principal goal, and should be clearly understood by all its members from day one. This may also involve organizing events (such as barbecues, parties, etc.) to which friends, family, and/or neighbors are invited. These activities inevitably involve new people who will join and expand the group.

MULTIPLICATION OR CLOSURE STAGE

The final act of a group is multiplication/closure. If a cell isn't growing, it's dying. Closure of the group is multiplication into newer and more manageable smaller groups that have the potential, vigor, and space to grow.

Multiplication is undoubtedly a difficult stage but, ultimately, the key measure of the cell's success. Careful consideration needs to be given to preparing group members for multiplication, and also planning who within the cell is to go into which group.

A cell can multiply through biological multiplication or through generation multiplication. Biological multiplication follows the growth principle of cell division/multiplication that's the natural growth process of a biological cell. The original cell splits and becomes two new cells, each made up of half the members of the original cell.

Generation multiplication grows as a family. Each member in the cell is prepared to go out and begin a new cell. Children from the parent cell begin a new "family." The "father" of the new family continues to be part of and receive support from the parent cell. Or, a combination of biological and generation multiplication can be used. Two or three mature Christians in the original cell form a core and begin a new "family."

THE CELL GROUP MEETING

Bill Beckham

The cell group meeting is only one part of cell life, but it's an important one. For Jesus, it wasn't enough to relate to his followers only in some kind of mystical or individual connection. Jesus met with them in various size groups for different purposes. He ate with them, prayed with them, played with them, taught them, and had special events with them. Jesus knew that bonding in physical community was essential for spiritual bonding. That's why Hebrews 10:25 warns us about "forsaking our own assembling together."

The cell meeting is a special time when all the members are physically together with each other and with Christ. Since he is present, the experience isn't just a meeting; it's an appointment with the indwelling Christ. The life of the meeting is built around an intimate experience with the presence, power, and purpose of Christ. The cell meeting's format must allow Christ's life to flow in and through the group so that Christians in a cell experience the omnipresence of God the Father, in Christ the Son, through the Holy Spirit.

THE MAKEUP OF A CELL FOLLOWS 1 JOHN 2:12-14

Each cell group should form a family comprised of children, young men in the Lord and fathers in the Lord. These are not gender specific terms; rather they are inclusive terms drawn from 1 John:

> I write to you, dear children, because your sins have been forgiven on account of his name. I write to you, fathers, because you have known him who is from the beginning. I write to you, young men, because you have overcome the evil one. I write to you, dear children, because you have known the Father. I write to you, fathers, because you have known him who is from the beginning. I write to you, young men, because you are strong, and the word of God lives in you, and you have overcome the evil one.

Each cell has "little children" who know two things: they have a father, and their sins are forgiven. Little children may be new Christians, hurting Christians, and/or prodigal Christians. They're to be nurtured and developed by cell members.

Each cell has "young men" who learned as children that they have a father, and that their sins are forgiven. They also know they have an enemy, and have mastered him! Young men are developing Christians who can be trained to reach out to those who are interested in God. They focus on cultivating and witnessing to responsive unbelievers.

Each cell has "fathers" or parents. The "fathers" know God intimately and have produced spiritual children. They learned as children that they have a father, and that their sins are forgiven. They learned as young men that they have an enemy, and have mastered him. These are mature Christians who can be trained to reach out to hard-to-reach, unresponsive unbelievers.

The expectation is that every cell member will process through these three stages of spiritual growth at his or her own speed and timetable. However, the hope and plan is for every member to eventually reach maturity.

THE CELL GROUP MEETING AND THE FOUR WS

The cell meeting is an essential part of the community experience, because it provides the visible context for proper and meaningful relationships to develop. It's not only the place where people can gain encouragement and support, but also an important context where teaching, discipleship, and spiritual growth occur. In essence, the cell meeting enables the cell group church's core values to be realized in practice.

The cell meeting gives a structured and regular time for every member to physically come together as the most basic unit of Christ's body. All community activities are planned and coordinated through the cell meeting to help the group remain Christ-centered, encourage all members into ministry and maturity, maintain and nurture the emphasis on sacrificial love and community, and ultimately, to be the launching pad for ministry and evangelism.

Groups must maintain a clear focus during their meeting. One way of doing this is to use the four Ws as the meeting format: Welcome, Worship, Word, and Witness. While such a structure should never be adhered to rigidly, these four stages have helped cells around the world maintain and

Part	Focus	Aim
Welcome	Me to You	To build relationships among those within the group
Worship	Us to God	To focus attention on God
Word	God to Us	To allow God to guide and minister to us
Witness	God thru Us	To allow God to touch the unchurched through us

multiply the core values of cell life.

The basic approach of the four Ws can be summarized in the table below. In reality, the boundaries between each stage of the cell meeting won't be as clear-cut as the chart suggests. Clearly, relationships among members will not only be developed through the welcome but will also be further encouraged through collective worship. Similarly, God may begin to minister to us through worship as well as the Word.

THE FOUR WS ARE A PATTERN, NOT A LEGALISTIC FORM

This format is like a cake recipe. When learning to bake a new cake, it's best to follow the recipe exactly. After successfully baking the cake a few times, the cook can become more creative and can deviate from the recipe, though certain parts of the recipe must remain in the mix. For instance, flour is an essential ingredient in a cake. Different kinds of flour may be substituted, but some kind of flour must be used. Otherwise, because of the missing basic ingredient, the cake ceases to be cake.

This is true of a cell meeting. Welcome, Worship, Word and Witness are essential ingredients in the meeting. For instance, some kind of welcome time happens naturally when a group begins to gather. This may take many different forms, but it needs to happen. Also, a different flavor of worship may be used, but some kind of worship is central to coming together in a meeting where Christ is in the midst.

The Word can be approached in many different ways, but God's Word will always be a central part of a cell meeting. Witness is a natural outgrowth of cell life. The ingredients of a cell meeting can depend upon the maturity of the cell and the stage of its development, but they will be present in some form. The recipe may change, but the basic ingredients of the cake will remain.

My high school basketball coach taught us a very simple offense that had only six or seven basic plays. We ran those plays over and over. The guard dribbled the ball down the court and passed to the center. The guard would set a screen for the forward, who broke toward the goal. The center then threw the ball to the forward and he shot a basket. This play ran smoothly every time when there were no defenders.

However, in a real game, defenders don't cooperate. They get in the way when opponents try to run a play. Does this mean the play is useless? Certainly not! Even professional teams run plays, which are helpful patterns when flexibility and innovation are allowed. The "four Ws" are plays that allow for flexibility and innovation. Cell leaders don't abandon the basic nature of the play, but are flexible and innovative when the situation calls for it.

It's the underlying process—characterized by the change in focus as a group goes through these four stages—that's important to grasp. Leaders and groups learn there are many different ways in which the Welcome, Worship, Word, and Witness can be approached within the context of a cell, but the ultimate purpose of each remains the same.

Welcome

Our ability to focus on God, both individually and as a group, will be limited until we can feel secure and comfortable together. Thus, there's a need for us to 'get to know' each other. We need to know about each group member's life, so we can be sensitive to his or her needs. We also need to build trust and respect, so we can be open and honest with one another. Until we can relate effectively as a group, we're going to find it difficult to relate to God effectively together.

Each meeting should start with some form of 'icebreaker.' This not only helps individuals to begin to feel more comfortable in the group and to settle down in the meeting, but carefully chosen icebreakers can also help the group members learn more about each other as the weeks progress. Clearly, the time spent on icebreakers and the nature of the icebreakers will change as the cell group develops and becomes more established.

At the beginning of every meeting, the cell leader (or person designated) should welcome Christ into the meeting. Some of the following sentences could be used:

• Jesus said, "Where two or three gather in my name I am in the midst of them."

- We're here to experience the presence, power, and purpose of Christ.
- Jesus promised he would be with this group.
- We believe his promise, acknowledge his presence, and welcome Christ here with us.

The Holy Spirit will give other words or prompt brief prayers acknowledging Christ's presence. An experience with Christ in worship and the Word generally follows this acknowledgement.

Worship

Worship is an essential aspect of cell life, as it enables the group to focus on God and his glory, and to be able to put aside personal agendas. It's the key to cell groups becoming and maintaining a Christ-centered focus.

Moreover, until the group sets aside personal agendas and truly focuses on God, their ability to hear what he has to say (i.e. through the Word) will be severely limited. Worship provides the necessary required step to allow God to minister to the group.

Worship follows the 1 Corinthians 14:26 pattern of participation. It reads, "What then shall we say, brothers? When you come together, everyone has a hymn, or a word of instruction, a revelation, a tongue or an interpretation. All of these must be done for the strengthening of the church." Paul is describing what happened at the house churches of Corinth, where everyone participated in worship. Everyone felt an urgency to hear God and contribute.

Likewise, worship in a cell is more than singing. Paradigms of worship other than just singing a few songs must be introduced in cell meetings. Using the Psalms and other Scripture is one way for a group to learn to worship together. At the same time, singing is important and can be done with or without instruments.

Word

During the first part of the cell meeting, members must experience Christ's presence. Having focused our attention on God and invited him to dwell among us, we're now in a much better spiritual position and general frame of mind to enable God to minister directly to us.

During the meeting, the cell focuses on the power of Christ. "What does Christ wish to do in my life and our cell RIGHT now?" He wants to reveal my sins and needs, in order to change and edify me. Christ wants to identify spiritual, emotional, and physical needs in my life that need to receive healing.

During the Word time, discussion allows the Living Word to apply the written Word to the life of each person present. Through the work of the Holy Spirit, sharing and edifying happen during the Word time. These are two interdependent parts. First, through the Word, Christ reveals himself to me and identifies specific needs in my life. Then Christ edifies me by applying his power to the personal needs that are revealed in the sharing. Sharing is revelation, while edification is application and healing.

The Word section of a meeting can take many forms. It can include a more structured and planned format, in which the application of Sunday teaching takes place. It can also include more spontaneous moves of the Spirit, arising out of worship and/or prayer. However the Word time is organized, it provides the context within which the application of teaching and ministry can take place, and where group members can grow and mature in their calling and giftings through discipleship and edification.

The content of this portion of the meeting focuses on allowing Christ to speak to group members through the written Word and apply it to our lives. It can vary according to the need of the group, the approach of the church, stage of development of the cell, etc. The purpose of the Word time is for the cell to listen to Christ through some inductive Bible exercise or activity, so that needs are identified and revealed. Then, the Holy Spirit heals those needs through members in the cell.

Of course the cell would not be healthy and well rounded if it used only one type of activity every meeting. The Word activity can be chosen according to the:

- makeup of the members of the cell;
- special needs of the members;
- circumstances in the church body;
- stage of development of the cell; and
- special events such as birthdays or Christmas.

Activities for Word time can be chosen by cell leaders, the cell itself, or by church leadership. The creative activities during the Word time can be changed at any time in order to meet the needs of the group (even during the meeting). If the cell is never willing to change, then it reflects an unhealthy dependence on form. If the cell always changes, then it reflects an unhealthy reaction to form. God is a God of both order and freedom.

But the encounter with Christ at the point of his presence, power, and purpose NEVER changes during a cell meeting. If a cell experiences Christ in these three ways, then the cell has been "successful." The Word time is not the purpose of the meeting, but a time to prepare for the work of Christ in the life of individual cell members and the cell as a whole. Christ is the purpose of the meeting.

Witness

The closing of the cell meeting focuses on the purpose of Christ. How does Christ want to minister through me and the group this week? Of course, as Jesus taught, the cell group's greatest commission is to "make disciples" (Matthew 28:16-20). The success of any cell group therefore, requires it to simultaneously adopt both an inward and an outward focus. Alongside the need to encourage and support one another within the group, it's equally important that there's a clear focus on those outside the group—family, friends, neighbors, and work colleagues.

There's no doubt that through the Word, God will guide us as to how we can best reach out individually and as a group to those around us. It's only when we become obedient to God that he can work through us to touch the lives of others. Not surprisingly, there are many different ways in which cell groups can develop this outward, evangelical focus.

Some subjects will repeatedly show up during the Witness time of the cell meeting. Praying together for special matters will be a continuing "work" of the cell.

Equipping new believers for ministry will be discussed often, when a cell considers how God wants to use it during the week until the next cell meeting. Living out the "one anothers" in accountability relationships with members of the cell will be a frequent subject at the close of a cell meeting. Making plans to contact those in the sphere of influence of the cell members will be a central theme of the Witness section.

Ministering to the lost and hurting in the world will be a major focus. Then planning for growth and multiplication will become an increasing theme as the cell increases in maturity.

CONNECTING THE WORD IN CELEBRATION TO THE WORD IN CELL

John Wesley's movement used a very effective method in teaching the Bible that's used in some form by modern cell group churches. Wesley provided for cognitive instruction in his societies (large groups), but recognized the need for another experience with the Word. That other experience was in a small group setting. Michael Henderson notes that "the subject matter of a class meeting was personal experience, not doctrinal or biblical information."[30]

"For Wesley the locus of activity relevant to the Gospel of Christ was the experience or behavior of a person. To most of the Reformers the locus was in verbal or printed statements."[31]

Wesley tied his society or large group celebration to his "class" meeting (cell) in three ways:

1. The class (cell) was a subdivision of the society and its leaders were appointed by the leaders of the society and were accountable to them.
2. The design of the two groups tied together the function of teaching and behavioral transformation. The class meeting (cell) incorporated into the lives of its members what had been taught in the society meeting.
3. Active participation in the class meeting was the condition for membership in the society.[32]

The Christian life for Wesley was a "behavioral struggle." To Wesley, "it was not so much what one believed but something one did that made him or her a follower of Christ and a Methodist."[33]

Many cell-based churches around the world have discovered the power of connecting the content of the large group meeting with the discussion of the small group meeting.

CELL AND CELEBRATION WORDS

With an integrated large group and small group structure, a church can be part of a powerful New Testament experience in the Word of God. In large group worship, God expresses himself through the Word in a very special way. We associate special words with this time of large group worship:

See Chapter 39 for instructions on how to write effective cell group questions.

revelation, inspiration, celebration, information, and proclamation. These powerful words describe how Christians experience God in large group worship.

In a cell-based church, another essential set of words is associated with the Word of God. In small group life, Christians experience the Word in application, edification, sanctification, transformation, and affirmation. These are equally powerful words. When a church functions with both a large- and small-group setting, God is able to join these two sets of words together in spiritual synergism.

By tying the message on Sunday to the Word section in the cell meeting, Christians experience the full impact of God's Word. This arrangement completes God's Word. Someone has said: "Large groups, information; small groups, transformation."

If the small group meeting is just another Bible teaching or a rehash of the pastor's sermon, Christians miss the second set of words. A typical Bible study does not result in application, edification, sanctification, transformation, or affirmation of God's Word. The typical Bible study results in more information, but often lacks the powerful revelation, inspiration, celebration, and proclamation that happen in a large group.

Most cell-based churches find a way to tie the revealed Word to the applied Word. A pastor may develop three or four questions from the sermon. They should be why, feeling, or application questions. Discussing "what" questions about the facts of a Scripture passage has only surface impact upon our lives. Asking "why" takes us down to the roots of our problems and needs. Feeling questions force us to get out of our heads and into our hearts, where the Holy Spirit can identify sins and initiate sanctification and edification.

If a question can be answered with one word or with a yes or no, it's not a good question. The questions should facilitate discussion and introspection. The final question should lead to personal and group application of the message to life.

BENEFITS

What are the benefits of church leaders providing a cell leader with questions from the pastor's message? Tying the large-group Word time to the small-group Word time gives opportunity for application. The Scripture declares that it's not he who hears God's Word who pleases God, but he who does God's Word.

The modern church has done a much better job teaching members information about God's Word than teaching them how to apply God's Word to life. The problem with most Christians isn't that they don't know enough. The problem is that they don't apply what they know.

Tying the two together establishes God's anointed leader. God reveals a message through inspiration, and the pastor proclaims that message in the large group. Surely that message that was inspired by God is worth considering during the week by those who heard it.

Tying the large-group Word time to the small-group Word time gives focus to the cell's edification. Suppose God reveals to the pastor that the church needs to be edified at the point of gossip. The pastor knows this is a major church problem. If he preaches a "God-breathed" message on gossip, then application and edification about gossip can take place in the cells during the week. Without small group application, the pastor may preach a wonderful message on gossip, but few will have the opportunity to apply the message and experience edification and healing.

Tying the large-group Word time to the small-group Word time breaks the "Absalom spirit" of passive and silent rebellion. This spirit is alive and well on the planet earth and in our churches. The spirit of individualism blinds many Christians to this destructive spirit. Cell leaders expect and even demand the right to do their own thing in their small group. Many are incensed that one would suggest they follow the pastor's instructions for their small group. This is the spirit Jesus was trying to break in the disciples when he washed their feet and told them to have the spirit of humility.

Tying the large-group Word time to the small-group Word time frees cell leaders to minister. By using the pastor-provided teaching plan, cell leaders don't have to come up with their own teaching plan for every cell meeting. Without having to decide on a topic or on questions, the cell leader can give attention to the relationships in the meeting, and to application and edification of the truths of the message.

COMPETING MEETINGS

The greatest obstacle to the church returning to New Testament community life is its commitment to other good programs. Some churches have substituted Bible study programs for New Testament community. Other churches have replaced community with special meetings for experiencing the Holy Spirit. Both these types of meetings may fill a need in the church. However, they should not and cannot take the place of basic Christian community. Both programs (understanding the Word and experiencing the Holy Spirit) are weak in the areas of application and edification.

Application was the objective in the first century, not just assimilating knowledge or experiencing signs and wonders. Jesus desired "doers of the word and not just hearers." Paul warned about those who seek knowledge (Jews) and those who seek signs or experiences (Greeks) as the way to God. The power of the Gospel is the cross and the daily experience of the cross is New Testament community, not knowledge or signs.

Since the Reformation, the Word has been used as the central focus of the primary meeting of most churches around the world. As a symbol of the importance of God's proclaimed Word, the pulpit is either central or shares the stage with the Lord's Supper table in most churches other than the Catholic Church.

In addition to proclaiming the Word at the usual time of worship, the Sunday school program has been a popular way for churches to teach the Word, especially in the United States and countries evangelized by United States churches. It has been popular in Europe and some streams in the United States to study the Bible in conferences, seminars, and special meetings not directly connected to the main day of worship.

In the last decades, in addition to learning about the Bible, the church has sought to experience the work of the Holy Spirit as recorded in the Bible. Therefore, the study of the written Word has been supplemented (and at times replaced) with power encounters with the living Word (Holy Spirit). As an alternative to Sunday school, many churches in the United States and Europe experience the living Word of the Holy Spirit in exciting meeting venues led by dynamic and gifted leaders.

Maintaining all these meetings has exacted a material and spiritual price upon the church. The spiritual cost of changing from meeting in small groups in homes to meeting in large groups and buildings has been to change the focus of Scripture. Cognitive information received from a teacher or affective experience received from a gifted leader replaced transformation within community. Personal sanctification and group edification has been replaced with personal spiritual experiences and group excitement.

The material cost has been high as well, in maintaining all these meetings at the expense of small group community in homes. What's the cost of maintaining the Sunday school as the primary venue for studying the Word? By the time we count the outlay of money for the program, facilities, materials, training, the outlay of time and personnel to run the program, a sizeable percentage of the resources of a church are directed toward the Sunday school. If this much time, effort, and resources are going into this activity, then it must produce outstanding results. The cost for providing special meetings for conferences, seminars, and high-energy meetings is also expensive in terms of dollars and distraction.

The twenty-first century church must find a way to give priority to small group community. This is where application of the written Word (Bible) and transformation through the living Word (Holy Spirit) will sanctify the individual Christian and edify the body.

BODY LIFE IN CELL GROUPS

Bill Beckham

18

"What is terribly missing is the experience of "body life"; that warm fellowship of Christian with Christian which the New Testament calls *koinonia*, and which was an essential part of early Christianity."[34]

"THE CHRIST WHO DWELLS IN ME GREETS THE CHRIST WHO DWELLS IN YOU."

For years, Ralph Neighbour has expressed the important biblical truth of "body life" and *koinonia* in a greeting: "The Christ who dwells in me greets the Christ who dwells in you." This greeting expresses three simple but profound truths about the Christian life.

Truth One: Christ indwells me.
Truth Two: Christ indwells you.
Truth Three: Christ indwells us. (Christ relates through us to each other.)

In the first century church, *koinonia* or body life was the design of God, the life of Christ, and the work of the Holy Spirit. It was an essential part of early Christianity and was a kind of rhythm of life. "The Christians would gather together in homes to instruct one another, study and pray together, and share the ministry of spiritual gifts. Then they would go out into the world again to let the warmth and glory of their love-filled lives overflow into a spontaneous Christian witness that drew love-starved pagans like a candy store draws little children."[35]

To restore the first century experience of "body life," the twenty-first century church must return to two New Testament experiences: the source of body life which is Christ, and the context of "body life" which is small group community. Body life cannot be manufactured in the church with formulas for Bible study, the latest spiritual experiences, or new small group programs. If we're to experience New Testament body life, we must experience Christ together in community: his presence, his power, and his purpose. Body life is the spiritual body of Christ on earth living the life of Christ between the ascension and second coming of Christ.

NINE ELEMENTS IN BODY LIFE

New Testament body life is made up of nine elements: worship, prayer, community, Word, prophecy, gifts, edification, equipping, and evangelism. These nine elements fall into four natural categories: context (the place of God), communication (the presence of God), catalyst (the power of God), and synergy (the purpose of God).

The context for body life is *community*: small and large. Community is the wineskin, the vehicle, the framework, and organizing principle, around which all the elements of body life function. It's the environment and atmosphere that provides the spiritual living conditions necessary for the other elements to operate in New Testament body life. Community is the matrix that gives a framework in which God and man can interact, speak the same language, operate in the same environment, and pursue common goals. All the rules and principles of the nine body life elements operate within the community matrix. Community is the place of God with his people.

Worship, prayer, and the Word belong to the communication (presence) category of body life. Through these elements, God communicates with man, and man communicates with God. Man experiences the presence of God as Father, Son, and Spirit. These elements make it possible for man to know and relate to God. God and man connect, establish, and maintain contact through the communication elements.

Worship is the communication element that sets the boundaries and structures of man's relationship to God. In humility, awe, and reverence, man approaches God as created being to Creator. Worship is inherently a community experience. Even when we think we're worshipping alone, the Holy Spirit and angels praise God with us, and creation "declares the glory of God."

2   *Prayer* is the communication element that connects God with man. It's the most basic and fundamental experience between God and man. Prayer activates body life because it connects man to the source of life: God.

3   The *Word* is the communication element through which God reveals himself and his will to his body. The Word is written Word in the Bible and becomes living Word through the Holy Spirit.

The catalyst (power) category includes prophecy, gifts, and edification. These elements are the catalytic agents that transform communication (worship, prayer, and the Word) with God into practical body life of holiness and harvest. Through prophecy, gifts, and edification, the Holy Spirit energizes worship, prayer, and the Word.

4   *Prophecy* is the catalytic element through which God makes the Word personal, positive, and practical. God speaks special words of prophecy to ordinary Christians and addresses the personal and practical needs of individuals and the body. New Testament prophecy is positive, not harsh, judgmental, and negative. It edifies, consoles, and comforts. Practical prophecy makes edification more than personal opinions, past experiences, or counseling.

5   *Spiritual gifts* are the catalytic elements that extend and express the life and ministry of Christ. The Spirit shares the appropriate gift with every child of God. He multiplies and integrates the various gifts within community so that the cell functions as one body.

Prophecy and the gifts facilitate the catalytic element of *edification*. 6
Individual Christians and the entire body are built up and edified as God packages his Word into practical prophecy that's then channeled through special spiritual gifts to specific personal and group needs within the community. Everything is to be done for edification of the body.

The synergy (purpose) category includes *equipping* (holiness) and *evangelism* (harvest). Body life is not empowered or energized until equipping and evangelism is the focus of the other elements mentioned above. Body life only exists where the body is being equipped and is involved in evangelism. When prophecy, gifts, and edification activate communication with God within community, a powerful spiritual synergism takes place at the   7, 8 point of holiness and harvest.

God is able to maximize the internal growth and health of the community by equipping every member for the work of ministry. He is able to multiply and mobilize the external growth of the community through harvest. The saints are equipped for the work of ministry and for evangelism.

This kind of body life completes Christ's ministry and mission statement. "The Spirit of the Lord is upon me, because he anointed me to preach the Gospel to the poor. He has sent me to proclaim release to the captives, and recovery of sight to the blind, to set free those who are downtrodden, to proclaim the favorable year of the Lord" (Luke 4:18-19).

BODY LIFE IS FOR EVERY CHRISTIAN

Paul makes it clear that every Christian must participate in body life. "What is the outcome then brethren? When you assemble, EACH ONE has a psalm, has a teaching, has a revelation, has a tongue, has an interpretation" (1 Corinthians 14:26). "For you can ALL prophesy, one by one, so that ALL may learn and ALL may be exhorted" (1 Corinthians 14:31f.).

The word for "everyone" or "all" is *hytoskos*, which means all without any exception. It's used over and over again in the New Testament because there's no community without it.

All Christians are to participate in the life of Christ in all elements of body life. ALL must worship, pray, prophesy, apply God's Word, exercise spiritual gifts, edify, equip, and be equipped. ALL must witness and live in community with one another! Body life is the life of Christ lived together by all Christians.

CELL GROUP COMMUNITY IS THE TRAINING CENTER FOR BODY LIFE

The cell group is the individual's school to learn to live out New Testament body life with other Christians. Paul uses the analogy of the athlete and soldier to explain the Christian's individual and group experience of discipline, practice, and training. Maturity in the life of an individual Christian or a group of Christians doesn't happen automatically and easily. Practice and training are required to live a mature life. This is also true of community in the large group and small group expression of the church. All must practice and train in order to live together in New Testament body life.

Concerning him (Christ) we have much to say, and it is hard to explain, since you have become dull of hearing, for though by this time you ought to be teachers, you have need again for someone to teach you the elementary principles of the oracles of God, and you have come to need milk and not solid food. For everyone who partakes only of milk is not accustomed to the word of righteousness, for he is a babe. But solid food is for the mature, who because of PRACTICE have their senses TRAINED to discern good and evil (Hebrews 5:11f).

In small group community, Christians must be retrained to see, hear, and experience God and to practice his presence, so they help each other daily exchange personal plans for those of Christ. They must learn together how to interchange and share their lives with each other and with Christ in community.

BODY LIFE AND PROPHECY
Prophecy's Roots

Prophecy can be used in a foretelling sense and a forth-telling sense. In the predictive sense, biblical prophecy is foretelling the future out of a special revelation from God that's beyond human knowledge. In the non-predictive sense, prophecy is forth-telling the will and message of God because of a specific inspiration.

The Hebrew word for prophet, *nabi*, comes from a word meaning to boil up or boil forth, like some hot spring or fountain. The Hebrew phrase *N'um Yahweh* ("Thus says the Lord") is a marker or indicator that often introduces a word of prophecy. It's a helpful marker because true prophecy is always a word from God.

Mount Sinai is the prophecy model used in the Old Testament. Moses alone went into God's presence on the mountain and brought God's Word down to the people. In the Old Testament, prophecy was from above down to man. In the New Testament, prophecy was from above but also from within. The indwelling Holy Spirit spoke to and through all Christians in practical prophetic words.

The church today will be much healthier if it views prophecy in the New Testament way, rather than the Old Testament way. The church should focus on the verb "prophesying" rather than the noun "prophet." Old Testament prophecy often included the method and means by which prophecy would be fulfilled. For instance, in Old Testament prophecy, the method and means by which the Messiah would come were also mentioned. The Messiah would be born of a virgin in Bethlehem. General prophecy today is often detached from the methods and means by which it will become a reality.

The church and ordinary Christians are often overlooked as instruments for the practical and specific fulfillment of prophecy. However, the church living in community is God's instrument for fulfilling prophecy.

All Are To Prophesy

The New Testament teaches that every Christian is to prophesy, but that every Christian is NOT a prophet! "Pursue love, yet desire earnestly spiritual gifts, but especially that you may prophesy" (1 Corinthians 14:1). But one who prophesies speaks to men for edification and exhortation and consolation (1 Corinthians. 14:3). One who prophesies edifies the church (1 Corinthians. 14:4). "I wish that even more of you would prophesy" (1 Corinthians 14:5).

"And it shall be in the last days that I will pour forth of My Spirit on all mankind; and your sons and your daughters shall prophesy. And your young men will see visions. And your old men will dream dreams. Even upon my bondslaves, both men and women, I will in those days pour forth of My Spirit" (Acts 2:17-18; Joel 2:28-29).

It's obvious that the word prophecy, when compared to its use in the Old Testament, is used in a different, new, or additional way in the New Testament. In the Old Testament, only a few chosen people were prophesying. However, in the New Testament, everyone is expected to prophesy.

The word "prophecy" is made up of two words. Pro is used as in the word "pronoun," "in the place of." A pronoun such as "me" is used in the place of a noun, a real person with a real name. The last part of the word (phecy) comes from *phemi*, "to speak." A prophet is one who speaks in place of another. God said to Moses: "Aaron thy brother shall be thy prophet (mouthpiece)" (Exodus 4:16).

In the New Testament, the word "prophet" (Greek = *Propheteuein*) is used in the following four ways:

1. To announce a revelation from God (Matthew 7:22; Acts 19:6; 21:9)
2. To reveal what has been hidden (Mt. 26:68)
3. To foretell the future (Matthew 11:13; 15:7; 1 Peter 1:10)

4. To edify within community (1 Corinthians 11:4f; 13:9; 14:1, 3)

The fourth kind of prophecy is unique to the New Testament. This should not surprise us because "edifying prophecy" could only be experienced after Christ established his spiritual community on earth. "God, after he spoke long ago to the fathers in the prophets in many portions and in many ways, in these last days has spoken to us in his Son (in Sonship), whom he appointed heir of all thing; through whom also he made the world. And he (Jesus) is the radiance of his (God's) glory and the exact representation of his nature, and upholds all things by the word of his power (Hebrews 1:1f).

In the past God spoke through the prophets. In his Son, God has spoken to us in a new way (and continues to speak to us in this special way). Today we can participate in incarnation and community prophecy because of the work of the Trinity! This special relationship of the Spirit with the church releases the presence and power of God among his people and releases New Testament prophecy.

New Testament Prophecy and the Believer

Paul suggests three results of practical prophecy. "He that prophesies speaks unto men edification, comfort and consolation" (1 Corinthians 14:3). Words of prophecy that are "spoken unto men" are healing and positive, not judgmental, harsh, invasive, or critical.

New Testament prophecy edifies the believer. "And he gave some as apostles, and some as prophets, and some as evangelists, and some as pastors and teachers, for the equipping of the saints for the work of ministry" (Ephesians 4:11-12a). All these leaders and gifts are essential for effective ministry, including prophets and prophecy.

"To the building up (edifying) of the body of Christ until we all attain to the unity of the faith, and of the knowledge of the Son of God, to a mature man, to the measure of the stature which belongs to the fullness of Christ. As a result we are no longer to be children, but speaking the truth in love, we are to grow up in all aspects into him" (Ephesians 4:12b-15).

New Testament prophecy comforts the believer. "Blessed be the God and Father of our Lord Jesus Christ, the Father of mercies and God of all comfort; who comforts us in all our affliction so that we may be able to comfort those who are in any affliction with the comfort with which we ourselves are comforted by God. For just as the sufferings of Christ are ours in abundance, so also our comfort is abundant through Christ" (2 Corinthians 7:5-7).

New Testament prophecy consoles the believer. "If therefore there is any encouragement in Christ, if there is any consolation of love, if there is any fellowship of the Spirit, if any affection and compassion, make my joy complete by being of the same mind, maintaining the same love, united in spirit, intent on one purpose. Do nothing from selfishness or empty conceit, but with humility of mind let each of you regard one another as more important than himself; do not merely look out for your own personal interests, but also for the interests of others" (Philippians 2:1-5).

New Testament Prophecy and the Unbeliever

"If all prophesy, and an unbeliever or an ungifted man enters, he is convicted by all, he is called to account by all; the secrets of his heart are disclosed; and so he will fall on his face and worship God, declaring that God is certainly among you" (1 Corinthians 14:22-25). Prophecy is a powerful experience for an ungifted man or an unbeliever. If either person is present where the gift of practical prophecy is being exercised, he will be touched at three points: sin, self, and God.

Practical prophecy will cause sin to become real in his life and he will be "convicted by all and called to account by all." In practical prophecy the secrets of his heart are revealed, and God's light shines upon the darkness in his life. In prophecy, the unbeliever encounters God. He falls on his face and worships God and declares the presence of God.

Notice: This kind of prophecy happens naturally within the context and safety of community. The unbeliever and unlearned are not embarrassed or singled out. The experience presupposes some kind of cultivation and relationship.

Prophecy is from a personal God through a person and to persons. God always speaks out of his nature in order to demonstrate who he is! Prophecy is about Jesus! "For the testimony of Jesus is the spirit of prophecy" (Revelation 19:10).

We need each other in order to participate in this kind of prophecy. "But prophecy is for a sign, not to unbelievers, but to those who believe" (1 Corinthians 14:26). "What is the outcome then brethren? When you assemble, each one has a psalm, has a teaching, has a revelation, has a tongue, has an interpretation ... For you can all prophesy, one by one, so that all may learn and all may be exhorted; and the spirits of prophets are subject to prophets; for God is not a God of confusion but of peace, as in all the churches of the saints" (1 Corinthians 14:26, 31-33).

BODY LIFE AND SPIRITUAL GIFTS
All Gifts Are Extensions of Christ

Gifts are not independent and isolated talents, responsibilities, or powers that fall down from heaven upon certain special people. To understand spiritual gifts, we should always see them as an extension of the life and ministry of Christ and as a work of the Holy Spirit.

Christ is the source of every gift that's used in the church. Every gift is an expression of a concern or a care that flows from Christ to a hurt or need in the life of a real person. To understand this link, think of Jesus' three years of ministry. Imagine the number of special gifts and ministry that flowed out of his life to meet the needs of his disciples, his followers, and the crowds. Christ has all the gifts and wants to give them to all his disciples to touch the needs and hurts of people in our world today.

However, no one Christian can contain all or even a small part of Christ's life and ministry. Therefore, through the Holy Spirit, the life and ministry of Christ is given in separate parts as special gifts to each individual Christian in his (Christ's) body.

Now, consider the Holy Spirit and see him hovering over the body of Christ on earth and every Christian in that body. He carefully shares the life and ministry of Christ through individual Christians in special gifts to individual needs.

The Holy Spirit is the midwife for birthing Christ's gifts in individual Christians. He coordinates the work of Christ's gifts and channels the flow of Christ's gifts into the proper persons at the proper time. He teaches each Christian how to properly use each gift. The Holy Spirit conducts a gift orchestra so that each gift plays its proper part in the beautiful symphony of community and body life.

So, we see that spiritual gifts come from God the Father to the spiritual body of Christ the Son through the Holy Spirit. Gifts are not "spiritual merit badges" given to honor a spiritual accomplishment or to recognize outstanding spiritual merit. They belong to the church for the building up of itself for the work of ministry. The church is built up within the context of small group community life, because that's where the gifts can be applied, multiplied, and integrated.

Application of the gifts within small group community results in spiritual synergism, as all the gifts work together in the Spirit's power. When orchestrated in community, the gifts are "greater in total effect than the sum of their effects." This means our individual gifts exercised together in community by the Holy Spirit are more effective and powerful than the sum of our gifts when exercised alone.

Operating gifts in the Spirit causes humility and gratitude. It breaks the pride of ownership and the pride of ability in the use of gifts. We learn that gifts belong to God and the body, not to individuals, and that only the Holy Spirit has the power to exercise them. Therefore, Christians have no reason to be prideful about any gift God exercises through them.

Spiritual gifts increase character and holiness. The Spirit can operate a gift in the life of a new or immature Christian. Sin doesn't eliminate a person from being a vessel and instrument for the use of gifts. However, a person's character and degree of spiritual holiness will eventually affect how the Spirit uses the gifts in his life. This is why God "promotes" (uses someone in greater ministry) according to character, rather than gifts.

Spiritual Gifts in the Large- and Small-Group Setting

Part of the power and synergism of gifts in the church is how they operate in concert within large- and small-group settings. In the large-group setting of the church, the five-fold leadership gifts listed by Paul in Ephesians 4:11-12 are manifested to lead and equip the church. "And he gave some as apostles, and some as prophets, and some as evangelists, and some as pastors and teachers, for the equipping of the saints for the work of service, to the building up of the body of Christ."

Leaders with a title and position normally operate within the large-group setting of the church, because that's the place for leadership coordination. For instance, the church only needs a limited number of Christians who are set aside as evangelists. However, these leaders should be identified while they're doing the ministry of evangelism.

The office of evangelist operates differently in cell-based and traditional churches. In a traditional church, those with the title "evangelist" will probably spend most of their time outside the church that set them aside doing evangelism. In a cell-based church, the evangelist will "equip the saints for the work" of evangelism, by passing on the passion and skills for evangelism to the entire church.

The evangelist will model the gift of evangelism and identify those who are gifted to evangelize. He will help coordinate the gift of evangelism within the church and discern the gift of evangelism as it relates to other gifts. The evangelist will develop evangelism strategies and plan for mobilizing the entire church for evangelizing.

In a small-group setting, cell community is the place where evangelism is implemented and where the gift of evangelism is identified. The passion and skills of the evangelist is applied within small groups, where the work of evangelism and the number doing evangelism is multiplied. Within community, evangelism is integrated with all the other gifts so that divine synergism takes place and multiplication and growth result.

Multiplication and Integration of the Gifts in Body Life

When the Spirit distributes gifts, the life and ministry of Christ are both multiplied and integrated in community. Gift multiplication takes place because in community one person can participate in the life and ministry of Christ that he has given to others!

It is always helpful to visualize spiritual gifts within the life of Christ. The different parts of the body of Christ can be used to categorize and group spiritual gifts. The mind of Christ can represent the gifts of knowledge, wisdom, humility, obedience, and sacrifice. The eyes of Christ remind us of the gifts of worship, compassion, and mercy that come from seeing God. The mouth of Christ suggests the gifts of speech, communication, and prayer. The hands of Christ point to the gifts of ministry, service, healing, and helps. The feet of Christ allude to the gifts of evangelism and witness to Jerusalem, Judea, Samaria, and the world. The ears of Christ make one think of the gifts of discernment, prophecy, and interpretation that come in listening and hearing God. The heart of Christ is the gift of love that's the greatest gift of all.

Within community, the Holy Spirit reassembles Christ's life and ministry by bestowing his gifts upon members in the group. The cell then functions as his body, not as separate pieces and parts.

Paul describes this divine synergism in Ephesians 4:16. "The whole body, being fitted and held together by that which every joint supplies according to the proper working of each individual part, causes the growth of the body for the building up of itself in love." The life and ministry of Christ come together in the cell and the gifts begin to work together beyond the power of any one gift or combination of gifts.

Stage 3:
Assess Your Current Reality

CELL GROUP READINESS ASSESSMENT

M. Scott Boren

Based upon research performed on churches which have successfully implemented cell groups versus those which have not, there are four traits successful implementations possess. While these churches were far from perfect before they started groups, they rated higher in these four areas. They are:

1. Permission-Giving Structure
2. Leadership's Willingness to Change
3. Worship Services Where People Experience the Presence of God
4. Passion for God Expressed through Prayer

WHO SHOULD COMPLETE THIS ASSESSMENT?

The following questions will help you determine your strengths and weaknesses in these four areas. It's best for staff pastors and key leaders to complete this assessment. At the very least, the senior pastor must complete it.

HOW DO YOU COMPLETE THE ASSESSMENT?

Answer each of the questions based upon the current reality of your church. Each question should be given a number from 1 to 5, which indicate the following:

1=This statement does not at all describe your church.
2=On rare occasions, this statement might describe your church, but is an exception to the rule.
3=Sometimes this statement describes your church, sometimes it does not; it's a 50-50 proposition.
4=This is generally true of your church; sometimes things falter, but not too often.
5=This is consistently true of your church, almost without exception.

After rating each statement, total the scores for each page. Then transfer those totals to the last page of the assessment.

WHAT DO YOU DO WITH THE RESULTS?

After adding your scores, you can use them in the following ways:

1. Meet with other pastors, key leaders, or your cell vision team to dialogue about how they scored the questions. Compile the numbers to attain a composite total for each of the four sections.
2. Complete the graph on page 205. Upon completion, identify the area(s) that require improvement to establish a strong foundation for cell group ministry.
3. Identify specific questions that scored only a 1 or a 2. These will provide a trail to help you analyze some of the root areas of the weaknesses.
4. The cell vision team, along with the pastoral leadership team, should begin to develop areas that are weak, using some of the ideas presented in Stage 4 of the book, *Making Cell Groups Work*, and the *Navigation Guide*.

PERMISSION-GIVING STRUCTURE

Rating:

1. The senior pastor's role is one that provides him the freedom and time to hear God's vision and direction for the church. He's not bogged down with lots of administrative duties and meetings.

   1 2 3 4 5

2. The church's leadership team (i.e. elders, deacons, etc.) works in unity with the senior pastor, neither trying to control the other.

   1 2 3 4 5

3. Pastoral staff members work in unity toward a single vision. In other words, the church has one vision, not multiple visions with departments going in different directions.

   1 2 3 4 5

4. The pastoral staff members are committed to the vision of the church, as they've made long-term commitments to remain on the staff.

   1 2 3 4 5

5. The church's pastoral leaders focus on empowering others for ministry, as opposed to performing the ministry themselves.

   1 2 3 4 5

6. The church constitution or by-laws give permission for the senior pastor to hear God and set the vision for the church. In other words, a volunteer committee does not dictate the vision of the church.

   1 2 3 4 5

7. The senior pastor is a team player; he sets the course as the captain, but he's not a dictator.

   1 2 3 4 5

8. Previous experience in the church with small groups has been positive.

   1 2 3 4 5

9. Over the last five years, the church has not experienced traumatic setbacks (i.e. leadership immorality, financial scandals, etc.).

   1 2 3 4 5

10. Denominational overseers won't seek to shut down any initiative (such as cell groups) that varies from the status quo.

    1 2 3 4 5

11. The senior pastor has committed to leading the church for at least the next six years.

    1 2 3 4 5

12. The emotional reservoir of trust and confidence the church has in the senior pastor is full.

    1 2 3 4 5

13. The church structure isn't based upon committees. Those committees that do exist are functional teams that operate on an as-needed basis.

    1 2 3 4 5

Total: _____

LEADERSHIP'S WILLINGNESS TO CHANGE

Rating:

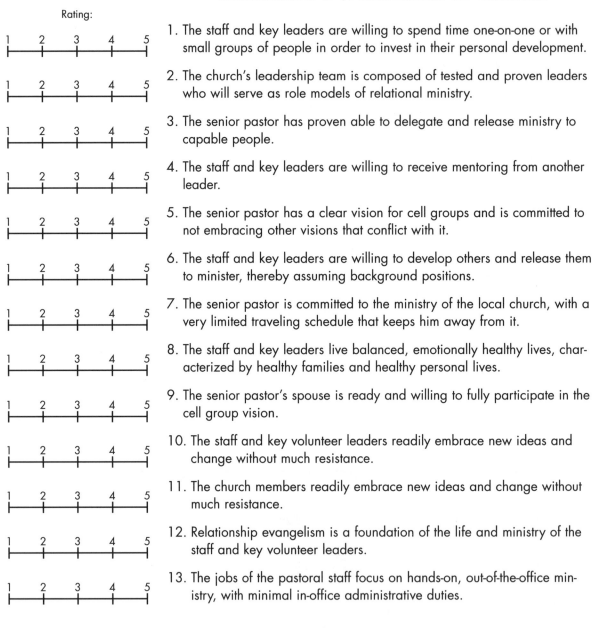

1. The staff and key leaders are willing to spend time one-on-one or with small groups of people in order to invest in their personal development.

2. The church's leadership team is composed of tested and proven leaders who will serve as role models of relational ministry.

3. The senior pastor has proven able to delegate and release ministry to capable people.

4. The staff and key leaders are willing to receive mentoring from another leader.

5. The senior pastor has a clear vision for cell groups and is committed to not embracing other visions that conflict with it.

6. The staff and key leaders are willing to develop others and release them to minister, thereby assuming background positions.

7. The senior pastor is committed to the ministry of the local church, with a very limited traveling schedule that keeps him away from it.

8. The staff and key leaders live balanced, emotionally healthy lives, characterized by healthy families and healthy personal lives.

9. The senior pastor's spouse is ready and willing to fully participate in the cell group vision.

10. The staff and key volunteer leaders readily embrace new ideas and change without much resistance.

11. The church members readily embrace new ideas and change without much resistance.

12. Relationship evangelism is a foundation of the life and ministry of the staff and key volunteer leaders.

13. The jobs of the pastoral staff focus on hands-on, out-of-the-office ministry, with minimal in-office administrative duties.

Total: _____

WORSHIP SERVICES WHERE PEOPLE EXPERIENCE THE PRESENCE OF GOD

Rating:

1. The church teaches and trains people in practices that support corporate and personal worship.

   1   2   3   4   5

2. The church makes room in meetings and gatherings for members to participate in the experience of worshipping God.

   1   2   3   4   5

3. Members participate in worship experiences with enthusiasm and joy.

   1   2   3   4   5

4. People express that they sense the presence of God when worshipping together.

   1   2   3   4   5

5. During worship, people obviously experience God's love and peace.

   1   2   3   4   5

6. People hear a clear vision from the church leadership that unifies their ministry efforts.

   1   2   3   4   5

7. The teaching in weekly large-group worship services challenges people to examine their values and calls them to realign their lives to participate in the Kingdom of God.

   1   2   3   4   5

8. People experience hope and victory as they celebrate what God is doing in their church.

   1   2   3   4   5

9. People view large-group worship services as a time when God meets them in their situations, and they have an opportunity to receive ministry.

   1   2   3   4   5

10. When unbelievers attend a celebration, they feel welcomed, and they experience something real and alive.

   1   2   3   4   5

11. There are no sacred cows that limit corporate worship.

   1   2   3   4   5

12. The senior pastor and worship leader work as a team.

   1   2   3   4   5

13. The senior pastor, staff members, and key leaders set the model by visibly participating in worship.

   1   2   3   4   5

Total: _____

PASSION FOR GOD EXPRESSED THROUGH PRAYER

Rating:

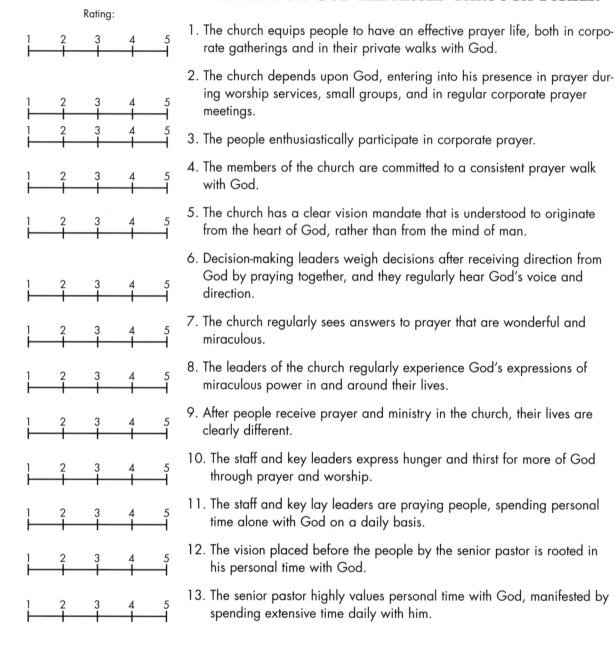

1. The church equips people to have an effective prayer life, both in corporate gatherings and in their private walks with God.

2. The church depends upon God, entering into his presence in prayer during worship services, small groups, and in regular corporate prayer meetings.

3. The people enthusiastically participate in corporate prayer.

4. The members of the church are committed to a consistent prayer walk with God.

5. The church has a clear vision mandate that is understood to originate from the heart of God, rather than from the mind of man.

6. Decision-making leaders weigh decisions after receiving direction from God by praying together, and they regularly hear God's voice and direction.

7. The church regularly sees answers to prayer that are wonderful and miraculous.

8. The leaders of the church regularly experience God's expressions of miraculous power in and around their lives.

9. After people receive prayer and ministry in the church, their lives are clearly different.

10. The staff and key leaders express hunger and thirst for more of God through prayer and worship.

11. The staff and key lay leaders are praying people, spending personal time alone with God on a daily basis.

12. The vision placed before the people by the senior pastor is rooted in his personal time with God.

13. The senior pastor highly values personal time with God, manifested by spending extensive time daily with him.

Total: _____

INTERPRETING THE SCORES

Total Scores for Each Section

Permission-Giving Structure: _____

Leadership's Willingness to Change: _____

Worship Services Where People Experience the Presence of God: _____

Passion for God Expressed through Prayer: _____

Grand Total: _____

Identify the group where your Grand Total score falls.

- 224-260 Move forward into the cell group vision. The church has a strong foundation upon which to build.

- 184-223 Proceed with the cell group vision, as the foundation is good. At the same time, there are a few areas that should be addressed to strengthen the foundation.

- 144-183 Weaknesses of the church should be addressed. If leaders feel God moving them into cell groups, they should do so with deliberation and caution.

- 101-143 Leadership should focus first solely on developing the weak areas of the church identified by this tool. After these areas have been improved, then the church can reevaluate the situation and determine the steps for moving into cell groups.

- 52-100 A church with this score has much about which to be concerned. Cell groups are not an option in the near future.

Cell Group Vision Team Exercise

Identify which of the four sections of the assessment reveal weaknesses in your church. Use the following scale:

- 56-65 Exceptional.

- 46-55 Strong but may have areas that need to be addressed.

- 36-45 Average. The vision team must work to improve these areas in order to improve the development of cell groups.

- 26-35 Weak. Must work on this area in order to secure the foundation for cell groups.

- 13-25 Very weak. Need to seek God diligently to determine the path to turn the ship around.

CHURCH PLANTING AND CHURCH RESTARTING STRATEGY

Bill Beckham

From a careful reading of the Gospels, I realized that God ministered on four different tracks to develop his movement. On the first track, God the Father made careful preparation to build his first church. He prepared a nation and the necessary political and social climate. He sent John the Baptist to prepare the way.

The other three tracks are seen in the direct ministry of God the Son. Jesus meticulously developed a step-by-step prototype of leaders for his church as he equipped his inner circle of Peter, James and John, the Twelve, the Seventy, and finally the 120. On another track, Jesus harvested broadly in order to gather the number of leaders and followers necessary to complete the prototype, reach critical mass, and to establish and expand his movement. This harvest track continued at Pentecost with the conversion of 3,000 and 5,000 new believers. On the last track, Jesus assimilated followers of many different levels of spiritual maturity, ethnic backgrounds, and social conditions. These four tracks are illustrated in the following matrix.

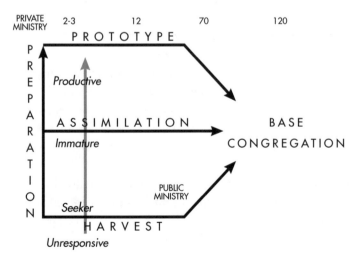

This matrix connects Jesus' four tracks into a grid that helps a vision team start new churches. It can help leaders solve one of the greatest frustrations in developing strategy for new starts and small churches: Blurring. Many times, the process of planting a church or restarting an old church can blur into one mass of activities. All the different parts run together.

Therefore, leaders find it difficult to determine what comes next and how the different parts relate to one another. Preparation is mixed into the other essential elements and consequently is generally shortchanged. Prototype, harvest, and assimilation merge into one blob that all looks the same. Lacking well-defined categories, leaders find it almost impossible to develop an effective implementing strategy.

This four-track matrix helps leaders visualize the relationship between the key elements of church strategy: preparation, prototype, harvest, and assimilation. It gives a way to arrange the simultaneous and sequential processes at work in a new start or restart. It gives direction, as all four tracks move toward the same objective of creating one base congregation of twelve to fifteen healthy cells.

WHO USES THE MATRIX?

This matrix is not a classroom theory but is designed for practical application at a local church level. Different kinds of churches will use this matrix:

1. *Church plants.* The leadership team of a church plant can use this matrix to understand its point of origin. Some teams are advanced and are ready to launch out into groups. Others have lots of preparatory work to do.

2. *An existing church preparing to begin a new church.* The leadership team of an existing church might have plans to start a new church. If so, this team should work through this matrix to determine its point of origin, so that a wise strategy might be developed that will produce the intended outcome.

3. *A small church looking to restart.* Many small churches are stuck. They need more than a transition. They need to restart. This matrix will help a small church see clearly where it is today and determine what it needs to do to restart.

4. *Mission-sending agency.* Mission overseers might use this matrix to determine a workable strategy to start new churches.

MATRIX QUESTIONS

After establishing a community center of gravity for the church, the leaders of a new start or restart should sit down and develop a strategy by applying the four tracks of this matrix. The matrix becomes a grid, in which the pieces and parts of the church process can be assigned to a proper place and sequence. By using the matrix, a team can then answer the following key questions about starting a cell group church or restarting a small church.

Preparation question: How will we effectively prepare to become a cell group church? Preparation is the first track of the matrix. It's important to build a team, agree on a vision, establish a culture, develop a strategy, and prepare all necessary materials. Essential elements must be put into place before starting the model. Notice the preparation arrow in the matrix chart is at the left side of the matrix and the other three tracks emerge from the preparation track.

Prototype question: How will healthy cell communities be developed into a quality prototype of twelve to fifteen functioning cells? The arrow at the top of the matrix represents this element. The prototype track can be visualized with the numbers used by Jesus in his ministry: 2-3, 12, 70, and 120. Jesus carefully developed his prototype over a period of three-and-a-half years, by forming these numbers of leaders into leadership units.

The prototype track develops the basic elements and momentum necessary to reach critical mass. A complete prototype consists of the basic implementing and ministry unit of the church (the cell), and the basic support and coordinating unit of the church (the congregation).

Harvest question: How will the team attract and gather a pool of productive believers necessary to build each stage of the prototype? The harvest track runs at the bottom of the matrix, and gives a way to develop strategy for gathering the initial team, organizing the prototype core, and establishing the base congregation.

Assimilation question: How will the team incorporate productive believers into the prototype without compromising the prototype with insincere seekers and immature believers? The assimilation track is in the middle of the matrix between the harvest track and the prototype track. The assimilation track protects the quality of the emerging prototype from uncommitted, immature, and dysfunctional members until the essential cell systems are operational.

PREPARATION INSTRUMENT

Jesus said, "I will build my church." This means Christ is the most important factor in creating his church. However, we can use the following human factors to help analyze the potential success in starting a new church or restarting a small church. These factors are applied to the initial leadership team, because starting a new church or restarting a small church depends upon the leaders. These eleven factors need to be carefully monitored during the preparation phase of a cell group church.

Factors	1	2	3	4
Culture	Outsiders in new culture	Able to adapt to culture	Members of the culture	Cultural team leaders
Vision	What church isn't	What church should be	Revelation vision	Implementing vision
Prayer	Activities-driven work	Formal praying	Prayer is the key	Prayer warriors
Support	Lone Ranger start	Traditional support	Creative church support	Cell group church support
Strategy	See no need for strategy	Want a strategy	Developing strategy	Implementing strategy
Team Size	One unit	2-3 units	At least 12 core leaders	Transplant of 70 people
Experience	No small group experience	Small group experiences	Member of a cell church	Started a cell church
Leadership	Cell level call & gifts	Supervisor call & gifts	Pastor call & gifts	Mega church call & gifts
Evangelism	Contact skills don't exist	Must learn contact skills	Contact skills	Contact plan & skills
Curriculum	No set curriculum	Traditional curriculum	Small group curriculum	Cell church curriculum
Response	No target group/s	Target needs, not response	Target one primary group	Responsive target group

Using the Classification Grid

If you're a pastor whose church is sending church starting teams, evaluate the potential of each team you're sending by using this grid. Or, if you lead a church of fewer than 200 members, apply this grid to members in your church who'll help you break through to critical mass. If you're beginning a new cell group church, use this grid to evaluate prospects for success in your new start.

The time of preparation should be used to strengthen the initial core in these eleven areas. Notice the four numbered columns in the classification grid. The columns in this instrument measure four levels of potential effectiveness in a team developing a cell group church. On a sheet of paper, write down the column that best describes your church project for each of the eleven factors.

Let me give an example. Suppose the team I'm evaluating consists of a Caucasian husband and wife who speak Spanish. A creative church is sending them to begin a new cell-based church in Mexico. They've helped start a cell-based church in another cross-cultural situation and are able to adapt to a new culture. However, no team members or leaders are from Mexico. The husband on the team has the gifts and call to at least lead at the one hundred level.

Just this information allows me to evaluate this team at the point of five of the factors: Factor 1, Culture; Factor 4, Support; Factor 6, Team Size; Factor 7, Experience; and Factor 8, Leadership. Using the Classification Grid, I'd evaluate this team in the following way:

- Factor 1, Culture: I'd put this team in Column 2, "able to adapt to culture," and would write the number "2" down beside the factor of "Culture."
- Factor 4, Support: I'd mark this church in Column 3, "creative church support," because the sending church is a "creative" church and not a cell group church.
- Factor 6, Team Size: I'd place this team in Column 1, "one unit," because only one couple makes up the team.
- Factor 7, Experience: I'd put this church in Column 4, "started a cell group church."
- Factor 8, Leadership: I'd rate it in Column 3, "pastor call & gifts."

More information is required to complete the other factors for this team. However, with just preliminary information on a project, several important factors about the start or restart can be evaluated.

After considering all eleven of the factors, the column numbers can then be added together in order to come up with one total number. The total number can then be compared to the Color Code categories (which I explain at the end of this chapter).

Factor 1-Culture: How indigenous is the team?

""Culture" as an evaluation factor measures the acceptability and adaptability of the core team to the cultural context. How does the team relate to the culture around it? Four cultural questions will help evaluate the potential effectiveness of a new start.

Factor	1	2	3	4
Culture	Outsiders in new culture	Able to adapt to culture	Members of the culture	Cultural team leaders

- Column 1: Is the initial leadership team comprised of outsiders in a new culture and lacking in cross-cultural experience? This is the worst cultural makeup of a team that wants to start a new church. A small church that wants to restart must also have a leadership team that's able to relate to its potential growth group(s).
- Column 2: Does the initial leadership team, though not necessarily of the culture of the new area, have experience in adapting to a new culture?
- Column 3: Are some of the members of the initial team part of the culture where the new start is beginning?
- Column 4: Are the leaders of the initial team part of the culture where the new start is beginning? This is the best cultural makeup for beginning a new church.

Which column best explains your project concerning culture?

Factor 2-Vision: Does one consuming vision move the strategy?

The initial core team must have the same revelation vision. A "revelation" vision is one that comes from the heart of God. It's not a statement on a piece of paper, but a consuming passion written on the hearts of leaders. Every member in the startup and test phases must own the same vision and values. Otherwise, the vision and values will be constantly under attack by well-meaning members who are gradually chipping away at the stated vision with their own personal agendas.

Factor	1	2	3	4
Vision	What church isn't	What church should be	Revelation vision	Implementing vision

Four statements will help evaluate the potential effectiveness of a new start in the area of vision and values.
- Column 1: The team understands little about the type of church it wants to begin. This creates a negative vision and is the worst possible vision base.
- Column 2: Core leaders understand what kind of church they want to be.
- Column 3: The leadership team has received a revelation vision from God. This revelation vision drives them toward the kind of church they want to be.
- Column 4: The leadership team has developed a strategy for implementing their revelation vision from God. This is the best vision context for beginning a new church.

Which column best explains your project concerning vision?

Factor 3-Prayer: Is prayer the force that makes things work?
This instrument evaluates the effectiveness of prayer by considering the prayer lives of leaders. It's wonderful if a small group of prayer warriors in the church pray, and it's commendable if a church meets for a prayer meeting one night of the week. However, a church will never rise beyond their leaders in prayer. Therefore, the leaders should establish a prayer base that's built upon their own prayer life.

Factor	1	2	3	4
Prayer	Activities driven work	Formal praying	Prayer is the key	Prayer warriors

- Column 1: The team operates more out of the ability of the team to do certain activities than out of prayer.
- Column 2: The team acknowledges the importance of prayer and practices prayer in a traditional way.
- Column 3: The team views prayer as the key to what will happen in the new start.
- Column 4: The team consists of prayer warriors who engage in prayer out of desperation.

Which column best explains your project concerning prayer?

Factor 4-Support: How much and what kind of support?

The best place to build a team is within an existing mother church. A new start that is sent out from an existing cell group church has greater potential for success.

A support church can be the preparation base, where the team is trained and gathered. Such a church can be a planning base, where the team is guided in developing an implementing strategy. A support church can model the tasks necessary to be an effective cell group church, and can be a resource base that helps a new work with seed resources, such as money and personnel.

In the startup phase, a mother church can be a prayer base, and a base from which to coordinate the new work. Therefore, the quality of the support church affects the quality of the new church. A small church that desires to restart must consider how the membership of the small church views and supports the leadership team in its effort to restart.

Factor	1	2	3	4
Support	Lone Ranger start	Traditional support	Creative church support	Cell group church support

- Column 1: The initial team is on its own without any support base. This is the worst-case scenario for beginning new work.
- Column 2: The initial team is sent out from a traditional church. This portends problems because support churches have a way of wanting a new daughter church to look like the mother church. The mother church will evaluate the daughter church from traditional values. Or, the small

church is traditional in vision and practice.

- Column 3: A creative church supports the team. A creative church is more flexible to new approaches and allows the daughter church to develop methods that reflect the values of the initial team. Or, the small church is creative.
- Column 4: A cell group church has sent the team out. This is the best possible support base. The new start will be living out the same values as the mother church.

Which column best explains your project concerning support?

Factor 5-Strategy: Is there a strategy?

God said to the prophet: "Write the vision down" (Habakkuk 2:2). God's vision to man is understandable and can be written as a strategy. The strategy should be a set of directions for arriving at the agreed upon destination. It's a road map to the vision and values, a description of what the project will be when it's operational.

Strategy should be specific and intentional. It should be value-based and vision-driven. The strategy should be practical, measurable, and transferable to ordinary members. Finally, the strategy must be comprehensive. It must cover all bases, fill in all gaps, and deal with all issues.

Factor	1	2	3	4
Strategy	See no need for strategy	Want a strategy	Developing strategy	Implementing strategy

- Column 1: The team has no strategy and has no one on the team who's interested in strategy or capable of developing an implementing strategy.
- Column 2: The team realizes the importance of a strategy but may not have a leader who can help develop an implementing strategy.
- Column 3: The team has a leader or leaders who understand how to develop a strategy, and the team is in the process of developing an implementing strategy.
- Column 4: The team has already developed a detailed implementing strategy before beginning the project. This is the best way to begin a new work. Develop an implementing strategy while still part of an existing cell group church.

Which column best explains your project concerning strategy?

Factor 6-Size: What size is the team?

The size of the initial team is important for beginning a new work. The quality of the team is also important. The quality is considered in some of the other factors, such as "experience" and "vision." But size determines what tasks can be done, how and when they'll be done, who'll do them, and how much momentum can be generated by doing them.

The size of the work represents stages of development. Jesus understood the importance of these sizes and built his base congregation upon them. Jesus' stages were: 2-3 innovators/visionaries; 12 core leaders; 70 support network; and 120 in his base congregation. In a restart of a small church, the size represents the number of members on the leadership team.

Factor	1	2	3	4
Team Size	One unit	2-3 units	At least 12 core leaders	Transplant of 70 people

- Column 1: The initial team consists of one unit, usually a husband and wife. This is the worst possible way to begin a new work. One person or couple cannot model even the most basic systems that are required to begin. A team of one unit must spend its initial time in trying to find potential members who'll eventually become leaders, so the basic tasks can be modeled.
- Column 2: Two to three units are large enough to encourage each other and to begin some kind of evangelism. However, a team of two to three units can still not effectively model the basic cell unit and the essential tasks. It's also difficult to establish a cell group church culture with this limited number of leaders.
- Column 3: Jesus began his church with a team of twelve core leaders. A team of this size can begin to model most of the tasks and systems necessary for an effective new start, and can quickly gather the initial pool of members and assimilate them into the prototype.
- Column 4: Cell group churches can transplant an embryonic church of thirty to seventy persons. This number of core persons is already a working prototype. The essential tasks and systems can be started immediately, and the team can aggressively begin to harvest. This is the best possi-

ble size to begin a new cell group church and to guarantee early momentum, growth, and eventual multiplication.

At this stage of the cell group church movement, a new church transplant, as described in Column 4, may not be a viable option. However, in the future, cell group churches will be able to send out a large enough initial core of members to "transplant" a new church from the original (see Chapter 71). When the movement reaches this stage, it's obvious that another level of growth has been reached. When a church is able to transplant a church, instead of planting a seed, exponential growth is possible.

Which column best explains your project concerning the size of the team?

Factor 7-Experience: Has anyone done this before?

The possibility for success dramatically improves when the initial team and core leadership have personally experienced the various systems they'll set up. This may not be possible during the early stages of a movement because models are still being developed. Therefore, in each new start, team members must learn to do the systems while trying to develop the systems. Eventually when a movement has many models, the experience level dramatically increases, because teams have already experienced the basic systems within the mother church.

In the meanwhile, until many functioning cell group churches are developed, a team can increase its potential for success by learning about cell group church in one of the early existing operational cell group churches.

Factor	1	2	3	4
Experience	No small group experience	Small group experiences	Member of a cell church	Started a cell church

- Column 1: The team has never experienced cell life, so the team must learn about community while trying to begin the work. This is the worst possible situation in beginning a new work. Becoming a cell group church is hard enough when we know what we're doing. But to try to learn while we're doing is almost impossible. It's like learning to drive an "eighteen-wheeler" on a busy freeway. It can be done, but it also can be extremely dangerous.

- Column 2: The leaders have lived in cell group life, but haven't experienced the support systems and tools they must establish.
- Column 3: The leaders have been part of a cell group church and have experienced all the systems and tools they'll implement.
- Column 4: The leaders have previously started a cell group church and have experienced the dynamics of setting up the necessary cell systems and tools.

Which column best explains your project, concerning experience?

Factor 8-Leadership: Are leaders called and gifted to do this?

What will your core team look like? It will look a lot like you. The team should have some members who are called to lead at the coordination and support leadership roles of one hundred and one thousand levels. The team needs innovators and visionaries who have the ability to think strategically and to develop an implementing strategy. These leaders should have a degree of spiritual maturity. Some of them may need to financially support themselves in the beginning of the new work. Members of the team should be team players with submissive servant hearts.

In an existing church that wants to transition to a cell group church, the senior leaders of the church must lead the transition.

Factor	1	2	3	4
Leadership	Cell level call & gifts	Supervisor call & gifts	Pastor call & gifts	Mega church call & gifts

- Column 1: The team has leaders who are gifted and called at the cell leader level but not at the fifty or one hundred levels. This severely limits the vision and the growth of the new start.
- Column 2: A leader or leaders are called and gifted at the fifty level and can oversee three to five cells. No leader feels called or feels he or she has the gifts to lead at the one hundred level of a congregational pastor.
- Column 3: At least one leader is gifted and called to function at the pastor level over one hundred. This leader can provide the support for up to twenty-five cells. This leader can also coordinate the large group wing of the church.
- Column 4: At least one leader is gifted and called to function at the coor-

dinating level of thousands. This leader can coordinate several congregations and can model leadership at each level necessary to be an operational cell church.

Which column best explains your project at the point of leadership?

Factor 9-Evangelism: How many relationship contacts are there?

The growth of a new start is directly proportional to how many contacts the team can establish with the lost and prodigals. Prepare for future expansion by evangelizing broadly through "super networking." Many of those Jesus touched in evangelism with the crowds in public ministry are the ones who came into the church after Pentecost. Use all the different kinds of evangelism methods that are available.

Factor	1	2	3	4
Evangelism	Contact skills don't exist	Must learn contact skills	Contact skills	Contact plan & skills

- Column 1: The team has few skills in evangelism and reaching the lost is not a passion. This is the worst possible situation to expect growth, because the growth of the new start is dependent upon how many contacts with lost people the team can establish.
- Column 2: The team has the desire to contact the lost, but lack the experience and skills in evangelism to successfully network with unbelievers. The team must therefore learn to contact through *oikos* relationships and groups. This limits the effectiveness of the team's early evangelism and may seriously affect the momentum of the new start or restart.
- Column 3: The team has the desire and skills to contact the lost, but has never actually experienced *oikos* and group evangelism in connection with a new start or restart.
- Column 4: The team has the desire, skills, and experience to contact the lost through relationships and groups. The team has been part of all these in an existing cell group church, or in a previous new start. This gives the greatest possibility for success in gathering the first harvest necessary to create significant early momentum.

Which column best explains your project concerning evangelism?

Factor 10-Curriculum: Are cell-based materials used?

The curriculum is one of the most important tools that can be used in beginning a new cell group church. Without a curriculum, the team is trying to "make bricks without straw." Pharaoh punished the children of Israel by withholding one of their "tools," the straw. If you want to punish yourself and your team while developing a cell group church, then begin without cell group church curriculum. Using only one systematic curriculum gives a clear track upon which the new start can run. A curriculum teaches and internalizes values and helps to quickly develop a common cell group church culture. An effective curriculum integrates the tasks and systems and provides a way to monitor quality control.

Factor	1	2	3	4
Curriculum	No set curriculum	Traditional curriculum	Small group curriculum	Cell church curriculum

- Column 1: The team begins without any kind of set curriculum.
- Column 2: The team is trying to use a traditional curriculum. This is better than not having materials at all, but will still not be totally effective. Good curriculum is based upon values and a philosophy of training. A traditional or small group church curriculum, though good in its own way, was not developed out of cell group church values and won't be as effective in internalizing these values and establishing a cell group church culture.
- Column 3: The team is committed to a cell group church curriculum, but hasn't yet decided on materials, or is trying to develop its own. Team member intentions are good, but they've put themselves into a "Catch 22" situation. They don't have cell group church materials early in the process and so can't properly model the tasks. They don't have time to give to developing the curriculum, because they're trying to implement the tasks without appropriate materials.
- Column 4: The team is using one cell group church curriculum. This is the best possible situation and will help ensure a good value base, will provide good quality control, will integrate the system, develop momentum, and help create a common culture.

Which column best explains your project concerning curriculum?

Factor 11-Response: Are responsive groups targeted?

A cell group church is able to relate to a broader geographical area than a traditional church. It doesn't view the church's work as a geographical "parish" that has characterized the traditional church for centuries. A cell group church is based on relationships and crosses geographical, political, and social boundaries.

Through homogeneous cells, cell group churches can penetrate a broad range of people groups. Every strata of society should eventually be reached. However, during the prototype building phase, several groups that are most responsive should be considered. Also, it's best to target groups that have some emotional and social health. These are the people who could be referred to as "productive believers."

Groups with a large percentage of insincere seekers and immature believers should be penetrated only after the cell infrastructure is in place to receive them. Insincere seekers and immature believers who come into the church during normal activities of the early stages of development should be assimilated through low maintenance large-group activities.

In the early stages of a cell group church's development, a general demographic survey may be helpful. After reaching the base congregation when the church is ready to begin exponential multiplication, a second more extensive survey may be required. At that time, additional target groups can be added and the church's geographical context can be expanded.

Factor	1	2	3	4
Response	No target group/s	Target needs, not response	Target one primary group	Responsive target group

- Column 1: The team hasn't identified any target group(s). "Everyone is the target" means no one is the target.
- Column 2: The team is focusing on needs, not response. The team sees certain groups of people who have great need of God, and is touched by their needs. These needy people are not the best group out of which to build a prototype. These groups can "eat the nets" thrown out to them and can destroy a new church start. These groups should become the focus of evangelism and equipping after the prototype is established with productive believers.

- Column 3: The team has one primary target group it's seeking to penetrate. A good percentage of those who are won out of this target group should be potentially productive believers.
- Column 4: The team has identified several target groups that are responsive to the Gospel. This team doesn't have "all its eggs in one basket," but has a broad enough target to harvest enough initial response to build up momentum.

Which column best explains your project in the area of response?

EVALUATION AND APPLICATION

Add the eleven column numbers. This is your classification number that will be used to help you evaluate the potential of your project. You'll use this information to learn to develop a strategy sequence appropriate for your situation.

I've developed color categories in order to evaluate the team that will develop a cell group church in the situations mentioned earlier:

1. An independent team desiring to start a new church
2. A team sent out by an existing church
3. A small church that desires to restart and become a cell group church
4. A mission-sending agency that is developing church planting teams

The total score from the different columns we considered above will fit into one of the following categories, which I've designated as blue, red, orange, and green. I've assigned numbers to each of these categories that represent levels of effectiveness and possibilities.

11 - 18 = Code Blue
19 - 27 = Code Red
28 - 36 = Code Orange
37 - 44 = Code Green

The lowest possible score is 11 and represents a team that falls into Column 1 in all eleven categories. The highest possible score is 44, if a team falls into column 4 in all eleven categories. Determine the category into which you fall by using your score from the above exercise. What is your potential success "number" from adding up the columns of the classification grid presented above?

In this section, we'll explore the positives and negatives for each category, and consider how these code numbers relate to developing the proper strategy sequence. This instrument is intended to help evaluate the potential success of a cell group church project. When combined with the matrix grid, the four color codes help to understand and plot the steps and sequence of a strategy.

A project may fit into more than one column. For instance, suppose a husband and wife team is beginning a new cell group church. They've started one in the past, but don't have a team around them. They might be evaluated at a high category (4) for the factor of "experience" because they've done it before, but a low category (1) for the factor of "team," because they don't yet have a team. However, the total number of all eleven factors can describe the overall potential for success.

These numbers represent a level of potential success in developing a cell group church. The sequence for becoming a cell group church changes depending upon the classification.

Code Blue Sequence (11-18)

Code blue means the project is already on life support. It may be DOA (dead on arrival) even before it begins. The ability of this team to successfully start or restart an operational cell group church is seriously in question.

A code blue classification normally means the leadership team is deficient. The team is normally too small with only one couple and probably has no pastor level leader. This type of team doesn't have enough people to model cell group life, and usually has little or no experience with the basic cell components of community, equipping, accountability, leadership, and evangelism. A code blue project generally will have no tested curriculum that's ready to be used.

A code blue team is so small that it has a narrow base for the evangelism effort necessary to contact and gather a group of potential members. Many code blue teams have no clear vision and values about what it means to be a cell group church. Often the leaders are reacting to what they don't like about the traditional church, but haven't yet decided what the church should be. Code blue teams are often Lone Ranger starts, without a church support base.

What can a team in this category do? Follow the numbers in the code blue sequence matrix and study the sequence of strategy in a code blue start.

Begin with #1 in the matrix above and follow the lines that connect the numbers within the context of the matrix. Code blue must go back to the start and spend time in preparation before it's ready to even start the project. The major challenge for a code blue classification is to gather enough people to build a leadership team. Look at #1 on the code blue sequence chart. It's placed at the lowest point possible under the preparation track. The second step, #2, is to move to the harvest track and evangelize in order to get some new believers who can be prepared to be part of the team.

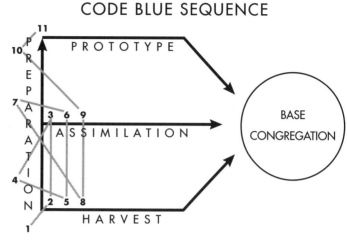

After bringing new people into the mix, they must be assimilated, so #3 is placed on the assimilation track. After the first group of members is assimilated, the project must go back to the preparation track with step #4 and begin to form the members into a leadership team.

At this point, more new believers are needed to enlarge the team, so step #5 is to go back to the harvest track and gather more potential team members. Then, what must be done with those who are harvested? They must be assimilated, so step #6 is to go to the assimilation track. At this point, the old and new members need to internalize the vision and values on the preparation track at point #7.

Most likely, the project still doesn't have enough productive team members to form an effective prototype. Therefore, more new members are needed. And what do we do when we need new members? We go back to the harvest track for step #8 and then to the assimilation track one more time for step #9. Now we're finally ready to form the team, up at step #10, in order to begin the prototype. Step #11 is to actually begin the prototype.

From the chart you can see that a significant amount of time is required to gather a core team large enough and mature enough for the code blue team to begin an effective prototype.

Code Red Sequence (19-27)

Code red means the project is operating under a big red danger signal. The team should stop and take inventory before proceeding. The project faces serious problems because of weakness at the point of almost every one of the eleven classification factors.

A code red may have one or two couples, but probably lacks a pastor-level leader.

The size of the team needs to be increased. The vision and values may be unclear because of a lack of practical experience in cell group church life. Therefore, a fuzzy understanding of the components hinders the effectiveness of community life. A pattern cell may not yet be experienced, and the small size of the team means the basic cell unit can't be effectively modeled. Code red may have a traditional church support base that wants to begin a new work. Often, the traditional base will expect the new start to look like the mother support base, even though the support base supports the use of groups.

CODE RED SEQUENCE

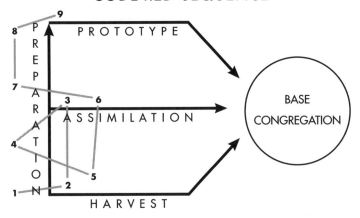

Code red suffers many of the same problems as a Code blue, even though it may be stronger on some factors. Code red must begin at an early stage of preparation. Therefore, notice the position of #1 in the Code red sequence chart. The first step is to increase the size of the team. The initial team must find a way to harvest at step #2. Then the team must assimilate (#3) the new Christians and new members who are gathered in the initial harvest.

After assimilation, the team must spend time in preparing the group to live out the vision and the values at #4. Now more members are needed, so #5 continues to gather new members through special harvest events and activities. After harvest, the team must assimilate one more time at #6. Now, the team is ready to continue to prepare the core team at #7. Probably another period of preparation will be necessary at #8 in order to complete the preparation track. The prototype can now be started at #9.

Code Orange Sequence (28-36)

Code orange means the team can be cautiously optimistic about the possibility of growth. The project has many positive characteristics that can result in a viable base congregation. A code orange classification has strong leadership at least at the pastor level of 100's. The team is large enough to begin to model the systems and has experience in doing the systems.

An orange team can do super networking with lost people and can assimilate them into the strong model. Leaders operate at every level of leadership: implementing (10's), supervising (50's), supporting (100's), and coordinating (1000's). The project is large enough to develop and maintain momentum. A mother church provides a good support base to encourage and support the growth of the work.

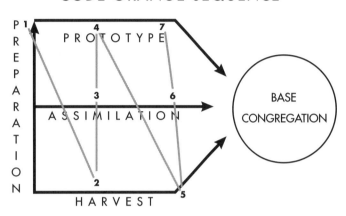

CODE ORANGE SEQUENCE

The strategy sequence used by a code orange team is significantly different from the first two. The team has a large enough core and the kind of quality necessary to immediately begin the prototype. In fact, the team is the prototype, so #1 is placed at the beginning of the prototype track. The project is ready to begin harvest immediately. Therefore, Step #2 moves directly to the harvest track.

After harvest, the team assimilates the growth at #3 and then incorporates the new growth into the prototype at #4. The project needs enough time to jell as a prototype and so can move back into harvest in order to increase the size of the support base (#5). Another period of assimilation (#6) should take the project to the point of critical mass (#7).

Code Green Sequence (37-44)

Code green means the team has enough members and enough systems and sub-systems in place to immediately model cell group church life and begin aggressive outreach. Code green is a full transplant. It has many of the same characteristics of the code orange but has a larger group and better strategy. A code green has proven pastor level leader(s) at the level of one hundred and one thousand. The mother church base has transplanted a working congregation out from itself. All systems necessary for growth are present and materials are in place. A code green project can begin outreach immediately and can model community and celebration.

Look at the code green sequence grid. This project begins on the pro-

CODE GREEN SEQUENCE

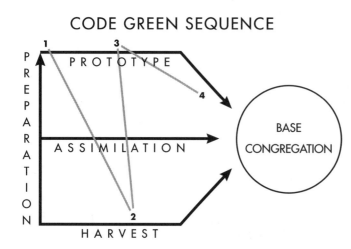

totype track (#1). The project needs to kick off its first growth cycle by harvesting (#2). Because of the strength of the project team, those harvested can be assimilated directly into the prototype (#3) and can move into critical mass (#4).

CONCLUSION

Jesus always builds the same size church: 120 base congregation. No matter how large or how small your situation, Jesus builds the church in the same way. He develops one base congregation. Then from that base congregation, he will grow your church to whatever size he desires. One person can become a team of three. A team of three can become a leadership core of twelve. A leadership core can become a support network of seventy. A support network can become a base congregation of 120. A base congregation can become thousands.

The key is the first base congregation! Apply Jesus' theology and matrix to your church project in order to develop a New Testament base congregation. The goal of a church planting cell group church is to send out strong teams of members who have learned to be Jesus' kind of church in the normal life of the church. This is church trans-planting.

LEADING PEOPLE THROUGH STAGES 4-8

Bill Beckham and M. Scott Boren

The cell group vision team has the job of guiding the church through the process of transformation into healthy and growing cell groups. Stages 1-3 focus on attaining the vision and developing a vision team. Stages 4-8 describe the practical things the vision team must do or help others do.

Moving through each of these stages is such a large task that the Cell Group Vision team will likely find overwhelming unless they are broken down into smaller tasks. The first step to breaking these stages down is to identify the key objectives for each stage. This is done in the section below. The second step then is to evaluate the progress made in accomplishing each of these goals. The second section below provides a tool for such evaluation.

The third step is to pray and, as a team, make plans based upon those prayers about the next steps in accomplishing these goals. Such planning involves setting deadlines, establishing boundaries, and assigning responsibility. The subsequent chapter provides a method for making such plans, called storyboarding.

KEY OBJECTIVES FOR EACH STAGE OF THE JOURNEY

There are twenty-two objectives that must be considered in designing a working strategy to develop effective cell groups. These objectives are not sequential, but do follow the process of the Strategy Template, as seen in the chart below.

This evaluation instrument should be used to develop the initial strategy. Then, leaders should use the evaluation periodically to determine the state of the project. The stage of development of the project must be factored into the evaluation. For instance, a church or group that's just beginning should score low in Stages 6-8, and much higher in Stages 4-5.

The comprehensiveness of the objectives keeps leaders from passing over important objectives and forces them to consider every important factor for a successful strategy.

STRATEGY TEMPLATE

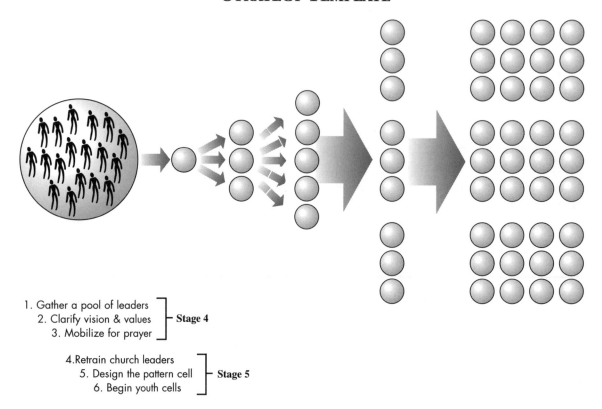

1. Gather a pool of leaders
2. Clarify vision & values   ⎤ **Stage 4**
3. Mobilize for prayer

4. Retrain church leaders
5. Design the pattern cell   ⎤ **Stage 5**
6. Begin youth cells

7. Develop accountability relationships
8. Establish an equipping track
9. Practice relationship evangelism   ⎤ **Stage 6**
10. Develop future cell leader training
11. Coach cell group leaders

12. Integrate children into cell groups
13. Set-apart overseers as cell group pastors
14. Change groups into cells
15. Cellularize calendar & budget   ⎤ **Stage 7**
16. Streamline programs
17. Establish a base congregation
18. Assimilate church visitors into cell groups

19. Promote penetration evangelism
20. Form congregational networks   ⎤ **Stage 8**
21. Develop a training center
22. Prepare for expansion

OVERVIEW OF OBJECTIVES FOR EACH STAGE

Stage 4 Objectives

1. Gather a pool of leaders
   The senior leader has identified, gathered, and shared the vision with key leaders who are now ready to do the vision.

   See pages 244-245 and Chapter 23.

2. Clarify the vision and values
   The senior pastor and leaders have prepared the whole church body for change by teaching biblical community values.

   See Chapters 15 and 24.

3. Mobilize for prayer
   Leaders and staff spend a significant amount of time during daily work in prayer that encourages the entire church to pray.

   See Chapters 26 and 44.

Stage 5 Objectives

4. Retrain church leaders
   Staff, leaders, and key influencers have been retrained to live in cell life and lead the church according to relational church values.

   See Chapter 29.

5. Design the pattern cell
   Leaders have received from God the dynamics and mechanics of a pattern cell that can be reproduced by all other cells.

   See Chapters 34 and 37.

6. Begin youth cells
   Young people participate in cell life, are equipped to lead cell groups, edify, mentor new believers, and reach their peers for Christ.

   See Chapter 42.

Stage 6 Objectives

7. Develop accountability relationships in cell groups
   Each member of the cell is assigned to a mentor/protégé relationship or to an accountability partnership.

   See Chapter 49.

8. Establish the equipping or discipleship track
   An equipping track is in place through which new members are trained in essential Christian beliefs and practices and prepared for life in the church.

   See Chapter 49.

9. Practice relationship evangelism
   Cell group members develop a friendship list, pray for these unchurched friends, and cultivate and witness to them.

   See Chapters 47, 48, and 69.

10. Develop future cell leader training
    Future leaders of cell groups are prepared through personal input, classroom training, and on-the-job mentoring.

    See Chapters 40 and 49.

See Chapters 50 and 51.

11. Coach cell group leaders
Coaches oversee and mentor current cell group leaders.

Stage 7 Objectives

See Chapters 65, 66, and 67.

12. Integrate children into cell groups
Christians minister and love God supremely through either children's cell groups or through intergenerational cell groups.

See Chapter 56.

13. Set apart overseers as cell group pastors
Oversight of the cell groups has been established with the development and hiring of cell group pastors.

See Chapters 58 and 59.

14. Change groups into cells
All old small groups have been changed into healthy cell groups that have embraced the values of Upward, Inward, Outward, and Forward.

See Chapters 62, 63. and 64.

15. Cellularize administration
Leaders operate from a yearly plan which prioritizes cell group activities in the church calendar, budget, and facilities.

See Chapter 37.

16. Streamline programs
Activities, programs, and ministries which compete with the life of the cell groups are identified, and reengineered, phased out, or replaced.

See Chapter 53.

17. Establish a base congregation
A base congregation is built with all the components in place to create critical mass.

See Chapter 61.

18. Assimilate church visitors into cell groups
Design and implement a plan to promote cell groups and envelop people into the cell groups.

Stage 8 Objectives

See Chapter 62.

19. Promote penetration evangelism
Equip people to reach those who are resistant to the Gospel through creative ministries and short-term small groups.

See Chapter 54.

20. Form congregational networks
Congregations provide leadership and training for cell group ministry and are formed around either geography or affinity.

See Chapter 70.

21. Develop a training center
The church has begun to train its own members to be pastors and missionaries through intensive in-house training.

See Chapters 71 and 72.

22. Prepare for expansion
The church has a plan for responding to exponential growth greater than what its human vision can conceive.

EVALUATING THE PROGRESS

Tool

Stage 4 Objective Evaluation

Degree of Completion

0% 25% 50% 75% 100%

1. Gather a Pool of Leaders

Senior Leader understands and carries the vision for cell groups.

Senior Leader has shared his vision with a group of key leaders.

The key leaders have embraced this vision for cell groups and are ready to enter into it.

2. Clarify Vision and Values

The people of the church have been taught about the vision and mission of the church.

The people of the church understand the difference between being busy with church activities and working as a part of God's mission.

The people understand that they're called to participate in biblical community and not just attend church meetings.

The people understand the role cell groups play in developing biblical community.

The people have been prepared to participate in cell groups through a cell preparation course.

3. Mobilize For Prayer

Leaders have modeled the importance of prayer.

Staff has set aside a portion of each day for prayer.

At every leadership meeting, lots of time is given to prayer and intercession.

An atmosphere of prayer dependence has grown in the church.

Members have learned to listen to God as an essential part of praying.

The church has learned to pray about things only God can make happen.

Members have participated in prayer and fasting.

Members have participated in church-wide prayer events.

4. Retrain Church Leaders

Church decision makers have embraced the vision.

Elders and staff understand the vision and have developed a strategy for cell group development.

Spouses have been included in the vision process.

Job descriptions for staff members have been adapted to fit the development of cell groups.

Key volunteer leaders have been freed from ministry positions so they can devote time to group development.

Stage 5 Objective Evaluation

5. Design the Pattern Cell

A predictable meeting format has been used by every cell.

Cell group lessons or agendas are written for cell group leaders to use.

Cell group lessons or agendas promote lively discussion, honest sharing, and vulnerability in the group meetings.

Cell group members have learned to edify each other at the point of the root problems.

Cell groups have experienced the process of community building, including conflict.

Degree of Completion
0% 25% 50% 75% 100%

Cell groups have experienced open and honest sharing.
Members have practiced the "one anothers" of the New Testament.
The homes of all members have been used for meetings.
The New Testament gifts have been released in groups.
The first cell groups have multiplied after a cell cycle.

6. Begin Youth Cells

A team to transition youth into cell groups has been appointed and has operated.
The youth pastor has a clear vision for cell ministry.
Teens have been selected to join a youth leadership team for mentoring.
Potential youth cell leaders have been identified and trained.
A youth targeted equipping system has been adopted and implemented.
The church has phased out old youth programs that limit the progress of cell groups.
All the youth are a part of cell groups.

Stage 6 Objective Evaluation
7. Develop Accountability Relationships

The senior pastor has set the example of New Testament accountability.
Cell group members have been partnered for the purpose of supporting one another.
Cell group leaders and interns work together in accountability relationships.
New cell members are mentored by experienced cell group members.
Cell group members have been trained to serve as mentors to new Christians.
Cell group members have accepted responsibility to mentor new members and new converts.
All cell group leaders have operated in an accountability network with other leaders.

8. Establish the Equipping or Discipleship Track

Someone has been appointed to develop an equipping system for every cell group member.
Cell member equipping materials have been selected that fit your church.
An equipping module for discipling new Christians has been adopted.
An equipping module for helping people enter spiritual victory and overcome sinful habits has been adopted.
An equipping module that will guide maturing Christians in the disciplines of a follower of Christ has been adopted.
An equipping module that prepares people to minister to others, including how to minister to the unchurched, has been adopted.
Cell leaders understand how the equipping system works, having gone through it themselves.
Cell members are working through the equipping system.

9. Practice Relationship Evangelism

Leaders have modeled relationship evangelism.
Reaching out to the unchurched is a stated priority for all cell groups.
Cell group members have been trained in relationship evangelism.
Cell groups have identified nonbelievers they're praying for.
Cell groups have planned low-key gatherings to invite unbelieving friends.
Relationship evangelism has become part of the lifestyle of the cell members.

Degree of Completion

0% 25% 50% 75% 100%

10. Develop Future Cell Leader Training

The future leader training has been tested to determine if it fits the church.

All current cell group leaders have been trained.

Cell group leaders have trained their interns through practical on-the-job training.

Training for new cell leaders is held at least twice per year.

After new leaders go through the training, they feel confident in their ability to enter into the vision of cell group leadership.

11. Coach Cell Group Leaders

Coaches (overseers of 3-12) groups have been developed.

Every cell group has a cell coach who's a proven, successful cell leader.

Cell coaches are mentoring and caring for their cell leaders on a weekly basis.

Cell coaches attend one cell meeting per week.

Cell coach training has been established and has proven effective.

Stage 7 Objective Evaluation

12. Integrate Children into Cell Groups

A pastor of the children's ministry has been commissioned.

The vision for children has been integrated as a part of the vision for the church.

Current children's staff members have experienced cell life.

All existing children's programs have been evaluated and integrated around cell life.

Cell leaders of intergenerational cell groups have been taught how to lead children.

A child link system has been established in each intergenerational cell group. Children's time during large group worship has been reshaped around cell values.

Parents have been recognized as the spiritual priests of their children.

Curriculum for children's cell groups has been adopted.

Curriculum for equipping children has been adopted and adults are trained to use it.

13. Set Apart Overseers as Cell Group Pastors

The roles of deacon and elder have become functions, not positions.

There's an appointed person who oversees and directs the cell ministry. (Even if this person is the senior pastor.)

Cell pastors are freed to focus on the cell ministry, having been released from any other administrative tasks.

Cell pastors spend most of their time relating to the people through personal visits, home visits, training, and mentoring. They don't administer the cell ministry from an office.

The cell pastors have developed a group of up to twelve cell group leaders they're mentoring in leadership and cell ministry.

A financial support base has been developed for cell pastors.

The cell pastors are effective at recruiting and training new cell leaders.

The cell pastors provide ongoing cell group leader support meetings at least monthly.

14. Change Groups into Cells

Leaders of old small groups have been trained in the vision and strategy of cell leadership.

These leaders have embraced this new vision.

A strategy has been developed for changing old small groups into cell groups.

Degree of Completion
0%   25% 50% 75% 100%

☐ ☐ ☐ ☐ ☐   All old small groups have been changed into healthy cell groups that have embraced the values of Upward, Inward, Outward, and Forward.

15. Cellularize Administration

☐ ☐ ☐ ☐ ☐   The budget has been developed out of cell values and vision.

☐ ☐ ☐ ☐ ☐   Cell group leaders have reports they complete and turn in on a weekly or monthly basis. The information from these reports is compiled into a database. Cell pastors evaluate this data and make ministry decisions based upon them.

☐ ☐ ☐ ☐ ☐   The annual calendar prioritizes the importance of the cell ministry.

☐ ☐ ☐ ☐ ☐   Cell leaders are honored through perks, paid retreats, and/or banquets.

☐ ☐ ☐ ☐ ☐   An office for cell ministry has been established to physically demonstrate the importance of cell groups.

☐ ☐ ☐ ☐ ☐   A place for mailboxes for all the cell leaders has been created.

☐ ☐ ☐ ☐ ☐   The budget reflects the importance of the cell group vision.

☐ ☐ ☐ ☐ ☐   The church provides ongoing resources, books, tapes, etc. (from the church budget) for the cell leaders.

☐ ☐ ☐ ☐ ☐   The budget covers all expenses for cell leader training.

☐ ☐ ☐ ☐ ☐   The budget subsidizes equipping resources and retreats for the cell members (complete subsidization should only cover those in financial need).

16. Streamline Programs

☐ ☐ ☐ ☐ ☐   All programs have been evaluated to determine how they fit into the new structure and vision.

☐ ☐ ☐ ☐ ☐   All good programs have been adapted to fit the new church structure or have been replaced with something better.

☐ ☐ ☐ ☐ ☐   A time line for adapting or phasing out outdated programs has been set.

☐ ☐ ☐ ☐ ☐   All programs and ministries are integrated into the cell structure.

17. Establish a Base Congregation

☐ ☐ ☐ ☐ ☐   Twelve-fifteen healthy cells have been established.

☐ ☐ ☐ ☐ ☐   All needed systems have been developed to support the cell groups.

☐ ☐ ☐ ☐ ☐   Significant momentum has been developed to propel the groups forward.

☐ ☐ ☐ ☐ ☐   Cells have begun to multiply spontaneously.

20. Assimilate Church Visitors into Cell Groups

☐ ☐ ☐ ☐ ☐   Visitors feel welcome when they attend celebration services.

☐ ☐ ☐ ☐ ☐   A "Welcome Gathering" has been instituted where visitors get to meet the pastor and key leaders and hear about the vision of the church.

☐ ☐ ☐ ☐ ☐   A clear follow-up strategy has been created and is in practice.

☐ ☐ ☐ ☐ ☐   A process has been established to connect new people with a cell group.

☐ ☐ ☐ ☐ ☐   Cell groups are promoted regularly by the senior pastor.

☐ ☐ ☐ ☐ ☐   A cell group board has been hung in the hallway with pictures of all the cell leaders and slots for information cards (with the cell leader's name and phone number and the night the cell meets) that visitors can take with them.

☐ ☐ ☐ ☐ ☐   Cell groups' stories are shared through the church bulletin or newsletter.

Stage 8 Objective Evaluation

Degree of Completion
0% 25% 50% 75% 100%

18. Promote Penetration Evangelism

Special harvest events (concerts, evangelistic speakers, plays) have been planned for the purpose of sharing the good news with the unchurched people with whom cell members have been building relationships.

Unreached segments of society have been identified and strategies have been developed for penetrating them.

Penetration ministries have been developed that are integrated into the cell group vision.

People have been trained to lead short-term interest groups to build relationships with the unchurched.

Short-term interest groups are successfully used as a penetration strategy.

International groups in the city have been targeted for penetration.

19. Form Congregational Networks

Pastoral leadership has a clear vision for developing congregational networks.

Pastors and cell group coaches have been identified and trained to oversee new networks.

New congregations are networked around affinities (i.e. geography, gender, age, etc.).

New congregations are established after ten to twelve cell groups have been developed within that affinity group.

Each congregational network has developed a mid-sized group event to meet the needs of that network (i.e. weekly youth service, monthly college student rally, monthly men's meeting, weekly Bible teaching).

21. Develop a Training Center

A mission statement for a training center has been developed.

A training center curriculum has been developed.

Students have experienced every leadership role up through cell pastor in training.

The first staff cell pastors have graduated from the training center.

The first missionary candidates have graduated from the training center.

22. Prepare for Expansion

The projected growth rate of cells has been calculated.

Plans have been made for developing leaders and pastors to oversee this growth.

Plans for planting new churches have been developed and implemented.

Mission ventures beyond the local church have been included in the vision.

The church has given sacrificially for missions.

TWO POINTS TO TRACK

To develop an effective strategy, the cell group vision team members must establish two points. They must know where the church is today, and must know where they want to go. Therefore, the difference between current church values and vision, and values and vision for the church they want to become, must be clearly defined. Chapters 19 and 20 help the vision team establish a starting point before launching cell groups, but this isn't enough.

The team must understand the concepts and values of a cell church, and be able to describe in detail what that church will look like when it's in full operation. Once a clear picture is established of the church three years from now, a strategy can be developed for becoming that picture. In addition, the team must continue to track where it is in the process to determine the crucial points it must work on.

Strategy is developed from the target picture back to the present. This is just the opposite from how we normally do strategy. The temptation is to start from where we are, and move forward to where we want to be. If we move from the present into the unknown future, we must anticipate the dangers and pitfalls ahead. And, we do a lot of wandering around because we don't have a clear destination.

Once we establish our destination point, we can chart our course back to where we are. For instance, if we know that three years from now our church should have twenty cells, then we can move backward from year three to year two and determine how many cells we must have at year two if we're to have twenty cells by year three.

Then we move back to year one and determine how many cells we must have at the end of that year, in

Cell Group Vision Team Exercise

Based upon the responses to the objectives, mark where your church lies on the following illustration.

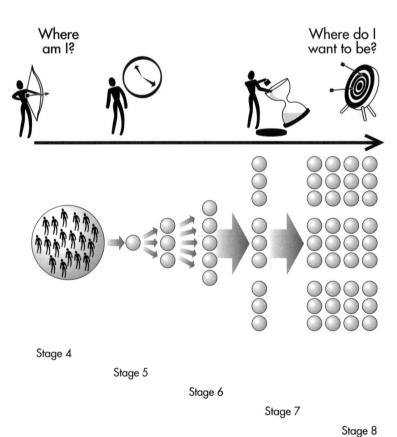

Where am I?

Where do I want to be?

Stage 4

Stage 5

Stage 6

Stage 7

Stage 8

order to have X number of cells at year two, in order to have twenty cells by year three. This process can be applied to every element in the church.

You must describe what your church will look like three years from now. And, you must be able to describe your church from several angles. Below, you'll see listed several elements of a church you should consider. The question that follows the element will help you give a complete picture of the church you're trying to become. When you consider these elements and answer these questions, you'll have a pretty good idea about your target.

Values: What core values will be lived out in your church three years from now?

Number of People: How many people will be part of the church?

Number of cells: How many cells will be functioning?

Number of clusters: How many clusters will be operating?

Number of congregations: How many congregations will you have?

Makeup: What will be the ethnic mix of the church?

Leadership: How will your leadership be organized?

Cells: How will a cell operate?

Equipping: How will new believers be equipped?

Growth: How will the church be witnessing and doing evangelism?

Training: How will you train leaders?

Sunday: What will be happening on Sunday and in your large group wing?

Government: How will the church be governed and how will you make decisions?

Finances: How will the church be financed?

Facilities: What kind of facilities will you have?

Pastor: Who'll be leading the church?

Special Programs: What special programs and ministries will the church develop and operate?

Networking: With what churches or organizations will you build network relationships?

22 CHARTING THE JOURNEY TO CELL GROUPS THROUGH STORYBOARDING

Bill Beckham

STORYBOARDING DEFINITION

Storyboarding is a simple strategy planning method first used by Walt Disney cartoonists. It was then discovered by the Stanford Business School and developed into a business tool for visualizing strategy.

Computers are now used to create incredible and lifelike animation. However, before the age of computers, cartoonists would draw action cartoons as individual pictures that became action as they were flipped or presented at high speed. These cartoonists would develop the major plot for a cartoon by sticking key pictures on a board in back of their desks. Then the cartoonists would develop the subplot pictures and stick them under the major plots. In this way they'd develop the story line for the cartoon. This method was copied and used to develop business strategy, and has proved to be one of the simplest and most effective ways to develop strategy.

"Storyboarding" is a management technique used to visualize a strategy in both its parts and its whole. It shows the critical paths along which a strategy will move. Properly done, storyboarding results in a practical strategy flow chart. Storyboarding elements include:

A vision statement
A value base
A large "board"
Major objectives
Specific action plans
Post-it® type sheets
Comprehensive factors

The following instructions will help you begin this process of storyboarding for a cell group church.

- Action Plans and Sub-Action Plans should be written to complete the sentence "We will ..."
- Action Plans and Sub-Action Plans should be stated briefly.
- Action Plans and Sub-Action Plans should be measurable and value based.
- At first, Action Plans and Sub-Action Plans should only contain a phrase. Later they can be crafted into more complete sentences.

STRATEGY TOOL: WE WILL ...

Most strategy planning sessions lack focus and turn into "rabbit chasing" hunts. Someone raises this issue. That issue makes someone else think of another related but distant idea. Then, another idea surfaces that causes the group to raise other marginally related ideas. Before long, the group has raised so many issues and opinions they're lost in a maze of unending paths and rabbit trails. And, each of these issues has danger points. Each gives opportunity for strong opinions that can divide rather than unify the group.

The end result is that a mass of ideas, some good and some bad, have been thrown on the table. An unmanageable and potentially dangerous brew is boiling in the middle of the group. It would take the wisdom of Solomon just to leave the meeting with everyone on speaking terms, much less to actually leave with some kind of workable plan.

This is why the result of most church planning is confusion and paralysis. Church leaders are often deceived by the idea of "brainstorming." Brainstorming is an essential part of strategy planning. A group must throw out ideas and creatively consider options. However, my experience has been that brainstorming without some stated objective is more "storming" than "brain." This leads to frustration in developing a strategy, and ineffectiveness in implementing the strategy that is developed.

It also can lead to stormy sessions of disagreement because, in chasing rabbits and brainstorming, the group gets emotionally further and further away from each other. A strategy-planning group needs some practical way to state the objectives that are already agreed upon by the group. At some point a planning group needs "brain-focusing," rather than "brainstorming."

A practical tool for stating objectives (brain-focusing) is to use the sentence "We will … These two words can turn "storming" into "focusing."

For months, our church had tried to pull together a plan to integrate our children into the ministry of the church. Several talented and motivated parents were involved in caring for the children and teaching them. Some older experienced members had actually set up and led children's ministries in the past. We had agreed upon our values for our children. We were using excellent materials.

An expert in children's ministry in a cell church led us in a conference that gave us a biblical context and practical suggestions. However, even with all these positive factors, our plan still wasn't working. Our workers were burning out. A great deal of confusion was evident, and dissatisfaction was boiling under the surface.

Notice the many positive factors we had going for us. We agreed upon the basic vision and values for our children, we had motivated and talented workers, we understood the basic implementing principles and needs, and we had experienced a wonderful conference about what we all wanted to do.

Surely, with all this working for us, a simple plan would quickly emerge. But, it didn't! Just when we thought everything was working, something would happen and we'd go back to our original point of confusion. We were unable to agree on a plan that satisfied everyone.

This has been my experience with church leaders in many countries and cultures about developing plans. Wonderful people, with wonderful ideas and wonderful values, are burned out, paralyzed, and confused when they try to develop plans. Once again, I saw this dynamic at work in the discussion about our children.

We called all the principal people together for a meeting. We gave everyone an opportunity to share. The discussion once again began to wander all over the page. We discussed this aspect and that aspect of our problem. It was obvious to me that we already agreed with almost everything being said. But we kept discussing and discussing and discussing. The more we discussed and brought up issues, the more tension and emotion arose in the meeting.

Finally, I listed four or five of the major issues we had talked about for the past hour. Then I asked the group to answer one question about each of the issues. What will we do about this? I insisted that we complete the sentence, "We will …"

Something amazing happened. All of a sudden the group was engaged in solving the problem, rather than just talking about it. Clear statements were developed for each need. The agreement that was always under the surface now was a stated agreement.

I've used this over and over in meetings and have found it to work. After an appropriate amount of brainstorming, lead the group to state the objectives by finishing the sentence, "We will …" Once the major objective is stated, then the specific objectives naturally emerge. And once specific objectives are stated, action plans will naturally follow: How will we do this? Who will do it? When will we do it? Where will we do it? Which will we do first?

This "brain-focusing" is desperately needed in a strategy planning session. The simple tool of asking a group to complete the sentence, "we will …" turns brainstorming into brain-focusing.

STORYBOARDING ELEMENTS

Storyboarding consists of the following planning elements: General Tracks, Major Objectives, Specific Objectives, Action Plans, and Sub-Action Plans. Strategies consist of large streams or directions.

The General Tracks are the eight stages. The Major Objectives are the twenty-two objectives identified in the previous chapter. Possible Specific Objectives include those listed under each Major Objective in the last chapter—though most churches will add or subtract from this list, depending upon their unique situations.

An Action Plan answers the questions of How? When? Where? Who? How are we going to do the Specific Objective? When will we do it? Where will it be done? Who will be responsible for doing it, and who participates in it? We ask "which" after all other questions have been considered, because "which" is about sequence. Which of the objectives is first in the planning calendar and what is the sequence of events?

Sub-Action Plans deal with the specific details necessary to complete the Action Plan.

STORYBOARDING STEPS

Preliminary Preparation: Develop the target picture of your church as explained at the end of Chapter 11. Then identify which of the eight stages your church is in at this point using the assessment in Chapter 21.

Tool

1. Write the first Major Objective on a large Post-it® Note and stick it to a wall. For instance, you might write, "Gather a Pool of Leaders."

2. Brainstorm the specific objectives related to each major objective. What specifically do you want to do in each of these areas? Write these on Post-it® Notes that are slightly smaller or a different color than the one used for the Major Objective. Place these in any order beneath the Major Objective.

3. Brainstorm the questions related to your Action Plans: How? When? Where? Who? Write down the Action Plans in simple phrases on a Post-it® Note that's either slightly small or a different color than those used previously. Don't worry about the grammar at this time.

4. Stick these Action Plans to the right of the Specific Objectives. Don't worry at this time about the sequence. You should have Specific Objectives, one under the other, placed beneath the Major Objective. And you should have Specific Action Plans in a row beside the Objectives. This will stretch across the wall.

5. Think about Specific Sub-Action Plans necessary for implementing the Action Plans.

6. Group the Action Plans and Sub-Action Plans under the proper Specific Objective or Action Plan.

7. Next determine your timeline. This is the "which." Which of the Specific Objectives and Action Plans come first? Don't work on your timeline as you're developing your Objectives and Action Plans. This will slow you down and distract from your brainstorming.

8. Finally, the specific tasks must be assigned to individuals to carry out. Therefore, each person would walk away with a list that describes who will do what by when.

At the end of this process, you should have a measurable strategy on the wall that you can visualize. The strategy is flexible and allows you to move the Objectives, Action Plans, and Sub-Action Plans around. And, you can easily and quickly add to it or change it. You should leave this up on the wall for a period of time, and use it to continue to develop strategy.

The following sections

demonstrate what the end result of a storyboarding process might look like for two of the twenty-two major objectives listed on page 228: Objective #1 and Objective #5.

OBJECTIVE #1: GATHER A POOL OF LEADERS CALLED A GIDEON GROUP

When God gets ready to do something big, he chooses a remnant. God never does big things through the majority. Nothing illustrates this better than the story of Gideon. God chose Gideon to lead his army against the Midianites, Amalekites, and "the sons of the east." The call to arms went out to Israel and something like 32,000 volunteers gathered to fight against the army of 135,000 (Judges 7 and 8).

The two armies were close enough to engage in the Valley of Jezreel when God began to choose his remnant. God began his preparation by reducing the number of his army. If Israel won the war, the people would say they won because of their abilities and numbers. God told Gideon the army was too large. "You've got to be kidding, Lord!" But Gideon sent God's word out to his volunteer army.

"Any of you who are scared, don't want to fight, and want to go home, can leave." Gideon almost got trampled, as 22,000 soldiers left for home "posthaste." But God had still not found his remnant. Those 10,000 left were still too many and would claim they were responsible for victory. The remnant test was applied once again.

God said, "Watch the soldiers as they go down to drink at the spring of Harod. Those that lay their spears down at their sides and get down on all fours with their tails in the air, vulnerable, send home. Those that go down to the water, alert because they know they are in the battle zone, and who reach down with their cupped hands and drink with their spears at their side, keep."

How many were keepers? Three hundred against 135,000. This was God's remnant. I've come to understand the power of the remnant. God was looking for a group that would depend upon him, his might, and his plan, without any question.

God had to have a committed and obedient remnant, because this was going to be his kind of battle. That night God, through Gideon, told the soldiers about the battle plan and the weapons they were to use. What were the weapons? A pitcher, a candle and a trumpet.

What would have happened if all the 31,700 soldiers who had gone home had been given those instructions? When Gideon told them they were going to fight a night action, there would have been murmuring. When he told them the weapons God had chosen for the battle, they'd have certainly rebelled and broken ranks, or gone to fight the enemy with conventional weapons and been defeated.

What did the 300 do? They didn't complain or rebel. They picked up those weapons and went to the battle. Why? They were such a small number by this time, it didn't matter what kind of weapons they used. They couldn't defeat 135,000 soldiers with bazookas. The characteristic of a remnant is that it's so small it must fight with God's plan and God's weapons, at God's time, with God's power. God's remnant is committed and obedient to doing things God's way.

God is calling out such a remnant today. You may be part of it. If you are, you'll be required to exercise great faith and courage. Many won't respond to the call, or measure up to the challenge. You'll be part of the remnant, not because of your spirituality or ability, but because of your commitment to the battle and your willingness to fight the battle with God's weapons, God's plan, at God's time, and with God's numbers.

Major objective for developing a Gideon Group: We will form and prepare a Gideon Group of seventy leaders to develop a working model of a cell church congregation that can be reproduced within the church as the implementing and coordinating ministry unit of the church.

SPECIFIC OBJECTIVE: We will meet regularly with the Gideon Group for vision casting, planning, and ministry.

ACTION PLAN: We will have a monthly meeting with the Gideon Group.

ACTION PLAN: We will use the monthly meeting to introduce and test out activities and materials that are essential for developing our Prototype.

Sub-Action Plan: At the first regular Gideon Meeting, we will introduce the four parts of the personal equipping track, give out the materials, and assign partners to help encourage the pastors, Gideon Group, and staff to complete the materials.

SPECIFIC OBJECTIVE: We will take all those in the Gideon Group through a special cell group preparation course.

ACTION PLAN: We will have this course in the early part of next year
  Sub-Action Plan: We will select leaders from the Gideon Group to attend this first course.
  Sub-Action Plan: We will select a place for this course.
  Sub-Action Plan: We will prepare the materials to be used in this course.
SPECIFIC OBJECTIVE: We will provide a way that all Gideon Group members can complete *Experiencing God* by Henry Blackaby.
SPECIFIC OBJECTIVE: We will choose a group from the Gideon Group to learn to reach seekers through Alpha.
SPECIFIC OBJECTIVE: We will use the Gideon Group to test out necessary encounters, such as formation, witness, victory, and cell leader training.
SPECIFIC OBJECTIVE: We will ask all Gideon Group members to complete the four-part personal equipping track: assurance of salvation, Journey debriefing, survival study, and living out Christian values.
  ACTION PLAN: We will form the Gideon Group into partner relationships (men with men and women with women) to encourage and support each other to complete the personal equipping track.
SPECIFIC OBJECTIVE: We will train members of the Gideon Group to lead a cell.
  ACTION PLAN: We will use the *Cell Group Leader Training* to plan a training retreat.
    Sub-Action Plan: The senior pastor will teach the first training and will train Support Leaders to facilitate the retreat in the future.
    Sub-Action Plan: The senior pastor will train Support Leaders to plan and teach the retreat in the future.
  ACTION PLAN: We will teach the material in *Cell Group Leader Training* to the Gideon Group.
  ACTION PLAN: We will train the initial cell leaders in practical on-the-job skills in the three preparation cell cycles: the alpha cell, beta cell, and gamma cell.

OBJECTIVE #5: DEVELOPING A PATTERN CELL

The objective is for the core leaders to receive from God a pattern community cell that can be reproduced in nature and design into every small group and cell God will form in this church.

I normally suggest beginning with one alpha cell group that goes through a cycle of twelve to sixteen weeks. However, the principle is to develop a quality pattern cell. How we do that can be flexible. Some leaders form two alpha cells: one for men and one for women. Or, a combination of a family cell and men or women cells can be formed. An early alpha cell can also be for youth. The principle of developing a quality pattern cell can be applied, no matter the makeup of the cells.

One way to quickly develop cells for men, women, and youth is to form an initial alpha cell of men, women, and youth leaders: four of each group. Then, after the alpha cell experiences community, dies to agendas, and decides on a cell agenda, form three beta cells: one for men, one for women, and one for youth.

This approach follows the strategy of developing an alpha prototype cell of leaders, before forming other cells. So, think of alpha and beta stages of the pattern cell. The makeup of the beta cells will be determined by the makeup of the alpha prototype cell.

Major Objective for establishing a pattern cell group: We will establish a pattern cell group that will model the vision and the values that will be replicated in future cell groups.

SPECIFIC OBJECTIVE: We will test out and receive confirmation from God about the dynamics and mechanics of basic Christian community in a first cycle cell experience (alpha cell).

ACTION PLAN: We will form men's and women's alpha groups of eight or nine selected leaders around senior leaders, and meet weekly for twelve weeks.

Sub-Action Plan: We will prayerfully choose the members of these groups and include representatives of the children's ministry and youth ministry.

Sub-Action Plan: We will use the sample agendas suggested in Chapter 36 for the meeting agendas.

Sub-Action Plan: We will follow the Four Ws meeting structure.

Sub-Action Plan: We will meet in homes.

SPECIFIC OBJECTIVE: We will test out and receive confirmation from God about the dynamics and mechanics of basic Christian community in a second cycle cell experience (beta cell) of twelve weeks.

ACTION PLAN: We will form six new cells from the original men's pattern cell and from the original women's pattern cell, that will meet for twelve weeks following the same procedures.

Sub-Action Plan: We will choose three new leaders from the alpha pattern cell to lead the new cells.

Sub-Action Plan: We will prayerfully choose other potential leaders from the Gideon Group to be part of the six cells (no more than nine per cell).

Sub-Action Plan: We will use the same twelve meeting agendas that were used in the first cycle.

ACTION PLAN: We will continue the meeting agenda and DNA used in the alpha cell.

ACTION PLAN: Leaders will model the role of a coach over the three cells under them.

Sub-Action Plan: The supervisors will visit the different cells frequently to observe. However, keep quiet and let the new leaders lead. Make corrections outside of the meeting.

SPECIFIC OBJECTIVE: We will form five test cells (gamma cells) to implement, for a period of six months, the pattern discovered in the alpha and beta cells and the five elements of the hand. (See Chapter 13)

ACTION PLAN: We will choose a leader and an intern from those who've been in the alpha and beta cells.

ACTION PLAN: We will form the ten cells out of selected members from the alpha and beta pattern cells, along with people from the Gideon Group. At the beginning, these cells will consist of no more than eight persons per cell. This gives a strong nucleus, but forces the cell to evangelize and bring in four to six new people over a six-month life cycle. (These cells should not be allowed to recruit people from the church. They should learn to reach the lost and prodigals. Cells should be formed with existing church members, by first sending them through a cell preparation class, and then forming them up into existing cells or new cells.)

ACTION PLAN: We will reorganize the gamma cells after a six-month cycle.

SPECIFIC OBJECTIVE: We will form a separate youth alpha cell during the adult beta cycle.

ACTION PLAN: The youth minister will choose eight potential leaders among the youth, and lead them in experiencing what the adults are experiencing for twelve weeks. (You can follow the adult pattern and have a boys' cell and a girls' cell, if you have a woman to help set the pattern with the girls.)

Sub-Action Plan: We will use the same twelve sample meeting agendas.

Sub-Action Plan: The youth minister will choose and train adults with a call to minister with youth to be youth cell coaches (maximum of three youth cells)

SPECIFIC OBJECTIVE: During the beta cycle, we will form a cell to test how children from the ages of birth through twelve will participate in inter-generational cells.

Stage 4:
Prepare the Church through Transformation

PREPARING YOUR PEOPLE FOR CELL GROUP SUCCESS

23

M. Scott Boren

The vision of multiplying cell groups has stirred many pastors so much over the last twenty-five years that some have made errors of impatience. They assume if they clearly present the vision of cell groups and people agree with the vision, that they'll be ready immediately to enter that vision. But there's a vast difference between catching a vision and preparing oneself for making the vision happen.

In *Making Cell Groups Work* (pages 199-211), it states that the people must be prepared to enter into cell groups. To throw people into groups without any preparation is a recipe for disunity or disaster.

THREE LEVELS OF PREPARATION

It's impossible to prepare everyone at the same time in the same way. There are three groups of people who should be prepared for the move to cell groups. The first group is comprised of key leaders who'll most likely serve as the first cell group leaders. Future cell group members form the second group that must be prepared. The third group is the crowd of people who'll eventually be part of cell groups.

The diagram on the next page demonstrates how these three levels of preparation occur at the same time. The goal is to prepare people for cell group participation and for cell group leadership in such a way that their vision and values line up with the vision and values that make cell groups effective.

Preparing the first leaders occurs first, as it focuses on preparing key leaders to become cell group leaders. The other two levels occur simultaneously. Cell group member preparation prepares churched people to be healthy contributors to cell groups. Crowd preparation develops the atmosphere of the church to fit with the values of relational ministry, and to feed people from the crowd into cell group member preparation.

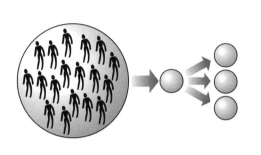

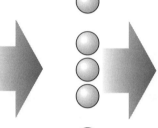

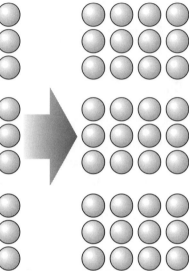

First Cell Group Leader Preparation

- Cell Group Vision
- Cell Leader Training
- Prototype Experience

Cell Group Member Preparation

- Cell Group Vision
- Cell Group Values

Crowd Preparation

- Values Transformation
  Prayer
  Relationships
  Commitment to Church

TIME

THE FIRST CELL GROUP LEADERS

Preparing the first leaders for success is one of the most important things a church can do to get groups started on the right foot. These first cell group leaders will most likely come from the current staff, volunteer leaders, and key influencers of the church. If key leaders aren't willing to embrace relational ministry, then the cell group vision won't get off the ground.

The first leaders need preparation in the vision for cell group ministry. This preparation includes a basic understanding of the vision and a call to commitment to relational ministry. One proven method for preparing these first leaders follows this pattern:

1. Gather a pool of leaders, including those who are potential group leaders of the first group and those who are potential members of the first prototype group or groups. Bill Beckham calls this a Gideon group.
2. Share the vision and strategy of cell groups with these leaders, using a tool like *Life in His Body*, by David Finnell, or teach through some of the chapters in this *Navigation Guide*.
3. Invite the Gideon group to a recruitment retreat (See Chapter 25).
4. Train the first cell group leaders (See Chapter 40).
5. Start the first group or groups, called a prototype group, with people from this Gideon group (See Chapter 36).

CELL GROUP MEMBERS

Cell group member preparation is especially important for people who have a lot of church experience. As the above diagram illustrates, the cell member preparation class feeds people into cells after the first leaders have been developed through the original prototype process.

In a Nashville church plant, the senior pastor and leaders felt they'd be able to reach a lot of Christians who were looking for a different kind of church. The problem they had to address was that people from this Bible-belt city had so much church experience that they wouldn't embrace the vision and values of cell group life. These people needed a preparation process to help them let go of their predetermined ideas about church and to embrace the relational vision of cell groups. This pastor called such a preparation process 'detox' for short.

Why does the average church member need a detox preparation process? First, many of them have no experience in relational ministry. They only know ministry that comes in the forms of programs, business meetings, and letting the preacher do the real ministry. These people require an introduction into relational ministry that occurs in cell groups.

The second reason is often more detrimental than the first. Many church members have had bad experiences in previous church small groups. They were burned by gossip. They were forced into a group by a strong pastor. They failed as a small group leader. These people need a place to talk about their previous experiences so they can deal with their fears in an honest and healthy way.

The third reason is that many people have good experiences in small groups at other churches. These people will import these experiences into the new cell groups every time. These previous experiences aren't wrong or bad, they're just different than the new cell group vision, which is unique to the time and place of each specific church. These people must learn what God is calling this church to do at this time, so everyone can flow in the same vision.

Detox preparation is designed for churched people before they actually join a cell group. Such preparation usually consists of a basic introduction to the vision for groups, along with exercises to help people embrace the relational values of cell groups.

People learn how the groups fit into the vision of the church. They discover how relationships are central to God's Kingdom. They practice praying for one another in small groups. They begin to pray for lost friends and relatives. They experience how the cell meetings are organized. They learn how to create a safe place where sin is confessed and forgiveness received.

Cell group member preparation usually comes in the form of an eight-week classroom experience. The number of people who can go through this experience will be limited to the number of people who'll fit into groups. The goal is to put every person who completes this course into a cell group as soon as the course is over. Therefore the course should be repeated two or three times per year until the church has been enfolded into cell groups.

New Christians don't require such preparation. They should be put into a cell group immediately because they don't have embedded ideas about what should or shouldn't happen in a group. In fact, many new Christians who are reached through cell groups are shocked when they learn that some churches don't have cells.

THE CROWD

Because every church member can't go through the cell group member preparation at the same time, there'll be many who require preparation on a different level, that of the crowd. Crowd preparation doesn't focus on the vision of cell groups. In fact, the crowd need not learn about cell groups until the cell groups are running and they have an opportunity to go through the cell member preparation class.

This doesn't mean cell groups are a big secret that should never be mentioned. It only means that it's very frustrating for people to learn about something they have to wait for a year to join. As people from the crowd embrace transformation through crowd preparation, they'll be fed into the cell member preparation course. This must be coordinated to ensure that those who graduate from the cell member preparation will be able to enter into a cell group. This means there must be room in those groups to enfold these graduates.

Crowd preparation focuses on transforming people's values. It calls them to live out the Great Commandment to love God and one another and the Great Commission to make disciples. It invites people to participate in the Kingdom of God and commit to God's body on earth, the church. Through this preparation, the crowd discovers the call to pray, the call to build relationships with other believers, the call to every member ministry, and the call to live a sacrificial life.

Methods for preparing the crowd include preaching the values of Upward, Inward, Outward and Forward, calling people together for special times of prayer, short-term courses that include small group activities, and dealing with unhealthy patterns of sin in the corporate body.

Such preparation doesn't guarantee success, because imperfect people are involved. However, when a church intentionally prepares people on these three levels, these imperfect people will be led to deal with their weaknesses and make changes in their lives that will contribute to more effective cell group ministry.

Written Resources

On pages 203-204 in *Making Cell Groups Work* there is a complete list of options for preparing the crowd that have proven effective.

CHANGING VALUES: MOVING BEYOND A NEW PARADIGM

Ralph W. Neighbour, Jr. and Randall G. Neighbour

Pastor Bob had done his homework. Over the course of the last year, he'd read a pile of books on cell church theology and methodology. He visited two different models, one in the Deep South and the other in an urban setting up North, taking key staff members and elders from his church along to catch the vision.

What impacted him most were his visits to the cell group meetings in these churches. The relationships were genuine and deep. The members cared to the point of sacrifice. The cell leaders were average people doing a great job of shepherding people and increasing the kingdom with relational evangelism. "This is what we must do at our church!" he thought.

Armed with knowledge and some exposure to cells, he set out to educate his staff, leadership, and congregation. He held Saturday seminars, preached his heart out, and taught Sunday evening classes on the importance of cell groups, community, and relational evangelism. But the folks who heard the message had a hard time letting go of the old to embrace the new.

Some members wanted to know more, but weren't willing to risk trying it. Others didn't want to show up to Bob's called meetings, but did it out of obligation, which put him at a disadvantage. And a few key leaders got mad—really mad. They were angry that Pastor Bob would try to change what they'd worked so hard to build over the years.

Numerous church leaders have implemented a new direction for their church, only to find it a hollow success at best. It's as if some of the leadership understand the vision, but don't implement it. Others begin to implement it, but don't stay the course and make the transition to living out the new vision. In order to help your church undergo significant change in a successful way, an in-depth understanding of values and how values are changed is required. Employing these principles will help you transform the very values by which your church members live, thus solidifying the new direction of your church.

EXISTING VALUES

It's important to understand a few key elements concerning a person's current value system:

- Values constantly change, albeit slowly. Facts, like the law of gravity, never change, but our values are under our control. We can modify, discard, and replace them at will. We don't change our values as easily as one changes his clothing, but it does happen when an overwhelmingly better value is presented or the existing value isn't valuable any longer.
- Values are often deeply rooted in emotion from the love or guilt relationships of our past. Example: "My parents sacrificed a great deal to make the educational facilities on campus a reality for us. Do you expect us to simply abandon the building to meet in homes for a small group experience?"

As you dive into the pool of value clarification and modification, remember one more very important thing: values are deep within people and can't be easily expressed or addressed. There are levels of learning and discovery, and if you only work on the top level, you won't see change. One has to be touched at the deepest level to see the kind of change that's required to shift a value from one way of life to another.

Pastor Bob received negative feedback from his leaders because he didn't understand that his church's structure was rooted in a closely held value system within his leaders. He shared information, but he never modeled the new behavior or helped a small group of leaders embrace the new and discard the old.

THE THREE DOMAINS OF LEARNING

Learning takes place within three areas: the psychomotor, cognitive, and affective domains of learning. While these are separate areas, they often overlap. Learning (change) in one area may result in learning within another area.

The psychomotor domain focuses on physical skills, such as running, walking, and catching a ball. Learning in the psychomotor domain progresses from repeated practice of a physical skill to mastery at the level of "doing without thinking."

The cognitive domain focuses on factual knowledge. Lower levels of cognitive learning include the ability to know and comprehend basic facts. Higher levels use these facts in application, analysis, synthesis, and evaluation within new situations.

The affective domain relates to emotions, attitudes, and values. Learning in the affective domain results in lifestyle changes. Because desired values are more often "caught" than "taught," modeling and mentoring are key elements in affective domain learning. Small group interaction is one of the most effective methods used in affective domain teaching.

Ask a group of children to pray. Without thinking, most bow their heads and close their eyes. They've learned, in the psychomotor domain, that prayer involves physical postures (though it is possible to pray in a variety of positions). Most begin their prayer with the words, "Dear Heavenly Father," because they've learned, in the cognitive domain, to address others by certain titles and names. Whether a child prays voluntarily without prompting shows us whether he truly values prayer as a way of communing with God. This value is part of a person's affective domain learning. Children tend to value what their parents or role models spend time doing.

Too often, churches don't see attitude and lifestyle changes within members, because they focus too much on cognitive learning by dispensing knowledge. Wise church leaders intentionally invest time, attention, and resources on affective domain learning experiences, because they want to see transformational change within individuals and their churches. Church members tend to value what they see their pastor and staff role models spend their time doing.

VALUES DON'T CHANGE BY PREACHING OR TEACHING ALONE

Many pastors attempt to teach a new value from the pulpit or in a classroom setting. Facts and biblical mandates were offered, and while these may have been received, no long-term change in the hearer's life was noticed. There's a big difference between hearing and doing.

The only way old values are changed is by repeat exposure to new experiences. The more recent the experience, the greater the impact it will have on a person. Experts say it takes several "layered" experiences to impact the affective domain. So, changing the day-to-day values of your church will take numerous experiences and successes with the "new way" of doing ministry.

Study carefully the ministry of Jesus. His teachings are quite limited in the four Gospels. Most of what we know about him are the experiences he had with his disciples. Note that Peter, James, and John were an "inner circle" who had special experiences with him that are carefully recorded.

The experiences you'll take your first cell members through should include:

- Doing an activity together of long or short duration, such as a prayer retreat or a hospital visit.
- Getting feedback: "What did this mean to you?"
- Evaluating the feedback. What additional experience is needed to strengthen this value?

Remember, several layers of experiences may be necessary before there's any short-term impact on a value system. Each layer will take the person toward another stage in the values change process, though change is not guaranteed.

THE FIVE STAGES OF CHANGING VALUES

For a new spiritual value to be internalized, you must take each individual and the church as a whole through the following important stages. In order for you to be successful, you must memorize these stages and the characteristics of each stage. Then, you'll be able to discern what stage people have reached and lead them into the next stage.

Stage 1: Unaware (Uncommitted)

At this first stage, the person has no awareness there's any difference between a traditional church and a cell-based church. The paradigm shift hasn't yet begun. It's important that there be no scolding or exhortations to "get involved" with the new ministry direction. This will only create a negative impression. The person's problem is not resistance, but ignorance.

When the time is right, you can do the following to bring your congregation from this stage to the next:

- Preach a series of sermons that will create awareness of the mission of your church, helping the membership see that it's not currently being fulfilled and that there is a better way.
- Worship services can include "small group" times to discuss and internalize the challenge set forth from the pulpit. While this may seem

Personal Exercise

Take time to list the experiences Jesus provided for his "cell group members." As you write out the various experiences he offered, consider how you can duplicate them in your own setting and culture.

highly unusual for a worship service, it's been found to be very successful because of this very thing.

- Existing small groups (Bible study groups, prayer groups, etc.) can be given carefully written material to use, to expose them to the contrast between what they're doing and holistic small group life (basic Christian community).
- Church bulletins, newsletters, etc., can be used to create an awareness of what a cell ministry is all about and how it would look in your church when implemented.

Stage 2: Aware (Still Uncommitted)

At this second stage, the person knows there's a difference between the two church patterns, but isn't interested in participating in a cell group:

- There's no motivation to do anything with the information received. The person sees this change as too much work. A passive attitude toward change is always the first response. "Why should I be moved out of my comfort zone?"
- What rewards await this individual if he/she agrees to adopt this new lifestyle? If the person doesn't value serving the Lord, seeing the lost come to Christ, and ministering to fellow Christians, there'll be no motivation to change.

Therefore, there must be strong preaching, presenting Kingdom values. Like the rich young ruler, some will go away sorrowful. Others will just stare back at you. With many, you can't do anything more at this stage. Not until some people are surrounded by totally committed Christians will they be impacted by this new way of life. While these may seem to be the darkest days in ministry, remember that a "remnant" in Israel was found when the nation was at its lowest ebb. There's always a remnant in every church. You must stir up those whose hearts are most tender and begin with them. It may take three or more years for others to move out of this stage.

Stage 3: Willing to Receive (Controlled Attention)

At this next stage, experiences are critical to the development of the person. Here are the two activities to carry groups through as they arrive at this point. The first activity is a prototype experience, where the first leaders learn how to lead a group by participating in a group together (See

Chapter 36 for more on this activity).

The second activity is a cell group preparation class, which provides experiences that will help people make the transition into cell group life (See Chapter 23 for more on this activity).

Stage 4: Committed (Conceptualization Completed)

At this stage, the person has become fully aware of the new lifestyle and is prepared. With guidance, a Stage 4 person can help others move through the previous stages.

Stage 5: Characterization (Integrated Lifestyle)

At this last stage, the person is oriented to a new lifestyle of living in community and building the kingdom through relational ministry. It's at this point that the person is fully capable of sharing the vision with others in the church. This person's influence begins to penetrate the lives of those who are still at Stage 1.

Pastors who've taken their churches through this process have indicated that it took a number of years to move the majority of members into Stage 5. Some have done it in as little as two years, but most have taken three to five years or more. Results vary by the degree of change required among the members, combined with the ability of the leadership to move people from one stage to another without abandoning the process when results are not instantaneous.

In summary, don't expect it to happen within a year at your church! You must be patient with people, and begin by working through these stages yourself. Simply moving to Stage 5 in some aspects of cell life and ministry may take a number of years for you personally!

YOUR PILGRIMAGE THROUGH THESE STAGES

Good news! You're most likely at least at Stage 3. You're willing to receive, and your attention is focused. This is a period in your life when you must lead others where you've never been. You'll have to journey with a special group of people, or what's called a core leadership group. Your life will be fully impacted by what happens in this "basic Christian community."

There'll be times when you'll feel like Moses in the wilderness, when the Israelites didn't understand the need for the transition, and longed for the

Personal Exercise

At what stage are you at this point in your journey toward cell groups? Make sure that you evaluate your point in the journey based upon your actual change in lifestyle and participation in cell groups, not on the fact that your are convinced that cell groups are the way to go for your church.

leeks and garlics of Egypt. You may desire the ease of the old as well! Your background will constantly be your enemy. Every time a new problem arises, you'll think of old traditional patterns you know well, and you'll try to solve the problem by implementing what you did in the past. Don't do it!

Should you find yourself tempted to revert back to what's comfortable, remember that new wine will require a new wineskin (Matt. 9:16-17).

Form a Core Leadership Group to Prototype a Cell Group

The purpose of this prototype is to prepare the first wave of leaders for the new church and demonstrate what you want the church to do. Create a prototype using your current leaders. Don't call it a "cell group." Instead, call it a "prototype cell." This will help all who are involved or looking on to understand that it's the first of its kind and will not be perfect.

Spouses of your key leaders should be included, with mutual ministry between families in mind. Limit this prototype's group size to twelve persons or six couples, and meet weekly for approximately six months.

Your prototype cell is the first structure fully inside the new paradigm called a "cell church." It operates as though the rest of the church structure did not exist. Refer to Chapter 36 on Prototype Cell Development for further clarification.

Phase Out Structured Programs over the Course of Future Multiplications

As your prototype cell multiplies, the leadership you've pulled into it will begin new cell groups with people from the traditional programs within your church. The natural relationships already established among them will generate confidence among the new people that this is a good next step.

QUESTIONS THAT WILL HELP YOU BEGIN THE CHANGE PROCESS

There are some things that don't need to be changed. These questions will help you see what must be done and what's valuable or a non-negotiable.

1. What do you value about your church as it now exists? Have you already transitioned into praise times from the old pattern of singing funeral-like songs from hymnals? Or, do you have an annual church

retreat that's a great blessing to all? Why change this?

2. What about the leadership? What do they value about this church that keeps them here? Among other things will be special friends. These clusters must not be disrupted, at least at the start.

3. What about the members? What's the value of the church to them? Is it the youth program for their teenagers? If it's going to change, the youth will have to be more excited about it than their parents!

There are also areas that must be changed, and these questions will guide you to the right decisions:

1. List the reasons why the church cannot continue as it is. Then, list the reasons why people will insist it remain as it is.

2. Why does the leadership want change? Ask them. See how close they are to what you're thinking. You must lead them; they cannot be driven!

3. What are your leaders' vested interests in the present structure? Who's gaining personal significance from a church office? How will this person lose his/her feeling of worth if the structure changes? (If a small child has scissors, you offer something more attractive and he'll relinquish the sharp blades. For many people in your church, you must develop a prototype they can see before they'll be secure enough to move to it. These leaders will not trade their significant role for undeveloped ones. They must be included in the early stages of the planning. They must feel like they're being "promoted," not laid aside.)

WHAT WILL HAPPEN TO YOUR MEMBERSHIP AS YOU CHANGE?

List all the people who attend only because they want to get their needs met and who have no interest in giving. You will lose them unless you can blend them into the cell groups. What can you do for them? Do you necessarily have to lose them? How can you crack through their self-centeredness? Does there need to be a time of cell group members befriending them to draw them from the periphery?

Who in your membership will be set free to fly into ministry, no longer being crushed by the program-based system that has no room for their ministry? Can you identify them? Pull them in quickly!

Face the reality that you may have some doctrinal views that will have to change. Your doctrine of what a true New Testament church is must change, but what about your church government? What about your view of the Holy Spirit and the availability of spiritual gifts for use by all believers?

As you can clearly see, the process of changing values within yourself is difficult and time consuming. Imagine taking on every member of your church! As you work with others in your prototype group, you'll see your values begin to change as a group. These prototype group members will join you in working with other key leaders in your church, moving them through each stage.

A shift in values takes multiple experiences with good outcomes to be successful. The journey is bound to be exhausting at times, but it's worth it. You're shaping a new set of Christian values within members who never knew living in basic Christian community could be so fulfilling and purposeful! Jesus preached personal transformation. Helping your members change from "pew-warmer" to equipped minister is the pinnacle of transformation!

RECRUITMENT RETREAT

Ralph W. Neighbour, Jr. and Randall G. Neighbour

A recruitment retreat is designed to introduce the first group of church leaders to cell ministry. This experience—if planned and executed properly—will help them see a new paradigm for the following:

- The power of basic Christian community to fulfill the church's mission
- The three basic levels of spiritual maturity
- The difference between a cell group meeting and a Bible study, fellowship group, etc.

• The path each cell group member will take to become spiritually mature.

This retreat will help the core "power people" within your church understand the way the vision team is directing the church body, and extend an invitation to be a part of the first experimental group, or prototype cell. This weekend retreat cannot instantly develop the transformational ministry that cell group life provides. But, it does "open the door" for a much deeper understanding of the church's new direction and the level of intimacy and participation required to make it work.

BE PATIENT!

A pastor will be taking his leadership through a paradigm shift. It's important to be patient with everyone. It may help to think of those who attend as blind people who are eventually going to receive their sight. He needs to see himself as God's healer, to remove the scales from their eyes.

One response to new things is anger. Behind all anger there's great fear. Seek to remain objective while working with the group. Expect this retreat to draw out true feelings. When they emerge, leaders mustn't become defensive. Remember that paradigm impressions can change!

PREPARATIONS

The outline below explains step by step what to do to have an effective Recruitment Retreat that's based on experiences, rather than on lectures. Study these instructions until they're internalized. Make any changes to adjust to the retreat setting, but don't tamper with the structure suggested until after it has been used once or twice.

1. Bring these things:
   A. All notes, books, or information to be shared in printed form
   B. An inexpensive, but appropriate, small notebook, pocket or Bible-sized, to be used as a prayer journal by each participant
   C. A goblet and a small loaf of bread for the Agape Feast
   D. Sports equipment for games
   E. One large adhesive nametag per person, labeled as follows, (varying the number based on group size):
      1. Cell leader (1 tag)
      2. Cell leader intern (1 tag)

3. Father (3 tags)
4. Young man (2 tags)
5. Little child (2 or 3 tags)
6. Broken wing (2 tags)
7. Senior pastor (1 tag)
8. Cell coach (1 tag)
9. Cell coach intern (1 tag)

F. Printed "Guidelines for the Cell Leader" (See web resource)

G. Material to lead Worship Time in the Simulation Cell Group.

2. Book a Retreat Setting

A. Book a retreat site for three days that's private, comfortable, and within an hour's drive from the church's campus.

B. Consider arranging for someone else to preach and do the three-day retreat over a Saturday, Sunday, and Monday. (Yes, this is that important!)

C. If possible, let the church pay for this retreat. If this isn't possible, be sure no one stays at home because the cost is too great.

D. Begin the retreat with lunch on the first day, close at 3 p.m. on the final day.

3. Select Potential Leaders to Attend

A. The Vision Team should pray over a list of "power people" in the church. Evaluate each person and his/her spouse. Which ones have potential to lead in the new cell ministry? If some of these are carryovers from the past and are unable to provide true leadership, is this a time to help them find a new position more suited to their capacities? Have the heart of Christ as he prayed all night about which men would become part of The Twelve.

B. The team should select no more than fourteen people to go on the retreat. If a larger church has more than fourteen people to work with, it will need to do a series of two, four, or more retreats. It's important that each retreat provides small group intimacy.

C. Personally invite each person to participate, face to face. (No phone calls!) Explain that the purpose of this retreat is to evaluate potential leadership for the first cell group, which will be a developmental prototype group. If some decline, don't attempt to coerce them. They may be the kind of people who need to see the concept in action before they can make a commitment to participate.

D. For those who've accepted the invitation and have children, ensure that they have friends or family who'll adequately care for the children while they're at the retreat. (This is very important ... off-site child care will make all the difference at this event because the parents will be able to focus on the experiences without interruption or concern about their children.)

4. Assign Advanced Reading for Participants

A. A product written and signed by the Vision Team, which is appropriate to the specific situation and missional direction of the church body. Keep it under twenty pages. Preparing this will focus the Vision Team on what to communicate about cell ministry as it will exist within the specific church. (Feel free to insert material from any TOUCH publication to get the job done.)

B. Add chapters on basic Christian community from one of these excellent resources:
1. *Making Cell Groups Work*, Section 2.3
2. *Where Do We Go From Here?* Chapter 5
3. *Life In His Body*, Chapter 2

RECOMMENDED AGENDA

A complete agenda for a three-day retreat which includes training sessions, instructions for activities, and a sample cell group agenda is available as a free download from <www.cellgrouppeople.com>.

DEBRIEFING THE RETREAT

Web Resource

Pastors need to be looking for leadership potential throughout the entire retreat. Watch participants during group discussions, meal times, cleanup times, and breaks. Often the best servant leaders work quietly behind the scenes. They model in ways that "stand out in the crowd" leaders don't. People will show leadership within their areas of gifting or expertise.

Who spontaneously leads in prayer when people share needs? Who shares scriptural insights when appropriate? Who nurtures and mentors naturally? Who "serves" even without a title? Who worships without inhibition? Who organizes others and delegates tasks? Who listens carefully and actively to others?

BASING CELL GROUPS ON THE FOUNDATION OF PRAYER

Larry Stockstill

Larry Stockstill has been on staff at Bethany World Prayer Center in Baker, Louisiana, since 1977 and became senior pastor in 1983. His ministry emphasizes prayer, cell groups, and missions. The church has over 10,000 members who meet in "Touch Groups" throughout the Baton Rouge area. Larry and his wife, Melanie, have six children.

We changed our name from Bethany Baptist Church to Bethany World Prayer Center because of our conviction that prayer had to be our focus. In 1983, we began a Saturday morning intercessory prayer meeting from 9-10 a.m. God spoke to us that our church was to be a center for intercessory prayer for the nations, and we established a twenty-four hour "World Prayer Center" to pray for our missionaries, pastors, and government leaders. This center has been in operation round-the-clock ever since, except for a brief period of remodeling.

In the summer of 1991, we established Gideon's Army, a 500-member prayer force. We sensed that the cell strategy was from the Lord, but that it must be birthed in prayer. In the very beginning, we established cells which met every other week for edification, and every other week for evangelism (members would bring friends). But these cells were made up of people from Gideon's Army who were praying diligently through each step in the process.

It was after this foundation of prayer was established that we ventured forth aggressively into the cell structure in April 1993. Over the next eighteen months, more than 250 cell groups were established. We believe this is because we showered every move in prayer, we knew God had spoken at each level, and we were determined that prayer would be the heart of it.

But there were practical, biblical reasons for this emphasis on prayer. Let's look together at six reasons to base your cell ministry on prayer.

1. PRAYER BIRTHS THINGS GOD WANTS TO DO

Prayer has the power to "birth" things. The church of the New Testament was birthed at upper room prayer meetings. I feel no church can transition into revival and the immense changes of cell structure without a prayer base.

I'm not alone in this. Many great moves of God in history were birthed in prayer: the Moravian missions phenomenon, the Methodist church and its emphasis on praying, small groups, etc. Someone once said that we've gone from the upper room agonizing to the supper room organizing. Prayer is the birthing power of the church, for "as soon as Zion travailed, she brought forth her children" (Isa. 66:8). "Substance before structure" is a guiding maxim that reminds us that revivals are "prayed down and not worked up."

All the cell structure does is divinely contain and protect the harvest—but cells will not provide the harvest. One trip to Korea and Prayer Mountain should be enough to convince any pastor that cells don't bring the revival, they hold the revival. To see thousands of Korean intercessors at Prayer Mountain in the middle of a weekday on their faces praying for souls, or to pass by a little prayer grotto and see a pair of shoes outside while a powerful intercessor inside is crying out for revival, will be enough to reveal to you in what direction we should move.

2. Prayer Helps Isolate the Committed Core of Your Cell Ministry

Think about it: what activity in your church trims down the attendance more than a prayer meeting? I've learned that the strongest disciples are those who long for the presence of God. Though you must occasionally endure some who lack that commitment, it's reasonable to say that your prayer warriors are the committed core of the church.

They're also the most sensitive to the changing direction of the Holy Spirit in a church and most aware of the spiritual warfare necessary to birth something that's a major threat to Satan's kingdom. Therefore, they'll be the least resistant to change and the most resistant to demonic efforts to thwart the fledgling effort. Teaching your prayer core the principles of intercession and spiritual warfare equips them to be the leaders and reapers of the cell dynamic.

3. Cells have the Ability to do Strategic Spiritual Warfare in Prayer

Located geographically, they provide the natural "command post" to do spiritual "reconnaissance" for their particular area and engage those spiritual forces in intensive prayer battle. Much material has been written recently on how to do spiritual warfare for city blocks, neighborhoods, city zones, etc. Cell groups can do "prayer walks" and other intercessory activities to begin the process of loosening the strongholds of darkness over their area.

Who better knows the particular spiritual strongholds of a neighborhood than those who live there? However, when most churches pray, it's for "the city," and is not informed, intelligent prayer for specific areas, like a street. Not so within the cell groups. Each group can pray over a targeted area of the city or over a specific group of people. There'll be a group committed to interceding for that place or people daily. This strategy has been very effective in Argentina and other countries which are experiencing great revival through "prayer cells."

4. Praying Cells Mean the Church-wide Prayer Load is Evenly Distributed

We've discovered that a cell structure works because it brings "shared responsibility" instead of "volunteerism." In the prayer area, we share the load by assigning a section of three to five cells to be in our prayer room during each service, praying for the presence of God and for unbelievers to be saved. The cells draw closer together as they intercede together. Then they actually provide the "altar workers" needed to reap the harvest at the altar call!

Also, the cells are each assigned to provide a "prayer covering" for one missionary family and one staff pastor (their District or Zone Pastor) through daily intercession. In this way, we know all our missionaries and pastors have several groups calling out their needs continually before the Lord and aren't lost in the shuffle without adequate prayer covering.

5. Cells can Focus on Specific Prayer Objectives

As the senior pastor, I have the vision of the current state of the church and the challenges we're facing in a particular month. The leaders hear the specific goals and urgent prayer needs that will affect the entire congregation from my vantage point and then communicate those prayer objectives to their cell groups. This means the pastor has hundreds of focused prayer warriors who are praying for the very burdens he's continually lifting up before the Lord. Breakthroughs come quickly, and progress is never impeded.

6. CELLS CAN INTERCEDE FOR THE HARVEST

In our cell group meetings, the members not only pray for each other's needs, but they break into "prayer triplets" and focus on three unbelievers each. The prayer triplets covenant together to pray for those nine names and then invite each to the "evangelism" meeting the following week. This prayer of agreement for the lost speeds up the harvest process.

Soon after we started our cell groups, God brought an unexpected revival among us as the cells prayed weekly for unbelievers. A drama team came for a three-day performance in February and one thousand people came for salvation on the first night! The meeting went on for twenty-one nights, and a total of 18,290 people came forward for salvation and filled out decision cards. This was twice the harvest of the Baton Rouge Billy Graham Crusade!

Our cell groups went quickly into action, each day following up the massive harvest and directing them to other area churches from which they had come, or placing them in cells if they had no church. Some pastors, who didn't even attend the dramas, baptized 25-30 new converts into their churches!

This abundant harvest showed us the power of intercession for unbelievers and the crying need now in America to "get the nets ready." Harvest is coming to this generation as we've never seen or known, and we pastors had best be spending our time preparing our leadership to hold and conserve this coming massive harvest.

I challenge every church and every pastor to seek the Lord for a fresh outpouring in America before it's eternally too late. The dynamic of prayer when God moves in power is truly the only hope for this world. Prepare your church to be an engine of prayer that will open heaven over your city!

How to Multiply Your Ministry

Ralph W. Neighbour, Jr. and Randall G. Neighbour

In 1996, a denominational church launched a cell-based ministry within its traditional Sunday school model in hopes of making a successful transition over time. While this was a 50-year-old Bible Belt church, it had a number of young, healthy families who desired to live out kingdom values. A handful of these families, along with a staff pastor, formed the first prototype cell group, led by the senior pastor.

According to a self-assessment, the senior pastor did an excellent job leading this first prototype cell. After all, this first group reached two families for Jesus! These new believers were invited to join this first group and were mentored by group members, providing the first cell members with experience in cell-based discipleship.

After eight months in this first prototype, the senior pastor sent out each family in the group to launch their own cell group with members from the church and unchurched friends. One group became six, led by a few existing church leaders, dedicated members, and even a couple who were brought to Christ in the prototype group. These six groups—coached by the senior pastor and the part-time staff pastor—grew primarily with church member assimilation, which was the first goal in the pastor's mind: Get as many church members into groups to further the transition.

Within a year or so, the remaining groups multiplied twice, populated with new church members and those who found their Sunday school to be non-relational. Assimilation was the goal. Just to tally the score, he had fifteen groups, four coaches, and about half of the church body in cell groups.

Then disaster struck. Groups were closed because the leaders were too immature for the task or still struggling with patterns of sin. Other leaders took better paying jobs out of town instead of living within their means and keeping their attention on building the kingdom.

Today, this church has a few struggling groups and has a declining membership. Many of the first-round cell leaders are no longer in leadership positions in any church, and some leaders are completely unchurched.

MULTIPLY LEADERS, NOT GROUPS

The typical "first-strike" for many pastors moving into cell ministry is to launch as many groups as possible to gain momentum for the new direction of their church. In the true story above, the pastor's first mistake was releasing prototype members to lead groups, but whose character and life's vision had not been shaped by a mentoring relationship with their cell leader, or in this case, their senior pastor. His goal was rapid assimilation. He didn't understand that cell ministry is about multiplying the number of empowered and equipped leaders—leaders who are consumed with the vision for basic Christian community and mentoring others.

Jesus' ministry provides simple and clear multiplication principles for producing leaders. Your ministry can be multiplied many times over by following his example. The kingdom principles of multiplication will yield unbelievable results, if you think people and not groups.

The four key principles Jesus used and taught are:

- Act! (Just do it!)
- Associate! (Do it with others!)
- Activate! (Have them do it!)
- Multiply it! (Release them to repeat the process around the world!)

ACT (JUST DO IT)

One of the most challenging questions posed to any pastor is, "How much time did Jesus spend in the office?" For cell ministry to work in your church, you must fight off the passive administrator role and stay in active ministry. Jesus never had an office or a laptop, yet his ministry changed the world.

Jesus' time and attention were consumed with extending the kingdom. His focus was on prayer and intimacy with the Father. He declared the kingdom to all who would listen, evangelized, ministered the power of God to people's felt needs, offered forgiveness, healed the sick, and accepted the outcast.

What will the "Act" phase mean for you?

- Radically and consistently encounter God in prayer. To do this, you may have to invest far more time each day on your face before God.
- Get out of the church office and do the ministry of Jesus with others. For many years, seminaries taught future pastors to distance themselves from people, to create authority and shield them from abuse. In cell ministry, authority is constantly earned and you must become close enough to people to know their lived-out values and shape them. Spend time with people and pastor them!
- Live a life of relational evangelism. Jesus' nickname was "Friend of Sinners." Pastors are some of the most insulated believers in the church. Make friends with unbelievers in your neighborhood, at your child's little league games, etc. If this doesn't work, find a neighborhood tavern and, along with another Christian leader, become a regular coffee drinker there. Invest a couple hours a week with the lost.
- Minister with power! If you don't have it, get it. Recent surveys show that non-Christians and children in Christian homes turn away from the church not because it's irrelevant, but because it's powerless. The Holy Spirit's presence and power was a tangible reality in the New Testament church and we're to carry out the ministry of Jesus with increased, not diminished power (John 14:12).

ASSOCIATE (DO IT WITH OTHERS)

Jesus did almost nothing by himself, which is a stark contrast to the typical American pattern of ministry, which embraces individualism. Anytime you do any form of ministry by yourself, you're on a dead-end street. When you die, that ministry dies!

Jesus used both the ministry and the everyday activities of his life to associate with others. He ate, traveled, and relaxed with others. You may think you're just not wired this way, but realize there's a difference between being an extrovert (or outgoing) and being relational. You must be relational to follow in the footsteps of Jesus. If you're non-relational, your church will be non-relational. There's no such thing as a non-relational New Testament church. Everything is based on relationships.

Jesus' Chosen

Jesus called rough, ordinary people who were potential future leaders to live in close relationship with himself. "Come, follow me!" was his call (Mark 1:17; Matthew 9:9; John 1:43). He appointed twelve—designating them apostles—that they might be with him … (Mark 3:14).

It's important to note that Jesus chose his disciples. After all, the vision, passion, and hard work lie squarely on the shoulders of the one mentoring, not the one being mentored. Therefore, you must choose those through whom you'll multiply your ministry.

Values Change Through Modeling

Jesus didn't ask his disciples to do anything he hadn't already done and demonstrated himself, which shows that values can be communicated most powerfully through modeling. The disciples' initial value systems were even worse than yours or the members of your church. Through modeling—in the context of community—their real motives and hearts were revealed and they were slowly transformed. Jesus modeled for us that values are more caught than taught.

Paul also realized this powerful multiplication principle of Jesus. He called others to imitate him (Greek: *mimeomai*) (1 Corinthians 11:1; 4:16). He calls would-be-leaders and others to communicate values by becoming models (Greek: *tupos*) (1 Timothy 4:12; Titus 2:4f; 1 Thessalonians 1:6-7). Paul modeled for Timothy and many others what Barnabas had previously modeled for him.

Modeling is the most effective method for communicating skills. The disciples caught the style and methods of Jesus' ministry through association. People can only replicate what they can clearly picture. They can only picture what they've experienced firsthand.

What will the "Associate" phase mean for you?

- Prayerfully select two or three leaders (or potential leaders) from your church whom you admire, trust, and respect. These should be men or women who understand the mission of your church and want to see it fulfilled. If they're not fully committed to Christ in one or more areas of their lives, don't discount them—develop these values within them. Let's call them your protégés.
- Invest time with each couple or person as a friend. Spend time togeth-

er eating, laughing, playing with your children, and living life. It will be during these moments that you'll discover the people behind the Sunday smiles, their dreams, hopes, struggles, and victories.

- Commit to a long-term relationship with those you mentor. Jesus invested three years into his disciples. Don't give up on a slow learner. Jesus' investment in Peter paid huge dividends.
- Take those you're mentoring with you when you minister. Ask them questions after the ministry time, to see if they were paying attention and catching what you were doing by watching.

ACTIVATE (RELEASE THEM TO DO IT)

Many pastors are anxious to succeed, releasing leaders prematurely. There's little involvement (or what we've termed association), and no long-term relationship where those being mentored undergo a transformational shift in values.

Jesus involved leaders before he appointed them (Mark 1:17; 3:1-4). They're to be selected carefully, in the context of ministry and prayer. In other words, you may not select leaders as well as you think! That's why it's so important to involve them in ministry and watch them carefully before appointing them as leaders.

The Activate portion of the mentoring process takes the most time. It will require that you remain keenly aware of what you're modeling and what your protégé is learning.

The process of releasing others to do ministry requires incredible faith in the Holy Spirit at work in others. God does the extraordinary through very ordinary people. The greatness lies in the Spirit's working and power, not in the people we're involving and releasing in ministry.

A pastor visited a cell group one evening and met a first-time visitor. He spent quite a bit of time with this man after the meeting, getting to know him on a personal level. Later that night, the pastor called the cell leader and said, "I really enjoyed visiting with Frank tonight. He's going to make a great pastor!"

The cell leader was puzzled, because Frank was not yet a professing Christian. But the pastor saw something in Frank that the cell leader did not—potential. Two years later, and with a great deal of mentoring and deep friendship, Frank felt the call into missions! It's all about the activity of the Spirit within an ordinary person, and laying hold of a vision for giving away your ministry to others.

Mentoring Pattern:

1. I constantly look for leaders. (Act)
2. I call you to involvement. (Associate)
3. I do, you watch. (Activate, step 1)
4. I do, you help. (Activate, step 2)
5. You do, I watch. (Activate, step 3)
6. You do it by yourself and we talk about it. (Activate, step 4)
7. You repeat the process. (Multiply it)

What will the "Activate" phase mean to you?

- Your protégés must view your ministry as one of giving away what you have. It may take repeat exposure to help them deeply understand what you're doing and why you're doing it.
- Challenge your protégés to recap the teaching moment and discuss what they would have done differently, if anything. (This will help you learn a great deal about the way he or she thinks).
- Allow your protégés to learn by failure, the best teacher! Drill it into their heads: "Failure is good, failure is good!"
- Encourage profusely. Your protégés will need to know they're loved unconditionally, and that failure is the way people learn.
- Watch those you're mentoring, after they've taken the ball and are running with it. Don't assume they've gained the skills or maturity to be independent just because they take responsibility.
- Always remain willing to let go when the time is right. Others must do what you've been doing up to this point, and with the power of the Holy Spirit, they may even do it better than you do.

MULTIPLY IT

The vision Jesus gives us is a huge vision, and it's much greater than the little dreams and visions we create (Matthew 28:18-20; Acts 1:6-8). Set your sights on global conversion! With a plan to multiply yourself in others and release them, completing the Great Commission can be achieved in our lifetime.

Years ago, a pastor sat down with a calculator to determine how powerful mentoring leaders could be in the life of his church and world. Being a conservative thinker, he assumed his failure rate with multiplying leaders might be as high as fifty percent. With this in mind, he began to multiply the number of leaders he would create year after year, and the number of leaders they too would create year after year. Each leader was to lead a holistic small group to win the lost and disciple them to do the same.

His final calculation shocked him. In just twenty-three years, the population of the world at that time would have been reached for Christ by his leader multiplication strategy. Remember, this calculation was solely based on a fifty-percent success rate!

There's power in mentoring and releasing others into ministry, even factoring in our humanity. God wants to multiply his life through you around the world and through generations to come!

Personal Exercise

MENTORING QUESTIONS

Following is a set of questions to help you consider all you've read here, and to write down your initial thoughts. Wrestle with these questions and ask God to give you his answers!

1. Are you willing to say "yes" to him in "just doing it," even if you don't know what all that will mean? Are you willing to move forward and not look back?

2. Do you want to minister the manifest power of Jesus?

3. Are you willing to move into close relationships of sharing and ministry with other believers, to experience "Acts 2 Christianity" in a deeper way than you ever have before?

4. Are you willing to release ministry and let Jesus and others become the primary ministers in your church?

5. Who will be your first disciples? How can you pastor them at this point in their lives?

6. Who are the lost people into whom you'll invest time each week?

THE PASTOR'S INNER LIFE

Ralph W. Neighbour, Jr.

"The LORD said, 'Rise and anoint him; he is the one.' So Samuel took the horn of oil and anointed him in the presence of his brothers, and from that day on the Spirit of the LORD came upon David in power" (1 Samuel 16:12-13).

As you examine the cell group churches in our generation, one fact should become obvious. While there are many churches that have chosen to enter basic Christian community as a way of life, only a few hundred have truly exploded with growth. While all cell churches use relatively similar structures, not all of them harvest the unreached world to the same extent. Why?

The answer is found in part by examining the pastors who are guiding the growing cell group churches. One word describes their greatest trait: anointed!

"If the anointing which we bear comes not from the Lord of Hosts, we are deceivers, since only in prayer can we obtain it. Let us continue instant, constant, fervent in supplication. Let your fleece lie on the threshing floor of supplication 'Till it is wet with the dew of heaven."
—Charles Haddon Spurgeon

AN ANOINTING FOR A LEADER

In 1990, Ruth and I finalized our affairs in the United States and moved to Singapore. There I served Lawrence Khong as Senior Associate Pastor for almost five years. In my first visit with him after our arrival, he told me in a voice deep with emotion, "Ralph, I am anointed for this task!"

If most men had said such words to me, I would have recoiled, thinking, "What an egotist!" However, I'd already known Pastor Khong for fifteen years and I knew his heart. He was sharing with me from the depth of his spirit. His statement wasn't braggadocio; it was an acknowledgement that he would become a leader of thousands, because of the anointing of God upon his life. He was saying, "Leading this church for me is not an option: it is an assignment from God!"

What I sensed in that moment with him I had sensed years before as a 23-year-old working for Billy Graham. He, too, knew his work was the direct result of the Spirit's anointing.

Anointed leadership is found throughout the Bible and church history. Moses, David, Paul, Luther, Wesley, and Spurgeon are among those special men who discovered that their ministry controls them, that they do not control it.

Exposure to significant cell church leaders like Mario Vega of El Salvador, Dion Robert of the Ivory Coast, Yonggi Cho of Korea, and Cesar Castellanos of Colombia, reveals a special anointing that has caused them to energize others through the anointing God has given to them.

More often than we wish to admit, pastors and Christian workers are faithfully serving the Lord without a special anointing for what they're doing. One quickly grasps the difference when the presence of the Holy Spirit reveals they have received an anointing for their work.

The significance of this anointing is found in 1 Samuel 16:13: "From that day on the Spirit of the LORD came upon David in power." Power for ministry: that's just one of the attributes an anointed man displays.

AN ANOINTING FOR THE BODY OF CHRIST

The anointing isn't just upon one man, but upon the whole body of Christ. Anointed means "set apart." When a church composed of cell groups receives the Spirit's anointing for ministry, it moves from the mundane and mechanical to the flow of mighty power.

In Pretoria, South Africa, the Hatfield Christian Church has seen its cell groups multiply over and over. When in the midst of them, a person feels their burning zeal, their worship and their ministry times are filled with the Spirit. This anointing carries into all the cell groups, where with boldness they pray for healing, for salvation for the lost, and for direction for ministry.

HOW DOES THE ANOINTING COME?

Several years ago, I took a group of pastors to visit the cell conference conducted by Yonggi Cho. Although we expected to be greeted by Pastor Cho at the central church, we were instead taken by bus to Prayer Mountain. There, in the "Ark" that has been built on the side of the mountain, Pastor Cho greeted us. "I asked you to come here first," he said, "because this is the reason our church has grown to be so large."

Over two million visits a year are logged into the registration of Prayer Mountain. That means the members of Yoido Full Gospel Church come and pray an average of over two days, twice a year!

As I walked down the side of the mountain, I saw the "prayer grottos" inserted into the earth. They were originally built as snipers' nests during the war: tiny concrete bunkers too small for a person to stand upright. There's a charcoal fire pot in each one, and a swinging wooden door to keep out the snow in winter. All were full and as I passed by, I noted the earnest prayer taking place.

One of those grottos is reserved only for Pastor Cho. He told us how he would come to stay on a Friday through a Saturday in his grotto, his only "comfort" a bamboo pad. There he would live before the Lord, all distractions put away. "When I am sleeping, I am also in the Lord's presence," he said to us.

It's in that grotto that Cho receives the continuing anointing for the massive work he has started around the world. It's in the grotto the Lord gives him the number of converts he can expect during the next year. Pastor Cho receives a continual anointing through prayer.

One day of the conference, I had a scheduled appointment with Pastor Cho. At the end, he said, "I have another appointment now. It has been good for us to visit." When I left his office, I sat down immediately outside it to record my thoughts from our conversation. Strangely, although he was anxious for me to leave promptly, I saw no one else enter his office. Fifteen minutes later, I went to his secretary and said, "Dr. Cho told me he had an important appointment to keep after I left him. But I haven't seen anyone enter his office!"

The secretary replied, "No, Ralph, he just didn't tell you who his appointment was with. At this time every day, he spends one or two hours alone with the Lord. He never misses that time. He is inside praying."

As their leader set the example by his own presence in the prayer grotto, his pastors also learned the importance of prayer. All the District and Zone Pastors make regular visits to Prayer Mountain. They wear banners over their shoulders that say "Hallelujah!" The staff prays because their leader prays.

One day, while walking across a trail on the mountainside, I saw below me a wooden bench, with a woman crying out at the top of her voice. She was in travail as she prayed. Two hours later, I passed by that place again and saw she was still praying. She repeated Korean words over and over. I stopped one of the pastors and asked, "What is she saying?" He listened for a moment and replied, "She is crying out to God for a wayward daughter."

An anointed cell church is one filled with constant prayer. The anointing begins with the senior pastor, who gains his vision and strength from the Holy Spirit, and flows out through the church body. Like the anointing oil poured upon David's hair dripped down his body and touched his toes, even so Israel found its King's anointing flowing from him to the edges of the kingdom.

Here's an important lesson: in the cell church prayer must become the focal point, not a marginal activity. It's through prayer that the anointing, the wisdom, the power, and the harvest take place!

ACTIVITY FOR DEVELOPING THE PASTOR'S INNER LIFE

Personal Exercise

Question...

Answer the question below without thinking much about it. Let your response flow from your first thoughts and feelings. The "right" answer at this point is what easily comes to your mind.

Who are you?

A Pattern for Empowered, God-Centered Ministry

What factors are significantly controlling your time and ministry? (Check all that apply.)

❑ Urgent needs

❑ The expectations of those you serve

❑ The expectations of colleagues or co-workers

❑ The expectation of family members (past or present)

❑ A desire to please those immediately around you

❑ A crystal clear sense of God's calling and direction

❑ Other: _____

Jesus was constantly buffeted by needs and conflicting expectations, but he was never controlled by them (Mark 1:32-39). His life offers a pattern for empowered ministry that's fully God-centered.

• His life demonstrates an amazing security. (John 13:3-5)

• He walked in a confident freedom. (John 5:19; 8:28)

• His short life and mission were marked by clarity of purpose. (John 17:4)

Ministry Begins with Empowering and Identity

Jesus was empowered for ministry by the Spirit.

1. What power source(s) are you mainly relying on? (Check all that apply.)

   ❑ Self-confidence

   ❑ Skills

   ❑ Education

   ❑ Experience

   ❑ The energy and direction of the Holy Spirit

   ❑ Other: _____

2. Are you desperate for God's empowering to serve others?

If you're thirsty, Jesus offers a never ending stream of living water, if you simply come and ask!

- God's empowering is an ongoing experience. Peter apparently leaked because he had to be filled over and over again! (Acts 2:4; 4:8; 4:31)
- If you're hungry for more of God's power, get alone with God and talk it over with him. Let him remove any obstructions and ask for the free gift of his empowering presence.

Jesus' identity was declared at his baptism, the onset of his ministry. "You are my Son, whom I love; with you I am well pleased." (Luke 3:22)

- In baptism, your allegiance and identity are declared. (Matthew 28:19)
- Your significance doesn't come from what you've done in the past or will accomplish in the future. It's based solely on God's love for you and his acceptance of you in Christ.
- Throughout Scripture, God repeatedly is communicating who we are.

Who Are You?

Read the statements below aloud, pondering their truth:

- I have been put right with God by faith and have peace with him. (Romans 5:1)
- I have been saved by Christ's life. (Romans 5:10)
- I have died to sin. (Romans 6:2)
- I now have no condemnation. (Romans 8:1)
- I am called into fellowship with Jesus Christ my Lord. (1 Corinthians 1:9)
- I will put on immortality. (1 Corinthians 15:53)
- I am comforted by God. (2 Corinthians 1:22)
- I have received mercy. (2 Corinthians 4:1)
- I have a house not made with hands in the heavens. (2 Corinthians 5:1)
- I am a new creation in Christ. The old has gone, the new is come. (2 Corinthians 5:17)
- I am Christ's ambassador. (2 Corinthians 5:20)
- I am holy and blameless in God's sight. (Ephesians 1:4)
- I am God's child. (Ephesians 1:5)
- I am a citizen in God's kingdom and a member of God's family. (Ephesians 2:9)
- I approach God with confidence to find grace and mercy. (Hebrews 4:16)
- God will never leave me nor forsake me. (Hebrews 13:5)
- According to God's great mercy, I have been born again into a living hope through the resurrection of Jesus Christ from the dead. (1 Peter 1:3)
- I have been given an inheritance which is imperishable, undefiled and unfading—kept in heaven for me. (1 Peter 1:4)
- I was not redeemed with perishable things like silver and gold, but by the blood of Christ, like a lamb without blemish or defect. (1 Peter 1:18, 19)

Reread these statements, underlining those that stand out as important for you right now.

Based on these truths, write down, in your own words, who you are.

What Unchangeable Values Shape Your Decisions?

Jesus' anointing for ministry was followed by an intense time of testing where his values were galvanized. Ministry is typically preceded by extreme testing where God clearly leads us into a place of desolation. When we're empowered by the Spirit, we're tempted to:

- Use God's gifts for our own comfort, rather than in service to others. (Luke 4:3-4)
- Compromise and build our own kingdom rather than God's. (Luke 4:5-8)
- Bring attention to ourselves instead of God. (Luke 4:9-12)

Determine Your Unchangeable Priorities and Values

- What are two or three ways you think Satan may likely attempt to ruin your life and ministry by sabotaging your values?

- Imagine that you only have three years to live. What will be your top priorities in the next three years?

- Write a paragraph or list of statements outlining the values you choose to guide your life.

What Is Your Mission?

Jesus began and continued his ministry with a clear sense of mission. Take the time now to discern and outline your mission.

- Pray, recommitting all you are and all you have to God.

- Imagine you have only three years to live. Write down in a short paragraph the things you feel God wants you to accomplish in those three years.

- Revise the paragraph above as needed to form a mission statement encapsulating God's call on your life.

- Write down the six to eight primary roles you have in life. (For example: child of God, loving spouse, parent, pastor, cell leader, friend of sinners, etc.)

- Now write each role down, one at a time. Below each role write down two goals and for each goal put down two specific actions to fulfill in the next year to help accomplish those goals.

Choose to Live a Life of Prayer

Jesus' heart for the Father is within you. Jesus, the person of prayer, is alive in you. Get away for extended times with God. I recommend two days at a time. Remember:
- At least once a year Jesus took an extended time for prayer.
- The call of the lovers in the Song of Songs is, "Come away with me."

Begin each day with God. (Mark 1:35) You get to pick when your day starts, evening or morning (Jewish or Roman), depending on what prime time is for you.

- Take special times with God in the midst of your weekly activities and schedule.
- Take a weekly Sabbath. (If you're not taking a weekly Sabbath, take time to identify what gods are controlling your time.) At that time, or at the end of each week, review your identity, mission, and goals to focus your life for the week ahead.

TRANSITIONING CHURCH STAFF

Ralph W. Neighbour Jr. and Randall G. Neighbour

In any successful church transition, the pastor must give time and attention to help staff make the dynamic shift of abandoning the old way for the new. Staff must model the new paradigm for ministry.

HOW PEOPLE MAKE DECISIONS

Our ability to understand why individuals make certain decisions or advocate certain actions is greatly enhanced when we understand their presuppositions, those beliefs held in advance of a new decision.

John Gray's book, *Men are from Mars, Women are from Venus*, describes a scenario surrounding a strained interaction between a married couple. A wife approaches her husband with a problem, and he immediately responds with a logical, straightforward solution, with little or no dialogue.

In this illustration, the wife did not want a decisive decision made by her husband after a brief description of the situation. She wanted to dialogue about the problem to process her feelings, making a decision based on the process of interaction surrounding the issue. In her mind, she needed a thoughtful sounding board that would help her come to her own conclusion.

The husband, on the other hand, assumed a problem wouldn't be brought to his attention if his tactical, analytical disposition was not required. He had an instant solution to her problem and became frustrated when she didn't quickly latch on to it and drop the long, exhaustive explanation.

In this illustration, both persons could have been far more effective in their communication by exploring the other party's presuppositions and sharing their own beliefs and feelings in advance. Moreover, by stating his or her own presuppositions, the person makes a dynamic shift in how the idea is presented and has a newfound clarity as to his or her position concerning the subject matter. Often, the greatest hindrance to communication is that the communicator doesn't truly understand his or her position before attempting to explain the idea to another person.

PRESUPPOSITIONS

Pastors of churches that are transitioning to cell ministry must face their own presuppositions. Following are common realities of bringing about radical change within churches.

1. Personal Change will be Required

When casting a vision for a cell-based ministry, staff and power people must be approached in a way that will yield the best results. To be successful, pastors will be challenged to:

a) Change presentation style to match listeners' reference points and feelings.

b) Lay down defensiveness and remain open to their concerns and feelings.

c) Love people through the transition process, realizing everyone learns new things differently.

d) Give staff (and members) sufficient time to "catch the vision." People adopt a new value system at differing rates.

e) Work as hard and long as necessary to retain every member and love sheep individually. (While a decision to transition "regardless of who stays or leaves" may be noble in the minds of a visionary leader, it carries with it an inherent danger. A pastor must first be willing to challenge and change those unbiblical values within. This conscious decision to do whatever it takes to move the church in a new direction must first move him to address his own leadership deficits, allowing God to change him.)

2. Redefine "Effective Communication"

In real estate, the motto is "location, location, location." To effectively transition a church into a cell-based, mission-driven congregation, leaders must adopt the motto "communication, communication, communication."

Communication is a dialogue, not a monologue. A pastor's level of effective communication is gauged by asking those around him to describe in their own words what they heard him say. If they don't understand his current line of thinking and communication, he must change his approach as many times as is needed to bring them to a point of understanding.

The typical pastor finds this difficult. Pastors often work with people who live under a cloud of fear or intimidation, and won't share what they're thinking and feeling. It may be caused by the pastor's disposition as a strong, determined, and demanding leader.

While one's choice of words and delivery is important, the best way to communicate is through actions. Jesus came proclaiming and demonstrating the will of God. To effectively transition the staff and church people into a life of community and outreach, the pastor must live out the values himself, not just communicate them verbally.

3. Communicate Through Actions

It's not unusual for people to get excited about something new and talk to others. But if they don't put into practice what they're teaching, their words seem hollow and without true passion.

Though difficult, a pastor must begin to live out the values necessary for biblical community to flourish in his church. His daily duties must shift from paperwork and meetings to deep relationships with staff, family, and the lost. As the senior leader, the pastor must first model the new lifestyle, before writing off others as "not having the vision or commitment to go the distance." When moving into the transition process, a pastor will come to understand that the real issue is one of values and lifestyle change, not structural change.

4. Adjust Leadership Style to Make the Transition Work

In any profession, the best leaders are those who are willing to adjust or change their own leadership style in order to motivate others to change and adapt. The extent of the adaptation is based upon what will motivate a particular group of followers. The effective leader "becomes all things to all men" that he might be able to win some.

Some of the most rigid, immovable, unadaptable, and hardheaded people are pastors! Transitioning to a cell-based ministry will require breaking out of molds and becoming the leader God destined. The leadership style a pastor has previously employed to motivate church leaders in traditional forms of church life will most certainly need modification.

PRESUPPOSITIONS HELD BY PAID STAFF

Grasping the other party's current beliefs is as important as coming to grips with one's own. Here are a few presuppositions paid staff (and unpaid

Personal Exercise

Make a list of all staff members. Write out the biggest barrier to each one entering into the cell group vision.

leadership) may have about the pastor and any kind of change he wants to make.

1. "Cell-based Ministry Is Yet Another 'Church Growth' Gimmick"

There's always a new and innovative way to increase attendance and participation in the local church. Any church leader who's been around for five years or more has seen them come and go. For many, transitioning to a cell-based ministry will not be viewed as a significant shift away from yet another program, regardless of how it's described. If a church has introduced numerous evangelism and church growth programs in the past, cell-based ministry will be categorized in this way until the differences are demonstrated through immersion experiences (i.e. weekend retreats, short-term cell group experiences, etc.).

2. "Others Have Tried Cell Groups and They Don't Work"

It's true that many churches have tried cell groups and were unsuccessful. But upon further examination, what's often found is that these same churches saw cell groups as a quick fix for problems, or a church growth tool. The pastor must help staff members understand that the shift toward relational ministry through cell groups is based on fulfilling the mission God has given the church. Leaders need to understand that when ministry becomes highly relational, inherent problems between people, and in the current system, will be brought to light so they can be addressed.

3. "I'm Too Busy for Cell Ministry!"

Staff members may not be wrong on this issue. When transitioning to cell-based ministry, the pastor must work with staff members individually to help them transition into their new roles. As growth occurs, he must release them from old responsibilities to work in new ways. They'll need assurance that new duties won't be added to their routine without careful review and a regular assessment of their time usage.

Pastors must follow through by reserving time with each staff member to discuss their perspective on the transition and help them with time management, keeping the future as a priority. Becoming an excellent listener and working with them, versus telling them what to do, is essential.

KEY QUESTIONS TO HELP TRANSITION THE STAFF

1. Is the pastor living the vision or simply talking about it?
2. Staff members don't merely want to be told what to do, they want to be shown. What are some ways the pastor can "walk the talk?"
3. How one uses his time reflects commitment. What schedule adjustments must be made to make relationships a priority?
4. Transparency, accountability, and mentor-based discipleship are three of the foundational values of cell ministry. How will the pastor become more transparent? Submit to accountability? Sacrifice to make disciples?
5. Living out the values is the best way to transition staff. When can a UIOF (Upward, Inward, Outward, Forward) cell group be launched for staff members and spouses?
6. What reading material can be given to staff members to help them catch the vision?
7. What thriving cell church in the area or denomination can the pastor and staff visit? How will this trip be budgeted?
8. Over the years, a pastor has created an "emotional bank account" with staff. How much emotional credit does he have with his staff members? If there's little credit or substantial debt, what will it take to earn the credit required for this major shift in ministry? (If a pastor has made numerous or radical changes in the past, only to leave them for the next idea, he may need to repent! Is he willing to do this?)
9. How has the pastor expressed care for staff in the past? Are they confident he has their best interest at heart and not his own?
10. Is the pastor a true friend to staff members? Can they disagree without fear? Does the staff get together for fun times as well as church business? Does the pastor know their families well and interact with them regularly?

CLOSING THOUGHTS

As a senior pastor, one can neither delegate nor legislate a transition to cell ministry. While he has the spiritual authority to lead in the transition, he must lead by speaking and living out what everyone in the body (including staff) is expected to live out. If future cell members are expected to make a radical commitment to basic biblical values, the staff must be radically committed to them first! Two final points to remember.

First, remember that paid staff members need as long a period of time to transition their paradigms and values as it took the pastor to do the same. This is one important reason that a transition can take three to seven years. Values don't change overnight.

Secondly, expecting staff to embrace change when they sense that key church leaders oppose such change is problematic. While they may wish to support their pastor, they're torn by loyalty to those holding ultimate authority within the church. They'll most likely give verbal assent to the pastor, yet live out values of those in opposition. This sets up a passive-aggressive block to progress towards transition. The pastor and staff members should discuss this openly and deal with it together prayerfully.

THE PASTOR'S WIFE IN A CELL GROUP CHURCH

Twyla Brickman

Twyla Brickman works with her husband Les for Strategic Cell Ministries International as a trainer and consultant for cell-based churches.

Wives have jokingly been called "the necks that turn the heads," but can a pastor truly lead those within his church through transitional change if he can't convince his wife? In a cell group church, the role the pastor's wife plays is critical! The pastor and his wife are partners in leading their church through the process of transformational change.

Transformed values permeate every area of a pastor's life—public and private. Modeling is a key ingredient for both daily living out biblical Christianity and impacting change within a congregation. Therefore, it's imperative that the pastor and his wife be in agreement as they face the challenge of living transparent lives. Wise pastors who desire to succeed in church transition know the value of bringing their family alongside them on this journey.

This article assumes that the senior pastor is male. While there is a growing number of women pastors in North America, the vast majority remains male.

What makes a cell group church's mold different for a pastor's wife? Just as the "job description" for a cell group church pastor radically differs from how a pastor may have functioned previously in a more traditional setting, so the paradigm has shifted for his wife.

BREAKING THE TRADITIONAL MOLD

In most cases, churches collectively, and church members individually, possess a set of expectations regarding what the pastor's wife is, or is not, supposed to do and to be. Those expectations may be conscious or unconscious. They may include everything from appropriate age to correct dress, hair, children, career, activities, and personality. They may focus on how she spends time inside and outside the church. Unfortunately, not all members agree on their list of requirements!

Traditional church life attracts a wide spectrum of pastors' wives. Some remind their pastor husbands that he's the one hired and should be pleased as long as she attends worship. On the other end, some churches find their pastor's wife enjoys her role as "first lady," with its power, prestige, and prominence. Pastoral counseling offices are full of pastors' wives who are tired, disillusioned, and wounded. These women are hungry for real down-to-earth Christian living without the masks.

In the traditional church, pastors' wives may feel pressured to "entertain" by inviting groups for dinners, hosting tea parties, or providing lodging for visiting evangelists. As we live in biblical community, we learn what it means to practice hospitality with one another. The pastor and his family model biblical hospitality by opening their home and their lives. Cell members learn they don't need to own a huge house, know how to prepare gourmet food, or become spotless housekeepers to extend God's love and welcome.

Hospitality isn't about what we have or how much we have. It's about what we do with what we have. Church members will be blessed as they watch the pastor's family open their home to lost friends and neighbors, cell groups, and those leaders they're mentoring.

Christianity is about relationships—to God and to each other. Living in biblical community is all about relationships. In the cell group, we don't just talk about loving, praying for, accepting, forgiving, and forbearing with one another. Instead, we're challenged to live that out in demonstrable ways.

The good news for pastors' wives in a cell group church is that they're encouraged to be themselves. Pleasing God, instead of people, is the focus. In a cell group church, each individual (even the pastor's wife!) is encouraged to take off his or her mask. In fact, the more the pastor and his wife model transparency, the more other church members will feel it's safe to be real.

The church needs a living, breathing, flesh and blood model like Paul, who says, "Follow me as I follow Christ." Christians, (including the pastor and his wife), sin, repent, cry, get discouraged, and find new faith. They model for a lost world simply what it means to be a Christian. A model, though imperfect, simply goes before.

FINDING A PLACE AT THE FOOT OF THE CROSS

The cell group church values the priesthood of all believers. The hard and fast traditional distinctions between clergy and laity have faded and blurred. In practical terms, this means all members are ministers. Some who minister are supported financially by the church, thereby enabling them to minister full-time. Others minister while working full-time jobs. There are no super saints. No one has to be perfect. Since all are ministers, the pastor and his wife no longer should be put on a pedestal. As one individual noted, "The ground is level at the foot of the cross."

The cell group church operates with a "gift-based" philosophy of ministry. God has set each one of us in the body functionally, just where he desires. Based on gifting, a believer must discover the ministry into which God is now releasing him or her. All members, including the pastor's wife, are free to find the place in church where the Lord wants them to minister and serve.

In the traditional church, the pastor's wife may have felt she needed to serve on several committees, play the piano, teach Bible classes, and sing in the choir. However, in the cell group church, the pastor's main role is equipping the saints to do the work of the ministry. His wife is one of those saints being equipped! When one hundred percent of the body is functional, one person won't need to take on five or ten different responsibilities!

WORKING TOGETHER IN MINISTRY

If cell groups were just another program, another gimmick, or only one facet of church life, a pastor's wife could choose either to be or not be a part of them. Leading a cell group church isn't something one man can do alone. He can't live out biblical values without the support of his wife and family.

What roles can pastors' wives fill as they support their husbands?

Service opportunities for pastors' wives and women in general will vary from church to church and denomination to denomination. In many cell group churches, most notably in South Korea, many ministry opportunities have opened up for women. These include women extending personal ministry to individual women, leading cell groups, supervising zones, and serving in pastoral ministry, as well as serving as interns at every level.

Some cell group churches are encouraging women to minister in these ways, but limit their sphere to women only. That's particularly true in countries or locales having gender-specific cell groups. Others are allowing ministry from women to men, especially if the groups are heterogeneous. Some denominations believe women may serve as deacons, elders, and even senior pastors, while others believe the Scriptures teach there are limits to how much authority a woman may exercise in the church.

What is shared ministry for pastors and their wives? Some wives will determine that shared ministry means primarily meeting their husband's needs and being active in a cell group. Other wives will participate in ministry activities, as their spiritual gifts are released in ways that complement their husband's gifts. In some cell group churches, pastors and their wives even serve as co-pastors.

THINGS FOR THE PASTOR TO CONSIDER

Pastors can make the transition process smoother for themselves, their families, and their churches by considering these simple, yet important actions:

Discuss with your wife how your own role will change, how you feel about these changes, and how these changes may affect your home and marriage.

Personal Exercise

Discuss your wife's current and future roles, spiritual gifting, ministry calling, personal and family needs, personality, fears, and desires. Listen carefully as she gives input.

Spend time together regularly with your wife reading the Bible and praying. Allow her to be your spiritual partner in ministry by praying together for your church. Provide the opportunity for your wife to share in ministry, while sparing her all the details and burdens.

Work on open communication and transparency in your marriage. Don't exclude your wife from your problems, fears, anger, or concerns. Give her the chance to minister to you personally.

Share with your wife what you're learning from reading, talking to other pastors, spending time with God, and experiencing through daily activities. Bring her along on the journey with you as you share insights, questions, ideas, and plans. Ask what God is teaching her. If you do, you'll see her bloom as a fruitful vine (Psalm 128:3).

Really listen to your wife! She can act as "iron sharpening iron" as she challenges, quizzes, and even points out weaknesses in your plans. Allowing her to turn them upside down and inside out looking for problems can save a lot of public defeat and embarrassment as she helps refine the vision in private. Ask for and receive her counsel.

Receive your wife as a gift from God. Accept her as she is, with the spiritual gifts given to her by the Holy Spirit. Don't limit her ministry to keeping the house clean, doing the laundry, taking care of the kids, cooking the meals, and meeting your sexual needs. She's a greater gift than simply an unpaid cook, maid, nanny, and mistress!

Release and free your wife; being her spiritual head doesn't obliterate her own personality or ministry. Allow and encourage her growth and development. View her as your sister in the Lord with whom you are joint heirs and co-laborers in the kingdom. You'll be the beneficiary, as "an excellent wife is the crown of her husband."

Minister to your wife as much or more than you'd serve any other church member. In your zeal and excitement to get cell groups started in your church, don't neglect your own family. Be sensitive to "seasons" of ministry. Raising godly children is very time-consuming. Setting reasonable expectations for yourself, your wife, and your children during this demanding period will yield long-term fruit without inflicting burnout.

Guard your home and marriage. Guard your heart from sexual temptations and any counseling or ministry to those of the opposite sex who could place you in a position for either temptation or accusation. Guard your family as you engage in spiritual warfare prayer on a regular basis.

A pastor's true spiritual ministry begins at home with his own family and then flows from there out to others. As pastors take these practical steps to include and equip their wives, God's kingdom and their own ministries will be multiplied.

QUESTIONS FOR THE PASTOR'S WIFE

Think about your answers to the following questions. Share your insights with your husband.

- How are you already ministering alongside your husband in natural, practical ways, (such as building relationships with couples in the church, being present during counseling sessions with women, exercising hospitality, or participating in cell group life)?
- How do you serve "behind the scenes" in quiet, supportive ways, (like listening to him, challenging his ideas, sharing your insights, and encouraging him)?
- What are your spiritual gifts? How do your gifts complement your husband's gifts and benefit his ministry? (For example, are you administrative in such a way that you help keep him organized and on schedule?)
- What's your calling? Do you feel equally as called to the ministry as he is? To what extent and in what roles are you willing to serve?
- If you have children, how old are they? What do they need from you and your husband at this stage of their development?
- Without adverse affects on your home life, how much time can you realistically give to sharing ministry with your husband? Is now the proper season for ministry to the larger body of Christ?
- Are you spiritually submitted to your husband and his pastoral authority? Being a married woman functioning under your husband's headship, what ministry will he release you to do?
- Are you truly supportive of your husband's ministry? How do you demonstrate your support in your attitudes? Do you honor your husband and his call before your children and church members?
- Describe your personality. Are you part of the key leadership team that God is putting together in your church? How do your personality and spiritual gifts fit together with your husband's gifts and those of others who serve on the team? What role(s) do you sense God wants you to play within your cell group church and within your cell group?
- How do you and your husband function together spiritually? Do you regularly pray and read the Bible together? Why or why not? How can you improve in the area of growing spiritually, both individually and together?

DEALING WITH COMPETING VISIONS AND PROGRAMS

M. Scott Boren

Dion Robert, pastor of the 150,000-member Works and Mission Baptist Church in the Ivory Coast, states, "Where there are two visions, there is di-vision." The church is the body of Christ. In order for a body to work properly, it must operate in unity around a single vision. Christ as the head provides the vision for the body. The body parts do not provide the vision for Christ.

Sadly, churches have operated with each body part having a different vision. This results in churches going in many different directions, so busy doing what they think is God's work that they have no time to stop and ask what God wants them to do.

Bill Beckham writes about barriers that keep churches small. One of these barriers he calls the "fragmented vision barrier." He writes:

> Churches remain the same year after year, not because they have no vision but because they have too many visions. One church has a vision for Bible study, another for women's work and still another for worship, and for discipleship and for children's work and for youth work and for prison ministry or a marriage ministry or a particular gift or a political or social cause. The many good visions keep small churches small and ineffective churches ineffective by standing in the way of a unified vision.
>
> Each vision establishes its own kingdom and each kingdom has a king or queen. To encroach upon another kingdom means war. Or the church allows all kingdoms to stake out territory and for the sake of peace to control that particular part of the church. This is the "balkanization" of the church. This multiple kingdom, multiple vision approach keeps the church fragmented and weak.[1]

In order for average North American churches to develop an effective cell group system, pastors must lead their people into unity around God's vision for the church. Here are a few steps that will serve as a guide.

DETERMINE THE VISION

One of the primary reasons churches are infested with multiple visions that compete with one another is that people have not had a compelling vision that's large enough to get behind and draw them into unity. Therefore, pastors feel like they're relegated to being a caretaker of others' visions.

Ephesians 4 states that leaders are set in the church "to prepare God's people for works of service, so that the body of Christ may be built up until we all reach the unity of the faith ..." Apostles, prophets, evangelists, pastors, and teachers are set in a church to prepare the people for ministry that leads them into unity. They're not called to facilitate a worship service for a crowd of individuals who are going about their disparate personal visions.

One church had many strong Christian leaders who attended, but they didn't get involved beyond attending weekly worship services. Instead they were committed to various parachurch ministries in the area. When the senior pastor talked with them about their involvement in these ministries and their lack of involvement in the church, it became obvious that the key factor was vision. These parachurch ministries had a compelling vision. This specific church did not have a vision that was any bigger than getting people to church on Sunday morning. These leaders wanted to be part of something with a vision to transform people's lives.

Before the competing visions in a church can be addressed, a big vision must capture the leaders of the church, specifically the senior leader. Until this vision gets in him and compels him to new ways of being the church, it will prove impossible to get other visions aligned around a unified vision.

IDENTIFY OTHER VISIONS

In many churches, members have become so accustomed to the reality of competing visions that it has become the *modus operandi*. Most don't even see the competing visions anymore, because they've become part of the flow of church life. For instance, choir practice has been held for the last twenty years on Wednesday night. Also on Wednesday night, the youth meet for a youth worship service, the pastor leads an adult Bible study, and various children's programs are held.

Each of these has an individual vision, but no one quite knows what that vision is. These activities just happen, whether or not they fit into a larger vision. Eventually the vision becomes: "to keep the activity going." Someone must determine the current vision for each activity in the church. Here are some key areas where the visions must be identified:

What's the youth pastor's vision? Is it to create a biblical community of young people? Is it to entertain young people so growth can occur and he can eventually get a job at a bigger church? Is it to serve faithfully, using youth ministry as a stepping stone to become a senior pastor?

What's the vision for children? Is this an effective ministry that's attracting young families? Is it stuck doing the same form of ministry developed fifty years ago? Is there anyone who has a vision for the children, or are people just filling positions?

What's the vision for Sunday school? Has anyone articulated the vision of Sunday School in the last five years? If so, who carries this vision? Or are people just going through the motions of doing what they've always done? If so, what's the unstated vision?

What's the vision for worship? Is there a stated vision for worship? Is the church fulfilling this vision? Or is it just singing songs and listening to the choir perform beautiful medleys?

What's the vision for the primary weekly service (usually Sunday morning)? The answer to this question might seem obvious at first, but most churches haven't articulated the vision of their Sunday morning service. They're stuck doing the same thing in their services, because they've done those things for the last fifty years.

What's the vision for secondary services (i.e. Sunday night and Wednesday night)? It's interesting to learn that the original intent of the Sunday night service was an evangelistic service to reach farmers who worked all day. In many traditions, Wednesday night was designed to be a prayer service. Do your secondary services have a vision? Or are they just repetitions of the Sunday morning service, done for a smaller crowd?

What's the vision for women's programs and men's programs? Many denominations have programs for women and men. If these are used, what's their vision?

What other visions have been developed?

EVALUATE THE VISION CARRIERS

Through the identification of visions, the people who carry these visions will become obvious. The volunteer music minister puts much energy into what he does with the choir every week. The Sunday school director has served the church in this capacity for the last fifteen years. The youth pastor is young and brought in a vision he saw working at the church in which he grew up. People like these are the vision carriers. Each has an investment in their visions.

Evaluate each vision carrier and determine which ones are the most open to a new vision. Ask questions like:

- Who thinks outside the box?
- Who's frustrated with the status quo?
- Who leads with a constant desire to follow God's new direction and is stretching the boundaries?

On a second level, evaluate each vision carrier to determine the one or two who influence the vision of the entire church. John Maxwell calls these people the E. F. Huttons—referring to the old commercial that stated, "When E. F. Hutton speaks, people listen." It's rare to find a church which doesn't have an E. F. Hutton. People wait for this person or persons to speak whenever it comes to something new. Pastors are wise to work with these people and get them on board.

EVALUATE CURRENT PROGRAMS

After identifying the various visions and evaluating the openness of the vision carriers, the next step is to list all the current programs in the church. This would include every committee, every ministry, every outreach, every singing group, even things like Vacation Bible School and missions trips. The pastor then should work with a team of key leaders (the Cell Group Vision Team would participate) to determine if these programs contribute positively to the new vision of the church. To help facilitate this evaluation, these leaders can use the following categories: dead, wean now, wean eventually, simplify, and keep and refocus.

The dead programs are those that can be eliminated now before the church starts cell groups, as they serve no purpose—a fact that's obvious to almost everyone. There are other programs that still have some life, but it's clear that they don't conflict with the new vision. These fit into the category of "wean now," and the church leaders can begin the process of de-emphasizing their importance.

A third category would include those programs that still have some life

**Cell Group
Vision Team Exercise**

1. List all of the ministries and programs that are now operating in your church.
2. Put each one into one of the following categories:
   Dead
   Wean now
   Wean eventually
   Simplify
   Keep and Refocus

and they conflict with the new vision. But many people feel deeply attached to them. Therefore, to eliminate them or de-emphasize them at this point would be detrimental, so leaders would wean these programs down the road, after cell groups are started.

The category called "simplify" includes those programs the leaders feel God is saying to keep, but they need to be retooled so they don't take up so much time and energy. In the last category of "keep and refocus" are those programs that are essential, but they need to be focused on the new vision of the church rather than the disparate visions of the past.

The goal of this evaluation isn't to eliminate everything now so cell groups can flourish. The guiding rule is "Never take something away until it can be replaced with something else." If the pastor terminates all programs, people will feel frustrated and lost, and most likely will leave. They won't understand the reason for the sudden change. Therefore the move from the old to the new would look something like this:

New Vision and Programs

Old Vision and Programs

TIME

BUILD CREDITS

Many pastors have caught a vision from God and have assumed that other vision carriers would readily embrace their vision. But such an attitude often results in feelings of pastoral control or even abuse. Such feelings most often occur when the pastor hasn't built up enough credits in the leadership bank account to deserve the trust of these vision carriers. A pastor low in credits won't have much ability to introduce a new vision, especially the vision of church transformation to cell groups. Therefore, he must invest in his people and build up the leadership bank account. Only then will he secure the trust of the vision carriers.

Credits are built on the organization level as the pastor demonstrates his ability to lead the church. On a deeper and maybe more important level, the pastor builds up credits on an emotional level as he befriends these vision carriers. As he demonstrates genuine care for them, he'll see open doors to begin to share his vision. In other words, the first meeting a pastor has with these people should not be to share his vision.

PRAY

Communicating new vision, especially one that's large enough to unify the entire church, should not be done recklessly. Some are ready to hear the vision. Others need time. And still others look unready on the surface, but God knows their heart. Pastors must depend upon God's leading during this time. This is no time for a pastor's desires to "get things done" to supercede his listening to God's direction.

ASK TO SHARE THE CELL GROUP VISION

As the pastor develops trust with these vision carriers, he'll discover natural ways to share his vision. He should ask permission to introduce a radical approach to ministry that the Lord has been revealing to him. By asking permission, he's demonstrating mutual submission to the other person, which will make the new vision feel less threatening.

In sharing the vision, the pastor should be careful not to overwhelm the vision carrier. He or she might not be ready to learn about everything. It might prove too overwhelming, especially if the pastor is so zealous for the cell groups that everything else seems like the handiwork of the enemy.

PRESENT THE NEW WAY AND DIALOGUE ABOUT NEW ROLES

As the vision carrier learns about the cell group vision, he or she needs to learn how it works. This might come through reading, a conference, or visiting a cell group church. In order to help the person process the vision, the pastor should enter into dialogue with him about how his role fits into the new vision. Of course, the pastor will have ideas about how his role will change, but it's best to discover together what the new role will look like, rather than having it prescribed by the pastor.

TRANSFORMING THE CHURCH CONSTITUTION AND GOVERNMENT TO RELEASE VISION AND MINISTRY

Joel Comiskey

A church board was seriously considering a transition and they wanted to know how to change their constitution to reflect a future cell church philosophy. One successful banker piped up, "I think we should radically change our existing constitution. Let's declare we're a cell church, rewrite the constitution, and move on." He referred to this approach as the "big bang" theory to changing the current constitution.

At first my heart united with his zeal, and I inwardly rejoiced in such a radical commitment. Yet, as I spent the entire week consulting with this church, I soon realized the board members weren't willing to live the values they wanted to write on paper. They were willing to change the constitution, but they weren't willing to do what they wanted others to do.

I told board members, "If you wanted to make a radical commitment to transition your church to a cell group church, it would mean far more than changing a piece of paper. A 'big bang' change would be for each of you to prepare to lead your own cell group. Such an action would shout loudly to the rest of the congregation that you're serious about your intentions." My banker friend didn't comment because he wasn't really willing to commit himself. Changing a constitution can't change people's values.

DO YOU NEED TO CHANGE THE CONSTITUTION?

Many constitutions are very generic and specifically avoid naming any one philosophy of ministry. Jim Clark, Executive Senior Apostle of the International Network of Local Churches—of which Bethany World Prayer Center is a part, says,

> The church constitution deals with governmental polity, doctrine, purpose and legal entities of church life, not with strategies, programs or methods, (if this were the case most churches would be changing their constitution on a regular basis) … I.N.L.C. has a generic constitution for all of our participating churches. Not one of them that I am aware of mentions "cell strategy" or "cell program" or even the church practicing "cells" in their constitution. … We have never found a need to name or define a "strategy" into a church constitution.[2]

Resist trying to change the constitution too early. These three stages represent slow, steady progress toward revision:

Stage 1: Develop a covenant of cell church values all key leaders should have, read, and embrace. The lead pastor would then push those values on every occasion.
Stage 2: Tweak the actual constitution to reflect leader and member cell involvement.
Stage 3: Change the constitution/bylaws to reflect cell church realities.

The exception to the above order is when a pastor is strapped with a constitution that hinders cell ministry. In this case, he must deal with the situation right away. One church had to "remove mandatory committees and other operational structures not compatible with a cell-based church" before they could even begin their transition.[3]

If the constitution/bylaws hinder cell-based ministry, the pastor should begin by talking to key leaders (e.g. elders, board members, etc.) on a conceptual level about how the cell group church will eventually affect the status quo. He must lead the power people in the church to a clear understanding of what the church will look like after transitions. Experts in the field of change recommend a retreat setting to sort through the issues.

During such a retreat the pastor should talk about the current constitutional roadblocks and get approval to remove those stipulations and proceed in a different direction. This doesn't mean the entire constitution needs to be rewritten. Dennis Wadley transitioned a small, traditional church with outdated bylaws into a large, dynamic cell group church in Santa Barbara, California. He suggests that pastors resist constitutional change until the cell church has been established:

> I would suggest that a constitution be changed when the cell vision of the church is functioning and stable and the old constitution no longer reflects who they are as a church. We were a couple of years into our cell transition when we realized that what was on paper was not reflected in who we were. We then wrote the constitution to reflect who we were and what God was doing. I wouldn't ever want to write a church constitution as a vision statement of what is to come ... that would become target practice in a congregationally run church.[4]

Most pastors have constitutions, bylaws, and forms of church government that grant enough wiggle room to begin cell ministry with the hope of transforming structures as people's lives are changed.

STEP ONE: MAKE A COVENANT OF CELL VALUES

On a micro-level, many cell groups make a covenant or agreement about what they want to see take place. Such cell group covenants often include commitments for weekly attendance, evangelism, discipleship, and multiplication of the group. In a similar way, but on a macro level, a wise pastor can begin by writing a cell church covenant that he shares informally with key leaders.

Dave Scott, pastor of New Hope Church in Chino, California, gently, slowly worked with his church staff and congregation to transition to the

Web Resource

See the sample statements of ministry values, available as a free download from <www.cell-grouppeople.com>.

cell model. He modeled cell-based ministry by leading a cell and multiplying it. As the vision caught among leadership, Dave didn't touch the formal constitution, but wrote a new covenant that captured the key values of his church. Pastor Dave concentrated on establishing cell values and seeing genuine transformation before dealing with the formal constitution. He taught these values to the key leaders of his church, which included board, cell leaders, interns, and staff.

The ministry value statement set forth the future direction of the church. Since the constitution in Dave's church didn't promote a philosophy of ministry, Dave didn't feel the need to change anything right away.

STEP TWO: GIVE THE EXISTING CONSTITUTION A CELL CHURCH TWIST

Most church constitutions cover doctrinal belief, the role of leadership (e.g., pastor's role, elders' role, board's role, and membership responsibilities), church discipline, and church government.

Becoming a cell church probably won't change doctrinal issues or your form of government. Successful cell churches around the world function in all kinds of church governments. (e.g., there's an explosion of cell church interest among the Anglican Church of England.[5])

A Presbyterian-type government is elder driven, whereas a Congregationalist government elects leaders through a democratic, congregational meeting. My own denomination, the Christian and Missionary Alliance, asks the annual church assembly, made up of church members, to elect the church board and elders, who will make authoritative decisions throughout the year. Independent and interdenominational-type churches take different approaches.

Larry Kreider, founder of the cell group church movement called DOVE Christian Fellowship, holds to the plurality of elders. He and three elders wrote an excellent book called *The Biblical Role of Elders for Today's Church*.[6] This book spells out the biblical requirements for elders. Beyond these basic requirements, Kreider writes, "We always recommend that anyone who desires to serve as an elder should first serve as a small group leader. This gives them an opportunity to learn how to lead in a smaller setting. It is best if they have been able to successfully train assistant leaders and have helped the group multiply into two or more groups."[7]

The first place you can give your constitution a cell church twist is to

Written Resources

Biblical Role of Elders for Today's Church by Larry Kreider, et.al.

make sure those serving in positions of leadership not only fulfill the Biblical qualifications (2 Timothy 3, Titus 1), but also are involved in the cell vision, thus showing their values by their actions. It's my conviction, for example, that an elder or board member should be currently leading a cell group as a prerequisite to serving in a governing role in the congregation. Dennis Wadley said,

> We set up a constitution that reflected our denomination's congregational structure, but only put ministry leaders in place who have risen up from among the cell ministry ranks … The key is that the only way to become an overseer is to first serve as a cell leader and then to move into a role of overseeing cells. With this restriction, the overseer's leadership is fully committed to the vision of the church.

Wadley's last two sentences reflect the goal behind this step in the process. The goal is to make sure those in leadership are one-hundred percent committed to cell ministry, not only by their words but by their actions.

Damian Williams guided Red Cedar Community Church (Wesleyan denomination) in Rice Lake, Wisconsin from a few cells and 200 people to 30 cells and 600 people. He established the rule that everyone on the board had to be leading a cell group. "This was one of the wisest decisions I made," he reported. "Everyone in key positions of leadership are leading cell groups and these same leaders want the new pastor to hold to those same cell church principles."

Some take cell group involvement beyond cell leadership. One denominational pastor spelled it out this way:

1. Within one year, every board member should be a member of a cell.
2. Within two years, every board member must be leading a cell.
3. Within three years, every board member must have multiplied a cell to remain on the board.

A Christian and Missionary Alliance church transformed its structure to reflect cell church values by adding additional bylaws that declared:

• Only those attending a cell are considered members of the church and are eligible to vote at annual assembly. They wanted to make sure every voting member was intimately involved in cell ministry by at least being an active participant in a cell group.

- Only those who are leading a cell group are eligible to be elected to serve on the board. This helped assure the pastoral team that those who were serving on the board, and making many of the key financial decisions, were in accord with the cell vision. Later in our cell church transition, the requirements stated: "Only those who are leading a cell group and have multiplied a cell at least once are eligible to be elected to serve on the board."

This assured that those serving on the board were in total agreement with the cell church structure. This also guards against individual board members from promoting their own agenda and leading the church away from the cell church philosophy.

These requirements would not be possible for someone just starting the cell church transition, but they can be future church goals. Beyond leadership requirements, the constitution should also spell out membership responsibilities. Faithful cell attendance should be a prerequisite to church membership. The bylaws at Dove Fellowship say, "The membership of the church shall consist of those persons who … shall be a member in good standing of a cell group."[8]

STEP THREE: REFORM THE ENTIRE CONSTITUTION

Steve Mack writes, "It is unwise to allow an obsolete constitution or bylaws to sit un-amended. Cell church pastors should swallow hard and take the steps necessary to make the changes to the constitution/bylaws, so they reflect the way the church is currently operating."[9] Once the majority of the church's elected leadership has embraced cell values and actively participates in cell life, it's time to reshape the constitution to reflect what's actually happening.

Revision of the Decision-Making Team

Many constitutions make pastors the employees of the church. Floyd Evers, pastor of Bear Valley Community Church, says, "While there are tragic examples of churches that have been blown up by autocratic, egotistical leadership, there are many thousands of churches that are small, having reached their peak or diminishing, at least in part, because of gover-

Web Resource

View sample church constitutions and bylaws from cell-based churches, available as a free download from <www.cellgrouppeople.com>.

nance issues."[10]

Rick Warren said, "What do the words committees, elections, majority rule, boards, board members, parliamentary procedures, voting, and vote have in common? None of these words is found in the New Testament!"[11]

When possible, pastors and key leaders should try to change or rephrase the constitution so that it's pastor/leader driven, rather than controlled by boards and committees.[12] In working with one denominational church whose superintendent has given the pastor complete liberty to throw out old bylaws and create new ones, he decided to convert his G-12 group into the elder board and key decision-making board. (A G-12 group is made up of cell leaders and mainly those who have multiplied cells.) This pastor will continue to have a separate group of elected board members to deal with financial/salary questions.

It's wise to maintain a separate board of leaders who can help make key financial decisions in the church. Pastor Lawrence Khong, pastor of Faith Community Baptist Church in Singapore, wrote,

> The church board has its place. Even the most anointed and God-appointed leaders will recognize their fallibility and need of others, so they will surround themselves with a team. Nevertheless, the board is not to rule, but to counsel. The board is not to dominate but to support. The board is not to restrain, but to release the pastor into God's purposes. Otherwise, we violate God's pattern of leadership.[13]

Doctrinal Changes

What about the doctrinal statement in the cell church? Ralph Neighbour, Jr. and Bill Beckham, working together to plant a church in Houston Texas, have transformed its doctrinal statement to reflect cell group church values.

The TOUCH Family Church affirms the basic tenets of the evangelical faith:

- We believe that there is one God, eternally existent in three persons: Father, Son, and Holy Spirit.
- We believe the Bible is the inspired and only infallible and authoritative Word of God.
- We believe in the Genesis account of creation.

- We believe in the deity of Christ, His virgin birth, His sinless life, His miracles, His vicarious and atoning death through His shed blood, His bodily resurrection, His ascension to the right hand of the Father, and in His personal return in power and glory.
- We believe that salvation is the free gift of God and is possessed by each individual who has, by faith, received Jesus Christ as Savior and Lord. We believe salvation is a finished work because of Calvary and is received in three stages:
   1. At the cross, the blood of Christ sets us forever free from the penalty of sin.
   2. Through the living Christ working in his body members, He sets us free from the power of sin.
   3. At His return, He will set us free from the presence of sin.
- We believe in the resurrection of both the saved and the lost, they that are saved unto the resurrection of life and they that are lost unto the resurrection of damnation.
- We believe "church" describes the "called-out people," baptized by the Holy Spirit to form the body of Christ on earth today.
- We want to make it plain that we believe the cell IS the church, the body of Christ! The church does not have a membership; it has body members. There is no membership in the TOUCH Family Church apart from active participation in a cell group.
- We believe in the present and living ministry of the Holy Spirit, who indwells and empowers every Christian for service. He imparts spiritual gifts to all as needed, so all will become agents of Christ's love and impart God's grace to others.
- We believe the Great Commission is a calling upon all believers and that every member must be fully equipped and released to fulfill their callings in ministry. This will be done through the community of the cell group, the "Basic Christian Community."
- We believe that every believer is accountable for the proper investment of time and income, and that we are to be responsible to and for each other as we live as a Christian family.

THE PROBLEM OF WINESKINS

God is moving in a new, powerful way through cell group churches worldwide. The problem is that most church constitutions navigate waters that no longer exist. While some churches have the luxury of creating new, fresh constitutions to match their New Testament vision, most do not.

If your church is in the latter category, I'd encourage you to start with a statement of vision and values as you begin the cell church transition. As you progress, tweak the existing constitution/bylaws to favor cell ministry and those involved in it. Later, as a full-blown cell church, you'll have little resistance and lots of help to reform your constitution to match your new wineskin.

IMPROVING CORPORATE WORSHIP

Twyla Brickman and Randall G. Neighbour

The second chapter of Acts tells that people met from house to house and in the temple courts. Those temple court meetings were important, and must have been exciting! Imagine the electricity in the air as the apostles preached the Good News, drawing the house church members together as one body to rejoice over what was going on in their midst. Because this was a public meeting in an open area, anyone near the group could join in and learn of the Messiah, and experience the power of the Holy Spirit teeming through the believers assembled there.

In his widely-used book, *Natural Church Development*, Christian Schwarz reveals—through extensive research among 2500 churches around the world—that "inspiring corporate worship" is one of the key characteristics of a healthy church. He writes:

> Whenever the Holy Spirit is truly at work (and His presence is not merely presumed), He will have a concrete effect upon the way a worship service is conducted including the entire atmosphere of a gathering. People attending truly "inspired" services typically indicate that "going to church is fun."[5]

Excellent corporate worship, or the kind of event that draws believers and unbelievers together in an exciting way, is vital to a growing cell ministry! To experience inspired worship to the level described by Schwarz, the following must be present:

- Everything is done for the glory of God. The praise and worship is directed toward God, making his heart glad because believers are gathered in his name.
- Outward expressions and inner motives that are shaped by God's Word, not by traditions that have died and withered, yet still remain.
- Praise and worship that's offered by those who've been set free to love God, to celebrate his goodness, and to express their joy without bondage, fears, or inhibitions.
- People attending feel a strong sense of celebration for all Jesus has done and is doing. The reality of his living presence is in the midst. In this environment, worship becomes a wholehearted response to the Lord.
- The lost can easily see and hear what our God has done for his followers. As songs of praise are lifted, unbelievers are amazed at God's realness, the great things he has done, and the abandonment with which people love him.

Here is a series of questions for the senior pastor and his team to discuss, followed by a statement revealing the reason for asking the question.

WORSHIP QUESTIONS

- Is worship a high, if not the highest, priority of your church? Why or why not?

The senior pastor's understanding of worship is critical. If he values worship, then resources, time, and personnel will be available for the worship ministry. There's no greater biblical priority than one's relationship with God. Worship is also eternal. Other ministries will pass away, but eternity will be filled with the continual worship of God.

- Are there doctrinal issues that must be addressed concerning worship?

Each denomination has 'do's' and 'don'ts' surrounding worship. Some are biblical and others are simply based out of tradition or what's comfortable to the leadership.

• Have church members made a paradigm and values shift toward more meaningful worship?

Most churches which have successful cell ministries have usually undergone a shift to dynamic, Spirit-led, corporate worship, leaving behind the traditions that were hollow, yet familiar. If your church members aren't flexible enough to adapt to changes in corporate worship, they'll find it even more difficult to make the greater changes required to live in basic Christian community and embrace the Great Commandment and Great Commission as a cell group team.

• Is the congregational worship leader empowered and released to do his/her ministry of leading worship? Is there coordination between the senior pastor and the worship leader?

The senior pastor should work closely with the worship leader to discuss and coordinate the congregational service. However, the worship leader must be free to be creative and give leadership to his/her ministry without being hamstrung by the senior pastor. Extreme time limitations, rules, inflexibility, and interruptions to the flow of worship during services will adversely affect what the worship leader can successfully facilitate.

• Does the senior pastor visibly participate in corporate worship?

His personal participation before the congregation is very important. When the congregation sees the pastor singing, lifting hands, kneeling, or dancing, it models freedom in worship. His worship underscores the value of spending time focused on the person of God, giving him worship.

TIPS FOR IMPROVING CORPORATE WORSHIP

Worship isn't simply singing a few songs, saying a few prayers, and moving on to the next item on the agenda, or "getting to the main part—the sermon." Here are some practical ideas and observations about corporate worship that are, as Schwarz states, "fun":

• Allow for a musical flow and focused attention on God.
• Create a sense of anticipation. The order of service need not always be spelled out in detail in a church bulletin. Be flexible and keep worshippers expecting that something new is just around the corner.
• An average worship time is about forty-five minutes. However, some churches worship an hour and others only worship thirty minutes.

- While there may be some intimate worship, the main focus is on a corporate experience. As a consequence, most of the music will emphasize celebration and exaltation. (The cell group meeting provides an atmosphere for intimate worship.)
- The congregational worship service is not a large cell group meeting. It's designed for very different purposes to meet the needs of a large number of people gathered in one place. Attempting to make the use of prayer, worship, fellowship, and release of spiritual gifts like a large cell meeting, guts the congregational service of its unique place and unwittingly limits the congregation's size.
- Items such as announcements, baptisms, greeting visitors, taking the offering, etc. are carefully placed before or after worship. If performed during the worship time, these must be woven seamlessly, as acts of worship themselves.
- Whenever the order of service is altered in a major way, consider how such a change will impact other ministries (i.e. children's church). Communicate with ministry leaders in advance.

As leaders teach their congregation how to worship, they must be patient and go slowly. The process of becoming a free worshipper of God is not an overnight event. Move members gradually into a new way of worshipping.

This is best done in a Sunday evening or mid-week service, allowing the effectiveness to "spill over" into Sunday morning services. It may be helpful to add a brief teaching on worship to the Sunday bulletin, explaining various ways people of God can express their gratitude in a corporate setting. As services begin, the worship leader can provide mini-teachings on worship to encourage the congregation to try something new. He may also wish to introduce a new form of worship through a workshop, or make recorded praise and worship available to members.

Inspiring and exciting corporate worship is vital to the success of cell ministry. Transitioning this part of the church is as important as any other, so carefully examine large group gatherings. Ask members if they come expectantly, and find it "fun." Work hard to move your congregation into a truly celebratory experience each week.

HOW WORSHIP TEAM MEMBERS PARTICIPATE IN CELL GROUPS

The following approaches have proven to work well:

1. All worship team members are part of different weekly cell groups. Their participation in the worship team is separate from the cell groups. They meet for practice at times that will not interfere with cell life, i.e. before Sunday worship services.

2. The worship team pastor serves as a cell pastor over cell groups that are comprised of worship team members. These cell groups meet on a separate night from worship team practice. The cell group meetings are open groups just like all of the other cell groups.

3. The worship team pastor serves as a cell pastor over cell groups that meet in conjunction with the worship team practices. These cell group meeting tend to occur 45 minutes to one hour before worship practices. Some churches have been able to make these cell meetings open and evangelistic just like other cell groups. Others have had difficulty doing so.

Stage 5:
Launch the First Groups with Kingdom-seekers

STARTING STRONG FOR FUTURE GROWTH

34

Bill Beckham

God created the world in seven days, not just one. The creative processes of each day were dependent upon his previous creative acts. God celebrated after each day and declared that it was "good." This means he celebrated the continuing process of creation, and not just the finished product. The church must learn to celebrate and use process rather than fearing it.

The unfolding story of the Bible is a process. God patiently moved the children of Israel through hundreds of years of process. The statement that Jesus came in the "fullness of time" implies a process moving toward a moment of completeness. We should not be surprised that Jesus used a step-by-step process to build the first church. However, the secret is to properly identify and apply the process.

THE "BIG BANG" THEORY OF STARTING GROUPS

One method of beginning a cell group church is the popular, but flawed, "big bang" theory. The "big bang" theory develops out of a cataclysmic event by which the church appears complete and fully formed. This theory is the opposite of the process principle Jesus used to build the first church, and it contradicts the factual evidence about how successful cell group churches have been developed. Every successful cell group church went through a process, sometimes for several years, and through several stages.

Church leaders, especially pastors of large churches, are attracted to the "big bang" theory because it seems to eliminate much of the pain and patience required in a step-by-step process. It promises to give instant gratification to vision. However, the "big bang" theory is a fatal attraction. It weakens the learning process of leaders and compromises the developing process necessary to strengthen the infrastructure.

Large cell churches may contaminate leaders with the "big bang" theory by teaching about the finished product, the cell group church, rather than the process that brought them to the finished product. In conferences, these cell group churches share exciting statistics and stories about current and projected growth. Leaders attending these conferences receive a revelation vision from God and an anointing to become a cell group church. However, when they go back home, frustration sets in because they can't ignite the "big bang." They're left with a "dud" because they don't understand the process that leads to the type of growth observed in these large churches.

These successful cell group churches teach an incomplete process by leaving out the early stages of their growth. They teach a "big bang" Pentecost experience and skip over the years of process through which Jesus carefully, patiently, and painfully took them. Their success actually covers up the process, and churches trying to "big bang" their finished product are doomed to frustration and failure.

A teaching cell group church must go back to the beginning and document the step-by-step process that brought them to the place of transition and growth. The beginning how-to process is what new cell group churches need to understand and is what an existing cell group church needs to teach.

A LEADERSHIP PROCESS

Process Circle

For years I searched the Gospels for the process Jesus used to build the first church. I know now why the process always eluded me. The Gospels were written from different perspectives, with different objectives, and with different chronological orders. Finally, during an extensive parallel study of the Gospels, the numbers jumped out at me: 2 or 3, 12, 70, 120, and 3000. I realized the same numbers are present in each of the Gospels and reveal Jesus' process for building his church and establishing the New Testament movement.

Jesus' process developed incrementally around leaders. In the process circle, Jesus first gathered a pool of potential followers and leaders from whom he would choose his initial core of twelve. This core of leaders was called to commitment and obedience. Jesus then tested his system with a group of committed leaders that grew from 12 to 70. He organized his church while the 70 grew to the coordinating unit of 120. Jesus consolidated and completed his model with the 120 in the upper room. At this point the church reached critical mass and expanded to 3000 and beyond!

The upper end of the numbers shows the potential size, not the required size, or even the preferred size of the church. A local church can be any size God desires, but it will operate with at least one base congregation like Jesus' 120.

A STEP-BY-STEP PROCESS

Let's consider the process Jesus used to build the first church within a ministry period of three to four years. That's the amount of time Jesus devoted to the process before "big bang" evangelism happened at Pentecost.

(Most churches today find that Jesus' timeline must be extended to at least seven years before experiencing exponential growth.) The following chart shows the leadership process, the structural process, and the tools process.

Some form of this process will be used in every attempt to establish a cell group church. The process applies to a new start, a small church that desires to break

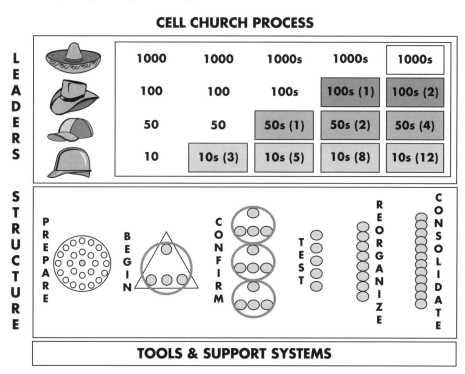

CELL CHURCH PROCESS

through stagnation, or a large church that needs to develop its first cell group church coordinating congregation. "A journey of a thousand miles begins with one step."

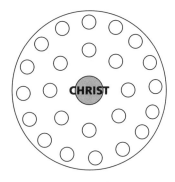

Jesus' Leadership Circle

What did Jesus do first in his process? Imagine a large circle surrounding Jesus as he began his ministry at the Jordan River.

This large circle was empty in the beginning. However, Jesus filled the circle with enough potential leaders to build the first stages of his movement. That leadership circle may have consisted of as many as seventy potential leaders who would be brought into his stages of development at the proper time. Out of this initial pool of followers, he identified, prepared, and called the twelve, and designated the three.

It's important to remember that Jesus' early followers didn't just "fall off a turnip truck." Like John the Baptist, their preparation as Jews prepared them to be part of Jesus' movement. They were trained in Old Testament Scriptures and biblical values. These were not dysfunctional people who had to be reeducated about normal life and behavior. The quality of Jesus' initial followers is an important factor to remember when a leader today begins a new church. The more mature the initial leaders, the better.

The leadership circle in the chart below is located between the first two process steps of "Prepare" and "Begin." The first step in the process is to follow Jesus' example. Choose key leaders to be part of a leadership circle.

In the transition of an existing church, this leadership circle should have representatives from the church staff, the governing body of the church, key influence leaders, and productive members. (Seventy is a good number to begin with in a large church). In a new start, the catalytic leader must gather followers to be part of the leadership circle before beginning the process. This is best done within the structure of a sending mother church.

If a new church is started by a small number of leaders without a team or a mother church, the early months must be used to contact and win potentially productive believers and prepare them in the leadership circle. Additional time and much patience must be allowed for this kind of solo start. In this scenario, initial followers must first be prepared and grow in maturity, before they can be used to develop a healthy pattern cell and establish a working prototype.

The purpose of the leadership circle is to introduce the concepts,

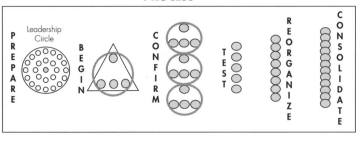

PROCESS

values, and vision to a key group of leaders. This can be done through one-on-one meetings, special vision retreats, conferences, and sharing books and materials.

Developing a commitment to evangelism should be a primary focus during the leadership circle stage. This initial stage is an excellent time for leaders to experience evangelism personally, which will lead to cells committed to new conversion growth. Share groups and interest groups of all kinds provide a venue to develop this evangelism commitment within the leadership circle.

Leaders should also experience a witness encounter in which one method of personal witness will eventually be learned by all members. Alpha, an investigative study of the life of Jesus, was developed in England for contacting and cultivating seekers. It's an excellent way to establish the value of evangelism among leaders during this initial stage.

Information is not the most important focus for the leadership circle. The issue is commitment: commitment to the vision, commitment to the values, commitment to evangelism, and commitment to the project leaders.

BEGINNING A PATTERN CELL

Jesus carefully modeled this basic ministry unit with his twelve because each stage of his process and all his activities were dependent upon basic Christian community.

The pattern cell must be started early in the process and then tested and adapted as the project moves toward critical mass. A pattern cell needs to live out community, equipping, accountability, leadership, and evangelism.

The pattern cell unifies the vision, sets up quality control, establishes spiritual authority, and integrates all systems. Core leaders must receive the cell DNA from God while living together in cell life. The leaders of the pattern cell must die to all personal agendas, discover necessary tools for implementation, commit to the vision, and have a reproducible pattern for the cell meeting.

In the process chart, the initial pattern cell is represented by a triangle with four circles. The circle at the top is Jesus and the three circles at the bottom are Peter, James, and John. Spouses should be included in this first cell experience.

Leaders responsible for developing a cell agenda don't have to rein-

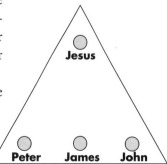

vent the wheel. A general cell agenda has emerged over the past several decades. It's explained in the materials of Ralph Neighbour, Jr., and is used by cell group churches around the world.

For most churches, the cell meeting agenda flows through four relationship experiences:

- You to me and me to you as the members bond in community
- Us to God in worship as the group focuses on Christ in their midst
- God to us in edification as application of the Word takes place
- God through us in ministry to reaching the lost and hurting in the world

This is the normal order of the agenda. The order may, however, be adjusted from time to time in order to help the cell in its growth process. For instance, the focus on the vision for reaching out (God through us) can be moved up if necessary, or the bonding element (you to me and me to you) can be extended when a new group is starting up.

The cell is too important to copy someone else's way of doing it. The pattern will be reproduced over and over. If the pattern is flawed, then all cells that are birthed out of the pattern will be distorted. Without a pattern cell, no quality control is possible.

Jesus

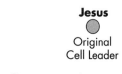

Original
Cell Leader

Peter   James   John

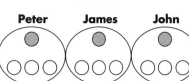

After completing the first "Peter, James, and John" cycle of approximately three months, leaders should enter into another cycle of three months with three more pattern cells. A new cell is formed around Peter, another around James, and another around John. Each cell should have three additional leaders plus their spouses. In the case of an unmarried leader, add another single, or let the cell have an odd number of members.

The leader of the original cell then steps back and supervises the three new cells. This second phase of developing the pattern cell uses what has been learned in the first cell. The goal is to listen to God about the DNA of the cell and to agree upon one cell agenda that will be used by all cells in the future.

CELL EVANGELISM AND THE PATTERN CELL

The initial pattern cell is different from the cells that will come after it in at least two ways. Not all the ministry tasks (community, equipping, accountability, leadership, and evangelism) will be operating at one hundred percent efficiency during the early phases of the prototype. It takes time to learn how to do these tasks and how to integrate them.

Also, the initial pattern cell is the only cell "closed" to unbelievers and new and immature believers. A healthy prototype cannot be developed with disruptive, rebellious, or functionally immature people. Therefore, the lost and new believers will not be brought directly into the initial pattern cell. This follows Jesus' model; he carefully chose those who would be part of his initial prototype and took care of others in different venues. Jesus' leaders weren't perfect. Thomas was filled with doubts, Peter denied Jesus, and James and John fought for position. However, these leaders, in spite of their weaknesses, were not severely disruptive, rebellious, or functionally immature people. They were mature enough to consider the claims of Jesus upon them. Jesus saw their weaknesses, but also their potential to lead his movement.

During the development of the pattern cell, the leaders must not ignore evangelism. Key leaders who are not yet in the pattern cell should continue evangelism in the leadership circle. During the first few months of the process, the lost and new believers should be cared for in other types of groups rather than in the pattern cell.

The purpose of the pattern cell is to receive confirmation from God. This will probably be the only opportunity for leaders to listen to God in a special way about the mechanics and dynamics of cell life.

THE IMPORTANCE OF A PATTERN CELL

The leaders of a cell group church establish a culture through a pattern cell. This begins by deciding on a basic cell pattern all groups and cells will follow and then by providing essential systems through which the culture can be lived out.

The pattern cell is affirmation of God's blessing upon the way the church will live in cell life. Leaders will not live and die for a method from a book or another person, but they will sacrifice for what they receive from God. The pattern cell must be revealed and confirmed by God.

Having one cell pattern establishes spiritual authority and neutralizes the seeds of leadership rebellion that plague many small group systems. The authority of God must surround the pattern cell so the leaders can assure their members that God is the source.

Suppose a leader on your team has always led groups by teaching a Bible study. You ask this leader to follow a certain cell agenda. The Bible teacher might respond with the question, "Why?" How will you respond?

You can respond by asserting your authority as leader: "You should do this because I say so, and I'm the leader!" Or you can assert the authority of a group of leaders: "You should do this because the leadership team wants it done that way." Or you can appeal to the experts: "You should do this because the cell group church experts tell us this is the way to do it." Some leaders who have their own agenda for a cell meeting will defer to these arguments, but not many. Many leaders believe they have a special word from God for their preference in cell life and will claim that leaders who expect conformity are "quenching the Spirit."

But suppose you respond in another way to the question, "Why should I use this pattern?" "You should do this because the leaders of the church have listened to God and this is the way we believe God wants to operate in our groups." Now you operate out of spiritual authority. In the first instance, you have a problem. That problem is how to convince this group leader to submit to your authority or the authority of a group of leaders. In the second example, that group leader has a problem. Will the group leader believe God has spoken to the church leaders?

The commitment of the core leaders strengthens the pattern cell, because God has affirmed it to the leaders so that the pattern isn't just a method learned from a conference or a book. The leaders become so committed to the pattern cell that they expect both existing groups and new cells to use this one pattern. Every cell leader and member will live out the pattern cell's DNA that God has revealed to the leaders. The leaders will then use the systems in the pattern cell as the quality control standard for all cells.

THE LEADERSHIP PROCESS

In a cell group church, four principles of leadership must function through four types of leaders before a church reaches critical mass. These leadership roles wear different hats. In a fully functioning cell group church, leaders will wear one of these hats and fulfill the principles of leadership associated with it.

The leadership process chart below shows five columns of leadership that correspond with the step-by-step structural development. In the beginning, the senior leader of the church will wear all four hats: coordinating, supporting, supervising, and implementing. The senior leader will lead the first cell and continue to coordinate, support, and supervise other areas of the church. His goal is to gradually put a hat on another leader.

During the second step, three leaders are leading pattern cells. This means the senior leader has now taken off the hat of implementing leader, but continues to wear the hat of coordinating leader, supporting leader, and supervising leader.

The third step of testing provides an opportunity to establish another leadership role. The senior leader now has five leaders operating as implementing cell leaders (tens). The senior leader now installs one of the previous leaders as a supervising leader (fifties) over the five cells. Let's suppose Peter, who led one of the original cells, is now the supervising leader over the five test cells (fifties). The senior leader now operates as the coordinating leader (thousands) and as the supporting leader (hundreds).

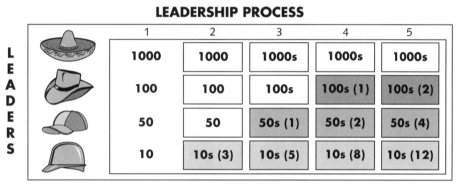

The fourth step of reorganizing moves the leadership development to another stage. More leaders are now operating as implementing cell leaders, and two supporting leaders (fifties), who were previously leaders over one of the cells, oversee the cells. The senior leader now installs a supporting leader over hundreds. This could be Peter, who has already served as a supervising leader of fifties. The senior pastor has now installed all the leadership roles.

Step five consolidates this leadership structure as the operating system of the church. The four principles of leadership are functioning through coordinating leaders (thousands), supporting leaders (hundreds), supervising leaders (fifties), and implementing leaders (tens). The process is complete and the church operates as a fully functioning cell group church.

WE MUST TAKE THE FIRST STEP

Jeff was pastor of a creative church that operated with small groups. On the first day of a conference, the cell group church vision captured his heart. On the second day, as I taught about the necessity to prototype a pattern cell, Jeff was having trouble with the idea. During a break he explained, "I have several groups that are already meeting. Do you think I should go back and prototype with a special leadership group?"

"Yes!" I replied. "That's what I would do!"

Jeff didn't like this advice. I knew he'd return home excited about God's vision, but would proceed without a pattern cell.

At a later training event, I once again taught about the need to use a group of key leaders to prototype the basic cell. Jeff showed me the strategy he had developed and confessed that he hadn't gone back and developed a prototype. This second time he had chosen once again not to prototype, hoping his existing groups would eventually become his working pattern. This same sequence of events took place four months later. Somehow in Jeff's thinking, forming a prototype meant retreat or wasting time.

Four months later, at the close of the third training event, I asked the group, "What are you going to do when you go back home this time?" Jeff stood up and said, "The first thing I'm going to do is repent and go back and develop a pattern cell." Jeff did eventually learn his lesson about the importance of the first step. Sadly, some leaders never learn!

HOW MANY GROUPS CAN YOU START?

M. Scott Boren

Starting a large number of cell groups is easy. Starting an equally large number of healthy groups is much more difficult. Training lots of leaders and inviting volunteers to participate in groups can happen quickly. But such a strategy doesn't guarantee the quality of group that will be started. There's no benefit to starting lots of groups when half of them will most likely end up stagnant and possibly cancerous.

Too many church leaders ask the wrong questions: How many groups can we start? Or how many groups do we have? Instead they should ask: How many people do we have ready to participate in a Kingdom mission? The answer to this question determines how many groups a church can start. The Cell Group Vision Team must determine how many Kingdom seekers, Kingdom-mentored leaders, and Kingdom-centered coaches are in their church.

KINGDOM SEEKERS

Kingdom seekers comprise the list of potential members of the first cell groups. These people are the cream of the crop. Most would identify them as potential leaders instead of potential members. Such an assessment is correct. All the members of the first cell groups must be potential leaders because they'll be leading groups very soon. In addition, the first groups must be strong groups. Strong groups birth future strong groups. If the first groups are weak, then future groups will be weaker.

Remember this: Sit-and-soak Christians are wet towels on cell group life. If such people are included as members of the first cell groups, then don't expect much life to flow out of them. They have little interest in living out the "one anothers" of the New Testament. They treat cell meetings just like any other church meeting. When they do come, they often hide behind religious phrases and "correct" answers. They demonstrate little passion to see the unchurched transformed through an encounter with Christ.

List people who are Faithful,
Available, and Teachable:

_____

_____

_____

_____

_____

_____

_____

_____

_____

_____

_____

_____

_____

_____

_____

_____

_____

_____

_____

_____

_____

_____

_____

_____

_____

On the other hand, those who've been identified as Kingdom-seekers have made an attitude shift that fits cell group life. They want to enter into relational ministry. They commit to minister to the people in the group, not just come to a meeting. They're willing to share their lives transparently and they long to see the unchurched reached.

Here are some questions to help the vision team identify potential Kingdom seekers:

Faithful:

- Has this person done things to undermine the authority of the pastor or other church leaders? (A negative answer here results in automatic disqualification, unless there has been clear repentance.)
- Does this person understand AND AGREE WITH the philosophy and vision of ministry, and does this person support it with consistent attendance and stewardship?
- Has this person undertaken other ministries and followed through to their success?
- Does this person have a heart for God and the fruit of the Spirit that's evidence of his active presence and life?

Available:

- Is this person involved in other areas of ministry that will keep him or her from effective cell group life?
- Are we able to release this person from current ministry responsibilities to serve as an initial member of a cell group?
- Do work or other outside commitments limit this person from being effective in ministry?

Teachable:

- Does this person respond positively when someone challenges his or her thought patterns?
- Does this person work well as part of a team?
- Does this person respond positively to and respect authority?

KINGDOM-MENTORED LEADERS

After determining the list of potential Kingdom seekers, it's time to determine how many leaders are ready to lead the first cell groups. These potential leaders are not the cream of the crop. They are the cream of the cream. These people have received mentoring in relational ministry. They've earned the pastor's high trust and are committed to walking in unity with him.

Most churches in North America will discover they have one leader who's ready to lead a group, the pastor. This is true because most churches have fewer than one hundred people. Some churches will have more, but the best advice is to err on the side of caution.

Review the names listed as Kingdom seekers and ask these questions about each one, to determine how many leaders are prepared to lead groups:

Trustworthy:
- Is this the kind of person you want other cell members to emulate?
- Is this person fulfilling the responsibilities in his or her personal life, family, and job?
- Has this person proven faithful in other leadership responsibilities?

Submitted:
- Does this person honor those in leadership?
- Does this person see himself/herself as a part of a bigger vision that God has given the church?
- Has this person responded positively in any disagreements with leadership?

Trained:
- Has this person been trained in cell ministry?
- Does this person understand the goal of the cell groups and is he/she committed to accomplishing that goal?
- Has this person proven effective in relational ministry in other settings?

List the names of potential leaders:

List the names of potential coaches:

—————————————————

—————————————————

—————————————————

—————————————————

—————————————————

—————————————————

KINGDOM-CENTERED COACHES

For churches that are looking to start more than three groups, it's crucial to determine who's available and ready to coach those new leaders. Churches that launch multiple first-round groups will only see success if they have coaches committed to provide hands-on mentoring and support for the leaders. Coaching these first group leaders will require a much higher commitment than after groups get going. Therefore, it's most likely that initial coaches will be staff members.

Review the list of potential leaders above and ask these questions about each person:

Prepared:
• Is this person experienced and fruitful in effective small group ministry?
• Has this person been exposed to other churches with effective small group ministry?
• Has this person been taught the principles of cell ministry that are specific to the church?

Available:
• Does this person have the time to mentor 3-5 cell leaders?
• Can this person visit one or more cell groups per week?
• Is this person accessible for cell leaders to approach and seek help?

Committed:
• Is this person passionately committed to the cell group ministry vision?
• Is this person called and committed to the ministry and vision of this local church?
• Does this person have the lifestyle values you want your cell leaders and cell members to emulate?

HOW TO INTERPRET THESE LISTS

To determine how many groups you can launch, the Cell Group Vision Team can take the liberal route or the conservative route. The liberal route would mean all the potential cell group leaders get to lead a group, and those listed as Kingdom seekers are placed in these groups. Those identified as coaches would be asked to oversee these groups.

To start strong groups, we recommend the conservative approach. When being conservative, the vision team should begin with the number of potential coaches. Multiply the number of coaches times three (unless there are no names listed). That's the maximum number of groups that can be launched.

For instance, the Cell Group Vision Team at First Church has two people listed as potential coaches and therefore should launch no more than six groups. (Note: a person can serve as both a coach and a cell group leader if time allows. In fact, it's often wise for the coach to do this at the beginning, in order to demonstrate how to lead, rather than tell people how to lead.) Calculate this number below.

From there, divide the number of Kingdom-mentored leaders by two. Because most are very gracious when evaluating people's ability to lead a group, it's best to partner these leaders with other leaders so they can learn together how to lead a group. This number represents the maximum number of groups that can be started. First Church has ten people listed as potential leaders and therefore should start no more than five groups. If there's only one potential leader, only one group can be started. Calculate this number below.

The next step involves dividing the number of Kingdom seekers by eight. This calculation represents the maximum number of groups that can be launched. First Church has identified 28 Kingdom-seekers, which means they can start no more than four groups. Calculate this number below.

Number of coaches x 3 = _____
Number of leaders ÷ 2 = _____
Number of kingdom seekers ÷ 8 = _____

The lowest number equals the maximum number of first cell groups a church should start.

MOVING TO CELLS: HOW TO DEVELOP HEALTHY CELLS VIA A PROTOTYPE

Laurence Singlehurst and Liz West

Laurence Singlehurst is a regular speaker and trainer on cell groups in the United Kingdom, with an emphasis on network evangelism within cell church structures. He is the author of *Evangelism Toolkit, Sowing Reaping Keeping, Loving the Lost,* and *Beyond the Clouds.* Liz West works with Cell UK as a writer and church consultant.

Written Resources

See *Making Cell Groups Work* pages 251-258 on three primary ways to prototype a cell group.

In seeking to become a cell church, we must keep reminding ourselves that we are in a process that starts where we are right now, and takes us to where we want to go. We call this the change process. This process is concerned with:

- What we believe.
- The values that we take from these beliefs.
- The structures that serve these beliefs and values.

Having heard something of the cell idea—perhaps read a book, or been to a conference on it—the temptation is to think, "Yes, I like this," and jump straight into it. This inevitably means that we violate the change process and end up implementing a new structure. We take our existing small group leaders, we train them in the dynamics of being a cell leader, we try to describe the vision to them, we introduce the idea to the church and we tell them that now all our small groups are cells. We have watched this take place many times and we call it the big bang process.

In one or two churches this method has worked well. But for many others, it has left them with a mixed bag. Some of the trained leaders have understood what is happening and are leading cells. However, many remain as small groups with a new name, and retain a lot of the old weaknesses. Inevitably, some of the leaders and congregation feel rushed into the process of becoming a cell church, so when the new vision does not appear to be fulfilling what has been promised, they become disillusioned.

So, we want to encourage a slower process which involves two levels of prototype cells and a period of teaching and preaching to the wider church on the values and visions.

The *Oxford English Dictionary* describes a prototype as "a trial model, preliminary version." This trial or preliminary version allows a safe environment to work through and grasp the issues to be faced in the final version. This, of course, applies to any area where a prototype is used—all car manufacturers spend huge amounts of time working with several prototypes before putting their new vehicle on the production line. They know that time invested at the prototype stage saves hours of recall once a model is on sale. The prototype is tested through all the conditions it will face in the real world. It would spell disaster for a car manufacturer to take the designer's drawings and go straight into production.

THE FIRST PHASE OF PROTOTYPE IS THE LEADERSHIP TEAM

The main leader of the church gathers together the senior leaders and their spouses (single leaders should be included), and for twelve weeks they experience a prototype cell. This will give them some understanding and experience of what they are getting involved in.

At the end of the prototype, these leaders need to pray and seek God, and ask if this is the way forward for their church. Therefore, this is not just the initiative of an enthusiastic leader since all the senior influences in the church are going to be involved in approving this new idea.

THE SECOND PHASE OF PROTOTYPE IS FOR POTENTIAL CELL LEADERS

These are the individuals whom church leaders believe have the necessary skills and character to lead these new cells, which require different skills and abilities to those needed for leading traditional house groups. We call this facilitating leadership. It still requires a level of maturity and leadership, but the leader is going to seek to lead through the people in the cell by a process of facilitation. And the group is as dynamic as the contribution and participation of its members.

These potential cell leaders will, therefore, have experienced what it is like to be in a cell. In the corresponding web resource are suggested cell outlines and the goals to achieve in these two prototypes. These potential cell leaders will—in addition to their twelve weeks in cells—probably need two days of further training. So when they come to lead a cell they will not be leading it purely out of a theory, but out of their own experience.

Health Warning!

To avoid concern from the congregation, explain that the leaders are experimenting with some new ideas. This is also important at the second prototype phase.

Health Warning!

We strongly recommend that the central leadership team lead a cell with the first phase of church members.

A note for small churches: in a small church, the people in the leadership prototype may actually be the people who also lead the first cells. This is fine.

GOALS FOR PROTOTYPE CELLS

While not exhaustive, the following list provides some general goals to work toward in the prototype cells. These goals should be outlined to the group in the early stages and each member's commitment to both the group and the goals should be sought.

- Gaining knowledge and understanding of cell values.
- Everyone practiced in leading the 4Ws—Welcome, Worship, Word, and Witness—taking each section at least twice.
- Feedback given on the leadership of the 4Ws section.
- Everyone experiencing edification.
- Understanding the need to create and cast vision.
- Experience the recognized development of small groups through the forming, norming, and storming stages.
- Understand the process of relational evangelism through cell.

One of the goals for the prototype cell groups is to challenge the future cell leaders to work together to change their values to those that undergird cell life. In this way, they will personally experience edification and can facilitate this in the cells which they will lead in the future. It is crucial that these leaders do not expect others to change if they have not already benefited from the process themselves.

Change begins with honest appraisal of the values that motivate these potential leaders. This honesty comes as a result of the trust that builds within the group. It also requires vision casting—the group needs to see, with the eyes of faith, how an individual and a group of people will look when they are totally motivated out of this biblical value system. They need to see that they can recapture the dynamic of the early church where building a relationship with God, and becoming like Jesus, is their life's calling—kindling a passion for Jesus and a gratitude for what he has done.

The following chart shows the significant changes that need to happen during the life of a prototype cell.

Value	**Change**
1. Jesus at the center (Upward)	• Priority of building relationship with Jesus and obedience to him as a lifestyle. • Knowing God, not only knowing about him. • Emphasis on hearing from God, resulting in character changing and Fruit of the Spirit growing.
2. Communities of honest relationships marked by sacrificial love (Inward)	• Closer relationships of openness and honesty means more commitment to people, not meetings. • Resulting conflict, when well managed, is seen to be welcomed as an opportunity for increased wholeness. • Change of the Sunday mind-set, whereby church is seen to be the Sunday meeting.
3. Everyone using their gifts in ministry (Inward & Outward)	• Leaders become facilitators, to enable everyone to make a contribution. • Each member discovers his or her gifts, and works to use them effectively to mobilize the body of Christ to work effectively both inside and outside the church.
4. Everyone making God known (Outward)	• Prioritizing time to build relationships with people outside of the church. • Working and praying together to create the bridge between Jesus and our friends. • We have been blessed to be a blessing to others, which is the motivation for outreach.
5. Everyone maturing (Forward)	• Expectation that hidden things will come to the surface, and change will happen through the ministry of the whole group. • Commitment to becoming like Jesus leads to a need for honesty and accountability. • The result is healing and freedom from the sin and the pain of the past. Each member becomes a witness with his or her own story to tell of God's goodness.

UNDERSTANDING THE 4Ws

As you have probably learned through books and conferences, most cells—within cell churches—have an internal structure. This structure exists to serve the leaders. It is there to ensure that the vision and the values actually happen. And in the future, where we have relatively young Christians (who do not have the maturity and experience that we have) leading cells, they will be greatly helped by the fact that there is a framework within which to operate.

The beauty of this framework is that it really does help us to experience the vision and the values of the cell. We are then able to train people since we know roughly what is going to happen. In previous house groups, there were not clear visions and values, and every group was shaped in the image of its leader.

As we look at these within the prototype cell, we are in some sense creating a false environment, but because the people involved are leaders, or potential leaders, this is fine. It is an important principle that we a) don't lead out of head knowledge and b) we don't ask our church members to go where we have not gone. Therefore, in this prototype we want to experience some of the things that they will experience so that their cell leadership training is reality-based.

The First W is the Welcome

One of the key values within the cell principles is every member in ministry. A second key value is honesty. When the cell meets, the first thing we want to do is to ask everybody an open question, which in our prototype cells we want to make fairly demanding. So we might ask a question such as, "Where did you hide as an adult?" Or we could ask, "What was your coldest physical experience?" Then follow this with, "What was your coldest emotional experience?"

What do these questions achieve? First, everyone in that cell has gone from being a spectator to being a participant the moment that each one speaks.

Second, community has begun to form. One of the key ingredients that binds together any group of people is knowing that they have experiences that are common only to them, and that they know things about one another that no one else knows.

I was with a group of leaders where I suggested that we do this. It was met with great disdain. "But we've known each other for years!" they cried. However, when they went around the room answering the question, "Which person most influenced you, for good or bad?" they learned things about one another that amazed them.

Third, honesty begins to develop, particularly when we go to real cells and the questions are a little easier at the start. We have to engage in a process where people learn to trust each other with the mundane, because people will probably not share the deep needs of their lives with others until they have learned to trust them with something of little value. We, as leaders, often preach about openness and honesty, but the fact is, we can be some of the most hidden people within our churches. So, for both our main church leaders and our potential cell leaders, this level of honesty is an extremely important part of our prototype experience.

The Second W is Worship

Meeting with Jesus and experiencing Jesus, and Jesus being at the center of our churches and of ourselves, is the major ingredient of church for the cell vision. It is the major ingredient of church that we love God. When it comes to worship within cells, we want to suggest some new and creative ways of doing this.

For many groups of this size, worship that is musical can be quite difficult, and may even be embarrassing. Many small groups don't have musicians or people who can really sing. So we want to encourage a mix where there will be some meetings in which we worship with singing as usual, but we also want to explore non-musical worship.

For example, we might ask the cell members to read John 3:16 and to think during a couple of minutes of silence about one thing that strikes them in this verse. Then ask them to share their thoughts. Finally, we could go into a time of open prayer where people give thanks for what they have learned and seen of the nature and wonder of God. In the cell outlines we have included some non-musical worship ideas. This kind of worship actually demands more creativity and participation from the members.

On Sundays, we then have the joy of worshipping God through singing and music which we have not used in the cell. But I believe that cell members who have gained confidence through praying and participation in the cell environment would, at a Sunday meeting, be far bolder not only to sing but also to pray aloud and to take part.

It has long been said within leadership circles that one of the greatest challenges is to get the group of leaders to worship. So one challenge of the prototype cells is to get the leaders and the potential leaders to become worshippers and to experience a new dynamic in the presence of Jesus.

The Third W is the Word

This is the hardest part to get right, because what we don't want within our cells and prototype cells is a formal Bible study. What we want to experience is more of our values at work. We want an environment for spiritual growth; for every member to be in ministry; for honesty and accountability. When we multiply the process later on, we will base the Word section on what is taught on a Sunday. It may or may not be possible to do this in the prototype process. And again, in the cell outlines, we have made suggestions.

There are three components to the Word section. First, there is something to understand. We want to grasp the Word of God. Second, having understood what was taught on Sunday, or what we're doing in our prototype, we want to ask, "What is its application today?" Go around the group and ask how a particular principle, passage, or idea makes an impact on the way we live.

Then we come to the most exciting and difficult part. We ask, "Who needs help to see this principle or idea at work in their own life?" We very much want to do this in our prototype cells, and hope that this will involve one of the main leaders or one of the potential leaders sharing a need they have—being honest about a problem or weakness, even confessing a sin. Then the rest of the group can gather around that individual, maybe sitting on a chair in the center, putting an arm on the shoulder, or whatever is appropriate, and every member being encouraged to minister.

This can mean several things. Some may pray, others may read an appropriate passage of Scripture. Others might have a gift of the Spirit, a word of knowledge, or a prophecy. We hope to see two things happen: the person receiving prayer meeting with Christ, and the people doing the ministry realizing, "Wow, God can use me!"

But we don't want to leave it there. Cells are not a meeting. It is a community and the leader of the prototype cell will, where possible, encourage practical support among cell members. For example, I was in a cell where a leader and his spouse had their elderly mother living with them. During a cell meeting the leader broke down and shared how hard it was, and how bitter he sometimes felt about having to care for her. He cried out loud to God for a new attitude, and a new heart, and was ministered to and prayed for. The prototype cell leader suggested that the group help him, by one or two members giving him a day from caring for his mother once a week or fortnight so he could get a little respite.

Following this theme to build community, the prototype cell leader should know when a member has a financial need and take up an offering for it. Or one of the members has a practical need and the leader wants to encourage the cell members to meet that need. We want to see these things happening in the cells, so we need to experience them in the prototype.

The Fourth W is Witness

The cell is here to empower its members into relationships with non-Christians. One goal in the cells is that each cell member will have three local, non-Christian friends and that during a one- to two-year period, these friends will have opportunity to experience Christ through friendship, prayer, and the moving of God's Spirit.

Now, in our prototype cell we cannot go through an entire cycle. But we want to at least experience some of this in terms of the main church leaders and potential cell leaders having a new passion for the lost. Many of us, as leaders, have very few non-Christians friends. In our cell outlines, we have made some suggestions for you to use in this section.

During the three months of the prototype cell, we want to cover the following areas:

First, we want to pray every week and ask God what, within our geographical area, are the four main factors that hold people back from giving their lives to Christ. And in each cell we want to spend five to ten minutes praying hard for the area where we live. We trust this will begin to give us a sense of God's heart.

Second, in one or two of the prototype cell meetings, we want to discuss, "what is evangelism?" We aim to come to the understanding that it is a relational process with a non-Christian, and that, through our lifestyle and works, we seek to win them to Christ. This, therefore, is something in which each of us can be involved. Having discussed that and, we trust, come to a common understanding, we want to address the next stage, which is how we will make local friends. Since we live in a commuting society, we often find that the friends we have at work live nowhere near our homes. Because they will not come to our church, we stop living our Christian life in front of them. We must continue to pursue our witness to them, but realize this is a missionary activity as far as their attendance at a local church is concerned.

Third, if we want to see our churches grow, we need to have local friends. How are we going to make these friends? The golden rule is that all friendships are made in the context of something else. In two or three of our cell meetings we want people to get into pairs or threes and think about which activity they can become involved in within their community so that they make non-Christian friends. For example, it might be joining a parent-teacher association or coaching a Little League team.

In the witness section of the last of our prototype cell meetings, we will ask people to share how they are going to make non-Christian friends. That is probably as far as we can go within the twelve-week prototype. But we hope both the main leaders and the potential cell leaders will not be asking or challenging their cell members to do something they've not begun to do themselves.

We are sure all of us want to lead meetings that are controlled by the Holy Spirit. It is our firm conviction and experience that having a little structure, such as the one we have outlined, does not limit the Holy Spirit. In some ways it actually helps because we are creating space for God to break in. And as prototype cell leaders, we want to go into each of these cells, having prayed and having called out to God, to take our ideas and ask the Holy Spirit to move through them.

CREATE HONESTY—HELP PEOPLE TO SHARE

When it comes to the ministry time, encourage people to reach out expecting a prophecy or a word of knowledge. I believe that we have, as a church, within our own nation, often seen God at work in large meetings. We saw the late John Wimber at work, or other people who have a tremendous anointing of the Holy Spirit. It is our belief and experience that God wants to move as mightily in these small groups of Christians gathering together in cells. And we want to see the Holy Spirit not only moving among us but also among our non-Christian friends in terms of winning them to Christ.

Last of all, we see God building genuine community among us and, we hope, transforming us into groups of Christians who love and care for one another.

SUMMARY OF THE PROTOTYPE PROCESS

The process we are outlining has a number of stages which can be summarized as:

- Gathering the central leaders to form an initial prototype cell that runs for twelve weeks, using the cell outlines available as a web resource.
- This group should experience:
  - facilitative leadership
  - a 4Ws structure
  - shared leadership with all participating
  - an open and honest environment where feedback is given
  - each member experiencing edification
  - understanding relational evangelism
- Pray and seek God to move forward.
- Identify and gather potential cell leaders.
- Use the central leadership team to run a second phase of prototype cells with potential cell leaders.
- Multiply the second phase prototypes into the broader church setting:
  - Ask people to join a group.
  - Or encourage cell leaders to invite people to join their group.

Warning

Do not systematically carve the church list into groups and instruct people to join them.

THE NEXT STEP—MULTIPLYING LEADERSHIP TEAMS

Toward the end of the life of the prototype cell group, the senior leaders should make plans for multiplying those in the cell into leadership teams. There are various options depending on the size of the church and readiness of the people to move into cell life:

1. The first prototype of the leadership team invites potential cell leaders to join in and create second prototype cells so that all the potential cell leaders have experienced cell life before leading one themselves. There may need to be several second prototype cells so that none exceeds twelve people.
2. Once the cell leaders have experienced cell life for at least twelve weeks, the rest of the congregation can join the cells. Initially these

Health Warning!

People leading your existing house groups—where a teaching focus has been dominant—may not always make the best cell leaders.

cells should aim to have eight members. This gives new cell leaders an easier job to establish cell life and gives space for growth with new believers. In smaller churches, this next phase could include the whole church. The new cell leaders repeat their experience of the prototype cell for the first twelve weeks before branching out to create their own outlines.

3. For larger churches, there will need to be several cell cycles before the whole church is involved. When allocating people to cells, it is helpful to identify leaders who can be developed and prepared to take on the next cells after multiplication. These potential leaders should be placed in cells where there will be a pathway into leadership after the next multiplication.

IDENTIFYING LEADERS

The role of the cell leader is crucial to the cell model, so choosing and developing leaders is a vital task for the church leadership. A cell leader is a facilitator. This role can be fulfilled by many different personality types with a variety of gifts. Organized around the three Cs, the following checklist is helpful when recognizing leaders:

Character

The cell leader needs to demonstrate godly character. It is more about who they are than what they do. Godly character can be described under the HIT principle:

Humble: Do they know their need of God?
Are they teachable?
Are they willing to serve?
Are they willing to promote others?

Integrity: Are they willing to be accountable to others?
Do they demonstrate a desire for holiness?
Are they working to overcome sin in their own lives?
Are they working toward being the same on the outside as they are on the inside?

Thankful: Do they show gratitude to God for what he has done?
Are they open to God for him to teach them?
Will they be reliant on God in their role as leader?

Competence

If people are teachable, then they can be coached into the role of leader. The process of developing leaders in cells has three parts: experiencing, mentoring, and training. The first stage of identifying leaders is to ask them to lead part of a cell meeting. Their reliability and understanding can be evaluated through this. If the culture in the cell includes positive criticism and feedback, skills can begin to be developed even before someone is approached to be a cell leader. The cell leader needs to become skilled at many tasks, including:

- Creating ownership of the cell by all the members.
- Affirming cell members at all times.
- Explaining what is happening to create security in the group.
- Using body language to encourage contribution.
- Using repetition to emphasize what God has been saying to the group.
- Positive listening, and well-expressed questions.
- Keeping the pace through the meeting.

Chemistry

It is very important for the cell leaders' group to be a place of safety where leaders can be open, knowing that there is complete confidentiality and support. If a potential cell leader is known to be negatively critical of the model, the vision, or the church leaders themselves, he will destroy the unity in the leadership team. Unless he can be moved to a place of acceptance and support, it is better that he does not become a cell leader, even if he is gifted.

Health Warning!

Those who fill the crucial role of cell leading need to be totally committed to the vision of the church and to have bought into the cell model.

ESTABLISHING CELL LEADERS' MEETINGS

As soon as the prototype cell has multiplied, the church leadership needs to set in place a support system for the cell leaders. The model that is generally adopted for this is a monthly cell leaders' meeting plus individual supervision for each leader. The cell leaders' meetings are the times where:

• The vision for the cell group is constantly revisited
• The cell leaders gain support for particular situations
• Issues from the cells can be tackled

These are usually run by the senior leadership team and regarded as a compulsory part of the job for cell leaders. Trainee cell leaders join this meeting when the multiplication of the cell is expected.

The role of the cell supervisor is to support the cell leaders, specifically, by meeting with them individually and by visiting the cell regularly. They are there to help choose and develop cell leaders and to help the cell leader through the cell cycle, making sure that the cell is working towards the values behind cell life and not swerving toward rot (i.e., missing one or more of the five cell values).

This implies that the cell supervisor is an experienced cell leader, and has, ideally, led a cell group through every stage of cell life to multiplication, has led someone to the Lord, and is developing the next leaders. Initially this role needs to be taken by the church leaders who will be the most experienced cell leaders, having led the prototype cell. It is difficult to lead a cell group and also supervise another one. It is also difficult to supervise more than three cells at any one time.

USING THE CELL OUTLINES IN YOUR PROTOTYPE GROUPS

Web Resource

There are twelve cell outlines for you to use as you run both the first and second stage prototype cells. These cover the five core values of cell church and are ordered to give a natural development in values change.

The value to be covered is at the top of each page, followed by the 4Ws sections. As a guide, the welcome should take twenty minutes, worship twenty minutes, word forty minutes, and witness twenty minutes. You will find that the timing of these sections varies enormously, and in the initial stages it will be important to spend an extended time with the icebreaker.

Remember, as you give the various sections to members of your group, it is important to give feedback on how they have done. You may want to phone them the following day or have a brief conversation with them before you depart.

COMPLEX PROTOTYPE

M. Scott Boren

37

Many churches launch their first cell groups by starting multiple groups at the same time. While this is a risky way to launch a cell group system, many churches have taken this approach with success. The key to achieving success with this approach is to understand the need for establishing a prototype or pattern cell group that will be reproduced throughout the church. Just because a church might start with fifteen groups, it shouldn't be assumed that all these groups are healthy. Nor should it be assumed that these groups are operating according to a pattern that should be reproduced in the future.

Other churches already have groups going. These may come in the form of traditional care groups. When a church desires to move such groups into the cell group vision, it must begin by establishing a prototype cell group.

Typically, the prototype concept is implemented by starting one cell group whereby the pattern cell is experienced and all the prototype group members can turn around and lead a group from their experience. This is called a Simple Prototype (See Chapter 36). When a church starts multiple groups, it will still need to develop a prototype or pattern cell group. It will just occur through a more complex process.

HOW THE COMPLEX PROTOTYPE WORKS
1. Identify the strongest groups.
When multiple groups are started, it will be very clear that some of the groups are strong, while others are weak. The strongest groups will have leaders who have vision and group members who buy into that vision. Usually these groups will have a few members who stand out as future leaders.

2. Cast the vision of UIOF cell groups to the leaders of the strongest groups.
Share the difference between the vision of traditional small groups and

UIOF cell groups (See Chapter 12) with the leaders of the strongest groups. See who catches the vision. Don't force people to embrace the new vision. For some people it takes time to embrace a new idea.

3. Key pastors should start a group.

The senior pastor (along with staff pastors working with cell groups) should start a group to develop the prototype or model cell group.

4. Focus coaching and oversight on the strongest groups.

The quality and quantity of coaching given to cell group leaders is the number one key to the success of a group. Because time is limited and most churches don't set up developed coaching structures when they start multiple groups, the coaching effort should not be spread evenly among the groups. Instead, coaches should focus their energy on the strongest groups. The goal is to work out the kinks in these groups to establish a pattern. The weaker groups should not be ignored, but focused coaching should be with the leaders of the strongest groups.

5. Multiply the strongest groups.

When these strong groups develop a workable pattern, new leaders should be trained and mentored in these groups. When new groups are birthed out of these strong groups, they'll reproduce the pattern the leaders experienced.

6. Raise the level of the weaker groups.

At this point, coaching should begin to focus more on developing the weaker groups. At that stage, the coaching system will be further developed and coaches will have more experience with how to develop leaders.

7. Recognize that some groups will not adapt to the pattern.

Some of the initial groups will grow stagnant and may even close down. Maybe the leader lacked the vision or ability to lead a group at that point. Maybe group members weren't willing to embrace the pattern of transparency. The goal is not perfection, but progress.

RAISING UP LEADERS IN PARALLEL PROTOTYPE OR TURBO GROUPS

Michael C. Mack

There is a process for spiritual growth in small groups. It involves: 1) knowing and loving God (Upward); 2) knowing and loving others (Inward); 3) serving and loving others outside Christ's church (Outward); and 4) developing and deploying new leaders (Forward).

The Bible teaches that stepping up to lead others is part of our own spiritual growth process. It should be a natural part of our spiritual formation. The writer of Hebrews made a straightforward connection between our spiritual growth and our stepping out to lead others. A mature Christian should be teaching others.

A Parallel Prototype (See *Making Cell Groups Work*, page 258) or Turbo Group is simply a small group in which every member is a leader-in-training. The purpose of this group, like every small group, is to send out trained leaders to start new groups. In this case, these leaders are usually all sent at the same time.

Michael Mack is Pastor of Leadership and Community Development at Northeast Christian Church in Louisville, Kentucky. He founded SmallGroups.com (the Small Group Network), an Internet-based ministry providing ongoing training and resources for cell group leadership. He is the author of several books and cell group guides including *Leading from the Heart*. He and his wife Heidi live in Louisville with their four children: Jordan, Dru, Sarah, and Annie.

TURBO GROUP PURPOSE

1. Discover and experience what authentic Christian community is all about.
2. Discover what it means to gather in the name of Jesus and experience him in the midst of the group (Matt. 18:20).
3. Discover and experience the five biblical values that lead to authentic Christian community.
4. Discover and experience how spiritual transformation occurs in a small group.
5. Prepare leaders-in-training spiritually, doctrinally, emotionally, and mentally.
6. Prepare leaders-in-training to lead a small group meeting, shepherd

people between meetings, facilitate intentional spiritual transformation in group members, and raise up and prepare new leaders from among group members.

TURBO VALUES

1. This group is a cell group. We will model what group life looks like by doing life together as we expect all community groups to do. We will show more than teach. We will meet in members' homes. (One person will be asked to be the official host, regardless of whose home the group meets in that evening. The host will make sure hosting specifics are taken care of.)

2. We want to reach the head (intellect, knowledge); the heart (emotions, love); the soul (spirit, will); and the hands (physical, external, skills).

3. We will use teachable moments to teach skills throughout the Turbo experience. We will list these skills and work them into specific meetings throughout the group life.

4. Group members will be active in the group. They will have opportunities to lead parts of meetings and then will receive helpful feedback.

5. Members of this group will be asked to make a commitment to the Turbo Group. This commitment includes commitment to attendance; commitment to complete any assignments, such as reading chapters from *Leading from the Heart* and chapters from other books or articles we may assign; and a commitment to fully engage in the life (community) of the group.

6. One apprentice will prepare to lead the next Turbo Group, so we can multiply Turbo Groups as well.

MOVING FROM MILK TO MATURITY

A Turbo Group is like any other cell group in that the goal is to produce spiritual growth in its members. The result of that growth is to step up and lead others.

My son Jordan is now 10 years old. When he was an infant, his diet consisted of only milk. He depended completely on his Mom for his food, and that was the most natural thing in the world for him. But as he matured, he was able to start eating more solid foods; in fact he became able to feed himself from the table. As he grew, he was able to fix his own food, simple things at first, of course, but that was a normal part of his growth. He became able to help prepare family dinners, whether helping to set the table or even helping Mom in the kitchen. Today, he can not only feed himself, he can and does help to feed his younger brothers and sisters. He makes them breakfast when asked, and helps in a variety of other ways.

We're preparing Jordan for adulthood, when he'll leave our home to form his own household. We look forward to that day, even though it won't be easy for his Mom and Dad! We know we've done our jobs in his maturity when he can step out to start his own family. If Jordan were to come to us at 30 years old and say, "I just need to be fed," we'd think something had gone terribly wrong in his growth. If he and his brother and sisters were still living at home as adults, still depending on us for their nourishment, my wife and I would consider ourselves failures.

Small groups are best described as spiritual families. One of our guiding values is that "family members (group members) grow up and leave home! Producing and sending new leaders is a natural occurrence in a healthy group." The "job" of the small group leader is to guide this spiritual family to spiritual maturity. Each member may be at a different place along the way, even in a Turbo Group. Relatively newer Christians may still need to be on some "pure spiritual milk" (1 Peter 2:2)—they need to learn, perhaps again, the basics of Christianity, led by more mature members of the group.

As believers grow, they become ready to eat solid food (1 Corinthians 3:2), studying the Word themselves regularly and participating in Bible study discussion and application. They're seeking to go deeper in their faith and as they do, the group teaches and admonishes one another with all wisdom (Colossians 3:16). That means everyone gets involved in the growth process!

As group members grow in their faith, they should be given opportunity to lead others. Small groups are teams that work best when everyone is involved. In a Turbo Group, everyone will take an active leadership and shepherding role. They may lead parts of the meeting or take turns leading an entire meeting, getting encouragement and feedback as they do. They also call or visit members of the group between meetings, following up and caring for people in the group.

HOW GROUP MEMBERS GROW

The best way for group members to grow is to not only study God's Word, but to be active in doing what it says together. Turbo Group members become active in teaching and leading other members and reaching out to those in their circles of influence who are not yet Christians. People grow best when they're involved, when they're teaching others, when they're sharing their faith with co-workers, neighbors, and friends. When they learn to love others and put their needs above their own, when they learn to serve others and build up others, the body of Christ is built up (Philippians 2:3-11; Ephesians 4:12-16).

The goal of all spiritual growth is to become more like Christ (2 Corinthians 3:18). Jesus was willing to leave his home in Heaven to take on human flesh as a man in his own created world. He was willing to suffer for our good. He came as a servant, putting our needs before his own. He said he came to "seek and save what was lost" (Luke 19:10). He said he had completed the work his Father had given him to do (John 17:4).

His mission was completed by teaching his small group of disciples, providing them opportunities to step out and lead, and finally giving them his mission to go and make disciples. Jesus came not only to teach, but to reproduce himself in others. That's why his church is called the "Body of Christ." He prayed to his Heavenly Father, "As you sent me into the world, I have sent them into the world" (John 17:18). The Christian life is by nature a life of being sent!

How to Develop and Deploy Leaders-in-Training in Your Turbo Group

Jesus gave us a simple yet ingenious plan for developing new leaders. In general, Jesus started the process by calling potential leaders into community with him and then moved them through logical steps before they were sent out.

Jesus' plan is simply a discipleship plan for all Christians! Spiritual growth leads to being sent out to lead others. Here is the plan spelled out in more detail:

1. Supplicate

"One of those days Jesus went out to a mountainside to pray, and spent the night praying to God. When morning came, he called his disciples to him and chose twelve of them, whom he also designated apostles" (Luke 6:12, 13).

As Jesus chose his leaders-in-training (a.k.a. apostles), he began with prayer. Prayer puts this important task in the right hands. It says we will let God do the actual choosing. As humans, we tend to look at outward appearances, which can fool us and produce bad fruit, but God looks at people's hearts. If Jesus found it necessary to pray before choosing his leaders-in-training, perhaps we should too!

Jesus prayed for his disciples not only before he called them, but also at the end of his earthly ministry (John 17:6-19)—and, undoubtedly, throughout the three years they spent together. Verses 18 and 19 are essential for the disciple-making leader. Jesus said that as the Father had sent him into the world, so he was sending them into the world. We have the awesome responsibility to prepare and send someone to lead a group, just as we have been sent to do. This is discipleship at its very heart. As you work with future leaders, you're a model of how a disciple-making leader is to be and act.

Send

↑

Provide regular feedback and encouragement.

↑

Delegate more and more leadership and shepherding roles to "leaders-in-training."

↑

Grow spiritually together. Spend time with Jesus by studying and applying His Word.

↑

Everyone in the group participates in community. Everyone has a role.

Before you even begin your Turbo Group, ask God to reveal to you who he wants you to disciple as leaders-in-training. The "harvest" for people who need to be in a small group "is plentiful, but the workers [leaders] are few." Jesus tells us to "Ask the Lord of the harvest, therefore, to send out workers into his harvest field" (Matt. 9:38).

2. Concentrate

After asking God to show you who should be in your Turbo Group, watch and listen attentively for who God is lifting up. Individuals won't walk up to you wearing "Future Leader" T-shirts! But God will reveal the person to you through conversations, group discussions, and perhaps a quiet leading from the Holy Spirit. Don't run ahead of God. Jesus modeled this for us: "I do nothing on my own but speak just what the Father has taught me … I do exactly what the Father has commanded me" (John 8:28; 14:31).

What do you look for? Jesus based the selection of his leaders-in-training not on outward appearances or skills; the first disciples were a motley crew of fishermen, tax collectors, and other assorted riffraff—in the world's eyes, at least. Jesus saw through to their hearts.

When we look for who we'll mentor as leaders-in-training, the easiest thing to do is to look at the outside of the person: skills, personality, education, ability to communicate. While those may be of some help, they're not what's most critical. "Man looks at the outward appearance, but the Lord looks at the heart" (1 Samuel 16:7).

The best future leader has a heart for God and a heart for people. He or she has a desire to live a life patterned after God's Word. They're growing in their relationship with Christ. Make sure they're Available, Faithful, and Teachable.

Available—Jerry was my first leader-in-training, and he had great potential: a Bible college degree, the gift of leadership, charisma, a wonderful ability to communicate, and good looks to boot. But he wouldn't make a time commitment to the group. His career and a number of multilevel-marketing moonlighting jobs kept him busy all the time. At that stage in his life, he was focused on accumulating wealth more than anything else, including shepherding a group. He was unavailable, which made for a difficult, if not impossible, on-the-job training. Finally, he stepped down as a leader-in-training, and we both breathed a sigh of relief.

Look for leaders-in-training who have the heart of the first disciples, who left what they were already doing to follow Jesus. You can't expect people to leave their jobs, of course, but you can make sure they have the ability and willingness to follow.

Discipleship is sacrificial. It may be costly. Jesus made that clear throughout the Gospels. But the rewards are sweet. Look for people who are willing to throw their lives into becoming a disciple-making small group leader.

Faithful—A future leader is first of all a disciple. Note that all the men Jesus called to be apostles (those who are sent) were already disciples (followers). Leaders-in-training have a growing, dependent relationship with God through Jesus. They have a quiet time with the Lord regularly. They show signs of maturity and a desire to keep growing. They regularly participate in worship, have been consistent and reliable in other areas in which they've been involved, and have been consistent in small group attendance. They have a heart for God, God's people, and people who don't yet know God.

Teachable—Leaders-in-training do not yet know it all and realize it. They have a hunger to learn more about the Bible, lead a group, shepherd people, and grow as leaders. Teachable leaders-in-training are humble. They're willing to listen, model, practice, give and receive evaluation. They're servants first, rather than leaders first. In other words, they'll step up to lead only when they see it's the best way for them to serve. They accept feedback, even when it involves areas of weakness.

At this point, you may be wondering if such a person even exists! Probably not. You're looking for someone who's in the process of growing in these areas. No one is one hundred percent available 24-7, or faithful or teachable all the time. So don't look for perfection. If that were required, you would never have made it as a leader—or as a child of God!

3. Initiate

As in any small group, from the time the Turbo Group begins, cast the vision for the group sending out people to start and lead new groups. This is a natural occurrence in a healthy small group. It's natural for members of a family to grow up and eventually "leave home." It's a biblical value. One of the first instructions to mankind in Genesis was to "be fruitful and multiply." When Jesus first called his disciples, he cast a vision as they cast their nets: "Come, follow me, and I will make you fishers of men" (Matthew 4:19).

Jesus' mission involved him sending these same disciples to go and make disciples. Regularly discuss the value of the group sending out members to form new groups. This will make it a norm for your group.

I've found that even Turbo Groups, whose purpose is to develop and deploy new leaders, lose the vision for doing this. They become satisfied in building community among themselves; they love the community itself more than the mission that community is meant to accomplish.

Each member should play a part in the "on-the-job" training, so that when individuals lead their first Bible-study time, for instance, the entire group will be pulling for them. A big part of the group's goal is to prepare to birth new groups, so everyone supports everyone else in their development.

4. Designate

Consider what you're calling the leaders-in-training to be. Jesus "appointed twelve—designating them apostles—that they might be with him and that he might send them out to preach" (Luke 14). The first part of the call was simply to be with him. They would spend a lot of time with Jesus and have the opportunity to watch him as he led.

The second part of the call was to be sent. This is what on-the-job training is all about! It begins with time spent together in a mentoring, discipling relationship, and grows to the point where the new leaders are sent out. The word apostle in the Greek means one who is sent, a messenger. Leaders-in-training are those who will be sent. They're like missionaries who prepare to be sent to multiply the ministry of the message of the Gospel.

While you may not designate a title to these leaders-in-training, be sure you designate the roles and responsibilities of a disciple and an apostle—one who follows and one who is sent. As your leaders-in-training grow and are being equipped to lead, you may officially designate the title of "leader-in-training" in order to prepare them for stepping out to lead their own groups.

5. Cultivate

It's helpful to include leaders-in-training in the planning of Turbo Group meetings, so they can witness what goes into preparation. Begin by asking them to evaluate a plan you've prepared; then have them do certain tasks, such as calling members between meetings; and then ask them to plan the actual discussion questions that will guide the upcoming group time together. Jesus often explained his parables to the Twelve, letting them in on the secrets of the Kingdom of God (Mark 4:10, 11, 33, 34). They learned from him and grew in their faith because of the time they spent with him.

As you involve leaders-in-training in leadership development naturally, continue to lift them up during your personal prayer times. Pray for their needs and their walks with Christ. Also, take time to pray with them regularly. Meet with them to lift up other members of the group, people who may be invited, the outreach efforts of the group, and you as leaders.

6. Demonstrate

More is caught than taught. Leaders-in-training will learn more from observing you than you might know. They'll watch and evaluate your demonstration of leadership skills, how you show people you care, how you lead different parts of the meeting, how you deal with negative situations, and a host of other tangible and intangible measures of your leadership. The apostles were always nearby as Jesus ministered to and taught people. They learned more from his actions than his words.

7. Communicate

Talk about Turbo meetings together. Ask leaders-in-training to evaluate your performance. This will help them to watch for the skills of leading a meeting. Continually discuss what you're doing and why, and encourage them to ask questions. Jesus often used questions to begin a discussion with his followers, so they could reflect on his words or actions. After washing their feet, Jesus asked them, "Do you understand what I have done for you?"

Evaluation is a skill that works several ways. It helps you strengthen the future leaders as you review meetings and evaluate performance. It also enables them to strengthen you by observing and evaluating your performance.

8. Simulate

One such tool for training leaders is role-playing, where you and the leaders-in-training act out situations they may be likely to encounter, and then evaluate their responses. Another tool is the "what-if" game—you throw out situations or conversations and ask them how they'd respond. Simulating situations allows you to train the future leaders in an environment in which mistakes won't be magnified, but can be corrected. Jesus used parables to simulate real situations the disciples would one day face. Some of his stories began with the word, "Suppose …" These stories enabled the apostles to put themselves into the situation in a learning environment.

9. Delegate

A step further than simulation is delegation. You can allow leaders-in-training to lead certain parts of the Turbo meeting. The first several weeks may involve reading Scripture. Then ask them to lead the prayer time or the opening activity. Finally, delegate the study time. In this way you can continue to add responsibility, authority, and opportunity until they can lead the entire meeting.

Notice this is Step Nine! Many leaders start here, and thereby rush the process. Or they have a leader-in-training lead the whole meeting, but never really follow up. This short-circuits the process and doesn't really disciple.

Of course, Jesus delegated responsibility when he sent out the 12 and the 72 (Luke 9 and 10). This gave them the opportunity to learn in a short-term situation.

10. Evaluate

After each Turbo Group meeting, meet with leaders-in-training individually, especially those who took a more active part in the meeting, and critique how they're doing. Be constructive with your criticisms and give lots of praise and encouragement for the things they're doing well.

Jesus did this with the apostles. After they'd returned from their first short-term mission, Jesus met with them in a solitary place so they could report what they had done (Luke 9:10). After the 72 returned from their ministry, Jesus met with them also and provided feedback and teaching (Luke 10:17-24).

11. Wait

Remember that discipling is a process which takes time, patience, work, and love. Both you and the leaders-in-training must be able to commit time to one another. Follow Jesus' example as a disciple maker. When you disciple people, you become actively involved in their lives: their stresses, choices, significant relationships, weaknesses, and strengths. Allow time for the Holy Spirit—the real change agent—to work. It took Jesus' leaders-in-training three years and the death of their leader before they were ready. It may not take your death or three whole years for your leaders-in-training—it may take only a few months for some who are already mature, growing Christians—but you certainly don't want to rush the process.

12. Educate through Experience

Be sure to teach the leaders-in-training some of the important beliefs and skills that are necessary for them to be successful leaders. But don't teach these things in a classroom environment or as "lessons." Instead, work them into your meetings together. There are many different options for providing such an experience. I list three below. To start all three, I always suggest beginning with a cookout at a member's home. Ask everyone to bring something. Introduce yourselves to one another; play an icebreaker game; set the vision for the Turbo Group. From there take one of these routes:

1. I designed my book, *Leading from the Heart*, to be used in a Turbo Group setting. It's divided into ten chapters, with discussion questions at the end of each chapter. All the group members should read the assigned chapter for the week and come prepared to share with one another and pray for one another.
2. I've also led Turbo Groups where *Leading from the Heart* is used in a different way. We'd begin each meeting with a 10-20 minute discussion about the assigned chapter and then we'd use cell group lessons written specifically for the experience of starting a new group.
3. Another option is to use *Leading from the Heart* for ten weeks and then meet for an additional few weeks to address core doctrines that are crucial for the leaders of a church to know.

13. Proliferate

When the leaders-in-training are equipped to lead a group, send them out as missionaries to start new small groups, perhaps sending another person or couple along with them to form core groups. Jesus sent his followers to go and make disciples of all nations. Throughout the Book of Acts, we see them continuing to go, spreading Jesus' Gospel throughout the world. That is our same mission today!

The Small Groups Office can help form new groups by sending postcards to neighbors for a Small Group Open House, promoting the new group on its list of "Small Groups Actively Seeking New People," working together with the Area Fellowship to help get people from the area into the group, and several other ways. Note that the Small Groups Ministry is a self-serve system. That means leaders are expecting people looking for a group to give them a call. Our mission is to make disciples of all nations—one home, one neighborhood at a time!

14. Advocate.

The relationship doesn't end when leaders-in-training step out to lead their own groups. When Jesus left his leaders-in-training with their mis-

Written Resources

Leading From the Heart by Michael Mack

Turbo Lesson Options:

- Living in Community, by Michael Mack. Available from <small-groups.com>.
- The prototype lessons by Laurence Singlehurst, available as a free download from <www.cellgroup-people.com>.
- Do some studies on core doctrines (about twelve weeks).
- End with a party as new small groups are formed and sent.

Possible Core Doctrines (LH=Leading from the Heart):

1. Nature of God (LH 1)
2. Man, created to worship God (LH 6)
3. Who Is Jesus? (LH 2)
4. The Holy Spirit (LH 3)
5. God's Purpose (LH 4)
6. The Bible: God's Word (LH 5)
7. How to Use the Bible in a Small Group
8. Grace; Faith: Belief, Confession, Repentance, Immersion (LH 7)
9. The Christian Life (LH 8)
10. The Lord's Supper/Communion
11. Theology of Community (LH 9)
12. Lordship, Surrender & Obedience (LH 10)

sion, he promised, "I am with you always, to the very end of the age" (Matthew 28:20). He promised his Counselor or Advocate, the Holy Spirit, who would stay with these new leaders in everything they would go through.

Remain available to give direction about leading a group. Even more important, coach/mentor the new leaders as they begin developing their leaders-in-training. They've learned how to develop and deploy new leaders through your work with them. Now they, with support from you, will develop people from their groups to become leaders—and on and on until Jesus returns for his church!

HOW TO WRITE GREAT CELL MEETING AGENDAS

Ralph W. Neighbour, Jr. and Randall Neighbour

For every kind of small group, there's a primary purpose that directs its activity. In a Bible study, the purpose is to help individuals within the group understand Scripture in depth. This group would be led by a gifted teacher, or a person with a solid understanding of a passage, a study guide, and the ability to facilitate the study. The Bible study would be considered a success if each person was faithful to the group and he or she grew in their understanding of the Bible.

In a discipleship group, the purpose is to help individuals become mature in their faith and deepen their personal walk with Christ. This group, led by a spiritually mature person, would use resources suitable for small group discipleship. This group would be considered a success if each person in the group completed the process and began a new group, or began the process again with a new believer.

While cell groups use the Bible frequently and disciple group members, cell meetings cannot simply be viewed as a variation of a Bible study or a discipleship group. The purpose of a weekly cell group gathering is to provide an environment where cell members can minister to each other powerfully through the Holy Spirit's leading. The meeting should also help each cell member embrace a revelation of God's call on his or her life.

For these goals to be realized and lived out, a cell group must interact transparently and live out New Testament values. Life between the meetings is just as important as the meetings themselves. In contrast to a typical Bible study or discipleship group, the topics discussed and the questions asked in a cell meeting must apply Scripture in such a way that the Holy Spirit has freedom to edify through the members. To achieve this goal week in and week out, the cell agendas must:

- Encourage each member to develop deep relationships and friendships with fellow members outside of the weekly meetings.
- Challenge the members to adopt and live out a lifestyle of reaching the lost for Christ as a team.
- Help each person gain a passion to know more of God's heart through prayer and individual study of the Word.
- Give members a strong spiritual purpose, seeing themselves as ministers, not simply members of their church's small group system.

CELL LEADERS LOVE CELL AGENDAS!

Years ago, I (Randall) was a cell leader in a church planted by Bill Beckham. He taught me many valuable things during those years, but the greatest thing he ever said to me was, "The cell leader's goal is to help his or her group experience the presence, power, and purpose of Christ each week." From that day forward, these three "Ps" became my battle cry in prayer before each meeting. Each cell agenda given to me was designed to bring us into Christ's presence, minister in the power of the Holy Spirit, and leave the meeting with a renewed sense of what Christ was calling us to do as a team to love one another and reach the lost for him.

As a cell leader, I love receiving a cell agenda each week and never find it too prescriptive. My pastor has given me the freedom to prayerfully make changes or even discard it if the Holy Spirit leads in a different direction.

A powerful cell agenda, given to leaders well in advance of the weekly meeting, will relieve the pressure to prepare a lesson each week. A cell agenda shows leaders they are supported, and partners in ministry. It also sets them free to pray, spend time with members, and become deep friends, ver-

Think about it...

Thoughtfully answer these questions. Your answers will help you find the right frame of mind to write a powerful cell agenda.

1. Think back to the last small group you were in where the Holy Spirit moved through others and true biblical edification took place. How did that evening impact you?

2. What did the facilitator do—or not do—to allow the Holy Spirit to speak through others?

3. What was the main focus of the evening?

4. If this was not a once-in-a-lifetime event and you've experienced it repeatedly, what was the common thread running through each encounter?

5. As you ponder how the meeting made you feel, would you invite your "seeker" unbelieving friends to the next meeting if it yielded the same results?

sus sitting at the kitchen table for hours on end fretting over which questions to ask.

DISCARD THE "PREACH IT AGAIN!" MENTALITY

In many cell-based churches, the cell agenda is shaped by the pastor's sermon, but it's not simply a list of discussion questions to drive home the points made from the pulpit. A good cell agenda helps the group members apply the truths shared, based on the leading of the Holy Spirit. When dovetailing cell agendas to the Sunday sermon, remember these goals:

- Cell members should interact with Scripture, not the sermon. Discussion of the sermon itself will make visitors and those who missed the sermon feel left out.
- Cell meeting facilitators are not to re-preach the sermon or use the evening as a teaching session where one person does all the talking. The focus should be on one Bible verse or paragraph and how it applies to our lives today.
- Praying for each other's needs and the lost should be given priority in each meeting. Questions provided to facilitators should lead the group into ministry to one another and a strong urgency to work as a team to win the lost through relationship building.

ESTABLISH A WORKING SYSTEM

The first step to create a system for producing good cell agendas week after week is to decide who should write the agendas for the cell groups each week. Though it's not hard to do and doesn't require hours of intensive work, some people are far better at it than others! Some senior pastors choose to write cell agendas themselves, because it's so vital to the church's direction and main ministry. Other pastors realize they're not good at it and a team member writes them. Regardless of who writes the agendas at your church, remember to keep the goal in mind and read cell group reports carefully: are you hearing and reading testimonies of how the Holy Spirit moved powerfully?

The second step is to determine your sermon themes and key Scriptures a month in advance (if possible). This allows cell agendas to be created, reviewed, and distributed to cell leaders in advance. When cell leaders have the agenda in hand while the sermon is being preached, the level of understanding is greatly increased. Some churches print the cell agenda right in the bulletin, so the entire cell group can begin to pray and think about the questions that will be posed at the upcoming cell meeting.

While distributing the first cell agendas, ask cell leaders for feedback as soon as they're able to give it. Calling immediately after the meeting would be best, but a conversation the next day will work, as long as the cell leader made good notes after the meeting. (Discourage any note taking during a cell meeting!) Ask them to jot down which questions made for a powerful time and how the various members answered. Also, inquire about the amount of member-to-member ministry and who did the most talking in the meeting. Clear answers to these questions will help refine the cell agendas to ensure each member is sharing and ministering, or put in other words, powerful and mutual edification has taken place.

WRITING EXCELLENT CELL AGENDAS:

Here is a step-by-step guide for writing your first cell agenda:

1. Place the date, theme, and Scripture clearly at the top. For example:

> Week of January 1
> "New Beginnings"
> Scripture: Philippians 3:7-14

2. Divide the agenda into the 4 Ws: Welcome, Worship, Word, and Witness.

3. Welcome

The Welcome is the icebreaker to connect people to one another. Wise cell leaders use icebreakers at the onset of the meeting, so even newcomers and introverts feel comfortable enough to participate in discussion. Vary the types of icebreakers. Here are some types and examples:

1) Tell us about your past:
   Where did you go to first grade?
   Who was your best friend when you were ten?
2) What if ...
   If you were moving and could only take two things with you, what would you take?

What's your idea of a perfect vacation?

3) How is it going?

What was the most important thing that happened in your life in the past week?

Describe your past week in weather terms? (Cloudy, stormy, foggy, partly sunny)

4) Tell us more about yourself?

What was the most difficult experience in your life?

What has been an important answer to prayer for you?

Written Resources

For more icebreaker ideas, see *303 Icebreakers*.

Consider using an icebreaker that fits the weekly theme or time of year. For the sample theme and date given above under #1 ("New Beginnings," Phil. 3:7-14), you might suggest an icebreaker like:

1) What's one thing God did for you last year?

2) What's one goal you have for the year ahead?

3) What's one thing you want God to do for you in the New Year?

4. Worship

Worship suggestions can be, but don't have to be, included in the cell agenda. The agenda is for the facilitator, and normally another person in the group should be responsible for worship.

a. Worship in cell groups should be brief. The time for extended worship is in the celebration service, not the cell group itself. When churches encourage cells to have extended times of worship, cell meetings become too long or there's not adequate time for prayer and ministry. Extended worship also makes groups harder to multiply because there are very few people who can effectively lead groups in long worship times.

b. Cell groups should use easy-to-sing worship songs that are part of the church's current repertoire. In other words, don't allow worship leaders to introduce a constant flow of new songs in cell meetings. This keeps people from focusing on the Holy Spirit's presence.

c. When choosing a worship leader for the group, the primary qualification is not that of a gifted musician, but a person who's a true worshipper. The person should be in a state of worship before the meeting and lead the rest of the group into a state of worship and acknowledge Christ's presence. (One of the best cell group worship leaders we know couldn't play an instrument and had a poor voice … but she was a woman of worship and took us to the throne room each week with a worship CD and prayer.)

d. If there isn't a gifted musician in a cell group, there are excellent CDs and tapes available to help cell groups worship.

5. Word

The Word portion of the meeting is the time for edification through interaction with Scripture, ministry, and prayer. [This time doesn't have to be facilitated by the cell leader if a mature believer or the intern (apprentice) understands the objectives of this portion of the meeting.]

This is done by creating three kinds of questions, which are described here. The first is closed-ended, have right answers, and shouldn't take up a great deal of discussion time. The second and third are open-ended, and provides an environment where powerful, member-to-member ministry can occur.

a. Observation Questions: These are questions about the passage that usually have one right answer, helping the cell members focus on the Scripture passage and understand its context. For example, in Phil. 3:4-7 you might ask: "Was Paul 'sold out' to God? What verse in this passage proves it?" (Only one or two observation questions are required to achieve a group's focus on a passage)

b. Interpretation Questions: These are questions about the passage, subject, or writer that further help the cell members understand the passage. Continuing with our Phil. 3:4-7 passage, you might ask: "For Paul to write like this, how do you think he lived his daily life? Why do you think Paul stated he surrendered his religious legalism and self-righteousness to attain Christlikeness?" (Questions like this have yet to apply this Scripture, but the cell members will begin to see its personal application. Once again, only one or two interpretation questions are needed.)

c. Application Questions: These are questions designed to move the conversation about the passage from the head to the heart. In this passage, Paul describes his knowledge of Christ to be so great that everything else has become rubbish in his eyes. Here are a few application questions for this developing cell agenda: "Can anyone share something they've given up to follow Christ?" After one or two cell

WholeHearted Worship has developed the "Worship for Small Groups" so that songs are organized into sets that work well in small group meetings. (Contact them by phoning 1-800-950-7288 or visit their website at: <www.wholeheartedworship.com>.

Written Resources

See Chapter 5 in *How to Lead a Great Cell Group Meeting* by Joel Comiskey for more on these three types of questions.

Another way of digging into a passage and making application is to ask these four simple questions:

• What stands out to you in this passage?
• What seems to be the main point?
• Can you illustrate this truth from an experience in your own life?
• What is God saying to you right now?

Just remember that you can't use these exact questions each week or the members will anticipate it and become shallow.

Written Resources

The Blessing List is a larger poster that helps facilitate praying for specific unchurched friends and relatives within the cell group meetings.

members share, a follow-up question might be posed: "What is God calling you to surrender to more fully follow him?" (Note: After asking a direct, heart-penetrating question like this, the facilitator must remain quiet and allow the Holy Spirit to speak to the individual cell members, let them "chew on it" for a moment and then speak. There could be one or two minutes of silence after this question is asked and between responses. That's ok!)

This will bring the group to a point of applying this passage to their lives and sharing transparently. Those who answer the application question above should be challenged to pray aloud and turn over those things (i.e., career, home, children, dreams, bitterness, secular beliefs, etc.), and proclaim that Christ is Lord over all! Then, other members should be encouraged to pray over the person, affirming that the Lord has heard their prayer, forgives them, and loves them unconditionally. Remember that every member of the group doesn't need to pray. One or two is fine, as long as they feel directed by the Holy Spirit to pray.

If the group is larger than eight people, it may be most beneficial for the cell group to break up into groups of three to answer the application question and pray for each other. This facilitates more transparency and can create accountable relationships to walk out what has been confessed and proclaimed in true repentance.

6. Witness

The final part of the meeting is the Witness portion that focuses on God's ministry through the group and its members to the unreached. Keep these things in mind as you create this part of the cell agenda:

Every group member should have one or two nonbelievers they're consistently praying for, and to whom they're demonstrating Christ's love. The cell should keep a list of these people (often called *A Blessing List*), so the group can make plans to get to know these people, listen to a brief progress report, and pray as a group over the list. The goal should be for each member to pray for these persons consistently throughout the cell cycle.

As you plan the Witness section of the meeting, use the cell agenda to bring awareness of any church-wide events, such as summer concerts, special Easter services, seeker-targeted sermon series, Christmas services, etc. The cell group should be lifting these events in prayer and making plans to invite unbelieving friends from their *Blessing List*.

This is the time in the meeting to notify and discuss equipping events or retreats available to the cell members (i.e., *Encounter God, Touching Hearts,* etc.) Challenge the groups to plan parties, cookouts, or other social times every four to six weeks for the people on their Blessing List.

For a Witness section corresponding to our sample cell agenda, you might have the group discuss the following questions in pairs, and pray together: "Who's one person you want to see come to Christ in the year ahead? What obstacles are keeping that person from Christ?" Instruct the group to take time to bring that person to God in prayer. Ask for the obstacles you've named to be removed. Invite the Holy Spirit to reveal to that person his or her need and the love and power of Jesus.

With the purpose of a cell group meeting in mind, try writing an agenda to lead cell members into ministry to one another and to a lost world.

Note: It's easy for this important portion of a cell meeting to get crowded out, since it's normally at the end of the evening. If your cell reports indicate that this portion has been omitted due to a lack of time, move the Witness portion in front of the Word portion for several weeks in a row. This is an effective way to make outreach front and center.

Personal Exercise

WRITE A CELL AGENDA

1. Imagine that four weeks from now the sermon will be based on John 15:5-8. Fill in the blanks below to begin your agenda:

   Cell Agenda for Week of _____
   Scripture: John 15:5-8

   Theme: _____

2. Now write down an icebreaker (Welcome). You may want to pick one that will fit with the passage or theme, or one that fits the time of year (four weeks from now).

3. Write down three to five questions you feel would help cell members dig into this passage and respond to God (Word).

4. Now write down instructions for a Witness time to move a cell group forward in outreach to those without Christ.

5. When you're done, ask someone on your team to read this article and then review what you've done here. Challenge them to give you honest feedback and help you see where it could be improved to provide an environment for member-to-member ministry and relational outreach.

TRAINING NEW CELL GROUP LEADERS

M. Scott Boren

Training is the process through which people attain the ability to perform skills they were previously unable to perform. Through mentoring, the trainer seeks to develop future leaders to use the methods and procedures that fit the vision and structure of cell groups. Many pastors have confessed their mistake of meeting with volunteer leaders for thirty minutes and then sending them off to lead groups. Other churches can learn from those mistakes and instead, implement the principle of thorough leader training from the beginning.

THE KEY TO TRAINING

Training courses provide an atmosphere where trainees discover new skills. Because pastors have been taught in Bible schools and seminaries to preach and teach, they often assume that the key to effective training will be found in an eloquent lecture. But the most ineffective form of training is that of a lecturer standing behind a lectern and launching into a monologue for sixty minutes. A lecture is not the same as training.

In training, trainees experience multiple mediums of learning. The trainer might introduce new information. Trainees might interact with that information through creative learning tools. They might experiment with the new concept by practicing what they learned. The trainer might suggest further reading on the topic discussed. People learn most when they interact with the new material. While it's true that a lecturer can introduce more information than a trainer, the trainer will always impart more skills to the trainee.

Written Resources

Cell Group Leader Training by M. Scott Boren and Don Tillman provides a comprehensive process for training up new cell group leaders.

Cell Group Leader Training has been developed to provide multiple mediums of learning. From visual stimuli through PowerPoint® presentations, interactive group activities, mini-teaching segments, optional reading assignments, and practicums, the trainee will have opportunities to experience the skills needed for leading a group through many different avenues.

EXPERIENCE REQUIRED

Training is not enough. When someone completes cell leader training, it's the equivalent of graduating from the eighth grade. Eighth-grade graduates aren't qualified to get a job. They are qualified to enter high school. In cell group leadership development, people enter high school when they receive mentoring by apprenticing with an experienced cell group leader. This might occur concurrently with the training course, or it might occur upon completion of the training course. But this must be clearly stated: When people complete training, they're not yet qualified to lead a group. They are qualified to receive mentoring to lead a group.

The exception to this rule is found in churches that have developed cell groups over a period of more than five years. In these situations, the cell groups have become a way of life and leaders are developed much more quickly. Since starting strong, healthy groups is crucial in churches that are beginning cell groups, cell leaders must be tested before being pushed out into the challenge of leading a group.

TRAINING YOUR FIRST GROUP OF LEADERS

A prototype group, or pattern cell, is the first cell group of church leaders led by the pastor. (See Chapter 36) The prototype group has the purpose of providing the experience of a cell group for those who'll be leaders of future groups. Many churches mistakenly use these groups to discuss the vision and structure of the cell groups and thereby provide a different experience than that of the future cell groups. Obviously, when a group spends its time discussing cell group methods and strategies, they're not experiencing the group life they want to reproduce in the church.

Yet at the same time, prototype group members need to process information regarding cell group strategy. Therefore, they need training that parallels their experience in the prototype group. When a church is starting its first cell group—a prototype group comprised of 8-10 future leaders—it will meet weekly for up to sixteen weeks as a cell group, while meeting at a different time for training. The training can be held either weekly or bi-weekly. Here's a twelve-step process for training the first cell group leaders through a prototype.

1. Identify your first group of twelve or fewer potential leaders. The reason is that these first leaders must be on the same page with the

Written Resources

This trilogy of books are excellent resources for training new leaders:
- *How to Lead a Great Cell Group Meeting* by Joel Comiskey
- *8 Habits of Effective Small Group Leaders* by Dave Earley
- *Leading From the Heart* by Michael Mack

vision, and this is very difficult to accomplish with more than twelve people.

2. Introduce the cell group vision to them. You can do this at a retreat or you can meet weekly and discuss a book. *Life in His Body*, by David Finnell, or *Reap the Harvest*, by Joel Comiskey, are good choices for casting the vision of cell groups.

3. Give each potential leader a *Journey Guide for Cell Group Leaders* and meet with each one individually for an interview.

4. Invite those who are ready to be a part of an initial prototype group. This will be a sixteen-week group that will experience all the various components of cell group life.

5. While the prototype group is meeting, it will also meet at a separate time to work through the eight sessions in the *Cell Group Leader Training*.

6. After the group has been meeting for eight weeks, it should go on an *Encounter God* Retreat. For more information on this retreat, see the resource section on <www.cellgrouppeople.com>.

7. After sixteen weeks of experiencing cell group life in the prototype group, start three second-generation prototype groups.

8. After these groups have been meeting for about five weeks, take all the group members on an *Encounter God* Retreat. Those who went on the first *Encounter God* Retreat will help you facilitate.

9. Recruit potential leaders from prototype groups and lead them through a *Journey Guide for Cell Group* Leader's interview.

10. Train potential leaders using the *Cell Group Leader Training Trainer's Guide*. *Participant Guides* are also available.

11. Train all cell group members in relationship evangelism and watch to see who actually embraces the call to love the lost.

12. After these groups have been meeting for about three months, lead the group members through the *Upward, Inward, Outward, Forward* Workshop, found in Part 2 of the *Cell Group Leader Training Trainer's Guide*.

Written Resources

Encounter God by Jim Egli helps people enter into spiritual freedom from past sin and current secret sin.

These twelve steps will guide you in the process, but they're not fixed. Your situation and the needs of your groups will require that you adjust the process.

Written Resources

Turning Members into Leaders by Dave Earley is an excellent resource for current cell leaders to use as they mentor up and coming leaders.

TRAINING INTERNS/APPRENTICES WHO ARE ALREADY PART OF THE CURRENT GROUP SYSTEM:

Interns and apprentices are cell group members who've been chosen because of their character, servanthood, love for people, and love for God to enter training for leading a future group. The ideal way to prepare these leaders is to give them weekly or bi-weekly training. Upon completing each training session, the trainees should be given an assignment to do with their cell group leaders or in their cell groups. (See the practicums found in Appendix B of the *Cell Group Leader Training: Participant's Guide.* These practicums are guides for implementing what was learned in the weekly session.)

If interns can't attend weekly training sessions, the church can organize a retreat or seminar. At the end of the concentrated training, the trainer should spend about thirty minutes introducing the practicums, explaining that their cell leaders will lead them through these activities each week and discuss the questions with them.

FREQUENCY OF TRAINING

Few churches have enough leaders once cell groups get off the ground. Regular training is an essential component for developing new leaders. Holding training at least twice per year is suggested, even if there are only two or three people ready for training.

41

OVERCOMING THE "I DON'T HAVE TIME" BARRIER

M. Scott Boren

"My people are overwhelmed with commitments," the pastor told me over the phone. "We live in the suburbs and between long commutes into the city, the activities of young families, and current Christian commitments, my people don't feel they have the time to commit to a weekly cell group."

At a recent conference, another pastor confessed, "I don't know if this cell group thing will work. My church is in a small farming community. In fact, some of my leaders are so busy preparing the fields for planting season that they couldn't take off today and come to this training."

Pastors everywhere complain that their people don't have enough time to participate in the life of the church they read about in the New Testament. Of course, each one believes his or her problem is unique, but time restraints impact every church, whether set in a city, the suburbs, or in small towns. People are just overwhelmed, over-committed, and over-spent. The idea of adding a weekly cell group meeting to their schedule doesn't sound appealing.

At the same time, biblical community in cell groups can't be ignored. The North American church doesn't receive permission to ignore the biblical commands to love and edify one another, just because life is so busy. No church would think it acceptable to hold bi-weekly services just because people don't have time to attend them every Sunday.

In order for the church to be the church, there are some non-negotiables. Pastors must understand the culture in which they minister, but must not waver from the call to be the church within that culture. To lead people within a busy culture into cell groups, pastors must take practical steps to guide people out of the frenetic life they lead and into the vision God has for them. Here are a few things I've observed churches doing to combat the time issue.

HELP PEOPLE BUILD MARGIN INTO THEIR LIVES

Dr. Richard Swenson has written a book entitled *Margin: Restoring Emotional, Physical, Financial and Time Reserves to Overloaded Lives*. He draws from the publishing industry to argue that life in the modern world lacks margin. Over the last ten years, I've worked as an editor, copywriter, and art director. When I first started in this field, I learned about white space, or margin, and the importance of it when designing a book or a magazine. Imagine trying to read this book if each page was filled with words from top to bottom and from left to right, leaving no margins. It would cause sensory overload.

We live in a world like that. In fact, this world celebrates the absence of margin. People feel guilty when they're not busy. If they're not busy with work, they fill the margin with the noise of television, entertainment, or the Internet. From the time the alarm goes off to the time the head hits the pillow, we fit as much as we can into our lives. To waste anything feels like a sin.

The first step to adding margin is to learn the need for margin. Because our culture emphasizes busyness, the church should help people recognize that busyness does not equal godliness. Some people are so busy doing "ministry" that they can't enjoy what they're doing. A pastor, feeling the Lord leading him to minister to someone struggling with alcohol, asked the person to come forward for ministry. He stated, "Don't be ashamed. Some of us are workaholics."

I wonder if God also wanted to minister to the Christian workaholics who are addicted to "ministry," while their personal and family lives fall apart. Ministry can easily become production-oriented work, modeled after corporate business life. Christians must discover the call to "live" and leave the tyranny of production.

The second step is to help people release the pressure of this busyness. One way churches have released this pressure has been to ask less of their people. They eliminate and shorten worship services. They create bi-weekly small groups. They don't teach people to obey the commands to tithe or invite people to serve in radical ways. They're so afraid of abusing people that they've swung too far and have become guilty of cheap grace.

Instead, the church must call people to make choices to create margin. Maybe the kids don't need to be involved in three different sports. Maybe earning less money is okay, if it means less overtime. They need less stuff than our culture tells us is so necessary. Church can't be squeezed into the demands of life. Church really only works when people create enough margin so they can hear God and listen to the way he wants them to serve him and relate to others.

People must learn to take their time and relax at church, the third step for building margin. Jay Firebaugh calls this wasting time with one another. Life with God and with one another should be fun. It should be free. It should be creative. Fun and freedom can't be forced. Creativity can't be rushed.

The church need not be about getting things done. God is at work in this world. The church need not be a frenetic, stress-filled place where it seems God has failed to do his job.

CALL PEOPLE TO THE VISION OF GOD'S KINGDOM

People don't commit to activities. They commit to vision. The reason parents cart their children to ballgames, gymnastics, and school club meetings isn't because they want to wear out their SUV. They have a vision for their children to be successful in life, and they believe these extra-curricular activities are necessary for them to go to college and get good jobs.

Many churches fail to recognize the difference between calling people to commit to activities and calling people to commit to vision. They ask people to come to church services, to attend cell meetings, to sit in committee meetings. In these activities, they find themselves busy, but lacking a clear vision for what they're doing.

While I was serving as a cell pastor in Canada, our pastoral team discovered many members who faithfully attended weekly church services, but they invested their heart and time in various parachurch ministries. These ministries had a vision to touch people who didn't know the Lord. Our church had traditionally only asked for faithful attendance. When we added cell groups, they saw them as just another meeting to attend. We had to reformulate the vision of the church and call them to a vision that was much bigger than attendance.

The vision of cell groups is not a weekly meeting. The vision of cell groups is to create an atmosphere where people encounter the presence of Christ, and he moves through the group to meet needs, touch hearts, and connect people with one another. Cell groups are only a structure, one that is not eternal. Cells are not an end. They're a means for experiencing the Kingdom of God

Pastors must call people into Kingdom living, not into cell groups meetings. Many caught in the web of a marginless life see church as a building where activities occur. Others see it as a purveyor of spiritual goods. They divide their lives into secular and spiritual activities. God's Kingdom doesn't work that way. The Kingdom infiltrates all of life. The church is to call people into this understanding of life in God. Cell groups facilitate this realization.

RELIEVE PEOPLE OF OTHER CHURCH COMMITMENTS

Those with the most obvious group leadership potential are most likely those who already serve in church leadership positions. They find their lives full of ministry and, if cell group leadership is added to their repertoire, the groups are destined for mediocrity. Cell leadership, especially when first learning how to lead a group, requires focused attention. Cell group leaders must be relieved of other responsibilities so they can focus on their new ministry.

When a church first starts cell groups, it can't immediately close old programs. In addition, some of the old programs will continue even after cell groups pervade the church (i.e. children's programs, nursery, worship team, greeters, ushers, etc.). To avoid overloading cell groups leaders, others must step up to serve in these roles. Though it will feel awkward at first for established leaders to let go of old roles, the church will not progress unless they do.

DEVELOP ATTRACTIVE CELL GROUPS

When I was a kid, I loved to play baseball. We lived in the country where no kids my age lived. If my Dad wasn't around to throw the ball, I had no one to play baseball with, but this didn't stop me. I threw the ball into the air and caught it over and over. I ruined our chain-link fence because I used it as my catcher. My parents bought me a contraption that would spring the ball back to me. No one had to tell me to practice. I couldn't get enough baseball.

Playing the piano was another story. I liked the idea of playing the piano, but I didn't like practicing. I'd put in as little time as possible. I still like the idea of playing the piano, but good ideas don't necessarily result in action.

The same is true for cell groups. If cell groups are just a good idea people feel forced into, they'll discover they don't have time to go to group meetings. Participating in cell groups can't be legislated by the pastor if he expects them to work. Yes, people will agree to give them a shot, but if they don't find them more attractive than other activities, then eventually they'll quit going, just like I quit playing the piano so I could play more baseball.

The best way to win the war against time is to make the cell group alternative so great that people can't stay away. Such an atmosphere can't be programmed, because it's a result of love and mutual support.

PRAY

We battle not against flesh and blood, but against principalities and powers in the heavenly places. Even the greatest sermons lack power to reorient the time priorities of those distracted by the spirit of this world. "I pray that the eyes of your heart may be enlightened in order that you may know the hope to which he has called you, the riches of his glorious inheritance in the saints, and his incomparably great power for us who believe" (Eph. 1:18-19).

Ultimately, how people spend their time reflects the state of their spirit and the flow of the Spirit in their lives. Changing this only comes through prayer and God's transformational power.

YOUTH CELLS

Joel Comiskey

A teenager approached me to share the great things God was doing through his small group ministry. "Your seminar is great," he said, "but you'd have to adjust if you wanted to reach my generation. We know all about information. We're accustomed to dealing with information, but what we really need is to experience God."

The postmodern generation is overloaded with information. They long for relationships. Youth cells provide an environment for youth to be transformed, to grow in a secure family environment, and to develop real relationships.

RESISTANCE TO STUDENT-LED CELLS

In many places around the world, student-led cells are exploding. The International Charismatic Mission has 9,000 youth cells meeting weekly in homes and campuses and 20,000 in the weekly youth rally. Yet many in North America resist the notion of student-led cell groups.

As I talked to several successful youth pastors about cell ministry, two common reasons for the resistance surfaced: tradition, and fear of losing control.

Tradition: Most courses or books on youth ministry don't even mention cell groups. Their focus is how to attract and keep a crowd of youth in a larger congregational youth setting. Since there's a dearth of literature on this subject, youth leaders tend to fall back on what they know best: speak-

Written Resources

Youth Cells and Youth Ministry by Brian Sauder and Sarah Mohler

ing events and a variety of youth activities.

Fear of Losing Control: Most youth pastors would never overtly confess to having control issues. Yet, covertly, many have imbibed the teaching that success in youth ministry depends on ministry plans and talent. Meeting in the church building simply makes it easier to control what's happening.

A NEW APPROACH

God began to speak to Kyle Coffin about a new approach to youth ministry while at Bear Valley Community Church in 1998. God showed him his main role was to prepare God's people to do the work of the ministry, rather than doing the work of the ministry for them. He started preparing key youth leaders in his home, modeling cell ministry, while continuing the Wednesday night congregational youth service. Then, as a transitional step, he asked those youth he was training to lead young people in the various classrooms after the youth service.

Eventually the youth (9th-12th graders) began leading weekly cells in homes throughout Big Bear, California. Fourteen cells were started with more than 140 in attendance. Kyle, believing team ministry was the best style, placed a girl and guy student together to lead mixed cells, although four of the cells were gender specific.

One of those leaders I interviewed spoke of the incredible spiritual growth he experienced in stepping out by faith and trusting God to help him prepare the lesson. Kyle maintained the weekly Wednesday night youth congregational service, which grew to record numbers.

John Church, junior and senior high pastor of Cypress Creek Church in Wimberley, Texas, started with one cell and currently has twenty-five junior and senior high cells. All the cells at Wimberley meet weekly in homes and are led by thoroughly trained students. The interesting difference between John Church and Kyle Coffin is that the cells at Cypress Creek are gender specific—boys meet with boys and girls with girls. Youth at Cypress Creek have a monthly youth service in the church.

Dove Fellowship, a worldwide cell group church movement, rediscovered the value of youth cells. Youth leaders at Dove write:

> We believe there is a vast, untapped reserve of youth cell leaders in
> our churches. This group could very well be the key for your youth
> ministry to prosper and grow. It has been overlooked for hundreds

of years by the church. Are you ready for the secret? The vast, untapped group of leaders in our churches are normal, average Christians! Most of our youth cell leaders are not super-gifted, charismatic, guitar-playing, solo-singing, Billy Graham-preaching, "Ken and Barbie" look-alikes. They are normal people who originally might not even have enough confidence to think they could help with a youth cell group. They need someone to come alongside of them and encourage them.[1]

CONNECTION WITH THE OVERALL CELL SYSTEM

There are certain principles youth cells must follow. One of those principles is that youth cells must be intimately linked with the rest of the church. They must never become a disconnected island. The youth pastor (or designated youth lay leader) should meet weekly with the senior pastor to talk about cell ministry.

Never allow the youth cell ministry to become a wandering star in its own galaxy. It should have the same characteristics as the church's other cell networks. When the ministerial team meets with the senior pastor (e.g., staff, G-12 group, elders), youth cells should be reviewed with the same rigor as the adult cells.

John Church uses the same training track as the adults at Cypress Creek Church, and develops leaders in a similar way. John said, "Many of our youth leaders are children of the cell leader parents. Having the same training track helps the parents to encourage their sons and daughters to go through it and eventually become cell leaders."

YOUTH CELLS AND INTER-GENERATIONAL CELLS

Some question whether youth cells should even exist. "Why not ask the youth to meet with the family cell?" some ask.

Daphne Kirk, the intergenerational cell expert, gives a balanced answer. She recommends that young people stay with the intergenerational (family) cell as long as they want, making sure they aren't forced to leave because of some age restriction (e.g., at fifteen, all youth must attend a youth cell, etc.). When youth cells are formed, however, Daphne encourages a link between the intergenerational cell and the youth cells—a coaching, mentoring relationship. She writes, "The intergenerational cell can be proactively involved with the youth cell, praying and supporting it through the involvement of the young person who is in their IG cell."[2]

Youth cell leaders from Dove Fellowship say, "The option of creating a new cell just for the young teens can be an excellent way to grow, adding new cells. In a cell of their peers, young teens can be themselves. Youth are shaped by their peer environment. Young teens can create an influential peer-to-peer environment where kids can mature spiritually."[3]

HOW TO START YOUTH CELLS

Those planting a cell church will most likely begin with family cells and pray that youth cells spring naturally from those family cells. The first youth cell leader would be cared for and discipled by the family cell group leader, becoming part of his or her leadership network (G-12 team). The young person would be held accountable to meet with his or her coach on a regular basis. Philip Woolford, a cell church planter in Australia, writes:

Two homogeneous cells (boys and girls) have now been established from this one adult cell. They are led by young people and they take pastoral responsibility themselves. The boys' cell initially met with the adults and then after Welcome/Worship left for their Witness and Word. It allows the young people to leave and establish their own cells while remaining connected to their 'family cells' for support, mentoring and family ties![4]

The youth at Dove Fellowship, where Larry Kreider is founding pastor, attended intergenerational cells until God birthed in them the desire to start their own youth cells.[5] Brian Sauder and Sarah Mohler describe Dove's experience:

Youth cells became an informal, casual place youth could take their friends. We were careful not to imply that these youth cells were better than the adult/family cells. As they expanded, we did not require [all] the youth to attend youth cells. They were given the freedom to go with their parents to the family cell or get involved in a youth cell, whatever met their needs best. We felt it was important that the youth felt affirmed and not forced into one pattern. Eventually, however, most of the youth got involved in the youth cells, along with some of their friends who got saved. A cell group of peers was just too exciting to pass by![6]

Many conventional churches already have separate youth ministries. To start youth cells in this setting, the best way is for the youth pastor (or key youth leader) to meet with the lead pastor in a prototype or model cell. After the youth leader has experienced how to lead a cell, he could then ask the first batch of potential youth leaders to meet with him for about six months. Each of these young people should have a commitment to leading their own cell group after the youth prototype cell is completed. These leaders become part of the youth leader's leadership team.

As youth cells continue to multiply, the traditional youth organization (e.g., president, elected officials) can be transformed into a ministerial team of youth cell leaders. The youth pastor or key youth leader should ask the most fruitful (those who have multiplied their cells) to meet regularly with him to plan, pray, and give oversight to the rest of the youth.[7]

WHAT A YOUTH CELL LOOKS LIKE

A youth cell is like a normal adult cell. It meets weekly. It focuses on evangelism, discipleship, and multiplication. It must remain small and intimate, and is normally led by a young person who's a bit older than the majority of the group members. (There are always exceptions to this rule.) The order of a youth cell meeting varies. The youth cells at the Highland Baptist Church of Waco, Texas are ninety minutes in length and follow this order:[8]

- Refreshments (15 minutes)
- Greetings and Announcements (5 minutes)
- Icebreaker (10 minutes)
- Brief Testimony (3 minutes-optional)
- Vision Sharing (5-10 minutes)
- Worship (10 minutes)
- Discussion (limit to 25 minutes)
- Prayer Time (15 minutes)

MEETING IN HOMES

It's best if the youth cell meets outside the church building. The best place is the home. Some youth groups have taken the first step of transition by breaking up in smaller groups within the church after the larger youth meeting, but this should only be a transitioning step and never the ultimate goal. The classroom atmosphere of the church doesn't compare to the family atmosphere of the home.

Brian Sauder and Sarah Mohler write, "The primary method that is used in youth groups is to have the youth cells meet in homes during the week and have a corporate youth gathering at the church facility on a regular basis."[9]

Kyle Coffin testifies about the blessings of kids meeting in homes. Parents were in the house but not in the room when the discussion was happening—although the parents did enjoy listening to the kids. John Church says:

> I think there needs to be a distinction between a cell group and a small group. Cell groups multiply. Churches that have a meeting at their church and then break up into small groups or cell groups is cool but their vision is as big as the building. Any successful youth cell ministry that is looked at as an example (MCI, Bethany, Elim, Korea Churches), the youth meet out of the church building. The ownership level and commitment of the youth/students increases greatly when they take their ministry to their houses and aren't dependent on the youth pastor to hold their hand as they lead. This puts the student in a position of faith. What a great place for teenagers to be. The youth pastor's job is to form leaders and model.[10]

UNIVERSITY CELL GROUPS

Faith Community Baptist Church in Singapore has one "university" network, dedicated to establishing cells on university campuses as well as military camps in Singapore. This district serves college/university age youth (18-25). The standard FCBC cell lessons are adapted, leadership commitment is often shorter, and more cells are planted. Every six weeks Pastor Lee gathers all the cell members in this network for a congregational service, which about 600 attend.

At the church I co-founded in Ecuador, some of our most life-changing cell groups met at universities. At one time we had over thirty cells meeting on university campuses in Quito, Ecuador.

When talking about her own experience with university cells, Jeannette Buller gives excellent advice, "We've changed from year to year depending on the students and the leadership available and willing. Be creative—do what works."[11] Cell ministry in general requires constant revision. Each youth ministry needs to find its own footing in what works for them.

CELL, CONGREGATION, AND CELEBRATION

Youth cell, congregation, and celebration work hand in hand. When I say congregation, I'm referring to the meeting in which all the young people are present. Some refer to this meeting as the celebration time, but I like to reserve that term for the Saturday/Sunday worship time, when the entire church gathers to worship God and hear his Word.

How often should the entire youth group meet? Most will probably start meeting each week, but many find, like we did, that weekly meetings were too time-consuming. We decided the congregational meeting should be once a month.

Some youth congregational groups have converted into a regular celebration event (i.e., the youth have their own "Sunday service"). The International Charismatic Mission is an example. In 1996, the Saturday night youth meeting was a congregational event—the youth on Saturday were also required to attend the Sunday worship service. By 1998, the church decided to make the Saturday night youth meeting one of the five celebration services. Yoido Full Gospel Church in Korea has two Sunday celebration services dedicated to youth.

EQUIP THE YOUTH LEADERS

A youth leader asked me, "Should there be a separate equipping track for young people? Youth today want things simpler and compact. Will it be wrong to compose a separate equipping track?" I wrote back: I think you should adapt your adult training track to make it relevant for youth. Make it more youth oriented, more concise, more dynamic, but it should have the same basic kernel of the adult equipping. Great adult cell church equipping tracks would be appealing to youth as well.

John Church has creatively adapted the training track of the International Charismatic Mission for youth. All youth go through the following steps:

- Pre-encounter (two weeks of training about the Encounter retreat)
- Encounter retreat
- Post encounter (eight weeks of basic teaching about the church, how to confront the world, the balanced Christian life, baptism in water, knowing God's will)

Written Resources

Other equipping resources for youth include those developed by Ted Stump, which have been modeled after the adult equipping resourced by Dr. Ralph Neighbour. These include:

Face to Face
The New You
The Bridge 1
The Bridge 2

• Level I school of leaders (eight weeks of teaching on salvation, repentance, Bible, prayer, evangelism, discipleship)
• Level II school of leaders (eight weeks of how to lead a cell group, including how to find the first three core members for the cell)
• Level III (eight weeks of character development for those leading a cell group. To enter Level III, it's assumed you'll be leading a cell group.)

Church says, "All successful cell group church youth ministries (International Charismatic Mission, Bethany, Elim, Korean churches) have an intentional equipping track that pushes students towards spiritual leadership. A major missing piece I've seen is lack of equipping in spiritual leadership. Without the discipleship/equipping track, the cell church will die. No leaders, no groups."

A NEW THING

The church that develops the next generation will win tomorrow's battles. Youth cells help release the next generation through evangelistic, multiplying cells. Youth cells give the next generation a chance to participate in significant ministry. God is doing a new thing among myriads of congregations today. This new focus is primarily concerned about developing leaders to reap the harvest through cell ministry, rather than solely focusing on running a youth program in the church building.

Stage 6:
Generate Cell
Group Momentum

STRATEGIC GROWTH FOR CELL GROUPS

© 2002 Missions International

Jim Egli

43

Jim Egli serves as the Small Group Pastor at the Vineyard Church in Urbana, Illinois. He and his wife, Vicki, oversee a growing small group system. Jim has authored fifteen books on discipleship, cell group ministry, and evangelism. He has a Ph.D. in Organizational Communication from Regent University. His doctoral research examined which factors in cell groups and churches create sustained cell group growth. His ongoing research is done in cooperation with Missions International, a mission agency committed to training pastors around the world in evangelism and church growth methodologies.

Even though church growth research has repeatedly shown that multiplying cell groups are the most effective way to reach new people for Christ and to grow vibrant, healthy churches, most churches aiming to create growing cell group systems have failed in their attempt.

Because of this, I began doing international research, in cooperation with Dwight Marable of Missions International, to identify the factors in cell groups and churches that produce long-term results. This research, which initially involved more than two thousand cell group leaders in sixteen countries, yielded new insights and also created a valuable assessment tool for churches wanting to improve their evangelism and cell group strength.

The results of this ongoing research have revealed many important things about how cell groups grow, what cell group health factors impact growth, and what elements must be present in a church for long-term growth.

HOW CELL GROUPS GROW—THREE DISTINCT GROWTH FACTORS

The research revealed three distinct growth dynamics in cell groups— evangelistic growth, assimilation, and group multiplication. In order for a cell group to consistently grow and multiply, all three of these dynamics must be present. People must be brought to the group and to Christ; they must be assimilated into the life of the group; and new leaders must be developed to launch new groups.

Good

As the diagram below illustrates, the three factors directly impact one another. Conversion growth leads to assimilation and discipleship, which in turn leads to group multiplication, which creates more conversion growth. These connections have been understood from years of general observation in churches around the world. But we're just beginning to understand what factors directly impact each of these three growth factors.

Interestingly, the research revealed that different group dynamics contribute to different growth factors. In other words, the cell group dynamics that bring people to the group and into relationship with Christ (conversion growth factor) are not the same dynamics that make them want to actually join the group (assimilation and discipleship factor). And a different set of group dynamics is at work to develop leaders and create new groups (group multiplication factor).

WHAT MAKES CELL GROUPS GROW?

The question "What makes cell groups grow?" can best be answered by a diagram that illustrates how church factors impact group factors, which in turn influence the three growth factors.

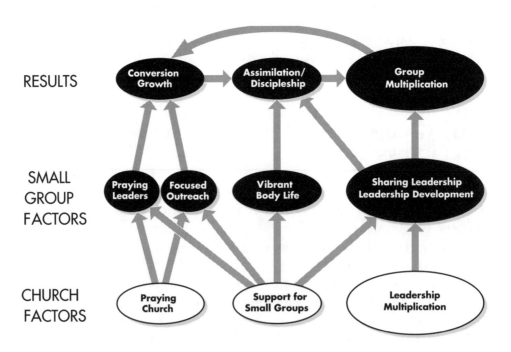

CELL GROUP HEALTH FACTORS

Four cell group health factors impact the three growth factors. The first is the small group factor called "Praying Leaders." Our research has concluded that when a cell group leader prays, the group will grow through conversions. Group leaders who don't pray are much less likely to see people come to Christ. The second factor, "Focused Outreach," also results in conversion growth. In other words, new people come to a group and to Christ when two dynamics combine in the cell group: cell group leaders pray and the group has an outward focus.

The third group factor must be in place in order for the people who are reached through conversion growth to remain in the group. A group that experiences "Loving Relationships"—a group that feels like family, a group where people genuinely love each other and pray for each other, and where people enjoy taking time with one another outside of their weekly cell group meeting—will assimilate new Christians much more quickly and easily than a group that does not. In addition, through the experience of "Loving Relationships," immature believers will be discipled.

The fourth group factor is called "Empowering Leadership." This factor directly impacts group multiplication. A growing group that is attracting new people and incorporating them into the life of the group will not automatically give birth to new groups, however. Group multiplication is fostered by other dynamics. In order to successfully raise new leaders and give birth to new groups, a group leader must continually involve people in ministry, be on the lookout for new leaders, send potential leaders to leadership training, and increasingly involve group apprentices in leadership. In addition, when a cell group leader demonstrates "Empowering Leadership" by involving group members in meaningful ministry within the group, it raises the factor of assimilation/discipleship.

These four factors relate to the four values of Upward, Inward, Outward, Forward. (I've written a training manual by that title.)

Upward=Praying Leaders
Inward=Loving Relationships
Outward=Focused Outreach
Forward=Empowering Leadership

See Chapter 12 for a complete explanation of Upward, Inward, Outward and Forward.

CHURCH FACTORS IMPACTING CELL GROUPS

It's not enough for a church to tell cell group leaders to raise these four factors and then see the resulting growth. There are also church-wide system factors that directly affect a group's ability to live out these four dynamics. The first church-wide factor is "Praying Church," which stimulates the group factors of "Praying Leaders" and "Focused Outreach." The third factor is called "A Culture of Multiplication," and it impacts the cell groups' abilities to share leadership within the groups and develop new leaders. This factor comes in the form of training new cell leaders.

I skipped the second factor for a reason: I want to highlight it separately from the other two. Our research revealed three critical church factors to cell group health, but this one is particularly important: "Proactive Coaching." Our research revealed that the one factor that influences everything about a cell group is the quality and quantity of support and coaching provided for the cell group leaders. When the church sets up a support system where each cell leader has a personal coach, the groups are much more likely to be healthy and grow. When active coaching is absent, our research revealed that groups are much less likely to be healthy and growing.

HOW IT ALL FITS TOGETHER

The Bible describes the church as a living organism. Understanding cell group growth is about organic, not mechanical, principles. For that reason the church dynamics illustrated above are perhaps best put in an organic picture that shows roots and fruits. One way to picture this is using the image of a tree.

FRUIT
• Conversion Growth
• Assimilation/Discipleship of New People
• Group Multiplication

SMALL GROUP FACTORS

Vibrant Body Life

Focused Outreach

Leadership Development

Praying Leaders

Shared Leadership

CHURCH FACTORS

Praying Church

Leadership Multiplication

Support for Small Group Leaders

HOW ARE YOUR CELL GROUPS DOING?

Many times, pastors look at the fruits of their cell groups and are frustrated. As a result, they put more pressure on themselves and their group leaders to reach more people and grow. They don't see the underlying issues that are limiting the production of fruit. By assessing the hidden root issues, pastors can then work on the root issues rather than telling people to produce fruit. Whether a church is large or small, or whether it has been doing cell groups for years or only recently begun its cell group journey, an assessment will reveal strengths and weaknesses that point to the next steps in improving its outreach potential.

Written Resources

Dwight Marable and Jim Egli's tool, *Strategic Growth for Small Groups*, will help cell leaders understand the group dynamics and will show pastors how well the church is doing to support the cell groups.

BECOMING A PRAYING CHURCH

Joel Comiskey

44

We thought we were prayer experts. Our pastoral team preached sermons and taught classes about the importance of prayer. We read all the material and knew the best ways to pray. However, we lacked one key ingredient: we were not praying.

We beat ourselves over the head time and time again. "We should be praying more. Prayer is vital to our church." Yet all our recriminations didn't change our priorities. We valued the ideal of prayer but we didn't value it enough to practice it. We depended on our programs and our personal efforts to make things happen. Despite this, God, in his mercy, blessed the work of our hands.

The programs in many churches are so effective and self-sufficient that there seems to be no need for prayer. As long as the worship team performs, the pastor preaches a relevant message, and the administration flows without a hitch, everyone feels satisfied. Dependence on slick programs is a North American norm. As you examine these churches, however, you'll notice a fatal flaw: the lack of transformed lives. There is no power. God seems to be controlled by the church's programs as well.

A church can be built without prayer and even grow numerically. But it will be a weak church that lacks power. Transformed lives will be the exception, rather than the norm. The only proven way to experience New Testament church life is through prayer. Would Jesus rebuke some of our churches today for their prayerlessness? Would he have to cast out some of the moneychangers who peddle programs, rather than God? Would he need to remind us, "My house will be called a house of prayer, but you are making it a 'den of robbers'" (Matthew 21:12)?

DEDICATE YOURSELVES TO PRAYER

Because the International Charismatic Mission (ICM) church has grown from 70 cell groups in 1991 to 20,000 cell groups today, pastors flock to that church, hoping to capture something that will make their churches grow. Pastor Castellanos says some pastors change their name to Charismatic, hoping the anointing of God will fall from heaven because of the name change.

Some copy the furniture or the precise administrative structure of the church. Those who try to copy the method miss the main point. The secret behind the amazing success of the ICM is its commitment to prayer. God is in the midst of its amazing success.

Only God can grant success. Cells are simply the instruments of God's mighty power. We mustn't trust methodology; rather, we must trust the living God. God uses the cell church, but he refuses to be used by it. We must humbly come to him, asking him to use us.

Paul wrote the Colossian epistle at the end of his life saying, "Devote yourselves to prayer, being watchful and thankful" (Colossians 4:2). The Greek word for *devote* literally means *to attend constantly*. To illustrate his point, Paul uses the example of Epaphras, "… who is always wrestling in prayer for you, that you may stand firm in all the will of God, mature and fully assured" (Colossians 4:12). Epaphras labored fervently and constantly for the believers in Colosse. We must continually cry out, "Lord, make us like Epaphras!"

Most people immediately agree that prayer is very important. But many don't understand how to create a church of prayer. Like one desperate seminar participant blurted out, "How do I make prayer the foundation of my church?" It's so much easier to talk about prayer than to pray. Here are a few suggestions.

FOLLOW THE LEADER

In 1998 our entire pastoral team visited ICM. We were privileged to eat lunch with Pastor César Fajardo and his wife Claudia. During the course of our conversation, Pastor Fajardo looked straight at my senior pastor and said, "Your church will never pray beyond your example, pastor." This not only sliced into the heart of my senior pastor but deeply moved each pastor present.

We left Bogota that year with a firm commitment to dedicate ourselves to prayer. We realized that if the generals weren't praying, the army wasn't going to go near the battlefield. Things changed. We stopped telling the troops what to do from behind comfortable desks. We, as pastors, started initiating prayer in the life of the church. Each staff pastor began leading a three-hour segment of weekly prayer in the church—including the senior pastor. Peter Wagner says it so well:

> The senior pastor must take direct charge of the corporate prayer ministry of the church. The day-to-day implementation of various aspects of the prayer ministry can be delegated to the church prayer leader and others, but if the pastor is not perceived by the congregation as the supreme leader of corporate prayer, it will not fly as it should.[1]

This doesn't mean the senior pastor needs to do everything related to prayer. Rob Campbell, the founding pastor of a dynamic, growing cell church in Wimberley, Texas called Cypress Creek Church, understood the importance of prayer from the very beginning. He not only exemplified prayer to the congregation through his personal example, but he also staffed the church based on the importance of intercession by bringing aboard a Pastor of Prayer. Cecilia Belvin, who has a wonderful gift of intercession, leads this church's vital prayer ministry.

PROMOTE A VARIETY OF PRAYER FORMATS

Concentrate on cell ministry. But remember, prayer is not another program. It is the life of the church. Prayer is the atmosphere where Jesus Christ lives and works. Promote prayer at every level of the church. Here are few suggestions for its implementation:

Twenty-four Hour Prayer Meeting

A twenty-four hour prayer meeting takes place within the church one day each week. Key leaders in the church take turns leading the various prayer intervals. Those who attend the church (both cell and celebration) are encouraged to attend at anytime during the prayer meeting. They might stay for fifteen minutes, a half-hour, one-and-a-half hours, or the entire three-hour time block. What matters most is that the pastors, the generals, are leading the charge to pray. (We've adapted to an eighteen-hour weekly prayer meeting because people simply didn't come between midnight and 6 a.m.).

It's important that key church leaders lead a prayer segment. Sheep follow the shepherd. If prayer is important in the church, the people with influence must demonstrate their commitment. Perhaps there's only one pastor in your church. If so, find key lay leaders who could fill each block. Cell leaders, preferably those who have multiplied their cells, could fill these posts.

As the church grows, staff members can be asked to fill each block. It's essential that the senior pastor take at least one segment and not delegate this area. The senior pastor must lead the charge, practically demonstrating the priority of fervent prayer.

The three-hour prayer block can be divided into worship, prayer for individual needs, prayer for church needs, and prayer for the country, the nation, and the world. Some pastors divide the larger group into smaller groups. Wagner's advice about praying in a group makes sense: "It is much wiser to stay with the least common denominator and keep the large group as a large group."[2]

Wagner acknowledges that breaking into smaller groups for the purpose of sharing intimate prayer requests can sometimes be beneficial, but it can also make the prayer meeting seem mechanical, and impose on people who would rather not break up into a smaller group.

There's no right or wrong way to lead these prayer segments. The right way is what works for your church. However, here are some suggestions:

- Make a list of prayer requests. These handouts can be distributed to newcomers.
- Individual prayer requests can be shared in the group, but don't allow the sharing time to become an end in itself. Limit sharing time and concentrate on prayer time. One way to avoid filling all your time

With six pastors in our church, each one leads a three-hour interval to complete the eighteen hours. Here's our example:

- 6-9 a.m.: Pastor 1 in charge
- 9-12 a.m.: Pastor 2 in charge
- 12-3 p.m.: Pastor 3 in charge
- 3-6 p.m.: Pastor 4 in charge
- 6-9 p.m.: Pastor 5 in charge
- 9-12 p.m.: Pastor 6 in charge

A prayer schedule utilizing lay leaders may look like this:

- 6-9 a.m.: Senior pastor in charge
- 9-12 a.m.: Key leader in charge
- 12-3 p.m.: Church board member in charge
- 3-6 p.m.: Key leader in charge
- 6-9 p.m.: Key leader in charge
- 9-12 p.m.: Church board member in charge

with personal prayer requests is to ask each person to pray his or her own prayer requests out loud and then recommend that one or two people mention those same requests in prayer. Be sure to keep moving on to additional requests. At all times, maintain the momentum of prayer.

- Make it the goal to pray eighty percent of the time and talk only twenty percent of the time.
- Try to pray and to worship non-stop for at least forty-five minutes. Before starting, explain to those present that you'll be praying without stopping for at least that long. Grant them liberty to pick a song, read a Scripture, pray more than once, etc.
- After a period of non-stop prayer, allow newcomers to introduce themselves. Some people will need to leave at this time. Normally, there's a flow of people as some enter and others go. The one constant is that the key leader or pastor remains.

Initially, we offered a 24-hour prayer vigil every three months, but we craved more of God's presence. If you plan to implement this strategy, consider starting slowly, meeting every quarter, and then easing into a monthly prayer time, with the goal of providing a weekly prayer watch.

Warning: You will not turn back the clock once you've tasted the benefits of a weekly prayer time.

Since converting to a weekly prayer watch, we experienced new growth, protection, and power in our church. God promises it: "If my people, who are called by my name, will humble themselves and pray and seek my face and turn from their wicked ways, then will I hear from heaven and will forgive their sin and will heal their land" (2 Chronicles 7:14).

God will provide new protection, new liberty, and a new atmosphere. Revivals start when God's people seek his face earnestly. He wants to do the same for you and your church if you will seek him.

Again, effective leadership is the key to making this work. The foot soldiers will follow their commanding officers, but they lose heart when leadership disappears. We made it a rule that our staff pastors must be present for their full three-hour block, unless sickness or death gets in the way. Delegation is important, but not in this area of ministry.

Pastors should turn off cell phones and cancel appointments during this time. Intercession is a serious undertaking, and we know Satan will do everything possible to distract, divert, and lead astray. Avoid being too rigid

and, under rare circumstances, a pastor might ask a layperson to replace him, but it's definitely the exception and not the norm.

This prayer methodology maximizes freedom and flexibility. The career person who rushes off to work in the morning can pray in the evening. The housewife who needs the extra time to prepare herself and her children in the morning can visit the church at midday, when the children are in the school.

We want as many people as possible to attend the all-day Friday prayer meeting, but this is one area where we emphasize quality over quantity. Even if only the pastor is in the church praying, God will answer his prayers and a new, fresh anointing will descend on the church.

We originally held these prayer meetings in the sanctuary, but circumstances caused us to change the location. We moved it to a designated room called the "prayer room." It can hold approximately twenty people and there are normally five to fifteen people praying during each three-hour segment.

The leader of each three-hour prayer segment must be directive: asking individuals to pray, waiting in silence, singing praise choruses, sharing Bible verses, and allowing various people to express their burdens. Over-structuring the prayer time is by far a greater danger than the fear of the unknown. Part of the prayer process is to allow the dynamic of God's Holy Spirit to break through and flow.

Morning Prayer Meeting(s)

In 1996, I visited the International Charismatic Mission in Bogota, Colombia for ten days. The church allowed me to stay in a converted sound room in the main sanctuary. During my visit, I didn't need an alarm clock. Every morning at 5 a.m., I woke up to Spanish worship choruses. Worshippers sang, "Jesus, I love you, I praise you, I adore you."

At ICM, prayer meeting starts at 5 a.m. every day. Another group of prayer warriors enter the church at 6 a.m. and another at 7 a.m. At 10 a.m., the last group finally leaves. Back in 1996, there were probably five hundred people who prayed every morning. That number is much larger today. ICM also hosts an all-night prayer meeting every Friday. The secret to ICM's success is dependence on God through prayer.

At Yoido Full Gospel Church in Seoul, Korea, the faithful arrive for prayer at 5:30 a.m. and have a similar rotation to ICM's. People are encouraged to come and pray every morning. One April morning when I visited their prayer meeting, it was below freezing and ready to snow. I bundled up and went down to the main sanctuary at 5:30 a.m. There I saw three thousand Korean saints crying out to God, "Give us Korea for Your Son Jesus, dear Lord." I was amazed. I realized the largest church in the history of Christianity is a praying church. This church is willing to pay the price in prayer, and God has mightily blessed it as a result.

Early morning prayer sessions are a great way to get your church praying, if you can mobilize your members to attend. The early morning schedule works well for many people, even if it means only staying for a short while.

Twenty-four Hour Prayer Sign-up

One way to make prayer convenient for church members is to allow them to pray at home in an organized fashion. A 24-hour per day sign-up promotes personal prayer, and ministers to congregational needs.

This type of prayer is especially effective when praying for specific requests—a harvest event in the church, reaching the goal of a specific number of cells, or just a fresh touch from God. Ask members to sign up on a list to pray for particular needs on a non-stop basis. Ask each cell member to pray for a half-hour, which means a total of forty-eight people are needed. Administration of the various time slots is easier if the list is posted during the celebration service, preferably at the cell information table.[3]

Spontaneous Prayer Chains

Prayer chains are an excellent strategy to promote prayer in your church. They're easy to start, work well in the background, and don't require individual church members to come to the church in order to pray. They work just as well at home, at work, or at school.

How do you make a prayer chain work? First, promote prayer chains at the cell group level. Each cell group distributes names and phone numbers. Then, when a need arises, one cell member will call another cell member and the cycle will continue until everyone is contacted. Unlike the twenty-four hour prayer sign-up, prayer chains are best administrated at the cell level.

All-night or Half-night Prayer Meeting

All-night prayer meetings were quite common among the cell churches I studied. Following the model of Yoido Full Gospel Church, most of the

Here is a basic format for a half-night prayer meeting:

8:00 p.m. Dynamic worship
9:00 p.m. Meditation from the
Word of God
9:45 p.m. Individual meditation and
confession of sin
10:15 p.m. Break into groups of
four to pray for personal needs
10:45 p.m. Pray as a group for
church needs
11:15 p.m. Pray as a group for the
nations
12:00 a.m. Repeat the process until
6 a.m.

growing cell churches in the world hold regular all-night prayer meetings. There are a wide variety of formats for this model, so use your creativity.

Prayer Retreats

The focus of prayer retreats is fervent prayer. Everything is centered around seeking the living God for his blessing. Yoido Full Gospel Church has built a prayer retreat on a mountain called Prayer Mountain, by converting a cemetery into a place of prayer and carving hundreds of individual caves into the mountainside. At the mountain they have a chapel—without seats (dedicated to prayer), lodging for those on prayer journeys, and a restaurant—to help you break your fast. YFGC takes the spiritual battle seriously and has prepared diligently to sustain the prayer dynamic over a long period. A bus leaves every half-hour from the mother church and transports prayer warriors (many who are fasting) to Prayer Mountain.

Promote Prayer in the Cell Group

Praying cell groups are effective cell groups. The first place to promote prayer is in the cell group itself. Cell group leaders need reminders that the cell group is not primarily a social time. Successful cell groups, rather, are flowing with the presence of God, which is the key to cell group success. Take a look at a normal cell group:

1. Begins with prayer.
   - The cell leader asks Jesus to fill the cell with his presence (or better yet, asks someone in the group to open in prayer).
2. Worship time draws members into God's presence.
   - Worship is a deep act of approaching the living God. It is also a form of prayer.
3. Prayer is interspersed in the worship and the lesson (Word time).
   - One of the best ways to get people praying is to ask them to pray between songs. Call on individual members, but not newcomers, to pray out loud between the songs.
   - Try to vary this time. Sing a few songs without interruption. Ask different people to pray out loud. Have a time of silent meditation. Don't follow a rote order, but rather depend on the Spirit of God to lead the group.
4. Members pray for one another during or after the lesson (Word time). God's Word often pinpoints areas of need.

- Be careful not to shorten the prayer time because of a long lesson. Prayer requests often naturally surface during the lesson time.
5. Participants freely share spontaneous prayer requests.
    - In one cell I visited, the leader asked each member to pick a favorite worship song. Theresa picked a song about renewal. Afterward, she began to sob, saying, "I picked that song because I desperately need renewal in my life. My non-Christian husband is talking about leaving me and he's treating me like dirt. I really need all of you tonight. Please pray for me." Immediately, the cell surrounded her and began lifting her up before the throne of God. Theresa left the cell group that evening completely renewed.
6. Members pray for newcomers to attend the cell during the vision casting time.
    - Bethany World Prayer Center in Baker, Louisiana and Faith Community Baptist Church in Singapore have popularized the practice of writing down the names of non-Christians and persistently praying for them to attend the cell group. A small white board or Blessing List can be used to write down the names of non-Christian friends and relatives. To avoid offending them, handle the list discreetly when those non-Christians visit your group.

Individual Prayer

Spiritually strong cell group leaders are the most effective leaders. Success comes not by might, nor by power, but by the Spirit of God. Cell leaders need to stop preparing the cell lesson at least a half-hour before the cell meeting starts so they will seek God and ask for his blessings on their cell groups.

True success in cell groups and cell group churches comes from God. The secret is not the cell structure, the cell order, or the cell pastor—it's the blessing of Almighty God upon the congregation. God spoke to Jeremiah saying, "But let him who boasts boast about this: that he understands and knows me, that I am the LORD, who exercises kindness, justice and righteousness on earth, for in these I delight" (Jeremiah 9:24). Churches should spot, develop, and release spiritual people—those who depend on God and know how to seek his face. Other leadership characteristics can help, but spirituality is the chief requirement.

A very successful multi-level marketing man converted to Christianity and happened to come in contact with one of the largest cell churches in the world. He felt he could build a large church because of his experience, but soon discovered he lacked the spiritual power to make it work. It wasn't about following the latest technique. When I spoke with him, he had failed miserably and was on his knees before God asking for guidance. He realized he had to pay the price in prayer to gain the needed power.

JUST DO IT

The most important thing isn't that you do it right, but that you do something. Some people criticized D.L. Moody for his bold style of evangelism. The evangelist responded, "You might be right, but I prefer what I'm doing to what you're not doing." Prayer methodologies and strategies abound. But none of them matters if you're not actually praying as a church.

TEN WAYS TO REFRESH YOUR CHURCH ATMOSPHERE

Ben Wong

Ben Wong is the founding pastor of Shepherd Community Church in Hong Kong, which has cell groups all over the city. He also developed the Hong Kong Cell Church Network, which consists of over 150 churches from 20 different denominational traditions.

Vibrant cell groups are life changing. Non-Christians meet Jesus and are saved. People find honest and healthy friendships, sometimes for the first time in their lives. Others discover the meanings of grace and forgiveness, and learn how to extend these to others.

Does this describe your experience in small groups? Or does your reaction fall somewhere between "ho-hum" and "I'm sure glad that's over?"

Being part of a small group, either for one visit or for the long-term, doesn't guarantee a great experience. Even churchgoers can come across as calloused or unfriendly. Cells are a way to organize a church body, but simply placing people in small groups doesn't mean they'll mature spiritually or become others-focused. If your church is dead, and you put a bunch of spiritually dead people into small groups, you'll be an organized dead church. If your church is alive in God and adopts his values, your groups will resemble breaths of fresh air.

What's the atmosphere like in your church? Take a "deep breath" in your Sunday service and in your cell group. Does the atmosphere attract others? Do outsiders look in and see something they want?

We sampled the air at our church, Shepherd Community in Hong Kong, after the cells started floundering. God revealed some poor "atmospheric conditions," and showed us that people were breathing polluted air that was choking the cells. We filtered and cleansed the air by applying some new values to our lives, and quickly saw change and growth.

Is your church's atmosphere as inviting as the fresh scent of a spring shower, or as repulsive as the stench of a stagnant swamp? By measuring your church with the following ten atmospheric conditions, you'll know how to bring new life to your group and church.

1. HAVE A POSITIVE FAITH IN GOD.

God continually challenges us to enter the realm of the unknown. You alone may not be able to do some things, but if your instructions are from the Lord, you can accomplish them with his help. As Christians with the power of Jesus Christ, we're not confined by man's potential. Paul said, "I can do all things through Christ who strengthens me" (Philippians 4:13 [NKJV]).

When a difficult situation arises, press into it. If you tackle only those things with which you're comfortable, you'll never mature spiritually. God grows us when we live outside our comfort zone. For example, if a person is asked to be a cell leader and accepts the position, believing he can lead by his own knowledge and power, then he ought to do something else or he'll stop growing. If, on the other hand, he knows he can't lead except by the grace of God, he should take the chance. If you face something and think, "I can't do it," then you must depend on Jesus to accomplish it through you.

God will lead you into tunnels with no light. So many times we focus on the darkness—problems, criticisms, fears—and we fail to hear the voice of God. He said, "I have told you these things, so that in me you may have peace. In this world you will have trouble. But take heart! I have overcome the world" (John 16:33). You will never do anything for God if you don't believe these words. He moves in the things you alone can't do, but you can boldly say, "Yes, I can, because God is on my side."

2. MAKE CHURCH FUN!

To make church or cell meetings boring is a sin. God is anything but boring. Church should be fun and exciting, reflecting God's nature. People want to bring friends and neighbors to a fun church, not to one where they'll fall asleep during the service. If newcomers enjoy your church, they'll come back, and bring others with them. If cell members leave a cell meeting wearing a bigger frown than when they arrived, they'll stop coming.

Learn to distinguish between being serious and being solemn. We can be serious about God and our ministry and be "wild and crazy guys," too. It's OK for Christians to have a sense of humor. Chinese churches, for example, are traditionally very solemn. This creates heaviness over people, and they return to church only out of guilt or hurt. A fun church atmosphere is to a nonbeliever what a free gourmet meal is to a starving man. Who can turn it down? Break out from your old church mold!

3. BRING OUT THE BEST IN PEOPLE.

Robert Rosenthal, a Harvard psychologist, and Lenore Jacobsen, a school principal in San Francisco, tried something novel. As primary school began, new teachers casually received the names of five or six students in their classes who were designated as "spurters," based on a test the year before. Though these students actually were chosen at random, the teachers believed they had exceptional learning abilities. The teachers described these selected students as happier, and more curious, affectionate and apt to succeed, than their classmates. The only change for the school year was the attitudes of the teachers.

The result: These five or six pupils in each class scored far ahead of the other students, gaining fifteen to twenty-seven points over the previous year's standardized test results. The study proved that the way we perceive people is the way we treat them, and that the way we treat them is the way they become.

Remember this important principle: You put people in touch with their faults when you assume a negative attitude toward them and reflect back to them only your perception of their weaknesses. Conversely, by assuming a positive attitude and concentrating on their strengths, you put them in contact with their good attributes. Their behavior inevitably improves. Proverbs 23:7 says, "For as a man thinks within himself, so he is."

4. ACCOMPLISH THE GREAT COMMISSION.

Jesus said in John 4:35, "Do you not say, 'Four months more and then the harvest'? I tell you, open your eyes and look at the fields! They are ripe for harvest." The fields Jesus referred to are in the world. The harvest is in the world, not in the church. Ideally, Christians go to church to get healed and encouraged so they can serve the Lord in the world, fighting the war against Satan. The church equips ministers to fight that war, and the world is the battlefield and our place of service.

Jesus told us in the Great Commission to "go." He didn't tell the world, "Come to church." People all around us—co-workers, neighbors, clerks, cousins, golf partners—live in darkness. How will they know about the Light of the World if we don't show it to them and tell them about it? Their bondage keeps them from coming to the place of truth. Therefore the church, YOUR church, YOUR cell group, must go to them.

A "go" atmosphere creates expectation and excitement, and transforms a dull Christian life into an action thriller. You find yourself waiting to see what God will do next. Start praying for, relating to, and inviting the pre-Christians in your life, and watch this aspect of your church attitude change.

5. BE A PEOPLE OF DESTINY.

People, including many Christians, are dying for something for which to live. Yet a large percentage of churches tell people to attend the Sunday service and the weekly cell meeting—period. Is this all there is to "church"? No! Everyone has a call on his or her life. God has called everyone into ministry. No one is excluded.

No one is in your cell by accident. Yet we often think people will reach their God-ordained destiny by accident. We get frustrated while waiting for people to grow up. Shepherd Community has learned to prepare people to find and then attain their destiny. We equip them to live victoriously in Jesus' freedom, and we teach them how to reach non-Christians. We disciple people within the context of relationships so they can discover their destiny, their "something to live for," in the Kingdom of God.

We challenge people with a big vision. When I was a six-month-old Christian, I started a weekly group meeting with six other young people.

Some well-meaning Christians told me I was supposed to grow up spiritually before I could help others grow. But I was being discipled by a friend named Peter, who showed me how to live the Christian life. Then I gave it to others. I saw God's vision for ministry very early, and I took the challenge, even though it was risky and some said I was wrong.

6. LEARN TO WORK TOGETHER, AS A TEAM.

I alone am not a good pastor. I need others, a community, around me. I must work smarter, not harder.

When I assembled my leadership team for Shepherd Community Church, I looked for people who were different from me. We're different in temperament and strengths, and we even look different. One has long hair and another prefers short hair. Some are modern, while others are more conservative. We have the jokers and the extra-serious.

God works through variety. Some in your cell group will be strong at prayer. Others will lead out in evangelism, or will have a deep knowledge of the Word. Learn to work with the diversity of giftedness surrounding you. Delegate tasks, and use people in their strengths. Don't try to do everything by yourself.

Shepherd Community succeeds because of the team, not because of one person, and certainly not just because I'm the senior pastor. For example, Tony Chan wrote me a letter stating that his purpose was to help me be the best senior pastor in Hong Kong. What support and selflessness! That's what makes a successful team. United we stand; divided we fall.

To work together in unity, the team needs to submit to the leader. The leader needs to shepherd with love, but the followers need to submit. Without this dynamic, teamwork doesn't exist.

7. LEARN TO FAIL WELL.

Fake people hide behind faces and masks. Real people outwardly reflect what's going on inside them. The key to relationships is to be real. The Bible tells us to "walk in the light," and this means to walk in openness, to let others see our failures and weaknesses.

Failure is a prerequisite to success. All successful people fail, even the great people in the Bible. (remember the mistakes Moses and David made?) Leaders who go to great lengths to hide failures are foolish and hypocritical. Strong people make as many mistakes, and just as ghastly, as the weak people. The difference is that strong people admit them, laugh at them, learn from them. That's how they become strong and gain the respect of their followers.

Some managers refuse to accommodate failure, and they fire employees who stumble. But the best managers expect their people to make mistakes. Instead of replacing staff members, they teach employees how to cope with failure and how to learn from their mistakes. Leaders who impart perseverance and tenacity, and help others learn from their errors, perform a vital service while creating a superior organization.

Abraham Lincoln was a great U.S. president, but look at this string of failures: failed in business in 1831; defeated for legislature in 1832; defeated for Speaker in 1838; defeated for Elector in 1840; defeated for Congress in 1843 and 1848; defeated for Senate in 1850; defeated for Vice President in 1856; defeated for Senate in 1858. If Lincoln had given up anywhere along the way, he may never have been elected President in 1860.

Where did Lincoln gain the ability to remain undeterred? From the people who believed in him when he lost, encouraged him when he despaired, taught him that failure isn't permanent and pushed him to continue. We must surround God's people with the same level of encouragement.

8. CONSTANTLY CHANGE FOR THE BETTER.

Our God is the God of change and the new. His "compassion is new every morning" (Lamentations 3:22-23). God promises that the old things will pass away. Isaiah 43:18-19 says, "Forget the former things; do not dwell on the past. See I am doing a new thing! Now it springs up; do you not perceive it? I am making a way in the desert and streams in the wasteland."

When Jesus comes into our lives, he transforms us. "Therefore, if anyone is in Christ, he is a new creation; the old has gone, the new has come" (2 Corinthians 5:17). Many people in your church or cell group can testify to the former and the current change in their lives.

A man once said, "I was a revolutionary when I was young, and my prayer to God was this: 'Lord, give me the energy to change the world.' As I approached middle age and realized that my life was half gone without my changing a single soul, I changed my prayer to this: 'Lord, give me the grace to change all those who come into contact with me; just my family and friends, and I shall be satisfied.' Now that I am an old man and my days are numbered, I see how foolish I have been. My prayer now is: 'Lord, give me the grace to change myself.' If I had prayed for this right from the start, I would not have wasted my life."

9. INCLUDE EVERYONE IN MINISTRY.

God desires each person to build up the body of Christ. When any one person doesn't fulfill his or her part, the body is incomplete. The "priesthood of all believers" is the community of God's people. A church is not a building or a program, but people living in love for one another and demonstrating the love of God to the world. This is why Jesus told us to love one another as he loved us.

A cell has no room for spectators. Members who don't fully participate in the life of the body are also not fully plugged into the life source. For example, Samantha and Peggy are members of the same cell and came to know the Lord at the same time. Both are from broken families and had many hurts expressed through bitterness. After about eight months in their cell, their leader asked each of them to care for a new believer.

Peggy accepted, but Samantha refused, saying she hadn't overcome her own problems. One year later, Peggy was growing by leaps and bounds, while Samantha was struggling with her same issues. When asked why, Peggy said, "Because I took the challenge to build up another person even through I was still very imperfect."

The church, as Christ designed it, has no pew-sitters. If you try to sit idly by and observe, others will nudge you, push you, pull you. You'll be forced to change your ways, either by participating or by leaving for another church.

10. DEPEND ON THE SUPERNATURAL GOD.

We are spiritual beings. Therefore, we're people of the supernatural and not just the natural. We must learn to operate in the supernatural, in the spiritual realm. The supernatural is the dimension of faith; the natural is the dimension of sight. We're told to live not by sight, but by faith (2 Corinthians 5:7).

This means we must have faith to believe God and to see with his eyes. Jerry had God's eyes for a new believer named Edward. When Edward first came to Shepherd Community, he had a bad temper and became especially angry when he felt dishonored. However, his life didn't deserve honor. He was lazy, undisciplined, mean, and couldn't hold a job. Even his parents had given up on him.

Through supernatural eyes, Jerry saw beneath the surface, prayed for Edward and spoke truth into his life. He and his cell saw a beautiful person inside, someone who needed help to surface. Through the love of the cell, Edward began to shock his family. He saw the dreams God had for his life. He became an effective minister. Now he's a cell leader who excels in helping other people who see themselves as failures.

Anyone can lead a cell meeting, but only God can touch someone's heart like this. A cell member can speak the truth in love, but only God can convict someone of unforgiveness or jealousy. A cell leader can visit and pray for a cell member in the hospital, yet only God can heal. God alone can restore marriages or turn selfishness into love. Only he can turn a prostitute into a church leader, or transform a youth on drugs into a worshipper.

This last condition can turn the tide of the other nine. If your cell group and church need an atmospheric change, begin with this value. Start with prayer and repentance.

Only God can turn death into life. He will touch those places that smell more like a dead skunk than a spring breeze. As your church adopts this culture of new values, a new way of living emerges. This culture creates a fresh atmosphere, and your church will become a magnet drawing people who need Jesus.

46

LIVING IN A NEW TESTAMENT LIFESTYLE

Les Brickman and Randall G. Neighbour

Les Brickman is the founder of Strategic Cell Ministries International, a worldwide ministry to cell-based churches. He holds a Doctor of Ministry degree in cell ministry and has served as an adjunct professor at Regent University. Les and his wife, Twyla, have three sons, a daughter, and three grandchildren.

Personal Exercise

Have you promoted cell groups like they are a program instead of a lifestyle?

The challenge of becoming a New Testament church comes not from altering the outward structure, but in changing the inward values which lead to a change in behavior. A pastor can form cells, preach on issues, eliminate programs and still have members attending Sunday services and cell meetings faithfully, without any change in values or lifestyle.

A LOOK AT THE ACTS 2 LIFESTYLE

Acts 2:42-48 is an excellent passage from which to draw compelling conclusions about New Testament values. The description of the daily activities of these early Christians can help us see what New Testament values look like when lived out. Here are the key factors used to make this statement:

1. Who were these people?—The people described in these verses could be divided into two groups. The first group of 120 had been eyewitnesses to Jesus' ministry, and had just experienced the confusion, disappointment, and agony of his crucifixion. This first group had also experienced the joy of his resurrection, commissioning at the ascension, and empowerment on the day of Pentecost. This first group was charged with discipling the second group of 3000 who were saved at Pentecost. Although the two groups differed in maturity, they were bonded together as the family of God and ready to follow Christ by laying down their lives to build his kingdom.

2. Time Factor—Several terms used in this passage tell us time is a critical factor to produce a New Testament lifestyle. Words such as "continually," "were together," and "day by day continuing," parallel what the writer of Hebrews stated in Heb.10:12: "not forsaking our own assembling together, as is the habit of some, but encouraging one another; and all the more, as you see the day drawing near." To achieve and expand a New Testament lifestyle, it will require that the people of a community spend time together between formal meetings, developing deep relationships.

3. Intentional Community—Verse 42 states that the early Christians continually "devoted themselves …" or set themselves apart for the task at hand. Community, as described here, was deliberate, purposeful, and intentional.

4. Equipping—It's evident that this group hungered to learn the things of God from the apostles, seizing every opportunity they could to learn from those "in the know." Equipping also happened while they were eating together and relaxing, not in a sterile classroom setting. It was an integrated part of their lives.

5. Commitment—These Christians participated in the breaking of bread, which often signified that the parties involved were entering into a covenant. The New Testament lifestyle obviously required a great deal of commitment, both to the Lord and each other.

6. Prayer—These early Christians knew how to pray, and it changed their world. Verse 43 describes the results of their prayer, which was a sense of awe, signs, and wonders. God began to do the same kind of miracles through these Christians that he did through Jesus.

7. "Koinonia"—This powerful Greek word shows up in verses 44 and 45 and indicates a fellowship that was sacrificial. While some have inaccurately interpreted this as "communal living," or communism, these verses describe a voluntary sharing of personal possessions with those who had nothing.

8. House to house AND Corporate Gathering—True New Testament lifestyle was lived out house to house and in the temple courts. There was intimate ministry to one another in homes and corporate celebration, encouragement, worship, prayer, and teaching in a large group setting. It wasn't one or the other—it was both!

COCOONING

This chapter in Acts describes a lifestyle dynamically different from what's experienced today in our Western society. Sociologists have coined a word to describe Western life today. "Cocooning" means we live our lives isolated from each other as we go from house to car to work and back again. Like caterpillars that have pulled into the safety of their cocoons, we avoid interaction with neighbors, strangers, and even friends.

We live complex, fast-paced lives, in which our labor-saving home appliances have provided us with more time to squeeze in additional activities, not deepen relationships with others. The Roper Organization con-

Cell Group Vision Team Exercise

What evidence of cocooning is there in your personal life?

What time barriers are hindering the building of community in your life?

List five ways and five times you spent with different people last week.

What are the normal expressions of care and friendship that the unchurched people of your town or city practice? Does your church exceed these practices.

ducted a survey of leisure time in America. It found that the average American has 10 hours less discretionary time per week in the 1990s than in the 1970s. It's questionable whether or not the quality of life has improved!

Coercing church members to add new cell group items to their already full lives won't work. Even if they faithfully show up for a weekly cell meeting, their commitment may not extend to the other six days and twenty-two hours in the week. The very roots of our value system must be examined and changed to reverse "cocooning."

MAKING IT HAPPEN IN TODAY'S SOCIETY

To foster a New Testament lifestyle in today's culture, it must be transferred from one person (or group of people) to others through accountable relationships and modeling. Preaching on it will raise awareness, but for a church to successfully make the transformation to missional, UIOF cell groups, the vision team must begin to live out the values and become excited enough to share it with others, just like the Christians described in the second chapter of Acts.

When the team is living in true community, fruit will abound. The team—functioning as the first cell group—will begin to learn about each other and how to be a true friend. Time together between meetings will become a priority, and sharing that time with unbelievers will draw them together to pray and testify to God's goodness. Deep, accountable friendships will be formed, because the task at hand is far deeper than just fellowship!

Inner healing and personal transformation will become typical instead of occasional or unusual. This fruit will bring about momentum and excitement, and other leaders should be invited to join and see the difference first hand, and adopt the new lifestyle of "outward-focused" community.

The most important variable in what has been shared here is time. It could take months or even a year to see this happen in the first cell group of team members. The length of time is dependent upon the current values of the team members and their ability to adopt New Testament values. If the team members love to spend time together, hold each other accountable, are reaching the lost for Christ, and discipling them today, the first cell group can be multiplied with key leaders from a church quickly.

But, if the team cognitively understands the New Testament values described in Acts 2, but isn't living them out, this must occur before others

Cell Group Vision Team Exercise

Ask cell group members how the sharing time in the groups could be improved.

❏ Do some of your group discussions tend toward being academic Bible studies?

❏ Do some of the cells turn into times of sharing prayer requests about the needs of people outside the group?

❏ Are some cell sharing times really impersonal discussions on general topics not related to how the Gospel impacts people's personal lives.

❏ Does ministry spontaneously occur as people share needs?

❏ Do people sense the presence of Christ in the midst of the group meetings?

can be invited to join. Patience and persistence are the keys to success. Rushing the process by multiplying the first group when a New Testament lifestyle isn't fully present will only yield hollow groups without passion, deep relationships, or a hunger to reach the lost, and disciple them to do the same.

A NOTE FOR CHURCHES WITH EXISTING CELL GROUPS

There are many churches that have launched cell groups and have a large portion of the church involved in groups today. But, in many cases, these groups aren't living out a New Testament lifestyle and have few testimonies of changed lives as seen in the second chapter of Acts. The group leaders may be discouraged, and group attendance is falling off.

In this situation, there are two choices. Begin a new cell group with the vision team as described above and allow the existing group leaders and members to join as biblical community is achieved. This would require the existing groups to close at some point.

Or, the vision team, pastoral staff, and coaches can begin to embrace the Acts 2 lifestyle with the leaders of the existing groups and help them "infect" their members, one by one. While this second plan is far less volatile, it may not work unless there's a strategic plan of action set in place. A plan to reform existing cells when leaders and members are unwilling to change must be considered when the time is right.

Creating and expanding a New Testament lifestyle is the foundation of a cell ministry. It's done through relationships and mentoring, not just through preaching or the reading of literature, and it doesn't happen quickly. Each person must be taken into the lifestyle deliberately, and helped to discard worldly values. And most importantly, the process must begin with the senior leadership of a church!

RELATIONAL EVANGELISM

Randall G. Neighbour

Bosworth sat in his bass boat, rod in hand, waiting for a fish to bite his artificial bait and hidden hook. He slowly cranked the reel, bringing the rubber worm over a prime spot where he sensed there might be a grand-daddy bass. He thought to himself, "If I could just catch a big one today, I could go home knowing this wasn't wasted time."

This man is an angler. He has spent thousands on a boat, rods and reels, and a wide variety of artificial lures, although he usually uses one or two favorites. He typifies the typical sport fisherman.

Allen and his friends, Frank, Susan, Emily, and Paul are fishermen too. Every day, they meet at the water's edge, organize their nets, and decide who'll work together for this day. This group makes decisions based on need—they have to eat, and they'll try any combination of people and techniques to increase their catch for the day. Most days, they catch just enough fish to eat that day. Some days they catch nothing. But they've found that working as a team, trying new things, and never giving up keeps them from being hungry day after day.

This small group doesn't know Bosworth, and have never seen a sleek bass boat and all his rods and reels. They couldn't imagine trying to fish the way he does, because it wouldn't feed their families. It might be fun to try for the sake of entertainment, but they don't have hours to spend developing the skills of a true sportsman. Fishing isn't an occasional thing for Allen's group; it's a way of life.

Many Christians see evangelism like Bosworth views his favorite hobby. "If I can just get the right equipment, and become an angler when I can find the free time to devote to the sport, I'll catch fish suitable for mounting on the wall." This isn't how God envisioned evangelism!

- God sees every Christian as equipped—we have his Holy Spirit.
- God wants more than free time—we have so little to give!
- God expects us to be obedient—to make disciples as his Word commands.

- God gave us community—so we can work together as many parts of one body.
- God desires to bless us—with an inheritance of seeing a harvest in our lifetime.

Is the Great Commission possible? Well, if we really treat it like a great "co-mission," we will find much success. Yes, if we work together as a team to reach out, instead of viewing our task as "sole anglers," with fancy equipment (or training), we will see the Great Commission fulfilled in our lifetime!

THE DREADED "E" WORD

Ask a group of your church members to tell you the first word that comes to mind when they hear the word "evangelism." If they're being gut-level honest with you, you'll hear names or phrases like "Billy Graham," "television evangelist," or "knocking on someone's door." Most Christians today don't have a positive, personal view of evangelism. They feel it's for a professional on a platform, and have a strong sense of fear about doing it.

Now ask the same group of people if they're happy they were evangelized. Everyone will say "Yes!" Truth be told, everyone is happy to have been brought to Christ, but fearful about bringing others to Christ, because they don't think they're called to it or have the right set of skills (or as a friend told me, an $800 suit and a TV show).

New Christians don't have this problem. The world is brand new and they're excited about their life in Christ. They want to share with everyone, and just need a place to bring friends who have questions they can't answer yet. The hard work comes in helping existing Christians move into a new paradigm, and then a new lifestyle of relational evangelism.

Here's one last question for your group. Ask them if they were led to Christ by a friend, family member, or total stranger. If your group is typical of most believers in the United States, nine out of ten will reply that they were led to Christ by a family member or close friend.

Why are Christians so fearful of evangelism? Probably, it's because they've been challenged to do it as a program of their church, instead of a lifestyle with other believers with whom they have a deep relationship. The challenge feels foreign and uncomfortable to them, so all but those who are especially good at stranger evangelism back out.

THE "OIKOS"

The word *oikos* is a Greek word used in the New Testament, which means "household" or "circle of influence." Each of us has an oikos of friends, family members, neighbors, and co-workers, with whom we spend most of our time. We've earned their respect and they've earned ours as well. It is among these people that we will find the most fruit when we share the Gospel.

New Christians are surrounded with an oikos of lost friends and family. Some long-term church members have an *oikos* filled with other churched believers and have little contact with unbelievers as true friends.

Some might think it would be far easier to evangelize with new believers. This is true. But, discipling the converts gained from new Christians can be hard if there are no mature believers to help. After all, we're commanded to disciple, not just make converts! So, the best environment is a small group of mature and new believers working together to reach friends and family for Christ, and discipling them as a team.

In a cell group, multiple people will be involved in reaching someone for Christ and discipling them to do the same. It's very relational!

Oikos (or relational) evangelism will probably be a new paradigm for believers who've been raised in a traditional church environment. For most, it's exciting because they've shared Christ with friends and family and one of two things has occurred:

1) The person came to Christ, but didn't join the church for one reason or another.
2) The person did not come to Christ.

Of course, there are certainly those who came to Christ and joined the church and grew like a weed in a garden, and for this we rejoice! But, the church isn't keeping up with the growth of mankind. We must find a better way to reach people for Jesus and disciple them to do the same! Relational evangelism offers the best solution for the challenge we face, and when it becomes a priority for a cell group, everyone grows and takes part in the process.

THE STRATEGY: HAVE SOME FUN!

The strategy behind relational evangelism is to create a family atmosphere where unbelievers are drawn like bugs to a porch light. When cell group members "cross pollinate" friendships with their lost friends, family members, and neighbors, the cell group's *oikos* becomes rich with unbelievers. Each member can be encouraged to befriend another member's *oikos* member to create a relationship. In this relationship, God's goodness and provision can be seen and shared in a non-threatening way.

The best way to make this strategy work is for cell members to simply introduce fellow cell members to unbelieving friends and family over coffee, a barbecue, or a night when the cell group gathers to play games or watch a ball game at someone's home. Through this interaction, hobbies and interests will be discussed. God always works in situations like this, and cell members find they have far more in common with some of the unbelievers than previously assumed.

If the group has fun together and shows genuine love for one another, the unbelievers will be drawn to it and will return to other parties and gatherings. When the time is right and group members know the unbeliever well enough to see there is interest, an invitation to a cell meeting or church-wide event can be extended. In this way, unbelievers become part of the cell before they actually come to Christ.

ARE YOU FISHING WITH A NET?

Cell-based evangelism is successful when a group of believers band together to share their lives with unbelievers around them. It's something they do together, and they pray for unbelievers by name. They strategically create fun times of rest and recreation where they can interact with lost friends and family to show them Christianity is a good thing. When one of these *oikos* members comes to Christ, the whole group supports that person as a new family member. The cell member who brought that person to the group takes on the discipling responsibility. However, if he or she is a new believer, a more mature Christian will help.

By embracing this kind of evangelism, cell members will become excited about the "E" word and it will become a natural part of their walk with Christ. It will also help them move into deep relationship with other cell members, because they're partnering to fulfill the Great Commission—a task God loves to bless!

Written Resources

Relating Jesus by Jim Egli
(Cell-based curriculum to help a group begin to pray and interact with lost friends and family members)

Are You Fishing With A Net? by Randall Neighbour
(Cell-based strategy for a game night and evangelistic cell meeting)

Touching Hearts Guidebook by Ralph Neighbour
(Discipleship resource for training believers how to share their faith with a modified bridge diagram, and training to determine the "man of peace" in their *oikos*)

CREATING EVANGELISTIC MOMENTUM

Joel Comiskey

Andrew Harper, associate pastor at Liverpool Christian Centre in Australia, pointed out that my seminar lacked any clear presentation of small group evangelism. I wrote in my diary the next day, "He nailed me." I had assumed that people would automatically understand the need to evangelize if groups were going to multiply. Yet, Andrew's comments stirred me to acknowledge that I had placed evangelism on the back burner, choosing rather to focus on other aspects of cell ministry. I realized the need to connect small group evangelism more pro-actively with cell multiplication and leadership development.

Some small group pastors are even more insistent about the importance of small group evangelism. Rob Reimer, for example, says,

> Something is unhealthy about cells that don't reach people. In my experience, everyone who tries to make a go at a cell church and fails, blows it on this major point. They compromise this principle and multiply cells through transfer growth. It is an unforgivable cell church sin. They end up with small groups that don't do evangelism.[4]

Pastor Reimer has taken his church plant from zero to 500 in secular New England society by emphasizing small group evangelism.

Randall Neighbour, president of TOUCH Outreach Ministries, transformed his own cell group by telling each member on the first night that each of them would see a friend, family member, or co-worker come to Christ before the cell multiplied at the end of the school year. Then Randall said, "My only role in your life will be to help you get this accomplished, so get ready to be challenged. You're about to grow."[5]

Previously, Randall prioritized shepherding the sheep in his cell group; his new purpose is to help each one get a friend, family member, or co-worker saved within six months.

Paul said to Philemon, "I pray that you may be active in sharing your faith, so that you will have a full understanding of every good thing we have in Christ" (verse 6). As a small group evangelizes, it experiences all those good things and begins to operate in the power of God. How does evangelism take place in the cell group? Here are a few suggestions.

PRAYER EVANGELISM

If we're going to see our friends, family, neighbors, and work associates won to Christ, we must pay the price in prayer. The Scripture tells us in 2 Corinthians 4:4 that: "The god of this age has blinded the minds of unbelievers, so that they cannot see the light of the Gospel of the glory of Christ, who is the image of God." Only prayer can break the hold of the enemy on people's lives. Satan and his demons have blinded people's minds, and they're unable to see the glorious Gospel of Christ.

Paul says in Ephesians 6:12: "For our struggle is not against flesh and blood, but against the rulers, against the authorities, against the powers of this dark world and against the spiritual forces of evil in the heavenly realms."

Effective cells and cell leaders recognize the most effective tool to win non-Christians to Christ is through fervent prayer. They take the words of Paul seriously: "Devote yourselves to prayer, being watchful and thankful" (Colossians 4:2).

Jim Pesce, founder and pastor of Harvest Family Community, regularly practices prayer evangelism. Jim and his wife, Debbie, have seen people healed from all kinds of dysfunctional behavior through fasting and prayer. They regularly participate in 21-day fasts and 40-day fasts.

Jim writes, "We also asked the Lord to grow our cells with new baby Christians during this fast. By faith, we set multiplication dates based on non-existent new believers, knowing only the Lord could empower us to reach these goals. All but one cell received new saints and were ready to multiply well before the multiplication dates."[6]

Cell evangelism begins and ends with fervent prayer. All the other suggestions pale in comparison with prayer. Let's fervently commit ourselves to prayer evangelism as our first and foremost resource to win lost men and women to Jesus Christ.

EVANGELISM AS A GROUP EVENT

"I'm the cell leader. I need to do all the work." Wrong! The cell leader is the facilitator, not the workhorse. Cell leaders orchestrate the work for the whole group to carry out. Remember the concept of net fishing versus pole fishing? It's the team that does the work. Everyone participates. The following are a list of group evangelistic ideas:

- Ask Members to Invite Non-Christians: Leaders who weekly encourage the cell members to invite visitors multiply their groups twice as much as those who do so occasionally or not at all. To be effective, cell leaders mobilize the entire team to invite new people. Dale Galloway writes: "To keep evangelism thriving in small groups, you must continue to push people out of their comfort zones by encouraging them to call on new people, putting the names of new prospects into their hands, and continually keeping the message of evangelism before them."[7]
- Video: During a cell meeting, watch an evangelistic video instead of having a Bible-based lesson, or rent a video and tie it in with biblical principles.
- Empty Chair: Place an empty chair in the cell meeting and have the members pray for the next person who will fill it.
- Special Outreach: Prepare a special outreach to one segment of society, such as police officers or teachers. (Bethany World Prayer Center used this approach with great success.) Dan Godard says, "We ask each of our groups to hold one social event every 4-6 weeks. The coaches hold the groups accountable for it. We give them lots of ideas as to what they could do, such as: go bowling, go for dinner, have a potluck, have a barbecue, have a games night (board games etc.), go to a local theater, or watch a movie together (especially a spiritually meaningful one)."[8]

EVANGELISM THROUGH HONEST TRANSPARENCY

Honest transparency is perhaps the most effective witness to win non-Christians to Jesus. My cell group experience in Moreno Valley confirms this. Our most effective evangelism has come through opening our own hearts and sharing honestly. We've noticed when non-Christians see other members of the group wrestling with the same normal day-to-day issues and how Jesus makes a difference, they hunger for more of God.

Remember that the cells of John Wesley were very oriented to sharing from the heart. Wesley's cells met only for one hour, and the main event was "reporting on your soul."[9] The meeting was built upon sharing personal experiences of the past week. Everyone was expected "... to speak freely and plainly about every subject from their own temptations to plans for establishing a new cottage meeting or visiting the distressed."[10] In other words, these groups emphasized transparency. Within this framework of "open sharing," many were converted. The hearts of sinners melted as they interacted with "saved sinners." Jesus Christ made all the difference.

FIND A NEED AND MEET IT

The Elim Church in San Salvador, El Salvador has grown to 120,000 people, meeting in 11,000 weekly cells, and has also planted more than 110 churches. Mario Vega shared the secret behind their successful evangelism:

> We make and strengthen friendships with non-Christians with the goal of serving them and giving testimony to God's love. We then continually invite non-Christians to attend the cells, while praying for the conversions of those we invite to the cell. We emphasize to the members of the cell that the goal is multiplication, which we achieve through the winning of people to Christ.[11]

The Elim cells personally care for the hurts and needs of those around them, winning the people to Jesus as a result. This is the same method that David Cho, pastor of Yoido Full Gospel Church in Seoul, Korea, has been so successful in implementing. In Cho's church, cell members are instructed to select someone who's not a Christian, whom they can pray for, love, and serve. They bring meals, help sweep out the person's store, or do whatever it takes to show they really care for them. After three or four months of such love, the hardest soul softens up and surrenders to Christ.[12]

Rob Reimer guides his own cell groups to "find a need and fill it; find a hurt and heal it; find a common interest and do it!"

SEEKER SENSITIVE SUBGROUPS FROM THE CELL

Another great way to increase the evangelistic momentum is to design outreach groups that are seeker-oriented. Seeker-sensitive groups specifically gear the cell lessons (Word time) to reach non-Christians. In these groups, there is little praying, singing, or talking about the church. The needs of the non-Christians are the priority.[13]

Ralph Neighbour, Jr. teaches cell group members to distinguish "Type A" unbelievers who are fairly open to Christian faith from "Type B" unbelievers who "... are not searching for Jesus Christ, and show no interest in

Bible study or other Christian activities."[14] For the "Type B" unbelievers, Neighbour designed "non-Christian type" groups called share groups. These don't replace the cell group but rather serve as an extension of it.

Believers who participate in share groups have the dual responsibility of attending their normal cell group as well as the separate share group. Neighbour writes, "This group should be free, informal, and spontaneous. … It's important for all share group members to feel they can be themselves."[15] Share groups allow cell groups to reach hard-core unbelievers who are not yet open to the Gospel, but who are open to friendships.

ALPHA COURSE IN CELL GROUPS

The Alpha Course is an introduction to the Christian faith, designed to instruct in a non-threatening way and inspire people who have little to no church background. It lasts eleven weeks and includes fifteen sessions. It's designed primarily to appeal to non-Christians and relatively new or immature believers. It began twenty years ago at a dying Anglican church in central London (Holy Trinity Brompton). Now there are close to twelve thousand courses being run worldwide in more than eighty denominations. More than one million people have gone through it. Some have called it the source of a renewal of the church in England.[16]

When I heard Ralph Neighbour was using the Alpha course as a tool of evangelism in his cell church plant in Houston, my ears perked up. I then began to discover that many cell churches are using Alpha as a tool of evangelism within their cell groups. In discussing how the Alpha course blended with his cell groups, Kenneth Behr says, "We used the Alpha Course at my church and the home cell groups … to lead discussion groups. Then it became very natural for some of these new and almost new Christians to start attending the groups."[17]

ZONE OR NETWORK EVANGELISTIC ACTIVITY

I visited one cell group church that works on the zone level to plan evangelistic activities, and each cell in the zone participates. The zone might present a Christian movie, a special speaker, or some type of servant evangelism. Each cell is encouraged to reach its neighborhood through zone-level events, and through special events the cell itself sponsors. Some groups might create cards inviting neighborhood mothers to a Mother's Day celebration. Or the cell might plan a dinner and invite those living in the neighborhood.

This has become more of an emphasis in the G-12 movement. The homogeneous networks come together occasionally to plan evangelism rallies and reach out to non-Christians. The men's network, for example, might have an all-men's rally. These are congregations (based on cells) that come together to reach a particular homogeneous group of people.

CELL HARVEST EVENTS IN THE CELEBRATION

One cell group church pastor had a harvest event in his church on the Sunday before Thanksgiving. The church put together a 36-hour prayer rally to prepare for the event. The cells participated in planning the event. Cell group members invited non-Christians and prepared parts of the harvest event (bringing food, setting up tables, renting a "moonwalk" bounce house for children's recreation, etc.). Pastor Harrell spent extra time in orienting his message toward non-Christians. The result was that forty-five new people showed up and several received Christ as their Savior.

One Southern Baptist pastor told me, "I train our cell leaders to be ready to pounce on every visitor in the church. Our cell leaders immediately try to assimilate the newcomers by inviting them to their cell groups. We've discovered here in North America people prefer to first attend a large celebration service and afterwards attend a cell group for fellowship and growth."

Rob Reimer said something similar, "Most of our evangelism growth occurs through the cells—that is, people from the cells, doing teamwork evangelism, bring people to church. But, usually their first exposure to a "church" experience is Sunday morning worship. They'll have gone to cell outreaches and the special events. But, usually they end up coming to a service with a friend before landing in a cell. I preach an evangelistic message on grace about 8-10 times a year."

DON'T GIVE UP

Effective leaders aren't necessarily talented, gifted, or outgoing. But they do have one thing in common. They're persistent. They don't give up. They keep encouraging cell members to reach out and invite people, even when the results are few. They keep on praying, even though the answer isn't immediate. Remember the Scripture in Proverbs 14:23: "All hard work brings a profit, but mere talk leads only to poverty." Such diligence will lead to success eventually.

COMMON CELL MEMBER EQUIPPING MODELS

Joel Comiskey and M. Scott Boren

When a church starts cell groups, the first cell group leaders are those who have proven themselves in previous leadership positions. These people embrace the vision and receive training to lead a group. Once the cell groups get going strong, growth comes. The cell group system gains momentum and more people would like to join.

The only way these people can be added to groups is by starting more groups. But most cell group churches complain they don't have enough leaders. They look at their current people and feel they've trained all who are mature enough to lead. Even though there are enough people who want to be added to the groups, they don't have enough leaders to lead these people. Therefore they either have long waiting lists or overflowing groups. This is a very frustrating place to be.

The cell group environment is a hothouse for growing leaders. Carl George calls small groups "leaders breeders." But plants don't grow in a hothouse just because they've been placed there. Likewise, cell group members don't magically grow just because they've been placed in a cell group. Disciples are made, not born. Leaders don't appear magically, they must be developed. Tomorrow's leaders are today's cell group members. Churches must recognize this and develop these people, equipping them as disciples, ministers, and eventually leaders.

EQUIPPING ON TWO LEVELS

Churches that develop cell group leaders the best train people on two levels. First they train those who are ready for cell group leader training. This is short-term training. Most churches that start cell groups understand this level of equipping. The problem is that this is short-term equipping. It only equips people who are already mature disciples.

The second level of equipping focuses on the future. Churches that produce leaders know their long-term success depends upon discipling people who have the potential to be a leader one year, two years, and even three years in the future. They realize tomorrow's spiritual leaders are today's spiritual children, spiritual adolescents, and spiritual teenagers.

Many churches, on the other hand, have failed to equip cell members for future leadership. After all, there are so many present pressures. It seems absurd to think beyond the present. It's even possible for a church to initiate a cell ministry and to immediately produce hundreds of cell groups. Further probing, however, often reveals that the initial growth was simply a changing of the guard. Established leaders who at one time maintained the cherished programs were relocated to lead cell groups. But without an established system for discipling current cell group members who'll become new leaders, the leadership pool dries up, bringing the cell ministry to a screeching halt.

Strong cell group churches, in contrast, develop equipping and training systems that carry the new Christian from the initial discipleship stage to leading a small group. Because the top leadership realizes training new leaders is the chief task, the entire church functions as a leadership production system.

THE PRINCIPLES OF EQUIPPING PEOPLE FOR MINISTRY

Many churches assume the magic lies in the equipping model. They can simply visit a church, copy its equipping curriculum, and immediately disciple their people. But there's no magic in the curriculum. Most churches pass through multiple revisions of their equipping track before finding the right fit. Initial failure often occurs because a church tries to copy another church's training model in its entirety. Most often, the church realizes the training model doesn't fit its unique context and identity.

Before going into the details about six prominent equipping models, it's crucial to understand the principles of equipping. These principles undergird effective equipping models, although the forms taken by different models are distinct.

Principle #1: Keep the Equipping Track Simple.

The equipping track should not be overly complicated. In the early days, the International Charismatic Mission developed a two-year equipping track that included homiletics, Theology 1, 2, 3, etc. By the time a

Written Resources

Read Leadership Explosion: Multiplying Cell Group Leaders to Reap the Harvest by Joel Comiskey for more information on this topic.

person graduated from that equipping track, he or she had lost contact with non-Christian friends. Most cell church equipping tracks prepare their leaders in the following four areas:

- Basic doctrine
- Inner-life development
- Personal evangelism and ministry
- Cell group leadership training

The first area is basic Bible doctrine. All evangelical Christians would agree that the teaching of God's Word is the foundation of the new believer's life. This doesn't mean the new believer must take systematic theology courses that take four years to complete. New believers need the milk of God's Word—the basic principles.

It's important to include basic teaching about God, sin, the person of Jesus Christ, salvation, the Holy Spirit, and the church. This initial training manual could include six, nine, or fourteen lessons, depending on how much biblical doctrine a church deems necessary for the new believer.

The second area, inner-life development, focuses on devotional life. The goal is to help new believers feed themselves. This step is summed up in the saying, "Give a man a fish and you feed him for a day; teach him how to fish and you feed him for a lifetime."

The first step provides an understanding of basic biblical teaching, while the second step helps the new believer nourish himself from God's Word. The teaching of this stage should also deal with confession of sin, forgiveness, and steps to freedom from past bondage. Christ wants to heal every sin and scar of the past, and the manual for this step should cover these issues. New believers should learn they have direct access to the throne of God because of the blood of Jesus.

The third area, personal evangelism, teaches the person how to share his or her faith. Each believer needs to learn how to lead someone else to Jesus Christ. This stage teaches the plan of salvation in a systematic, step-by-step process. Beyond learning the content of the Gospel presentation, the believer must also learn how to develop friendships with non-Christians (i.e., reaching his personal contacts—*oikos*). The effectiveness of small group evangelism is also highlighted, and teaching is given on how the cell functions like a team to evangelize non-Christians, as well as providing the ideal atmosphere for non-believers.

The final area covers how to lead a cell group. The manual for this stage should cover the basics of cell ministry, small group dynamics (e.g., how to listen well, transparent sharing, etc.), how to lead a cell group meeting, and characteristics of godly leaders. Teaching this manual in a home setting provides a small group atmosphere and gives the group opportunities to practice small group dynamics. This manual should include teaching about the order of a holistic cell group meeting (Welcome, Worship, Word, and Witness).

Principle #2: Provide Action Steps within the Equipping Process.

Each stage in the equipping process should be practical, including an action step. Beyond completing the action steps, all those taking training must be actively involved leading various activities in the cell group. In churches using the four Ws (Welcome, Worship, Word, Witness) as their meeting format, the trainee must lead each W, under the direction of the cell leader. One month, for example, the trainee could lead the Welcome time, another month the Worship time, etc.

Principle #3: As Part of Inner Life Development, Help People Walk in Spiritual Freedom.

Before a potential leader is trained in the methods of leading a group, he must walk in spiritual victory, exhibiting freedom from previous sin patterns, whether overt or secret. The amazing success of the International Charismatic Mission (70 cells in 1991 to 14,000 cells in 2002) has startled other churches to realize the importance of helping people deal with past patterns of sin and release them into spiritual freedom. This church uses Encounter Retreats as a major part of the inner-life development stage of their equipping process.

There are many different ways to lead people into spiritual freedom. One of the best is Jim Egli's, *Encounter God*. Others include: *7 Steps to Freedom*, by Neil Anderson, *Living Streams*, by Jack Hayford, and many others.

In the Old Testament, God gave the Israelites the Promised Land, and they conquered most of it. However, enemies gained strongholds in the land, places where God's people couldn't drive out the enemy. An Encounter Retreat helps people regain land Satan has taken in their lives.

Below are four basic action steps that could be included in a four-stage equipping track.

- Basic doctrine action step:
  Be baptized in water.
- Inner development action step:
  Have a regular daily quiet time.
- Personal evangelism action step:
  Witness to and invite a non-Christian to the cell meeting.
- Cell leadership training action step:
  Lead a cell group.

Written Resources

The *Encounter God* material, written for a retreat event, has proven to be one of the most effective. In the retreat sessions, participants work through the following topics:

- Understanding spiritual warfare (teaching on strongholds)
- From darkness to light (liberation from occult bondage)
- From bondage to freedom (liberation from the sins of the flesh)
- From impurity to purity (dealing with sexual strongholds)
- From brokenness to wholeness (learning to forgive others)
- From rebellion to submission (liberation from rebellious attitudes)
- From cursing to blessing (breaking curses over our lives)
- Living in victory (maintaining a close walk with Jesus)
- The filling of the Spirit (how to be filled with the Spirit of God)

The goal is liberation and freedom—not ritualistic legalism.

Before our church held Encounter Retreats, my wife and I (Joel) trained Nancy to lead a cell group by taking her through the various steps of our training track. However, she needed deeper help, unseen help. Our training ministry had an impact on her life while we were with her, but it was like the training wore off, and she'd fall back into depressive patterns, refusing even to come back to the cell group. "I have to work this through myself," she'd tell us over the phone. "When I have it all worked out, then I'll come back to the cell." Knowing this was Satan's trick to separate and destroy, I pleaded with her to allow us to help.

My wife and I noticed the training didn't free her from past bondage and depression. Since we as a church weren't offering Encounter Retreats, we decided to send Nancy to a Spirit-filled professional counselor. The counselor confronted Nancy on many hidden issues of past bondage and strongholds. Through intense bondage breaking, Nancy confessed, released, and cut loose past thievery, bitterness, and generational bondage.

After several sessions with this counselor, Nancy was forever changed. She was suddenly a bold Christian, ready to help others, and became one of our most effective cell leaders. She wrote the following testimony:

> Now I feel that God is in control of my life, and my life is so much better. I have a real joy, a happiness like none other, and an extreme confidence that God is with me and that every day is a new one. At times I can't control my tears. I now feel like a useful person for my God and also for society. Today, I'm a new creature, free from my bondages, in order to give my life to the one who saved me. My Lord overcame and destroyed my chains.

Most churches can't afford to send every member to professional, Spirit-filled counselors. Most churches, however, have many people like Nancy, who are enslaved to sin and strongholds.

An Encounter Retreat offers a way for a majority of church members to deal with past hurts and bondages. It gives them the opportunity to deal with obstacles, sinful habits, and strongholds that constantly come back to haunt them. An Encounter Retreat goes beyond personal counseling, by teaching Biblical principles on holiness and deliverance from satanic strongholds, which may or may not be present in a counseling situation.

Principle #4: Use a Variety of Methods for Equipping.

Because a pastor is trained to teach and preach, he falls into the trap of doing what he knows best. He assumes the best way to equip people is to get those people into a room and have them listen to him talk for an hour. Therefore, for new believer equipping, the senior pastor assembles new believers and lectures to them, over a six-week period, on the nature of Christ and his atonement. While such equipping is good, and better than nothing, it assumes that all people learn best through the lecture model.

A church's equipping method must take into account that not everyone learns the same way. Some learn by reading. Others learn through listening to someone talk. Most need to talk about what they're learning, in order to absorb the material. In other words, the equipping method should not be limited to an information dump. People need a place to process what they're learning. Therefore, most equipping models use a variety of methods, including:

- One-on-one mentoring from a more mature believer
- Support prayer triads (Often called Life Transformation Groups)
- Reading
- Small group processing
- Classroom teaching
- Retreat events

Written Resources

For a great resource for one-on-one mentoring see *How to Mentor Another Christian* by Ralph W. Neighbour Jr.

Some believe the only way to train new believers is one-on-one. Others disagree and train new believers in a group setting. During one seminar, I (Joel) mentioned that our church most commonly trains new believers in a group setting. One person shook his head in disbelief and said, "But isn't one-on-one discipleship in the cell group the only true way to equip new believers?" I reminded him that even Jesus didn't always use the one-on-one discipleship format. He trained the twelve disciples in a group.

Written Resources

For information on Life Transformation Groups see *Cultivating a Life for God* by Neil Cole.

The equipping methodology (where or how you train people) must not be confused with the equipping track (the steps of training.). In the fastest growing cell group churches around the world, there's a great variety of methodologies for equipping people (e.g., one-on-one discipleship, one-on-two or three, training after the cell group, seminars, classes, retreats, or a combination of these).

Principle #5: Provide Additional Equipping for Cell Group Leaders.

Many cell churches fall into the trap of over-complicating cell member training for cell leadership. They try to place too many steps of training for cell members before they ever become cell group leaders. Therefore potential leaders never actually arrive at the point of leading a cell group.

After people have been trained for leadership and are leading a group, they can then enter into more advanced training. The Little Falls Christian Centre in South Africa has developed an exemplary equipping system. It equips cell members through a clear, concise track that trains new believers rapidly to enter cell leadership. In 1999, 970 passed through this first level and were able to eliminate the cell leader shortage in their church. LFCC provides additional training for those who are leading a cell group, providing added biblical and spiritual nourishment for those most needing it—the front-line soldiers.

The Door of Hope Church, pastored by Al Woods, is another great example of second-tier training. This church has developed a leadership-training track for cell leaders and zone shepherds (overseers of three to six cells).

For cell group leaders, the church might provide additional doctrinal courses, a spiritual warfare course, teaching on spiritual gifts, etc. There's considerable room for creativity and many excellent courses and materials. One church decided to use its denomination's theological education by extension.

Cell leaders deserve special treatment because of their important, foundational role in the church. Treat them like royalty. Offer them all the help and training they need in order to be effective.

Some cell churches even offer a third and fourth level of training, leading to pastoral ministry. Faith Community Baptist Church features an extensive training program to prepare higher-level leaders (i.e., zone pastors). Bethany World Prayer Center hosts a three-year Bible school on its own property. Neither church requires higher education for cell leadership—it's simply provided for those who feel called to full-time ministry (and who've been successful in leading and multiplying their cell group).

Principle #6: Use Only One Equipping Track.

While allowing flexibility in the training methodology, a church should only have one training track. After deciding on a church-wide training track, (ideally both first and second levels), a church should require that all future leaders pass through the same training. This will assure that:

- All future cell leaders are biblically and spiritually trained.
- All are prepared to evangelize and lead a cell.
- All are in line with the leadership of the church.
- All understand the church's vision.

To guarantee long-term success, make sure every future leader has passed through the same process and has received the same training.

Principle #7: Encourage Every Cell Group Member to Enter the Equipping Track with the Goal of Eventually Leading a Cell Group.

Every believer should be equipped. Ideally, each new believer should immediately start attending a cell group and begin the equipping track. In reality, it often takes more time. However, the more a church closes the gap between idealism and reality, the more effective it will be.

The goal of the track is to train growing Christians to be cell group leaders. Don't pressure those who refuse to enter training to become cell leaders, but constantly promote it (both at the cell and at the celebration levels). Those who desire to follow the church's vision enter training to become cell leaders.

Principle #8: Continually Adjust and Improve Training.

A church should fine-tune the equipping system continually. Cornerstone Church in Harrisonburg, Virginia, led by Pastor Gerald Martin, has been working on its model for seven years. Dennis Wadley, a pastor in Santa Barbara, California, says their equipping track has been in a process of development for three years, as they've been creating and recreating the tools. Each church will need to adapt, adjust, and improve its training system after receiving feedback from members.

MODELS OF EQUIPPING
Equipping through One-on-One Mentoring Model

This model is based on the relationship between two cell group members—a mentor and a protégé. Each new believer in the cell group is assigned a mentor. With the help of the mentor, the new believer passes through the various levels of the equipping journey. Ralph Neighbour, Jr. instructs, "Assign each new believer to someone in the group who will help them become established in their walk with Christ."[18]

The mentor-protégé relationship lasts from three to four months. Then the relationship changes to partnership. It's during this transitional time that the mentor trains his protégé to become a mentor of others. The mentor focuses on the six leadership characteristics, which include listening, interceding, modeling, teaching, leading, and involving the disciples with other Christians.[19]

As a part of each stage of the journey, the protégé will work through an equipping book. Each week the protégé will meet with his mentor to talk about what he's learning. Between books, the protégé will attend a retreat to launch him or her into the next book or booklet.

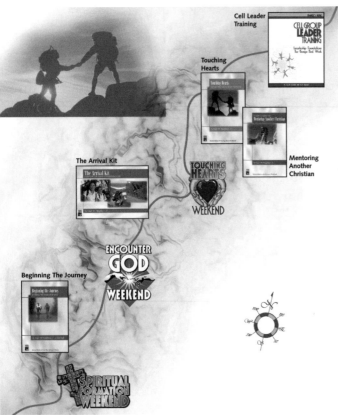

The main characteristic that separates Neighbour's training manuals from most discipleship booklets (i.e. Navigator or Campus Crusade) is that they're so intimately linked with the cell group. In the cornerstone booklet, *The Arrival Kit*, Week One, Day One, informs the new believer, "Small groups, or 'cells,' are forming all over the earth … Typically, one person will serve the group as the leader and facilitator. Some day, when you have matured, you may also shepherd others as a cell leader. There will never be more than fifteen in your family cell, and you will soon discover that each member is on a spiritual journey with you."[20] Not only does Neighbour introduce new believer training and cell group involvement simultaneously, he also plants the seed of small group leadership.

The Retreat Focused Equipping Model

Pastor Harold Weitsz of Little Falls Christian Centre in South Africa has taken the best of Ralph Neighbour's equipping track and then adapted it to his own context.

Every potential leader attends the training track, consisting of four weekend encounters spread over a four-month period. That's right—cell members move through the process of new believer to trained cell leader in four months! Preceding each encounter weekend, each member receives a process booklet with questions to answer. After completion of this booklet, the cell leader reviews and signs it, thus permitting the member to attend the encounter weekend. The booklet becomes the "entry ticket" for the appropriate encounter weekend and qualifies the person to receive the weekend training manual.

The four encounter weekends cover basic concepts of Christianity: spiritual freedom and victory, soul winning, and cell leadership training. Each weekend is held in the church, starts on Friday night, and finishes on Saturday. The member must faithfully attend his cell meeting to fulfill the assignments of the weekend. Once the course has been completed, the new leader is expected to attend the quarterly general leadership training weekend.

The weekend encounters are repeated continually throughout the year and enable each member to select four weekends suitable to his or her lifestyle and other commitments. One can therefore complete the four encounters in a four-month period or longer.

After becoming a cell leader, further training takes place. There is specialized training for cell group overseers, and a two-year course of the LFCC College must be completed by all who emerge as new potential pastors from the ranks of the cell overseers.

The Group-Focused Equipping Model

The bulk of the equipping in this model takes place in a classroom or retreat setting. In this system, very little training takes place within the cell. Rather, cell leaders ask cell members to take the training courses in the church and/or in a retreat setting that's administered and taught within each homogeneous department.

The most prominent cell group church using this model is the International Charismatic Mission, though other cell churches also train their leaders in a group format. ICM does not use one-on-one training in the cell. New believers are trained in a class setting, along with many others. The equipping at ICM takes approximately six months to complete. Although this is the average time, some homogeneous departments at ICM take less time, and others more.

The following steps outline the official process for every new convert. However, some new converts don't attend an Encounter Retreat immediately. Instead, they enter the School of Leadership and only later attend an Encounter Retreat. Flexibility, therefore, is possible within ICM's training.

Steps One & Two: Initial Follow-up and Life in the Cell

During the celebration services (entire church on Sunday) or congregational service (one of the homogeneous group gatherings), there's always the opportunity to receive Jesus Christ. Large numbers respond and are gathered into a separate room after the service. Trained workers present the Gospel once again in a more personal manner.

The information of each new convert is placed on cards, which are immediately entered into the computer system at ICM. This information is distributed to the different homogeneous departments, and within forty-eight hours cell leaders contact the new believers.

The new person begins the Christian life in a cell group. The new convert receives personal care and spiritual food within the group. In the context of the cell group, each person is pastored—but not trained. Within the cell group, the new convert will hear about a three-day retreat called an Encounter Retreat. Before attending this event, the new convert must take three preparatory lessons taught in a classroom setting.

Step Three: Pre-Encounter

A pre-encounter is a series of two to three classes that focus on preparing people for the Encounter Retreat. Because many who attend an Encounter Retreat are new to the work of God's Spirit, the pre-encounter classes will include teaching on basic Christian doctrine, and the need to be set free from sin. Each lesson is offered in a classroom setting in the church, taught by a trained teacher within the particular homogeneous group (one lesson per week).

I (Joel) learned the hard way about the importance of holding pre-encounter sessions to prepare the people for the retreat. During our first retreat, we noticed a lot of time was spent educating people about the importance of dealing with past bondages, and the need for confessing our sins to each other.

Because we didn't do this, some thought the retreat was a series of sermons or even a recreational event. I could understand why some resisted deeper-life teaching and why it took longer for the Spirit of God to break through.

Step Four: Encounter Retreat

Those who receive Jesus Christ as adults are often bound up by past hurts, dysfunctional behavior, and sinful patterns. The act of "accepting Jesus" saves them from eternal hell, but doesn't instantly change their behavior. The Encounter Retreat is a three-day event designed to help liberate the new believer from past bondage. ICM believes a three-day Encounter Retreat is equal to one whole year of attending the church.

An Encounter Retreat begins on Friday evening and finishes late Sunday afternoon. Between 70-120 people attend a retreat, held away from the city and routine schedules in order to concentrate fully on God.

The Encounter Retreat deals with four areas in the person's life. First, there's teaching on the security of salvation. Second, the participants experience liberation and inner healing. Designated leaders teach the true meaning of repentance and how to live in broken surrender before God. Third, the Encounter Retreat is a time to receive the fullness of the Spirit of God. Fourth, the new believer receives teaching about the vision of ICM. Those attending hear ICM's plans to use each one of them in cell ministry.

Step Five: Post-Encounter

The Post-Encounter takes place immediately after the Encounter Retreat and prepares the new believer to enter the School of Leaders. Sanctification is both a crisis and a progressive experience. This simply means a believer can experience quick spurts of holiness but shouldn't count on instant perfection. When we see Jesus, we'll be like him, but until that time, it's a continual journey.

Before ICM implemented the Post-Encounter, many people left the church immediately after attending the Encounter Retreat. ICM eventually realized it was a counterattack from Satan. After implementing the Post-Encounter lessons, ICM has seen its retention rate dramatically increase.[21] At ICM, the Post-Encounter consists of three lessons: Foundations of the Faith, Growing in Christian Service, and Christian Character, taught in a group setting (mostly in a classroom).[22]

Step Six: School of Leadership

After the Post-Encounter teaching, the young believer begins attending the yearlong School of Leadership. This consists of a two-hour weekly class that takes place among the different homogeneous groups.

César Castellanos has written a book for each semester. Encounter One (first semester) covers God's purpose for mankind, man's sinful condition, the person of Jesus Christ, and the uniqueness of Christianity. Encounter Two (second semester) deals with the cross of Jesus Christ. Encounter Three (third semester) teaches baptism, the devotional life, authority of the Scriptures, and the doctrine of the Holy Spirit.[23] Another manual, C.A.F.E. 2000 (a compilation of cell leadership training materials), is taught alongside the Encounter manuals, in order to prepare the person to lead a cell group.

Step Seven: Second Encounter Retreat

This second retreat is designed to reinforce the commitments made at the first retreat and to instill final principles in the potential leader before he or she launches a cell group.[24] The second retreat normally occurs after the first semester of the School of Leadership, immediately before the person starts leading his or her cell group.

Step Eight: Lead a Cell Group

It's important to remember that a person doesn't have to finish the entire School of Leadership before opening a cell group. Many, in fact, lead an open cell before attending a second Encounter Retreat. Often, the School of Leadership provides ongoing training for those already leading a cell group.

Step Nine: More In-depth Teaching

For those cell leaders who desire more advanced training, there's a graduate level training track that uses a series of materials entitled "Firm as a Rock."

Step Ten: School of Teachers

The School of Teachers is a course designed to train potential teachers to teach in the School of Leadership. Potential teachers learn various teaching skills and especially how to apply the teaching to the lives of their students.

Sunday School Equipping Model

This model is a version of the group-focused equipping model. Many churches that have a strong tradition of Sunday school have embraced this approach. Rather than the traditional age-graded education model, these churches use the Sunday school hour to equip people through the four stages of training identified under Principle #1 above. These courses are designed for people to graduate from them, and then move into the next course. This is in contrast to the old model of Sunday school, where no one ever graduates.

One church converted the 9:15 a.m. adult Sunday school into its equipping track for adults. Worship service began at 10:30 a.m. Everyone was encouraged to attend one of four courses, which ran simultaneously in different classrooms.

The Journey Guide-Focused Equipping Model

Ben Wong, founding pastor of Shepherd Community Church in Hong Kong, developed this model, desiring to create an equipping track that's flexible. He found that cell group members need different kinds of equipping because each one has different struggles. For instance, if an immature Christian is struggling with what it means to be a father and a faithful husband, it might be better for him to go through a book or a tape series to help with this struggle, rather than taking a generic inner-life development course. Or, if a single mom needs help in developing a budget and managing her money, she should work through some information that will help her take control of her finances.

To accomplish this, Ben Wong developed the Journey Guide-Focused Equipping Model. While the Equipping Journey by Ralph W. Neighbour Jr. uses the same Journey Guides, this model uses them differently. In the Neighbour approach, the Journey Guides are used to introduce a predetermined book. Ben Wong uses the Journey Guides to determine the needs of the person, and then the resources to meet those needs are chosen.

Ben Wong lists four purposes for the Journey Guides:

1. They give the person an opportunity to evaluate his life.
2. They introduce the person to new concepts that are important for the next stage of his journey.
3. They give a preview of the journey ahead.
4. They allow the mentor to know the present state of growth of the person.

One church with four Sunday worship services ran training courses simultaneously. For example:
- 9:00 worship service
  Basic doctrine
  Cell evangelism
- 10:30 worship service
  Cell leadership training
  Inner life development
- 12:00 worship service
  Basic doctrine
  Cell evangelism
- 6 p.m. worship service
  Cell leadership training
  Inner life development

There are three basic Journey Guides, *The Journey Guide for New Believers, The Journey Guide for Growing Christians*, and *The Journey Guide for Cell Group Leaders*. These Journey Guides help participants evaluate their progress on their journey, and then point to needs and resources that will take them further along the journey.

While this model is extremely flexible, it's not chaotic. It does provide a basic course or book for new believers that all new believers will take. Before or during the time a new believer is taking this course or working through new believer material, he will fill out the *Journey Guide for New Believers*.

Upon completion of that guide, the person will meet with a mentor and talk about how he responded to the questions in it. From the responses, the mentor will help the new believer establish two or three goals to address the needs that become obvious. This is done through the use of the Journey Map, which is the last part of each *Journey Guide*.

To meet the goals identified on the Journey Map, the mentor should be provided a list of resources by the pastoral team to address various needs. These resources form a type of library and can come in the form of Bible studies, books, booklets, articles, audio series, videotapes, websites, etc. The mentor need not come up with these things, because the pastor has access to many more resources and the time to identify those that are most crucial.

When the protégé works through the goals identified on the Journey Map, it's time to move to the *Journey Guide for Growing Christians*. New goals are identified and new steps are taken by the protégé. The process is repeated for the *Journey Guide for Cell Group Leaders*.

Pantego Bible Church has developed a similar pattern. The leadership has identified 30 core competencies that they feel are crucial to basic discipleship in the church. They have developed an online assessment to help individuals determine their areas of competency and the areas they need to work on.

The Huddle Model of Training

The Elim Church in El Salvador has taken a different approach in preparing cell members for cell leadership. Instead of a step-by-step process for walking a person through the stages of new believer, the various stages of maturity, and then into cell leader training, this church depends upon its mid-week expository Bible teaching services to provide foundational Bible training.

Written Resources

The Journey Guide for New Believers
The Journey Guide for Growing Christians
The Journey Guide for Cell Group Leaders

Web Resource

For more information on the core competencies of Pantego Bible Church, visit their website at <www.pantego.org>.

Then, when people are ready to enter into cell leadership, they go through a four-week training course. The District Pastor teaches this course, with the help of a Zone Pastor. Each district offers this course repeatedly throughout the year. The following table explains the content of this leadership training course:

In this system, there are very few initial requirements for becoming a cell leader. Instead, this system realizes that people learn and become equipped in the heat of the battle. Therefore, there's a heavy dependence upon a weekly huddle meeting, which provides ongoing supervision and training.

Once a person has become a cell leader, the supervisor is constantly coaching him or her, during weekly lesson preparation gathering and in the weekly planning meetings (the supervisor rotates among the planning meetings as well as the cell meetings). Even during the Saturday night cell group, the cell leader can expect to see the supervisor, even if it's only for five minutes. Because there's so much coaching, role playing, and discipleship, few initial requirements are needed.

FIRST WEEK	The Calling to Lead
	The Vision of the Cell Group
	The Reason for Cell Groups
SECOND WEEK	Requirements and Characteristics of Leadership
	Lesson Preparation
THIRD WEEK	How the Cell Groups Operate
	How the Cell Groups Multiply
FOURTH WEEK	Administration and Organization of Cell Groups
	Final Exam

Elim's care structure is divided geographically into sectors (a neighborhood unit), zones (a group of sectors), and districts (various zones). The weekly huddles take place on the zone level. Elim prepares the lessons in written form for the cell leader, and then diligently trains the leader on lesson delivery.

Little is left to chance. Encouragement, motivation, and vision are transmitted during these meetings. All cell leaders are required to attend the weekly huddle.

FOLLOW THE PRINCIPLES

Don't follow methods; rather, extract principles from the methods and apply them to the situation. Cell group churches that are serious about reaping the harvest invest heavily in future leadership. They invest in equipping systems for developing small group leaders for the harvest. Serious churches go beyond these models and look closely at the principles.

PRACTICAL STEPS FOR DEVELOPING AN EQUIPPING TRACK

The best equipping tracks highlight excellent material. The materials in these equipping tracks promote the basic doctrines of the faith (along with the specific vision of the church), spiritual life development, evangelism, and leadership training. They're concise, clear, and don't overwhelm the learner.

There are two major points to remember when selecting training material for your cell church. First, is it biblical? Does it reflect the pure doctrine "once delivered by the saints?" Second, is it connected with your cell church philosophy? In other words, is the training conducive to convert every member into a cell leader?

Most cell churches around the world have developed their own materials. It's wise to take advantage of their experiences. Remember the words of leadership expert Tom Peters: "The best leaders ... are the best 'note-takers', the best 'askers,' the best learners. They are shameless thieves."[25]

Peters recommends the title, "Swiped from the Best with Pride."[26] Someone has said that plagiarism is copying one man's material, while research is gathering the materials of many. On a more serious note, plagiarism is a sin and the law forbids us to make whole photocopies of someone else's copyrighted material. Churches can, however, use their ideas and synthesize them with their own. Here are the basic steps to follow in developing your equipping track.

1. Obtain Copies of Other Equipping Material.

Research what's out there. Obtain copies of the material from the best cell churches.

2. Test the Material.

After receiving materials from a variety of sources, review and test them to determine those that best fit the church. Some materials work better in more educated churches, while others are designed to equip those with less schooling. Evaluate the stance taken on specific theological issues to make sure they line up with the church's beliefs.

Many churches, while in the process of testing materials, combine materials from different churches. They might use a book from Ralph W. Neighbour, Jr. for new believers, a course from their denomination for inner life development, an evangelism course from a church down the road, and the cell leader training written internally.

3. Listen to God and Adapt.

Most importantly, listen to God. Each church must discover what's best for its own particular context. Include your specific doctrinal slant. God has been uniquely working in each situation. Adapt the materials according to needs. Over time, most churches establish their own materials because they fit better. God has made each church unique, with particular convictions and methodologies. It's best to reflect this uniqueness in the church's equipping material.

EFFECTIVE CELL GROUP COACHING

50

Joel Comiskey

The word "coach" comes from an old Hungarian term referring to the carriages and carts that were made in the village of the Kocs. On the American Western frontier, the large four-wheeled horse-drawn carriage was called a "stagecoach." The use of the term evolved in the 19th century as a part of university slang to mean an instructor or trainer, "the notion being that the student was conveyed through the exam by the tutor as if he were riding in a carriage."[27]

A cell coach equips cell leaders with the tools, knowledge, and opportunities they need to develop themselves and become more effective.[28] A cell coach encourages, nourishes, and challenges cell leaders to grow and multiply their cell groups. The word "coach" is descriptive of the role a per-

Written Resources

How To Be a Great Cell Group Coach by Joel Comiskey

son plays as he or she supports cell leaders under his or her care. It's not a sacred term. In fact, churches use many terms to identify the role played by the cell group coach: supervisor, section leader, G-12 leader, cell overseer, cell sponsor, even "L" (the Roman numeral for 50).

Just as the best athletes in the world require coaches to help them play their best games, so do the best cell leaders. No cell leader, no matter how gifted or how well trained, will be able to lead as effectively alone as he or she would with the help of a cell group coach.

THE STRUCTURE OF COACHING

One structure for coaching encourages a full-time pastor to oversee twelve cell leaders, while a lay leader envisions caring for three daughter cell leaders and continues to lead an open cell group. The goal of coaching three lay cell leaders is a more realistic and manageable number that gives lay volunteers a feasible goal: multiply the original cell three times and care for each one of those leaders, while continuing to lead the original cell.[29]

This coaching structure is called G-12.3 and uses all the principles from another popular coaching model called "the G-12 model" (i.e., multiplication without division, every member a cell leader, every leader a supervisor, etc.). It simply reduces the load on lay leaders to three. Steven L. Ogne, church planter and coaching consultant, says,

Most of the ideal systems you see described in small group seminars these days say the ratio should be one to five or even one to ten. I'll tell you what, in my experience in our busy society, coaches are much more effective when they're coaching one to three group leaders. It really does allow them to visit the groups. It really does allow them to have enough time to build relationships, and it reduces the stress on them … Go for the connections that work, not the pretty organizational chart.[30]

In this structure, a staff pastor would lead a G-12 (Group A). Each one

Written Resources

From 12 to 3: How to Apply the G-12 Principles in Your Church by Joel Comiskey

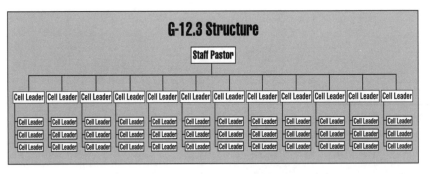

of the G-12 members would lead an weekly open cell group (Group C) and coach three other cell group leaders in a G-3 (Group B). The members of the G-3 would lead weekly open cell groups (Groups D).

Is Three a Sacred Number?

Although the number three is important in the Bible (e.g., Trinity, resurrection, etc.), gathering three cell leaders into a G-3 does not unlock the door to special blessing. Pastors might, in fact, decide to ask lay leaders to care for five cell leaders. Or they might feel led to develop a G-10.5 system (staff pastors care for ten cell leaders while lay leaders care for five multiplication leaders). The G-12.3 structure is principle-based, built upon observations of a realistic span of care between lay leaders and multiplication leaders.

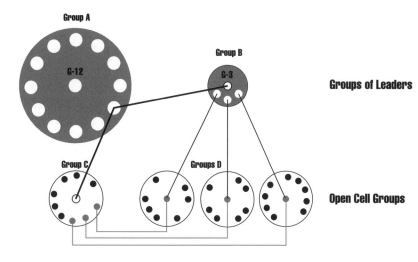

Three is a feasible number of groups for a volunteer leader to oversee. Lay people can immediately get their hands on it, and lay people training to become cell leaders can grasp the vision of multiplying a cell three times and caring for those three leaders much better than multiplying a cell twelve times.

Can the Group Go Beyond Three?

What if a lay person wants to care for more than three? If a lay leader wants to continue to lead his own cell and continue multiplying leaders beyond three, encourage him to "Go for it!" If a lay leader says, "I've already multiplied my cell three times and am caring for those leaders, but I plan on multiplying my cell again and want to supervise it too," encourage him.

Starting with a goal of three enables lay leaders to grasp the vision with firm purpose, without feeling overwhelmed. They can expand beyond three because they're in a leadership cell above them that provides guidance and support when they need it.

The number three simply reduces the coaching goal to reasonable proportions. It's not intended to be a legalistic straightjacket on a fruitful cell leader. On the contrary, it's intended to give practical hope that it's perhaps possible to fulfill the goal of multiplying three times and someday even surpass that.

HELP THE THREE FIND THEIR OWN THREE

True success occurs when a mother cell leader has multiplied three times, is leading his or her own cell group, AND is helping the daughter cell leaders find their daughter cell groups. Paul said to his spiritual son Timothy, "You then, my son, be strong in the grace that is in Christ Jesus. And the things you have heard me say in the presence of many witnesses entrust to reliable men who will also be qualified to teach others" (2 Timothy 2:1-2).

The person who's leading a cell group, caring for the daughter cell leaders, and also helping the daughter cell leaders multiply their own groups, has truly entered fully into this vision.

The goal, therefore, of a G-12.3 leader is to help his disciples find their disciples, while leading a healthy open cell group too. An effective G-12.3 leader won't be satisfied until those in his or her immediate group have spotted, developed, and released their own disciples.

WHO CARES FOR THE FOURTH CELL LEADER?

The fourth cell leader is a cell leader developed by a mother cell after that mother cell leader has formed a G-12.3. The fourth cell leader should be cared for by one of the parent cell leader's three disciples (daughter cell leaders). In other words, the fourth daughter cell leader would continue to stay in the family, but would not be cared for directly by the parent cell leader. This would put the fourth cell leader in the position of a grand-daughter to the parent cell leader.

This is the result of a trade-off between the ideal (the mother directly caring for the daughter) and the practical (the mother doesn't have the time or energy). However, everyone belonging to the mother cell leader's network would come together periodically for summit meetings, and the mother cell leader would continue to care for the one who's caring for the grandchild.

Four to five years down the road, if all leaders have multiplied their cells yearly, it may be necessary to reevaluate who supervises the original mother's new groups. At that time, the original mother cell leader might be mature enough to extend her own network to G-4, G-5, or even G-12! Better yet, this is the time to think seriously about asking this fruitful multiplication leader to join the full-time staff.

HOW LARGE CAN A NETWORK BECOME WITH ONE PASTOR?

We know that in the G-12 care structure (or an adaptation of it) degeneration occurs at lower levels. The farther away a disciple is from the original discipler, the higher the degree of degeneration. The original twelve understand the vision. The farther away a disciple is from the original discipler, the more the purity and intensity of the vision fades.

Experience has shown that a network of cells begins to decline in quality once it exceeds seventy-five cell groups. (Remember that each full-time pastor ultimately has twelve leaders under his care, as opposed to three.) This number comes from practical, common sense experience, as opposed to hard scientific data. Billy Hornsby, former staff pastor at Bethany World Prayer Center, suggests a lower number:

> In our own experience at Bethany, we first committed to add zone pastors as the number of cell groups grew at a 25/1 ratio. We have since discovered that with the principle of twelve, that ratio can be as much as one pastor for 50 cell groups or even more. You will know when it is necessary to add pastoral staff by the workload on the existing staff. The senior pastor should develop his "twelve" and only add staff as he needs to do so.[31]

Degeneration typically arises not by someone leaving his post, but rather by offering lower-quality care due to an overburdened load. In such cases, the senior pastor must step in to assure continued quality or risk future failure at the lower cell levels, because pastors can't continue providing care to so many cell leaders.

WHO WILL LEAD THE NEW NETWORK?

Maintaining relationships between mother cell leader and daughter cell leaders is one of the core values behind the G-12.3 care system. When the network under one pastor grows too large, intimate care and discipleship will suffer. Therefore, when one network reaches around seventy-five cells, it's time to multiply it.

Where will a church find the new pastor to care for half the network? Choose a qualified, successful cell leader from within the network and raise that person up to a full-time staff position. Doing so will maintain relationships, continuity, and authority. It's also a testimony to everyone else that higher-level leadership is an attainable goal.

INSTILLING THE VISION OF THREE EARLY

David Jaramillo, senior pastor of The Light, an exciting church in Quito, Ecuador, has a clear cell vision and knows how to raise up leaders. He's able to grasp the different aspects of the cell vision without losing his focus. Pastor David became convinced of the G-12.3 strategy and actively promoted it, but then he went one step beyond. He decided to instill the vision of leading a cell and multiplying it three times in the Encounter Retreat (a two-day spiritual retreat that's part of the equipping track and gives new believers victory from past bondages).

Even new believers in the Encounter Retreat would hear the goal of raising up three leaders. "God is going to free you and bless you. He wants to use you mightily. After you pass through the training track, which will take about nine months, you'll begin to lead your own cell group. But that isn't everything. You'll also go on to multiply your cell group at least three times and you'll care for those three new leaders! You'll not only lead a cell group, but you'll also be a coach of future cell leaders."

Pastor David began to instill in the new cell leaders the hope of one day leading a cell group and multiplying it. In fact, the vision-casting time was the culmination of the Encounter Retreat. Each new believer left the retreat with the vision of multiplication.

The number three is feasible. It's too easy to talk about "the twelve," when the majority of the people haven't even considered "the one" (leading a cell group). Start by setting feasible and realistic goals for your church members, and the new believers they'll reach through the dynamic power of the cell group church!

THE CONTENT OF COACHING

Habits are practices a person does without thinking about them. They become such a part of a person's character that no conscious effort is required. The best cell group coaches use seven common habits in their ministry and support of their leaders.

Receiving

Great coaches need in-depth wisdom and constant encouragement. The best way to get these is to go directly to the source: Jesus Christ. Meet with God before meeting with leaders.

Coaches have nothing of true value to give their cell leaders apart from what they're receiving from God himself. For their coaching to be effective and fruitful, they must be plugged into the power source. After spending time in God's presence, coaches will notice a new attentiveness to his presence in their daily activities.

Cell group leaders are frontline warriors and, for this reason, the devil levels heavy artillery at them. Coaches must protect their cell leaders by covering them with a prayer shield that can withstand even the fiercest assaults. Prayer is desperately needed to protect cell leaders from enemy attack. Praying daily for cell leaders is one area where Christian coaches, unlike their secular counterparts, can excel. The Spirit of God is at work between coaching sessions.

Listening

Listening involves intensive and earnest concentration on what a leader is saying. The human mind processes ideas and thoughts far faster than a person can speak them (by five to one), so it's easy to drift or daydream when someone's talking.

Before a coach can really listen to someone, he must prepare his heart. Since coaches face the same problems, difficulties, and fears that leaders face, they'll need a special touch from God in order to focus on the leaders' needs and not their own. "When you find yourself trapped in self-analysis—defending, judging, feeling annoyed ... your job is to get yourself unhooked. You've got to push all of that internal confusion out of the way ..."[32]

The only way for a coach to fully separate himself and focus on his leaders is through prayer and meditation. Only when a coach untangles himself through the Spirit of God can he fully listen to the needs of his leaders.

When a cell leader comes to a coach with a concern or problem, most coaches are tempted to give their expert advice. Telling the leader what to do seems like the quickest way to remedy the situation. But when a coach shares too much, he or she undermines the leader's story. Most leaders

Great coaches:
- Receive from God
- Listen to the leader
- Encourage the leader
- Care for the leader
- Develop/train the leader
- Strategize with the leader
- Challenge the leader

respond with a cold silence when their coaches spend too much time reiterating their stories. A good coach should hold back and help the leader discover the answer through carefully designed questions.

Encouragement

Cell leadership can be a wearisome journey. It's not for the faint-hearted. The fact is that members often don't show up, evangelism fails, babies get sick, events fill the calendar, and bosses require extra hours. Cell leadership involves making phone calls, developing new leaders, evangelism, and administration. In the face of so many tasks and problems, how can coaches keep leaders alive, well, and ready to follow God?

The answer is encouragement. A coach who encourages can make the difference between success and failure, between the leader continuing—and eventually multiplying the cell—or throwing in the towel. This ministry of encouragement takes on additional importance because it has the potential to have long-term, widespread impact on many people, not just on an individual cell group leader.

The writer to the Hebrews says, "Let us not give up meeting together, as some are in the habit of doing, but let us encourage one another—and all the more as you see the Day approaching" (Hebrews 10:25). Discouragement comes naturally to everyone. Introspection haunts people; they compare themselves to others and feel like they don't measure up. A word of encouragement can often make a huge difference.

A cell group coach should be the head cheerleader for his or her cell group leaders. Cell leaders who are supported and encouraged will serve above and beyond the call of duty. Those who wonder if they're appreciated or even noticed will eventually run out of steam.

Caring

A focus only on results will turn cell group leaders into cogs in a machine. Cell leaders will begin to feel used by the church to "produce converts," or to "grow a big church." Ministry is not an assembly line. Ministry happens through people who live lives. The life of a cell leader is a journey, a process. A coach is a person who walks with his leaders through that process over a period of time—not just a few days.

The coach must help leaders along their lifelong journeys. The coach might discover, for example, that the leader is out of control in financial spending, drinking, or pornography. Or perhaps there are issues of pride, rebellion, workaholism, ignoring children or wife, skipping church, or not tithing. The coach must care enough to confront.

Find the help your leader needs. Is it a training course? A bondage-breaking retreat? Professional counseling? The leaders you're coaching need wholeness, and this must be a top priority.

Developing/Training

Discover the vision your leader already has and shape it. Although a coach will want to expand the vision, he must first discover what the leader is already dreaming about. Then stir that vision, fan it into flame, and cause it to grow.

Coaching's goal, as opposed to that of training, is to help leaders become lifelong learners. A great coach, therefore, should make sure the cell leaders are reading books, attending workshops, and pursuing new ways to improve their leadership capacities. It's the coach's responsibility to help interpret the data, while meeting with leaders one-on-one or in the group/huddle setting. Bill Donahue says, "Coaches support each leader's ministry by connecting them to necessary resources, such as curriculum, training, or prayer support."[33]

Great resources will help coaches and cell leaders strategize better. It's up to the coach to put leaders into contact with the resources they need to succeed. Great resources will fill leaders' minds with the seeds necessary to get the job done. Coaches must become resource people in order to improve themselves and the leaders in their care.

At times, a coach will need to answer the questions and be the expert, but first the coach should try to draw from the leader's well. The leader must wrestle with the issues and exhaust his or her own understanding first. A great coach will then capitalize on the insight that came from the leader's own mouth and will constantly remind the leader that it was his or her own insight.

Strategizing

The strategic vision for cell groups is found in Matthew 28:18-20: Make disciples. Cell ministry is the best way to fulfill Christ's command to make disciples. Cell leaders will be living out Matthew 28:18-20 when they begin coaching the new leaders who've left their cells to start their own groups.[34] Thus, cell multiplication, which results in the multiplication of leaders, is the principal goal of cell ministry.

Although the strategic vision is cell multiplication, coaches must spend the majority of their time focusing on details: raising up new leaders, promoting evangelism and discipleship, and keeping the parent cell leaders healthy.

If a leader concentrates solely on cell group dynamics (e.g. the lesson, listening skills, etc.), leadership development will suffer. If a leader only focuses on discipleship, the group will grow inward and stagnate. If a leader centers on evangelism, many believers will slip out the back door. For a cell group leader to reach the point of cell multiplication, he or she must do a lot of things well and should be congratulated and honored accordingly.

One of the most important details is finding an apprentice. A coach should work with the leader to identify a potential apprentice who possesses a hunger for God and a faithfulness to attend and participate in the cell. Then the coach should help the leader approach and develop the apprentice.

Challenging

A coach is not a good coach if he allows the leader to get away with mediocrity or to meander down the wrong path. Speak the truth. Tell it like it is! Paul says in Ephesians 4:15, "Instead, speaking the truth in love, we will in all things grow up into him who is the Head, that is, Christ." The love part ensures that coaches will be sensitive when they dare to speak the truth.

Can you imagine a sports coach who didn't tell players when they needed to improve? A great coach will zero in on the players' weaknesses in order to improve them. Players expect this from coaches.

A coach should ask leaders for permission to confront them on a deeper level. Although there'll be those spontaneous break-ins when the coach just goes for it, it's best to ask before entering the private areas of a leader's life. One way to say it: "Jane, can I have permission to share with you something I'm seeing about your life?"

PASS THE BATON

At the end of his life, Paul exhorted his own disciple, Timothy, "And the things you have heard me say in the presence of many witnesses entrust to reliable men who will also be qualified to teach others" (2 Timothy 2:2). Notice the word "reliable." The work of passing the baton to successive generations of leadership mustn't stop due to a bad link in the chain. Leadership development must continue.

A cell leader's main task, therefore, should be to work his way out of a job by training cell members to lead the cell group. Far from losing a job, disciple-making leaders gain authority, new leadership, and cell multiplication. They eventually become cell coaches! By concentrating on leadership development, coaches help leaders multiply their ministry over and over and over.

OPTIONS FOR EFFECTIVELY COACHING CELL GROUP LEADERS

M. Scott Boren

While coaching is paramount to the health and growth of cell groups, the exact coaching methods used vary from church to church. Basketball coaches operate from similar coaching principles, but they have different methods of getting their jobs done.

This chapter identifies various systems used by churches to coach cell leaders. These systems combine the following three methods, usually giving more emphasis to one over the other two:

1. All-cell leader meetings: Regular gatherings of all cell leaders and interns to hear the vision, receive encouragement, and pray together. These are also called super-huddles by some.
2. Coaching Cluster Meetings: Small group gatherings of the coach with his cell leaders. Some churches call a cluster a "huddle."
3. Ad hoc, one-on-one mentoring: Coach initiates meetings and phone calls with individual cell group leaders.

As a church grows beyond five to ten cell groups, it's vital that the leadership determine a workable coaching pattern that fits the church. The following have been observed and have proven to work well.

Quarterly all-cell-leader meetings, with ad hoc mentoring

Description: All cell group leaders gather once per quarter to receive encouragement, vision, and training. There are no required coaching cluster meetings. Instead, each coach determines the needs of the cell group leaders and seeks to meet those needs as he or she feels best, through one-on-one meetings, phone conversations, etc.

Advantages: 1. This limits the number of official meetings required. 2. This allows coaches the flexibility to spend time with leaders one-on-one to target specific needs, rather than sitting in official meetings led by a staff pastor.

Disadvantages: 1. This requires the coach to be highly self-motivated, therefore limiting those who are qualified to coach. 2. If the coach doesn't demonstrate initiative, he'll lose track of what's happening in the groups, which can lead to problems like heresy, cell group splinters, and unmet pastoral needs. 3. This limits the effectiveness of the training received in the quarterly meetings, because there's little continuity. 4. Cell group leaders tend to lose the vision when they don't hear it every month from the visionary leader.

Works best when: 1. Group leaders aren't willing to commit to more. 2. Groups aren't expected to grow and reach out to the lost, but emphasize ministering to those already part of the church. 3. The church has lots of leaders who've bought into the cell group vision and understand what it takes to make them work. 4. The number of cell groups is small, allowing the pastor great flexibility for one-on-one mentoring.

Monthly all-cell-leader meetings, with ad hoc mentoring

Description: All cell group leaders gather once a month to receive encouragement, vision, and training. There are no required coaching cluster meetings. Instead, each coach determines the needs of the cell group leaders and seeks to meet those needs as he or she feels best, through one-on-one meetings, phone conversations, etc.

Advantages: 1. This limits the number of official meetings required. 2. This allows coaches to flexibly spend time with leaders one-on-one to target specific needs, rather than addressing leaders in weekly meetings with all cell group leaders, where the trainer must assume everyone has the same needs.

Disadvantages: 1. This requires the coach to be highly self-motivated, therefore limiting those who are qualified to coach 2. If the coach doesn't work hard, he'll lose track of what's happening in the groups. 3. This places a great deal of emphasis on the monthly cell leader meetings and requires the leaders to provide all the support and mentoring that's needed—an impossible task!

Works best when: Because this system is highly fluid, it works best when the number of cell groups is small, allowing the pastor a great deal of flexibility for one-on-one mentoring.

Weekly or biweekly all-cell-leader meetings with ad hoc mentoring

Description: All cell group leaders gather either weekly or biweekly to receive encouragement, vision, and training. There are no required coaching clusters, except for the breakout groups that are a part of the agenda of the all-cell-leader meetings. Instead, each coach determines the needs of the cell group leaders and seeks to meet those needs as he or she feels best, through one-on-one meetings, phone conversations, etc.

Advantages: 1. This provides a setting for cell group leaders to receive ongoing training after they've started leading a group. 2. It allows the senior pastor to have weekly direct contact with all the cell group leaders, thereby imparting his vision to them. 3. This allows better communication on a more frequent basis, either biweekly or weekly.

Disadvantages: 1. As the number of cell group leaders grows, it proves increasingly impossible to address the specific needs found in individual groups. While leaders might find such a meeting informative, it doesn't really help them. 2. Such meetings tend to focus on teaching information, and provide little time for discussion about what's happening in the groups. 3. This schedule adds additional meetings cell leaders must attend. 4. Because cell leaders are committed to attend more training meetings, there's less time for their cell coach to mentor them in a one-on-one or small group basis. 5. This assumes all cell leaders learn how to lead groups the same way, i.e., through large group training.

Works best when: 1. The church is first starting groups, so the pastor can put the vision before the leaders, either weekly or twice a month. 2. The number of cell group leaders is small, so the meeting can have a relational, not a classroom, atmosphere. 3. The church doesn't require cell leaders to attend more than two weekly worship services, or lots of other ministry activities.

Weekly coaching cluster meetings

Description: Cell group coaches meet weekly with the cell group leaders they oversee. This is the basic strategy of the G-12, where the G-12 leader meets with his cell group leaders (up to twelve in number) on a weekly basis. This strategy has been adopted by other churches that don't require the group to grow as large as twelve. Therefore, the cluster is usually three to seven cell group leaders in size.

Advantages: 1. The cell group leaders receive much more hands-on mentoring from the coach. 2. It provides a formal setting for the cell group leaders to talk about what's happening in their groups every week. 3. The coach can address specific problems that arise in the groups, and this group can pray about specific needs on a weekly basis.

Disadvantages: 1. There's no place for ongoing training from the senior pastor, therefore requiring the cell coach to be a good trainer, in addition to being a mentor. 2. The vision can become watered down, as the cell leaders have little direct contact with the senior pastor. 3. This assumes all cell leaders should be mentored the same way, i.e., through a small group meeting.

Works best when: 1. A church is implementing the pure G-12 model as it was developed in the International Charismatic Mission. 2. Cell leaders have committed to the cell group vision, see its value, and are ready to make the commitment to an additional meeting every week.

Biweekly coaching cluster meetings

Description: Cell group coaches meet every other week with the cell group leaders they oversee. This is the basic strategy detailed in Joel Comiskey's book, *From 12 to 3.*

Advantages: 1. Cell group leaders receive much more hands-on mentoring from the coach. 2. It provides a formal setting for the cell group leaders to talk about what's happening in their groups every other week. 3. The coach can address specific problems that arise in the groups, and the group can pray about specific needs on a biweekly basis. 4. Because meetings are biweekly instead of weekly, more time is created for the coach to mentor his cell leaders on a one-on-one basis.

Disadvantages: 1. There's no place for ongoing training from the senior pastor, therefore requiring the cell coach to be a good trainer in addition to being a mentor. 2. The vision can become watered down, as the cell leaders have little direct contact with the senior pastor.

Works best when: 1. The church appreciates the core principles of the G-12 model, but feels the need to adapt the specifics of the G-12 strategy.

Monthly all-cell-leader meetings and monthly coaching cluster meetings

Description: All cell group leaders gather once a month to receive encouragement, vision, and training. Cell group coaches meet with their cell leaders once a month in a cluster meeting, at a different time than the all-cell-leader meetings.

Advantages: 1. This provides a place where leaders hear the vision from the pastor and receive training on a monthly basis. 2. It facilitates a formal setting for a coach to discuss with his or her leaders what's going on in their groups, pray for specific issues, and encourage the leaders. 3. It provides time for the coach to also do one-on-one ad hoc mentoring outside of the official meetings.

Disadvantages: 1. This adds two meetings per month to the cell leader's schedule. 2. It requires self-starting coaches to mentor the leaders outside of official meetings.

Works best when: 1. The number of cell groups grows to more than fifteen. 2. The cell leaders can't commit to weekly coaching cluster meetings, or weekly coaching cluster meetings are deemed unnecessary.

Monthly all-cell leader meetings and weekly coaching cluster meetings

Description: All cell group leaders gather once a month to receive encouragement, vision, and training. Cell group coaches meet with their cell leaders every week in a cluster meeting, except for the week of the all-cell group leader meeting.

Advantages: 1. This provides a place where leaders hear the vision from the pastor and receive training on a monthly basis. 2. It facilitates a formal setting for a coach to discuss with his or her leaders what's going on in their groups, pray for specific issues, and encourage the leaders. 3. This promotes dealing quickly with issues that arise in the cell groups, because they meet every week. 4. The weekly coaching cluster meetings can be a place for the coach to model how to lead that week's lesson, (but most churches don't use their weekly coaching meetings in this way).

Disadvantages: 1. This adds four meetings per month to the cell leader's schedule. 2. It requires self-starting coaches to mentor the leaders outside of official meetings. 3. It could limit the ad hoc one-on-one mentoring because of time limitations and the commitment to lead the additional coaching clusters.

Works best when: 1. The cell leaders are highly motivated and committed to the cell group vision. 2. The cell group leaders require lots of mentoring. 3. The church started lots of groups very quickly, and the cell leaders are making lots of mistakes because of their lack of experience.

CELL GROUP FORMS

M. Scott Boren

Information is key to effective strategy. Without a clear picture of what's happening in cell groups, pastors will find it almost impossible to develop and implement an effective cell group strategy. Cell leaders possess the information regarding the groups and the people within those groups, and churches must determine a way to pass that information from the cell group leaders to the cell group coaches and finally to the pastoral leaders.

In my research of churches, I found three types. The first depended heavily upon information transfer through forms. Cell leaders were required to complete forms every week. These churches had detailed data in computers. Pastors analyzed this data and reported it to their team. I call these churches Form Dependent.

The second type was just the opposite. One pastor told me if he needed cell leaders to complete a form every week, it just revealed that the coaches and cell pastors weren't doing their jobs. Instead of depending upon forms, these churches transferred information through relationships. Coaches and cell pastors would gather information about what's happening in cell groups through personal interaction with cell group leaders. These churches are Relationally Dependent.

A third type is a combination of the two above extremes, depending upon the use of forms and relational communication. When churches over-estimate the ability of forms to communicate information, the system can become stale and lifeless. On the other hand, in placing their sole emphasis on relational communication, information can easily slip through the cracks as a church becomes larger.

Therefore, churches usually find that some forms are required. Almost every church will develop forms that fit the church. The following forms are not included to be prescriptive. Instead they provide options for you to adopt and adapt for your setting.

TYPES OF FORMS

The forms on the next few pages* are broken up into types of forms. These include:

- Forms for cell group leaders to complete
- Forms to cell group coaches to complete
- Reports for cell group pastors to complete

Web Resource

All of these forms are available as a free download from <www.cellgrouppeople.com>.

---

*These forms are offered by Jim Egli, Dave Earley, and Randall Neighbour.

CELL GROUP LEADER FORMS

Cell Leader's Report

Cell Leader: _____ Intern: _____ Cell: _____
Date of Meeting: _____ Actual start & ending times of meeting: _____
Location: _____ Total Persons Present: ___ Adults ___ Teens ___ Children

Projected number of converts for the remainder of this cycle: _____

Rate and give brief description of what happened:
(1 = Poor 2 = Below Average 3 = Average 4 = Above Average 5 = Excellent)

( ) Welcome & Worship

( ) Word

( ) Witness

Attendees: (first names are ok):

Visitors (first and last names, address and phone. After 3 visits, consider them members)

Accountability Partners: (fill in initials and circle Y if they met last week, N if they didn't)
__/__ Y N   __/__ Y N   __/__ Y N
__/__ Y N   __/__ Y N   __/__ Y N
__/__ Y N   __/__ Y N   __/__ Y N

Call Report: (please list who you met with or telephoned, the date, and the outcome)

Home Group Leader Weekly Report

Shepherd: _____ Week of _____ to _____
Intern: _____ (Sun.) (Sat.)

Zone Pastor: _____ Zone Supervisor: _____ Meeting Day ____

Name List all members and visitors	At Meeting	Current Base	Name List all members and visitors	At Meeting	Current Base
1.			11.		
2.			12.		
3.			13.		
4.			14.		
5.			15.		
6.			16.		
7.			17.		
8.			18.		
9.			19.		
10.			20.		

Covenant Membership ( ) Present ( ) Visitors ( ) Birth - 17 ( ) **Total Present** ( )

H.E.A.L.T.H. CHECK UP & EVALUATION: _____

Home Group Report: (written evaluations, testimonies, and problems).
Report prepared by: _____
_____
_____
_____
_____
_____
_____
_____
_____
_____
_____
_____
_____

Salvations/Baptisms this week: (names) _____
Location, date & time of next meeting:
_____

Small Group Quality Assurance Report

Name: _____ Date: _____

P R A Y E R

1. Did you average 30 minutes a day in PRAYER this month?

   A. If not 30 minutes, how much time did you average?

   B. Are you praying through a list for those you oversee by name?

   C. Who are you praying for?

   D. What are you praying about?

I N V I T E

2. How many INVITATIONS did you make this month? The goal is four!

   A. How many people did you invite to your group?

   B. How many people did you invite to the Sunday services?

   C. Who did you invite to Sunday Services?

   D. Who did you invite to your group meetings?

C O N T A C T

3. How many CONTACTS did you make this month? The goal is every member twice!

   A. How many calls is your goal for the month?

   B. Who did you call and what's going on?

   C. What is the mood of those you oversee?

   D. Did you make any visits this month? To whom?

M E N T O R

4. Who are you MENTORING? The goal is every apprentice weekly!

   A. With whom did you meet?

   B. What did you discuss?

   C. Are you casting vision for those you oversee?

   D. Who has potential in your circle of influence?

Weekly ACTS Group Report

Your name _____ Group Name _____ Today's Date _____ Meeting Date _____

Number of Adults at this meeting ____ Number of Children ____ Did the children take part in the meeting? Y N
_____

In the four categories below, describe your meeting with as much detail as you would like to include.
Rate the strength of each area using a number between 1 and 10 (10 = the best ever; 1 = non-existent)

___ **Upward** (Development of hunger and intimacy with God) Discuss the time your group spent in prayer and worship this week, in and out of your meeting:

___ **Inward** (Development of community/family and discipleship) Discuss the fellowship and one another ministry (edification) between members during the week and at your meeting:

___ **Outward** (Kingdom expansion/outreach... being God's Army) Discuss the time your group devoted to reaching the lost this week:

___ **Forward** (New leadership development) Discuss the ways you have trained and are releasing your intern for ministry to others in your group this week:

About You This Week (check one from each area):
☐ I spent time with God each day ☐ I spent time with God most days. ☐ I'm struggling in this area.
☐ My family would say I spent quality time with them. ☐ I spent time relaxing or enjoying my hobby.
☐ My work week was productive and not terribly stressful ☐ My work week was stressful, but I didn't lose perspective.
☐ My work week interfered with my spiritual purpose (family life and my ability to be a good ACTS leader)
How can your coach and pastor pray for you or your family this week? _____

About Your Ministry This Week (check one from each area):
☐ I prayed for each of my members daily. ☐ I prayed for my members a couple of times. ☐ I'm struggling in this area.
☐ I spent time with at least two members. ☐ I couldn't spend time with them, but I called. ☐ I'm struggling in this area.
☐ I encountered ministry challenges with group members, and together we worked it out and were victorious.
☐ I encountered ministry challenges with group members, and I need pastoral help. Please call me.
What specific needs within your group can your pastor be praying for? _____

About Your Future (check one from each area):
☐ My group members are spending time with unchurched people and inviting them to meetings/gatherings. We're growing.
☐ My intern and I spent time together this week to plan and pray together. ___ My intern is in charge now, and delegating to others.
My group members are moving through the discipleship process ☐ With Ease ☐ With Difficulty ☐ Poorly

COACH FORMS

Coach's Report Form

September-October, 2003

Name _____   Email _____

Upward
How would you like your head coach or Small Groups Pastor to pray for you?

Are you spending daily time with Christ?

Are you praying consistently for your leaders?

Inward
Did you attend VLT(s) and/or hold another huddle meeting?

What you have you done to build relationship with and between your leaders in the past two months? (Have you done anything to build relationship with your sub-zone?)

What one-on-one meetings or contacts have you had with leaders?

Outward
Are you consistently praying for non-Christian friends, neighbors and relatives?

How have you helped connect others to body life at the Vineyard?

What have you done to build relationships and serve non-Christians?

Forward
Are you praying for the multiplication of leaders?

What are the names of some potential leaders that you see in your groups? What would you recommend as the next step to encourage their growth?

What small groups should consider multiplication in the coming months?

Please give copies of this report to your Head Coach and Small Groups Pastor. Thanks!

Vineyard Small Groups
Coach's Monthly Report Form

Coach(s) _____   **Month** _____

Date Turned In (due first Sunday of the Month) _____

Leader(s):   **Status:**

_____   _____
                     _____
                     _____
                     _____
_____   _____
                     _____
                     _____
                     _____
_____   _____
                     _____
                     _____
                     _____
_____   _____
                     _____
                     _____
                     _____
                     _____
                     _____
                     _____
                     _____
                     _____
                     _____

Small groups attended this month:
_____
_____

Vineyard Small Groups
Coach's Small Group Visit Report Form (page 1)

Why are you visiting groups?
• To get to know small groups and their members better
• To see how the group is doing. What are its strengths and weaknesses?
• To make the group and its leadership feel supported and connected.
• To help identify and befriend future leaders.

Suggestions:
• Arrive early and get to know people as they arrive.
• Introduce yourself and learn individual names.
• Express appreciation and pray for the small group leaders at the onset of ministry time.

Coach(s) _____   **Date of Meeting** _____

Leader(s) _____   **Start Time** _____

Intern(s) _____   **End Time** _____

Name	Present	Other	Name	Present	Other
1.			11.		
2.			12.		
3.			13.		
4.			14.		
5.			15.		
6.			16.		
7.			17.		
8.			18.		
9.			19.		
10.			20.		

Who did what? Indicate above in the "other" column using the legend below:
H= Hosted   W = Led Worship   I = Led Ice Breaker   S = Led Study   M = Led Ministry   O = Other _____

Overall Observations: (Note additional questions on following page)

Vineyard Small Groups
Coach's Small Group Visit Report Form (page 2)

1. Would you like to see more small groups like this one? Why?

2. What encouragements do you want to offer to the leader(s)?

3. What is one suggestion that you want to give the leader(s)?

4. Are there any needs or concerns that require attention from the pastoral staff?

5. What potential leaders do you see in this group?

CELL PASTOR REPORTS

**Quarterly Summary
of Cell Group Leader's Weekly Report
by Zone**

For the months of January - March, 1994

District: __NORTH__   Zone: __BISHAN__   Zone Pastor: __James Challander__

No.	Description	Jan	Feb	Mar	Average
1	Number of Cell Groups	12	11	11	11.33
2	Number of Groups Not Met	4	14	3	7.0
3	Number of Meetings	44	30	41	38.33
4	Percent of Meetings	91.7	68	93	84.34
5	Number of Cell Members on Record	124	138	138	133.33
6	Average No. of Cell Members on Record Per month	10.3	13	13	11.81
7	Cell Group Attendance	316	239	342	299.00
8	Average Attendance per Cell Group	7.18	8	8.3	7.83
9	Total Visitations	3	1	2	2.0
10	Average No. of Visitations per Cell Group	.25	.1	.2	.17
11	Total Salvations	0	0	2	.67
12	Average No. of Salvations per Cell Group	0	0	.2	.06
13	Number of Current Interest Groups	0	0	0	0.0
14	Number of Completed Interest Groups	0	0	0	0.0
15	Number of First time visitors	5	4	2	3.66

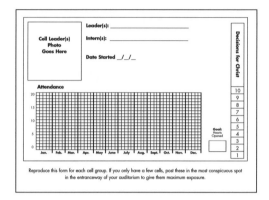

Reproduce this form for each cell group. If you only have a few cells, post these in the most conspicuous spot
in the entranceway of your auditorium to give them maximum exposure.

Stage 7:
Establish the Hidden
Systems that Support Cells

CRITICAL MASS

Bill Beckham

Pentecost is an illustration of the explosive power and energy released by God through the church. "And there were added that day about three thousand souls. And they were continually devoting themselves to the apostles' teaching and to fellowship, to the breaking of bread and to prayer. And everyone kept feeling a sense of awe; and many wonders and signs were taking place through the Apostles. And day by day continuing with one mind, in the temple, and breaking bread from house to house, they were taking their meals together with gladness and sincerity of heart, praising God, and having favor with all the people. And the Lord was adding to their number day by day those who were being saved" (Acts 2:41-47).

Christ hasn't called us to visualize the church at the size of thousands. He uses one critical number to model the church we see in Acts. He wants to use us to develop a base congregation of 120 as a new start, or as a prototype within an existing church. This first hurdle is the biggest one. When the base congregation comes together, everything that's necessary to be the body of Christ is in place.

WHY IS 120 IMPORTANT?

The first reason for the importance of 120 people is that Jesus modeled the church at this size. Jesus had promised he would "build his church." And, the first church he built was one base congregation of 120 members in the upper room in Jerusalem. The life and dynamics of Jesus' base congregation of 120 assured the success of the church when it grew to thousands.

We know from the biblical accounts that the broader group in the first church was probably five hundred followers, including men, women, and children. Around this five hundred were the crowds who attached themselves to the movement during his three-year ministry. But the foundational core of his first church was made up of 120 followers.

Second, the 120 unit is the point of critical mass. Critical mass is the minimum amount of fissionable material necessary to produce a chain reaction. In building a cell group church, critical mass indicates the size when the working unit and the coordinating unit fuse together in an integrated whole that can reproduce itself. Divine synergism kicks in at the point of 120, when the total operates in a more powerful way than the sum of the individual parts.

Third, the number is not magical; rather, it's the number when the essential qualities and tasks of the church can begin to operate as one unit. A group of seventy to 120 adults must be living out these spiritual elements before a healthy base congregation will function properly:

**Cell Group
Vision Team Exercise**

How close is your church to seeing these things occur in your 120 people? You can use the assessment on page 373 of *Making Cell Groups Work* to evaluate your progress.

- Listening to God in prayer
- Worshiping in spirit and truth
- Hearing and doing the Word
- Operating in the power of gifts
- Submitting to Kingdom authority
- Living together in community
- Caring for new believers
- Nurturing accountability for each other
- Raising up spiritual leaders
- Reaching out to a lost and hurting world

When these qualities come together within the context of the basic working unit and the coordinating unit of the church of 120 members, critical mass is experienced.

Fourth, building a church at the size of 120 is attainable. One base congregation is doable in a new church start. A pastor can make plans to grow to 120 in the upper room, and can also get a handle on a remnant of 120 within a large existing church. He can conceptualize the infrastructure necessary to support one base congregation, while the structure of a church of thousands is beyond his grasp.

Fifth, the church at this number is able to withstand the attacks of Satan. Jesus promised that "the gates of hell will not prevail against my church." Jesus' church was established with 120 followers. Satan knows the importance of a church operating at the optimum size of Jesus' model. Therefore, he draws the battle line at some point before the church reaches optimum size. Satan then marshals his energy and effort so leaders and methods will not result in enough momentum to break through the single congregation barrier.

Sixth, a church of this size can birth other churches. This is the reproductive size and maturity of the church. With an initial group of 120, a church prototype can be established. The basic ministry unit (cell) of the church can be modeled and the basic coordinating unit (congregation) can be modeled. When the ministry and coordinating units of the church are operating, the church is able to expand.

Seventh, the dynamics of 120 allows the church to grow much larger. Inherent within one base congregation is the infrastructure to be a church of thousands, or tens of thousands. No other structure is required and no new strategy is necessary to grow to a larger size. One base congregation has everything in place for a church to have 1,000 members, or 5,000 members, or 50,000 members. Just keep multiplying the same kind of congregational unit.

Carl George observed that a church that organizes into congregations and groups of approximately ten people, as its "spiritual and emotional center," never has to be reorganized. "It can accommodate every church size from 50 to 500,000. Churches can maintain quality and meaningful care giving no matter how many of these spiritual kinship groups comprise the whole church."[1]

CRITICAL MASS DEVELOPS FROM A PROTOTYPE

Critical mass doesn't happen automatically but is the result of a process that leads to a working prototype. A prototype is a small model of a larger project. In a prototype, the viability of a total concept or system can be tested out. The Gospels reveal how Jesus developed critical-mass momentum by carefully forming a prototype. With 120 committed followers, Jesus modeled the smallest implementing unit of a cell and the larger coordinating unit of a congregation.

At the beginning of the twentieth century, in Glasgow, Scotland, two men formed a partnership and began a furniture company. In the early years, the company did very well in a market characterized by easy-to-please customers who wanted large basic furniture.

The next generation formed two associated family companies out of the original business. Business was much more difficult during the second generation and customers were harder to please. However, both companies survived and were passed on to the third generation. Today, the grandchildren of the founders own two separate furniture companies in Glasgow.

One of the third-generation companies invested heavily in new equipment, brought in top-level management, and hired skilled designers from various successful companies. This company reorganized its system around a prototype shop, where every piece of furniture was developed and assigned detailed specifications. The company called these specifications and drawings "the bible."

No one started an assembly line without reading all the memos and drawings related to that section of "the bible." Problems could be identified and quickly corrected because of the prototype procedures. This company has shown significant growth since its reorganization, and is now one of the largest furniture manufacturing companies in Scotland.

The other company poured its money into large and impressive-looking buildings, but never developed a prototype shop. Consequently, this company has no standard system for controlling the quality of each piece of furniture. Without prototype drawings, responsibility for and correction of a problem has been next to impossible. When a problem comes up on an assembly line, the foreman typically blames other departments.

On more than one occasion, the owner of the struggling company brought in experts for consultation. Always the same suggestion was made: "You must prototype the furniture you're selling." But, up to this point, the company has been unwilling to stop long enough to develop a system for prototyping. It continues to fall further behind the growth of its sister company.

We learn from this story that a prototype is important. We also learn that some leaders resist going back and completing a prototype. This is true in the business world as well as in the church.

Two Types of Prototypes

The prototype concept is used in two ways in the development of a cell church. Prototype can mean a base congregation of 120 members that's operating with all essential systems. This is the model of the support and coordinating unit of a cell church. Prototype can also refer to the pattern cell from which all other cells will grow. A prototype cell is the building block of the prototype base congregation. The prototype cell is the model of ministry and implementing unit of a cell group church.

Jesus developed his prototype congregation incrementally around several leadership stages. These different leadership stages can be understood by studying the numbers associated with them. The numbers—two to three, twelve, seventy, and 120 represent leadership stages in Jesus' strategy.

The "two to three" were Jesus and John the Baptist, and then Peter, James, and John. Then the three became twelve and the twelve became seventy. This prototype was completed with the 120 leaders in the upper room. Each stage became part of the next size of the prototype. The twelve were part of the seventy and the seventy were part of the 120. The 120 represented the completed model for the thousands who followed.

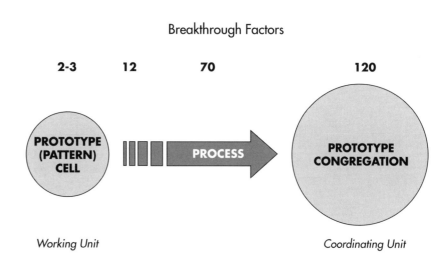

Breakthrough Factors

| 2-3 | 12 | 70 | 120 |

PROTOTYPE (PATTERN) CELL

PROCESS

PROTOTYPE CONGREGATION

Working Unit

Coordinating Unit

This diagram shows these two essential units as they relate to each other. A cell group church organizes and operates around them. It's imperative for a church to develop a healthy prototype model of both units. These two units are essential for reaching critical mass and establishing a church that lives in continual revival.

BANGKOK URBAN STRATEGY

I learned the lesson of the base congregation and critical mass the hard way. Between 1976 and 1984, I was part of a church planting team in Bangkok, Thailand. The team was built around veteran missionary Judson Lennon, and eventually grew to five, as new missionaries were assigned to the project.

The vision was conceived in my heart in Texas, but born on top of the 26-story Chokchai Building in Bangkok in 1975. Judson Lennon, Bill Smith, and I stood on the tallest point in Bangkok with our Area Director, his assistant, and our Mission Administrator. Looking out over the city of millions, we dreamed of developing a comprehensive church planting strategy for Bangkok. The effort was named Bangkok Urban Strategy and later shortened to BUS.

Every week we met for prayer and planning. A 52-week neighborhood strategy began to take shape. The plan was for a neighborhood team made up of a missionary and national Christians to witness to Thais, bring them to conversion, form them into groups, and use the groups to begin a

Cell Group Vision Team Exercise

Rate your progress toward the development of a prototype cell group on a scale of 1 to 10.

Rate your progress toward the development of a prototype congregation on a scale of 1 to 10.

church. The team would follow the same steps each week:

- Learn essential concepts of neighborhood cell ministry
- Implement those concepts in a target neighborhood
- Evaluate what had happened
- Go through the process again

During the first three years the strategy was tested, indigenous materials were developed, and methodology was put in place. The initial three-member team became four with the addition of Bill Hitt. In another year Floyd Kendall joined the team. We continued to refine the strategy and to develop indigenous materials.

OPPOSITION TO CHANGE

Eventually, the natural process of change produced opposition. I now know we should have anticipated opposition and planned for it. However, we were consumed with the vision and believed it would eventually prove itself. Opposition centered in the missionary community and then surfaced as doubts among the nationals.

The Bangkok Urban Strategy team believed that "comprehensive" meant that all of the missionaries and institutions in Bangkok in our organization would eventually operate within the context of the strategy. This definition of "comprehensive" touched the lives and ministries of every missionary in Bangkok and every institution associated with us. This ultimately doomed the vision because criticism toward the project increased in direct proportion to how comprehensive the strategy was expected to be.

I'm sure the team could have done a better job in preparing for the change. We didn't realize the extent of the radical nature of the vision, the level of commitment to the old way, and the depth of the resistance to change. For whatever reason, the effort began to polarize at several points. Urban and rural missions became an issue, as more and more church planting missionaries were assigned to Bangkok. The question of church planting and institutional missions became a problem, because the mission had several large and well-staffed institutions in Bangkok that had their own separate visions. The strategy even began to touch on personal missionary issues such as housing, because BUS wanted to get missionaries off missionary compounds and into Thai neighborhoods.

Because BUS was initiating the change, it was increasingly seen as the problem. BUS was charged with the ultimate missionary sin of being "uncooperative." Because of this polarization, the BUS team felt that after the initial testing it was essential to broaden the strategy as much as possible to silence the opposition and convince the doubters it would work.

A FATAL MISTAKE

We decided to begin five different church plants in five different areas of Bangkok through five different existing mother churches. We fell right into the Devil's trap of dividing and conquering. We had fragmented our strength and split our forces.

With five separate projects, we could never build up enough momentum to prove the system to the satisfaction of the silent majority and to those in authority. In hindsight, we should have focused all our personnel and resources toward developing one strong and viable base congregation. Then we could have transplanted other base congregations into target areas of the city.

Some good things happened in the project. For the first time in two decades, our organization began several new churches in Bangkok. Relationship evangelism was introduced and shown to be a viable method. Small groups were established as an essential element in the church. The importance of penetrating neighborhoods was accepted. A boldness in evangelism emerged. Today some of these principles are still evident in Bangkok.

However, almost a decade after our rooftop experience at the Chokchai Building, the painful decision was made to let BUS die a natural death. During one of our weekly meetings, the team pronounced the obituary over BUS and buried it as a structure, with the hope that it would continue to live as a movement. Unfortunately, it continued in Thailand only as a blip in the yearly statistics and as some isolated methods and concepts.

LESSONS FROM FAILURE

The experience in Bangkok was like death to me. For eight years I had dreamed of developing an urban church model. My greatest regret has been that the strategy came very close to working, in spite of our mistakes and the opposition to change.

Though painful, the experience taught me several important lessons about change, the base congregation, and myself. The situation in Thailand forced me back to the basics. Response to the Gospel was so slow in Thailand that a strategy had to go back to the essentials and the power of

God. Nothing could be taken for granted and all bases had to be covered.

In the process, I returned to the New Testament to understand how Jesus developed the first church. My theology was clarified in the trenches. My concept of the presence, power, and purpose of Christ was learned in the neighborhoods of Bangkok. I was tested in the fire of failure. Out of failure I learned that God could still use me in his Kingdom. In hindsight, I can't imagine my ministry today apart from my painful experience in BUS. Simply stated, the lesson I learned in Bangkok about the base congregation is: concentrate your strategy, don't fragment your forces, and transplant from strength.

How Long Will It Take?

Human nature is the same in every new endeavor. The standard American corporate questions about change are: "What do we do? (But keep it simple)," and "How long will it take? (But keep it short.)" These are the same two underlying attitudes I sense from church leaders interested in changing to the cell group church way. Always there's a desire for immediate results and simple (and painless) strategies.

Change doesn't happen that way! When business consultants address the second question: "How long will it take?" they say, "The rest of your life, but—here's the good news—you should start to see results in three to five years."

In the development of a cell church, one year of preparation is necessary to internalize the vision, values, and commitment in a core of selected leaders. In addition to the first year, becoming an operating cell group church stretches into a two-year, five-year, and seven-year process.

One year is required for preparation. Then it takes at least two years to learn how to do it and to put the basic systems in place. Another two years are required to assimilate the rest of the church body into the cell culture. And then, another two years are required before unusual growth associated with many operating cell group churches is experienced.

CONGREGATIONAL NETWORKS

M. Scott Boren

In his 1976 book, *Your Church Can Grow*, Peter Wagner wrote about the 3 Cs: Celebration, Congregation, and Cell. In fact, Wagner combined these three into a formula: Celebration + Congregation + Cell = Church.

In the cell group church, the first and last have been emphasized. Joel Comiskey writes, "Celebration participation and cell attendance are two sides of the same coin. One is not sufficient without the other, and both are essential for success in the cell group church. The meaning of the phrase 'cell group church' implies cell and celebration working as equal parts of the cell system."[2]

Bill Beckham illustrates the cell-celebration structure of the church by talking about the two-winged church, one wing being the small-group structure, and the other the large-group structure.

These two are highlighted because they're the most visible. Both the cell and celebration are weekly meetings. The format for the cell and celebration is relatively consistent among cell-based churches around the world. And the size of these churches is measured in cell group attendance and in celebration attendance.

Congregation is the lesser-known middle child of the three Cs. Congregation meetings tend to be less frequent than the other two. Churches are quite inconsistent in the organization of their congregational networks. Thus, it's not used much for statistical purposes when assessing the size of a church.

At the same time, when the most effective cell group churches in the world (both large and small) are rightly understood, it becomes clear that the middle C is crucial to the life of those churches.

WHAT IS A CONGREGATIONAL NETWORK?

A congregation is a network of connected cell groups that facilitates relationships between members of different cell groups in a mid-sized group format. The phrase "congregational network" is used to communicate the interconnectedness between groups and the people within those groups.

Congregational networks will have leaders who minister to those in the cell groups and organize the life of the networks. For instance, if the groups are organized geographically, there'll be a staff cell pastor overseeing groups within that geographic region. The same would be true for men's networks, youth networks, etc.

ADVANTAGES OF A CONGREGATIONAL NETWORK

1. Facilitates relationships beyond the cell groups. While cell groups facilitate close relationships between cell members, these relationships should never become exclusive. People need to connect with those outside their groups and learn what's going on in their lives. Because this is difficult to do in the weekly celebration services, mid-sized congregational network meetings help facilitate the building of these inter-cell group relationships.

2. Connects old cell group mates with one another, decreasing the fear of multiplication. When groups multiply, cell group members develop a fear that they can never relate to cell group members who are no longer part of their group. By creating mid-sized group congregational network meetings, the church facilitates connections between those of old cell groups, thereby alleviating some of the fear of change.

3. Provides a forum for teaching by those gifted as teachers. Old small group Bible studies required the leaders to be gifted Bible teachers. The cell group model requires leaders to be facilitators of discussion and ministry, not teachers of biblical information. At the same time, the church needs strong teaching. Of course, people will receive good teaching in the Sunday celebration services, but many churches use the mid-sized congregation meetings to teach the Bible in a way that applies to the specific group being addressed.

4. Facilitates activities that can't be organized well on the cell group level. While cell groups have the ability to embody the life of the church, there are some activities that require more organizational effort and skill than can be done by an individual cell group. For instance, a network of cell groups might work on a special outreach event. Or a network of groups could take a retreat together. In such cases, the overseeing network leader would organize the groups and oversee events.

5. Assimilates disconnected celebration service attendees into cell groups. Because the congregation meetings are smaller, people who haven't connected relationally in large group worship will meet people in these

mid-sized group meetings, opening the door for an invitation to a cell group.

6. Provides an additional door for the lost to enter the Kingdom. Some people will be introduced to church life by coming to a cell group first. Others will attend a weekend celebration service first. Some will be intimidated by both these experiences. They'll see the cell group as too intimate, and the celebration service as too much like traditional church. The mid-sized congregational meeting provides a doorway that's non-traditional but God-focused, where the unchurched can hear the Gospel and develop relationships in a non-threatening environment.

How Congregational Networks are Organized

There are different ways to network these groups. Some churches do so geographically. Pantego Bible Church uses school districts to mark boundaries of how groups will network with one another. For instance, a cell coach might oversee the groups within the geographic area of one elementary school. Then a staff cell pastor might oversee all the groups within the geographic area of one high school.

Cell Group Vision Team Exercise

What current congregational networks are already in place? How can they be connected to the cell groups?

Other churches build networks around gender. Churches that have men's and women's cell groups that meet separately often have men's network meetings and women's network meetings.

Still other churches develop networks around age groups. For instance, most churches have a youth congregational network. Some larger churches have a junior high network and a senior high network. Churches that minister to a significant number of college students will have a college congregational network. Children's church is an example of a network gathering. Networks for young married couples, middle-aged couples, and retirees could be created. If cell groups meet based on age groupings, the church can create congregational networks for the various age brackets.

Most churches develop congregational networks around a variety of the above groupings because they have different kinds of cell groups.

Congregational Network Models

I've observed four basic models. The model a church chooses should fit into its overall vision and should fit the culture in which it's set. None of these models is perfect. But they each illustrate different ways the mid-sized congregational network can operate. As more churches develop growing cell group systems, I'm sure more congregational network models will arise. The following four models are listed in descending level of emphasis.

Congregationally Focused Churches

In this model, the emphasis of the church lies on developed congregations of cell groups that are no larger than two hundred people. These multiple congregations are connected together under one larger church-wide structure. While the congregations meet weekly for Sunday worship, they're not autonomous churches. Periodically (usually quarterly), these multiple congregations will come together for joint worship celebrations.

Even within these congregationally focused churches, there might also be additional networks which follow one of the following three patterns.

One derivation of this model is a new approach called micro-cell-based house churches. Such house churches meet weekly for worship and teaching in a home. In addition, they meet in cell groups throughout the week. Instead of having a goal to become large, these micro churches seek to send out people to start new micro house churches. Usually these churches are connected together under one overseeing leadership team.

Weekly Teaching Networks

This model focuses on developing congregations of fifty to seventy-five adults, comprised of three to seven cell groups. These people meet weekly for Bible teaching on Sunday mornings at the church building during the traditional Sunday school hour. Overseeing this network will be a cell group coach. Additionally, a gifted Bible teacher provides the teaching each Sunday.

Alongside these adult networks are networks for children and youth, where they receive teaching from someone who's gifted to teach on their levels. Youth cell groups might meet in homes throughout the week and have a weekly youth network service one night of the week. Many churches use the same pattern when ministering to college students. For children, the meeting usually occurs on Sunday mornings in the form of children's church.

Monthly Network Meetings

Those who've followed the principles of the Groups of 12 model have adopted some form of this approach, but other cell group models can follow this pattern. It works like this: once a month, a network of cell groups gathers for a meeting to address specific needs of that group. For instance, men's cell groups gather monthly to receive encouragement as men. Women do likewise. Many times, this comes in the form of a Saturday morning breakfast gathering.

Invisible Congregational Networks

Of the four models, churches in this category place the lowest emphasis on their mid-sized congregational network. The purpose of the network is oversight and organization. The cell pastor who oversees each network has a clear picture of the cell groups he oversees. He gathers cell coaches within his network for encouragement and training. He calls together cell leaders in his network to minister and to equip them. He tracks the growth of his network with charts and computers. For the most part, the networks are relatively invisible.

The exception is found in ad hoc gatherings he might organize for his network. He might organize a prayer event for his cell groups. He might prepare a special training event. He could invite all his cell groups to a retreat.

Cell Group Vision Team Exercise

Which of these network models best fits your church? What components will you adopt and what will you adapt?

WHEN TO DEVELOP CONGREGATIONAL NETWORKS

Small church pastors may wonder why they should develop congregational networks. They might question the necessity of midsized group gatherings when the church is small enough for people to connect to one another on Sunday mornings. Contrary to popular opinion, congregational networks aren't only for mega-churches.

When a church starts developing cell groups, the leadership should focus on supporting and growing those groups. But as the groups gain momentum and start growing, the Cell Group Vision Team must consider how these groups will be connected to one another. Some churches with as few as ten groups have developed monthly congregational network meetings for the men and the women. These meetings feed the groups and support the work of those leaders.

Churches with up to 120 attendees usually find that all of them are connected to one another and that cell and celebration are all they need. But when they grow beyond that, disconnection sets in. Therefore, a church should start experimenting with its congregational network strategy no later than when it has twelve to fifteen cell groups. At this point, there are enough groups for multiple networks, requiring multiple people to oversee their development.

THE ROLE OF THE VISIONARY SENIOR PASTOR

Joel Comiskey

A church of 150 purchased a huge piece of prime property. The massive building engulfed this little flock inside a hollow behemoth that continually reminded them of their mistake. Adding insult to injury was the weighty debt the outside organization expected the church to pay. Now they wanted to become a cell church. What could they do?

Surprisingly, the debt wasn't the church's major problem; its pigmy mentality, rather, caused the most grief. Church members believed the senior pastor had to visit, preach, teach, and do everything else. Although an associate pastor helped bear the load, the church insisted the senior pastor perform most of the work. Changing to the cell structure didn't immediately help the congregation overcome this mentality. The church figured the senior pastor would visit and pastor all the cells, and continue his Sunday morning responsibilities.

This senior pastor weathered those initial storms. He nourished his vision, sought help, envisioned the big picture, and then worked diligently on the details. His church, which had failed to grow for 20 years, is breaking growth records for Jesus. It's a model of how to grow in quality and quantity. The following principles will help pastors lay hold of the vision and implement it practically.[3]

STAY CLOSE TO THE FIRE

Senior pastors have one chief priority: give attention to prayer and the ministry of the Word. The Bible says in Acts 6:1-4

> In those days when the number of disciples was increasing, the Grecian Jews among them complained against the Hebraic Jews because their widows were being overlooked in the daily distribution of food. So the Twelve gathered all the disciples together and said, "It would not be right for us to neglect the ministry of the word of God in order to wait on tables. Brothers, choose seven men from among you who are known to be full of the Spirit and wisdom. We will turn this responsibility over to them and will give our attention to prayer and the ministry of the word.

Personal Exercise

See the personal exercises on pages 283-286.

Even well-known, highly publicized cell church pastors have lapsed into moral failure. Jesus, not cell ministry, must be the most important focus of a senior pastor. We must remember that personal godliness is the senior pastor's badge of authority and power. Trust is the glue that binds people to the pastor. If that trust is broken due to moral failure, it's sometimes impossible to fix.

If there's any question about the pastor's moral character and leadership, he'll be a crippled leader for life. People might follow the pastor warily, but hidden doubt will reside just below the surface. The pastorate, unlike other jobs, requires moral authority. The credibility of a pastor revolves around his personal life—who he is in the dark.

SEE THE BIG PICTURE—AND THE SMALL ONE

Some senior cell church pastors are more effective than others. One trait that distinguishes the best pastors is their ability to focus on the big picture while working on the details. Put another way, successful cell church pastors refuse to major on one minor item to the neglect of the others. They won't allow one aspect of the cell church to drain their time and attention.

Take Encounter Retreats. God is using them in a powerful way, yet, it's possible to become an Encounter Retreat pastor and forget that it's part of the bigger picture of training cell leaders. Encounter Retreats are not an end in themselves.

Some pastors are enamored with discipleship, to the point of seeing everything through discipleship eyes. The danger is forgetting about cell reproduction and evangelism. Others become celebration focused, allowing the cell vision to diminish.

The best senior pastors know what the end results will look like. They nourish that mental blueprint until it becomes part of their present reality. They see with certainty what others dismiss as fanciful daydreams. Yet, they don't only live in the land of dreams. Their dreams compel them to master the details of the cell group church system.

Very few succeed in combining the big vision with the present details. I've known the dreamer-type pastors who launch lofty goals and do little else. Then there are those pastors who confuse the trees for the forest. They get lost among the trees, never quite knowing if they're in the right forest.

David Jaramillo is very effective as a cell group church pastor because of his passion and clarity for the cell church vision AND his attention to details. He understands the big picture but then works weekly—and even daily—on those details that will make the cell church system work. Other cell church pastors tend to meander here and there. Like a cow preoccupied with the present patch of grass under its nose, some pastors fail to see the whole picture, getting bogged down in one or two cell church details.

Can any pastor lead a cell group church? Some pastors have a personal charisma that attracts people to the teaching or preaching event on Sunday morning. These pastors feel fulfilled and successful when large crowds gather to hear them.

The cell church pastor is different. His primary effort isn't directed toward the celebration. His primary effort is growing the infrastructure. His success is determined by the number of cells multiplied and whether or not he's caring for the cell system—not primarily whether or not a huge celebration crowd has gathered. Sunday attendance is the result of growing the infrastructure. Cell church pastors don't place the cart of attendance before the horse of cell growth and multiplication.

Effective pastors stay on top of their cell system, carefully analyzing weekly reports and knowing exactly what's happening. They help the church stay focused on cell ministry and don't let competing programs, building issues, etc. distract them. To successfully lead a cell group church, a pastor must possess an aggressive balance. He must have the ability to see where he wants to go and then move intelligently in that direction. Effective cell church pastors DON'T expect cell church success to simply happen. They make it work. To lead effectively, pastors must:

• Catch the blueprint, the exciting vision of the cell group church

- Master the details that make it work
- Run with fire toward the vision, while managing the various details, refusing to over-emphasize one detail to the exclusion or neglect of the others.

EXPERIENCING CELL

Dale Galloway reported that every pastor and staff person at New Hope Community Church led a cell group—even when the church had 6,000 members and 600 cell groups. He asserted that it's foolish to expect others to follow what the senior pastor fails to model.[4]

Someone might argue, "Shouldn't the senior pastor delegate as much as possible? Shouldn't he rotate among the various groups instead of concentrating on one?" These arguments have their merits, but they fall short. The benefits of leading a cell group far outweigh the shortcomings.

Laxness and apathy develop in cell churches where the senior pastor is far removed from personal involvement in cell ministry. Over time, the cell church operates like a giant machine—without proper lubrication.

One particular church tried to transition but got stuck somewhere between theory and practice. The pastor waxed eloquently about the superiority of the cell church ministry but then trusted in programs to bring success. He really didn't understand cell church—only the rhetoric that accompanied it.

When leading a cell seminar in his church one year later, I noticed little change in his leadership and even fewer positive results in the church. Another year later, I taught a cell church course in a nearby seminary. This same senior pastor audited the entire course. The one principle from the course that transformed his ministry was his need to lead and multiply his own cell group.

When I visited his church for a third seminar, this pastor was on fire for cell ministry. He was now walking the talk. Excitedly, he introduced me to a few of his disciples—former cell members of his own group who were now leading their own cells. Not only was his own perspective transformed by leading a cell group, he tripled his authority with the congregation. His life shouted, "Cell ministry is so important to me that I'm leading my own cell group. I've also multiplied it. I won't ask you to do anything I'm unwilling to do."

This pastor's cell church rhetoric suddenly had a practical ring. He was no longer directing a program called cell group church; he was now

Personal Exercise

What kind of cell group would you enjoy leading?

involved in that ministry and demonstrating how others could be successful. Notice the benefits of leading a cell:

- Deeper cell church vision
- Increased pastoral concern for cell leaders
- Insight into which cell lessons actually work and which ones don't

Above all, it declares in a million different ways that cell ministry is so important that even the senior pastor is willing to lead one.

The pastor of a 3,500-member transitioning church immediately knew it was right for him to lead his own cell. For too long, he had felt the inadequacy of announcing that everyone needed to be in a cell and even in the training route to lead one, when he himself wasn't doing it. He found six professional couples who were not in cells and began leading them, excited about the growth he knew would take place. He multiplied that cell within one year. He was a pastor who was passionate to practice what he was preaching.

A pastor can go to Elim's yearly cell conference, visit Bethany World Prayer Center, fly to Bogota for International Charismatic Mission's annual G-12 conference, or become immersed in David Cho's ministry in Korea. Yet, the long-term success of cell ministry depends on adjusting cell group church principles to each church's own reality. The best laboratory is personal involvement. When a pastor leads a cell group, he captures the weekly benefits of cell ministry and can empathize with fellow cell leaders in the church.

Leading a cell group is costly in time, spiritual stamina, and pastoral care. And we all know no one has extra time. When the senior pastor leads a cell group, it sweeps away the common arguments of the laity. The pastor's actions declare to the rest of the church that cell ministry is not optional; it's the very life of the church.

"I'm just too busy," many pastors say. Yet, lay people also have crazy, crowded schedules. "I'm called to lead others on a macro-level, not on a micro-level," a pastor might reply. Yes, but that's the point. A pastor can't understand macro thinking unless he knows what micro thinking is. Since the essence of the cell church is to convert the pew sitter into a harvest worker through cell leadership, shouldn't the senior pastor know how to lead a cell?

Clarence Day once said, "Information's pretty thin stuff, unless mixed with experience."[5] Leading a cell group, as opposed to attending a cell group, allows the senior leader to experience the need to invite new people, train the next leader, prepare the study, and even shepherd those in need. And what better place for the senior pastor to determine if his own cell lesson (based on his Sunday morning message) actually works!

Granted, there are times when the senior pastor will no longer lead a cell group. Many senior pastors of the world's largest cell churches don't personally lead a cell group. These churches have reached another level, and most likely the senior pastor has worked his way through the ranks and thus might not lead a cell now. There are also time periods in which a senior pastor won't lead a cell, only to enter the fray later on.

The norm of leading a cell group always has its exceptions and there's probably a time when this rule should be broken. Do so, however, with great care. Resist the temptation to supervise without personally leading a cell as long as possible.

FEED THE VISION

To understand how to feed the cell group church vision, here are several recommended steps:

First, a pastor should be a cell church student. A pastor's library should have the latest small group/cell church books: *Successful Home Cell Groups*, by David Cho; *Where do We Go from Here?* by Ralph Neighbour, Jr.; *Prepare Your Church for the Future*, by Carl George; *The Second Reformation*, by Bill Beckham; and even a few of my own! Successful cell church pastors study and restudy the cell church literature to solidify their vision.

Cell seminars will also help a pastor grow in knowledge. Yet, the primary role of a cell seminar isn't to teach a pastor how to do cell ministry, but rather to fan the flame of vision and to encourage the pastor to press on. The most popular seminars are filled with inspirational stories and miracles from Almighty God. With such a diverse audience and so little time, the seminar speaker must paint broad strokes, knowing each situation is different.

I've heard of pastors who repeatedly attend the great cell church conferences around the world in order to keep recharging their vision. I applaud such effort.

The second most important thing is for pastors to network with other cell church pastors. Pastors can learn from each other's successes—and failures. Our cities are full of hungry pastors who long for a helping hand to

Written Resources

Basic cell group books that every senior pastor should read:
- *Where Do We Go From Here?* by Ralph W. Neighbour Jr.
- *The Second Reformation* by Bill Beckham
- *Reap the Harvest* by Joel Comiskey
- *Home Cell Group Explosion* by Joel Comiskey
- *Making Cell Groups Work* by M. Scott Boren
- Books that address specific cell group models.

guide them in the process. Cell group church networks provide that link. Meeting with other pastors to share ideas and pray together is a bonding experience that refreshes.

Perhaps the most famous is the cell church network of Hong Kong, under the direction of Ben Wong. He primarily directs the HK Cell Church Network, which links approximately 160 cell churches to share ideas and resources to more effectively reach the remaining unreached people groups. From the Hong Kong network sprang an international gathering of cell church pastors that meets in a different country each year.[6]

There are also formal networks that link professional coaches with pastors who are transitioning to the cell group church model. A formal network connects an experienced, successful coach with an inexperienced pastor.

One of the best ways to feed a cell group church vision is to actually visit a cell church. If a pastor can combine a visit to a cell church with a cell seminar, it's even better. The best cell church seminars take place in cell churches, allowing participants to see practical examples of what they're hearing.

FROM THE INSIDE OUT

The effective cell group church pastor knows that if he can mobilize the laity to lead cell groups, those attending the church will receive personal care. The major statistic for a cell church pastor is how many cell groups are functioning in the church, as opposed to how many people are attending the worship service.

A lone pastor in a small church will take longer to arrive at this point than a pastor in a large church. The goal is the same, however. Carl George says, "I challenge pastors to be minister developers, and then to measure every other effect in the church by that standard—not by how impressive is the sermon but by how many ministers are made. Measure not by how available or busy the pastors are but by the extent to which the paid staff contributes to the making of ministers."[7]

The cell group church strategy is primarily a leadership strategy. The very essence of the cell church is developing new leaders. Cell groups are leader breeders. The primary function of the group is to develop new leaders, not to provide an atmosphere for cell attendance.

Successful cell group church pastors see success as how many pew sitters can be converted into cell leaders who'll pastor home groups that will, in turn, pastor and evangelize. The real work is caring for the current leaders (G-12) and then training the future ones (training track). The celebration is important, but it's the RESULT of the real work that takes place during the week.

The cell infrastructure focus helps align the pastorate with New Testament truth—remember that Ephesians 4:11-12 says the job of the pastor is to train the lay people to do the work of the ministry. This new focus also helps rescue the pastor's role from the star of the Sunday celebration to chief trainer and disciplemaker. Instead of asking about how to make the celebration attractive enough to keep people coming back, he asks, "How can I prepare and release lay workers into the harvest by developing them to lead dynamic cell groups?"

Like Jesus and his disciples, the lead pastor will primarily care for and minister to his ministerial team (G-12, staff, etc.). The senior pastor must pour his life into his key leaders. He must build relationships with them outside the official team gathering. Jesus, the ultimate G-12 leader, revealed how he developed relationships with his disciples: "I no longer call you servants, because a servant does not know his master's business. Instead, I have called you friends, for everything that I learned from my Father I have made known to you" (John 15:15).

Lead pastors may find it helpful to read my book, *How to be a Great Cell Group Coach* (Houston TX: Touch Publications, 2003), and apply those principles with key leaders. In that book, I recommend the following coaching order:

- Receive from God
- Listen to the leader
- Encourage the leader
- Care for the leader
- Develop/train the leader
- Strategize with the leader
- Challenge the leader

Written Resources

How to Be a Great Cell Group Coach by Joel Comiskey

The senior pastor will never fully meet the needs of his disciples in the weekly group meeting. He must spend personal time with each key leader outside the leadership meeting.

MINISTERING TO THE MINISTERS

The following agenda is recommended when the senior pastor meets with his paid staff or key volunteer cell leaders (G-12 group):

Word and Prayer Time

"For the Word of God is living and active. Sharper than any double-edged sword, it penetrates even to dividing soul and spirit, joints and marrow; it judges the thoughts and attitudes of the heart" (Hebrews 4:12, NIV). A wise pastor begins with the Word of God. Often the senior pastor will give a brief explanation of the passage and then ask application questions.

Prayer naturally follows ministry time in the Word. The senior pastor must make time for his key leaders to share their burdens and receive prayer.

Review of Cell Ministry

Before we transitioned to the cell group church structure, we started our ministerial meetings with a review of the various programs, ministries, and worship service concerns. Since becoming a cell group church, we start our meetings by talking about the heart of the church—cell groups.

The beauty of the cell group church is that it's possible to know what's really happening in the church. In a program-based church, the emphasis is on how the programs are functioning. In the cell group church, the focus is on how each cell is doing. Each cell leader turns in a report to his or her supervisor that might look like the sample on the following page. Utilize the back for prayer requests or information you deem important to communicate with your coach/pastoral staff.

Those reports are collected and summarized, so each pastor can see the results. Each pastor (or lay leader) reports on what's happening in his or her network of cells. This includes struggles, number of leaders visited during the week,

---

WEEKLY LIFEGROUP REPORT

Please return to LifeGroup mail slot in church workroom by Sunday.

Leader:_____Attendance: _____Date: _____

Conversions: _____

Topic/Theme of gathering: _____

Multiplication date: _____Multiplication Leaders: _____

Contacts of members/visitors: _____Visitors: _____

How many in Training Track: _____Meeting with Coach: _____

groups that have closed or are in the process of closing, victories, conversions, number of people in the training track, plans, why certain groups didn't meet, etc. As each key leader reports on his or her network, there's a sense that the church is truly pastored.

In the initial stages, we covered these reports quickly, but when we grew to 250 cell groups, we had to take longer. I believe the team should take as long as necessary, remembering the Proverb, "Be sure you know the condition of your flocks, give careful attention to your herds" (Proverbs 27:23). Cells are the heart of the church, and the place where the church is pastored.

Celebration Concerns and Other Matters

Since cell ministry drives the cell group church, it's best to cover cell ministry before celebration. After fully covering cell ministry, it's important to review the celebration service and everything connected with it.[8] During this time, the team discusses areas of need, worship, ushers, preaching, children's ministry, or any other aspect of the Sunday celebration. The team might talk about a future planning meeting, retreat, finances, or whatever relates to the church and vision.

Promoting the Vision

Promotion and vision casting can't be delegated. I made a mistake in 1993 when I personally assumed the role of the cell minister—even though I wasn't the senior pastor. I made cell ministry happen. The senior pastor administered the various visions at the church. To justify my position, I even wrote in my training manual, "The head pastor ... doesn't necessarily need to be in charge of this ministry. However, it is necessary that he is in total agreement with a cell-based vision for the church." I've changed my thinking since then. I now believe the senior pastor must be the cell minister.

No one else can take his place. George Barna reiterates this point saying, "The role of the leader/pastor is to provide vision, motivation, mobilization, direction, and resources to the laity. The role of other staff is to reinforce motivation, facilitate team building, and disseminate resources strategically."[9] Only the senior pastor can promote the vision effectively enough to make it work.

Dale Galloway understood this truth in 1984 when he wrote:

One mistake I made about three years ago was looking for someone from the outside to head up this ministry in our church, much like one might look for a music man or a youth pastor. This is the wrong approach. For the cell system to be successful it can never be delegated to someone else as a separate ministry. It must come out of the vision and heart of the Senior Pastor who is in charge. It must never be another ministry but must be central for the entire body. It is not to be like a music ministry, youth ministry or some other ministry that you hire an associate to do. If it is to be successful, it must be the vision, desire, and passion of the leader of the church.[10]

I encourage lay people in my seminars not to attempt to transition to the cell group church philosophy. They must, rather, pray for their pastor to catch the vision, as well as invite him to attend a cell seminar, provide literature, etc. A church will never go beyond the level of a church with cells unless the senior pastor is sold on the cell church vision and is openly promoting it.

SAYING NO TO THE MYRIAD OF PROGRAMS

The Titanic was supposed to be unsinkable. The builders didn't even bother to provide sufficient lifeboats because of the unsurpassed toughness of the ship. No one imagined it could ever sink. Yet, one tragic night, the Titanic met its match in the form of a rock-hard iceberg. The impossible turned into tragic reality.

The subtlest iceberg in cell ministry is when the senior pastor becomes enamored with new techniques, visions, and ministries. Seminars abound promoting new techniques that promise incredible results. Magazine articles and books promote the latest church program. Church members push—and sometimes demand—their favorite outreach or plan. In a strictly democratic situation, each proposal would receive equal billing and attention.

Such equality, however, will sink the cell group church transition. Be leery of the argument, "This program will help our cell ministry." This argument could be repeated for virtually every program on the market today. Everything "potentially" could help your cell ministry. Yet in the process, you'll drain your scarce people resources and fail to do "this one thing" well.

If you expect your people to multiply cell groups, oversee those new groups, and attend your church activities, you must not expect them to involve themselves in a variety of additional programs. Only the senior pastor can successfully navigate around the hidden icebergs of church programs and keep the cell group church transition on track.

INCLUDING CELL MINISTRY IN THE SERMON

When the person in the pew hears the senior pastor using illustrations from cell groups, this transmits the vision "loud and clear." Larry Stockstill makes it a point to include one cell illustration in each Sunday morning message. In a cell-based church, the experience of the cell should be the lifeblood of each member. Visitors should immediately know that involvement in the church means active participation in cell ministry.

Hearing it from the pulpit will do one of two things: draw the person to participate in a cell, or turn the person against cell ministry. The senior pastor must not capitulate to those who'd rather not participate in cell ministry. Although there'll always be those who choose to sit and soak, the senior pastor must choose to focus on the active, involved segment of the church. In our church, we made the rule that only leaders of cell groups are permitted to participate on the church board, thus removing the possibility of those not involved in the vision to rule in the church.

FREEDOM

The end result of cell ministry for the senior pastor is freedom. He's set free from the heavy load of pastoring everybody, being everywhere, and doing everything. It's the same freedom Moses must have felt when he accepted Jethro's advice and reorganized around groups of ten, one hundred, and one thousand.

Establishing the church around groups of ten requires hard work. The rewards, however, of seeing a church of lay ministers, lay pastors, and lay evangelists brings relief, freedom, and joy to the heart of God.

Staffing the Cell Group Church

Joel Comiskey

Lots of churches make the change to cell groups, but they continue to organize their leadership and staff around the old way of doing church. A pastor introduced his pastoral team to me. "This is John. He's over Christian education. Jack is over missions. Judy leads our worship. This is Tim. He's over all the cell groups in our church." Then the senior pastor began to talk about how they had made the transition to cell group church ministry, but that he wanted to learn more.

Hearing that a staff pastor, instead of the senior pastor, is over cell ministry shows me the church has a long way to go in its understanding.

Since the pastor openly asked me for counsel, I told him he needed to directly lead the cell ministry—not Tim. I told him all staff pastors needed to directly lead a network of cells, as well as take responsibility for a ministry in the church (e.g., Christian education, missions, and worship). Before leaving, the senior pastor said, "We were trying to get our congregation to make the cell group church transition that we as a staff were not yet willing to make."

Transitioning the Staff First

Don't expect the congregation to make the cell church transition before the pastoral team. Full-time staff members are called to wrestle with a wide variety of ministry-related issues. While many lay people are just as dedicated to the work of God, they haven't, as a general rule, worked through all the philosophical issues of church ministry.

Any church desiring to become a cell group church must first make the transition at the pastoral team level. Don't try to convince the congregation before the pastoral team is starting the journey.

STAFF MUST BE SUCCESSFUL IN LEADING AND MULTIPLYING CELL GROUPS

If a staff pastor hasn't multiplied a cell group, or worse yet, isn't currently leading one, authority and effectiveness will be greatly diminished. Reverse the situation! Some cell group churches fall into the error of separating staff from cell leadership. The leaders distance themselves from personally leading a cell group and winning souls for Christ. It's then easy to lose touch with non-Christians and cell ministry. Larry Stockstill says:

> North America has moved away from middle management. Some cell structures emphasize this middle management and set up a corporate type structure. The three levels are just supervising and not winning souls. All levels should be winning souls. No one should just sit back and do nothing. Everyone in the church should be winning souls. Everybody.[11]

If you're just starting the cell group church transition and have staff members who aren't leading a cell, ask them to lead one, multiply it, and shepherd a network.

All the largest cell churches in the world operate this way. They won't elevate anyone into higher positions unless the person has demonstrated success at the lower levels. Yes, calling and personal qualities were taken into account, but the ultimate test was past success as a cell leader, supervisor, etc. For the most part, Bible school training was not a major factor in elevation to top leadership.

It's also best to raise up staff members from within the church. In their book, *Built to Last: Successful Habits of Visionary Companies*, James C. Collins and Jerry I. Porras did an excellent job of analyzing how leadership was developed in the successful companies around the world. They concluded, "The visionary companies were six times more likely to promote insiders. Of the 113 CEOs in the visionary companies, only 3.5% came from outside."[12]

This was the pattern in leading cell group churches worldwide. These churches didn't have to look beyond themselves to fill their top leadership positions. All leaders had to go through the normal channels of ministerial experience, ministerial success, and leadership training within the church before being lifted up to higher positions.

Cell Group Vision Team Exercise

What keeps current staff members from leading a cell group?

EACH STAFF PASTOR A CELL GROUP LEADER

The senior pastor should take the role of cell minister. Each staff pastor, including the senior pastor, leads his or her own cell group and develops a network of cell groups.

Each staff pastor should continue to direct his or her ministry as well, although the ministry assignment would be greatly streamlined. But the chief identity of each staff pastor should be "overseer" of a network of cell groups.

A staff member might oversee the music ministry, for example, but that same staff member would also have a network of cells, and would be expected to multiply that network, just like everyone else on staff.

THE MAIN STAFF TASK: LEADERSHIP DEVELOPMENT

Carl George says, "The role of the church staff is to effectively manage the leadership development structures."[13] The main role of pastors isn't to manage church programs, but to develop, manage, and care for cell leaders.

I consulted one cell group church whose staff focused week after week on the Sunday service. It was a clear case of a pastoral staff existing for the Sunday event. I spent the weekend with the staff, encouraging each one to be over a network of cell groups. I counseled them to start the pastoral meeting by examining each network of cells, and only afterward to focus on the celebration service.

The senior pastor and pastoral team were willing to prioritize cell leadership development and care as the main task of the church. After they worked on this shift of focus, the senior pastor wrote to me,

> … our staff is totally on board and committed to the philosophy [cell church] and a large part is because they are seeing the results in people's lives. They also like the fact that they have a very specific ministry approach to follow and directions on how to make it happen: i.e. get people through the training, work with leaders, get apprentices, etc. It is less nebulous than a generic "get people to come to your events"—or "build a ministry"—it is training lay people for a very specific role, and now they have a plan on how to do it.

The reason for having pastors on staff in the cell group church is to produce new leaders to reap the harvest. All aspects of the cell group church are designed to produce, care for, and encourage cell leaders.

WHAT DO STAFF PASTORS DO?

When thinking about what a staff pastor does, it's important to keep three principles in mind. First, the staff pastor's major responsibility is his network of cell groups, and afterward his ministry responsibilities.

Second, a staff pastor is guided by the goal of how many cells his network will have at the end of the year. Having a clear-cut goal for cell multiplication means the staff pastor must concentrate on leadership development. Developing new leaders goes hand-in-hand with caring for the existing leaders.

Third, the senior pastor must give each staff pastor sufficient liberty to fulfill the overarching goal of multiplication without trying to micromanage each step. The senior pastor must realize the role of staff pastor isn't primarily about punching time clocks, sitting behind a desk, or fulfilling rigid requirements. Rather, it's all about growing a network of cells, which means caring for unique individuals with particular situations. It's more like having your own business than administrating the business of someone else.

Fourth, the staff focuses together on developing new leaders. On each weekly report, include how many are taking each level of training. Create a form with a column for each level on on the training track (B.D:-Bible Doctrine; PAN: Panorama of the Bible; EVAN: Cell Evangelism; C.L.: Cell Leadership). The pastor of each network should give a report on how many people are being trained to become cell leaders. If you have a second level of training for existing cell leaders, it would be good to include it as well.

STAFF PASTORS PERFORM THE PRIMARY PASTORAL FUNCTIONS

Although we're all called to minister, certain church functions are reserved for staff pastors. Weddings, funerals, difficult counseling, and baptisms require training beyond the level of normal cell leadership.

While some cell group churches allow cell leaders to baptize, the vast majority do not.[14] Most cell group churches also ask that staff pastors perform the baptisms within their own particular network of cells. Often the cell leader prepares the person for baptism, but the staff pastor actually baptizes him.

Most states require that an ordained pastor perform weddings. Funerals also require some knowledge of funeral procedures, and training in dealing with the bereaved. While the priesthood of all believers is a core value for cell group churches, some functions are best left to trained pastors.[15]

VISITATION AND CONTACT

Some have predicted the day of the virtual church. As valuable as e-mail, web pages, and other Internet features are, they'll never replace personal relationships.

Staff pastors must meet with their cell leaders and personally minister to them. The most effective staff pastors I know visit their leaders regularly. Some cell churches even require their staff pastors to spend afternoons visiting. Such visits are then noted.

A staff pastor will use the Internet to make contact and talk about appointments. Yet, the bottom line is that a pastor must make personal contact with his people, getting to know them on a personal basis. He must visit their cell groups, help them in their problems, and disciple them.

The only way to produce long-term results is to effectively pastor. The best pastors spend time with people. They are full-time in the ministry, and their people know it.

The major principle here is that people will follow the pastor's lead. If the pastor only calls, but never visits, those under the pastor will do the same. Paul could say in 1 Corinthians 10:33, "Follow my example, as I follow the example of Christ." The example, more than words, is what a staff pastor must model.

GOAL SETTING

Joel Comiskey

Most have heard the age-old story of the archer who shot the arrow, found where it landed, and then drew a bull's-eye on that exact spot. We chuckle when hearing this illustration, but it's the sad reality in many churches that prefer to wait until December to draw circles around their natural accomplishments. True, this methodology avoids stark failure, but it accomplishes little. Human nature tends to look for the lowest denominator, so it's important to make the goal(s) beforehand. Setting clear goals separates the record-breaking cell group churches from those that limp along year after year.

Many cell group churches are led by committed senior pastors, hold to a proper view of the cell, and concentrate on cell ministry. In other words, they do everything else perfectly. What makes the difference? One of the key differences is that some cell churches are guided by clear-cut goals for cell multiplication and some are not.

David Cho, the pastor and founder of the largest church in the history of Christianity, is a very goal-oriented pastor. Listen to his words: "Many people criticized me because I was giving goals to my people, then encouraging them to accomplish the goals. But if you don't give them a goal, they will have no purpose to being in the cell."[16]

He goes on to say, "Many churches are failing in their cell system because they do not give their people a clear goal and remind them constantly of their goal. If they have no goal, then the people will gather together and just have a grand fellowship."[17]

Ted Engstrom, president emeritus of World Vision, and an expert on leadership, observes, "The best leaders always had a planned course, specific goals, and written objectives. They had in mind the direction in which they wanted to go."[18]

Both goal setting and making plans are God's will. The writer of Proverbs said: "We should make plans ... counting on God to direct us" (Prov. 16:14, TLB). The same writer goes on to say, "Any enterprise is built by wise planning, becomes strong through common sense, and profits wonderfully by keeping abreast of the facts" (Prov. 24:34, TLB).

Some leaders obscure the process by setting goals too high or too low, not setting goals, or lacking an accountability structure while setting goals. Having made all these mistakes and learning the hard way, my goal for this chapter is to offer practical advice that will help your ministry.

WATCH THE MOTIVATION

It's hard to promote a worthless goal. A Christian salesperson could sell fifty cartons of cigarettes a day and condemn himself afterward. When setting goals, a leader must ask the why question before determining the what question. Why should we set this goal? What's the motivation? Is it for the glory of God? Will this goal help us advance the kingdom of God? The congregation will only respond to a goal that moves their souls, stirs them to greater heights, and accomplishes greater things for God's glory.

Some cell group churches reject goal setting as carnal and numbers-oriented. Some pastors feel that projecting a numerical goal is sinful and worldly, but the only proper motivation for setting a goal for multiplying cell groups is to glorify God and advance his Kingdom. Pastors need to ask God to give them a higher motivation for goal setting.

Donald McGavran said it well: "It is essential that Christian leaders align their basic purposes with the eternal purpose of God to save unbelievers through faith in Jesus Christ. This is the first step in the consequent growth and development of the church. Goal setting helps implement such alignment."[19] When a leader doubts the validity of goal setting, he or she needs time to reflect on God's will and to align his own purposes with God's.

Once that alignment has taken place, the leader needs to constantly remind people, "We're not setting a goal today just to have a more successful church or so that the pastors can impress others. No, we want to double the number of cell groups this year because people are going to hell and we desire to reach our city for Jesus."

I can never justify a preoccupation with success. In my view, it's always wrong to seek personal success in ministry. Whenever I'm preoccupied with personal success, I'm sinning. Whenever, I want my superiors to notice how "successful" I am, I'm guilty of personal ambition. Yet, personal success and ambition have nothing to do with God's desire to grow his church. I've now come to realize that an ambition for church growth is literally God's ambition for a lost world. He's not willing that any should perish but that all might come to repentance.

As a young pastor, I wrestled with the motivation issue. I knew my quest for church growth was to succeed. I wrestled with my own carnal motivation for success when setting a numerical goal.

It wasn't until later that I realized that Jesus Christ is extremely concerned with numbers. It's not God's will that anyone should perish. The apostle Peter says: "But do not forget this one thing, dear friends: With the Lord a day is like a thousand years, and a thousand years are like a day. The Lord is not slow in keeping his promise, as some understand slowness. He is patient with you, not wanting anyone to perish, but everyone to come to repentance" (2 Peter 3:8-9).

Paul wrote to his disciple Timothy: "This is good, and pleases God our Savior, who wants all men to be saved and to come to a knowledge of the truth. For there is one God and one mediator between God and men, the man Christ Jesus" (1 Tim. 2:3-5). God desires to save ALL men and to bring them to the knowledge of the truth. I can never justify personal ambition.

God finally convinced me that he wants his church to grow more than I ever will. I now see goal setting as part of his perfect plan, but I still wrestle with unworthy motives. I still have to resist carnal motivations of self-promotion and success, calling them what they are: sin.

Yet, my own sinful tendency must never stop me from working toward his greater glory—the salvation and discipleship of a lost world. When by God's grace you move beyond that lower level thinking and realize God himself is intimately concerned with the salvation of his creation, you'll then be encouraged to make goals, so more people will be saved and enter the kingdom.

THE INADEQUACY OF ATTENDANCE GOALS

I co-founded a church that grew from 150 to 550 in four years. Yet before transitioning to the cell group church philosophy, we uncovered glaring weaknesses. An exceedingly small percentage participated in prayer, training, and other ministries. Without realizing it, we were proclaiming, by our goals and values, that it was okay to just attend church on Sunday morning. Our Sunday emphasis also attracted the crowd of church connoisseurs who loved to taste something new.

I attribute much of my zeal for celebration attendance to church growth theory, though not all church growth theorists point to Sunday morning attendance as the primary or only way to measure church growth. Peter Wagner teaches his students to combine worship attendance, membership, and Sunday school attendance to arrive at a composite membership. Practically, however, for most pastors, Sunday attendance is the primary indicator of church growth success.[20]

The Sunday attendance focus can subtly produce inactivity among church attendees who feel they've fulfilled their purpose by attending the Sunday morning service. There's always a danger in aiming too low, and aiming at Sunday attendance is too low (just like aiming at cell attendance instead of the next leader is inadequate).

Another problem with Sunday celebration goals is the lack of accountability. It's easy to set a yearly attendance goal, but in the end, who's responsible? It's easy to proclaim an attendance goal to the entire congregation, but who in the congregation is responsible for the goal's fulfillment? What if the goal isn't met? Who's responsible? The entire congregation? Is it the pastor's fault? The board's?

Larry Crabb addresses a similar issue in his book, *Encouragement*:

A goal may be defined as a purpose to which a person is unalterably committed. *He assumes unconditional responsibility for a goal, and it can be achieved if he is willing to work at it.* A desire may be defined as something wanted that *cannot be obtained without the cooperation of another person.* It is an objective for which a person can assume no responsibility, *because it is beyond his control. Reaching a desire must never become the motivating purpose behind behavior, because then a person is assuming responsibility for something he cannot fulfill on his own* [italics my own].[21]

Celebration attendance goals fall into the category of desire because, in the long run, no one person can be held responsible. Christian A. Schwarz arrived at a similar conclusion in his book, *Natural Church Development*, and even discovered that only thirty-one percent of the growing churches actually have a precise attendance goal.[22] While an attendance goal isn't wrong, attendance should be the result of clear, concise goals to grow the infrastructure.

GROWING THE INFRASTRUCTURE

Growing cell group churches around the world prioritize the development of new cell groups as their primary goal. In other words, the one driving goal in the cell church should be *how many cells we will have at the end of the year.*[23] These churches expect harvest to occur as a result of their hard work in the cells. They concentrate on developing and releasing new leadership (which requires cell multiplication), and the result is increased church attendance.

With this approach, a church can concentrate on multiplying the infrastructure—new leaders—and be assured of quality and quantity growth. Outreach and evangelism are core values in this approach. A church that's constantly multiplying cells is penetrating the city with red-hot evangelistic fervor and diligent leadership development.

This concept is straightforward and simple: concentrate on developing new leaders through constantly multiplying cell groups, and they will in turn reap the harvest. Wasn't this Christ's strategy? We read in Matthew 9:35-37 that Christ:

> … went through all the towns and villages, teaching in their synagogues, preaching the good news of the kingdom and healing every disease and sickness. When he saw the crowds, he had compassion on them, because they were harassed and helpless, like sheep without a shepherd. Then he said to his disciples, "The harvest is plentiful but the workers are few. Ask the Lord of the harvest, therefore, to send out workers into his harvest field."

Then in Matthew 10:1-2ff, Jesus fulfills his own strategy: "He called his twelve disciples to him and gave them authority to drive out evil spirits and to heal every disease and sickness. These are the names of the twelve apostles …" According to Jesus, the way to harvest wasn't to call crowds into a big building. The most effective way to harvest was to raise up workers to reap the harvest.

Jesus believed so much in this strategy that he spent a lifetime developing leaders to reap the harvest after his departure. He accomplished his purpose, leaving behind twelve leaders who stood up to the entire Roman Empire and won.

This is the principle behind the mighty harvest these huge cell churches are experiencing. They've learned the secret of converting the multitude into workers who reap the harvest. Dale Galloway, a pioneer of cell church philosophy in the U.S., understood this well. He wrote, "The concept is that first you build leaders. The leaders build groups. Out of these groups come more leaders and a multiplication into more groups."[24]

WARNING: MULTIPLY LEADERS, NOT JUST CELLS

Cell multiplication is the motivation for cell ministry, but only as cell multiplication means new leadership development. In exceptional circumstances, one leader might lead two cell groups. However, this is the exception, not the rule. The clear goal must be one leader per cell.

At the International Charismatic Mission, many leaders led two or three cells. In fact, leaders were expected to have at least two cells. In this way, they were able to arrive at a large number of cell groups, when in reality they only had half that many leaders (20,000 cell groups with 10,000 leaders).

My own church was so concerned about meeting the goal that we allowed key leaders and pastors to lead more than one cell group. Yet, as the months and years went by, we had to confront the reality of a leadership shortage. Each succeeding year, we had fewer leaders, and it became harder to reach the goal. We finally had to bite the bullet and realize it's dangerous to allow a cell leader to lead more than one group. The burnout might not show immediately, but it will eventually stall the system.

We fell into this trap. Many of our leaders led more than one group and were tired. They couldn't produce any more. We saw the writing on the wall and made a firm commitment to one cell per leader. We ask our cell leaders to personally shepherd their own daughter cell leaders, and realized we were asking far too much of them to lead more than one cell group.

When setting a goal for cell multiplication, just remember that implicit in the goal is the idea that each cell group will be led by a different person. Otherwise, the cracks will begin to appear in succeeding years, as has been the case with the International Charismatic Mission.

PUBLIC GOALS VERSUS PRIVATE GOALS

The major public church goal should be the total number of cell groups by the end of the year. Additional goals, such as baptisms, conversions, and number of leaders, are important as well, but it's best to keep these goals among the leadership. Confusion reigns when the congregation hears ten goals simultaneously. Proclaim the one goal—cell groups—and then privately work towards the sub-goals throughout the year. A church might decide to make the following sub-goals for the year:

- 25 baptisms
- 75 conversions
- 50 leaders trained

The public goal is for the number of new cell groups, but this inherently means new conversions, new baptisms, and new leaders trained. The sub-goals serve the greater goal of producing new cell groups, which ultimately produces church growth. The church above set the goal to train fifty new leaders, yet the greater goal was that each one of those fifty would graduate from the equipping track by actually leading a cell group (since each cell leader must pass through the entire equipping track before leading a cell group).

Baptism can be seen in a similar light. Many churches won't allow a person to lead a cell unless he or she is baptized; again, this is a sub-goal that promotes the major goal of cell leadership.

The public goal should be the number of new cell groups, but to fulfill that goal, the leadership team must focus on conversions, baptisms, pastoral care, and leadership development.

THE TWO KILLERS: IDEALISM AND INDIFFERENCE

Year after year, one cell group church failed to reach its cell goals or grow in celebration attendance. The senior pastor seemed to have captured the cell vision. His cells were defined accurately. Yet, something was missing.

For two consecutive years, the church established the goal of one hundred cell groups and both years failed to even come close. When the church launched this goal, only thirty or so cell groups existed. Idealism birthed the goal of one hundred and then fed it. The goal might have initially inspired the congregation to expect something great, but it failed to motivate and inspire throughout the year. Adding insult to injury, the leadership acted as if the goal didn't exist—a forgotten paper tucked away in a dusty filing cabinet. The goal, bred in idealism, inspired people for a moment, but soon lost its luster and became useless.

The second killer in this church was indifference. The goal of one hundred wasn't owned by the congregation, because it was never officially announced (nor proclaimed in a public way through the use of banners). The pastor paid lip service to making goals, but was indifferent to enforcing them. The next year, he didn't even bother to set an overall goal for the number of cell groups. Idealism and indifference encourage each other.

They both oppose reality and diligence in goal setting.

BALANCE BETWEEN QUALITY AND QUANTITY

Cell multiplication goals must always take into account two things: the urgency to reach a lost world without Christ (rapid multiplication of cells), and the long-term commitment of the church to reach this lost world (quality cells that endure over time). It's important to strike a balance between quality and quantity with regard to cell groups. If the goal is too high, the danger is producing weak cells.[25]

Meeting goals is important, but it's also essential to multiply healthy cells. There's a danger of multiplying too fast, and reproducing weakness. A company that releases a product too early might need to recall it later. If a new cell group starts too quickly, it might fulfill the goal, but will also close unexpectedly. This is particularly true in the G-12 system, in which individuals leave the mother cell to plant new cells with only one or two people.[26]

THE NUTS AND BOLTS OF GOAL MAKING

Pastors might agree with the principles presented thus far, but may not understand how to set multiplication goals. The next few points will help to apply these truths in practical ways.

Determine a Yearly Goal

Although it's not the only way to set goals, it's best to initiate the new goal in January and finish it by December.

One large cell church in Tegucigalpa, Honduras, called Love Alive Church, purposely has only one official multiplication date per year. In other words, cell groups at LAC multiply at the same time and on a predetermined date each year. This isn't to say a cell group at LAC can't multiply beforehand if it's ready to give birth. However, these new births are the exceptions. Only about ten percent of the new groups open at various times during the year. They purposely wait for one year because they believe the cells need a period of solidification.[27]

There are some problems with having only one multiplication date. First, the church misses the excitement of seeing new cell multiplication throughout the year. I've come to believe (through experience) that waiting a whole year for one huge multiplication slowly drains away excitement throughout the year.

Second, it places too much pressure on top leaders at one particular time of the year. When pastors or key leaders are concentrating on too many leaders at one time, some leaders will fall through the cracks.

Third, if the multiplication date is near the end of the year (November, for example), some leaders will say, "I'm just going to wait until January to multiply." We all know December is filled with Christmas activity, so some will think, "Why start a group only to close it for Christmas break?"

Divide the Goal into at Least Three Periods

There are positive points about dividing the goal into distinct time periods throughout the year. First, top leadership is focused from January onward. Rather than thinking, "I have ten months until my groups multiply," the pastor or leader over a network of cells is working right away, knowing a portion of his small groups will multiply in March, for example.

Second, it alleviates end-of-the-year pressure by spreading the commitment throughout the year.

Divide the Goal According to the Readiness of Each Cell

If the goal is seventy-five cells by the end of the year and the church currently has fifty cells, the divisions might look like this:
- By March: 55 cells
- By July: 65 cells
- By November: 75 cells

The reason for proposing three checkpoints instead of four is because it's very difficult to multiply small groups beyond November. When a small group opens in December, for example, it immediately closes for Christmas and New Year's break. Notice that the above numbers aren't evenly divided. That's because each key pastor or leader over cells needs to determine what cells are able to give birth in each of the three time periods.

The key is to divide the goal according to the readiness of the groups, rather than a mathematical calculation. In other words, don't grab a calculator in order to divide your yearly goal into three precise sub-goals. This doesn't work!

It's best to decide the checkpoint goals during the yearly retreat time with the key leaders who are over cells (pastoral retreat, if you have full-time pastors, or ministerial retreat, if you depend on key lay people). This retreat would normally take place in December, thinking about the upcoming year.

Each pastor or leader of a network of cells should come prepared to propose which cells will multiply at each specific checkpoint. This means giving specific names of cell leaders who'll multiply at each particular time period, rather than general numbers of groups.

Determine the Goal Before the Year Starts

Make your goals for the following year in November and December. This avoids a slow start in the next year. Starting in November and December stimulates the thinking process.

Thinking about next year's goal, when the current year's goal is not yet fulfilled, can be bothersome. In order to avoid hassling your hard-working leaders with new goals when they're busily working to fulfill present ones, it's best to keep this discussion at the ministerial team level.[28]

Make Sure the Goal is Reachable

In order to reach the goal and celebrate its fulfillment, make sure the goal is achievable. This is a common error among pastors. Suddenly, a pastor feels the urge to make goals (perhaps due to an irritated church board), so he launches an incredible goal that makes him look good for the moment ("People will think I'm a man of intense vision") but has no real chance of fulfillment. Some like to take out their calculators and piously assert, "If each member could just win one more member and each cell leader could just raise up two new leaders we could have nine hundred cells." Easy! Presto!

In reality, it doesn't work that way. Leaders quit. Excitement wanes. Cells close. People are busy.

A Miami pastor of 150 people said before a large congregation in March, "Our goal is to have fifteen hundred attending the church by the end of the year." It's hard for a congregation to grasp such a goal, let alone participate in its fulfillment.

There's a huge difference between casting a long-term vision (hope) for incredible growth and the short-term yearly goal. A pastor needs to paint an exciting long-term vision. He or she could say, "In ten years we hope to have five thousand people attending this church." This is far more stimulating than a logical, risk-free statement; "In ten years we hope to have two hundred people in our church." The higher number stimulates vision and purpose, while the lower one reveals the pastor's lack of vision.

A short-term goal, however, should be practical and concise. People think in one-year time frames, whether contemplating family planning, annual payments, or work goals. When the members hear a one-year goal, they can envision how the fulfillment of that goal will look in the church. A ten-year goal, on the other hand, is almost incomprehensible. It's difficult to think practically when hearing it. Think of inspiration when launching a long-term goal, and think of realism when introducing the short-term goal.

For years, the Elim Church in El Salvador automatically set its goals based on one hundred percent growth. Each district, zone, and sector had to double every year. The problem was that the church never expected to double. Rather, pastors and leaders were placed on a list in the order of how close they came to arriving at the goal of doubling. Those highest on the list often only reached twenty-two or twenty-four percent of their goal to double. Finally, Elim changed this system because it simply wasn't based on reality.

Base Your Goal on Church Health

When trying to determine a goal for the next year, examine the infrastructure. For example, if an equipping track isn't in place, it will be very difficult to produce new leadership. In the beginning, a church can draw from the old pros, those who've taken loads of Sunday school classes or have been involved in various programs for a number of years.[29] Yet, that pool will soon run dry, and the church must depend on the new leaders who've passed through the equipping track.

Remember the exhortation of Proverbs 27:23: "Be sure you know the condition of your flocks, give careful attention to your herds." If your herd is tired, pressured, and goal-weary, be very careful about demanding another record-breaking year. To know the state of your flock, it's best to use information on weekly reports from cell leaders.

Pastors need to hold cell leaders, coaches, and network pastors accountable for collecting reports. Place someone in charge of having exact statistics from all the cells by the time the pastoral team meets.[30]

If a group doesn't meet for six weeks, it's wise to delete that group from the statistics. That group might reappear at a different date, but it's a great mistake to count a group that's not actively involved in meeting. What are the results?

1. Reality. The key leaders are aware of what's really happening. This is hard but necessary.
2. Healthy Groups: The purpose of statistics is to maintain healthier groups.
3. Plans for the Future: The church can now better plan for the future.

Start staff meetings with prayer and then ask each pastor to give a report about the state of his network. Each pastor will give a verbal report, based on a written report of all the cell statistics for that week from all the cell reports.

Since every pastor has a written copy of the report, while one pastor is talking, the others can follow along. Each is free to ask questions like, "John, I noticed Mary's cell group hasn't met in awhile. Is she still leading the group?" Godly peer pressure keeps everyone on track. Since there's a global goal for the number of cell groups, if one pastor fails, everyone fails.

Here's a sample report:

| | Actual Cells | Cells That Met | Leaders w/o Reports | Cell Attendance | Conversions | | Cell Goals | Cell Visits | Leader Contacts | |
					Acum.	Actual			Tel.	Personal
Pr. Hans Vera	48	44	0	229	33	1	50	3	15	8
Pr. Denis Fiallos	81	49	0	231	12	4	90	2	8	10
Pr. Vincent Gonz.	46	35	1	202	29	2	57	2	5	7
Pr. Javier Silva	48	26	0	171	45	8	63	2	8	10
Pr. Jon Prado	38	29	0	223	9	6	50	5	5	4
Total	261	183	1	1056	128	21	310	14	41	39

If you're just starting, here is a sample report from a smaller church:

| | Actual Cells | Cells that Met | Attendance | Conversions | | Leaders | | Goals | | Visitors in Cells | Contact of Leaders | |
				Acu.	Act.	Act.	Meta	Trim.	Annual		Pers./Telf.	G-12 Meeting
Pastor David Sanborn	15	12	79	2	0	12	17	17	30	3	7	7
Pastor Earl Clugh	22	15	109	0	0	14	27	27	40	7	10	4
Pastor Tom Scott	6	6	40	1	1	5	7	7	10	4	2	3
Total	43	33	228	3	1	51	51	51	80	14	19	14

The overarching goal is the number of cell groups. From that goal, each staff member gives a report on cells that actually met in his network, the attendance in his network, conversions, how many cell groups he visited, his contacts with cell leaders by telephone, and his personal contacts with cell leaders. Above and beyond this general summary report, each network has a more extensive list that includes individual cell groups (attendance, conversions, etc.).

Why bother with reports? Accurate statistical reporting preserves quality control. It also keeps goals and ministry on track.

The above reports are only examples. Make your own. Decide what aspects are most important to your church and pastoral team. Just make sure everything the staff person does and reports on leads to the ultimate goal of cell multiplication, which means developing new leaders.

Make Sure the Goal Challenges and Demands Sacrifice

Goals must excite people. If the goal is super safe (ten to twelve cells in one year) it's doubtful anyone will get behind it. Why even bother setting a goal? Most likely two out of ten cells would multiply in one year anyway, so such a goal is more of a scientific statement, rather than a target to stimulate progress.

James C. Collins and Jerry I. Porras studied some of the most successful companies on the face of the earth (e.g., Sony, IBM, Disney, etc.) and compared them with companies that started at a similar time but weren't as successful. Along with other discoveries, these Stanford researchers revealed that although the successful companies might appear safe to outsiders, they make big, hairy, audacious goals in order to stimulate progress.[31]

These researchers define a big, hairy, and audacious goal this way: "A BHAG engages people—it reaches out and grabs them in the gut. It is tangible, energizing, highly focused. People "get it" right away; it takes little or no explanation."[32] The key to a BHAG, according to these researchers, is whether it stimulates the organization to forward progress, whether it creates momentum, gets people's juices flowing, and if people find it stimulating.[33] Make sure your goals stimulate others to work hard, without killing them in the process.

Work as a Team to Decide the Goal

So how exactly do you arrive at the goal? Here are some principles:

• Cell Members

Cell leaders should talk in cell group meetings about the goal to multiply. Since reproduction means members will be involved, with one or two actually leading the new group, there's absolutely nothing to hide. So the goal starts with the cell members.

The Love Alive Church in Tegucigalpa, Honduras follows this process for making its reproduction goals:

- The cell leaders communicate their goals for multiplication to the area supervisors.
- The area supervisors tell their zone pastors how many cell groups under their care will be ready to give birth.
- The zone pastors tell the district pastors how many possible new births to expect in their zones.
- The district pastors communicate their goals and visions to the director of the cell groups.
- The director of cell groups, in coordination with the district pastors, establishes a multiplication goal for the year.
- The pastoral team then approves this goal.

- Cell Leader-Coach

The coach/supervisor should know right away when the group will multiply and who's preparing to be the next leader.[34]

- Network of Supervisors-Staff Pastor

The network of supervisors (the twelve disciples of the staff pastor) meet at least once a month for skill training, vision casting, prayer, and also to confirm the details of cell reproduction. At the end of the year—or at the latest, the beginning of January—the staff pastor asks all key G-12 leaders to set an annual goal for their sub-networks. There'll be some give and take between pastor and supervisor.

- Pastoral team

Working as a team to develop goals is a rigorous task that demands tough skin, lots of feedback, and prayer. During a pastoral team meeting (as described above), each pastor will present his or her group vision for the year. One leader might promote a conservative goal—just a few more than last year, while another suggests reaching the entire city for Christ in one year. The senior pastor usually must mediate between the various opinions, always reserving the right to make the final decision. It's best if the leadership team can slip away for one day to pray, debate, analyze, and project the yearly goal for cell groups (as well as any other goals for the church). The final decision might come a week or so later in an official meeting. (Let the leaders sleep on it for a few days.) The pastor must lead the charge, while treasuring team participation.

- Pastor

It's unwise for a senior pastor to dictate God's goal to everyone else. Dictated goals dampen team spirit. The senior pastor, however, must ultimately decide what the goal should be.

Distribute the Goal among Leadership

After arriving at a general goal for the church, break it down and delegate the goals to those responsible. If you're a church planter with five cells, the yearly goal might be ten cells (and maybe even to start your first weekly celebration service by the end of the year). In this scenario, the five cell leaders will be responsible to help reach the goal of ten. After you've reached ten, you'll appoint two supervisors who'll each care for a cluster of five cells (if you're using the 5x5 system). These supervisors will primarily be responsible for the next year's goals. When you hire your first staff member, place him over a network of cell groups and hold him responsible to multiply new groups.

Avoid Spiritualizing the Goal

Watch out for the phrase, "If the Lord wills, I will multiply my cell." This phrase is deadly and can kill the best initiative. Here's a typical scenario: The ministerial team decides on a particular goal. The entire year, each pastor is working hard to fulfill the goal. Each week, there's accountability and everyone is enthused about meeting the goal. During the last months, however, the reality of the situation begins to sink in. Some cell leaders have quit. Others who've promised to multiply their cells will begin to say, "I'm not ready to lead a new cell. It's better to wait until the next year." Expect this to happen.[35]

Yet when it does happen, the goal will seem daunting, unreachable. At this moment, some members of the ministerial team will say, "If the Lord wills, I will fulfill my projected goal." Watch for this mentality and avoid it like the plague. I like to say to those who make such statements, "Yes, the Lord wills for this cell to multiply. What are you doing about it?" We made this a rule among our ministerial team (although it often turns into a time of laughter) that when someone uses the phrase, "If the Lord wills," we all retort, "yes, the Lord wills."

It's easy to hide behind spiritual language. It eases the pain of not fulfilling the goal, and even makes a person appear spiritual—"I'm trusting the Lord, brother." Yet, people respect someone much more who just acknowledges failure and says, "I'm struggling because I'm not sure if I'm going to make my goal." Be honest and real. If you're not going to meet your goal, admit it. Most likely your failure will stir you to work much harder the next year and to start much earlier to prepare your leadership.

Remember also to give yourself margin in reaching your goal. Privately, you should over project the goal by a few cell groups. For example, if your public goal is to reach ten cells by the end of the year, privately aim at developing thirteen cells. Most likely three of the thirteen groups will make excuses, experience an expected tragedy, or transfer to another city.

Proclaim the Goal Publicly

There's no such thing as a hidden goal. Goals by their very nature are public. We learned from other successful cell churches about the importance of using banners to proclaim the cell goal. Each year we proclaim our yearly goal through huge banners that hang down on either side of the pulpit. The banners not only proclaim our goal but also declare our cell group church philosophy. Every Sunday, the entire congregation stares directly at our goal for the year. If we fail, we'll admit it, but we refuse to hide by not setting a goal.

Measure Progress Continually

For the last several months, I've vigorously tried to lose weight. I've discovered that my best friend is my bathroom scale. I force myself to get on it every morning because I know my friend will tell me the truth—the reality of my situation. In some of my heavier moments, I've avoided my scale like the plague.

One of the main reasons to maintain and review weekly cell statistics is to mark progress toward the yearly goal. Statistics provide the necessary shock treatment, forcing us to see the reality of the situation—"You mean Susan's cell has also closed!"

Time flies. Twelve months might seem like an eternity in January, but December will soon be here. Those churches that fail to fulfill their goals also do a poor job of measuring their goals throughout the year. Think of how quickly a year flies by:

1. First quarter (January-March). These are mop-up months from the previous year. Some cells are weak and need lots of encouragement. Yet, mature cell churches begin training people in earnest during this time period, knowing twelve months pass very quickly.

2. Second quarter (April-June). These should be the most fruitful months to train, disciple, and cast the vision, yet it's common for pastors and leaders to take a break during this period. Everyone's tired and often very little transpires.

3. Third quarter (July-September). In many places around the world, these are vacation months. We never close cells, but we also realize it's hard to get lots of work done when people are busy or on vacation.[36]

4. Fourth quarter (October-December). This quarter suddenly arrives and each network pastor (or district pastor) must give an account. This quarter is the make-it-or-break-it time. The amount of work done previously will determine the amount of work the pastor performs during this time period.

The regular review of statistics keeps the state of the flock continually before the pastor and the ministerial team. The accurate reporting of cell groups will expose weaknesses as well as initiate action.

Fulfill the Goal

Failure—the word everyone avoids. It's possible that your church won't reach the goal. Admit your disappointment, acknowledge it before the congregation, and by all means learn from it. Respect this mindset far more than the justifying, excuse-making mentality of some. Use the failure to calculate next year's goal with more precision and then run toward it with all your energy.

Try to develop the habit of fulfilling your goals each year. First it will build confidence in the congregation. When a goal isn't reached—or worse yet, ignored after not reaching it—the congregation stops listening to next year's goal. "We've heard that before," they say under their breath as the pastor proclaims the new goal.

Second, it produces assurance among the leadership team that next year's goal will also be reached. With this comes a seriousness to set the next goal. Success breeds more success. No one wants to taste failure after feeding on success. This is the mindset that will prevail in the leadership team.

Pastors and key leaders will begin to think to themselves, "Our senior pastor takes these goals seriously. I better plan now to fulfill them." Everyone will wholeheartedly analyze and debate the goals for the next year in November and December, knowing fulfillment of the goal is the norm. It stirs the ministerial staff to work extremely hard to make it happen.

Celebrate the Fulfillment

Give your leaders a break. They're the volunteer stars who've sacrificed the whole year for Jesus Christ. Shower honor upon them. It's the least you can do. We always hold a cell recognition dinner in December to honor the most important people in our church—the cell leaders. We go out of our way to prepare a first-class meal, special gift, and slide show that highlights their accomplishments.

THE DILEMMA OF MINISTRIES

Joel Comiskey

One pastor transitioning to the cell church wrote: "Would a community center offering things like a drop-in coffee shop, counseling rooms, relationship-training and other courses be considered under 'programs' if undertaken by a growing cell church?"[37] Questions like this weigh heavily on the minds of most leaders considering the cell church. "Are all programs evil?" many wonder, thinking the cell church teaches this.

A pastor from a seeker-targeted church in the U.S. concluded that the cell model didn't work. Upon further inquiry, the pastor had wrongly interpreted the cell group church model. He thought the cell group church consisted only of cells, with no children's program or children's pastor. He believed the cell performed children's ministry on a rotating basis. Likewise, he felt cell groups did everything else in the church.

Much of the resistance toward the cell group church comes from wrong interpretations. "Cell group churches are against everything except cells," some imagine.

PROGRAMS IN CELL CHURCHES?

What is a program? According to the dictionary, it's simply a system of procedures or activities that has a specific purpose.[38] Synonyms include plan, agenda, and curriculum. The cell group church movement rightly downplays the over-emphasis on programs, believing the main focus must be the cell.

Let's be careful, however, not to throw out the baby with the bath water. Even the fastest growing cell group churches have more than cell groups.

Bethany World Prayer Center features a children's Sunday school, worship team ministry, Saturday morning prayer meeting, youth ministry, and college and career ministry.[39]

At the International Charismatic Mission in Bogota, Colombia, you'll find the ministries of worship, spiritual warfare, TV, radio, counseling, ushers, follow-up, social action, pastoral care, accounting, video, sound ministry, bookstore, and more.

Yoido Full Gospel Church, where the modern cell group church movement was founded, highlights a number of ministries, like Elim Welfare Town, a village for both the elderly and delinquent young people. This facility is considered the largest welfare facility in the Far East. Delinquent young people are trained with practical skills, and the elderly gratuitously find housing. YFGC also spawned off the Soon Shin University, with approximately one thousand graduate students. Karen Hurston adds,

> Each of YFGC's more than twenty outreach fellowships targets a different segment of society, offering a wide variety of activities. Whether a person has a heart to help struggling churches, is a professional actor looking for a way to spread the gospel through drama, or is concerned for the homeless and disabled, an outreach fellowship invites involvement.[40]

Faith Community Baptist Church in Singapore, a world-renowned cell group church, reaches out to the physical needs of the Singaporeans through day-care centers, after-school clubs, centers for the handicapped and deaf, diabetic support groups, and legal counseling. They call this TOUCH Community Service Center. It's a nonprofit organization, which receives eighty percent of its support from FCBC, and most of its staff members belong to the church. The range and depth of ministry at TOUCH Community Service Center is staggering.

The 150,000-member Works and Mission Baptist Church in Ivory Coast, West Africa, has developed an intricate departmental system. Every member of the church must be involved in some kind of ministry. These ministries include visitation, casting out demons, ushering, tape ministry, etc. Ralph Neighbor, Jr. said Pastor Dion Roberts' ministry structure is top-notch, and wondered why more North American churches weren't doing something similar.[41]

Neighbour also said, "Realistically, perhaps it is best to say that in the cell church very few additional programs exist."[42]

THE WORD "MINISTRY" AIDS UNDERSTANDING

The word ministry comes from the Greek word *diakone*, where we get our English word deacon. Ministry speaks of humble acts of service for others. The word program, in contrast, often carries the idea of self-perpetuation—something that has a life of its own. Ministries serve and sustain both the celebration and cell structure; programs divert the attention away from cell life. Ministries add to the success of the cell system; programs compete for time and activity. Ministries refer to such activities as prayer, ushering, the follow-up of new converts, missions, children's ministry, nursery, etc.

Those planting a cell group church shouldn't be burdened with adding ministries. Follow the policy of adding new ministries only as the need arises. But don't imagine that the cell church is only a worship service, a cell meeting, and nothing more.

KEEP IT SIMPLE

Leonard Sweet, in his book *Soul Tsunami,* looks at our culture (postmodern or pre-Christian) and suggests that traditional Christianity, with the heavily institutionalized church structure, conveys the wrong kind of message in our culture. He concludes that most in our culture, while turned off to "religion," are very much tuned into "spirituality." While people might yawn and tune out if someone wants to talk to them about Christianity, most people will actually tune in if we identify ourselves as "disciples of Jesus Christ."

Sweet says the state of society is such that we have tremendous opportunity to advance God's kingdom, but only if we start doing things differently, or simply get back to the basics. His arguments are threefold: 1) let Jesus be the message, not "Christianity," nor religious traditions; 2) "lose control," as church ministry becomes decentralized, and ministry structures become horizontal instead of vertical/hierarchical; and 3) acknowledge the spiritual—recognize there is something mystical about Christianity, that one can actually experience the presence of God in their lives.[43] Sweet's analysis of modern culture sits well with the cell group church philosophy, which is a call back to the simplicity of the New Testament.

Don't add unnecessary ministries. Allow your church to maintain a New Testament feeling. Don't try to harmonize all ministries by using elaborate graphs or globes. Often these attempts complicate more than they clarify.[44]

DON'T CONFUSE MINISTRIES WITH CELL GROUPS

Some churches, trying to integrate small groups and programs, label any group that's small a cell. This might include Sunday school classes, prison ministry task groups, church boards, choir groups, usher groups, etc.

One recent book on small groups defined the small group as a "a face-to-face meeting that is a sub-unit of the overall fellowship."[45] This author goes on to say, "Any gathering of less than a dozen people is a small group."[46] Small groups are defined by some as cell groups, home Bible studies, Sunday school classes, deacon boards, AA groups, pulpit committees, or prison ministry task groups.[47] We're told simply to recognize that our church already has existing small groups.[48] A faulty definition of a cell could lead a person into thinking a cell is a board meeting, a choir group, a task force, or something else.

Cell group churches place a high priority on the cell group. They believe participation in a cell is just as important as the celebration meeting. To live the abundant Christian life, we need both. If the cell is distorted, a believer will likely be weak, lacking discipleship. Likewise, a cell must evangelize and multiply, or face certain stagnation.

In all the worldwide cell group churches I studied, the cell could be defined as:

> A group of four-fifteen people that meets weekly outside the church building for the purpose of evangelism and discipleship with the goal of multiplication.

There might be other groups in a church that are not cell groups (Sunday school classes, boards, choirs, parking lot groups). But a person would need to attend a real cell, and could also be participating in another ministry group. The danger is that a person might be lulled into thinking involvement in a choir group or Sunday school class is an adequate replacement for a life-giving cell group. It isn't!

CELL AND CELEBRATION

Cell (small-group wing) and celebration (large-group wing) make up the two wings of the cell group church. Both are important. Ministries, therefore, should be connected to one or both of the wings. If a particular ministry doesn't fit with either, be very careful about adding it.

I consulted with one transitioning church whose pastor had received a vision while looking at a monument that had five pillars. He thought God spoke to him saying, "Your ministry will have five pillars." He tried to connect the number five to everything he did in ministry and eventually erected five programs to somehow connect with the vision he saw. When the pastor attempted to transition his church to the cell model, he refused to kill the five-headed beast, preferring to feed and nourish it. I returned a year later for further consultation and found the pastor at the end of his rope. He was finally ready to slay his dragon.

I counseled him to emphasize a two-pronged church, one that emphasizes cell and celebration. He suddenly understood how to integrate his ministry pillars with the cell church structure and the problem was solved. This church is now a thriving cell group church model.

CELEBRATION MINISTRIES

Practically, celebration in the cell group church is very similar to vibrant celebration in the conventional church. Such celebration services require:

• Inspirational Worship

Great cell group churches feature lively, contemporary worship where participants worship without interruption, rather than having to sit, worship, stand, worship, shake hands, worship, look at the bulletin, worship. Worshippers get involved with God and each other and have fun.

Admittedly, there's no one way to worship in the cell group church. Each church's tradition and background will dictate the style in which it worships.

• Preaching-Teaching Ministry

The cell group church should have a strong preaching ministry, teaching people from God's inerrant Word.

• Children's Ministries

Don't shortchange children in the name of cell church. Every single cell group church I studied offered great children's teaching during the celebration service. The main difference between children's ministry in a cell group church and in a conventional church is integration. In a cell group church, the Sunday morning children's hour is often connected with the children's cell during the week.

• Care for Babies

Don't expect mothers to care for their children during the worship service—just because you're a cell group church! Provide them with the best nursery care possible, so they can freely concentrate on the biblical message.

• Ushers

Ushers help provide order, information, greetings, and they collect the offerings. The key difference is that ushers could be chosen from cell leaders, or those in the process of becoming cell leaders.

Cell Group Vision Team Exercise

Make a list of all current ministries tied to the weekly celebration. Evaluate each one to make sure they line up with the vision of the church and do not compete with cell group participation. Develop a strategy to make necessary changes.

• Administration

As the celebration service begins to grow, administration questions take on new significance. Who'll count the offerings? Who'll sell the books? What about the parking lot attendants?

• Sacraments/Ordinances

Most cell group churches serve the Lord's Supper (Communion) on Sunday. To make this happen, someone must prepare cups and trays and afterwards clean them. The same is true for baptism. There are always people behind the scenes who help in these areas.

This list isn't complete, so churches need to fill in the gaps. Notice how the above ministries are integrated into the large-group wing of the church, called celebration.

CELL MINISTRIES

• Equipping Track

New cell leaders don't just appear. They're developed. Effective cell group churches rely on extensive training to make it happen. Many cell churches have converted their adult Sunday school into their equipping track, along with other training formats.

• Pastoral Care Structure

Cell leaders become tired. When they fail to receive care and attention, they quickly fade away. Cell group churches must develop a first-class care structure (5x5, G-12, combination) to assure long-term success.

See Chapter 49 for a complete discussion on developing an equipping track.

• Various

Who'll prepare the cell lesson? How about administrating weekly reports? Who'll provide worship choruses for the cells? A cell secretary is ideal, but when starting, someone will need to help.

To help people understand that cells are not the only thing in the cell group church, a coworker suggested using the term "cell-based church," rather than cell church. Perhaps this will help people to see that the cell is the base of the church, but it's not the only thing in the church.

See Chapter 39 for instructions on how to write good cell group lessons.

Some churches think they know what it means to be a cell group church, when in reality they think the cell group church is only the cell. Because of faulty definitions, some churches never make it, because they don't have the permission to experiment and to adjust on the fly.[49] They're locked into one way of doing cell group church, and they don't realize they have the freedom to act creatively and integrate ministry within their cell system.[50]

OTHER MINISTRIES?

Where do you place the extensive radio ministry of Elim, or the television ministry of Bethany? Bethany World Prayer Center also has an extensive counseling ministry that's open to the community. Nor is the social outreach of Faith Community Baptist Church directly related to the celebration. In all endeavors in life, there are exceptions to every rule. Because of these exceptions, don't discard the rule, but for the most part, ministries should be connected to cell and celebration.

In these churches, the cell group church philosophy has been thoroughly formulated as part of the warp and woof of the church. These ministries aren't seen as competitive when everyone on staff understands where they fit.

CELL-BASED CHURCH WITH INTEGRATED MINISTRIES

Joel Comiskey

We who are constantly using our computers know the dangers of mixing and matching software programs that aren't compatible. Since I began using personal computers in 1984, I've experienced countless crashes, because Windows or Norton didn't integrate with my newly installed software.

Integration in the cell group church functions a lot like a computer operating system handling application programs. In the cell-based church, there's only one operating system. The ministries are like the application programs on the computer.

A lot has been written about the different types of small groups ministries (e.g., Meta versus cell church, etc.),[51] but very little has been written about how to integrate small groups with ministries within the church. While this can be helpful, my purpose is not so much to classify, as to explain how your church can integrate your current ministries into the cell group church philosophy.

Let's look at the various ways churches integrate small groups. The first two (non-integration and faulty integration) are common in churches with cells, while the last two (member integration and cell leader integration) should be your goal if you plan to transition to the cell group church.

Non-Integration	Faulty Integration	Member Integration	Leader Integration
Church with Small Groups	Church of Small Groups	Cell-Based Church	Cell-Based Church
• Cells are one ministry. • Some in cells; some in other ministries. • No attempt to integrate cells and ministries.	• Faulty definition of a real cell group. • All groups are cell groups (Sunday School, Choir, Cells, etc.) • Integration is the acknowledgement that the church already has small groups.	• Cell attendance is just as important as celebration attendance. • Clear definition of a cell group. • Only those already attending a cell group can be involved in official church ministries.	• Cell attendance is just as important as celebration attendance. • Clear definition of a cell group. • Those leading a cell group or in training to lead a cell group are involved in the official church ministries.

NON-INTEGRATION: PROGRAMS AND SMALL GROUPS

Non-integration compartmentalizes small groups from the rest of the programs in the church. Members choose among various ministry options—one of them is cell ministry. Some will be in the choir, or teach Sunday school, while others will be in the cell group ministry.

In non-integrated churches, if someone wants to start a new ministry, the pastor says, "Go for it." Free choice reigns. Integration isn't an issue. The senior pastor simply blesses all the programs and hopes it will all work out. Someone said, "If you chase two rabbits, both will escape." The non-integrative approach chases both ministries and cells. The two run off in different directions, creating a competing programmatic structure.

Some churches use programs and ministries to connect people to the church—even non-Christians. Sometimes a ministry (e.g., usher, greeter, etc.) works like an outreach tool to convert the person. "People will stay in the church once they're involved in a task," these gurus say. After hooking the person into a ministry, some churches might try to get that person into a small group—if and when the person feels the need for further discipleship.

I call this the funnel approach. The sad reality is that often people never get funneled. Small groups remain one rusty option. The problem with this approach is that it prioritizes the one-wing church (celebration).

I consulted one of these churches in which the pastor truly wanted it to become a small group church, but failed to realize that his entire focus was the celebration wing. Fewer than one-third of those who attended the Sunday celebration funneled down to the small groups. This pastor ideally wanted more people in small groups, but cell and celebration weren't on the same level.

The cell church, in contrast, asks everyone to either be in a cell, in the process of leading a cell, or leading a cell, before taking part in a ministry in the church. Ministries are present (and perhaps even abundant), but should not operate as independent planets following their own orbit. In the cell group church, church growth means the church is growing both in cells and celebration.

Don't pander to the weakest link—worship attendees. Concentrate on small groups and especially small group leadership. As the infrastructure grows, so will the worship service.

FAULTY INTEGRATION: ALL GROUPS ARE "CELLS"

With this view of integration, a person simply recognizes that the church already has existing small groups. These groups might be Sunday school classes, the choir, elders, committees, ministry teams, outreach teams, worship-production teams, sports teams, recovery groups, or women's circles, etc.[52] One expert promoting this view said, "The phrase cell groups refers to an encompassing care system that includes Sunday school. Sunday school is simply a centralized, on-premises cell system. Churches should have as many Sunday schools as they can afford."[53]

This might seem like one way to integrate everything, but it creates confusion by saying a ministry is a cell, when in fact it is not. I've noticed an adverse effect on the cell-based system when all small groups are embraced in the cell system and given equal priority. This mentality cheapens the cell vision by saying a small group ushers' meeting in the church has the same priority as a home-based small group. In fact, the two are worlds apart, due to the setting and the purpose. The lack of quality control in this smorgasbord approach eventually weakens the entire system.

Is there only one type of group in a cell church? No. Actually, there might be a variety of groups (e.g., governing board, worship team, point of entry groups, leadership groups, classes, missions group, ministry groups, etc.). It's not that the cell church doesn't have usher groups, or groups that visit the homeless mission. Rather the key difference lies in the fact that those involved in those ministries are ALSO participating in the base life of the church—the cell group.

At one time, my church bought into the faulty view of integration. We had a particular women's ministry that studied the Bible in the church. These were semester-oriented Bible studies that had six levels. Each level used a different Navigator book. After completing one book, the class would graduate to the next level. The groups were closed to non-Christians at the higher levels.

At the time, we were trying hard to make cells the base of our church, and we heard that some churches were simply calling all small groups "cells." So we decided to label these church-based Bible studies cell groups. We told people that if they were involved in a women's Bible study, presto—they were in a cell group.

This decision cost us dearly later on. It caused confusion of vision. People found it hard to swallow that a closed Bible study was a cell group. These groups weren't evangelizing, weren't multiplying, weren't meeting in the home, and were bound to their own curriculum.

When we proclaimed our small group vision from the pulpit, we suddenly had to proclaim that the women's Bible studies were also cell groups. It was like we had injected a virus into our system.

We finally admitted our mistake. However, the women who were running this ministry liked the idea that they were cell groups and didn't want to change. It took two long years, but we finally converted these church-based Bible studies into our equipping track.

The women continued to meet together as groups, but we asked them to start using the church's equipping track material rather than the Navigator studies. After the last class, we expected the ladies to lead a home cell group.

I counsel pastors to refuse to call everything that's small and a group a cell. Cell group churches want to know that those attending a cell will experience community and have a chance to invite their non-Christian friends. Cell group churches believe that labeling everything a small group will actually water down the cell philosophy.

CELL MEMBER INTEGRATION: CELL-BASED CHURCH

With cell member integration, every person in the church attends a cell group before becoming involved in the official ministries of the church. Of course, all believers should use their gifts at work, school, and the cell group. Cell member integration is simply saying that official ministries in the church are privileges that belong to those who are involved in the life of the church—cell ministry. Cell member integration prevents ministries in the church from developing a life of their own and becoming programs in competition with cell ministry.

The underlying philosophy of cell member integration is that small group attendance is just as important as Sunday morning worship. The reasoning goes like this: Since a person who didn't attend the Sunday celebration wouldn't be allowed to perform a ministry, the same is true with cell attendance. Attendance in a cell group is a minimum requirement to be involved in a ministry.

In a cell group church, there'll also be other types of groups (e.g., Sunday school, board, choruses, parking lot groups), but I consider these other groups as ministries. Cell member integration encourages everyone to be in a true cell group before being involved in additional ministries.

The suggestion that a person attends a cell group before being involved in an official church ministry sounds time intensive. I'm not suggesting, however, that a person must be involved in an official church ministry. However, the person who chooses to be involved in a church ministry must also attend a regular cell, since the cell is the heart and soul of the cell group church—the place where people can experience the true church. Our tendency in the western world is to get involved in task-type ministry before relationship. The cell group church cuts across that grain.

The 150,000-member Works and Mission Baptist Church, in Ivory Coast, West Africa, promotes cell member integration. Everyone must be in a cell to participate in one of the departmental ministries. Cell attendance is necessary for ministry involvement. Everyone is placed in a ministry according to gifting. While forty to sixty percent of the members at WMBC actually lead a cell, not everyone is expected to lead one.[54] Cell leaders report to the house church department, while those in other ministries have their own departments. The key is that everyone must faithfully attend a cell to participate in a ministry.

Another growing cell church, Love Alive Church, in Tegucigalpa, Honduras, has chosen this option. It considers itself a cell group church with specific ministries. In this church, everyone must participate in a cell group before choosing a ministry.

René Peñalba, the senior pastor of this church, reflected back to 1980, when cell groups were just one program among many. However, in 1982, the Love Alive Church made cell ministry the very base of the church. Since then, it has not been afraid to add specific ministries to meet the needs of the church.

CELL LEADER INTEGRATION: CELL-BASED CHURCH

The record-breaking cell group churches ask everyone to enter training. They believe everyone can make disciples who, in turn, make disciples. These churches believe facilitating a cell group is the best way to make disciples. The goal of these churches is for everyone in the church to eventually congregate their friends and relatives and lead a group of people.

The Elim Church, in San Salvador, El Salvador, finds all its workers for the various ministries through the cell districts on a rotating basis. All workers for every type of ministry must be cell leaders. In this way, there's no competition between church ministries and the cell, which is the heart of the church. It's also logical that those who are in the battle would also have the privilege of serving on Sunday. Lon Vining said:

> I think that those who have advocated an equipping track that ends in "everyone becoming a cell group leader" have done so with the idea of raising the bar. I think they are trying to say, in essence, that instead of cell group leadership being "for highly-trained ministry specialists," or "super-spiritual Christians," (an elite few), that instead, cell leadership (and the type of disciple who fits that profile) is something much closer to the NORM of Christian life as one matures. The track ending there also indicates to the general congregation that it's a spiritual goal that is reachable by many, not just a few.

Many cell group churches start with cell member integration and move into cell leader integration. Asking everyone to eventually lead a cell group will maximize leadership development and more rapidly multiply cell groups. Churches emphasizing cell leader integration don't permit church ministries to become an end in themselves. Everyone involved in a ministry (e.g., worship, etc.) must be preparing to facilitate a cell (in the training track), or is actually leading a cell.

What if a Person Doesn't Lead a Cell Group?

There are no second-class citizens in God's kingdom. All those in Christ have received Christ's righteousness and God's favor. There's a danger in making a person feel second-class if he's not leading a cell group.

The role of leadership is to cast the vision and watch God work. Casting the net that everyone can lead a cell group and enter the equipping track will launch many (not all) into ministry.

In cell leader integration, those who decide not to enter the training track to eventually lead a cell group continue to exercise their spiritual gifts at work, at school, and especially in the cell group. The key point in churches that emphasize cell leader integration is that official church ministries are reserved for those who have fully entered the vision of the church—making disciples who make disciples.

What about the Gifts of the Spirit?

Some object to this type of cell leader integration because of the gifts of the Spirit. "It's not scriptural," one man said to me. "Doesn't the Bible teach that every believer possesses particular gifts of the Spirit? Shouldn't we allow individuals to develop their own gifts and talents, and thus start the ministry of their own choosing?"

It's important to remember that when Paul wrote the three major gift passages (1 Corinthians 12, Romans 12, and Ephesians 4), he was writing to house churches, not congregations meeting in a church building. Paul knew that those in the small group (house church) were able to exercise their particular gifts. Thus he could say, "When you come together, everyone has a hymn, or a word of instruction …" (1 Cor. 14:26).

There's no better atmosphere for the exercise of one's giftedness than in a cell group. Only in the intimacy of a small, closely knit group will many Christians ever be able to exercise their spiritual gifts. Neighbour says,

> All are to exercise spiritual gifts to edify others. The early church did exactly that! Recognizing there cannot be total participation by every member when the gatherings are only made up of large, impersonal groups, the people of God moved from house to house in small groups. By moving among their residences, they became intimately acquainted with each person's surroundings.[55]

As more people lead cells, it also gives more people the chance to exercise their gifts (both in the direction of the cell and in the participation within the cell). Integrated cell churches help church members exercise their gifts in the cell group. Those attending a cell will eventually discover his or her gift, and have opportunities to exercise it more fully. We have some cell leaders who exercise their gift of teaching in the training track (basic and advanced level). Others exercise their gift of mercy in the social action ministry. Others might be led into missions, counseling, or worship.

GO FOR IT!

In summary, cell group churches are in one of two categories: cell member or cell leader integration. Churches with small groups fall into the non-integrative or faulty integrated category.

Cell leader integration provides the greatest multiplication of cell groups. Yet, it might not be the best option for everyone, especially right away. In a very traditional church that's just beginning to make the transition, it's best to apply the cell member integration option, and even that option will require a transition period.

Integrating ministries within the cell church won't come overnight.[56] It takes time.[57]

THE INTEGRATION OF CELEBRATION

Joel Comiskey

While speaking in Cambodia to a cell group that was only lightly connected with an Assembly of God church, the hostess made an interesting comment about her local church. "We're not worried that our church isn't a cell group church because after all, our cell is the church."

I responded by stating that if they believed that the cell, all by itself, is the church, then there was no need to attend Sunday morning services. Their home group meeting would serve as both their celebration and their cell group. Their cell, then, would be a house church.

The house church movement may be preferable to the cell group church movement in some countries. The lines are becoming increasingly blurred between the two movements. However, the preferred strategy of the primitive church was cell and celebration (Acts 2:42-46) and, in free countries, it's best to emphasize both cell and celebration. The celebration fulfills certain needs and the cell fulfills others.

It helps to use terminology that clarifies this reality, such as: "The cell is the church and the celebration is the church. Both are needful in the life of the believer." J. I. Packer says something very similar: "I go around telling people that if they're not with the whole congregation on Sunday, and in the small group somewhere during the week, their Christian lives are unbalanced."[58]

Don Davidson, a cell church pastor, put it this way, "The cells are the church, and the congregational gatherings are the church, and the worldwide Christians are the church ... it isn't an either/or proposition, but a both/and proposition."[59] Often the phrase, "the cell is the church," is more of a practical statement than a theological treatise. One cell church pastor explained it this way:

When we say, "the cell is the church" what we mean is that the cell is where most of His work in and through us is done and that when the cells meet for weekly celebration they do not cease to be cells and the celebration becomes "the real church." The rhetorical emphasis is for a reason. We do not want the cell members to be confused into forgetting that the cell is the place the Lord" actualizes being church in and through us." The Saturday/Sunday celebration is where we celebrate what He is doing through the cells and when we also hear His vision cast for us through the sermon.[60]

Although the early church was birthed in the atmosphere of the home, the modern cell group church movement is relatively new. The ingrained understanding of the church today is that Sunday morning worship is where the church meets. When we talk about church today, the common understanding is that we're talking about the Sunday worship service.

DON'T OVEREMPHASIZE CELEBRATION

A large part of the church's anemic state today is due to our preoccupation with celebration. Pastors often measure their success by Sunday attendance figures. According to one study that examined why people attend the fastest growing churches in America, the number one reason given was: "so they could remain anonymous."[61] Many celebration services in today's church exist for these anonymous people.

This must change. It's time to stop measuring our success based on Sunday morning figures. Many of the great cell churches around the world don't even count Sunday worship attendance. A church must be cell driven. That is, the main concern of church leaders is to grow the church from the inside out. Celebration attendance is the result of a healthy cell infrastructure. While both wings of the cell group church are equally important, the cell wing should drive the celebration wing and not vice versa.

DON'T UNDEREMPHASIZE CELEBRATION

Some would have us underemphasize the celebration service. Some in the cell church movement emphasize the phrase, the cell is the church, but are hesitant to emphatically say, the celebration is the church. Affirming only the former make it sounds like cell is more important than celebration. In truth, celebration is a vital part of the Christian life and must be emphasized accordingly.

PURPOSES OF THE CELEBRATION

Balance

One of the key reasons for the celebration service is balance. Trying to mesh everything together in one house meeting (both cell and celebration) doesn't quite fulfill either necessity. Most house churches have thirty-plus people. This group is too large for cell intimacy and too small for dynamic celebration.

Worship

Large-group celebration is the time to focus on worshipping the living God. John writes about worship in heaven:

> And I saw … those who had been victorious over the beast and his image and over the number of his name. They held harps given them by God and sang the song of Moses the servant of God and the song of the Lamb:
> "Great and marvelous are your deeds,
> Lord God Almighty.
> Just and true are your ways,
> King of the ages.
> Who will not fear you, O Lord,
> and bring glory to your name?
> For you alone are holy.
> All nations will come
> and worship before you" (Revelation 15:2-4).

You can feel the electricity in this heavenly multitude worshipping the living God. The worship celebration can grow as large as possible—the bigger the better! It's like watching a professional basketball game. Larger crowds contribute to the excitement.

Granted, it's harder to grasp the feeling of a great multitude when there are only fifty people in church. (The average-sized church in North America has between fifty and seventy-five people.) Yet, whether in a crowd of thousands or dozens, the primary purpose of a celebration service is to extol God's greatness.

One person wrote, "If the body of Christ doesn't attend celebration services, how will they practice for when they get to heaven? They'll feel a little out of place when those who have practiced know what to do and they don't."[62]

Instruction

This is also the time to receive biblical instruction. The early church gathered daily to grow in the faith. We read, "Day after day, in the temple courts and from house to house, they never stopped teaching and proclaiming the good news that Jesus is the Christ" (Acts 5:42).

In those early days, God appointed gifted teachers to feed the entire flock. We read that the early believers devoted themselves to the "apostles' teaching." Early Jewish believers needed clear teaching concerning how Christ's teaching related to the Old Testament. With enemies from within and without ready to pounce on the tender church, those believers needed a firm foundation.

Going through a book of the Bible on Sunday mornings is recommended. Expository preaching assures that the church hears the full Gospel and feeds the saints a steady diet.

Harvest

In the early church celebration, where instruction and worship were a priority, God granted a gigantic harvest. Three thousand were added on one occasion, five thousand on another, and we read in Acts 2:47, "… the Lord added to their number daily those who were being saved."

Peter Wagner, in his excellent book, *Churchquake*, notes that the fastest growing churches in the world—including the U.S.—promote dynamic worship and powerful preaching. Wagner notes the power for evangelism in dynamic worship.[63]

Effective cell group churches have an inviting worship service that reaches the unsaved. Bethany World Prayer Center invites people to receive Jesus in nearly every service. Pastor César Castellanos gives an invitation to receive Christ every Sunday and hundreds come forward. They are immediately integrated into the cell system.

Likewise, the Elim Church gives salvation messages in its worship services, with comparable results.[64] In most cell group churches, the majority of conversions happen at the cell level, but these churches aren't limited to cell group conversions.

ATMOSPHERE OF THE CELEBRATION IN THE CELL CHURCH

"What a relief it is to celebrate in the cell church!" I remember the earlier days of our church. When we started in July 1994, our entire strategy depended on the Sunday morning service. What a hassle! As pastors, we ran around trying to perfect every detail of the church, because we wanted the people to come back. For us, success depended on how many people would return the next Sunday.

We switched strategies and became a cell group church. The real hard labor comes on a personal level through the cells. The church's true organization takes place on that level. The Sunday service is primarily a place to celebrate victories experienced in cell ministry. The celebration service is the gathering of all cells to worship, hear God's Word, participate in the Lord's Supper, and reap the harvest.

This isn't to say the celebration is any less qualitative. The Holy Spirit makes a service exciting, but he expects diligent planning from us. An excellent worship service requires hours of sacrificial preparation. In the fastest growing cell group churches around the world, everything is well planned—ushers, greeters, announcements, special music, and the general atmosphere.

AVOID THE BIG-CELL MENTALITY

A visiting speaker highlighted the need for fellowship in the church by asking someone in the front row to stand. Then he called on another person from the back row to stand. He asked, "Do you two know each other?" When they acknowledged that they didn't, he said, "This is my point. We as the church should know each other. We should know each other's names if we are truly the body of Christ."

Wrong! It's not necessary to know each other in a large, growing congregation. In fact, it's impossible. Don't gear the celebration service as a warm time of getting to know each other.

In another example, the senior pastor of a three hundred-plus church asked those visiting to stand up and share. I felt so sorry for the visiting family who had to get up and bare their souls. In front of this multitude, the poor husband had to share his life.

This goes against everything group dynamics teaches. In a large group, only the most confident personality would feel comfortable. The vast majority shake in their boots. Just because the preacher has overcome many of the initial fears of speaking before a large group, he shouldn't expect others to do so, especially if he wants them to come back!

A celebration service is the opposite of the cell. It's a time when the anointed man or woman of God shares a well-prepared biblical message in order to feed the people of God. It's not meant to be a warm family time.

When I visited the Yoido Full Gospel Church in Korea, I noticed that the celebration time was brief and orderly, yet very powerful. It could even be called impersonal, yet it fully met the needs of the 25,000 who attended each service.

ENCOURAGE CELL RELATIONSHIPS
IN THE CELEBRATION

The beauty of fellowship during the celebration service is that often cell members will look for fellow members. Often they'll sit by each other during the service.

After every celebration service at the Love Alive Church in Tegucigalpa, Honduras, the leadership team meets together! The supervisors and cell teams (leader, assistant, treasurer, and members-at-large) gather in designated locations to pray, plan, and dream together. Supervisors take attendance of the leadership teams present; zone leaders take attendance of the supervisors present; and district pastors take attendance of zone leaders who are at each service.

The cell factor makes the celebration experience more enjoyable in cell group churches around the world. Although it's difficult to prove scientifically, it makes sense that when dozens, hundreds, or even thousands of cells meet during the week in homes, the sum total of them will strengthen the general fellowship of the church.

DIVERSITY IN CELEBRATION, HOMOGENEITY IN CELL

"In our church," the transitioning pastor began, "we're having problems with two classes of people. There's a middle-upper class and a lower class. What should I do?" I counseled him to do absolutely nothing. The homogeneous problem is a mute one in the cell group church.

The cell-celebration paradigm is an ideal strategy for gathering ethnic groups in distinct cells and then asking all the various groups to celebrate together on Sunday morning. Encourage a rich variety of homogeneous cell groups to meet during the week in your church. Make sure you invite them also to gather in a common Sunday celebration service.

The beauty of the cell group church is that it welcomes all of God's rich creation. Those same homogeneous cells that meet during the week come together for a weekly Sunday celebration. Festive moments in the celebration of a cell group church echo the words of John, the apostle. "And they sang a new song: You are worthy to take the scroll and to open its seals, because you were slain, and with your blood you purchased men for God from every tribe and language and people and nation. You have made them to be a kingdom and priests to serve our God, and they will reign on the earth" (Revelation 5:9-10).

ASSIMILATING PEOPLE INTO GROUPS

Joel Comiskey

How do you assimilate your people from celebration to cell or from cell to celebration? Some ideas are more radical than others. For example, Jeff Green wrote:

Each Sunday, using a small squirt bottle, we secretly mark first-time visitors with a scent undetectable to humans but very favorable to dogs. Immediately after the celebration service, we loose several ferocious dogs from the back of the auditorium. In less than five minutes, they find all the visitors and back them into a corner, barking, snarling, and baring their teeth. This affords a very opportune moment in which to get a commitment from each visitor to attend a cell meeting during the week. After receiving the commitment, we call off the dogs and the visitor is allowed to leave. Our retention rate is nearing 100%.[65]

Most churches take less threatening approaches to connecting people with their cell groups. The churches that best assimilate their people through cell ministry do at least these five things well:

- Activate Cell Leaders to Reach Newcomers and New Converts
- Identify Newcomers
- Distinguish Those Who Receive Christ
- Establish Immediate Contact
- Disciple Them in the Cell Group

ACTIVATE CELL LEADERS TO REACH NEWCOMERS AND NEW CONVERTS

While it's the goal to fill the cell group with unsaved friends and neighbors, many cell group members and future leaders will come from within the celebration service. Cell groups made up primarily of non-Christians are very difficult to multiply. The reason? You can't depend on a non-Christian to attend the group faithfully. It also takes time for the non-Christian to convert, receive discipleship, and enter the equipping track.

While the majority of new cell members might come from the mother cell group, many new cell groups are planted with one to three people from the mother cell group. People from the celebration service who are not yet attending a cell can help form the cell nucleus. Cell leaders and cell members should proactively recruit newcomers from the celebration to the cell.

Wise cell leaders work on Sunday morning, looking for new prospects to join their group. All it takes is simple hospitality. "Hi, my name is Joan. Is this the first time you've visited our church? How did you like it? I'm the leader of a cell group in the north end of town on Wednesday nights. It's a small group of eight people. Here's my phone number and address. We'd love to have you attend."

Though there might be reasons why a person can't attend (time, work, etc.), there are also many newcomers and new Christians who'd jump at the chance! This communicates that your church is comprised of friendly, caring people who want to include others. Wouldn't it be great if five cell leaders approached the same person on Sunday?

As the cell group church gathers momentum, most first-time visitors will hear or see something in the celebration that makes them aware that cell groups are a vital part of the church—the very base of the church (e.g.,

announcement from pulpit, bulletin insert, etc.). Some cell group churches display pictures of all their cell group leaders. They provide take-home
cards for visitors that include leaders' phone numbers and areas where the
groups meet. Therefore, it won't be alarming when a cell leader or member
offers an invitation.

IDENTIFY THE NEWCOMERS

To assimilate celebration newcomers into cell ministry, you first need
to know who those newcomers are. How do you identify the newcomer?
Many churches have successfully used a tear-off section within the bulletin.
The person making announcements asks everyone to take a moment to fill
in the information and drop the card in the offering plate.

One reason everyone fills out a card is to make visitors feel more comfortable. Another reason is to gather prayer requests and needs from church
members. In some churches, right after the worship, the pastors greet newcomers by asking them to raise their hands for a brief moment, while everyone claps.

Never embarrass the newcomer in order to gather information. This is
always counter-productive. Don't have the newcomer stand, say his name,
and then share a testimony. The person will not only be traumatized, but
won't think too highly of your church or cell ministry.

DISTINGUISH THOSE WHO RECEIVE CHRIST

The most effective churches not only clearly articulate a salvation message, but also gather the saved for further counseling. Some churches ask
those accepting Christ to meet in another room for coffee and to receive a
special gift. The International Charismatic Mission has been highly successful by asking those who raise their hand to come forward. These people are whisked into another room for discipleship.

In this room, the leader always gives another invitation to receive Jesus
Christ. Then counselors give individual attention to each convert. During
this personal time between counselor and new convert, instruction is given,
and the counselor asks for prayer requests. The counselor then prays for the
new convert and asks him to record his or her personal information on a
card. Another counselor will then confirm the information on the card:
"Okay so you're name is _____, and you live where?" Part of the reason
for ICM's success is carefully identifying and separating the new converts
for immediate follow-up.

ESTABLISH IMMEDIATE CONTACT

One larger church positions a welcome team outside the worship center with a sign posted "Visitors' Table." Visitors fill out cards and the information is processed on the same day.[66] By the end of each service, a cell leader is assigned to personally care for the visitor. By Monday, the cell leader calls or visits the new person, in order to initiate a personal follow-up program that's closely connected with the cell.[67]

The core principle is to make contact with the newcomer/new convert as close to the celebration event as possible. Herb Miller declares:

> No other single factor makes a greater difference in improving annual membership addition than an immediate visit to the home of first-time worshippers ... When laypersons make fifteen-minute visits to the homes of first-time worship visitors within thirty-six hours, 85 percent of them return the following week. Make this home visit within seventy-two hours, and 60 percent of them return. Make it seven days later, and 15 percent will return. The pastor making this call, rather than laypersons, cuts each result in half.[68]

One of the best ways to initially visit is with a loaf of bread. One cell group church pastor writes:

> I suggest ... something similar to the approach used by Bethany World Prayer Center. BWPC has contracted with a bakery to make fresh loaves of French bread. Within just a few days of the initial visit to BWPC celebration, the previous week's guests are visited by persons belonging to a cell within the geographic region and presented with a free gift of a freshly baked loaf of French bread and are extended an invitation to attend cell.[69]

Cell Group Vision Team Exercise

Outline a process of assimilating visitors into cell groups.

Obviously a personal visit is the best. If this proves too difficult for your situation, make a phone call. The principle is to make immediate contact.

DISCIPLE THEM IN THE CELL GROUP

The cell group is the place where true follow-up takes place. This is where progressive sanctification happens. As the new person attends the cell, information will turn into transformation. The new convert will learn to apply God's Word to daily life. Cell involvement, however, is only the beginning. If new cell members are going to grow, they must enter the equipping track. Cell leaders need to encourage each cell member to receive further training while attending the cell group. Assimilation continues to cell leadership and beyond.

RESTRUCTURING CHURCH FACILITIES

Randall Neighbour

As a church makes a shift in styles of worship and ministry, the facilities must change to accommodate the new way of doing church. Many churches have modified their platforms to make room for worship teams where robed choir members once stood. Others have renovated their adult Sunday School classrooms to make room for children's church. As a church expands its cell ministry, facility changes must take place as well.

Years ago, I heard a senior pastor of a growing cell church make a fascinating comment. As he took me on a tour through its newly renovated facility, he quietly whispered, "I never should have given my staff pastors comfortable, large offices. They stay in them too much! I should have used the building monies to give them a cell phone and a fuel and meal allowance."

This pastor realized that the role of staff pastors in a cell-based church was to spend a majority of their time with cell leaders and coaches, not hanging out in an office doing administrative tasks.

When a church launches a cell-based ministry and begins to replace programs with member-driven cell life, the church office must also undergo alteration to ensure that communication between pastoral staff members and lay leadership remains high, as well as productive.

CUBICLE, SWEET CUBICLE!

As I tour various cell-based churches around the world, I've found the most productive cell church offices have the following:

- Small cubicles for full-time cell group pastors. Most of these cubicles were occupied for just an hour or so each workday to answer e-mails and make a few phone calls. In some churches, two or more pastors shared cubicles.
- A small, enclosed office for the pastor who oversees the cell pastors. This allows for private meetings with the staff. Many churches have put windows in all their enclosed offices, and in doors, to prevent accusations of improper conduct.
- A large, multi-use open area. The best cell church office layout I saw had an area where all the pastors could meet for prayer regularly, leaders could meet for meetings, or training could be offered. The space was reserved through the secretary.
- A central secretary's desk. This is the central nervous system for the cell ministry. (The person at this desk answers the phone for all the pastoral staff, keeps a current copy of their schedules, etc.)
- A counseling room with a couch and two chairs. This was a common, shared room for any pastor who wanted to counsel leaders or members, reserved through the secretary. Windows in the door and interior walls were common.

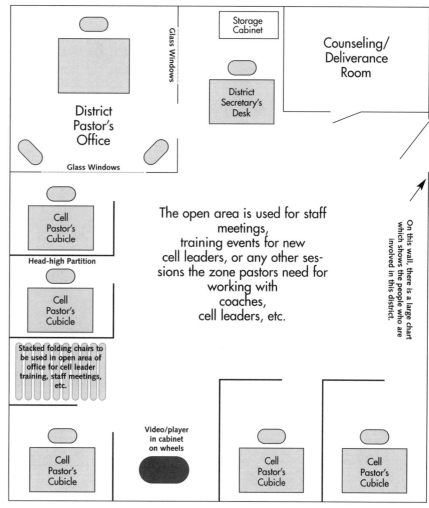

FORM FOLLOWS FUNCTION

As a church transitions to a cell-based system and structure, the role of the staff pastor changes as well. He or she is not in the office much, and therefore doesn't need a big office with all the decorations and furniture. The role is that of an equipper, or one who stays in the community with present and future leaders of the cell ministry. An excellent cell pastor has lunch with coaches and leaders often, visits groups once or twice a week, and has developed deep friendships with those he or she serves.

Administrative tasks must be kept to a minimum to allow time for this, and the time required to be in the office must be reduced. In some cell churches, staff pastors don't "punch the clock" until early afternoon, due to the evenings they spend mentoring leaders and visiting groups.

OTHER FACILITY CONSIDERATIONS

Cell-based churches can grow rapidly, making facilities management a daunting task. This rapid growth doesn't affect the office layout as much as it will affect the more public areas of a church's facility. As your cell ministry grows, keep these expansion ideas in mind:

- Celebration (sanctuary) space will need to be expanded.
- Rooms will be needed by cell groups which can't use a host home (teens, college students, special needs groups), or for those whose homes are too small for meetings.
- Space for a training center. As a cell church grows, training church planters, missionaries, and new pastoral staff members become a priority. Even the smallest church should keep this in mind as its cell ministry grows.

Some of what has been discussed here may seem unrealistic, or something to be considered at a much later date. But, as mentioned above, cell churches grow quickly! Don't let a slow, determined transition plan lull the church into thinking a restructured facility isn't in the near future. As the first cells multiply, ensure that the staff pastor(s) who are overseeing the groups have an office environment that plainly states: "Stay out in the field developing leaders!"

Cell Group Vision Team Exercise

What facility changes need to be made to propel the cell group vision?

RESTRUCTURING THE CHURCH CALENDAR

Randall Neighbour

63

Making changes in a church calendar isn't easy. Much like restructuring the budget, the ever-important calendar defines the direction and priorities of a local church. As a church leadership adopts cell ministry as the most effective way to fulfill the mission of the church, events must be added to the calendar. When these events are added, they will compete with other events and programs, which must be justified as being missional and supportive of the new direction of the church.

The kinds of events found in most cell-based churches are designed to train cell leaders, members, and coaches; help new cell members become set free from strongholds; and provide times of refreshing for hard-working volunteers. Harvest events are designed to provide a large-group activity for unbelievers who are connected to cell members. Some of these events are Saturday events, weeknights, or Friday to Sunday retreats off the church campus. While each cell-based church does things differently, they all have one thing in common—cell ministry events are calendared and given high priority.

ENTER CONFLICT, STAGE LEFT

Years ago, I was a leader in a sixty-year-old denominational church in the beginning stages of a transition to cell-based ministry. Everyone was fully aware of the renewed mission of the church, and that it would be done through cell ministry. The deacon body unanimously approved the new vision statement two years before, and it was plainly stated in bold type on the front page of the Sunday bulletin every week.

One day, the senior pastor met with me and asked me to meet with cell leaders each week for eight weeks, encouraging them to love their group members, and learn from a book we'd study together and discussed. I was all for it, but mentioned that if we didn't provide childcare, there'd be few if any leaders present each week. He agreed, and suggested we hold the training on Wednesday nights, which had established childcare for many years, due to the traditional Wednesday night meal and devotional the church offered. He encouraged me to contact cell leaders and interns as soon as possible.

It was great to hear that cell leader training and support was given priority! I started making calls and put a paragraph in both the Sunday bulletin and the monthly newsletter.

Two days before our first meeting, I received a call from the minister of music. He was calling on behalf of the choir, which had moved its practice time a month before to the same time as cell leader training, but didn't ask or even announce it to the pastor's secretary. Many of the choir members were also cell leaders or interns, and would have to make a choice as to which event to attend.

While the choir wasn't a driving force in fulfilling the mission of this church, the ten choir members and a handful of elderly people in the church loved it dearly. While cell leader training went forward, only a few of the choir members showed up and when they did, it was out of duty, not to learn and become part of a team.

You may be thinking this was a simple case of poor communication, but the roots were far deeper. For this church's calendar to reflect the new direction of the church with any success, the "hot button" areas like choir practice had to be addressed first. What this church had not done successfully was to create a multi-year process of transitioning the calendar—and the programs that filled the present calendar.

IT'S A PROCESS!

Consider the huge leap from a calendar full of traditional programs, versus a calendar with numerous cell-based ministry events. These two calendars are 180 degrees apart for most churches. So, the shift in the calendar must happen slowly, as the mindset of the church makes a shift and the cell ministry needs more time. Consider your church's current calendar, then look at this sample planning process:

Year One—Catalytic Calendar Planning

In your first year, don't remove anything from your church's calendar. Just add up to ten percent with events for cell ministry training and expansion. Yes, you read it right! The first year, your calendar will have 110 percent of what it had last year. Why? This will create a sense of urgency within the decision-makers to find something to cut next year to make it less hectic. The kinds of cell ministry events you'll be adding will be vision casting events and leader identification times.

Year Two—First Calendar Planning

If you created a sense of urgency to do away with the old and bring on the new last year, your team will be able to change up to twenty percent of the existing calendar, keeping eighty percent intact. The changes your leaders will make will be to bury dead programs, and protect the time needed for the vision team to live in cell life during the prototype phase. At this point, the vision team members who've served on existing committees, teams, or ministries should examine their involvement. Are these supporting the cell ministry or hindering a deeper involvement with it?

Year Three—Second Calendar Planning

If your leadership buried dead programs last year and is beginning to talk about programs that aren't dead, but don't fit the new vision, then you can increase the amount of change in your calendar. Your new values reflect it. Up to fifty percent of the calendar can be changed to release prototype cell groups into secondary groups. When this occurs, equipping and spiritual freedom (deliverance) weekends must be established to handle the flow of converts coming into groups, in order to maintain individual group health. You may also want to add your first harvest event near the end of year three, and focus on the unbelievers attached to the first cell groups.

Year Four—Third Calendar Planning

Once again, if you've been able to do what's described above, you can now modify far more of the original calendar. Up to ninety percent of what you began with four years ago can be modified. In this sample scenario, all programs and activities can be reengineered to fit within the cell ministry calendar (in previous calendars above, cell ministry was fit into the existing calendar—this year, it's the opposite).

This sample scenario is quite concise and assumes everything in a transition to cell-based ministry moves along at an exciting pace. Some churches can shift their calendars in three to four years without much concern, because the leaders and members are mission-minded and there are few programs that would interfere with the shift.

Others can't change a thing without lengthy discussions, prayer, and fasting for breakthroughs, and possibly some hurt feelings. These churches have leaders and members who've found their significance in the programs in which they lead or are involved, and hold that significance as more important than fulfilling the mission of the church.

The more mission-minded the congregation and leadership become, the more change will be expected and welcomed. Many pastors assume that their church will have no problem making the shift quickly, and work with leadership to radically change the calendar, ending programs that are dearly held by members. It's far better to add a few events to an existing calendar and move into the shift slowly, "taking the pulse" of the church frequently to see how accepting they are of the new direction.

COORDINATED PLANNING

Some friends of mine were planning a family, and sat down to make a strategy. They'd begin to save extra money for the needs of a newborn, and they decided to move out of their small home in the city and buy a larger home in the suburbs, where the schools were better.

To cut down on traffic time, this required my friend to move his business closer to where he planned to live. This would take a year, so they decided not to have children for at least two years, to make it all work right. Today, they live in the suburbs, his business is close by, and they have a newborn baby. The plan worked well.

This example is quite fitting for a church "birthing" a cell ministry. Closely study the sample calendar below. In this church calendar, you'll find a series of calendared events that have been strategically placed throughout the year, driven by the harvest events, which are corporate gatherings designed to draw in and involve unbelievers attached to the church body.

Calendar Key:
Church-wide Harvest Events:

Special Easter Sunday services; Independence Day barbecue and fireworks display; Special Christmas Eve service. These events are designed to give cell members an invitation to bring friends and relatives to a non-threatening corporate function where testimonies and the plan of salvation will be shared.

SAMPLE CELL CHURCH CALENDAR

Month	CHURCH-WIDE HARVEST EVENTS	LEADERSHIP EQUIPPING EVENTS	CELL GROUP EVENTS	CELL MEMBER EVENTS
JAN.	SUPERBOWL ON THE BIG SCREEN IN AT THE CHURCH	CELL LEADER HUDDLE		SPIRITUAL FORMATION WEEKEND; ACCOUNTABILITY & MENTOR-DRIVEN DISCIPLESHIP
FEB.		CELL LEADER HUDDLE	"UPWARD INWARD OUTWARD FORWARD" WORKSHOP	ENCOUNTER GOD RETREAT; ACCOUNTABILITY & MENTOR-DRIVEN DISCIPLESHIP
MARCH		CELL LEADER HUDDLE	"RELATING JESUS" SERIES IN CELL MEETINGS	ACCOUNTABILITY & MENTOR-DRIVEN DISCIPLESHIP
APRIL	EASTER HARVEST EVENT	CELL LEADER HUDDLE; CELL LEADER TRAINING	HALF NIGHT OF PRAYER	ACCOUNTABILITY & MENTOR-DRIVEN DISCIPLESHIP
MAY		CELL LEADER RETREAT	GAME NIGHT (OUTREACH)	ACCOUNTABILITY & MENTOR-DRIVEN DISCIPLESHIP
JUNE		CELL LEADER HUDDLE		ACCOUNTABILITY & MENTOR-DRIVEN DISCIPLESHIP
JULY	4TH OF JULY HARVEST EVENT	CELL LEADER HUDDLE		ACCOUNTABILITY & MENTOR-DRIVEN DISCIPLESHIP
AUG.		CELL LEADER HUDDLE	BARBEQUE (OUTREACH)	SPIRITUAL FORMATION WEEKEND; ACCOUNTABILITY & MENTOR-DRIVEN DISCIPLESHIP
SEPT.		CELL LEADER HUDDLE	"UPWARD INWARD OUTWARD FORWARD" WORKSHOP	ENCOUNTER GOD RETREAT; ACCOUNTABILITY & MENTOR-DRIVEN DISCIPLESHIP
OCT.	"HARVEST" PARTY FOR CHILDREN (OCT. 31)	CELL LEADER HUDDLE		ACCOUNTABILITY & MENTOR-DRIVEN DISCIPLESHIP
NOV.		CELL LEADER HUDDLE	HALF NIGHT OF PRAYER	ACCOUNTABILITY & MENTOR-DRIVEN DISCIPLESHIP
DEC.	CHRISTMAS HARVEST EVENT	CELL LEADER HUDDLE		ACCOUNTABILITY & MENTOR-DRIVEN DISCIPLESHIP

Leadership Equipping Events:

Monthly Cell Leader Huddle: Each month, the pastoral staff will meet with the coaches, cell leaders, and interns for vision casting and to minister to one another.

Cell Leader Training: Eight weeks of training with practical application (homework) for interns. Implementing what is being learned and taking ownership of their present group is the objective.

Cell Leader Retreat: A crucial event where coaches, cell leaders, and spouses are honored and encouraged at a first class retreat center or hotel. This event is geared to build up and recharge the cell leaders. Do not fill the time with long meetings and teaching times.

Coaching Retreat: This retreat is designed for coaches over groups. The time will be invested in discussing which members should be approached for cell leader training as new interns, and skill training in how to raise up leaders, and work with existing leaders and groups to achieve their goals.

Cell Group Events:

UIOF Day: This is a gathering of all the cell group members and leaders on a Saturday to make a strategic plan of action for the next four months using the four basic values of cell life: Upward (prayer), Inward (community), Outward (evangelism), Forward (discipleship and leadership development).

Relating Jesus Series: This five-week resource will help a cell group adopt a lifestyle of relational evangelism, and is used as curriculum during the cell meeting itself.

Half-night of Prayer: Each cell group will schedule a four-hour meeting to focus on prayer for the church, the group, the lost, each other, etc.

Cell Member Events:

Spiritual Formation Weekend: All church members who wish to join a cell group and new believers who have not yet attended will be invited to this event. It makes cell membership "official" and gives the staff an opportunity to share the mentor-driven discipleship path and cast a vision for "every member a minister and leader."

Encounter God Retreat: Provides a safe environment for new cell members to be set free from spiritual strongholds. Should be offered within four to six weeks of joining a cell. (Designed for believers only.)

Accountability and Mentor-driven Discipleship: The church's unified discipleship process is ongoing throughout the year and, with the help of a mentor, leads a new believer into maturity (which include adopting Christian values, walking free of strongholds, reaching a friend for Christ, and finally, enrolling in cell leader training).

Before harvest events, new cell leader training must be completed for existing cell group interns. This gives these new leaders enough time to gain experience and build confidence. This is strategically scheduled before the harvest event because people will come to Christ and the groups will swell. The conclusion of the eight-week leadership training cycle before the harvest event will allow these larger cell groups to multiply.

After strategic harvest events, a new member class or "spiritual formation" weekend event must follow to assimilate all new believers. Shortly after the spiritual formation weekend, an Encounter God retreat is scheduled for new believers.

A solid cell church calendar considers the potential outcomes of a harvest event and what will make the planned events successful in the long run—with the expansion of the cell ministry as the motivating factor. Because each harvest event is the launching part of a process of discipling members, training leaders, and expanding groups, the vision team should make the church calendar a priority.

CLOSING THOUGHTS:

Here's a list of important things for churches to keep in mind as they move into cell ministry:

- Significant change is occurring when the church calendar is modified.
- Change values in leaders and members before changing calendar items.
- Never drop/stop, replace, or significantly change an old calendar item until new values are caught and the change is justified.
- Fit calendar events into the new vision and values of the church's mission.
- Christ should minister in every kind of meeting or event scheduled.
- Govern the church through a detailed calendar.
- Invest three to seven years to shift the church calendar slowly toward your goal.
- Let participants set the time and place of their meetings (cell leader

huddles, etc.).
- Keep weeknights free for family and cell member-to-member ministry.
- Eliminate traditional evening services to allow cell members to schedule and practice a new lifestyle of relational evangelism.
- Double up on meetings (i.e. Meet with leaders before a Sunday service, thus reducing the number of trips leaders need to make to the church facility.)
- Eventually "pull the plug" on all competing programs.
- After the first year or two, begin the calendaring process with a blank sheet of paper. Schedule the most important cell-related events first and fit the rest in.
- Give priority to learning how children can be incorporated into cell life. This will reengineer children's corporate activities, such as teaching time on Sunday morning and special programs during the week.

TRANSITIONING THE CHURCH BUDGET

Ralph Neighbour, Jr. and Randall Neighbour

Editor's Note: Please read "Restructuring the Church Calendar" prior to reading this article. A church's calendar and the annual budget are intertwined and should not be viewed separately or developed by separate groups, but as interwoven elements in a transition strategy.

In order for the transformation to cell-based ministry to occur, a church's budget must be slowly shifted from its present state to the primary goals of equipping the saints (a church's membership) for the work of ministry via discipleship, leadership training, missions, cell ministry staffing, and harvest events.

These funds will come from increased giving by cell group members and funds made available from programs that have been carefully integrated into cell ministry or prayerfully eliminated when the time is right (if they don't fulfill the renewed mission of the church). As one can imagine, this won't be an easy task, even if the mission of the church is kept in mind at all times.

(By the way, cell group churches that emphasize stewardship as part of their equipping track find that cell group members are excellent tithers.)

Church budgets can easily bring a team, committee, or the staff to a boiling point. Why? Because where the money is spent shows where the church's priorities lie. For this reason, the vision team must be integrally involved in creating a budget for the upcoming year, just as they've helped to shape the calendar. This is critical, and many churches have stalled in their transition early in the process by allowing a group of church leaders to create a "non-missional" budget that sacrifices little or nothing for the emerging cell ministry.

Strategically, budget modifications occur at the same rate as the shift in the church's calendared events. Logically, if the following year's calendar has a new cell leader training weekend, and the church leadership has adopted a new equipping system to lead cell members into leadership, funds will have to be made available for the need. So, budgeting should always follow the calendaring process to ensure that cell ministry is given the percentage of priority it deserves.

ROADBLOCKS

The budget may be the first place a church finds substantial opposition to cell ministry in favor of existing programs. Usually, this occurs when one or both of these issues are present: First, there is a lack of understanding of the mission of the church and how it will be achieved through an expanding cell ministry. Second there is an imbalanced financial obligation for facilities, staffing, or both.

If the first occurs, the task of making an assessment of the current reality must be made more effectively, to encourage decision-makers to put money into the new direction of the church. The stronger the urgency to do something differently to achieve better results, the better! The second, however, is a different issue altogether.

Recently, we visited with a pastor and his small group coordinator concerning the expansion of their small group ministry. Both saw small groups as the weakest part of their church and knew that the existing groups should become far more holistic and missional to take the church in the direction God had called them.

The leadership team behind these two staff members felt the same way, but made an excellent point when the staff members approached them concerning the addition of a simple vision-casting day for the existing small groups. Due to the financial burden of the building program, there were simply no funds available, regardless of need.

For this church to make its existing small groups a mission-fulfilling priority, training events and printed resources would have to be funded through the church's budget. Huge financial sacrifices were already being made by the church membership, and until the debt could be refinanced or the giving levels increased, the small group ministry would have to make due within the diminished budget it was given. This church made the decision to move into the new facility and refinance the debt prior to beginning its transition to a holistic small group ministry, and had to pay for this commitment before it could move forward.

Other churches are financially strapped due to excessive staffing. One church we surveyed had half a dozen staff pastors who trained and prepared volunteers for various programs, many of which did not help the church fulfill its mission. By shutting down these programs, it was able to trim its staff and free up precious financial resources for the growing cell ministry. Later, staff members were added to oversee twenty-five to fifty groups, and the funds necessary to pay their salaries were derived from the groups they oversaw.

HYPOTHETICAL CELL CHURCH BUDGET (CHURCH SIZE, 100 MEMBERS)

This sample budget is not ideal by any means, but shows how cell churches make staffing, equipping, and training a high priority, as a percentage of an overall budget.

Income Available from Cell Groups (rough estimate):
10 cell groups, averaging 10 members per group = 100 cell members
Each person averages $25,000/yr in salary.
6 persons from each group tithe 10% on average ($2500 per year)
3 persons from each group contribute 3% on average ($750 per year)

Total Annual Income from 1 Cell group	$18,000
Total Annual Income from 10 cell groups	$180,000

Budget Allocation of Income

Giving to Missions (10%)	$18,000
Senior Pastor's Salary (total package)	$40,000
Staff Pastor's Salary (total package)	$32,000
Administrative Secretary's Salary (part time)	$18,000
Property	$42,000

Benevolence	$5,000
Equipping & Training Resources	$12,500
Capital Expenses	$4,000
Sunday Celebration Expenses	$8,500
Total Expenditures	$180,000

THE BOTTOM LINE

A transitioning church's budget will change from year to year as cell ministry becomes more prominent and non-missional programs are eliminated or integrated into the life of cell groups. This shift should be gradual, and budgeting must be done with a determined, long-term mindset. Minor modifications are made the first year, followed by an increased reallocation of funds in future years. Coordinating the budget changes with the modifications made to next year's church calendar is the best approach.

Vision team members must help shape the budget, helping the financial team or committee to make solid changes with the mission of the church in mind, versus maintaining existing programs.

In fully transitioned cell-based churches, the budget is designed to release as many members for ministry as possible. This includes cell leader training, missions opportunities for cell groups, harvest events, and printed resources that may be required to disciple new believers, just to name a few.

While many cell-based churches have extensive facilities, the church's focus is on discipling people for ministry. The percentage of the budget given to buildings is small, compared to staffing for cells and the needs of groups.

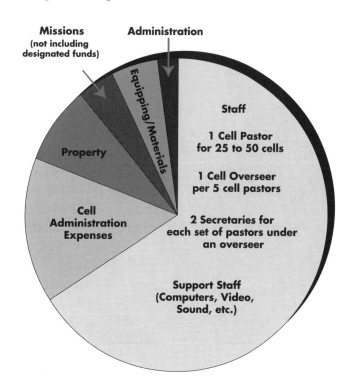

ONE CHURCH, ONE VISION: ADULT, YOUTH, AND CHILDREN

Daphne Kirk

Daphne Kirk travels the globe working with cell-based churches to help them develop a vision and strategy that incorporates children into cell groups. She is the author of over ten titles on the subject.

Written Resources

Reconnecting the Generations by Daphne Kirk

ONE VISION

Effective leaders will always be clear about the God-given vision for their local church, continually keeping that vision before the people, with strategies to enable it to come to pass.

It's been said that two visions create division, yet many churches have three visions—one for adults, one for young people, and one for children—with their own strategies to go with their vision. A united church must have one clear vision and be mobilized with clear united strategies.

Vision is for everyone! So who is "everyone?" "Everyone" is adults, young people, and children—all understanding, all working together, all being empowered. The outworking of this vision means every child, every young person, every children's or youth pastor, and every family, will be moving in the same direction and living out the same core values.

I often go into churches where the vision statement is clearly written on a wall or on handouts. Yet when I ask if the children and youth understand this vision and are an integral part of it, the leaders give me blank looks!

Pastors, when God gave you a vision, it probably came from a "dream" you had. You "saw" your church and were excited. I encourage you to go back to your dream and see every member of your church living out that vision. See families, children, young people, and adults fully participating! The gates of hell will tremble when a church is so united.

I once had a picture of a train leaving the station. The engine was called "cell group church," and the railroad cars were called "cells." In the cars were adults and, in some, were young people. I looked at the station from which it was leaving and saw it was named "Sunday school." On it, children stood, watching the train leave. As I travel around the world, I see this in action. People tell me they're a transitioned church, but when I ask what the children are doing, they reply, "The children are in Sunday school."

Whether discussing vision, strategy or values, the principle is the same: "one for all and all for one!" The vision for cell groups must be applied throughout the whole church. Every member of the church is to be the presence of Jesus within his or her small community. Every man, woman, young person, and child is to reveal Christ's power to the lost and hurting world around them.

ONE SET OF VALUES

With this in mind, the cell value that says, "All are called to minister," means that every child, young person, and adult is given the opportunity and is discipled to be a minister. This simple principle will bring transformation throughout the whole church.

- All (adults, young people, and children) are ministers.
- All (adults, young people, and children) are called to serve.
- All (adults, young people, and children) are called to win others.
- All (adults, young people, and children) have cell as a priority.
- All (adults, young people, and children) are empowered for service.
- All (adults, young people, and children) participate fully.
- All (adults, young people, and children) are receivers and givers.
- All (adults, young people, and children) are hearers and doers.

ONE STRATEGY

The implementation of the vision and values for a united body of believers must be through one set of strategies.

- Cell is the basic community for adults, young people, and children.
- There are two wings for the cell group church (large-group wing and small-group wing), including two wings for children and young people.
- An equipping track for discipleship will be put in place for adults, young people, and children.
- If the church is running encounter retreats for adults, children and young people need them too.
- Cell leaders and coaches need to be equipped and trained to lead adults, so cell leaders and coaches need equipping and training for leading children and young people also.
- Target groups to reach out to those who don't know Jesus are impor-

tant for adults, children, and young people.

- The 4 Ws (Welcome, Worship, Word, and Witness) provide a framework for adults, young people, and children in their cell group meetings.

... And so the list continues.

ONE SET OF GOALS

Some churches are goal-oriented, but in meeting those goals, they put all the weight on adults, instead of every generation pulling together to ensure that those goals are achieved. A pastor who says, "This year we're believing God for twelve new cells," can inspire the young people to believe for four new cells, for the children to believe God for four, and for the adults to do the same. How much easier to achieve our goals when every generation is playing its part!

ONE MESSAGE

When the senior leadership hears the Word or direction of the Lord for the "church," it needs to be clearly understood as a message for every person of every generation who believes in Jesus. So when the Lord says the church needs to enter a season of prayer, he means the whole church. So often the adults hear and are instructed to pray, yet the young people are left to deal with relationships, and the children are left to learn about the fruit of the Spirit! Children and young people are prayer warriors, too, and must be included!

Throughout Scripture, we see every generation moving together toward one vision, with one set of values, one goal, and one message. Jehoshaphat called everyone (adults, young people, children, and babies) to pray in a time of crisis. In the early church, every age group met in their homes. A young lad called David came onto the battlefront and gave the nation a breakthrough. Every man, woman, and child moved together from Egypt to the Promised Land, with no one left behind! Children and young people are integrated and vital throughout Scripture.

It's time to return to our biblical roots and, as a united people, advance against the powers of darkness with one army, one vision, one Commander, one strategy, one set of values, connected heart-to-heart to fulfill the prayer of Jesus, "that they may be one."

Take some time and check through every age group of your church and see how united you are as you transition. Are your children's and youth ministries integrated parts of the mandate for your church? Is every member of your church (adults, young people, and children) being given the opportunity to be equipped and trained to live out cell values? Is cell the basic community for children and young people, where the presence, power, and purpose of Jesus are manifest? Are they being made into disciples of Jesus and are they making disciples?

- Every generation is called to love God.
- Every generation is called to love one another.
- Every generation is called to love the lost.

ONE CHURCH, ONE VISION, ONE STRATEGY!

Today the Holy Spirit is reuniting the generations to release a powerful move of God. All over the world, God is raising an army of children and young people to be on fire for Jesus. They'll have a heart for missions and evangelism. You can be part of raising this younger generation to become that army, as you incorporate children and young people fully into the cell group vision.

Radical leadership will respond to the sound of the prophetic voice as it's declared across the earth. It will seek to be on the cutting edge of what God is doing, taking people where God is moving, putting them in the way of his Spirit as it blows like a mighty wind.

Leaders today must look beyond the confines of their own sphere of influence and hear what the Spirit is saying to the churches throughout the earth. One of the things resonating throughout the earth is that God is raising up a radical, prophetic, passionate generation of children and young people, such as has never been seen in history.

No longer can children and young people be confined to a department that's seen as the training ground for greater things. No longer can they be quietly taken out of sight, or told stories until they're old enough to "enter in." They're a major part of a move of God. They're being brought to center stage and will ignite the revival for which we're all crying out.

Today's leaders must embrace this army and must be prepared to make radical changes that will release them. Leadership will raise leaders, not only from their own peers, but also from boys and girls who will stand in these troubled days. We cannot focus only on adults anymore, as if they're the only ones who truly matter, and as if the future is in their hands.

A revolution is taking place! Chad Taylor says, "Certainly from this

Cell Group Vision Team Exercise

How do the children and youth fit into the vision of the senior pastor?

generation is springing up an army of prophets and prophetesses. A vanguard that hears the beat of his heart and march to its rhythm ... that has counted the cost of discipleship, have plunged into the deep and cast their nets on the other side of religion, ... and such will declare his heart to the masses."

STRATEGIES FOR CHILDREN IN CELL GROUPS

Daphne Kirk

As church transitioning begins to take place, it's essential to have an overview of the biblical place and potential for children, and to understand the place every member of each generation is commanded to play in raising and equipping them. The following ideas will help you know how and where to start as you consider the transitioning process in relation to children.

PREPARATION

Initially, and throughout the ongoing transition process, there needs to be:

1. Foundational preparation of the senior leadership, and as many of the church leaders and members as possible through conferences, reading, consulting, training, and seeking the heart of God for his children. Each member of the senior leadership team needs to live out God's model of family and the discipling of his or her own children.

2. A challenge to remember God's heart towards children and young people. Through the ministry from the pulpit and through cells, challenge everyone to understand how serious God is about the place of young ones in his body.

The vision of the biblical and prophetic place of children and young people must be carried by the senior leadership and imparted at every level. The whole church needs to understand God's purpose and plans for the children of the nations, and adults must come to a place of repentance for attitudes that prevent us from releasing children into their God-given destiny (Matthew 18). In this way, the spiritual atmosphere of the church will be changed and strategies can be released through prayer, under the power of the Holy Spirit.

3. A review of church policies, so that the place of children is clearly written and understood in relation to baptism, communion, and without fail, a cell-based child protection policy. Check with local childcare agencies and officials to become familiar with laws regulating child safety. Meet and exceed standards pertaining to facilities requirements, background checks for those who work with children, and appropriate discipline methods. Avoid legal entanglements by knowing the laws and training workers to follow health-related procedures, such as diaper changing and hand washing techniques and mandated child abuse reporting.

4. Strategic ongoing prayer for children, young people, and families.

5. Preparation for children, young people, and parents, so they understand and have the opportunity to ask questions about the part they have in the vision and implementation of cell group church.

6. Assurance that there are people on the senior leadership team who have a heart for children and young people, so their voice is clearly heard, and they're part of decision-making that will affect every generation.

7. Training all cell leaders, regarding their role in discipling children, (both their own and those of their cell members). Help cell leaders understand the place of their own children in their ministry, so they can equip group members to disciple, and include their own children appropriately.

8. A discipling equipping track for children. Every adult needs to understand the biblical place of parental discipleship and one generation's responsibility to disciple the next, so that parents proactively are restored to disciple their own children. This can be achieved by integrating the children's track into the equipping track the church already has in place.

TRANSITIONING THE CHILDREN'S MINISTRY TO CHILDREN'S CELLS

The children's ministry needs to transition into children's cells for the following reasons:

Written Resources

What Shall We Do with the Children by Daphne Kirk is a training course that lays the foundation for incorporating children into the cell group vision. Audio tapes are also available.

- so every child has the opportunity of experiencing cell group life
- to raise peer leadership
- to prepare children to take their place in cells with their parents
- so children have a model to take into their schools, their streets, and wherever they have the opportunity of winning their friends and discipling them
- to birth children's cells as a result of a large children's outreach harvest event

Eventually adult cells may start their own children's cells as they reach out to children. Intergenerational cells may birth children's cells as a strategic move when they find that, because of evangelism, they have too many children. (This would be a temporary move until multiplication of the parent cell.)

Sunday school teachers will need a paradigm change as they begin to understand the facilitating role of a cell leader. This can be achieved as they take their place in cells themselves, and as they attend cell leader training. The basic principles are the same, whether leading children, adults, or a mixture of both.

Sunday school is generally built on a school model, with all the language that goes with it: teacher, class, lesson, grades, graduation, etc. Transitioning gives the opportunity to transform into a ministry that reflects kingdom values that are based on relationship. As children are put into cells, they can be in three-year age bands, so that the competitiveness of a single age group changes to caring within a mixed-age group.

While cells multiply through evangelism, the cell leader can remain with those children as they grow and relationships can be maintained (just as in cells with adults). No adult has to change cell groups on reaching a certain age! The same words can be used for the children as with the adults: cells, cell leader, etc.

In these cells, through the 4 Ws, the children will be relating to Jesus, each other, and the cell leader, as they worship Jesus, apply the Word of God to their lives, while also being challenged and held accountable to win their friends for Jesus.

Ideally, children need to hear and apply the same message as the adults. This means one message is going into the homes, and one message to the whole body of Christ. This may seem like an impossible challenge, but application of the Word is ageless! The senior pastor can designate a children's cell agenda writer who'll add creativity and send it out to all children's cells each week. He should give this writer the following three points from his sermon:

- The main Scripture (For example, John 3:16)
- The theme of the message (God loves the world.)
- The challenge of the message (Do we love those around us as God does?)

If children's cells meet in one room, then the following pattern could be used, with the children's pastor facilitating all the cells from the front:

1. Children go straight to their children's cell group where their cell leader is waiting to welcome them, and chairs for their cell are set out in a "U" shape open to the front.
2. In their individual groups, they have their Welcome time of refreshments and sharing together.
3. All cells do their icebreaker (as given on the cell agenda).
4. An anointed worship leader leads from the front of the room. Children remain in their cell groups, where the group leader facilitates worship and the gifts of the Holy Spirit are encouraged to flow.
5. A short "Word" (Bible teaching) is given from the children's pastor to all the cells.
6. In their cells, the chairs are closed to a circle and the Word is applied to their lives. (Questions will be on the cell agenda given to each cell leader.) Ministry takes place among the children.
7. The cells then move on to the Witness time, (as given on the cell agenda).
8. All cells close with prayer. Parents pick up children from their cell groups.

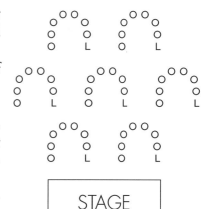

If children's cells meet in individual rooms, then a cell leader will be responsible for that cell's 4 Ws. They still have, and follow, the agenda given to all the children's cells.

As children become familiar with cell life and the cell is formed, it will become clear that there are children who are capable of leading the cell themselves. These children can be raised into leadership by modeling, training, and gradually releasing them. This must always be within the confines of the cell-based child protection policy.

I have a dream "that parents will raise soldiers and bring these soldiers to the body of Christ which forms them into an army to win the lost." Cells are this army. Gradually the vision will see children forming cells wherever they're winning their friends to Jesus, supported and resourced by the children's ministry and intergenerational cells.

This is our goal: to send young people out, equipped and empowered to disciple their friends; to take cells into their communities and go where adults cannot go; and to reach those we cannot reach with the Gospel of Jesus.

Written Resources

Heirs Together by Daphne Kirk

INTERGENERATIONAL CELLS

Cell values can also be lived out by all generations together. In intergenerational cells:

- Children are bought into the center of our lives together.
- The generations are united, bringing about a community that will demonstrate to the world that "they are my disciples, when they have love for one another," regardless of generational differences.
- There's a return to the generational flow of blessing in which God intended us to live (Psalm 78:3-6).
- Parents are empowered with their children, and families are released to love God, one another, and the lost. It's the most natural thing in Scripture to see the church of the household and home. Acts 2:46 gives a wonderful picture of homes enjoying the resurrection life of Jesus when "they met together in homes, and shared their meals with great joy and generosity—all the while praising God and enjoying the good will of all the people."
- Older women can relate to and pour themselves into the lives of younger women (Titus 2:4). Today there are so many struggling younger women with families, needing the support of those with more wisdom and experience.
- Older men can be there for younger men, and older married couples for younger married couples. Children can have spiritual aunts and uncles, cousins, and grandparent figures. God's rich tapestry of relationship and support can begin to be woven.

In most church settings, the family as a unit does not come into a place of vulnerability together, to be exposed to the presence of Jesus within the community of believers. They don't see each other confessing their sins, giving, or receiving ministry. Children were created to learn by seeing things modeled in the context of family (Deuteronomy 6:49). In this intergenerational setting of church, children see their parents being vulnerable, and parents have the joy of seeing their children's lives maturing among the community of believers.

All around the world, people are recognizing that children have much to offer. What's sadly lacking is awareness that we can be together. Throughout Scripture, children are integrated into the community of which their family is a part. The intergenerational cell restores that biblical lifestyle to the body of Christ, offering families life within the body together, and an environment where there is family for everyone—whether they have children or not! This will take a renewing of our minds and values—but cell demands that of us anyway!

My prayer is that every church setting out on the path of transitioning will at least prayerfully consider what God is doing in intergenerational cells. Don't travel too far down the track, leaving families divided and children isolated any more. Jesus prayed that we would be one ... that includes families and generations!

Here are some basic guidelines:

1. Prototype your first intergenerational cell with visionaries who are healthy adults and healthy children. Ideally these need to be a mixture of singles, couples, and families. In this early stage, it's important that other church members can see this is about the generations, not just about families, or children. From this cell can come a source of support, help, and encouragement in the early days of transitioning other cells.

2. Give the whole church opportunities to develop values that underpin intergenerational cells. These include:

- A biblical understanding of God's purposes and plans for the generations
- Parents restored to their role as primary disciplers of their children
- The biblical mandate of "fathers for the fatherless" (of all ages)
- Singles restored as "He puts the solitary in families"
- The generational blessing passed to children who were created to receive it.

3. Take plenty of time to thoroughly research good models through reading, conferences, and consultation. Many of the mistakes churches make could be avoided with more thorough preparation. Prepare children within the children's ministry as they transition into children's cells.

4. Always start a newly formed cell with a "Kid's Slot." The time when children (or adults) go into a different room after the Welcome and Worship time to continue with the cell group meeting is generally called a "Kid's Slot." Every adult cell member takes a turn to facilitate the Word and Witness time for children. Initially, each adult will need to see it modeled by someone who has experience. (Be sure to train adults to comply with your church's Child Protection Policy.)

5. Find good, tried and tested cell meeting materials to use. This will prevent the cell from becoming too childish or too academic. Either of these will be inappropriate for both children and adults! When all ages are being challenged and fruit can be seen in every age group, then you know you've "pitched it" right. (These may vary according to the age mix of the group.)

6. Implement a cell agreement and keep it operational. From the beginning, it's important for children and adults to have ownership of an agreement that can be regularly reviewed. This agreement focuses on such issues as: how each member will respect hosting homes; how they'll respond to other members; how the issue of discipline will be addressed; and anything else where people have different standards and boundaries. Children can discuss independently of the adults, and then everyone compares ideas and reaches an agreement. If this is kept alive and reviewed at regularly stated times, e.g. every two months, then many unnecessary conflicts can be avoided.

7. Give children some ownership of the cell. Ask their opinions and advice, give them appropriate responsibility, and have faith for them to move in the gifts of the Spirit and minister to other age groups. Creating space and having the expectation that this can happen will benefit everyone.

8. Remember the principle "as with adults." Although children have

some unique needs, anyone can facilitate an intergenerational cell. If, in any situation where they're unsure, they ask, "What would I do if an adult was in this situation?"

For example:
- If a child is sick, visit him (as with adults).
- If a child doesn't want to go to the meeting, spend time talking with him to assess the problem (as with adults).
- If a child doesn't participate, break into twos or threes so he can be drawn out (as with adults).
- Have an expectation that the children will be active participants of the cell (as with adults).
- Disciple, equip, and empower children to reach the lost (as with adults).

9. Equip parents to be disciplers of their own children. Implement the equipping track and model this through the life of the cell.

10. Pray and fast. This is spiritual warfare! During an intergenerational cell meeting, one member was absent with a migraine headache. The cell leader asked a child to pray for her. The child prayed, "Dear Lord Jesus, please make her better, take away the pain, and don't let her die. Amen." The adults chuckled to themselves and spent some time reassuring the child that the sick member would not die. Later, the cell leader called to check on the absent member. "Haven't you heard? I had meningitis." And she did not die.

Never underestimate God's desire and ability to speak to children and use them in his service! We need each other. We were created to be generationally interdependent just as Eli and Samuel were. Intergenerational cells give us that opportunity!

DISCIPLING CHILDREN IN CELL GROUPS

Daphne Kirk

Go into all the world and make disciples of all nations! (Matthew 28) This was Jesus' command as it has resonated through the centuries. This is our commission: to make disciples of Jesus! He didn't say, "Get them born again and hope for the best." Jesus said, "Make disciples who will walk this earth as I have walked it." He didn't say, "Teach them every week," though he did say, "Teach them to obey everything I have commanded." In other words, "Be doers of the word and not hearers only."

Jesus didn't say, "Make sure they're happy and entertained." He said, "Take up your cross and follow me." This is the heart of discipleship. Jesus' commission was for all nations—every adult, every young person, and every child throughout history.

So we have to ask ourselves … are we "making disciples" of our young people and our children, or are we prepared to settle for something less? This youngest generation is called to be a voice crying in the wilderness, to prepare the way of the Lord, to prepare for the return of Jesus—a generation that will blaze like John the Baptist. And we're called to train them, to make them disciples! They were born for such a time as this!

DISCIPLESHIP THE ANTIDOTE!

So much focus placed on teenagers today is to try and maintain their place in the kingdom, and prevent them slipping away. We address crisis after crisis, which so often resulted from cracks that appeared during childhood, not suddenly appearing overnight.

If children are discipled, these issues will raise their heads far less during teenage years. Their foundations will be secure, a "24-7" lifestyle of accountability and relationship will be in place, and they'll be launched into their adolescence with the fire of the Holy Spirit already burning in their lives. They'll have a passion for Jesus flooding them, and will already be making disciples of Jesus themselves.

WHY CHILDREN NEED DISCIPLING

Children need discipleship for the same reasons as adults! Each child is a unique, profoundly precious individual in the eyes of God. That individuality needs to be recognized. Children need someone who knows where they are in their relationship with Jesus, and the challenges they're facing. They need someone who'll nurture them and hold them accountable in every area of their young lives.

Children's soccer coaches don't just sit and teach them. They train children, giving them opportunities to be coached, to make mistakes, to go onto the field and participate, etc. The same principle applies in the kingdom. We're told to "TRAIN" up a child in the way he should go! God has a unique plan for each one of them!

ONE GENERATION TO DISCIPLE THE NEXT

When one generation fails in its responsibility to the next, Judges 2:10 describes the results: a generation grew up without knowing God. The Bible is very clear that every one of us is responsible for the next generation; we're all called to win and disciple them. This cannot be abdicated, any more than any other command from the throne of heaven. God is pouring out his Spirit that a generation of fathers (Malachi 4) will rise up for a generation of children. Young people across the nations will "go and make disciples."

PARENTS THE PRIMARY DISCIPLERS

Deuteronomy 6:4-9 instructs parents, "Hear, O Israel: The Lord our God, the Lord is one. Love the Lord your God with all your heart and with all your soul and with all your strength. These commandments that I give you today are to be upon your hearts. Impress them on your children. Talk about them when you sit at home and when you walk along the road, and when you lie down and when you get up. Tie them as symbols on your hands and bind them on your foreheads. Write them on the door-frames of your houses and on your gates."

This is the lifestyle discipleship Jesus lived out with his own disciples. This lifestyle flows from the hearts of parents who are passionate. A father who's passionate about a sport will spill that passion all over the children so they become supporters of the team. How much more with Jesus!

When parents are totally sold out for Jesus, the result will be that Jesus

Written Resources

Hand in Hand by Daphne Kirk explains how an adult mentor disciples a child.

becomes a member of the family and is included as such: never ignored, always included, talked with, and never hurt by the things that happen in that family. This is the foundational discipleship of every child and young person. To have God's results, we must disciple our children God's way!

Passionate parents will raise passionate children! How passionate are we, as parents, about Jesus?

WHY PARENTS DON'T DISCIPLE

I've asked parents why they're not discipling their own children. In any culture, the conclusions are the same. Primarily, parents say no one told them how important it was; they're too busy; they were never discipled themselves; and without any modeling or resources, they don't know how to go about it. Many parents have not been discipled even in adulthood, and so the cycle has continued to their children.

Sadly, the church has continued the cycle, though for the most commendable reasons. The church has taken upon itself the primary task of overseeing children's spiritual development. Parents are left feeling inadequate and dependent on the church's children's workers. They don't see themselves as God's chosen and anointed for the task.

Then there are many parents who never consider that their children need discipling. Parents are happy that their children have been born again and presume that everything else will now safely wait until they're older. It's quite remarkable that this principle isn't applied to other profoundly important areas of their children's lives. Sadly, they haven't been told or understood the value of discipling, and the scriptural command to pass on the lifestyle that's based on Godly values!

EQUIPPING

Most cell group churches focus on the discipleship of adults, developing an equipping track. How many churches have included a track for discipling children? Every adult should be discipling his or her own children before being released to disciple another adult. Why do we send people out to "feed" others, when their own children are "starving?"

So, integrated within the adult cell members' discipleship track, there needs to be a time, quite early on, when the focus is on their children. They must be held accountable for their children's discipleship as part of the cell lifestyle. It's a biblical command that parents disciple their children (Psalm 78:1-8, Deuteronomy 29:29).

Written Resources

The Living with Jesus Series by Daphne Kirk is a set of eight books that equip and disciple children in the foundations of the Christian faith.

It would be unthinkable to release cell leaders, coaches, pastors, or worship leaders who were stealing, lying, committing adultery, etc. Yet we release them when they're breaking a clear command to disciple their own children.

We must restore this biblical command to our pulpits. The church must train and equip families and cell groups for their biblical role in discipling future generations.

LEADERS

Among the church's leadership, there must be a clear message given both in word and deed. As leaders are seen to be including their children in their ministry, blessing their families with their ministry, taking time for their children and honoring them, so they'll be empowered in an even greater way to pass this on to others within the church.

All leadership training needs to help leaders envision the place their own children have in their ministry, so that the days of children being harmed by the ministry of their parents is forever behind us. God gave that call to ministry to the parents in order to bless the family, not to harm it.

LIFESTYLE DISCIPLESHIP

The lifestyle of the cell is about discipleship. Jesus looked for, raised, and left disciples. The vision is for each child of God to be a disciple of Jesus twenty-four hours a day, seven days a week!

Children's Cells—Making Disciples

To make disciples will mean breaking the "meeting mentality!" The cell leader will be a discipler not only during the cell meeting time, but throughout the week. Relationship building with the child must always be in the context of also building a relationship with the family.

Contacts made through the week (by phone calls, visits, letters, or going out together) will help to maintain discipleship of children through their daily lives. Things will have been shared in the cell meeting that need following up. Decisions made will need accountability and encouragement.

Intergenerational Cells

Within the intergenerational cell, develop the value that parents take responsibility for the discipleship of their children. Encourage this to be the lifestyle of the cell group. Naturally, children need others in their lives. Other adults add to that discipleship dynamic, but never detract from supporting and equipping parents as the primary disciplers.

CHILDREN AS DISCIPLERS

Children, too, are called to make disciples. A discipled child (or adult) will disciple another naturally. However, just as adults need encouragement, empowerment, resources, and training, so do the children.

Today, children are making disciples in their schools and their communities. But the most effective result has been where this is an intentional, proactive strategy and culture of the church. Let's disciple this generation to disciple others—just like Jesus!

Stage 8:
Expand the Cell Groups To Reach the Unreached

Penetrating "Type B" Unbelievers Through Target/Share Groups

Ralph W. Neighbour, Jr.

> I am made all things to all men, that
> I might by all means save some.
> —1 Corinthians 9:22

During the first stages of cell group life, members are made aware of many responsive unbelievers within their circles of influence, or *oikoses*. These are called "Type A" unbelievers, described in Luke 10:6 as "men of peace." Included in the "Blessing Lists," they're harvested through prayer and relationships. Because there's often a steady flow of these easy-to-reach converts, a cell group may fail to consider harvesting those who are "far off" (Isaiah 33:13).

A church will see its harvest diminish if it doesn't train cell group members to reach those who are not responsive or open to the Gospel. The above diagram labels these people as "Type B" unbelievers.

Experience over many years has demonstrated that not all cell members are equally qualified to harvest the resistant. The "little children" and the "young men" are not yet acquainted with the way the Holy Spirit draws unbelievers. They seem to exhibit a "God-shyness" that decreases their

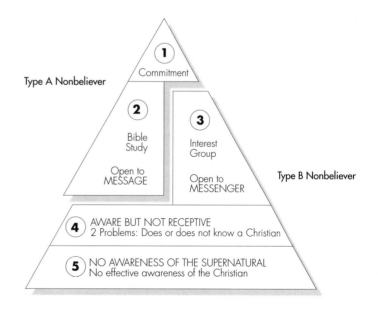

ability to reach the resistant.

As a cell group matures, there will be "fathers" who've experienced reaching responsive unbelievers. This group can be prepared to harvest unresponsive "Type B" people, because they've experienced how the Spirit brings conviction to the lost.

Three "fathers" are needed to form a team from the cell. The rest of the cell will participate through prayer support and introducing team members to resistant people they know. At the close of the short-term outreach, there's a gathering which includes all the cell members and some of the oikos members of the "Type B" unbelievers.

LISTENING TO THE SOILS OF THE HEART

In Matthew 13:1-24, Jesus shares a long illustration about "Type B" people. A farmer is sowing grain in his fields. Oddly, he seems oblivious to the soils as he scatters the seed. It seems foolish for him to take good seed and throw it on the hard path, on rocky soil, on earth filled with thorns.

The disciples asked, "Why do you always use these hard-to-understand illustrations?" He explained that what seems foolish in the natural has another dimension when seen through the values of the Kingdom of God. He explains that hearts that are fat and heavy, and eyes that are dull, don't see what God sees. "Blessed are your eyes, for they see; and your ears, for they hear," he said.

We must not pay so much attention to the surface soil. Jesus knew that beneath the roadbed, rocks, and weeds, was sub-soil that would readily accept the seeds. It's mandatory that we listen to the soils of the heart!

Jesus was teaching that we must not see the resistant unbeliever with human eyes, but with Kingdom of God eyes. What in the natural seems to be irrational is very different when the power of Christ is present in the sub-soil. Cell members must learn to listen to the soils of the heart, not to the defensive crusts protecting the surfaces of life! Thus, we must realize that spending time with "Type B" unbelievers must precede sowing good seed into the sub-soils of their lives.

This is the greatest flaw in contemporary evangelism! We act too much like the salesman whose only interest is in getting his product sold to a "prospect." (The very use of the word "prospect" by Christians referring to unbelievers is repugnant!) Jesus saw the sub-soils in tax collectors, prostitutes, and thieves. He spent time with winebibbers and sinners. We must do the same!

CULTIVATING COMES BEFORE SEED SOWING, NOT AFTER IT!

In 1 Corinthians 9:20-23, Paul explains clearly the way he went about reaching "Type B" unbelievers:

> When I am with the Jews I seem as one of them so that they will listen to the Gospel and I can win them to Christ. When I am with Gentiles who follow Jewish customs and ceremonies I don't argue, even though I don't agree, because I want to help them. When with the heathen I agree with them as much as I can, except of course that I must always do what is right as a Christian. And so, by agreeing, I can win their confidence and help them too. When I am with those whose consciences bother them easily, I don't act as though I know it all and don't say they are foolish; the result is that they are willing to let me help them. Yes, whatever a person is like, I try to find common ground with him so that he will let me tell him about Christ and let Christ save him. I do this to get the Gospel to them and also for the blessing I myself receive when I see them come to Christ. (TLB)

The major ingredient to be invested in reaching the resistant is spending time with them. I often share a great truth about those who are planning marriage: they first meet! People don't marry someone they've never met. Our lack of harvest results from not relating to the unreached.

Some years ago, a Polish sociologist was asked to evaluate the way Americans relate to each other. After much evaluation, she reported that in this culture people are divided into three groups.

First, she observed the majority of people are treated as landscape. Like the mountains and the highways and the buildings, they're simply observed as objects. Without any concern for them, further contact isn't possible.

Second, she observed that a limited number of people are treated as machines. These people are a necessity because they serve us in some manner. Even as we're careful to keep oil in the transmission of our automobile, we also "oil up" these people with polite courtesies: "How are you today?" (But please don't tell me, because I don't really care!)

Being polite is necessary to get good service from the "machine people," but there's zero interest in sharing intimacies with them. In a restaurant, it's amusing to view the way the customer and the waiter treat each other as "machines." Observation reveals that most of the time they don't make eye contact. The waiter concentrates on the order pad and the customer views the menu. Conversation is limited to the necessary words to get the order to the cooks.

Third, she observed that only a few people, perhaps no more than eight for the typical person, are treated as equals. This limited community is cherished, honest dialogue takes place, and intimate issues are shared. This group is limited by trust factors that have been established over time. To meet a stranger who seeks to share confidences too early causes us to be on guard, to become defensive. One must earn the right to be treated as an equal.

It's obvious that Paul realized all this when he wrote the passage we've just read. In his days as a tentmaker in the marketplace, he had many opportunities to evaluate people who came to look at canvas. Always in the back of his mind was the desire to become whatever was required to move from being a "machine" to an "equal." He developed a skill to do that for the sake of the harvest.

The typical Christian doesn't consider the importance of cultivating. It's not as much taught as it is caught. It's a compassion that's created through multiple experiences, not just one event.

Two Types of Soil Among the "Type B" People

In working with the unconverted, the cell team will confront both those with a "modern" worldview and a "post-modern" worldview. It's important for the "fathers" to be prepared to respond properly to both.

The "Modern" Worldview
- Everything can be explained.
- The more we study, the more we learn.
- The more we learn, the more we'll understand.
- The more we understand, the more control we'll have.
- The more control we have, the better world we can create.
- Scientific theory will create a better world.
- There's no need for supernatural intervention.
- Even if God exists it makes little difference.

The "Post Modern" Worldview
- Began in the 1960s. Everything is relative.
- Skepticism about, or outright rejection of, Christian worldview and trust in science as a source of truth.
- Pluralism: nothing is "ultimate truth."
- Authority and knowledge aren't respected.
- Self-developed religious convictions are authoritative only for the person.
- "If it makes you happy, it can't be half bad."
- We can never really know whether we know what's true.
- Ultimate truth doesn't exist. Be tolerant of all views.

The shift between these two worldviews is important to understand:
• Postmodern: truth is conditioned by what we are, developed by our personal culture.
• Meaning is found in the context of life.
• Rejects the modern view that there's a right interpretation of any text.
• All reality is filtered through individual senses and is not the same for all.
• Christianity is a rigid interpretation of truth that's no longer valid. It may be mixed with many other concepts.

Thus, the "fathers" cannot expect to pass on their convictions as "true truth." Because they're based on personal experience, they can't be handed down. It's necessary to help unbelievers generate their own convictions. If we don't, we'll downgrade our convictions into unabsorbed belief systems for others. Then, the next generation will transform beliefs into opinions!

What do we say to the person who says, "I'm unsure God exists. If he does, the only way I can know is to experience him. How does one experience God?"

The answer is found in John 13:35: "They will know you are my disciples by your love." Post-moderns aren't concerned about whether something is true (that's a "modern" value). They're asking, "Does it work?" The share or target group strategy for reaching the sub-soils is to demonstrate compassion.

OUR STRATEGY: THE INITIAL CONTACT

It all begins by providing experiences to impact the resistant person:

1. Have a need, not an answer. This is precisely the approach Jesus took with the woman at the well in Samaria.
2. Earn the right to be trusted. This is done by serving the person, not seeking to control or persuade. For many years, Ruth and I supported a YWAM young woman in Amsterdam who visited prostitutes to serve them cookies and tea. She had a huge harvest by just listening to their heart soils until it was time to plant the seed of Christ's presence in them.
3. Probe for the bee sting of sin. Unresponsive people will quickly respond when we minister to their true needs. But they won't emerge until we've moved to a deep trust relationship.

Providing new experiences with the "Type B" unbeliever will create a bond of trust, making it possible to probe for their interest in knowing more about Christ through an investigative Bible study. Here are suggestions for creating new experiences with them

1. Experience: How can you serve?
2. Experience: How can you encourage?
3. Experience: What can you share?
4. Experience: What can you learn?
5. Experience: What can you lend?
6. Experience: What can you write?
7. Experience: What can you fix?

Imprinting these values within the lives of the spiritual "fathers" in the cell group will not only change the way they reach out, but will also be reflected into the less mature cell members as they receive the weekly reports from the ministry of the outreach groups.

TWO WAYS TO CONNECT TO "TYPE B" UNBELIEVERS:

Share Groups

The group is made up of three "fathers" and no more than six "Type B" unbelievers. When reaching into the oikoses of the cell members, many "Type B" people will be discovered. They have one common ground: they like to share about what they're doing. Thus, by visiting in each home and letting every unbeliever host the meeting and share his or her interest, bonding takes place between team members and the group. Thus, the agenda is set by the person hosting each session. One advantage is that the "fathers" are participants and are not seen as controlling the activities. A period of cultivation must precede the proposal to launch the sharing sessions. The group lasts up to nine weeks as each home is visited.

Target Groups

The group is made up of three "fathers" and no more than six "Type B" unbelievers. In this ministry, the "fathers" select a group within the community who share a common hobby, interest, need, or problem. The target group is contacted through appropriate advertising. Personal visits or interviews link those who respond to the "fathers." When six people are enlisted, the group begins to meet. The group usually lasts six weeks.

A PROJECT TO DISCOVER HOW TO REACH "TYPE B" UNBELIEVERS

Dear Co-Worker,

You're taking this course because you have a passion to reach "Type B" unbelievers. Too many Christian workers are content with learning "how to" without ever experiencing the actual ministry being presented.

This course has a critical requirement: you must actually experience either a Share Group or a Target Group in order to receive credit. We don't have "audits."

When you complete your project, TOUCH Glocal will feel comfortable in recommending you as a "workman who does not need to be ashamed."

First of all, read through this list of directions now. Then, as you complete certain modules, reread the directions that are linked to them. In your syllabus, there'll be a panel telling you which suggestions to review.

This module of your Glocal training requires you to be a member of a cell group. As you're taking the module, you will include two other "fathers" in the cell. In addition, your project at times will include the "little children" and the "young men."

Web Resource

The following is taken from the unique Distance Learning Module, now available from the TOUCH Glocal Training Center (course CL 202) <www.touchglocal.com>. Those receiving this training are mentored as they develop these ministries.

Written Resources

Building Bridges, Opening Hearts (Order 3 sets.)
Building Groups, Opening Hearts (Order 3 sets.)
Building Awareness, Opening Hearts (Order one for every cell group member.)

Direction 1: Select your team members now!

As you take this course, you'll be forming either a Share Group or a Target Group. This requires at least three "spiritual fathers" to create a team. (A "spiritual father" is a fellow Christian who has already harvested at least one unbeliever.)

You'll reach about six "Type B" unbelievers. (A "Type B" unbeliever is one who's not yet responsive to receiving Christ as Lord.)

Pray about who you'll involve in your project.

Select two other "fathers" in your cell group to form a team. Explain that they'll complete the three Daily Growth Guides with you.

You may invite them to view the online course presentations with you. They don't have to enroll as a student to view them, but if they choose to do so, they can also get TOUCH Glocal credit.

Each of the team members will form friendships with two "Type B" unbelievers. They'll then join you in a six-week group and learn to cultivate and harvest.

When you've selected them, post their names in your project folder on the web site.

Direction 2: Complete *Building Bridges, Opening Hearts* with the team.

At this time, present *Building Bridges* to the two "fathers" you've selected to form your team. Ask them to complete the Daily Growth Guides each day. Meet with them weekly, perhaps before or after your Cell or a Celebration service, to review the contents.

Direction 3: Form either a Share or Target Group.

In Part 4, you'll learn the difference between a Share Group and a Target Group. After you understand the difference, meet with your "fathers" and decide which of the two groups you desire to form.

Your local situation will make that decision easy. If you all have friends who are "Type B," you may well enjoy a Share Group. If you don't, then "target" a segment of the community by meeting their needs or focusing on their interests.

You'll find this course has far more value as you implement these steps. Instead of theory, the content becomes reality and it gives you opportunity to share your results in the cohort sessions with fellow students.

Your professor is always available to help you with problems, questions, or suggestions. Remember: your tuition gives you opportunity to contact us at any time! We are here for you!

Direction 4: Bathe this outreach with prayer!

In Seoul, Korea, there's a Baptist cell church growing at such a rapid rate that it has the potential to become the largest church on the face of the earth within the next ten years. What's its secret? Its pastor, Rev. Seok-Jeon Yoon, prays eight hours a day, some of that time leading the 14,000 cell leaders in intercession from 10 p.m. to midnight, Monday through Friday. Its Prayer Mountain, located outside Seoul, has space for thousands of cell groups to retreat for extended times of prayer. He states frankly, "The missing ingredient in the harvest of lost souls is the lack of intercessory prayer by Christians. When our prayer lives are shallow, the harvest is not reaped!"

Can you revise your daily schedule to pray at least one hour for this ministry to "Type B" unbelievers? It will change everything.

Direction 5: Cultivate the "Type B" unbelievers.

Paul said, "I have become all things to all men so that I might win some of them." You should now be cultivating the "Type B" unbelievers you'll invite to a target or share group. Here's a tip to share with your team:

- Have a Need: Jesus opened his contact with the woman at the well by asking her to help him.
- Serve a Need: What's the "bee sting" of sin that's painful to the unbeliever? When you pay attention to the problem, he or she will treasure your assistance.
- Share an Opportunity: Do you have two tickets to an event that would appeal to your friend? By sharing that time, you're bonding to each other.
- Offer Assistance: Can you offer a ride, help to paint a wall, participate in a project important to the unbeliever?

Direction 6: Prepare your entire cell group for the coming party.

Create an awareness in your cell group about their participation in the party you'll sponsor at the end of the target or share group experience.

You're about to enter the module explaining how to create a Share or Target Group. Ask your cell leader for time to explain to your entire cell group what your team is about to do.

You've selected the "spiritual fathers" from your cell to be your partners. Together with them, you can make a great impact upon the "spiritual young men" who've not yet harvested an unbeliever, and the "little children" who look up to you as an example of a mature believer.

A part of your ministry is to prepare these fellow cell members for a party you'll invite them to attend at the close of the Share/Target group. Explain to them that after the six weeks of cultivation, all the cell members will have opportunity to meet people from the oikoses of the "Type B" unbelievers who'll attend your group.

Alert them to the coming opportunity they'll have to make friends and cultivate these new people. Answer any questions they may have and pray for the outreach. Include prayer for each of the unbelievers by adding them to your *Blessing List.*

Written Resources

A Blessing List is a large poster on which a group can list names of unchurched friends, co-workers, neighbors, and family members. The cell group can use this list as a reminder to pray for those people.

Direction 7: Relate to the families of each "Type B" person.

In your next team meeting, meditate together on Luke 10:5-6. Be aware that your contacts with the "Type B" unbelievers may lead you to a member of their family or a friend who is the "man of peace," searching for answers to life's questions. Don't focus only on the one person you'd like to invite to your group. Get acquainted with all the people in each *oikos.* How? Ask the Holy Spirit to show you the way to visit in each household!

Direction 8: Conduct a "dress rehearsal" with your team.

Your team will now study the Daily Growth Guides in *Building Groups, Opening Hearts* as you view Part 9 in your course. Get your team together and have a "dress rehearsal."

If possible, do this with the cell group. It will further expose them to the procedures that will take place in a Share Group and prepare them for the time when they, too, will become "spiritual fathers" and reach out to "Type B" unbelievers.

A vital part of this course is the cohort meeting. You'll find it helpful when you face a problem or need a suggestion.

Direction 9: Conduct a team half-night of prayer.

With your team, list different areas of prayer that need to be included:
- Needs in your own life;
- Needs in the team's lives;
- Warfare prayer related to strongholds in the lives of the "Type B" unbelievers with whom you're working.

Direction 10: Use your one-minute testimony.

How soon do you share your witness with "Type B" unbelievers?

Discuss this in your team meeting. The sooner, the better! Only after you share your one-minute testimony will unbelievers connect your actions with the Christ who dwells in you. When will you know when the time is right to share? It will be soon after you first meet and a bond is established.

Remember—you're sharing something deeply personal. Don't wait too long, but wait until you know the person knows you well enough to respect what you say.

Wait for the Spirit to "tap you on the shoulder," and tell you, "This is the time! Now!"

Always remember that a witness is a report of something you've experienced. It's not a sermon. It's not a sales presentation. It's simply telling someone else what has happened to you. No one's offended when you do that.

Read 1 John 1:1-3. Note how John shares his witness:

Christ was alive when the world began, yet I myself have seen him with my own eyes and listened to him speak. I have touched him with my own hands. He is God's message of life. This one who is life from God has been shown to us, and we guarantee that we have seen him; I am speaking of Christ, who is eternal Life. He was with the Father and then was shown to us. Again I say, we are telling you about what we ourselves have actually seen and heard, so that you may share the fellowship and the joys we have with the Father and with Jesus Christ his son. (TLB)

Direction 11: Advertising is a cell group task.

(Note: This section applies only to the formation of a Target Group. In a Share Group, you will select people from your *oikoses*. Thus, there's no need to advertise.)

How will you advertise your target group?

Brainstorm with your team members. Ask cell members to assist you, if you're going to put out leaflets or posters. Their involvement will be important in bonding them to your mission to harvest the unreached. Remember—the more information you release, the greater will be the response!

May God anoint you for this time of learning how to harvest "Type B" unbelievers!

CELL-BASED HARVEST EVENTS

Ralph W. Neighbour, Jr.

When you admire a tree in bloom, you see its leaves, its flowers, and how its branches reach upward. Never, unless you're a botanist, would you think about the root system that produces this beauty. However, if you were to consider a tree's roots, how large do you think the circumference of the root system would be? Do you think the roots pierce the earth below exactly as deep as the tree is tall? Or do the roots spread under the earth exactly as wide as the branches have spread from the trunk?

The latter of the two choices is correct. If a tree develops a proper root system, it will be filled with strong branches and will bear fruit to reproduce itself in kind. The same applies to the church. A church only looks as good as the root system that supports it. In the cell-based structure, strong emphasis is placed upon helping every cell member become a part of its "root system," as he or she is learning to reach another person for Christ soon after joining a group. Each person then can be encouraged to sow, cultivate, and expect a harvest time in a continuing cycle.

Harvest events help develop this root system. If people know the church expects and plans for a harvest, it's easier to commit time to it. Cell members know to look forward to what God will do in the lives of the lost.

HARVEST EVENTS AS CELL GROUP CHURCH TRADITIONS

Think of harvest events as part of the traditions of your cell group church. The word "tradition" may be seen as a derogatory reference to program-based churches that say, "We have our traditions. We never tried it that way before!" (See *The Seven Last Words of the Church*.) Nevertheless, there's a need to create new "traditions" in the cell group church that are positive, leading to annual harvesting events.

In America's Southland, there once were two traditional evangelistic meetings each year, called "revivals." One was in October, the other in March or April. Around the beginning of the 20th century—without radio, TV, or transportation—these revivals were spectacular events that drew even the town atheist to the public meetings. For example, the famous evangelist, Sam Jones, used to have a special seat for the town atheist on the front row of his meetings, and rousing debates would take place between him and the one who dared to sit in it!

In the past thirty years, revivals have failed to produce—attracting few, if any, unbelievers and bringing little or no edification to the faithful core who dutifully attended and put their love offering in the plate for the visiting evangelist. Times changed. People adjusted to a culture saturated with multiple TV entertainment channels, and the attractiveness of attending a revival died.

As we think about lifestyles of people today, we recognize there must be a new approach to harvest events that attract the lost. Entertainment is no longer in short supply and this will not attract people to Christ. The church cannot out-entertain Hollywood.

What will draw people to Christ? What can the church do better than anybody else? Relationships! As Christians, we have the power to love and reach out to people. Today's society is made up of lonely people. Most walk in inner despair, hungry for true friends.

In America today, the Promise Keepers movement has exploded into existence. Tens of thousands of men gather in huge stadiums for rallies. These major events are fed from hundreds of small groups—each with three men who meet together and become accountable to and for each other. While it's primarily a gathering of Christians, many unbelieving men have been swept into the Kingdom by its impact. What's the drawing power of this movement? It offers intimate relationships.

Body life evangelism is a method that can best be utilized by the cell group church movement. By building relationships with the lost, cell members will have the right to minister to them, leading them one step at a time to the Father. If this root system of cell groups is put in place, there should be times for harvesting the results as a formal activity of the church. These events should form the basis of the annual church calendar.

The stronger the cell group church grows, and the more cell members are reaching out to the lost, the more critical it will be to focus on harvest events. The sign of a mature cell structure is the schedule of traditional harvest events.

Because each community has its own distinctive needs and population mix, it's best to present models to stimulate planning. Let's examine several illustrations of effective harvest events.

HARVEST EVENTS USED SUCCESSFULLY BY CELL GROUP CHURCHES
Come Celebrate Christmas

For several years, Faith Community Baptist Church (FCBC) sponsored a special Christmas program for the people of Singapore. Every year, the 12,000-seat Singapore Indoor Stadium was reserved four nights for the performance put on by hundreds of cell members. On some nights, hundreds were turned away! The conversions through that single harvest event numbered in the hundreds.

Heaven's Gates, Hell's Flames

This is a drama that's put on by the members of a church. Reality Outreach has produced the script and sends a producer/team to direct the rehearsals for the church. The response to this nine-part drama has been phenomenal! Bethany World Prayer Center, in Baker, Louisiana, presented this for twenty-one nights in February-March, 1994, and had 18,290 recorded decisions for Christ. In Modesto, California in 1995, there were 25,000 decisions when the presentation ran in a local church there.

Parents' Banquet

This event drew hundreds of Buddhist parents of FCBC young people to a special twelve-course Chinese banquet held in a hotel ballroom. A Chinese movie star from Hong Kong who has accepted the Lord was the drawing card: she'd been seen in movies by the parents for years. Many conversions were recorded on decision cards placed at each table.

Crusade

In El Salvador, the 110,000 member Mission Elim Cell Church packs out the largest soccer stadium in the nation for an evangelistic crusade. Cell members bring guests who are either unsaved or on the verge of making a commitment.

Stadium Rally

Each year, Dion Robert gathers the people who are in the cells of the *Eglise Protestante Baptiste Oeuvres et Mission* in Abidjan, Ivory Coast, for a harvest time. In the past, there have been so many decisions during this event that the church systematically multiplies all its cell groups prior to the meetings, so converts can be properly assimilated into the body. People come days in advance to fast and pray in preparation for their ministries of deliverance. A team of more than two hundred sets up a kitchen to feed all who attend. Miraculous healing constantly takes place. Some of the highest government officials in the land sit on the platform, and many of them have been saved through attending this rally.

Holiday Excursion

When the Abidjan church had only 9,000 members, Pastor Dion took the members and their unsaved friends by buses and boats to an offshore resort island. There the Holy Spirit began to draw the unbelievers who lived with the cell members. On another occasion, this church rented trains and took thousands of people from Abidjan to Bouake, the second largest city in the nation, for a special harvest event there. Unbelievers were glad to share in such an adventure as a trip to Bouake, and hundreds were saved in the meetings.

One-Day Community Event

Fifteen years ago, a Florida pastor envisioned impacting Fort Lauderdale by sponsoring the feeding of 5,000 people on the church property. Newspaper ads publicized the date, inviting all who were poor or hungry to come, to be fed roast chicken and many other dishes. The entire church participated, as all the food was prepared in the homes of the members. Men with counting machines clicked those who received free meals, and true to their promise, 5,000 people were fed on that day! The impact of this loving group caused many people to seriously investigate the claims of Jesus Christ. The impact made on the area was powerful.

MAJOR CHURCH-WIDE HARVEST EVENTS

The Billy Graham Evangelistic Association employed me as a young college graduate. At that time (1950), Dr. Graham was forming his crusade team and needed guidance about crusade development. He contacted a man who'd been with Billy Sunday years before. This gentleman spent several months with the Graham organization. One of the lessons he taught us was that great stadiums were filled only when the crusade preparations involved at least one person for every ten who were needed to fill the stadiums. Thus, Cliff Barrows began to organize crusade choirs of 1,000-2,000 voices. The counseling training involved hundreds of people sitting in the stands. For several years, as I worked in this crusade ministry, I saw the proof of his premise.

In order to successfully pull off church-wide harvest events, follow these guidelines:

1. The calendar for the cell church should include at least one major church-wide harvest event each year.
2. This should be well planned to maximize involvement. At least forty percent of the total cell group membership should have responsibilities in preparing for the event. For the event to succeed, this high percentage must be honored, because it creates high ownership. The cells are to be prepared to actively participate in the activity in every possible way.
3. Develop as many tasks as possible to involve people. Here's a list of ways cell members and cell groups have been involved by cell churches:
   a. Musicians: Bands, orchestras, dancers, drama groups, etc.
   b. Counselors: Prepare them by conducting an Encounter God weekend in advance of the event.
   c. Ushers: Use more than you need to build the percentage of involvement.
   d. Prayer Warriors: They might sit in a group. Have them begin to fast and pray one day a week for three months prior to the event.
   e. Greeters: Prepare shoulder sashes to identify them at the

entrance doors.

    f. Technicians: Have volunteer crews of teens or young adults assist in moving props and microphones, etc.

    g. Parking Teams: Using flashlights, the teams will help guide cars to parking spots.

    h. Food Support Teams: Arrange for food to be served to either performers or event participants.

DISTRICT/COACHING CLUSTER EVENTS
Home-made Ice Cream Social

Tom Glymph was a coach over cell groups in Houston, Texas. His cluster of five cells came together to penetrate a low-cost housing project. Tom deliberately moved into an apartment among these people to establish a Christian presence for them. The cells rotated, spending Sunday afternoons among the residents. The coaching cluster purchased two ice cream makers and each week homemade ice cream was made in the middle of the courtyard in full view of all residents. It was then given away to all comers, and even taken in plastic cups to the doors of the apartments.

After a couple of weeks, some of the unbelievers came out to "help turn the crank," and brought bananas and peaches for the mix. Out of this, the zone saw two new cell groups formed from converts. (That coaching cluster would highly recommend this technique as a harvest event for you to try!)

Wild Game Night

One adult coaching cluster in Houston, Texas asked all the members who went hunting or fishing to donate a tithe of their game for a special banquet. The evening was called "A Wild Game Night," and it brought many chuckles as unbelievers were invited to participate. A film showing a "camera hunt" in Africa was presented, several men gave testimonies, and many decisions were recorded.

Foods of the World

In a coaching cluster with many different ethnic groups, there have been very successful events called "Foods of the World." The cell members in a cluster invite all the friends of other ethnic communities. All participants are given the option of preparing an ethnic dish or providing a recipe, as their "ticket" to attend. All the foods are placed on a long table and people are invited to taste as many varieties as they wish.

Little placards are put beside each dish, giving the name of the dish and the country/ethnic group it represents. Wearing one's national clothing is encouraged, and get-acquainted games can be built around the different customs for doing common things (pointing with the fingers, greeting salutations, etc.)

Valentine Party

Special preparations for a valentine party include "icebreakers," decorations, etc. Couples seated around tables in groups of six share details of how they met, fell in love, etc. Toward the close, a speaker may share about the qualities of love and fidelity.

National Holiday Gathering

Some countries have a national day that attracts everyone's attention. This is a perfect time for a cluster or groups of coaching clusters to have a special meal or party in connection with a parade, with floats, etc.

CELL GROUP EVENTS

"Mini-Harvest Events" will make a cell group come alive with vision for what can be done to win lost people to the Lord.

Evangelistic Cell Meetings

Located in the context of a nation with significant poverty and unemployment, the Elim Church in El Salvador has an astonishing record of conversions. It's grown to 110,000 members in less than a decade, from approximately 3,000 at the time it transitioned. The pattern is very straightforward:

- All cells multiply at 12-15.
- Each Zone Pastor has monthly "retreats" for his cells. This means they come to an all-night session, which includes times of praying and times of marathon teaching. Most of those attending are grassroots people who don't learn by reading.
- Every cell leader is tightly monitored by the Zone Supervisor and he/she is often involved in visiting the lost with the cell leader, cell intern, or even cell members, as evangelistic visits are made.

• The cell meets twice weekly. The first meeting of the week is for edification; the second gathering of the group is strictly for outreach. Every single week, the group plans the activity that will put them in contact with unbelievers they know. This constant weekly cell group outreach is the main reason they're growing so rapidly. They have a weekly harvest event in all of their cells!

Monthly Birthday Parties

Cell groups have at least one occasion each month when there can be a party—someone's birthday! Surprise birthday parties are always fun for both those who give them and the one receiving. When the person having the birthday is an unbeliever, there's a special impact made by the thoughtfulness of the cell group that sponsors the party.

A cell group threw a surprise party for one of the young women. All her friends were invited, many of whom were unbelievers. After the big "Surprise!" was over and cake was being served, the cell leader said, "We'd like you to give us a report of your past year and what your dreams are for the coming year." As the "birthday girl" shared, one of her co-workers began to think deeply. On the way home, she said, "Tonight I saw my need to think about where I'm going. I was deeply moved by this evening. Thank you for inviting me!"

Celebrations at the Close of Share/Target Group Cycles

We recommend that cell groups sponsor at least one Share or Target Group annually. At the close of the ten-week sessions, the special "celebration" is conducted. Each person in the group invites two friends. The three from the cell who've sponsored the gathering will invite all the other members of the cell to participate. This activity can often lead to a harvest of people so contacted.

TGIF

At FCBC in Singapore, they developed an annual cell harvest event for Good Friday. Because Friday is a time to relax after a hard week, it's a good opportunity to share with unbelievers why Good Friday means so much to Christians.

The format of "Thank God It's Friday" takes on a party atmosphere. In fact, the first half of the gathering is called "Happy Hour." During the

Happy Hour, the cell members and invited guests participate in some ice-breaker games, eat together, play some more games, and then sing karaoke.

The second half of the evening is called Agape Hour. This time is clearly scripted for the master of ceremonies to explain why Good Friday is so important to Christians. Then a short video is shown of the death and resurrection of Jesus. After this, everyone's invited to commit his or her life to Christ.

A time of counseling follows. Group members divide up with the guests and minister to them. During this time, everyone's invited to come to the shepherd group meeting the following week.

This kind of harvest event takes a lot of preparation to equip the cell groups to effectively pull it off. Yet it can be a powerful time of sharing Christ through relationships that reveal to the lost the love God has for them.

Harvest events should be planned at every level of a cell-based church throughout the calendar year. The leadership of the church should hold at least one large venue event each year, where cell group members can bring their lost friends to hear the Good News. Coaching clusters should band together and create events that will draw lonely unbelievers who crave new friends.

Cell groups should hold monthly game nights or barbecues to interact with the lost oikos members attached to the group. By working on all these levels simultaneously, the value of reaching the lost through relational teamwork will become your church's most cherished tradition!

TRAINING FUTURE STAFF PASTORS

M. Scott Boren

70

As the number of cell groups grows, so does the need for pastors to oversee those groups. Staff cell pastors are needed to support the cell group leaders, to minister to special needs of cell group members, and organize congregational network meetings or activities. More than anything, these pastors are needed to pray for the leaders and members who are under his or her care.

Churches that have a plan for cell growth also have a plan for training and releasing new cell group pastors.

WHERE DO STAFF CELL PASTORS COME FROM?

For centuries, raising up pastors has been the job of seminaries. Aspiring ministers follow the pattern of receiving the call to ministry within the church, but going off to receive training for ministry outside the church. When they graduate, they look for a job as an associate pastor.

See the traits of potential staff cell pastors in *Making Cell Groups Work* pg. 356-357.

Another place to look for cell pastors is from other churches. When a position opens, the church announces the position to other churches within the denomination or looks within other churches to find the right person.

Hiring pastors from seminaries and other churches are viable options. Many churches must hire the first staff cell pastor through one of these means, because the cell group system hasn't been fully developed. But churches that become Stage 8 cell-based churches take a different approach. These churches look at their current cell group leaders and cell group coaches as their future staff cell group pastors.

THREE ELEMENTS OF TRAINING

The training of future staff pastors should take a holistic approach, by emphasizing appropriately the three domains of learning: cognitive, psychomotor, and affective.

The cognitive domain has received the primary emphasis in traditional forms of pastoral training. This in no way faults the godly professors who have sown into our lives. I cherish the information I received from them. But an overemphasis on the cognitive domain produces pastors who know how to teach information, following the pattern of their professors. Staff cell pastors need to be equipped for more than teaching information.

The psychomotor domain relates to physical skills needed to perform certain tasks. Skills such as walking, throwing a ball, typing, and painting are related to this domain, because they require repetition in order to learn how to do them. One might assume this domain has relatively low priority when learning to pastor, but that's far from the truth.

Staff cell pastors must learn skills, such as how to lead a training meeting, how to speak clearly to a group of people, and how to encourage potential cell leaders to enter cell training. While none of these skills is purely psychomotor, they require practice and can't be learned from a book.

The last domain is the affective domain, which includes things like emotions, attitudes, and values. Those being trained as staff cell pastors should already have their basic values in line, or they wouldn't have been recognized as potential pastors. Even still, as a potential pastor moves into the new calling and responsibility, his or her values will be challenged. The Holy Spirit will shape his or her spirit to fit the call. Small group experiences are the best format for helping people process how they're being reshaped.

The three components of cell pastor training are intertwined with one another.

Mentoring

Mentoring occurs when a current staff pastor adopts a future staff pastor as his spiritual son or daughter. Many staff pastors get so caught up in their current duties of pastoring people and training cell leaders that they're too busy to multiply themselves among potential staff pastors.

The only way someone learns a job is from someone else in that job. I remember when I graduated from college. I was working with my father for the summer and we were meeting with a salesman. When he realized I'd just graduated, he said, "You really don't know how to work when you graduate from college. You only learn that from experience." My immediate response was anger, but over the years I've learned how right he was.

If new pastors are going to be developed, then current pastors must realize their job description includes mentoring. They must give away their ministry. They must see their job as working themselves out of a job.

David Summerall, a pastor of a very large cell-based church in the Philippines, believes in this principle so much that he's given it a special name, "shadowing." If he plans to send out a pastor to serve as a senior pastor, he asks him to "shadow" him for a couple of months. Wherever the senior pastor goes, he has a shadow, someone who's learning the daily grind of his job. He doesn't just learn the theories of what a pastor does. He learns the struggles, emotions, schedule, and process of being a senior pastor. This is the stuff that can't be written in a book. It can only be caught from observation and experience.

Pastor Summerall's principle of shadowing is implemented at all levels of pastoral training. All cell pastor trainees are connected with a mentor, and become the shadow of the mentor. They learn the job of a cell pastor through observation. They have the opportunity to ask questions about what they see. The mentor begins to give away some of the responsibilities the shadow has observed, and then the mentor provides feedback.

Such a process is more work today for the mentor. He'll have to choose to give up some of his current ministry responsibilities, but the long-term payoff is incredible.

Information

Even though mentoring is the primary means for training future cell pastors, they still require cognitive training. Luckily, this training can be attained through many accessible sources. For instance, a trainee could attend classes from a local seminary or Bible college, while being mentored by a current staff pastor. There are many online courses available. Extension courses are also an option. The trainee may or may not work toward a specific degree. The goal should be to take the courses that will prove most helpful to being a cell pastor, not completing a degree just for its own sake.

Many large churches operating in Stage 8 are starting schools for developing future pastors. Some smaller churches are partnering together with other churches of like vision to start such schools. Many of these churches offer courses as elective training for those who've proven themselves as cell group leaders, without the expectations that they'll join the pastoral staff.

The courses provided should include:

Web Resource

GLOCAL is a cell-based training institute located in Houston that offers both resident courses along with internet-based courses. Visit <www.touchglocal.com> for more information.

- Old Testament Survey
- New Testament Survey
- How to Read and Interpret the Bible
- Theology Survey
- Jesus Christ: Basic Christology
- Introduction to Counseling
- Biblical Leadership and Mentoring
- Promoting Cell Group Health and Growth
- Building Cell Group Community
- The Role of a Cell Group Pastor
- Cell Group Evangelism
- Hearing God in Prayer
- The Flow of the Holy Spirit and His Gifts

Of course, each church tradition will add or subtract courses from this list, which is only intended to illustrate topics that will prove the most useful to those in the role of a staff cell group pastor.

Learning Cohorts

In addition to mentoring and information, trainees need a place to process what they're learning. While I was working on my master's degree, I met weekly with three other students over coffee. In this meeting, we'd talk about our insights from a book we were reading, and then process what we were learning from our other courses. While I learned much from the lectures, the papers I wrote, and the preparation for exams, I must admit that this group process experience proved to be the most fruitful learning experience of all. And it was free. Granted, without the lectures, papers, and exams, we wouldn't have had much to discuss, but this process took our learning to a new level.

Trainees should be connected with one another in peer cohorts of four or five, with a requirement to meet once a week and discuss what they're learning. With the Internet, the group members can live in different cities and still meet weekly as a group.

Through the combination of an experienced mentor, information from lectures and books, and peer cohorts, trainees will be cultivated in an environment that will prepare them for effective ministry.

TRANSPLANTING TO JUMP-START NEW CHURCH PLANTS

Bill Beckham

In Israel, the tall palm date trees near the Dead Sea are gradually being replaced with shorter ones. These shorter trees are easier to care for and to harvest. In a desert country that treasures every tree, the taller trees are dug up and transplanted in the cities.

Transplanting trees is also a common practice in Houston, Texas. Almost all the trees that are less than thirty years old are transplanted. The original trees are removed to develop a housing subdivision. Then new trees are transplanted around the houses.

Special equipment is required for transplanting trees. A huge machine that looks like jaws is attached to a large truck. These jaws are placed around a tree, and a large segment of earth is dug out of the ground, with the tree and its roots in the middle. Using this method, very large trees can be transplanted, if someone's willing to pay the price for instant shade and beauty.

I first learned about transplanting trees while in high school. One of my projects in a vocational agriculture class was to plant a thousand slash pine seedlings. I again experienced transplanting trees firsthand when my father retired and planted a peach orchard with a thousand trees.

Orchards are not planted from seeds but from transplanted trees that are two years old. These trees have been carefully selected and cared for in a nursery. A transplanted tree is larger, stronger, and reproduces more quickly than a planted seed. Transplanted fruit trees are also healthier, because they're grafted into a special stock that's resistant to root disease.

SEED PLANTING STRATEGY

For decades, the church has operated with a seed-planting mission paradigm. One person or one family goes out into a new area to plant a new church. The seed-sowing planting strategy has resulted in what I call a "margarine mission strategy:" spread it just as thin and as far as it will go.

Churches and mission agencies spread new starts as thin and as evenly as possible, all over the world.

In a northern city of the United States, a denomination with the margarine parish paradigm had three churches within a four-mile radius of one another. Two were new church starts. Each church was struggling to build enough momentum to break through to critical mass. The leaders of the three churches wanted to join together as one cell group church and establish a strong base, so eventually they could transplant other churches.

The leaders of these churches prayed about the problem and developed an excellent prospectus of how they could join together, reach critical mass more quickly, and then begin to reproduce themselves. It looked like an excellent strategy. The plan was presented to the denominational committee responsible for new church starts that helped support the salaries of two of the three pastors.

They turned them down. Why? I have no doubt they were operating in good faith with their paradigm of church planting. They made a decision from a "margarine mission strategy" and their "dots on a map" tracking system. In their annual report, three green dots on a map look a lot better than one dot, especially if last year you had three dots. It doesn't matter if the dots represent small, struggling churches.

I've concluded that this is the most difficult and ineffective of all church starting strategies. Little margin for error is possible in this approach. It's almost impossible to develop momentum, leaving the church plant under attack from all directions. The result is often a church that's stunted and unproductive. This may explain why more than eighty percent of the churches in the world never grow beyond fifty to one hundred adult members.

The number of churches isn't always the best indicator of the strength of the church in a country or area. Wales has more churches per person than any other country in the world, but the average size is less than fifteen members per church. The size and quality of the church must be considered when evaluating the strength of the church.

This strategy is so popular because territory is easier to sell back home than quality. Spreading the Gospel everywhere feels good, seems fair because the church is responding to need, looks good on world mission maps, and makes for wonderful human interest stories for raising money.

In some cases, the church can't be transplanted, but must be planted as a small seed with one missionary. However, the seed-planting strategy method hasn't been just an option to church planting. This approach is the strategy of choice the church has used for more than a century.

JESUS USED A TRANSPLANT MODEL

The New Testament model of starting churches is transplanting a tree, not planting a seed. Jesus developed a strong strategic church in Jerusalem, from which new church starts would be transplanted all over the world. Paul followed this strategy as he transplanted churches from his home base in Antioch. Paul selected target cities and concentrated as much personnel and time in those areas as possible. Even when he was thrown out of a target area, he continued to send his support leaders back as often as possible to strengthen his bases.

Think of Jesus' stages of the church as a growing tree, (as presented in the chart below.) The sending church on the left side represents a strategic church, large and strong enough to begin another church. One unit would be a seed (one person or a couple). Two or three innovators would represent a small seedling. A group of twelve would be a small tree with a good root system and the possibility of fruit in a year or so. Jesus' thirty to seventy person support network is a growing tree mature enough to produce fruit immediately. A base congregation of 120 is a young full-grown tree that can begin to transplant other trees very quickly.

The traditional church has used adaptations of the transplant model. In the hive model, forming new churches in a new area involves transplanting a leader and a portion of the original church. In the mission model, a mother church sends out a number of leaders and members to establish a new mission.

Church Transplanting

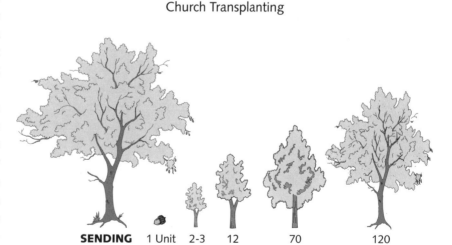

| SENDING CHURCH | 1 Unit | 2-3 | 12 | 70 | 120 |

With the popular satellite model, large churches begin a satellite church on a new church campus in a growing area of a city.

The senior pastor of the mother church often preaches at both churches until a choice is made about which campus will become the central church. Both sites eventually become strong independent churches.

Unfortunately, these models haven't been used as frequently in traditional overseas mission situations, and they have been used to begin traditional staff-based churches, instead of community cell-based churches.

ADVANTAGES OF A CHURCH TRANSPLANT

A transplanting strategy has several important advantages over the old seed planting method. Transplanting a church has the advantage in the areas of vision, maturity, experience, momentum, vigor, leadership, evangelism, flexibility, multiplication, and options.

First, the new start has a support base with the same vision and values. In fact, the vision, values, and culture have formed within a mother church so that a cell culture is in place. Those coming in with hidden agendas are met with an existing community culture that's protected by a strong core.

Second, the larger and more mature a tree when planted, the stronger it will be and the sooner it will produce fruit. This is true about beginning churches as well. The larger and healthier the church planting team, the stronger the new church will be, and the sooner it will produce fruit. In a transplant, the "tree" is large enough to quickly take root and to grow.

Third, because an experienced and trained team is beginning the new work, the team members are strong enough to model the basic life of the church. A transplant provides tested cell structures and an understanding of the infrastructure of a cell church.

Fourth, momentum can be developed and maintained in a transplant. Essential operating systems can be put into place because cell church infrastructure already exists. Therefore, cells can be set up that can immediately model for new members what it means to live in this kind of church life.

Fifth, a transplant has growth vigor that helps it resist disease and adversity. Peach growers complain that every disease known to man will attack a peach tree. Fruit trees need as much health and vigor as possible to survive and be fruitful. This is also true of a new cell church. A transplanted church has a better ability to overcome adversities than a seed planted with a few Christians.

Sixth, a transplant has enough experienced leaders to model ministry through the life of the cell. Leaders on the team can operate at the four essential leadership levels: coordination, support, supervision, and implementation.

Seventh, evangelism contacts are accelerated. Every team member can lead a special contact group. This gives the team the potential for rapidly increasing the number of people connected to the new start. This potential for accelerated contacts also provides the structure for assimilating the new converts into meaningful and productive community life.

Eighth, a transplant gives flexibility in relation to political and religious opposition. A cell church can begin with high or low visibility and exposure, depending upon the strength of the opposition. A cell church can even be transplanted into a hostile situation.

Ninth, a transplant can begin to multiply much more quickly. Transplanting a cell church greatly accelerates the growth of a new start. The principle of multiplication applies to all areas of church life. "Just as the true fruit of an apple tree is not an apple, but another tree; the true fruit of a small group is not a new Christian, but another group. The true fruit of a church is not a new group, but a new church. The true fruit of a leader is not a follower, but a new leader. The true fruit of an evangelist is not a convert, but new evangelists."[1]

The life of a tree is in a new tree, not in the tree's fruit. The purpose of a tree isn't to produce fruit. The fruit is a secondary benefit for trees. The purpose of a tree is to produce another tree from the fruit. In the bigger picture, the fruit of a tree is an orchard of trees.

Ten, a transplanting model gives a church the option of supporting congregations as part of the mother church, or of transplanting a new church. I began to understand this several years ago when the pastor of a strong growing church presented the case study of his church to me.

The pastor explained that his church had operated for years as one church with several integrated congregations. The congregations were all serviced from the same administrative and logistical structure. The church leaders decided to form the congregations into independent churches (missions) in order to promote more growth. Therefore, leaders were assigned, facilities were developed, ministries were duplicated, and administrative structures were set up in each new church.

The pastor showed me a chart of growth. It revealed a steady increase for several years, but after implementing the independent-congregation strategy, the overall growth immediately leveled off. The pastor commented that they killed their growth "as dead as cold meat."

Why? The support system of administration, logistics, and facilities in the mother church had originally served all the congregations. When these congregations became separate churches, the support system had to be duplicated for each new church. The energy and effort of the new churches was directed toward support systems, rather than toward evangelism and growth.

The support system of administration and coordination in a cell church is like an umbrella that stretches over the church. Internal growth can take place by developing new congregations that are supported and protected by the administrative umbrella of the church. A cell group church can also grow externally by beginning a new church that has its own administrative and logistical umbrella.

Instead of stretching new church starts as thin as possible, the cell group church has the option of stretching the support umbrella over dynamic congregations that focus on evangelism and edification. Then, at the proper time and place, a cell group church can transplant another separate church from its own support umbrella.

In the twenty-first century, after the first wave of cell group church models, I believe cell group churches will be transplanted. Imagine what will happen when cell group churches begin to transplant dynamic churches. This is why there can be such optimism in the face of the population explosion. At a certain point, cell group churches will begin to transplant churches exponentially.

A Transplanting Church Model

Antioch Church in Waco, Texas is a classic example of a church transplant. This church was birthed out of the vision of its pastor, Jimmy Seibert. As a young Christian, he made a request of God. "Lord, if you have a special dream in your heart, dream it through me. And if there is something no one else is willing to do, do it through me."

The vision was birthed in the womb of Highland Baptist Church in Waco, Texas as a college congregation. For a decade, Highland provided a safe environment in which the dream could grow. Jimmy Seibert and this student-centered congregation have been driven by six passions: a passion for prayer, a passion for worship, a passion for cell community, a passion for holiness, a passion for ministry, and a passion for evangelism and missions.

First, prayer has been the driving force that has moved the congregation. Second, the congregation has moved into the presence and glory of God in worship and praise. Third, the congregation was organized into a pure cell structure. Fourth, the congregation used a one-year training course called Master's Commission to develop a committed core of leaders who were "willing to live and die" for Christ. Fifth, the congregation targeted students, one of the groups most responsive to the Gospel. Sixth, the congregation created a dynamic sending arm called Antioch Ministry International.

Effective integrated systems were developed through which these passions could be lived out. Members of the congregation worshiped and prayed passionately. University students and young singles were won and nurtured through the cells. Potential leaders were prepared through short-term mission projects and an intensive discipleship program. Members learned sacrificial ministry in cell life. Finally, these committed Christians were sent around the world to begin new cell churches. This has proved to be a powerful combination.

Highland Baptist Church and the college congregation (including a significant number of older adults) decided to send the college congregation out as a separate church. Antioch Church was transplanted June 6, 1999. Before its first service, the leaders and core members raised $150,000 to purchase an abandoned supermarket near the low-income neighborhoods where the congregation would focus its local ministry. More than 500 people attended the first service at its temporary location at the Heart of Texas Coliseum.

On the first Sunday, the new church sent out a team of twenty members on a mission trip to India. The church began with missionaries in fifteen different countries. By the end of 1999, more than a thousand were participating in worship and cell life. This is a transplant of a church tree of huge proportions that will quickly be able to transplant other churches. I believe the mother church, Highland Baptist Church, will quickly return to its previous size.

Antioch is now applying the transplant principle to its mission strategy. For instance, the church formed a strong team of fourteen leaders who went to Turkey. The strategy of the team is to establish a strong base congregation in one of the population centers of Turkey. This is an example of a transplanted church that's now transplanting other churches. I believe God has prepared this church to transplant trees—and orchards.

CELL GROUP CHURCH MISSIONARY STRATEGY

Bill Beckham

Standing by a small graveyard near Lake Victoria in Kenya, I was deeply moved by the sacrifice of the early missionaries who were buried there. Those graves caused me to think about thousands of missionaries who left the comfort and safety of home to take the Gospel to the remotest corners of the world during the past two centuries. Their lives are a testimony of dedication, courage, and sacrifice.

To expand in the twenty-first century, the church needs the courage and commitment of those early missionaries. However, a different mission paradigm must be used today. It's not enough to change only the practices of missionaries, because churches, denominations, and mission agencies are responsible for missionary strategies. These sending groups must develop new strategies for indigenous missions.

William A. Smalley, former professor of linguistics, defines an indigenous church as one in which "the changes that take place under the guidance of the Holy Spirit meet the needs and fulfill the meanings of that society and not of any outside group."[2]

Smalley believes anything less than a totally indigenous church is a form of paternalism, "because we do not trust the Holy Spirit to adapt the church to culture." He maintains that "we are treating the Holy Spirit as a small child with a new toy too complicated and dangerous to handle. Our paternalism is not only a paternalism toward other peoples; it is also a paternalism toward God."[3]

THE WATER OF LIFE IN FOREIGN CUPS

A story from Indian evangelist Sadhu Sunder Singh illustrates the importance of presenting the Gospel in an indigenous and cultural way. A high-caste Hindu fainted from the summer heat while sitting on a train in a railway station. A train employee ran to a water faucet, filled a cup with water, and brought it to the man. In spite of his condition, the Hindu refused to drink. He would rather die than accept water in the cup of some-one from another caste.

Another person noticed the high-caste passenger had left his own cup on the seat beside him. He grabbed it, filled it with water, and returned to offer it to the panting victim. Immediately he accepted the water with grat-itude.

Singh's comments about the story go to the very heart of indigenous missions. "This is what I have been trying to say to missionaries from abroad. You have been offering the water of life to the people of India in a foreign cup, and we have been slow to receive it. If you will offer it in our own cup … in an indigenous form … then we are much more likely to accept it."[4]

The following four interrelated principles are essential in order for the church to offer the water of life in indigenous, rather than foreign, cups. We'll look at each principle in detail in this chapter, and use them as foun-dational principles for developing mission strategy.

- An indigenous sequence is essential.
- Nationals are the best indigenous missionaries.
- Cities are the proper place to begin indigenous missions.
- Strategic churches are the greatest hope for indigenous expansion.

AN INDIGENOUS SEQUENCE IS ESSENTIAL

In Acts 1:8, Jesus gives the direction and the sequence of the Gospel. Jesus' followers and the Gospel are to go to "Jerusalem, Judea, Samaria, and the world." This phrase has both a geographical and cultural connotation. However, the presence of the word "Samaria" suggests that culture is important to how Jesus used the phrase. His Gospel is to penetrate every geographical area, people group, and culture.

The follow grid helps us visualize the indigenous sequence of the church. The left circle suggests that the most culturally forgiving mission context is to share the Gospel in a major city, a Jerusalem. The right circle suggests that the least culturally forgiving mission context is a village out in the world, because witnessing must cross major barriers of language, cul-ture, prejudice, finance, and distance.

Jesus strung the sequence of Jerusalem, Judea, Samaria, and the world together for a reason. Each point becomes more culturally distant from the preceding one. To go directly from "Jerusalem" to the "world" is too great a distance, both geographically and culturally. In the chart below, I've added the bottom sequence of a major city, a city, a town, and a village. This sequence also reflects distance between each place that's too great to ignore. A great distance separates a major city from a village, and that distance is important in developing an indigenous strategy.

The chart also includes Ralph Winter's wonderful insights on three types of witness he identifies in Acts 1:8: E-1 Witness, E-2 Witness, and E-3 Witness.4 Winter's teaching supports the importance of sequence in missions, and provides a way to chart a mission journey.

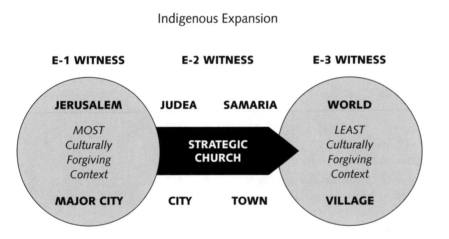

Indigenous Expansion

1. Penetration into Jerusalem and Judea is E-1 witness. E-1 is "near neighbor" witness and only needs to penetrate one level: the level of communication. E-1 is "near" witness.

2. Penetration into Samaria is E-2 witness. E-2 is "bridge" witness that must cross over the level of communicating the Gospel, plus the level of prejudice and culture. E-2 is "close" witness.

3. Penetration into the "world" is E-3 witness. E-3 is "cross-cultural" witness, is utterly different in language and culture, and is the most extreme of all witness. E-3 is "far" and foreign witness.

Winter believes "the easiest, most obvious surge forward in evangelism in the world today will come if Christian believers in every part of the world are moved to reach outside their churches and win their cultural near neighbors to Christ. They are better able to do this than any foreign missionary."5

The New Testament church "turned the world upside down" with E-1 evangelism when the first converts returned home and witnessed to their friends, families, and fellow countrymen.

The old foreign missionary strategy has had a measure of success, until it's measured against the New Testament church. The New Testament church was able to maximize E-1 witness and E-2 witness. Many different people groups were in Jerusalem on the day of Pentecost. However, they received an E-1 and E-2-witness from Jews of the same religion, language, and in many cases, culture. Maybe in the beginning this wasn't an intentional strategy on the part of the Apostles. It was certainly God's strategy for the expansion of the church.

Winter suggests that four out of five of the lost people in the world can't be reached with E-1 "neighbor" witness or E-2 "bridge" witness. Given the old foreign mission paradigm and strategies, this may be true. It's very difficult for the traditional large group church to participate in New Testament E-1 expansion.

The church is restricted to use E-3 witness, where foreign missionaries are sent to witness to people in culturally distant areas. These strategies for sending foreign (E-3) missionaries have been more popular than strategies for preparing and sending national churches to nearby areas. To send nationals out from indigenous churches is E-1 and E-2 witness.

However, a cell-based transplant model can maximize E-1 and E-2 encounters and minimize the dependence upon E-3 encounters for church growth. The goal of the church in every mission opportunity must be to give the water of life in indigenous (E-1 and E-2) cups.

NATIONALS ARE THE BEST INDIGENOUS MISSIONARIES

The church must develop strategies to use nationals in close-cultural missions that complement its cross-cultural mission strategy. Let me state this national "close-cultural" principle. The greater the distance from Jerusalem, the more indigenous leaders are needed to help establish strategic bases. This indicates that E-3 witness is the most difficult of all the witness types.

Winter concludes that "E-1 evangelism ... where a person communicates to his own people ... is obviously the most potent kind of evangelism."[6] The challenge is to find strategies that multiply quality E-1 encounters.

In 1997, Cesar A. Buitrago, pastor of a growing Spanish-speaking cell church in San Jose, California, traveled to Spain on a mission trip. On the first part of the trip, Cesar trained cell group leaders. Toward the end of the trip, he visited Morocco.

During the four-hour ferry ride from the Spanish coast to Tangier, Morocco, Cesar noticed hundreds of Moroccans travelling to Tangier with large briefcases and electrical appliances. These Moroccans lived in Europe and returned to Morocco once a year.

After returning to Spain, Cesar met a pastor who had been trying to begin a church in Morocco for seven years. During those years this pastor had only three converts. He was betrayed by one of these "disciples," jailed, and finally expelled from the country for witnessing to Muslims. He now lives in Spain, but his burden is still to reach the Muslims in Morocco.

Cesar was deeply touched by the story of this pastor. He wondered, "In light of this kind of resistance to the Gospel by the people and government of Morocco, how can God possibly reach that Muslim country?" Then, he remembered the hundreds of Moroccans he had seen on the ferry traveling from Europe to Tangier. He made the strategy connection. "The most natural and easy thing to do would be to plant a Moroccan church in Spain, where we have total religious freedom among these Moroccans who already speak Spanish, and later, send national Moroccan missionaries to their own country."

Cesar concluded, "We need a paradigm shift in missions. Very sadly, many outside groups are still trying to reach the Muslims in Morocco, while thousands of Muslims in Spain have no Christian witness." In other words, Cesar realized that E-3 witness was ineffective in Morocco. But, he also realized that E-1 and E-2 witness was possible with the Moroccans who lived in Europe. The European Moroccans who become Christians could become E-1 witnesses to family, friends, and fellow countrymen in Morocco.

Cesar left his mission ferry ride with a new mission revelation. Unfortunately, most Christian leaders get off their mission ferry rides with the same old mission paradigm. Consequently, foreign missionaries continue to be sent to countries and people groups that are difficult to penetrate by outsiders.

CITIES ARE THE PLACE TO BEGIN INDIGENOUS MISSIONS

In the nineteenth century, most of the first Christian missionaries to

Thailand traveled north by boat from Bangkok as far as they could go. Then they rode elephants into the jungles. Then they walked or took canoes into the tribal areas of the country.

These animistic tribes tended to be more responsive to the Gospel than the thousands of Thai Buddhists these missionaries passed on their journey to the jungles. However, these tribes were also the most culturally extreme segment of Thai society. Because of cultural differences, it was impossible for the early missionaries to use the Christians in the tribes to evangelize the other native Thais.

In fact, Christianity was stereotyped as a simple religion that could fool the uneducated tribal people, but couldn't compete with the sophisticated philosophy of Buddhism. Consequently, for more than 100 years, an indigenous Thai face was not given to the Gospel. As a result, Thailand remains one of the least Christian nations in the world.

What would have happened if the first missionaries in Thailand had established indigenous urban bases in Bangkok and other principal cities? We can only speculate about the results, but I believe there can be no speculation about what the New Testament strategy would have been. Jesus or Paul would have penetrated the major people group in an urban center.

Jesus understood the importance of cities and established the flow of missions out from them. A major portion of his ministry was committed to Jerusalem. His sequence of mission expansion took the Gospel from major cities to smaller cities, to towns, and finally to villages.

Paul also made the city the geographical and cultural epicenter for the expansion of the church. According to Roger Greenway, in Apostle to the City, Paul's strategy was to reach the cities. The early church built base churches in the major cities of Ephesus, Antioch, Damascus, Corinth, and Rome.

The city must be the staging point for indigenous missions in the twenty-first century. Of the six billion people who presently live in the world, nearly three billion are urban dwellers. Over 200,000 new urban dwellers are added daily and seventy-eight million annually. This is the equivalent of adding a new Dallas every five days, or a new Thailand each year. Migration is producing up to sixty percent of the urban growth, with the rest coming from natural increase.

During the life of William Carey, the father of "modern" missions, five percent of the world lived in cities. By the year 1900, approximately nine percent of the population were urban dwellers. Today, fifty percent live in cities. In 1995, seventy percent of the people in the U.S. and Europe lived in urban areas. In fifty years, it's estimated that eighty percent of the people in the world will live in a city.

This is why the strategy for church expansion in the New Testament is so significant. In a primarily rural world (at least ninety percent in rural situations), the first century church had an urban to rural strategy and not a rural to urban strategy. Why? The city offers the best opportunity for neighbor and bridge witness.

I'm not advocating the neglect of rural areas in the world. I am calling for an emphasis upon New Testament urban missions to birth a movement that can eventually penetrate the towns and villages with E-1 and E-2 witness.

STRATEGIC CHURCHES ARE THE GREATEST HOPE FOR INDIGENOUS EXPANSION

In order to expand the church in the twenty-first century, strategic churches must be developed in population centers where people who are culturally different work and live. Notice the strategic church arrow between the two circles in the Indigenous Expansion Grid. A strategic church is the connecting link in the expansion of the church from Jerusalem to the world and from cities to villages.

I call these "strategic churches" because of where they're located, and because of the kind of churches they are. They're located in population centers where people who need to be reached by the Gospel live and work. These strategic churches are reproducible cell-based churches that have the capacity to train every member for holiness and harvest.

The following steps are involved in developing strategic churches:

- Begin with a church in a major population center.
- Target and win converts from groups that haven't received the Gospel.

- Train these "bridge" Christians.
- Send those nationals back to their own smaller cities to establish other indigenous strategic churches.
- Strategic churches in the smaller cities send nationals to towns where strategic churches are built.
- From the town base, surrounding villages are evangelized by villagers won in the town.

This strategy process gives the church a way to maximize its E-1 witness encounters, and to escape missions at the cultural extreme of E-3 far and foreign missions. In other words, it maximizes quality E-1 and E-2 encounters by building indigenous churches in strategic mission areas.

A strategic church strategy is practically indigenous, because it uses a mother church to coordinate the extension of the Gospel to the most distant people groups. It's culturally indigenous, because it sends indigenous teams to witness to those who are most like them. Establishing strategic churches is financially indigenous, because each strategic church is able to support the startup of other strategic churches in smaller cities and towns. It's strategically indigenous, because it can gradually adapt the cell group church strategy to all types of cultures.

Of course, there are always exceptions, where E-3 foreign missionaries are the only way. However, our goal in the twenty-first century must be a "near and close" missionary strategy.

An exception to the strategic church approach may be more isolated tribes that are small in numbers, cut off from the culture around them, and have no written language. Special mission groups such as New Tribes have been called to this unique mission role. However, even in these situations, national Christians who are connected to these tribes in trade, marriage, or proximity may be a better alternative than sending foreign missionaries.

A more indigenous approach would be for an outside expert in linguistic skills to train a local national "bridge" Christian from a nearby strategic church. Then send that "bridge" Christian to live with a tribe, translate the Bible into its language, and begin a strategic church that can penetrate the rest of the tribe.

PAZ: INDIGENOUS MODEL IN THE AMAZON

A ministry in Brazil that works in the Amazon River Basin is a good example of this strategy. Paz International is a ministry founded in 1976 by Luke and Christine Huber. It's headquartered in the city of Santarem in northern Brazil. Over a period of twenty years, Paz has started more than 250 churches in the Amazon Basin, as well as in Japan, Portugal, and Mozambique.

Paz International represents all the exciting and good things associated with frontline missions. First of all, Paz is centered in the Amazon Basin. This river system has ten separate basins, each as large as the Mississippi River Basin in the United States. The Amazon Basin consists of seventeen million people who live in an unexplored frontier, covering 2.3 million square miles of rainforest, lakes, and tributaries.

Paz people build boats, outfit them, and send them up and down the tributaries of the Amazon. In addition to their boats, they fly into inaccessible areas. Paz is involved in educational ministry. Under local church supervision, Christian elementary schools are functioning in many of the cities and towns along the rivers. Paz's medical boats help river people with health care, food, clothing, and other forms of social assistance. Paz also helps construct wells up and down the rivers.

I first came into contact with this ministry in 1997. Paz's vision hasn't changed over the years. Its vision is to plant 100,000 churches focusing on the Amazon Basin and to fuel a nationally-led movement to establish God's Kingdom in a great harvest field across the world. Luke Huber, the mission's late founder, wanted to see at least one church in each of the Amazon's estimated 80,000 villages.

God has changed and adjusted the method for the vision to be implemented. The ministry now thinks in terms of strong strategic churches in the population centers of the Amazon Basin. The vision begins in cities and moves to villages, instead of beginning and ending with villages. Paz envisions strong base cell group churches that will be centers for training, supporting, financing, and sending teams into towns, and from the towns into the villages. Paz has divided the Basin into fifteen strategic areas, each with an existing or proposed base of operation.

In the past, Paz worked more from the traditional mission base paradigm. A mission base consisted of a team of missionaries in an area who train, plan, and send missionaries into towns and villages to plant churches. Now, they've begun to think more in terms of church bases. The strategy is to develop strong Antioch-type cell group church bases in strategic areas. These base churches will then be responsible for implementing the church planting/transplanting strategy into surrounding cities, towns, and villages.

Jeff Hrubrik, Director of Paz International, expressed the strategy of this ministry in a recent update. "We want to strategically move into each municipality beginning with the key cities. Although our ultimate goal is the river villages, we have learned that we need a strong base to raise up local leaders, prayer covering, and financial support to then spread out to the 'uttermost parts' or the hidden river villages."[7]

HOPE OF BANGKOK: INDIGENOUS URBAN MODEL

Over the past two decades, Hope of Bangkok Church has grown to be one of the largest churches in Thailand. It has the most aggressive and successful expansion strategy of all church groups in that Buddhist nation.

This cell group church began as a "vacuum cleaner" model, and sucked up many members and leaders from other churches in Bangkok and the surrounding regions. To be completely fair, most of the earlier successful churches in Bangkok also used this same approach. However, Hope of Bangkok was more successful at it and continued to court leaders and members from other churches for a longer period of time.

Hope of Bangkok went another step beyond the other "vacuum cleaner" churches. Not only were members and leaders from other churches recruited to be part of the early core, but entire churches were allowed, if not encouraged, to change the name on their church sign and join Hope of Bangkok.

This aggressive proselytizing led to an ugly schism between Hope of Bangkok and other churches in Thailand. In one of the least Christian nations in the world, the church polarized. Today a large percentage of the members of this church and its daughter churches are new converts, but old suspicions and feelings still remain.

The traditional churches in Thailand compounded the mistakes made by Hope of Bangkok, by overreacting to the perceived threat of the new church. It's difficult to see how revival can break out in Thailand until this wound is healed. (Please join with me in prayer for the reconciliation of the church in Thailand.)

However, these mistakes should not negate the lessons that can be learned from this model. In one of the most difficult countries of the world for Christianity to grow, this church has grown significantly. It has grown for several reasons:

- This church has a dynamic cell-based ministry.
- This church is indigenous (founded by a Thai leader who became a Christian while studying in Australia).
- The movement has an urban strategy of beginning churches in regional cities.
- From its beginning, this church has had an intentional and aggressive growth strategy.

We learn from this flawed but powerful model that urban, indigenous cell churches with a strategy will grow, just as they did in the first century.

END NOTES

Stage 1

[1] Ralph W. Neighbour, Jr. *Where Do We Go From Here?* (Houston: TOUCH Publications, 1990), 92.

[2] David Yonggi Cho with Harold Hostetler, *Successful Home Cell Groups* (Gainesville, FL: Bridge Logos, 1981), 17.

[3] Karen Hurston, "A Day in the Life of a Staff Pastor: A Study in Contrasts." Hurston Ministries accessed on 3/12/03. <http://www.hurstonministries.org>

[4] Ralph W. Neighbour, Jr. *Seven Last Words of the Church* (Nashville: Broadman, 1973), 25.

[5] Karen Hurston, *Breakthrough Cell Groups: How One American Church Reaches People for Christ through Creative Small Groups* (Houston: TOUCH Publications, 2001), 25-26.

[6] Jean Vanier, *Community and Growth*, Revised Edition (Mahwah, NJ: Paulist Press, 1989), 99-100.

[7] Gregory Nazianzen, *Oratoines*, 40.41 in T.F. Torrance, *The Christian Doctrine of God: One Being Three Persons* (Edinburgh: T & T Clark, 1996), 112.

[8] Francis Schaeffer, *The Church at the End of the Twentieth Century* (Crossway Books, 1994), 47

[9] Didache reads regarding baptism, "The procedure for baptizing is as follows. After repeating all that has been said, immerse in running water 'In the Name of the Father, and of the Son, and of the Holy Ghost.'"

[10] James H. Rutz, *The Open Church* (Auburn, MA: Seedsowers), 11,

[11] H. G. Bosch, "He Left No Vacancy," Our Daily Bread, May 1974, quoted in James F. Engel and H. Wilbert Norton, *What's gone Wrong with the Harvest?* (Grand Rapids: Zondervan Publishing House, 1975), 156.

[12] Christian History Magazine, Issue 60, Vol. XVII, No.4; p. 36.

[13] An Ancient and Undying light, Giorgio Bouchard, Christian History, Volume VIII, Number 2, Issue 22, p. 8.

[14] Martin Luther, *Luther's Works*, vol. 53, Preface to the German Mass and Order of Service, gen. ed. Helmut T. Lehmann, trans. Paul Zeller Strodach (Philadelphia: Fortress Press, 1965) 63-64.

[15] Michael Henderson, *John Wesley's Class Meetings*, (Evangel Publishing House, 1997), 132.

[16] Ibid., 94.

[17] Ibid., 28.

[18] James S. Stewart, *The Strong Name, Scribners*, 67-69.

[19] Peter M. Senge, *The Fifth Discipline* (New York: Currency Doubleday, 1994), 223-224.

[20] Stephen R. Covey, *Principle-Centered Leadership* (New York: Simon and Schuster, 1992), 314.

[21] Senge, 209.

[22] Robert E. Coleman, *The Master Plan of Evangelism*, 37.

[23] Stephen E. Ambrose, *Citizen Soldiers* (New York: Touchstone, 1997), 332.

[24] Coleman, 21.

[25] Ibid.

[26] Ibid., 33.

[27] Ibid., 34.

[28] Ibid., 35.

[29] Ibid., 109.

[30] Ambrose, 473.

[31] Ibid.

Stage 2

[1] John C. Maxwell, *The 17 Indisputable Laws of Teamwork* (Nashville: Thomas-Nelson, 2001), 49.

[2] Adapted from John P. Kotter, *The Heart of Change* (Boston: Harvard Business School Press, 2002), 46.

[3] Robert Wuthnow, *Sharing the Journey: Support Groups and America's New Quest for Community* (New York: The Free Press, 1994), 49.

[4] Church growth specialists who advocate small groups include: Peter Wagner, Carl George, Christian Schwarz, Robert Logan, Donald McGavran, Gary McIntosh, and Eddie Gibbs.

[5] Bill Beckham, *The Two-Winged Church Will Fly* (Houston: TOUCH Publications, n.d.)

[6] Ralph W. Neighbour, Jr. *Where Do We Go From Here*, Revised Edition (Houston: TOUCH Publications, 2000), 220.

[7] Beckham, 27.

[8] Joel Comiskey. *Reap the Harvest* (Houston: TOUCH Publications, 1999), 109.

[9] Robert E. Logan, *Beyond Church Growth* (Tarrytown, NY: Fleming H. Revell Company, 1989), 124.

[10] Billy Hornsby, *Becoming a Cell Church: Transition*, Tape 4: The Successful Cell Group, audio tape.

[11] This list is based on the original research of Joel Comiskey that has been clearly presented in the book *Home Cell Group Explosion* (Houston: TOUCH Publications: 1998).

[12] *Victory Cell Leader Manual and Training Notebook*, pages 40-41, and cell conference tapes.

[13] Bill Donahue. *The Willow Creek Guide to Leading Life-Changing Small Groups* (Grand Rapids: Zondervan, 1996), 82.

[14] Bill Donahue and Russ Robinson, *Seven Deadly Sins of Small Group Ministry* (Grand Rapids: Zondervan, 2002), 154.

[15] Ted Haggard, *Dog Training, Fly Fishing, and Sharing Christ*

in the 21st Century: Empowering Your Church To Build Community through Shared Interests (Nashville: Thomas Nelson, 2002), 23.

[16] Ralph W. Neighbour, Jr., *Where Do We Go From Here*, Revised Edition (Houston: TOUCH Publications, 2000), 294.

[17] Ken Hemphill, *Revitalizing the Sunday Morning Dinosaur: A Sunday School Growth Strategy for the 21st Century* (Nashville: Broadman & Holman, 1996), 87.

[18] E. Stanley Jones, *The Way* , 272.

[19] Deitrich Bonhoeffer, *Life Together* (San Fransisco: Harper and Row, 1954),?

[20] Ibid., 111-121.

[21] Ibid., 119.

[22] Henderson, 107.

[23] *Civilization and its Discontents* (New York: W. W. Norton & Company, 1962, 24.

[24] Bonhoeffer, 93.

[25] Elton Trueblood, *The Company of the Committed* (New York: Harper and Brothers, 1961), 76.

[26] Bonhoeffer, 88.

[27] Ibid., 86.

[28] Elizabeth O'Connor, *New Community*, 83.

[29] Bonhoeffer, 90.

[30] Henderson, 102.

[31] Ibid., 104.

[32] Ibid., 107.

[33] Ibid., 132.

[34] Ray Stedman, *Body Life* (Ventura, CA: Regal Books, ?), 107.

[35] Ibid., 108.

Stage 4

[1] William A. Beckham, *Redefining Revival* (Houston: TOUCH Publications, 2000), 141.

[2] Personal email sent to me on Tuesday, June 10, 2003.

[3] Personal email from Steve Mack on Wednesday, June 11, 2003.

[4] Personal email sent to me on Saturday, June 07, 2003.

[5] The following three books are written by Anglican pastors about the cell church movement among the Anglican church in England. You'll notice how recent these books are.

> Howard Austin, *Body and Cell: Making the transition to the cell church—a first hand account* (Mill Hill, London: Monarch Books, 2002), 174.
> Phil Potter, *The Challenge of the Cell Church* (Oxford, England: The Bible Reading Fellowship, 2001), 175.
> Michael Green, ed. *Church without Walls: A Global Examination of the Cell Church* (Great Britain: Paternoster Press, 2002), 133. Each chapter is written by a different Anglican pastor.

[6] Larry Kreider, Ron Myer, Steve Prokopchak, Brian Sauder, *The Biblical Role of Elders for Today's Church* (Ephrata, PA: House to House, 2003).

[7] Ibid., 53. Tom Brunner, pastor of Hope Church, has been transitioning a 100 year old CMA church in Indianapolis, Indiana. He writes, "Currently all our board are in cells, all the elders are cell leaders, the one non-elder board member is a cell intern. This has made a huge difference in our board discussions since everyone is involved in leading cell meetings, taking people through our equipping track and mentoring someone, building/praying/working blessing lists."

[8] Ibid., 246. Many churches also require members to tithe. Ted Haggard says, "Members shall be all people who contribute financially to the Cooperation (church). Membership is granted and recognized with voting powers when a person has attended the church long enough to receive an annual contributions statement. A contribution statement is the certificate of membership. Should one year pass without a record of contribution, membership is automatically terminated (Ted Haggard, *The Life Giving Church* (Ventura, CA: Regal Books, 1998), 225).

[9] Personal email from Steve Mack on Wednesday, June 11, 2003.

[10] Personal email sent to me on Friday, June 13, 2003.

[11] Peter Wagner, *Churchquake* (Ventura, CA: Regal Books, 1999), 89.

[12] Many boards view the pastor as:
> • Pastors are paid a salary to minister as an employee of the church.
> • Pastors come and pastors go. (Southern Baptist tenure is 2.3 years; U.S. Methodist is 4.3 years).
> • Pastors are subject to performance reviews

Lyle Shaller wrote a book called *Tattered Trust* in which he emphasizes how denominations have replaced personal relationships with the rules and regulations. The manual that sets forth the rules and regulations in the Christian Missionary Alliance, contains 83,500 words. The Nazarenes have one that is 96,000 words and that the minutes alone of 1993 annual council of the Assemblies of God contained 555,500 words (Peter Wagner, *Churchquake* (Ventura, CA: Regal Books, 1999), 83, 89). The constitution of Chuck Squeri, senior pastor of Fellowship Christian Church of Cincinnati, Ohio, reads: "SENIOR PASTOR – as President of Corporation, and Head of All Ministries chooses the Philosophy of Ministry, and FIRST AMONGST EQUALS amongst the Elders ability to Discipline Members." Chuck tells me that before the constitution was rewritten his church was unable to act because of multiple visions for ministry.

[13] Lawrence Khong, *The Apostolic Cell Church: Practical Strategies for Growth and Outreach from the Story of Faith*

Community Baptist Church (Singapore: Touch Ministries International, 2000), 108.

[14] Christian A. Schwarz, *Natural Church Development: A Guide to Eight Essential Qualities of Healthy Churches* (St. Charles, IL: ChurchSmart Resources, 1996), 30.

Stage 5

[1] Brian Sander and Sarah Mohler, *Youth Cells and Youth Ministry*, (Ephrata, PA: House to House, 1997), 45.

[2] Daphne Kirk wrote these words on cellchurchtalk on 1/1/2003.

[3] Sander and Mohler, 20.

[4] Philip Woolford [pkwool@iprimus.com.au] wrote to cell churchtalk on Thurday, January 02, 2003.

[5] Sander and Mohler, 19.

[6] Ibid., 20.

[7] Our youth pastor, Dennis Fiallos, formed a G-12 group of youth cell leaders. Since we used a G-12.3 pastoral care structure (staff coach twelve cell leaders and lay leaders coach three), each of these key lay leaders seeks to multiply his or her own cell three times, while caring for the new daughter cell leaders. The youth pastor should feel the liberty to replace members of his G-12 group with more fruitful members as time goes on. In other words, it's not a permanent G-12 group. This should be clear from the beginning. Fruitfulness, faithfulness, and above all dedication to God must always be the reason why someone participates in the inner circle.

[8] Written by Highland Baptist College Ministries, *Reaching College Students through Cells* (Houston, TX: 1997), 127.

[9] Sander and Mohler, 24.

[10] Personal email from John Church on Wednesday, June 11, 2003.

[11] Jeanette Buller wrote these words on cellchurchtalk, an email chat group on 3/24/2001.

Stage 6

[1] Peter Wagner, Churches that Pray (Ventura, CA: Regal Books, 1993), 114.

[2] Ibid., 121.

[3] I recommend that every cell church have a cell information table. This table functions during the celebration service and provides the cell lessons, equipping track manuals, cell information (dates, times, locations), weekly cell reports, etc. A cell volunteer (preferably a cell leader) should be available at the table to answer questions. If you have a cell secretary, he or she should be available at the table during the Sunday worship services.

[4] Rob Reimer sent me this email on 7/25/2002.

[5] Randall Neighbour, "The Goal is Clear: Live our Your Purpose," *Cell Group Journal*, Vol. 9, no. 2 (Spring 2000): 16.

[6] Jim Pesce, "Fasting for Results," *Cell Group Journal*, Vol. 9, no.

2 (Spring 2000): 30.

[7] Dale Galloway, *The Small Group Book* (Grand Rapids, MI: Fleming H. Revell, 1995), 62.

[8] Dan Godard wrote to Small Groups Network, http://www.smallgroups.com/ on 4/05/2001 at 18:05:50.

[9] Howard A. Snyder, *The Radical Wesley and Patterns for Church Renewal* (Downers Grove, IL: InterVarsity Press, 1980), 55.

[10] David Sheppard, *Built As A City: God and the Urban World Today* (London: Hodder and Stoughton Publishers, 1974), 127.

[11] Mario Vega sent to me this email on 11/22/2002.

[12] David Yonggi Cho, *Successful Home Cell Groups* (Miami, FL: Logos International 1981), 59.

[13] A great tool for such groups is ???

[14] Four booklets of the Track Pack (Houston, TX: Touch Publications, 1996) focus on teaching the new believer to reach out to non-Christians. Also in *The Shepherd's Guidebook: A Leader's Guide for the Cell Group Church* (Houston, TX: Touch Publications, 1992), 27, Ralph Neighbour Jr. deals with the different classes of believers.

[15] Ralph Neighbour Jr., *Building Groups Opening Hearts* (Houston: Touch Publications, 1991), 60.

[16] Steve Porter wrote this comment on cellchurchtalk on 4/7/99.

[17] Kenneth Behr on <mailto:smalltalk@smallgroups.com> smalltalk@smallgroups.com, 4/7/1999.

[18] Ralph W. Neighbour Jr,. *The Shepherd's Guidebook* (Houston: TOUCH Publications, 1994), 26.

[19] Neighbour, *How to Mentor Another Christian* (Houston: TOUCH Publications, 2001).

[20] Neighbour, *The Arrival Kit*, Revised Edition (Houston: TOUCH Publications, 2001), 11.

[21] Castellanos says that before teaching these Post-Encounter lessons, 70% of the people left the church in two to three months after attending an Encounter Retreat. Since the Post-Encounters, Pastor Castellanos says that they now conserve 100% of the fruit (César Castellanos, cell seminar in May 1998 in Quito, Ecuador). This percentage appears extremely high to me, nor can I be sure of its statistical validity. It is, however, an actual quote from César Castellanos.

[22] One year ago, ICM offered four lessons that dealt with how to deal with temptation, spiritual warfare, how to live a holy life (especially as it relates to dealing with non-Christian friends), and how to administer finances.

[23] Mercedes de Acevedo, *Formando para Formar*, Audio tape.

[24] In October 1996, attendance at a second Encounter Retreat was only a requirement for the youth cell group leaders. By March 1997, the whole church required the second retreat. It is common knowledge at ICM that the ministry of the young people is the most effective in the entire church. I heart from

several leaders that ideas and methods are first proven among the young people and if they work they are implemented in the entire church.

25 Thomas Peters, *Thriving on Chaos* (New York: Harper Perennial, 1987), 284.

26 Ibid.

27 John Ayot, *Dictionary of Word Origins* "Coach" (New York: Arcade Publishing, 1990).

28 David B. Peterson and Mary Dee Hicks, *Leader as Coach: Strategies for Coaching and Developing Others* (Minneapolis, MN: Personnel Decisions International, 1996), 14.

29 If you are coaching the daughter cell leader from your own cell, I would encourage you to continue to lead your cell group. The leader under your care will respect your counsel in a new way, knowing that it comes from someone who is living the life. Some coaches see their role as graduation from the hands-on ministry in the cell group. This could not be further from the tr0uth. In order to encourage cell leaders, a coach must be able to say, "I've been there." At a minimum, coaches should participate in a cell group to continue experiencing cell life so that their lives speak as models. It is even better if coaches can continue leading a cell group while coaching. (This can usually be done when coaching three leaders or fewer.)
The best coaches are those who have successfully led and multiplied a cell group. Why? Because they know what it's like to experience the pain of giving birth, the joys of ministry, and the struggles of evangelism. They can offer a fresh word and relevant counsel to those they're coaching.

30 Steven L. Ogne. Audio tape. *Empowering Leaders through Coaching* (ChurchSmart Resources, 1995).

31 Billy Hornsby, *The Cell-Driven Church: Bringing in the Harvest* (Mansfield, PA: Fire Wind: 2000), 79.

32 Laura Whitworth, Henry Kimsey-House, Phil Sandahl, *Co-Active Coaching* (Palo Alto, CA: Davies-Black Publishing, 1998), 99.

33 Bill Donahue, *Building a Church of Small Groups* (Grand Rapids, MI: Zondervan Publications, 2001), 146.

34 You might even be reading this book to discover how to coach those leaders under you who are also coaching others (those who have multiplication cell leaders under their care). If you're in that situation, I would encourage you to train those coaches under your care in the principles highlighted in this book. The chapters in this book will help them to more effectively coach their own cell leaders

Stage 7

1 Carl George, "What is a Meta-Church?" *CellChurch Magazine*, vol.2 issue 2, 5.

2 Joel Comiskey, *Reap the Harvest* (Houston, TOUCH Publications, 1999), 51.

3 Lawrence Khong says, "The cell group church is vision driven. It needs a strong leader to rally the people toward the God-given vision. Because it is also structured like the military, it calls for a strong commander to instill a sense of strict spiritual discipline to complete the task" (Lawrence Khong, *The Apostolic Cell Church: Practical Strategies for Growth and Outreach from the Story of Faith Community Baptist Church.* (Singapore: Touch Ministries International, 2000), 108).

4 Galloway said this to a group of pastors at the Republic Church on Thursday, June 29, 2000.

5 As quoted in Thoene, Bodie & Brock, *Writer to Writer* (Minneapolis, MN: Bethany House Publishers, 1990), p. 58.

6 For more information, please contact Neville Chamberlin at nevc@hknet.com or goodhews@csranet.com. You can also visit their web site at http://www.ln.com.ua/~emmanuel/ccmn.html or http://www.ccn.org.hk/english.htm

7 Carl George, *How to Break Growth Barriers* (Grand Rapids, MI: Baker Book House, 1993), 104.

8 Part of the reason that we start by reviewing cell statistics rather than the celebration needs is to change our conventional paradigms. Before becoming a cell church, we spend the vast majority of our time talking about programs in the church. Cell ministry, as one of those programs, received some attention. Now as a cell church, we've made it the goal to start with this focus and to always keep it central.

9 George Barna, *The Habits of Highly Effective Churches* (Ventura, CA: Regal Books, 1999), 62

10 Dale Galloway, *20-20 Vision* (Portland, OR: Scott Publishing House, 1986), 156.

11 Larry Stockstill, "G-12 System," Holding the Harvest Conference, November 1998. Audio Cassette.

12 James C. Collins & Jerry I. Porras, *Built to Last: Successful Habits of Visionary Companies* (New York: HarperCollins Publishers, 1994), 173.

13 Carl George, *Prepare Your Church for the Future* (Grand Rapids, MI: Fleming H. Revell, 1992), 60.

14 Of the eight case study churches, only Faith Community Baptist Church allowed their cell leaders to baptize. They serve communion and baptize. The cell is the church and the cell leader is the pastor. I have always felt that such pressure was unnatural and unnecessary. None of the cell churches in Latin America allowed the cells to serve communion nor baptize (Living Water Church sometimes allowed their cell leaders to baptize, but it wasn't the rule). Nor does Yoido Full Gospel Church, the forerunner of the modern cell movement, allow cell leaders to administer the sacraments within the cell. Again, it seems to me that such an immense leadership responsibility is unnecessary.

15 This is another weakness that I find in the house church model. The pastor of a small house church is expected to do everything: pastor, teach, marry, bury, counsel, etc. The cell church asks each member to facilitate a small group of believers, but also provides trained pastors who are able to handle more difficult pastoral functions.

16 David Yonggi Cho, *Church Growth. Manual No. 7.* (Seoul, Korea: Church Growth International, 1995), 18.

17 Ibid.

18 Ted W. Engstrom, *The Making of a Christian Leader* (Grand Rapids, MI: Zondervan Publishing House, 1976), 106.

19 Donald McGavran, *Understanding Church Growth*, 3rd Edition (Grand Rapids, MI: William B. Eerdmans Publishing Company, 1990), 265.

20 All churches can measure weekend attendance, and thus it's a common standard in measuring church growth success. Membership definitions vary from church to church and not all churches have Sunday school. Thus, attendance is normally used to measure church growth success.

21 Larry J. Crabb, Jr. and Dan B. Allender, *Encouragement: The Key to Caring* (Grand Rapids, MI: Zondervan Publishing House, 1984), p. 52).

22 Christian Schwarz, *Natural Church Development* (Carol Steam, IL: ChurchSmart Resources), 44.

23 You can see from the below list that these churches are constantly breaking records:
- Yoido Full Gospel Church (25,000+ cells)
- Bethany World Prayer Center (900 cells)
- International Charismatic Mission (20,000 cells)
- Elim Church (11,000 cells when counting children's cells)
- Christian Center of Guayaquil (2,000 cells)
- Love Alive Church (1,000 cells)
- Living Water Church (900 cells)
- Faith Community Baptist Church (600 cells)

24 Dale Galloway, *20-20 Vision* (Portland, OR: Scott Publishing House, 1986), 155.

25 I started my cell network with five cells in 1997. My wife and I set the goal of twenty-one cells for 1998, and we exceeded that goal by two. We sensed the joy and accomplishment of victory, but we were also painfully aware of weaker cells within our network. For a variety of reasons, we as a pastoral team decided to set a huge cell goal for 1999: 250 cell groups. My wife and I were responsible to grow our network from twenty-three cells to sixty cells in one year. We grudgingly accepted, but looking back from the advantage of hindsight, I now realize that we should have said no. The goal of forty-five cells would have been far more realistic and feasible. Wanting to carry our weight on the pastoral team, we accepted. We felt driven to meet the goal of sixty cells,

and we did meet the goal. However, many of our cells lacked quality. In January 2000, Celyce and I turned over our network of cells to national pastors. In the process approximately twelve of our cells died. They were just not healthy enough to stand the transition. As we look back, the goal of forty-five would have been challenging but realistic. Sixty was out of the ballpark.

26 I've seen the International Charismatic Mission change their cell statistics from 24,000 to 18,000 for this reason. Bethany World Prayer Center, using the G-12 model, skyrocketed from 300+ cells to 900 cells in two years. Yet, in the year 2000 they reduced the number from 900 to 600. Why? Billy Hornsby wrote to me, "Spring Cleaning! We "consolidated" about 200 groups. Some of the groups were not really a "G-12" prototype and had no real chance to multiply and for some other reasons others didn't meet the criteria that we expected. So, we closed them. However, we are up and at it full strength and expect some major growth this year." (E-mail sent to me on 2/22/2000).

27 The reasons that LAC multiplies on one date are:
1. The top leadership is able to think and plan together more concretely concerning future goals.
2. The training of new leadership teams can take place at the same time in the church.
3. Leaders of sectors, zones, and districts are able to consolidate their time and energy by focusing on one particular time period of multiplication.
4. There is more support for the new cell groups when they open together. It's harder for weaker groups to fall through the cracks.
5. The church can better focus its attention on prayer and support when there is simultaneous multiplication

28 At the Republic Church we've always believed in team ministry and have worked with a multiplicity of pastors from the very beginning of our church. If you are the only pastor in your church, you can think about including your board or key leaders in the planning of next year's goals. Ideally, those planning the goals should be those totally involved in cell ministry or there is the danger of setting the goals too low.

29 In my first cell ministry, I didn't even have to worry about establishing an equipping track because the church (El Batán) had a strong teaching ministry. The problem in that church is that those taught had very few significant places to serve. Starting a cell ministry met a deep felt need among those already trained—the need to serve. My job was to identify these trained people and convince them that they needed to lead cell groups. I train them in cell principles and offered ongoing Summit Meetings, but I didn't have to worry about the entire equipping track. In this manner, we grew from five cells to fifty-one in two years.

[30] It boiled down to two options: Option One: That the cell secretary become totally responsible to produce the report for our Wednesday pastoral meeting (to the point where she could not say that the "pastors weren't giving her data). With this option the cell secretary could receive help from the pastors, but ultimately she would be responsible. Option Two: The pastors becoming totally responsible to make sure that the reports were completed—with the penalty of paying five cents for every cell group that was not reported on. With this option, the pastors could ask help from the cell secretary, but ultimately she would be responsible. After much debate, we decided on the second option, making the pastors responsible. We decided to fine a pastor five-cents for every missing report (lack of information from a cell group).

[31] James C. Collins & Jerry I. Porras, *Built to Last: Successful Habits of Visionary Companies* (New York: HarperCollins Publishers, 1994), 9.

[32] Ibid., 94.

[33] Ibid., 95.

[34] If a G-3 cell leader (explained in chapter on coaching) has found all three of his daughter cell leaders, he should know when each one of them plan on giving birth to a daughter cell. The rule of thumb is that each cell must multiply in one year.

[35] I believe that it's helpful to set a higher goal than the one officially given. When leaders fail to fulfill what they said a year earlier, when groups close, or when circumstances hinder the opening of a new group, you'll have more groups than you need. For example, as pastor of a network of cells, my goal for 1999 was to go from twenty-three cells to sixty cells. In order to do so, I projected seventy cells, knowing that several of my groups would fail to bring forth fruit. I knew that at the last minute, one particular leader would decide to wait until the next year to open a cell. Sure enough, I discovered that I desperately needed those extra cells to meet the goal of sixty groups.

[36] When I first started a cell ministry, I believed that it was essential to give all the cells a break for the summer. I wrote this in my manual: "Do the cells meet all year? In our system the cells do not completely dissolve each year, but there are several 'breaks' during the year: a. One month break from the 1st week of December to the 1st week of January b. Two week break during the Easter season 3. Two month break during the summer time." I had it all figured out. Once again, however, I learned from the fast growing cell churches around the world that it wasn't necessary to program in such breaks. I believe that cell groups will take naturally breaks throughout the year, but you don't have to legislate such breaks. Some will want to meet while others will not. Each case will be worked out between pastor, supervisor, or

G-12 leader. For example, if your church legislates that cell groups will not meet during Christmas break, you might quench the family spirit of some groups who really want to do something special right around Christmas time. The same holds true for the summer break. Most groups will want to meet and maintain contact, while some will take short breaks. Every situation is different and is worked out between cell leader and director (pastor, G-12 leader, etc.). My point here is that it's far better NOT to legislate at the level of the entire church what the various networks of cell groups (or geographical districts) should or shouldn't do.

[37] Ian Russell, Monday, May 22, 2000, cellchurchtalk, , http://www.cell-church.org/list/highlights.html.

[38] *Encarta® World English Dictionary* © & (P) 1999 Microsoft Corporation. All rights reserved. Developed for Microsoft by Bloomsbury Publishing Plc.

[39] Bethany runs their youth and college and career ministries through cell groups; nevertheless, they don't ignore the needs of these age specific groups.

[40] Karen Hurston, *Growing the World's Largest Church* (Springfield, MO: Chrism, 1995), 125.

[41] Neighbour commented about this during Les Brickman's doctoral defense on the Works and Mission Baptist Church. Neighbor cited Victory Christian Center in Tulsa, Oklahoma as an example of a church with multiple ministries.

[42] Ralph Neighbour, CellChurchTalk, http://www.cell-church.org/list/highlights.html, Tuesday, May 23, 2000.

[43] Leonard Sweet, *SoulTsunami* (Grand Rapids, MI: ZondervanPublishingHouse, 1999). I'm grateful for this summary given by Ralph Neighbour on cellchurchtalk,

[44] In George's book *The Coming Church Revolution*, he spends most of the time describing his mapping strategy called the Meta Globe. According to George its a way of analyzing your church by placing all of the ministries into various categories. This categorization is supposed to help a church examine their real structure. However, I have found the concept more confusing than helpful. Dale Galloway mentioned the same thing to me at his cell conference in Columbus, Ohio (Oct., 1995)..

[45] Carl F. George, *Nine Keys to Effective Small Group Leadership* (Mansfield, PA: Kingdom Publishing, 1997), 11.

[46] Ibid., 24.

[47] Ibid., 11,12,23.

[48] David Limiero, "Meta, Model, or Martyr? Three Approaches to Introducing a Small Groups Ministry in Your Church," July 1996. http://smallgroups.com/models07.htm. Accessed: Friday, May 22, 1998.

[49] It's a misnomer that all programs flow from the cell. One pastor who tried to transition to the cell church said, "It's

impossible for all things to flow through a cell. As the church grows, certain extra items must occur. For example, worship ministry is a vital aspect of any Vineyard. While some Cell Churches claim they have a zone of worship people, it still leaves the uninvolved spouses needing to be covered in another cell strategy. In reality, it generally works better to have a worship team apart from the cell strategy. The same is true with assimilation and enfold. Boomers are not good at simply following up on people where something is not organized. Ministry teams after a service also are something that doesn't fit well in the context of a cell. Someone must train the workers. Thus, while this principle sounds good, it has a number of issues that must be covered in order for the church to function" (Hap Leman, "Frustrations of a Cell Church Pastor," Research Paper presented to Regent University on 5-19-98).

[50] Take the example of David Cho. He did not have a definition that told him he had to be some way. He had to figure out what would work within the basic confines of the general vision. In other words, he understood the basic definition of the small group then did whatever it took to make it work.

[51] Karen Hurston, for example, provides a helpful chart that describes the levels of integration among of small groups in churches in *Growing the World's Largest Church* ((Springfield, MO: Chrism, 1995), 203.

[52] David Limiero, "Meta, Model, or Martyr? Three Approaches to Introducing a Small Groups Ministry in Your Church," July 1996. http://smallgroups.com/models07.htm. Accessed: Friday, May 22, 1998

[53] Carl George, *The Coming Church Revolution* (Grand Rapids, MI: Fleming H. Revell, 1994), p. 284.

[54] This statistic came from the research of Les Brickman for his doctoral dissertation at Regent University. Comments made during the doctoral defense on Friday, December 15, 2000.

[55] Ralph Neighbour, *Where Do We Go from Here?* (Houston, TX: Touch Publications, 1990), p. 41.

[56] We at the Republic Church consider ourselves a strong cell church. We rejoice in maximum integration. Yet, not everyone is in agreement, even among our church board. Our pastoral team had to have a meeting with his board member and clearly explain our philosophy. We told him that if he wasn't in agreement, he was free to look for another church. He agreed not to manifest his resistance (he does lead his own cell group).

[57] In my book *Reap the Harvest* (Houston, TX: Touch Publications, 1999) I talk about steps to a successful transition (chapters 14 & 15).

[58] Quoted on the Small Group Network, http://www.small-groups.com/quotes.htm. Accessed Saturday, May 23, 1998.

[59] Don Davidson, cellchurchtalk, July 13, 2000, http://www.cell-church.org/list/highlights.html.

[60] David C., cellchurchtalk, July 12, 2000, http://www.cell-church.org/list/highlights.html.

[61] As quoted in Rick Diefendefer, ""The CellChurch and the Six Spiritual Needs of Disillusioned Americans." PowerPoint® Presentation. www.committed.to/cellchurch

[62] Stephen Csaplar, cellchurchtalk, 11/5/2000.

[63] Peter Wagner, *Churchquake* (Ventura, CA: Regal Books, 1999), p. 180.

[64] A team from our church in Quito, Ecuador recently visited the Elim Church. They said that some 50 people receive Jesus Christ in each of the six worship services.

[65] Jeff Green, Sunday, September 17, 2000, cellchurchtalk - www.cell-church.org.

[66] The church that uses this method is Love Alive Church in Tegucigalpa, Honduras. In 1996, LAC received approximately 150 first-time visitors each month.

[67] The member of the cell group (or the leader) meets with the person once per week to cover one of the four lessons contained in the pamphlet, "Your New Life In Christ." The pamphlet covers the person's new life in Christ, spiritual growth, and finally the importance of the cell group. A form is completed, each time the leader meets with the visitor. The last page of the pamphlet contains a final report of the visitation process.

[68] Herb Miller, *How to Build a Magnetic Church*. Creative Leadership Series. Lyle Schaller, ed. (Nashville, TN: Abingdon Press, 1987), 72-73.

[69] Rick Diefenderfer wrote on cellchurchtalk on Sunday, September 17, 2000.

Stage 8

[1] Christian Schwarz, *Natural Church Development* (Carol Stream, IL: ChurchSmart Resources, 1996), 68.

[2] William A. Smalley, "Cultural Implications," in *Perspectives on the World Christian Movement*, ed. Ralph D Winter and Steven C. Hawthorne (Pasadena, CA: William Carey Library, 199), 476.

[3] Ibid., 479.

[4] K. P. Yohannan, *The Coming Revolution in World Missions* (Altamonte Springs, Fl: Creation House, 1986), 142.

[5] Ralph D Winter, "The New Macedonia," in *Perspectives in the World Christian Movement*, 339.

[6] Ibid., 345.

[7] Ibid., 344.

INDEX

GREAT VISION TEAM BOOKS

MAKING CELL GROUPS WORK
by M. Scott Boren

These resources break down the transition process into eight manageable parts. If your church is just beginning its transition, these materials will help you focus on building cells on a sure foundation. If you are in the midst of developing cell groups, it highlights where to focus your energy. No matter where you are with your church, these resources will help you identify your current stage of cell development and articulate a plan to address that stage.

THE SECOND REFORMATION
by William A. Beckham

Don't jump head-first into a cell church transition or church plant without reading this book! Beckham brilliantly walks you through the logic of a cell/celebration structure from a biblical and historical perspective. He provides you with a step-by-step strategy for launching your first cells. This wonderful companion to Neighbour's material will ground you in the values and vision necessary for a successful transition to cells. 253 pgs.

WHERE DO WE GO FROM HERE? THE 10TH ANNIVERSARY EDITION
by Ralph W. Neighbour, Jr.

With updated data on new cell church models, new information on equipping and harvest events and practical teaching on how to begin a transition, this book will continue to stir hearts to dream about what the church can be. You will find hope for the church in North America and discover the new things that Dr. Neighbour has learned over the last 10 years. Share this vision with a friend. 400 pgs.

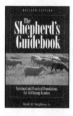

THE SHEPHERD'S GUIDEBOOK
by Ralph W. Neighbour, Jr.

With over 100,000 copies in print, this tested guide will equip and train your leaders to develop community and lead people into relationship evangelism, by learning to listen to God's voice on behalf of their flock. Cell leaders will gain tools for leading a cell meeting, and learn pastoring skills that will multiply the ministry of your church. 256 pages.

LIFE IN HIS BODY
by David Finnell

Communicate the vision of the cells to everyone in your church with this simple tool. The short chapters followed by discussion questions clearly define cell life for your leaders and members so that they can catch a lifestyle of prayer, community and evangelism. This book will give your church hope and vision as your members discover the possibilities of the New Testament community. 160 pgs.

Order Toll-Free from TOUCH Outreach Ministries
1-800-735-5865 • Order Online: www.cellgrouppeople.com

GREAT VISION TEAM BOOKS
By Joel Comiskey

GROUPS OF 12

This book clears the confusion about the Groups of 12 model. Joel has dug deeply into the International Charismatic Mission in Bogota Columbia and other G-12 churches to learn the simply principles that G-12 has to offer your church. This book also contrasts the G-12 model with the classic 5x5 structure and shows you what to do with this new model of ministry. 182 pgs.

FROM 12 TO 3

There are two basic ways to embrace the G-12 concept: adopting the entire model or applying the principles that support the model. This book focuses on the second. It provides you with a modified approach called the "G-12.3." This approach presents a workable pattern that is adaptable to many different church and cultural contexts, including your unique environment. 184 pgs.

REAP THE HARVEST

This book casts a vision for cell groups that will work in your church. Based on research of the best cell churches around the world and practical experience by the author, Reap the Harvest will reveal the 16 proven principles behind cell-church growth and effectiveness. It will also provide you with a strong biblical and historical foundation that anyone can understand. Great to share with key leaders as you transition to cell groups. 240 pgs.

HOME CELL GROUP EXPLOSION

This is the most researched and practical book ever written on cell-group ministry! Joel traveled the globe to find out why certain churches and small groups are successful in reaching the lost. He freely shares the answer within this volume. If you are a pastor or a small group leader, you should devour this book! It will encourage you and give you simple, practical steps for dynamic small group life and growth. 152 pgs.

LEADERSHIP EXPLOSION

Cell Groups are leader breeders. Yet few churches have enough cell leaders ready to start new groups. In this book, you will discover the leadership development models used by churches that consistently multiply leaders. Then you will learn how to create your own model that will breed leaders in your church. 208 pgs.

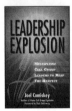

Order Toll-Free from TOUCH Outreach Ministries
1-800-735-5865 • Order Online: www.cellgrouppeople.com

ENCOUNTER GOD!

Encounter God is a simple, easy-to-use weekend resource to help you walk your church through a spiritual freedom experience.

Spiritual strongholds in the life of a Christian are dark areas of bitterness, unforgiveness and secret sin that keep him from seeing his own worth, leadership potential and purpose in life. If your church members resist discipleship, and/or have no passion for the lost, a spiritual freedom weekend experience will help them see areas of their heart where they need healing and give them a safe environment to receive ministry. *Encounter God* is also a wonderful tool for helping new converts overcome old flesh patterns and beginning their new walk with increased spiritual freedom. Believers who are set free from the grip of sinful habits and attitudes enjoy a fruitful, purpose-filled life!

The materials we have designed make preparation as easy as possible! *The Instructor's Guide* is very clear on how to present the materials yourself or use the video. *The Video Series* contains seven hours of professionally created sessions that you can use to prepare or show during the actual retreat. *The Retreat Guide* will help you choose a good location, select from a variety of possible schedules, and answer frequently asked questions.

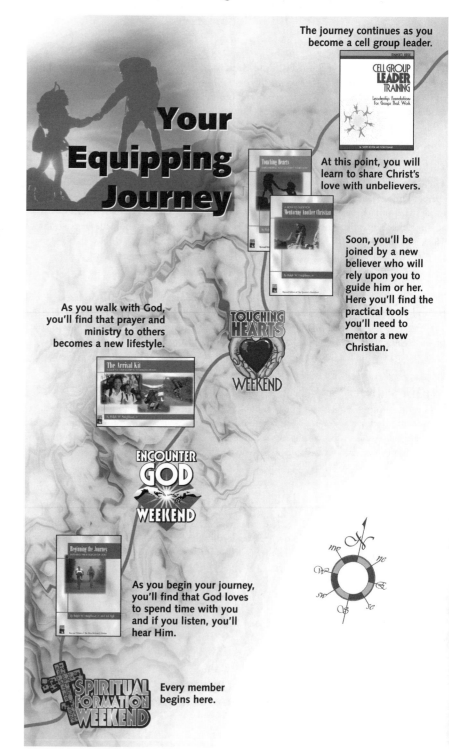

The journey continues as you become a cell group leader.

At this point, you will learn to share Christ's love with unbelievers.

Soon, you'll be joined by a new believer who will rely upon you to guide him or her. Here you'll find the practical tools you'll need to mentor a new Christian.

As you walk with God, you'll find that prayer and ministry to others becomes a new lifestyle.

As you begin your journey, you'll find that God loves to spend time with you and if you listen, you'll hear Him.

Every member begins here.

Cell Group Leader Tools

303 ICEBREAKERS:

At last . . . 303 ways to really "BREAK THE ICE" in your cell group! You will never need another icebreaker book. This collection places at your fingertips easy-to-find ideas divided into nine categories, such as "Including the Children," "When a Visitor Arrives" and "Lighthearted and Fun." This is a needed reference for every cell meeting. We've included instructions on how to lead this part of the meeting effectively. 156 pgs.

OUR BLESSING LIST POSTER

Growing cell churches have proven that constant prayer for the lost yields incredible results! Use this nifty poster to list the names of your oikos and pray for them every time you meet. 34" x 22", folds down to 8.5" x 11" and comes with a handout master, equipping track and a master prayer list. Pack of 10.

ARE YOU FISHING WITH A NET?
by Randall G. Neighbour

Lead your group into team evangelism. These proven steps will prepare your members to reach out effectively as a group. 12 pgs.

ANSWERS TO YOUR CELL GROUP QUESTIONS,
by Randall G. Neighbour

As your cell leaders face new challenges, it's comforting to know there's a resource they can turn to when they need answers to specific questions and issues. "Answers to Your Cell Group Questions" covers the entire gamut of cell life and leadership and is written by Randall Neighbour, a seasoned cell leader and President of TOUCH Outreach Ministries.

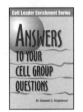

This book is an invaluable resource for you and your leaders! Topics include: working with difficult or hurting people, how to facilitate a meeting the right way, working with children, training interns and releasing the ministry to them, jump-starting a cell group that doesn't care about the lost, etc.

THE JOURNEY GUIDE FOR NEW BELIEVERS

Launch your cell members on a journey of freedom and ministry to others! This tool helps a new believer understand his past and determine the steps leading to growth. It will guide new believers to deal honestly with their struggles and share them with those who can love them through the healing and growing process of discipleship.

THE JOURNEY GUIDE FOR GROWING CHRISTIANS

This tool is designed for growing believers in your cell groups. It will affirm how God has used them in ministry, challenge them to move forward in their Christian walk and set a workable course for their future ministry.

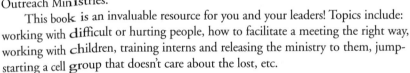

Order Toll-Free from TOUCH Outreach Ministries
1-800-735-5865 • Order Online: www.cellgrouppeople.com

CELL GROUP LEADER TRAINING

CELL GROUP LEADER TRAINING:
by Scott Boren and Don Tillman
The Trainer's Guide and Participant's Manual parallel the teaching of Comiskey's How to Lead a Great Cell Group Meeting. Through the use of teaching, creative activities, small group interaction, and suggested between-the-training exercises, this eight-session training will prepare people for cell group leadership like no other tool. The Trainer's Guide provides teaching outlines for all eight sessions and options for organizing the training, including different weekly options and retreat options. The Trainer's Guide also has bonus sections, including teaching outlines for the Upward, Inward, Outward, Forward Seminar and detailed interview discussion guides for The Journey Guide for Cell Group Leaders. This comprehensive training tool will establish your group leaders on a sure foundation.

UPWARD, INWARD, OUTWARD, FORWARD WORKBOOK
Improving the 4 Dynamics of Your Cell Group, by Jim Egli
You can now take your cell leaders and interns through the same strategic planning workshop TOUCH® offers across the country!

This easy to use workbook, combined with the facilitator's presentation (a FREE download from our website) will help your cell groups grow in the four basic dynamics of healthy cell life. Upward: Deepening your relationship to the Father; Inward: Deepening community between cell members; Outward: Reaching the lost for Jesus successfully; Forward: Developing and releasing new leaders. 72 page student workbook

THE JOURNEY GUIDE FOR CELL GROUP LEADERS
This tool will help your interns and cell leaders evaluate their leadership abilities and determine their next steps toward effective group leadership. It will help you as a pastor or trainer identify the needs of your future or current leaders so that you can better train and mentor them.

HOW TO BE A GREAT CELL GROUP COACH
by Joel Comiskey
Research has proven that the greatest contributor to cell group success is the quality of coaching provided for cell group leaders. Following in the footsteps of his bestselling book, *How to Lead a GREAT Cell Group Meeting,* author and church consultant Joel Comiskey provides a comprehensive guide for coaching cell group leaders. Chapters include: What a Coach Does, Listening, Celebrating, Caring, Strategizing, Challenging, and more. This book will prepare your coaches to be great mentors, supporters, and guides to the cell group leaders they oversee.

CELL GROUP LEADER BOOKS

HOW TO LEAD A GREAT CELL GROUP MEETING . . .
. . . So People Want to Come Back
by Joel Comiskey

Joel Comiskey takes you beyond theory and into the "practical tips of the trade" that will make your cell group gathering vibrant! This hands-on guide covers all you need to know, from basic how-to's of getting the conversation started to practical strategies for dynamic ministry times. If you're looking to find out what really makes a cell group meeting great . . . this book has the answers! 144 pgs.

LEADING FROM THE HEART
by Michael Mack

Recharge your cell leadership! Powerful cell leaders share a common trait: a passionate heart for God. They know their priorities and know that time with Him is always at the top of the list.

Do your cell leaders attract others? Is their cell ministry central to their lives? This book will renew their hearts, refocus their priorities and recharge their ministry.

If you have a sense that your leaders are tired of ministry or frustrated with people, this title will help! And, if your leaders have great attitudes and you want to help them move to the next level, this book will move them into new fields, white for harvest!

8 HABITS OF EFFECTIVE SMALL GROUP LEADERS
by Dave Earley

Are your cell leaders truly effective in changing lives? They can be! After years of leading and overseeing growing small groups, Pastor Dave Earley has identified 8 core habits of effective leaders. When adopted, these habits will transform your leadership too. The habits include: Dreaming • Prayer • Invitations • Contact Preparation • Mentoring • Fellowship • Growth. When your leaders adopt and practice these habits, your groups will move from once-a-week meetings to an exciting lifestyle of ministry to one another and the lost! 144 pgs.

TURNING MEMBERS INTO LEADERS
by Dave Earley

The development of new cell leaders is the key to growing cell groups. The best way to raise up new leaders is through mentoring current cell group members within cell groups. Pastor Dave Earley has observed that cell leaders employ some basic steps when successfully raising up new leaders. The steps include Dream • Demonstrate • Discover • Deepen • Describe • Determine • Develop • Deploy. When current cell group leaders use these simple steps in mentoring future leaders, they will discover that their ministries are multiplied and new cell group started.

Order Toll-Free from TOUCH Outreach Ministries
1-800-735-5865 • Order Online: www.cellgrouppeople.com

Make Cell Groups Work Online!

Our website was designed for pastors just like you!

Complete archives of *CellChurch Magazine* & *CellGroup Journal*.

Fast and secure online resource purchases.

Enjoy streaming video and audio from our A/V resources.

Discover other churches with cell groups in your area or denomination in our networking area.

Post your resume or search for a new staff member in our cell-based classifieds area.

Free downloads of leader's guides, presentations, and software to track cell growth.

Interact with other pastors and experts in our bulletin board forum.

Ask questions of cell group church experts in a forum setting.

Interact with other pastors in the online forum around the eight stages.

Access exclusive articles only available to *Navigation Guide* users.

What are you waiting for?

Grab a cup of coffee and visit us now...

www.cellgrouppeople.com